Enhancing Supplier Relationship Management with SAP® SRM

 PRESS

SAP PRESS is a joint initiative of SAP and Galileo Press. The know-how offered by SAP specialists combined with the expertise of the publishing house Galileo Press offers the reader expert books in the field. SAP PRESS features first-hand information and expert advice, and provides useful skills for professional decision-making.

SAP PRESS offers a variety of books on technical and business related topics for the SAP user. For further information, please visit our website: *www.sap-press.com*.

D. Rajen Iyer
Effective SAP SD
2007, app. 384 pp.
ISBN 978-1-59229-101-4

T. Götz, S. Safai, and P. Beer
Efficient Supply Chain Management with SAP Solutions for RFID
2006, 104 pp.
ISBN 978-1-59229-081-9

Jochen Balla and Frank Layer
Production Planning with SAP APO-PP/DS
2007, app. 336pp
ISBN 978-1-59229-113-7

Martin Murray
Understanding the SAP Logistics Information System
2007, app. 336 pp.
ISBN 978-1-59229-108-3

Sachin Sethi

Enhancing Supplier Relationship Management with SAP® SRM

Galileo Press

Bonn • Boston

ISBN   978-1-59229-068-0

1st edition 2007

Editor Jawahara Saidullah
Copy Editor John Parker, UCG, Inc., Boston, MA
Cover Design Silke Braun
Layout Design Vera Brauner
Typesetting SatzPro, Krefeld
Printed and bound in Germany

© 2007 by Galileo Press
SAP PRESS is an imprint of Galileo Press,
Boston, MA, USA
Bonn, Germany

To my parents whose incessant sacrifices to "do the right thing" no matter how tough the path always inspires me to make the right choices.

To my wife Ekta for her unconditional support, boundless understanding, and infectious energy. Her endless efforts helped me bring this book concept to life.

Contents at a Glance

Contents

PART III: SAP SRM IMPLEMENTATION, INTEGRATION, AND UPGRADES

Appendix 623

Contents

"We're at the beginning of one of the most important revolutions in business. The Internet will forever change the way business is done. It will change every relationship, between our businesses, between our customers, between our suppliers. Distribution channels will change. Buying practices will change. Everything will be tipped upside down. The slow become fast, the old become young. It's clear we've only just begun this transformation."
— Jack Welch, Chairman GE; Fortune Magazine

Preface

In the spirit of the axiom that change is the only real constant, procurement has undergone its full share of renewal. Paradigms shifted, rules changed, and boundaries disappeared. In the 1990s, with the advent of the Internet, e-procurement burst on the scene, ushering in a new era. Simply stated, e-procurement is the business-to-business exchange of goods and services over the Internet that provides means for organizations to automate their internal purchasing processes. E-Procurement forced organizations to redefine their processes in preparation for a new, highly competitive, boundaryless economy.

As procurement processes in organizations matured and software solutions offered by vendors improved, the need to enhance e-procurement followed. This book addresses that need and aims to provide an in-depth understanding of SAP's Supplier Relationship Management (SRM) solution offering: SAP SRM. According to SAP, the SAP SRM application tightly and cost-effectively integrates strategic practices for supplier qualification, negotiation, and contract management with other enterprise functions and their suppliers' processes through a single analytical framework and support for multi-channel supplier enablement.

The contents of this book are inspired by my consulting engagements with some of the leading companies on the landscape today. This book extends beyond configuration. It strives to fill the need for a comprehensive guidebook on strategies in the areas of content management, workflow, integration to financials and SAP Human Resources, security management, business intelligence, enterprise portals, et al.

Since SAP introduced its first e-procurement solution in 1999, it has enjoyed explosive growth and evolved into what we know as SAP SRM. Today, SAP SRM is the market leader in its field. SRM enjoys the incongruent distinction of being both an industry term and the name of a host of software solutions.

This book clarifies both aspects and attempts to empower the reader with the information and tools needed to understand and implement SAP SRM. After reading this book, readers will possess an overview of the industry term SRM, an understanding of what is the SAP SRM solution, and have a comprehensive guidebook to use for developing strategies in implementing the SAP SRM solution.

Who This Book is For

This book targets SRM project managers, consultants, cross-functional leads, technical teams, and support leaders who want to deploy SAP SRM successfully in the real world.

It is organized into five logical parts, enabling readers to delve directly into the part most relevant to them. However, readers new to SRM will find it more valuable to start with Part I, which provides an overview of SAP SRM.

Experienced consultants familiar with SAP SRM and its core functionality might be drawn to Part III, which deals with implementation, integration and upgrades.

The content and capabilities in this book are based on SAP SRM 4.0 and SAP SRM 5.0 releases. In addition, I have provided a "What's New" section in various chapters to highlight major functionality included in SAP SRM 5.0 or planned for SAP SRM 6.0 release.

I recommend that this book be used in conjunction with SAP SRM training, release notes, and the help guide available in the Service Marketplace. This book does not aim to replace any of the other content provided by SAP.

About This Book

Let's get a quick look at what the various part of this book contain, so you can get an idea of how to best use it for your needs. Some of you might read it from beginning to end. Or you might use it as a modular resource, dipping into specific chapters as to needed you. Let's get an idea of what is included in this resource.

Part I: How SRM fits within an Organisation

This part gives an overview on Supplier Relationship Management (SRM). It answers the question: "What is SRM?"

Part II: What is SAP SRM?

This begins with an introduction to SAP's supplier relationship management solution, SAP SRM. It them provides a detailed understanding of the three supply processes within SRM: operational procurement, strategic sourcing, and supplier anablement. "What is SAP SRM?" and "Where does it fit in the overall SAP solution landscape?" It then guides you through the detailed functionality and capability of SAP's supplier relationship management solution, SAP SRM.

Part III: Implementation, Integration, and Upgrades

This part outlines valuable and relevant tools for implementation, integration, and upgrade processes. It guides you through finer points that cannot be learned from SAP training alone. Most of these insights are based on my real-life implementations and experiences.

This part also offers knowledge that would distinguish configuration consultants from process consultants and answers to key project questions such as the following:

▶ "We are considering SRM/EBP for global eProcurement along with a global SAP R/3 project. What are the decision criteria for selecting a scenario? How do scenario decisions affect the communication to the supply chain?"

▶ "There seem to be a lot of different options for catalogs. Should we merely implement punch-out catalogs? What is the SAP solution for catalog management?"

▶ "How does SRM integrate with the SAP financials? We're using the SAP funds management solution; what integration touch points should we be aware of?"

▶ "We are looking at upgrading from EBP 3.0, which currently fronts SAP 4.6c MM. I am looking for some summary documentation setting about the functional and technical pros and cons for upgrading to EBP3.5.5.0."

▶ "We are implementing SRM with BW and SAP R/3. Is there a guide to assist us with the security knowledge?"

Part IV: Industry Solutions

This part highlights the new goverment and public-sector solution offering from SAP — Procurement for Public Services (PPS) — based on SAP SRM. Originally branded as Government Procurement (GP), this solution focuses on the unique requirements for government entities but can also be implemented in other public-sector companies.

Part V: Selected Configuration in SAP SRM

This part arms the reader with selected solution configuration information. While not a step-by-step cookbook for configuration, it discusses key setup and configuration areas in SAP SRM.

Appendices

The appendices contain valuable extras that readers will find extremely helpful in their projects: SRM functionality matrix, job scheduling, Business Add-Ins (BAdIs), customer fields, a quiz to test your SRM knowledge, and more.

Summary

In this preface, I tried to give you a general idea and overview of the book. I hope that the contents of this book, along with the examples I have chosen to illustrate important concepts and processes, furthers your understanding of how you can use SAP SRM to enhance procurement in your company.

Let's now move on to Chapter 1, where I will give you a general understanding of supplier relationship management and its important concepts.

Special Thanks

When I embarked on the journey to write this book, I had no idea how, when and where I would find the time between running Brite Consulting, working on client engagements, completing my EMBA and trying to be a good husband and father. It is during times like these that we are amazed by what true support from friends and family can do. I have been fortunate to be blessed with incredible relationships whose support made this book possible.

I am indebted to my friend, Abhijit Umbarkar, for his unstinted and unparalleled efforts in this endeavor. He spent countless hours reviewing every chapter and providing his expert advice. I am extremely thankful to him for his contributions in the Integration to Financials chapter.

I thank my extraordinary colleagues and friends who spent numerous hours combing through the chapters of this book and provided invaluable reviews – Susan Benkowski, Maria Gregg, Debbie Jackson, Hari Krishna Nalluri, Thang Ngo, Miroslav Oborny, Varun Ratta Patricia Sadowski, Raji Sankar, Sudhakar Stephen-Rolance, Amogh Umbarkar, Raghu Rao Vallam, Jeanne Young, Stuart Zimmerman, and members of my family.

My initiation in SRM started at SEAL Consulting. I will always be thankful to my friends at SEAL for their continual support.

To SAP PRESS for giving me this wonderful opportunity and a special thanks to my amazing editor, Jawahara Saidullah for her relentless patience, belief and dedication in making this book a reality.

PART I
How SRM Fits Within an Organization

Supplier relationship management (SRM) is rapidly developing as a key business priority for companies as they look for tangible savings and enhanced collaboration, communication, and visibility in the procurement life cycle.

1 Introduction to Supplier Relationship Management

The ever-changing economy, globalization, reduced product margins, and offshoring of manufacturing and services have all promoted and elevated the need for a tighter and more robust integration of business partners throughout the value chain. The new customer–supplier relationship involves not just the procurement and supply of goods and services but a relationship that demands true partnership.

Today organizations are learning that the way to gain the most value from their business partners is by enhancing their collaboration throughout their supplier base. Internet connectivity has defined new ways to identify, negotiate, and engage with suppliers and partners worldwide, while other data-aggregation and enrichment tools are providing greater insight into procurement trends and best practices.

This is where supplier relationship management (SRM) provides value for organizations. SRM aims to streamline all the processes and communication channels between an organization and its supplier base.

Example

Organizations used to take 10 to 15 days to requisition and processes a purchase order. They can now process a purchase order in one to two days using SRM processes and applications. Supplier organizations have greater visibility into the customer processes. Suppliers can, for example, view their invoice status and payment information by logging into supplier portals provided by customer organizations implementing SRM.

Let's begin the next part of this chapter by talking about the evolution of procurement and about how SRM has matured over the last five years.

1.1   E-Procurement and SRM

Some form of communication and collaboration between the buyer and the supplier has always existed, so procurement in its basic form has been around for a long time According to procurement services provider ICG Commerce, the term *procurement* refers to the process of managing activities associated with a company's need to procure the goods and services required to either manufacture a product (direct) or to operate the organization (indirect). Breakthrough inventions in communication and collaboration technologies like the telephone, fax, and Internet have had a significant impact on the procurement process over the years. Figure 1.1 illustrates the evolution of procurement in a simple way.

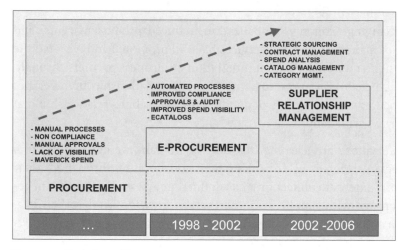

Figure 1.1 Evolution of Procurement

Until the late 1990s, most organizations still had manual, costly, and inefficient procurement processes. Limited standardization in the requisition-to-order process, no approvals or manual approval processes, none or minimal visibility into spending, along with no strategic sourcing capabilities, all worked to create a largely manual and highly inefficient procurement environment.

This is why the advent of the Internet and e-commerce gave birth to e-procurement (the term for electronic procurement), which became the buzzword for buying and selling of products and services using the Internet. E-procurement was adopted by organizations to assist in automating their largely manual procurement processes, and reducing costs by directing spending on primarily indirect goods to negotiated supplier catalogs.

Ariba, i2, SAS, and Commerce One were some of the pioneers in the industry that actually started the e-procurement marketplace. And their entire solution offering was branded as e-procurement. Interestingly most of these software providers were niche players and none were major ERP software providers. Companies like Ariba were too far ahead for any ERP software providers to provide a competing product for e-procurement.

A number of Fortune 500 companies implemented Ariba and Commerce One solutions, touting these as best of breed. Over the past four to five years, the big ERP software providers have finally caught up and developed a very compelling solution offering for customers. Not only have they built "best-of-breed" solutions, but also have the advantage of possessing a front door into all the large key customers that for years have implemented the ERP solutions in their organization. Furthermore, the ERP solution providers offer the great benefit of integrated solutions.

Another key development over the past few years has been that customers have begun demanding more than automation of processes. Organizations came to realize that e-procurement tools by themselves were not enough to provide the cost reductions and savings that were projected by the market. Other drivers, such as sourcing, contract management, reporting and analytics, were all equally important in gaining the true benefits promised for e-procurement. This is where the industry shift has given birth to SRM, which is broader in scope as than e-procurement and represents the next step in the evolution of procurement.

SRM applications take a comprehensive approach towards managing an enterprise's interactions with the organizations that supply the goods and services it uses. SRM manages the flow of information between suppliers and purchasing organizations and ensures the integration of supplier information in the procurement process. The goal of SRM is to make all the interactions between the enterprise and its suppliers streamlined and effective. Some of its key objectives are to optimize the processes designed for acquisition of products and services, to replace inefficient paper trails, and to maximize on savings by using companywide supplier contracts.

A simple Google search on *supplier relationship management software* provides more 2.43 million results. Interestingly, a search on *e-procurement software* provides around 3.03 million results. The question arises whether the shift from e-procurement to SRM has really happened. The answer is **yes**, because SRM is not just a re-branding of e-procurement, but rather an umbrella term for a suite of tools, one of which is procurement or e-procurement. **Catalog Mgmt.**, **Sourcing**, **Contract Mgmt.**, **Spend Analysis**, and **Supplier Enablement** are all tools within the SRM umbrella (as illustrated in Figure 1.2).

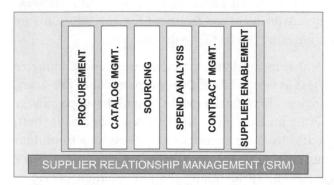

Figure 1.2 Supplier Relationship Management Suite

As illustrated in Figure 1.3, procurement is very much a core part of the SRM suite, accounting for 52 % of the suite. Market studies show that procurement solutions are still the leader in revenue share in the overall SRM market segment. There is no mystery behind this growth, because at its core e-procurement is the automation of the requisition-to-order process. Every organization that ventures down the path of SRM has to overcome its first challenge of automation.

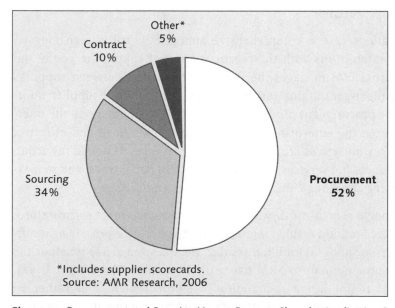

Figure 1.3 Procurement and Sourcing License Revenue Share by Application Segment, 2005

SRM is more than just about cost savings; it is also about value generation. Leading organizations understand that their business partners can be a key element in their overall success. Together, they can improve business processes, share information to reduce wasted time and resources, and improve overall margins.

The value proposition for SRM allows companies not only to reduce costs, but gain considerable competitive advantage. Figure 1.4 illustrates some of the benefits that buying organizations and suppliers gain by implementing SRM solutions and processes.

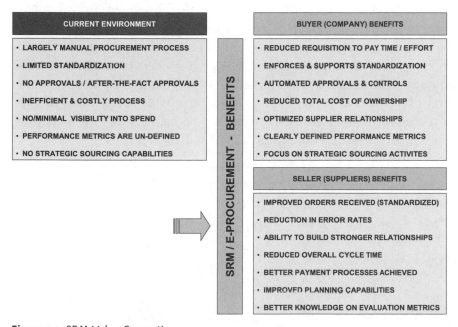

Figure 1.4 SRM Value Generation

SRM reaches beyond just the automation of business processes and the reduction in operating costs gained by this automation. This was best expressed by Bill Knittle, global procurement pirector for downstream procurement at BP International: "SRM is about much more than cost reduction…it's about ensuring continuity of supply and obtaining collaborative value from a select group of strategic suppliers. The key is to focus on the right suppliers in the first place, and then to work with them in a structured and disciplined manner. We have implemented a formal process of segmenting our supply base to choose the appropriate engagement approach for each supplier, and we're continuing to put structure and discipline around relationship and performance management."

Section 1.1 discussed the evolution of procurement to SRM. In the next two sections, 1.2 and 1.3, we will briefly discuss about the SRM vendor landscape and introduce why SAP with the SAP SRM solution is the market leader for SRM applications.

1.2 The SRM Vendor Landscape

In 2002, Frost & Sullivan identified SRM as a promising growth area, forecasting a compound annual growth rate (CAGR) of 18 percent over the 2001–2006 period. This growth was more than sustained, and in 2006 a leading supply-chain research organization, AMR Research, projected that the SRM market segment will experience a CAGR of 8% through 2010. This provides a market opportunity for software providers to continue to build efficient and cost-effective SRM solutions, and for customers to have a wide array of solutions to choose from. This section provides an overview of some of the leading SRM solution providers in the market and shares industry research on the leaders dominating the SRM market.

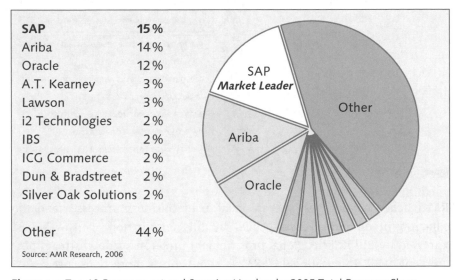

SAP	**15%**
Ariba	14%
Oracle	12%
A.T. Kearney	3%
Lawson	3%
i2 Technologies	2%
IBS	2%
ICG Commerce	2%
Dun & Bradstreet	2%
Silver Oak Solutions	2%
Other	44%

Source: AMR Research, 2006

Figure 1.5 Top 10 Procurement and Sourcing Vendors by 2005 Total Revenue Share

According to leading research firm AMR Research, the market for SRM software providers is led by **SAP** with **15%** of the overall procurement and sourcing market, with **Ariba** and **Oracle** at a close second and third place with 14% and 12% respectively. It is interesting to note that most of the other players have a very small proportion of the overall SRM market; however, the percent growth change from the previous years is fairly high for some of the vendors such as **ICG Commerce**, which grew by 26%. Figure 1.5 illustrates the top 10 procurement and sourcing vendors by 2005 total revenue share.

1.3 Why SAP SRM?

In a market with so many best-of-breed solution providers, organizations ask themselves why they should implement SAP SRM, the supplier relationship management solution from SAP.

SAP introduced its initial e-procurement solution in 1999, calling it Business-to-Business procurement (B2B). This happened at a time when market leaders such as Ariba were years ahead of the SAP solution. It was also an era when e-commerce was the leading buzzword, and ERP vendors had missed the boat on *e* or web-based commerce. Many organizations that had existing implementations of the SAP ERP solution, SAP R/3, opted to implement *best-of-breed* e-procurement solutions such as Ariba.

This has since changed considerably. Over the last six years, SAP has drastically improved its SRM application and become a leading solution provider. The current solution is branded as SAP SRM, and everything from the user interface to its functionality for operational procurement, strategic sourcing, and supplier enablement provides a highly competitive offering for customers. SAP SRM has been the fastest growing SAP application in two of the last three years prior to 2006, and SAP has been adding significant investments in the overall SAP solution.

Figure 1.6 provides results from a 2005 SAP Annual Report for investors in which the SRM solution gained 20% in revenue. Notice that, compared to the other solutions including ERP, SRM had the largest percentage change compared to any SAP single solution offering.

In addition to being a very competitive solution as compared to Ariba and others in the market, SAP SRM has a big advantage in its tight integration to the core SAP R/3 or ERP software. A recent survey conducted by Accenture (with findings illustrated in Figure 1.7) concluded that the most important deciding factor for organizations that are evaluating SRM software solutions is the functionality available in the software. The second most important factor is the ease of integration with existing ERP systems.

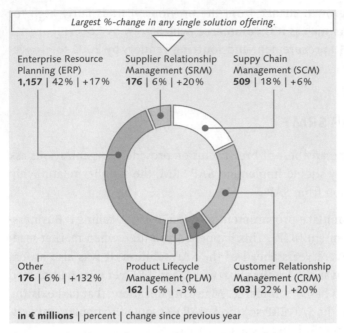

Largest %-change in any single solution offering.

Enterprise Resource Planning (ERP)
1,157 | 42% | +17%

Supplier Relationship Management (SRM)
176 | 6% | +20%

Suppy Chain Management (SCM)
509 | 18% | +6%

Other
176 | 6% | +132%

Product Lifecycle Management (PLM)
162 | 6% | -3%

Customer Relationship Management (CRM)
603 | 22% | +20%

in € millions | percent | change since previous year

Figure 1.6 SAP SRM Software Product Revenue Breakdown

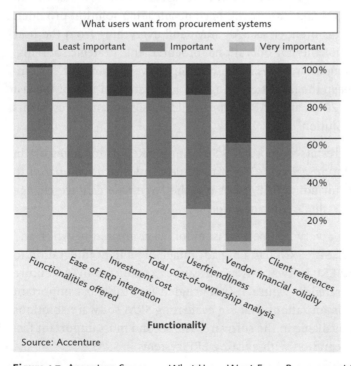

What users want from procurement systems

■ Least important   ■ Important   ■ Very important

100%
80%
60%
40%
20%

Functionalities offered
Ease of ERP integration
Investment cost
Total cost-of-ownership analysis
Userfriendliness
Vendor financial solidity
Client references

Functionality

Source: Accenture

Figure 1.7 Accenture Survey on What Users Want From Procurement Systems

The Accenture survey results are further strengthened with the testimony of customers that have implemented the SAP SRM solution illustrated in Figure 1.8. SAP conducted research across a number of its SAP SRM customers and published an SAP SRM customer reference book.

The companies listed in Figure 1.8 are just a few of the many listed in the survey reference book. It is important to notice that four out of the six companies listed cited leveraging their existing investment and integration as their key deciding factor for choosing to implement SAP SRM.

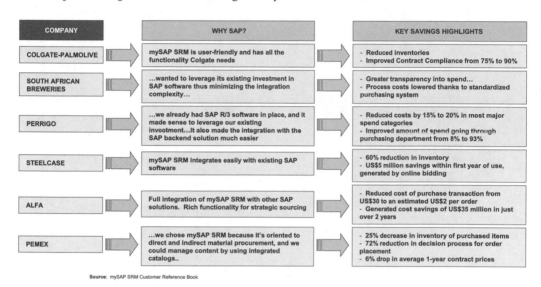

Source: mySAP SRM Customer Reference Book

Figure 1.8 Why Organizations Chose SAP SRM

As illustrated in Figure 1.8, companies like **STEELCASE** have chosen SAP's SRM solution for its ease of integration with their existing SAP software. They have been able to attain results of more than 60 % reduction in inventory along with a $5 million savings generated by using the SRM bidding solution.

1.4   Summary

In this chapter, I introduced the term Supplier Relationship Management (SRM). We talked about the evolution of procurement into e-procurement and then into today's SRM. We also briefly discussed the current SRM vendor landscape and how SAP is today the market leader in SRM with 15 % of the overall procurement and sourcing market.

In Chapter 2, I will introduce SAP's supplier relationship management solution, SAP SRM. The goal of the next chapter is to help readers answer the question: What is SAP SRM, and where does it fit into the overall SAP solution landscape?

PART II
What is SAP SRM?

"With the SAP Supplier Relationship Management (SAP SRM) solution, we want to enable our customers to unleash the value potential of a holistic and strategic approach to purchasing and supply management by offering a purchasing platform for continuous savings and value generation" — Peter Kirschbauer, General Manager, SAP AG, SAP Applications

2   SAP SRM — An Introduction

2.1   Evolution of SAP SRM

SAP introduced its e-procurement solution in 1999. Since then, the solution offering and its acceptance have seen tremendous growth. The SAP SRM solution has been the fastest-growing SAP application in two of the last three years, up to 2006. Customers that were early adopters of this solution remember the solution branding as Business to Business Procurement (BBP) or Enterprise Buyer Professional (EBP). Over the years, the solution has grown from a web-based catalog requisitioning solution aimed at operational excellence to the solution today that offers complete supply management. Figure 2.1 provides a chart that shows the progression of this solution from B2B to SAP SRM.

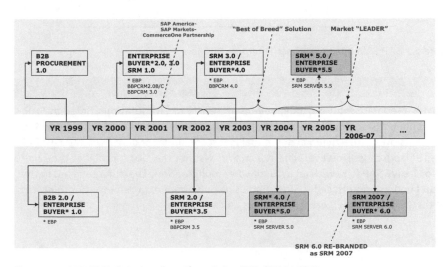

Figure 2.1 SAP SRM Solution Growth — From B2B–EBP to SRM

In 1999, SAP introduced the B2B Procurement 1.0 solution and has since re-branded the offering from BBP to EBP to the solution available today as Supplier Relationship Management (SRM). The solution release generally available to customers today is SAP SRM 5.0. Recently SAP has announced plans to rebrand the SAP SRM 6.0 release as SRM 2007. Based on current information SRM 2007 (or 6.0) will be generally available towards the third quarter of 2007, until which time it will remain in ramp-up mode with selected customers.

2.2   SRM and SAP Enterprise Applications

The SAP SRM solution integrates seamlessly with enterprise resource planning (ERP), product life-cycle management (PLM), and supply chain management (SCM) applications to ensure an effective implementation of cross-application business processes (see Figure 2.2).

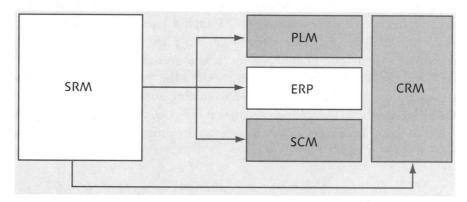

Figure 2.2 SAP SRM Integrates Cross-Enterprise Business Processes

> **Note**
>
> SRM is a separate solution, independent of the R/3 or ERP solution offered by SAP. It is common for people to forget that SAP SRM is installed and implemented within its own three-tiered architectural landscape, independent from the SAP R/3 or ERP landscape. However, it is still an SAP system; the GUI for SRM is the same as for native SAP R/3, with an IMG for core-configuration. The difference lies in the actual end user interface for SRM. End users only require a Web browser to access all the transactions. Figure 2.3 provides an example.

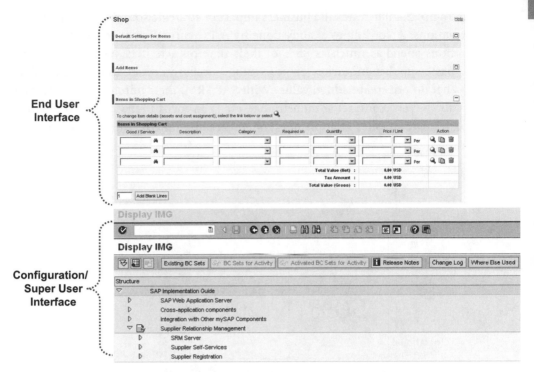

Figure 2.3 SAP SRM User interface — End User and Configurator

Note
Until SAP SRM 5.0 the user interface was based on ITS or BSP technology. From SRM 2007 (or SRM 6.0) onwards SAP will phase out ITS and BSP by introducing a portal user interface for SRM based on Web Dynpro.

2.3 Benefits of SAP SRM

Often it's not easy to clearly understand the business benefits within a solution offering or a new business process unless at some level we're able to understand the underlying business challenges within the organization. Once we as users realize and understand the challenges faced, we then can be open to hearing about the solutions. We frequently question why we need to change our current system or business processes. It is advisable for organizations to review the challenges faced by their internal business systems and processes and then review the business benefits offered by SAP SRM.

Figure 2.4 illustrates the business impact of strategic sourcing within organizations. According to a study done by A.T. Kearney, procurement organizations spend as much as 85% of their time on activities such as answering basic supplier inquiries, or processing purchase orders and change orders that do not create added value. With SAP SRM, their purchasing professionals (buyers, contract administrators, etc.) can focus their efforts on building strategic supplier relationships and streamlining the procure-to-pay process.

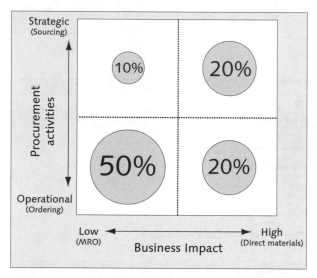

Figure 2.4 Operational Procurement Focus vs. Strategic Sourcing Opportunity

Example

Organizations using SAP SRM empower end users to keep track of their orders using real-time status checking. Requisitioners do not have to call the purchasing department to find out the status of their shopping cart request; they can use the Check Status application in SRM to monitor the status of their order. Using the Biller Direct application, your organization can enable suppliers to view the status of their invoices and view in real time what payments have been disbursed. This reduces drastically the time spent by the purchasing and accounts payable departments in handling end user and supplier calls.

2.3.1 Opportunities and Business Benefits Within SAP SRM

Solutions driven solely by technological enhancements only provide a siloed response to the competitive and strategic needs of organizations today. World-class business solutions need to use advancements in technology as a strategic advantage to provide solutions that cater to the unique business processes that exist in organizations.

Organizations that are leaders in their markets and industries are better at using IT to enable business strategy. The SAP SRM solution provides benefits that exist in three realms, which are listed as follows and illustrated in Figure 2.5:

▶ Process benefits

▶ Technology benefits

▶ People benefits

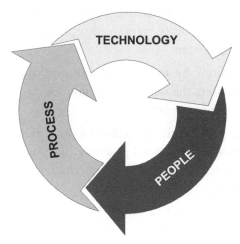

Figure 2.5 The Three Realms — Process, Technology, and People

2.3.2 Process Benefits

SAP SRM is based on SAP best practices that stem from proven business and industry expertise. In addition, with the SAP SRM solution, SAP provides a wide range of pre-configured business scenarios that organizations can quickly deploy and benefit from with improved efficiency in their business processes. Let's examine some process benefits now:

▶ Overall reduction in requisitioning, order processing, and supply-management cycle time are a direct result of the streamlined procure-to-pay processes within SAP SRM.

▶ Efficiencies in business process eliminate costly process-related errors and increase productivity by implementing adequate internal controls.

▶ SAP SRM replaces manual procurement processes with a streamlined requisitioning and approval process. Delays caused by lengthy manual approvals are replaced by faster electonic workflows and online status displays.

▶ Web-based catalogs provide a quick and easy mechanism for finding nego-tiated goods and services, comparative prices, and required attributes. Additonally, catalog-based selection ensures compliance with approved vendors.

▶ An Internet-based request for proposal (RFQ) and bidding process reduces the source evaluation cycle time.

▶ Greater visibility of the historical spending data reduces the source deter-mination time. Purchasing professionals can optimize sourcing decisions based on such criteria as past supplier performance data to determine the best source for goods and services. This helps to continously enhance the sourcing knowledege within the organization.

▶ Synchronization of back-office functions by integrating with corporate finance and ERP systems. SAP SRM offers the capability to integrate with one or many SAP and non-SAP back-end systems.

▶ Improved contract compliance and governance are achieved by driving spending towards selected suppliers with negotiated products and prices. Spending analysis within SAP BW matches contracts with purchase trans-actions to monitor off-contract spending

2.3.3 Technology Benefits

SAP SRM provides real-time integration with ERP as the backbone, ensuring real-time data validation across SAP modules like Financial Accounting and HR. Let's take a look at some technology benefits:

▶ Web-based requisitioning, bidding, and supplier interaction provide ease of use and increased collaboration across the supply chain.

▶ Out-of-box, ready-to-use workflow templates promote reduce implemen-tation efforts.

▶ SAP SRM replaces paper approvals with online approvals, reducing the processing time drastically. It also provides greater visibility and aware-ness with an electronic audit trail.

▶ Email integration with standard mail clients such as Microsoft Outlook or Lotus Notes provides greater productivity and user acceptance.

▶ Pre-delivered Business packages within SAP Enterprise Portal provide end users with a single interface for all purchasing needs.

▶ Better on-demand reporting and improved compliance.

▶ Flexible and scalable architecture and implementation scenarios provide organizations the opportunity to configure for their specific business requirements.

▶ Integration technologies such as XML and Supplier Networks promote opportunities to standardize supplier adoption.

▶ Users only require a Web browser to access the functionality in SAP SRM. This in turn reduces end user maintenance costs with a lower total cost of ownership (TCO).

2.3.4 People Benefits

Benefits for the organization's users are listed here:

▶ Streamlined Wizard and *Extended Form* requisition navigation in SAP SRM provide a solution for both casual and power users.

▶ Online *check status* provides users with real-time visibility on the status of their requisition and reduces time-consuming follow-up.

▶ Professionals within the purchasing organization can focus on strategic supplier relationships and contract negotiations instead of requisition processing.

▶ Online supplier catalogs in SAP SRM ensure that users can quickly search for goods and services. This greatly reduces the need for intervention by purchasing professionals for negotiated goods and services ordered from these catalogs.

▶ An intuitive Web-based interface provides the similarity of online applications like Office Depot and Grainger, easing change management and training.

▶ A single interface to all the procurement functions allows users to focus on their tasks and activities improving productivity. Additionally, Business Packages for SAP SRM provide the ability to direct information to different user group on an individual basis, which increases productivity and enhances user acceptance.

In SAP's recently published *SAP SRM Statement of Direction 2005*, SAP outlines the business benefits of SAP SRM and describes how SAP SRM addresses the business challenges faced by organizations today. Table 2.1 is an excerpt from the document.

Capability	Business Need	Business Benefit
Sourcing	Gain visibility into and actively control more spending categories and manage demand; ensure compliance across business units and supply base	Better sourcing decisions that optimize overall value contribution from suppliers
Procurement	Simplify, standardize, automate, and integrate the procure-to-pay process	Streamlined procure-to-pay process with less administration and more efficiency, resulting in elimination of errors, increased productivity, reduced cycle times, and lower processing costs
Supplier Enablement	Enable the supply base to collaborate and work more effectively	Increased adoption of e-procurement practices through scalable supplier-connectivity capability

Table 2.1 Some Business Benefits of SRM

Organizations interested in reading the statement of direction can download a copy from SAP's website at *www.sap.com/solutions/business-suite/ srm/brochures*.

Now that you are familiar with the key benefits of SAP SRM, let's use the next section to further dissect the SAP SRM solution. In Section 2.4 I will introduce three key concepts, which are:

▶ Core supply processes

▶ Business scenarios

▶ Technology components

Let's proceed with this now.

2.4   Dissecting my SAP SRM

There are a few terms and concepts that we need to define in order for you to properly understand the makeup of SRM. SAP constantly changes the SRM framework and often introduces new concepts for arranging the constituents SRM. Fundamentally there three key concepts to understand: core supply processes, business scenarios within each core process, and underlying technology components that enable the business processes.

It should be noted that for the implementation of each business scenario, one or more SAP components or third-party applications might be required. For example, the Supplier Enablement business scenario is powered by a number of underlying technology components, such as, Supplier Self Services (SUS), Biller Direct, Enterprise Portal, Inventory Collaboration Hub (ICH), to name a few.

2.4.1   Core Supply Processes

SAP defines three core supply processes that collectively make up the SAP SRM solution, which are:

▶ Operational procurement

▶ Strategic sourcing

▶ Supplier enablement

Chapters 3, 4, and 5 are dedicated to each one of these core supply processes.

2.4.2   Operational Procurement

Each core supply process has multiple business scenarios that I'll describe here:

▶ **Self-Service Procurement**
Indirect procurement enables your employees to create and manage their own requirement requests. This relieves your purchasing department of a huge administrative burden while making the procurement process both faster and more responsive.

▶ **Plan-driven Procurement (direct procurement)**
This automates and streamlines ordering processes for regularly needed core materials. Because SAP SRM is integrated with planning, design, and order-processing systems, you can link your procurement processes to a plan-driven strategy that gets you the materials you need for core business processes exactly when you need them. Plan-Driven Procurement integrates seamlessly with back-end systems such as enterprise planning and production. The scenario allows you to integrate operational procurement with your existing supply-chain management solution.

▶ **Service Procurement**
E-procurement has produced great opportunities for saving costs in the purchasing process. However, companies generally fail to extend cost saving measures to services, even though services amount to more than 50%

of annual purchasing volumes. The Service Procurement business scenario within SAP SRM covers a wide range of services such as temporary labor, consulting, maintenance, and facility management.

2.4.3 Strategic Sourcing

It is estimated that sourcing accounts for up to 75 % of the total opportunity for procurement savings within an enterprise. The following business scenarios enable the strategic sourcing capabilities within SAP SRM to fulfill supply needs, negotiate supplier contracts, and evaluate supplier performance:

- ▶ **Catalog Content Management**
  This scenario provides a solution for creating, maintaining, and managing catalog content within your e-procurement application. This concept will be discussed in detail in Chapter 6.

- ▶ **Strategic Sourcing and Contract Management**
  This application in SAP Enterprise Buyer provides professional purchasers with a wide range of actions and information to help them source their requirements. As a purchaser, you can use the interface to process the requirements and determine the best source of supply. Once you have done this, you can create a purchase order or contract directly from the sourcing application or SAP Bidding Engine. Save it either locally or in the back-end system, depending on the technical scenario you are using (Classic, Extended Classic or Standalone).

- ▶ **Spend Analysis**
  This is a decision-support application that enables you as a purchaser to analyze your total spending across system and organizational boundaries. You can perform the analyses per supplier, per product or per product category.

2.4.4 Supplier Enablement

Supplier Enablement provides a quick and easy process for suppliers and customers to collaborate along the supplier relationship lifecycle. Supplier organizations can connect to a customer-hosted portal to communicate across a number of supplier related activities. Let's examine them here:

- ▶ **Supplier Self-Registration**
  With this application, organizations can provide a simple Web-based self-registration process for potential suppliers. The main aim for this process is to allow strategic purchasers to identify new suppliers for doing busi-

ness; accepted suppliers can then participate in strategic sourcing events such as bidding and auction events.

▶ **Design Collaboration**
This scenario allows organizations to involve suppliers beginning with the product design stage which enables collaboration on design objects like specifications and bills of materials. Organizations using the product lifecycle (PLM) application can use C-folders to invite suppliers to participate in the design aspect of acquiring specialty products and services.

▶ **Order Collaboration**
Organizations can use the supplier self services (SUS) component to exchange business documents with their suppliers. Purchase orders, purchase order acknowledgements, invoices are examples of some of the business documents that can be exchanged with suppliers using a Web-based application hosted by the customer. Suppliers only require a Web browser to log in to the application and receive purchase orders and can collaborate on all procurement-related activities.

▶ **Collaborative Replenishment**
Collaborative replenishment optimizes the supply-chain performance by enabling suppliers to access customer inventory data and making them responsible for maintaining the inventory levels required by customers through exception-based replenishment.

2.5 SAP Components

SAP components are the underlying technologies that enable the SAP business scenarios. The key SAP components are listed below and described in some detail in the remainder of Section 2.5:

▶ SAP Enterprise Buyer (SAP EBP)

▶ SAP Bidding Engine

▶ SAP Supplier Self-Services (SAP SUS)

▶ SAP Catalog Content Management (SAP CCM) or SRM-MDM Catalog

▶ SAP Business Information Warehouse (SAP BW)

▶ SAP Exchange Infrastructure (SAP XI)

▶ SAP Enterprise Portal (SAP EP)

Let's explore these in more detail now.

2.5.1 SAP Enterprise Buyer (SAP EBP)

SAP EBP promotes *self-service* procurement. It is a Web-based solution that provides the complete procurement process for the procurement of both direct and indirect goods and services. The process begins with the creation of a *shopping cart* and ends with the entry of an *invoice*. SAP EBP is the execution hub for the majority of processes within SAP SRM, as shown in Figure 2.6.

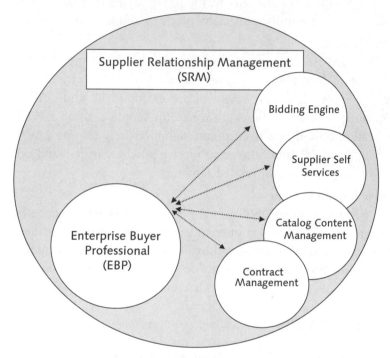

Figure 2.6 Enterprise Buyer — Execution Engine in SAP SRM

Most organizations initiate their supplier-relationship management journey with implementing the EBP component in SAP SRM. Once implemented, EBP acts as a catalyst for all the other components. For example, the SAP CCM component is not used by itself; instead, users creating shopping carts or purchasing professionals creating purchase orders in EBP use catalogs to quickly search for and order products and services.

2.5.2 SAP Bidding Engine

The Bidding Engine is an Internet solution that provides organizations the ability to strategically source and obtain optimal prices for goods and services. Tools such as RFx, Auctions, Reverse Auctions, and Bid Evaluation enable organizations to create and process bid invitations and Auctions to source products and services. Suppliers access the bid invitations using a Web browser where they can submit bids and access all the details of the bid.

As an example of how organizations might use the Bidding Engine capabilities is as follows, let's say your company wants to replace all the existing computers because they're getting outdated and wants to purchase state-of the-art laptops for all 5,000 users in the organizations.

This type of a purchase could cost an organization anywhere from $75,000 – $100,000 just in equipment purchase, apart from the services and maintenance cost. Organizations could use the SAP Bidding Engine to invite a select group of suppliers such as Dell Corporation, IBM Corporation or HP. to a Bidding Event where they would get competitive bids electronically. Your company can then evaluate the bids received in an electronic manner based on a number of different criteria and select the most suitable supplier to contract the purchase.

2.5.3 SAP Supplier Self-Services (SAP SUS)

Supplier Self-Services, or SUS, is a hosted Internet solution that provides an integrated application for organizations to collaborate with their business partners. A Web browser such as Internet Explorer is all that is required for accessing SAP SUS. This offers smaller and mid-sized suppliers the opportunity to electronically integrate the procurement processes without the need for their own sales systems. SUS provides hosted order-management capabilities, including purchase-order processing, goods-receipt confirmation, invoice entry and the ability to view the payment status.

Organizations can invite strategic suppliers that are smaller in size and those that do not have the capability to exchange business documents electronically using XML or EDI. By enabling smaller suppliers with supplier self-services capabilities, your organization can ensure that documents are delivered to the supplier electronically via a hosted solution. Supplier organizations can assist in order collaboration and can acknowledge the PO receipt and delivery of the goods and services electronically, alleviating the manual efforts required by your purchasing department.

Also, suppliers can enter invoices electronically using SUS, and these can then be sent to the appropriate individuals in your organization for proper approvals using workflow prior to payment. This can reduce the manual efforts for your accounts payable department to enter invoices.

2.5.4   SAP Catalog Content Management (CCM)

SAP CCM is a new solution offering as of release SAP SRM 4.0 that enables organizations to manage enterprise and supplier content. Users can search for products and services using a robust search tool with added flexibility to search cross-catalogs, comparisons, and get detailed information on products or services. SAP CCM is a competitive offering to the widely used BugsEye and Emerge products offered by Requisite. SAP support for Requisite products expired in 2005. This means that organizations that have been using the Requisite applications with the previous SRM releases will have to decide whether to implement SAP CCM or enter into a new independent contract with Requisite.

Additionally, your organization might need to evaluate whether it will implement SAP CCM or NetWeaver Master Data Management (MDM), given that SAP has announced the strategic shift in content-management strategy in May 2006. SRM- MDM Catalog will be the strategic content-management offering by SAP beginning in Q4 2006, and all new SRM customers are being advised to implement SRM-MDM catalog instead of SAP CCM. There will be some confusion for customers on the selection of the right catalog solution. Chapter 6 will help clarify this for you.

2.5.5   SAP Business Information Warehouse

Business Information Warehouse (sometimes shortened to Business Warehouse or BW) is a packaged, comprehensive business-intelligence (BI) product centered around a data warehouse that is optimized for (but not limited to) the R/3 environment from SAP. SAP BW is an integral component of the SAP suite of applications with an added advantage of being a software package that can be used in both SAP and non-SAP environments.

It is important to note that all analytics in SAP SRM are powered by the business warehouse. This is one reason why SAP's BI solution is integrated as a component within the SAP SRM solution offering; organizations really need to implement to enable analytics in SRM. The positive aspect for organizations is that they can quickly use more than 100 reports and queries that are provided via the standard content in BW for SAP SRM. SAP pre-delivers these reports for SAP SRM that can be used out of the box.

2.5.6 SAP Exchange Infrastructure (SAP NetWeaver Exchange Infrastructure)

SAP NetWeaver Exchange Infrastructure (SAP XI) provides open integration technologies that support process-centric collaboration among SAP and non-SAP applications, both within and beyond enterprise boundaries. SAP XI is a middleware solution that organizations can use to exchange data between SAP SRM and business partner systems or electronic marketplaces, over the Internet. SAP XI is used in SAP SRM, to integrate processes between SAP EBP, SAP SUS, and SAP CCM.

Organizations that want to exchange business documents such as purchase orders, acknowledgements, and invoices electronically via XML or EDI with their suppliers need to implement the SAP XI component.

2.5.7 SAP Enterprise Portal (SAP NetWeaver Portal)

SAP NetWeaver Portal unifies key information and applications to give users a single view that spans IT siloes and organizational boundaries. With the SAP NetWeaver Portal, you can quickly and effectively integrate SAP solutions, third-party applications, legacy systems, databases, unstructured documents, internal and external Web content, and collaboration tools.

2.6 Summary

Thus far, we have talked about supplier relationship management in general and have briefly defined the SAP SRM solution. In this book, we will try to describe in detail the functionality available in SAP SRM. Chapters 3, 4, and 5 focus on SAP supply core processes: operational procurement, strategic sourcing, and supplier enablement respectively.

In Chapter 3, we discuss in detail operational procurement, which is primarily enabled using the EBP component. We will introduce the concept of the shopping cart in SRM, which is similar to a requisition in SAP R/3. In addition, we discuss in detail the business scenarios: Self-Service Procurement, Plan-Driven Procurement, and Services Procurement.

The aim of operational procurement is to effectively manage the procurement activities in organizations from purchase to payment.

3 Operational Procurement

Let's begin this chapter by defining procurement and then operational procurement. We defined procurement in Chapter 1 as the process of managing activities associated with a company's need to procure the goods and services required to either manufacture a product or to operate the organization. The process of procurement typically differs from one company to another.

> **Note**
>
> Procurement processes within a government institution may have unique regulatory requirements, which might be different compared to a non-governmental company such as Intel. However, the need to purchase is the same across all the organizations; to efficiently support the company business.

Procurement activities are often divided into two distinct categories, which are:

- Direct: Production-related goods
- Indirect: Non-production-related goods and services

When we talk about direct procurement, we are referring to raw materials or production goods that directly affect the production process within an organization. An example of raw material would be coal. Coal is primarily used to generate electricity. Therefore most energy companies purchase coal as a raw material to produce energy in one form or another.

In contrast, indirect procurement deals with the purchase of goods and services to support maintenance, repair, and operating (MRO) activities within the organization. Indirect procurement also encompasses procurement of capital goods and services for the organization as well. Some examples of indirect procurement would be the purchase of spare parts for a shop-floor machine, office supplies such as paper and pencils, and an MRI machine for a hospital.

Operational procurement refers to the effective management of all procurement activities within an organization, both direct and indirect. However, most organizations that have implemented SRM solutions or are evaluating these solutions have initially targeted management of their indirect spending.

Most organizations that have already implemented SAP SRM or are planning to implement it in the future begin with the process of automating their core procurement processes. It is amazing to see many large organizations that are leaders in their industries having largely inefficient internal procurement processes within their organization. It seems as though they have been so busy trying to gain a competitive edge over their competition that they've worked on everything but controlling their internal spending and laggard processes.

In Figure 3.1, you can see an example of what the core procurement process still looks like at many organizations today (or used to for companies that have already moved ahead with SAP SRM).

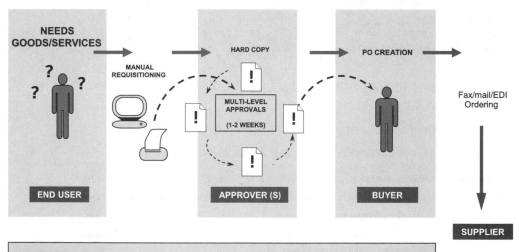

Figure 3.1 Traditional Procurement Process

In the process illustrated in Figure 3.1, the requisition-to-delivery time amounts to days and sometimes weeks, making the overall procurement process very inefficient. Because of the manual processes involved, the visibility to the end user and the buyers is very poor. In most organizations, delays happen because movement of paper-based requisitions require multiple levels of authorization and budgets and commitments either have to be checked manually. In non-public organizations, there may be no budget checks at all.

Organizations implementing an operational procurement solution expect the following key benefits:

▸ Elimination of inefficient processes; standardized and automated procure-to-pay processes

▸ Reduction in overall procurement costs; control over maverick buying

▸ Reduction in the overall requisition-to-pay cycle time

▸ High user adoption via a simple easy-to-use procurement application

▸ Reduced dual entry and error rates

▸ Increased user and regulatory compliance

According to a study done by the Warwick Business School, some organizations spend a whopping $84 in requesting and processing a purchase order (PO). The same study found that this number could be reduced to approximately $31 if an efficient e-procurement system and its processes were implemented. Figure 3.2 illustrates this finding.

Function	Traditional Process	E-procurement
Requisition Generation	66.76	29.2
Requisition Distribution	7.36	0.0
Order Generation	8.87	1.5
Order Distribution	1.87	0.0
Expediting	0.91	0.3
Goods Receipt	3.83	1.5
Invoice Processing	10.40	0.7
TOTAL	**100.0**	**33.2**

The above table, taken from a report by Warwick Business School, highlights the administrative costs of a traditional procurement system compared with the costs of e-procurement (using the manual system costs as the base index (= 100)

Figure 3.2 Administrative Costs of Traditional Procurement Systems vs. e-Procurement

The procurement capability of SAP SRM automates purchasing transactions for goods and services. It is designed to help companies reduce costs by automating and streamlining the purchasing process, connecting buyers and vendors, and controlling corporate spending. Figure 3.3 illustrates at a high-level the procurement capability of SAP SRM.

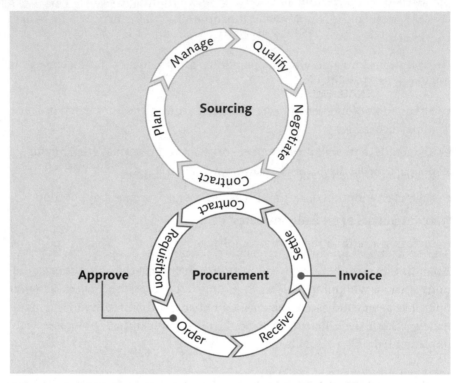

Figure 3.3 SAP SRM Closes The Loop Between Procurement and Sourcing (Source: SAP America)

Within operational procurement there are three main business scenarios, illustrated in Figure 3.4. Note that when we talk about operational procurement in SAP SRM, we are primarily referring to the Enterprise Buyer (SAP EBP) component. SAP EBP was introduced in Chapter 2.

In the remainder of this chapter, we will discuss in detail the functionality available within each of the three business scenarios illustrated in Figure 3.4: self-service procurement, services procurement, and plan-driven procurement.

Let's now move on to learn about self-service procurement.

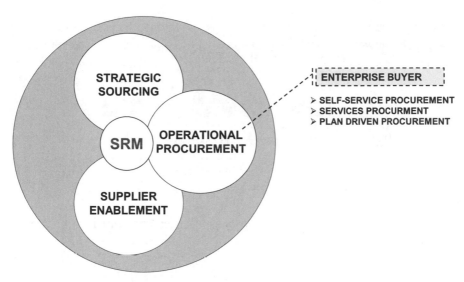

Figure 3.4 Operational Procurment in SAP SRM

3.1   Self-Service Procurement

The self-service procurement business scenario is designed to empower users in the organization to be self-sufficient in ordering day-to-day goods and services without buyer intervention. It provides end users with the appropriate tools to find the items they need via easily searchable product catalogs that have been pre-negotiated by procurement professionals.

Self-service procurement enables your employees to create and manage their own requirement requests. This relieves your purchasing department of a huge administrative burden while making the procurement process both faster and more responsive. It ensures compliance and reduces process costs by decentralizing the procurement process while maintaining central control, allowing purchasing professionals to focus on managing relationships instead of transactions. The main objectives for self-service procurement are as follows:

▶ To increase the speed of procurement and reduce overall costs

▶ To provide an integrated purchasing environment

▶ To foster and maintain compliance

Simply put, the self-service procurement process can be described by five easy steps illustrated in Figure 3.5. We will discuss each of these process steps in detail in the subsections that follow.

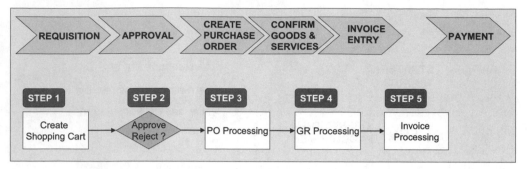

Figure 3.5 Self-Service Procurement Process

Let us begin with Step 1 of self-service procurement, which is to **Create Shopping Cart**.

3.1.1 STEP 1: Create Shopping Cart

Many organizations are still using manual paper-based forms for their requisition process. Even those that are using electronic media still seem to be separating, their requisition applications from their purchase-order creation application. This prevents users from accessing any pre-negotiated contracts or supply sources in ways that could reduce unnecessary administrative work by the procurement departments. SAP SRM streamlines this procurement process. Let's start by reviewing the requisitioning process in SAP SRM, as illustrated in Figure 3.6.

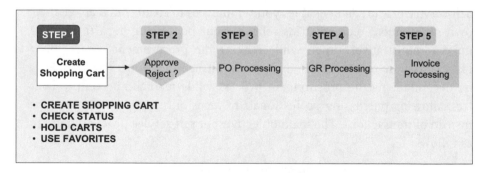

Figure 3.6 Requisition Process — Creating Shopping Carts

There are many definitions of a purchase requisition, but in its simplest form a requisition is *a written, printed or electronic request for something that is needed*. In SAP SRM, a requisition is created using a shopping cart. The shopping cart application is split into a number of different areas so let me begin by describing some of these.

As of release SAP SRM 3.0, the user interface for the shopping cart application has changed considerably from previous releases. SAP has created flexible options for organizations to choose from when it comes to creating a shopping cart.

In the *Shop* application, three user interfaces have been developed with different types of user in mind. These three user interfaces are called Wizard, Extended Form, and Simplified Form. Before we dive into explaining these three different shopping cart forms, let us talk about some of the global functions within the shopping cart application that are independent of the shopping cart form. Understanding these will help when discussing the details of the shopping cart.

User Settings (my Settings)

The settings function allows users to review and set their personal settings such as email address, address information, and assignment of attribute defaults. These settings act as default values that are automatically entered in each new shopping cart created by the user. In the shopping cart, the user still has the ability to override these defaults if needed. Figure 3.7 illustrates the settings application.

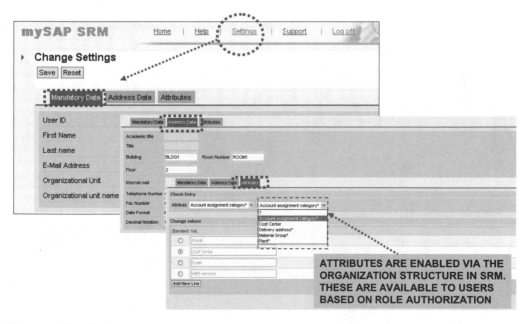

Figure 3.7 User Settings

The **Mandatory Data** tab allows users to review and set information such as First Name, Last Name, and E-Mail Address. The **Address Data** tab allows users to set a default Building, Room Number, and Floor, which can then be used as a default in the shopping cart. The **Attributes** tab allows users to set a default value for attributes that are available in the Attribute drop down.

For example, in Figure 3.7 the user has selected **Cost Center** as the default Account assignment category. This means that when this user creates a shopping cart, the default account assignment category will always be a **Cost Center**. Attributes are enabled via the Organizational Structure in SRM. The attribute concept is discussed in detail within Chapter 8.

Extended Details

As a part of the overall design of the Shopping Cart, Check Status, Approval, and other applications within SAP SRM, SAP has provided the **Extended Details** option. This enables the user to expand the screen to view additional details for that section. In standard use, the details are hidden and if the users want they can click on **Extended Details** to expand this section for additional information. This is shown in Figure 3.8.

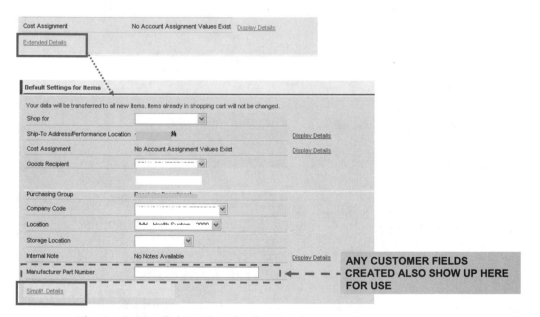

Figure 3.8 Extended Details in the Shopping Cart

Search

Users can use the search function in the various SRM applications to search for documents, using criteria such as document number, description, etc.

The search function is always constructed in the same way and can be displayed as **Simple Search** or **Extended Search**, as illustrated in Figure 3.9. The Simple Search generally contains the most commonly used fields that you can use to specify your search criteria. The Extended Search provides additional search criteria that you can use to target the information you require more precisely. The selection of entry fields available depends on the chosen application and on the role assigned to you. For example, in Figure 3.9, a user cannot search using a shopping cart number in the simple search Only the extended search provides the number of shopping cart field.

Figure 3.9 Search Function

Approval Preview

As a part of the overall design of the shopping cart, confirmation entry, PO, invoice entry, and other applications, SAP has provided the **Approval Preview** function. This allows users to preview who needs to approve their shopping cart (or other documents), and users can additionally add reviewers or approvers to influence the approval process.

The example in Figure 3.10 shows that there are multiple approvers for this shopping cart. The first approver is **APPROVER1 — MANAGER**, and the next approver will be **APPROVER 2 — COMMODITY**. The ability to view all those in the approval chain promotes a self-service approach and allows the end user to be more knowledgeable. The user can also add additional approvers or a reviewer using the **Add Approver** and **Add Reviewer** buttons.

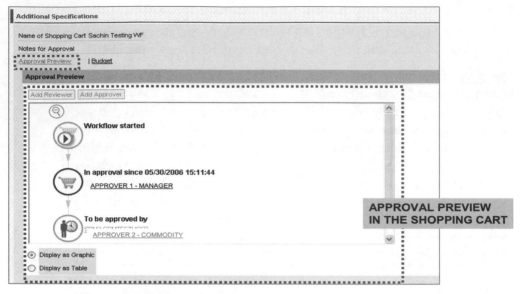

Figure 3.10 Approval Preview

> **Note**
>
> Figure 3.10 shows the approval preview displayed as a graphic. As of release 2007 (SRM 6.0) the graphical view is no longer available, only the table view is provided.

Hold Functionality

The Hold functionality allows users to temporarily save a document for processing at a later time or date. This is helpful if users are creating documents such as a shopping cart and adding multiple items. If the user has not completed a shopping cart, he or she can put it on Hold so that it can be accessed at a later date and time.

One example would be a situation where a user is awaiting response from the vendor on a particular quote for items within the shopping cart. Figure 3.11 illustrates this functionality. The held shopping carts can be accessed using the Check Status application. For example, in Figure 3.11 the shopping cart Number 1000121225 has a **Status** of **Held**. You can click on the magnifying glass in the Action column to access this shopping cart and make any further changes.

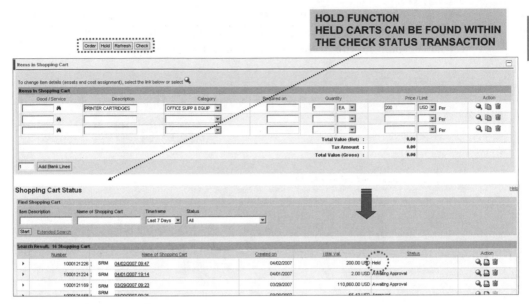

Figure 3.11 Hold Functionality

Check Functionality

The Check functionality was introduced in the SAP SRM 3.0 release, and works to check the documents for errors. These checks could be standard system checks provided by SAP, or organizations can use their own business rules to include checks for documents.

One example of the standard system check is for *Cost Assignment*. A shopping cart cannot be completely saved if the user has not specified a valid Cost Assignment. Therefore, if the G/L account or cost center is invalid, the system will issue an error message. An example of a check that an organization might want to include is whether shopping carts with zero dollar values are allowed. In the standard design, shopping carts of zero value can be created.

The check's results are displayed either in the bottom of the screen or on the top of the screen, depending on the type of document. In the shopping cart, the checks are typically provided on the top of the screen, however in the PO they are in the bottom of the screen. A message with a red icon indicates an error, a message with a yellow icon indicates a warning, and a message with a green icon is an informational message.

Figure 3.12 illustrates checks within the shopping cart. In the shopping cart the end user can click on the **Check** button to determine whether the shopping cart is completed free of any errors. In our example in Figure 3.12, a system message is issued with a red icon **No G/L account was entered. Enter a G/L account**. This indicates that the user has not provided a general ledger (G/L) account in one of the line items in the shopping cart.

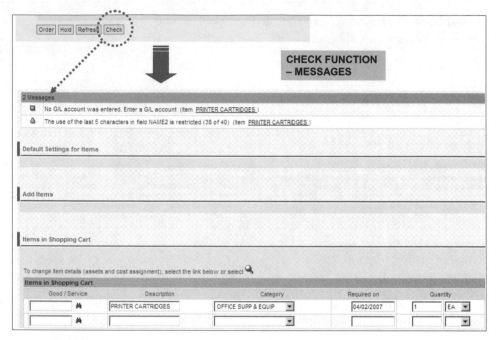

Figure 3.12 Check Functionality

Save or Order Functionality

In all documents created in the SRM system, once the document entry is complete the end user needs to either select the option to **Save** or **Order**. The Save and Order buttons perform the same function. For example, in the shopping cart, users click the **Order** button once they have completed their shopping carts and are ready to order. However, during approval of a shopping cart the approvers click on the **Save** button to complete their action of approval or rejection.

Change Functionality

The change functionality allows users to change the documents such as shopping carts, PO that have already been created. This allows you the flexibility to make changes to these documents while they are in approval. However, it is very important to know that document changes can only happen until a particular point.

For example, the shopping cart can be changed while it is in approval, but once all approval steps have been created, the shopping cart no longer can accommodate any changes. Many organizations expect the shopping cart to be changed even after a PO has been created, but this is not possible. Once a PO has been created, any further changes are only allowed in the Purchase Order application; the shopping cart can no longer be changed.

For example, if the requisitioner finds out from the vendor that they can only deliver half the quantity within the specified delivery date, assuming that the PO has been created, at this point the end user cannot make any change to the shopping cart, only users that have authorization to change POs can make further changes.

The **Change** button is found at the bottom of the shopping cart screen, and at the top of many other documents such as the POs or contracts (see Figure 3.13 for illustration). Note that, based on user authorization, approvers can make changes to the documents as well. For example, if an approver needs to make a change to the Cost Center used in a shopping cart, he or she can make changes to the shopping cart during the approval process as long as he or she has the appropriate authorizations.

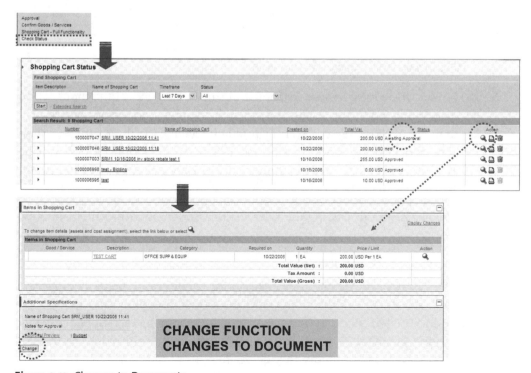

Figure 3.13 Changes to Documents

Once changes are made to the document, a change history is created in the shopping cart, which is especially useful from an audit perspective. Figure 3.14 illustrates this capability.

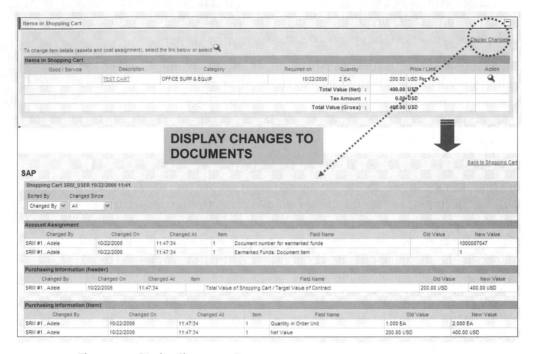

Figure 3.14 Display Changes to Documents

Now that we have an understanding of some of the global functions within a shopping cart, let us discuss the different shopping cart forms that are available in SAP SRM. We will start by briefly reviewing the three different shopping cart interfaces and then discuss in detailed the various areas available within the shopping cart application, such as **Default Settings for Items**, **Add Items**, and **Item Details**.

We begin with discussing the Wizard-based shopping cart form.

Shopping Cart: Wizard

The Wizard is the default user interface for employees. It helps employees to find, select, and add goods or services to their shopping carts quickly and easily. This wizard interface is ideal for casual shopping cart users, those who request goods or services occasionally. This interface provides users with three easy steps to follow that guide them in completing their request for ordering goods and services. This allows the user to view graphically the particular stage of the purchasing process they have reached, as illustrated in Figure 3.15.

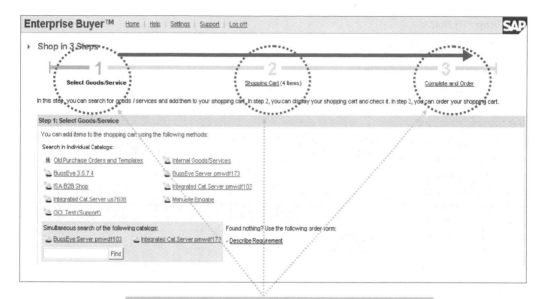

Figure 3.15 Wizard-Based Shopping Cart (Source: SAP America)

Each of these three steps in the Wizard-based shopping cart is explained in the following bullet points. In Step 1, you can search for goods or services and then add them to your shopping cart. In Step 2, you can display your shopping cart and check it. In Step 3, you can order your shopping cart. Let's take a closer look at these three steps now:

1. **Select goods or services**

   This step allows users to select goods and services and add them as items in the shopping cart. Users can add one or more items within their shopping carts from a variety of sources such as electronic catalogs, **Old Purchase Orders and Templates** and **Internal Goods or Services**. If users are unable to find required goods or services, then they can simply describe their needs using the **Describe Requirement** option. This is sometimes referred to as *free-text* or *free-form text* shopping cart where a user simply describes their requirement, as illustrated in Figure 3.16. In the figure, we show that the end user can click on the **Describe Requirement** link, which opens a new section allowing the user to provide a **Description**, **Quantity**, **Price** and **Required on** date for the requirement.

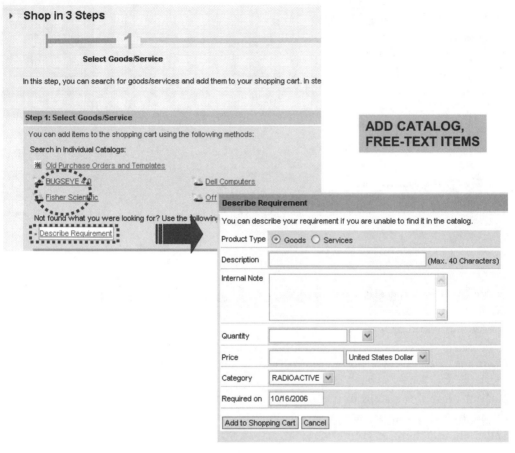

Figure 3.16 Wizard Shopping Cart — Free Text Item

2. **Shopping cart**

   In this step, users can review their overall shopping carts and make any changes, such as update quantities in the Quantity field. Additionally in Step 2, users can review the details of each line item and provide additional details such as account assignment information, attachments, or notes to buyer or suppliers, as illustrated in Figure 3.17. In our example, there are two line items in the shopping cart with a total value (Gross) of $200.93 USD.

The end user can make additional changes in the Item Details section within the Basic Data, Cost Assignment, and other areas as illustrated in Figure 3.17.

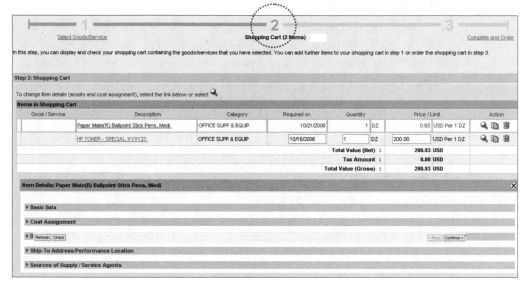

Figure 3.17 Wizard Shopping Cart

3. **Complete and order**

The user has completed their shopping cart and is now ready to place the order, as shown in Figure 3.18. At this point he or she has the option to check if any approval is needed for this order by clicking on **Approval Preview**. Also, the user can enter any notes for the approver in the Notes for Approval section.

Figure 3.18 Wizard Shopping cart

Now that we understand how the Wizard-based shopping cart works, let's discuss the Simplified form of creating a shopping cart.

Shopping Cart: Simplified Form

The Simplified Form allows users to create a shopping cart in one-single form interface, where the navigation style is vertical. This navigation interface has been created with the frequent user in mind. Instead of creating the shopping cart one step at a time, the user can quickly create a shopping cart in a single step, as illustrated in Figure 3.19.

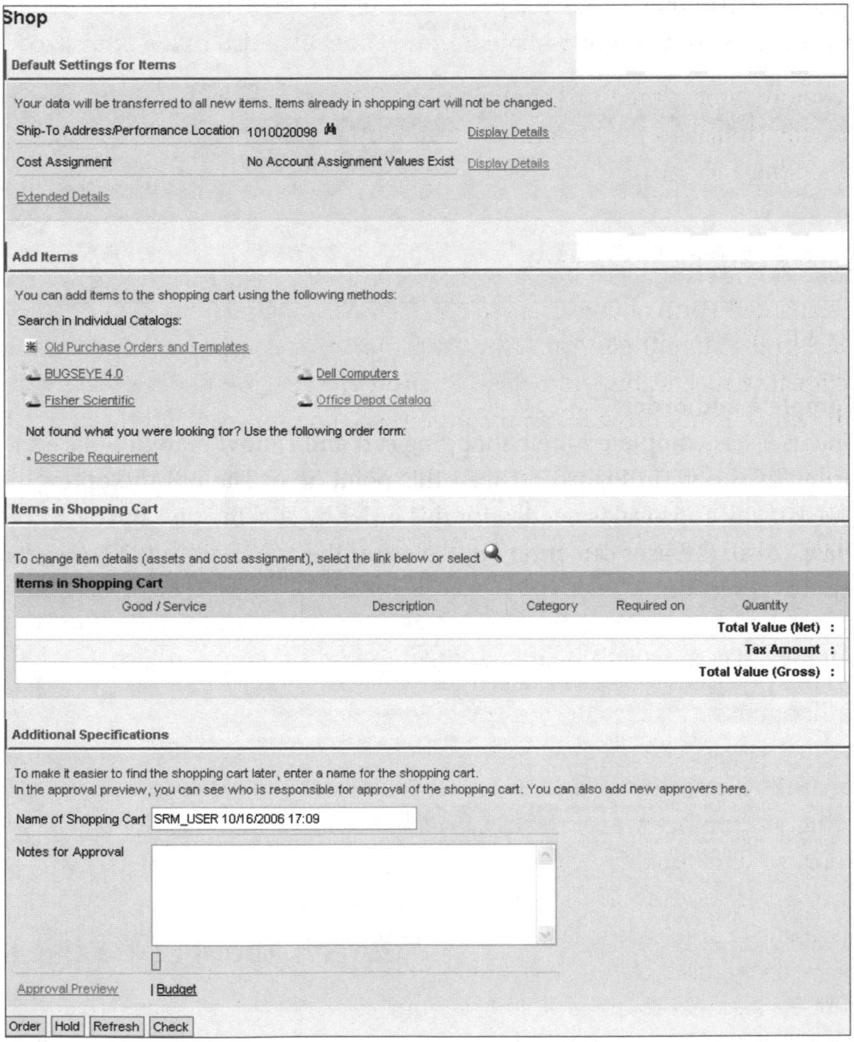

Figure 3.19 Simplfiied Form — Shopping Cart

The end user is able to view the **Default Settings for Items** section, which was not available in the Wizard form. They can use the **Add Items** section to **Search in Individual Catalogs**. As they add items to the cart, users can view the line items in the **Items in Shopping Cart** section. They can look at the **Approval Preview** or add notes for the approver in the **Additional Specifications** area of the form.

However, this navigation style does not provide users the functionality to create shopping carts for ordering services using **Create with Limit** (discussed later). Additionally, the Simplified Form interface does not allow users to create shopping carts using products (material master) on the overview screen. Another disadvantage of the Simplified Form is that it does not allow users to use the **buy-on-behalf of** functionality, also called **Shop For**.

Let us now discuss the third shopping cart form, the Extended Form, which is visually similar to the Simplified Form but provides much more functionality for the end user.

Shopping Cart: Extended Form

The Extended Form allows users to create a shopping cart in a single screen similar to the simplified form. However, this form also provides additional functionality such as buy-on-behalf, **Request external staff,** and **Create with Limit**, which is not provided in the other two shopping cart interfaces.

The Extended Form is suitable for users that are fairly comfortable with online shopping. These users like the ability to create multiple line items in a single screen without going back and forth as in the Wizard interface. Also, users working in professional form can quickly access the four sections within the shopping cart:, **Default Settings for Items**, **Add Items**, **Items in Shopping Cart**, and **Additional Specifications**, as illustrated in Figure 3.20.

The shopping cart is displayed as a table-style list that includes an easy entry form that is particularly useful for items that a user might enter regularly. Figure 3.21 illustrates the additional capabilities available to end users when creating a shopping cart using the Extended Form. They can use the **Requests** and **Order** functionality within the **Add Items** section to request external staff or other services. They can use **Create Limit Items** in order to create a shopping cart line item with a fixed maximum amount for a product or service. Also, the user can quickly enter a material or product number in the **Good/Service** field to create a line item using the product master (material master) in SRM.

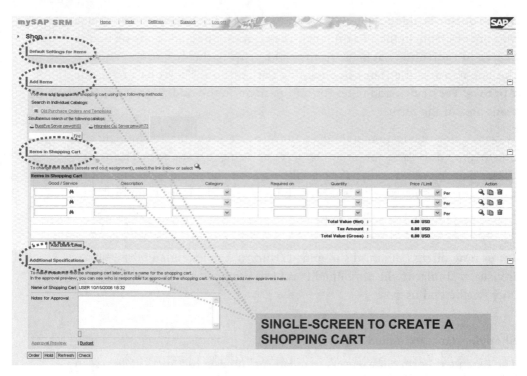

Figure 3.20 Extended Form — Shopping Cart

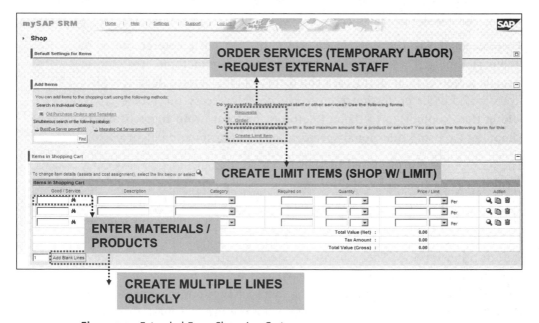

Figure 3.21 Extended Form Shopping Cart

SAP SRM allows organizations to enable all three user interfaces within a single production environment. Each of the interfaces has its own transaction in SRM, namely: BBPSC01, BBPSC02, and BBPSC03. Based on roles and authorizations, the business can decide which users get access to the Wizard, Simplified Form, or the Extended Form. It is important to note that, although this is technically feasible, most companies do not enable all three shopping cart forms. There are multiple reasons for this, training and on-going support being the most frequent.

These different shopping carts user interfaces are assigned to users via roles in SAP SRM (e.g., employee user, secretary, professional purchaser).

Depending on the role assigned to a user, that user can access the appropriate forms. Review Chapter 11 on security to understand how roles and authorizations impact a user's access within SAP SRM. Additionally, review Appendix D on custom development and BAdIs to see what other options organizations have to override the standard user-interface settings provided by SAP.

So far, readers have learned that the shopping-cart application has three different forms: Wizard, Simplified Form, and Extended Form. Now we will dive deeper into the shopping cart application by discussing about the different areas within the shopping cart. The shopping cart application is divided into four distinct sections: **Default Settings for Items**, **Add Items**, **Items in Shopping Cart**, and **Additional Specifications**. Let's begin our discussion with the **Default Settings for Items** section.

Default Settings for Items

This section of the shopping cart provides users assistance with quick data entry; entries that you make here are copied to the shopping-cart line items. This is useful for users when creating a multi-line shopping cart because it ensures that the same information is not keyed in multiple times. As an example, let's say you needed to order some office products: printing paper, toner, and notepads. You need to charge the costs of these goods to your department in the **Default Settings for Items** section (see Figure 3.22). You can enter the **Cost Assignment** for your department, and when you add the three line items (paper, toner, and notepads) the Cost Assignment is automatically copied to all three line items, assisting the user in quick data entry.

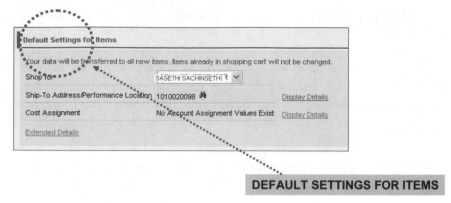

Figure 3.22 Default Settings for Items

> **Note**
>
> Once you have started to create line items within the shopping cart, any changes to the default settings do not affect the shopping cart. Only settings made prior to adding items in the shopping cart are copied to all line items.

The default setting also provides the functionality to order products on behalf of other users. In previous SRM releases, a separate transaction was available for this function, called *Buy on Behalf of*. The functionality offered is still the same but is accessed via the **Default Settings for Items** section instead of an entirely separate transaction.

The Buy on Behalf of functionality is also called **Shop for**. This functionality allows authorized users the ability to purchase goods or services on behalf of their colleagues or managers. The approval process invoked in the system is based on the Shop for user, therefore compliance is still achieved. Additionally, users for whom the order is placed can still continue to create the confirmation and the invoice for the products bought on their behalf. Figure 3.23 illustrates the **Shop for** functionality.

> **Note**
>
> The users for whom individuals can shop must be specified as values in the attribute REQUESTER in the Organizational Structure. This is further explained in Chapter 8.

As a standard, the **Default Settings for Items** section is only available within the Extended Form shopping cart. However, organizations using the other forms: Wizard or Simplified Form can activate the Default Settings for Items section via the Change Display in Shopping Cart BAdI (BBP_SC_MODIFY_UI).

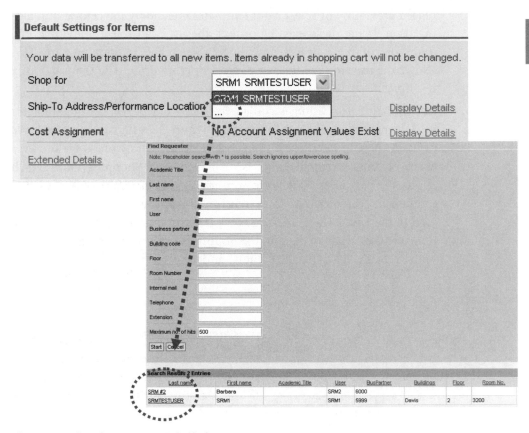

Figure 3.23 Shop for or Buy on Behalf of

Project teams interested in this functionality should work with their development teams to activate and code this BAdI. Also review Section D.2.1 in Appendix D to get more information about this BAdI. Let us now discuss the Add Items section of the shopping cart.

Add Items

In the Add Items section of the shopping cart, the requisitioner can select goods and services using a few different methods such as **Old Purchase Orders and Templates**, **Search Internal** and **External Catalogs**, and using the **Describe Requirement** function. The following bullets points explain these methods in further detail:

▶ **Old Purchase Orders and Templates**
  Once the user is in within a shopping cart, he or she can click the **Old Purchase Orders and Templates** function to search for orders that were

placed previously or select from templates created by the central purchasing team. Using these existing orders, the user can select individual line items or complete orders and quickly re-create a shopping cart. This allows the user to save time and effort in re-entering data that can easily be copied.

All relevant information is copied from the old purchases or templates into the new shopping cart line item(s). Figure 3.24 illustrates an example of using the **Old Purchase Order and Templates** function. Once the user clicks on this, a search screen is displayed **Find Shopping Cart**, which allows the user to provide search criteria. In our example, we've selected the default search criteria to search for all **Approved** shopping carts created in the **Last 7 Days**. In the **Search Results** area we select the **test** line item and then click on the **Add to Shopping Cart** button. The **test** line item with at total value of **10 USD** will be added to our new shopping cart.

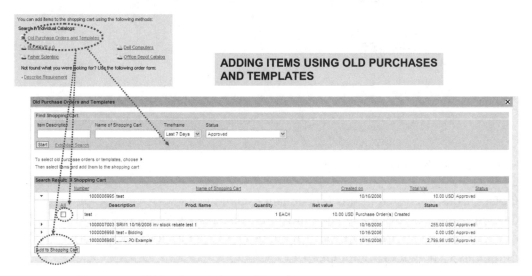

Figure 3.24 Old Purchase Orders and Templates

A template can be used as a reference when creating and processing shopping carts. Individual items or entire shopping carts can be transferred from old POs and templates to a new template or shopping cart. These are usually useful when processing recurring procurement transactions.

For example, suppose a department administrator orders a set of products from an office-supply vendor on a monthly basis. In such a case, purchasing professionals can define templates that can be used by employees as references when creating and processing their shopping carts. In the standard design, users need the Purchasing Assistant or Purchaser role assigned in order to create templates.

The template creation process is very much like creating a shopping cart with small differences. For instance, there is no cost assignment functionality when creating a template because it's supposed to be generic for use across all departments that have access, as illustrated in Figure 3.25.

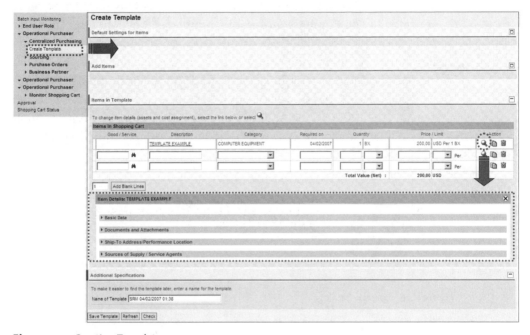

Figure 3.25 Creating Templates

▶ **Search Internal and External Catalogs**
Users can search both internal and external catalogs to quickly and efficiently search for negotiated goods and services. The benefit of these electronic catalogs is multifold. Users can quickly find products and services using rich search capabilities provided by the catalogs, and once they find what they need, all the information about the product or service is seamlessly transferred back to the shopping cart line item(s). The user does not have to re-type information.

▶ **External Catalogs**
External catalogs are typically maintained by your suppliers and hosted on their systems; users can access these catalogs via the Internet. An example of an external catalog could be Office Depot. Users can seamlessly log on to the Office Depot catalog directly from within

the shopping cart, search for goods, and then bring all the information for the product back to their shopping carts as line items. In Figure 3.26 I illustrate how a user can click on **Fisher Scientific** link to launch the external catalog and search for products.

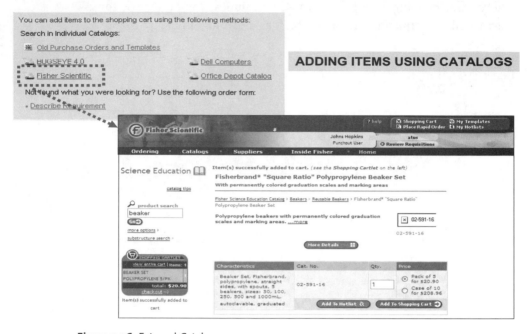

Figure 3.26 External Catalogs

▶ **Internal catalogs**

Internal catalogs are catalogs that are created and maintained by your organization. These could be items that are a part of your existing material master or products that your suppliers have provided you for listing in your catalog. Chapter 6 will introduce readers to the concept of catalog and content management and explain in detail how organizations can use catalogs to drive efficiency in their overall procurement process. Both internal and external catalogs are explained in detail in Chapter 6.

▶ **Internal goods or services**

These are products that are housed within the SRM system (Product Master). The product master represents either a material or a service master. If you have a material or service master in another system, it can be replicated to the SRM system as well.

For example, if you use a SAP R/3 Materials Management (MM) system that contains material masters, you can replicate the material master items from R/3 into SRM as products. Users can search for these products using a selected set of criteria including the Product ID, Product Description, Category, etc as illustrated in Figure 3.27.

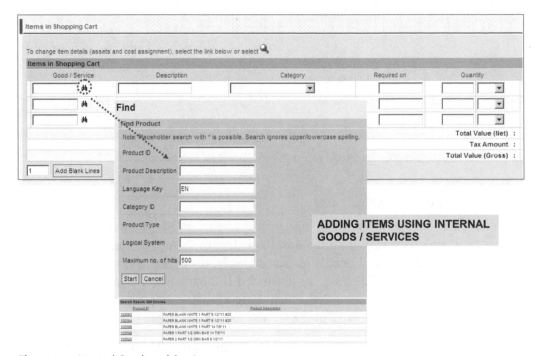

Figure 3.27 Internal Goods and Services

▶ **Describe requirement**

If the requisitioner is unable to find the goods or services they wish to procure in any of the catalogs, a text description can be entered in the shopping cart. Users can click on **Describe Requirement** in the **Add Items** area to enter a free-form text description of what they need. The user needs to provide enough information to the purchasing team so they can find the appropriate vendor and price. Figure 3.28 illustrates the **Describe Requirement** function. Often the requisitioner might actually know the price and vendor who can supply the goods or services and therefore can provide this information in the free-text order.

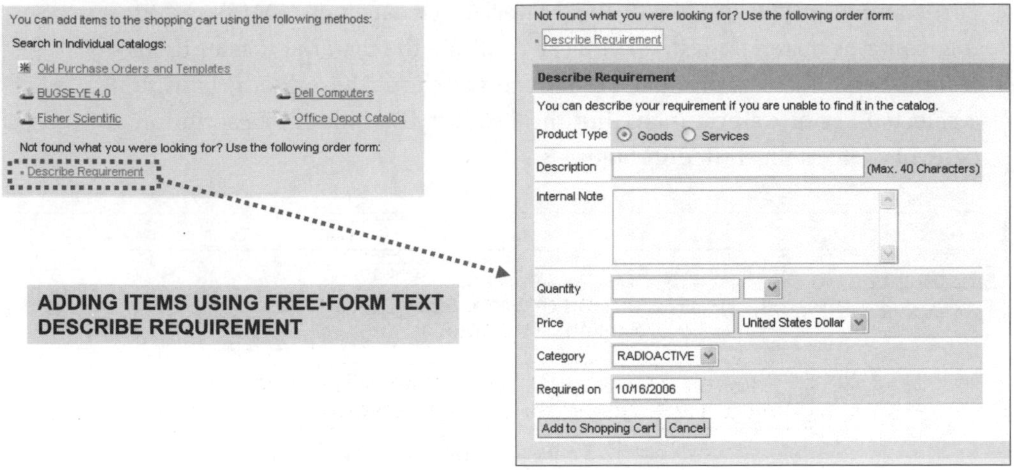

Figure 3.28 Describe Requirement — Free-Form Text Requisition

Items in Shopping Cart

This section of the shopping cart provides users with a running list of items they have added from the **Add Items** functions such as catalogs or old purchase orders and templates. For example, if the requisitioner launched the **Fisher Scientific** catalog as illustrated in Figure 3.26, selected three items from Fisher's catalog, and added those to their shopping cart, then all three items will be available in the section **Items in Shopping Cart**.

In the Extended Form version of the shopping cart, the requisitioner also has the flexibility to directly create line items in the Items in Shopping Cart section. As a default, three blank lines are available for entry in this area and the requisitioner can use them to quickly enter the appropriate product number or item description in the available fields.

Let us use Figure 3.29 to illustrate the Items in Shopping Cart section. The first line item was created by the requisitioner by just entering some information of the required product in the **Description** field. In addition the user can select an appropriate product **Category**, **OFFICE SUPP & EQUIP** in our example. Additional information can be entered in the **Required on**, **Quantity**, and **Price** fields.

The second line item in Figure 3.29 was created by simply entering a product ID **3425** in the **Good/Service** field. This allows the user to enter multiple product numbers in the open line items and quickly create a multi-line shopping cart.

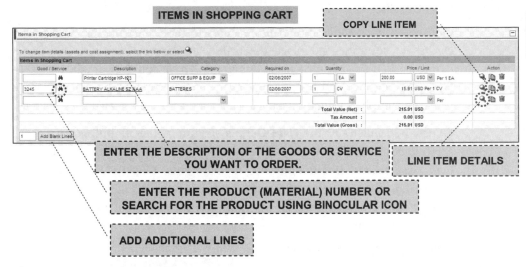

Figure 3.29 Items in Shopping Cart

This is useful when the requisitioner knows the product IDs in the SRM system. Alternately, he or she can click on the binocular icon to search for products or services available within the SRM system.

The requisitioner can also simply copy a line item by clicking on the copy icon in the **Action** column. This is especially useful when the user might want to create multiple line items with the same basic information but with small changes such as **Quantity** and **Required on** date.

In situations when a user needs to provide additional information for the shopping cart line items, such as entering the vendor part number, adding a vendor note, or changing the account assignment details, they can go to the line item details by clicking on the magnifying glass icon in the Action column. The Item Details section is discussed in greater detail in the next section.

Additional Specifications

Once the user is done with adding all items to the shopping cart, he or she can provide some additional information within the **Additional Specifications** section. The Additional Specifications section was illustrated in Figure 3.20. To make it easier to find the shopping cart later, the user can enter a unique name in the **Name of Shopping Cart** field. The user also can view whether an approver is needed for the cart. The Approval Preview functionality was discussed and illustrated in Figure 3.10.

Item Details

Once users have added one of more items to their shopping carts, they can choose to continue and place the order, or they can provide additional details related to their individual line items. These could be details on specifying the location, cost assignment, notes or attachments, or specifying the source of supply for goods or service.

Figure 3.30 illustrates the **Item Details** section of the shopping cart. There are five sections within the Item Details of the shopping cart: **Basic Data**, **Cost Assignment**, **Documents and Attachments**, **Ship-To Address/Performance Location**, **Sources of Supply / Service Agents**, and the **Availability** section. We will discuss each of these sections in detail using the bullet points that follow:

SHOPPING CART LINE ITEM DETAILS

Figure 3.30 Shopping Cart Line Item Details

▶ **Basic data**

This section allows the end user to review and provide additional information pertaining to the shopping cart line item. Figure 3.31 illustrates the fields available on the **Basic data** section of the cart. Notice that the users are unable to select the Purchasing Organization in the shopping cart; this is similar to a purchasing requisition in SAP R/3. If there are multiple purchasing organizations, only the buyer has the ability to select the purchasing organization in the *Process Purchase Order* application.

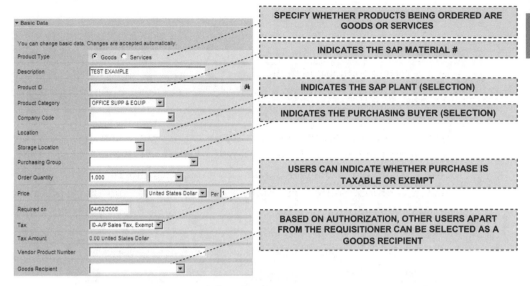

Figure 3.31 Basic Data Section in the Shopping Cart

▶ **Cost assignment**

This section allows users to provide information on where the goods or services being purchased are going to be charged. Users can allocate costs towards a variety of cost assignments available in SAP FI (SAP Financial Accounting). This functionality is defined in detail within Chapter 9, where we discuss integration to SAP Financials. Figure 3.32 illustrates the fields available on the **Cost Assignment** section of the cart. Notice that for ease of use there is a clipboard available to quickly copy and paste the cost assignments. Also, costs can be split across multiple cost allocations by **Percentage**, **By Qty**, or **By Value**.

For each cost assignment, additional detail can be accessed using the magnifying glass in the **Action** column. This could be necessary if your organization is also using a public sector solution and needs to use the **Fund** or **Grant** account assignments fields. Also, if the cost assignment is an **Asset**, the **Subnumber** can only be assigned in the cost assignment details area. Figure 3.33 illustrates the details of the account assignment.

▶ **Documents and attachments**

This section allows users to add **Texts** and **Attachments** to individual line items in the shopping cart. The **Texts** section allows the user to add an **Internal Notes** or **Vendor Text**.

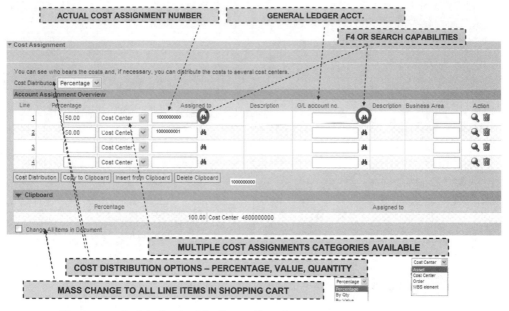

Figure 3.32 Cost Assignment Section — Overview

Figure 3.33 Cost Assignment Section — Detail

The Internal Notes are intended for providing additional information to the buyers and approvers within the organization. These are not printed on the corresponding PO. However, the **Vendor Text** is intended for the use of the vendor or supplier and by default is printed on the PO sent to the vendor or supplier.

Figure 3.34 illustrates the **Documents and Attachments** section of the shopping cart. The **Attachments** area allows the user to attach documents such as Word, Excel, or PDF. **Attachments** can be internal or external, and can be identified using the **Internal** check box. The internal attachments would be for the approvers and buyers internal to the organization and the all other attachments would be sent to the suppliers as information that needs to accompany the PO, such as a copy of the estimate or quote.

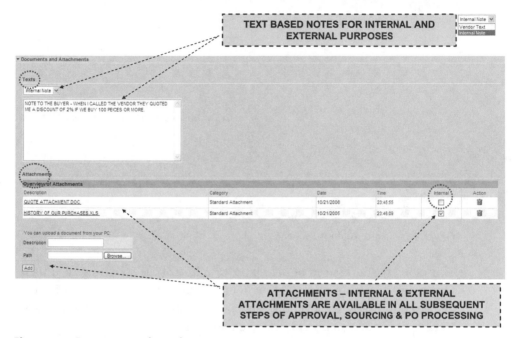

Figure 3.34 Documents and Attachments

▶ **Ship-to address/performance location**
This section allows users to provide a shipping point where the goods/services are to be delivered. Typically, a default ship-to address is populated in the shopping cart. This is based on the Organizational Structure or whether a **delivery-address** attribute was maintained in the **Settings** application illustrated in Figure 3.7. The user can change this ship-to address in certain cases. A list of existing delivery addresses is available to the users based on their organization, or the user can enter a one-time ship to address. Figure 3.35 illustrates the ship-to address section.

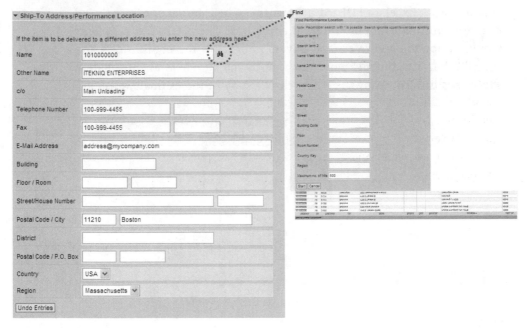

Figure 3.35 Ship-to Address Section

This delivery address can be set up on each line of the shopping cart; therefore users can create multiple line item shopping carts where each is being delivered to a separate location. The plant or location identified in the **Basic Data** section can also provide a default address.

▶ **Source of Supply/Service Agents**
This section allows users to select from pre-defined sources of supply or specify a source to purchase from. Use of pre-defined sources of supply allows the shopping carts to automatically convert into a PO after all approvals are complete and no further buyer intervention is needed. Purchasing organizations utilize this process to alleviate buyers from the non-value processes of creating POs.

If there are contracts or agreements that the organization has set up with vendors for specific products or product categories, those contracts and vendor lists can be available for end users to use seamlessly. This promotes compliance, process improvement, and cost reduction. The following sources of supply are considered fixed in the SAP SRM system. This typically means that buyer intervention is not required if the goods and services are provided using these following sources of supply:

- ► Catalogs
- ► Contracts
- ► Vendor lists

Figure 3.36 illustrates the **Contract** and **Vendor List** as fixed sources of supply. If no pre-defined source of supply is found, users can search the vendor database in SRM and suggest a vendor from which to purchase the goods or services being ordered, as shown in Figure 3.36. In this scenario, the system creates an incomplete PO (locally) or purchase requisition (in the back-end).

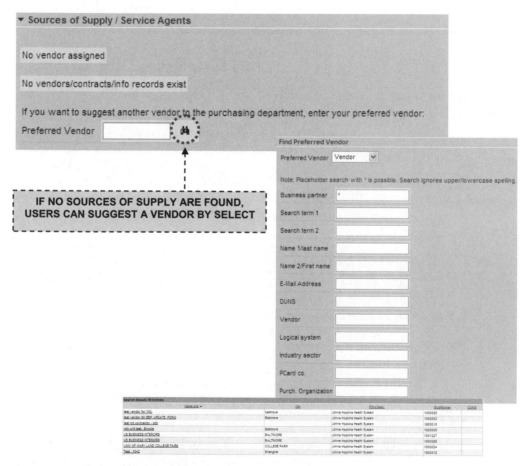

Figure 3.36 Source of Supply — Assign Manually

The SRM system provides all valid possible sources of supply (local sources available in SRM or the SAP back end) for the product or free- text items. If a unique source of supply is found for a product or service, it is automatically assigned; otherwise the user can select from a list of other pre-defined sources. If you do not want to use the source assigned, you can replace it with a preferred vendor. However, these purchases are then sent to the professional buyers to review and complete.

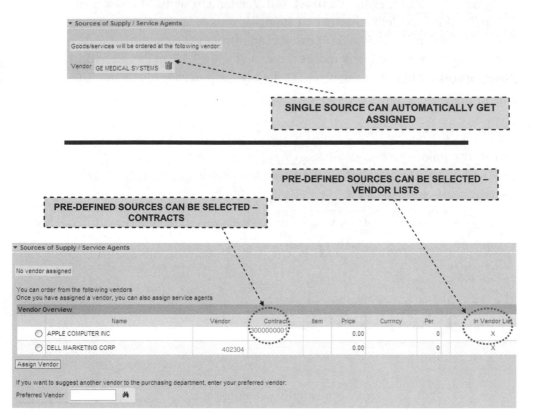

Figure 3.37 Source of Supply — Pre-Defined

Depending on the Customizing settings, the system displays either all vendors or just those in a vendor list. It is important for users to know that when they change a product category, company code, or plant field in the shopping cart, sourcing is re-determined.

▶ **Availability**
This section allows users to review the availability of products; they can check whether the quantity required is available by the requested delivery date. However, this functionality is only valid for product-based purchases; i.e., material master items.

The SRM system provides the ability to check the availability of the products across multiple plants. A list is returned from the check showing the quantity available and date. For example, 100 pieces are available now, and in four days 250 pieces will be available. You can select the plant that can provide the required product quantity.

Now that I have described the Item Details section of the shopping cart in detail, let us learn about how users keep track of the shopping carts they create, using the **Check Status** application.

Check Status

One of the key capabilities of SAP SRM self-service scenario is the real-time access users have to the status of their orders and what stage the orders have reached in the business process. In the Check Status application users can review the follow-on documents that have been created for the shopping cart, such as requisitions, POs, confirmations, invoices, or payment status. Users can use a variety of search criteria available to find their shopping carts, such as the Shopping cart name, number, or status, as illustrated in Figure 3.38.

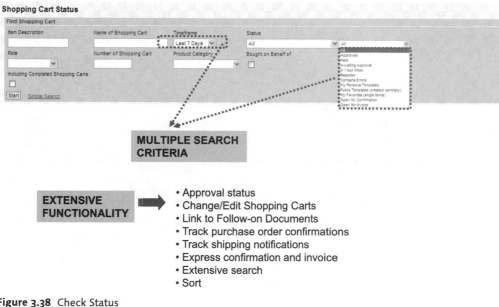

Figure 3.38 Check Status

Users can also check their document status based on Buy on Behalf of functionality or their role as an approver, as shown in Figure 3.39.

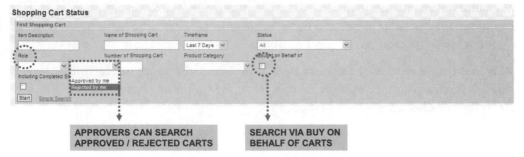

Figure 3.39 Approvers Search for Approved or Rejected Carts

The shopping carts can also be printed via the Check Status transaction. Users can print the shopping cart by selecting the print icon on the shopping cart header, as illustrated in Figure 3.40. Use PDF format when printing a shopping cart.

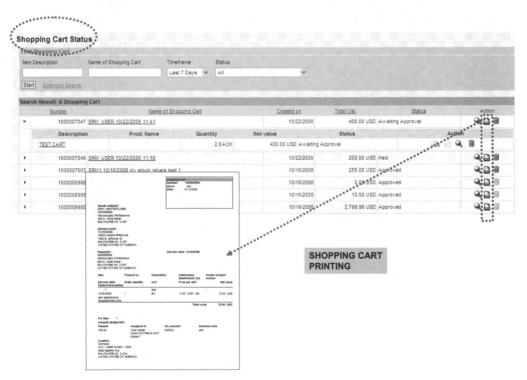

Figure 3.40 Shopping Cart Printing

In addition to the status, users can also execute confirmations and invoices directly from the Check Status transaction (illustrated in Figure 3.41). This functionality was added in the SRM solution beginning in SAP SRM 4.0. These are referred as *Express Confirmation* or *Express Invoice*.

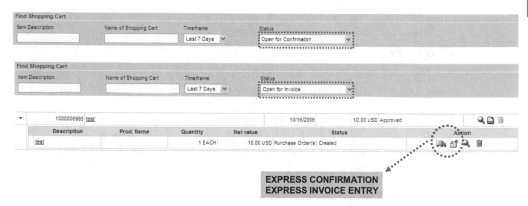

Figure 3.41 Express Confirmation and Invoice Entry

The shopping cart order history is available in a graphical or tabular format within the line item details, as illustrated in Figure 3.42.

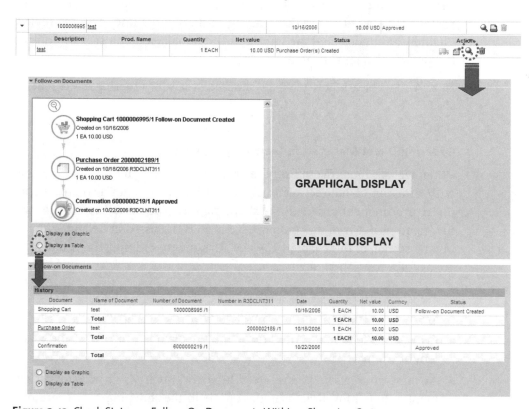

Figure 3.42 Check Status — Follow-On Documents Within a Shopping Cart

As a standard in SAP SRM the following PO types are created as follow-on documents to shopping carts:

- **ECPO PO**
  This is for all Expense item purchases
- **ECDP PO**
  This is for all POs with stock items that need to be received into inventory in SAP R/3 (also called *direct procurement*)
- **Requisitions**
  These can be created for all shopping carts of ECPO document type (given that the classic implementation scenario is configured and a requisition instead of a PO is desired)
- **Reservations**
  This is forfor all shopping cart line items that contain materials or products subject to inventory management, irrespective of whether stock is available in SAP R/3

Organizations can determine what type of document is created in SRM or the SAP backend based on the Customizing settings in the IMG. You can review Chapter 7 to understand the impact of the implementation scenario on the follow-on document creation.

Next, You will learn how to create shopping carts for ordering direct materials.

Ordering Direct Materials in the Shopping Cart

When we talk about the self-service procurement, we typically associate that with ordering of indirect materials. In SAP SRM, we can also create spot direct procurement orders in the shopping cart. The overall direct procurement and plan-driven procurement scenario is discussed in detail in the following section of this chapter. The key attributes of ordering direct materials are as follows:

- This only makes sense for material- or product-based shopping carts.
- When ordered, those products will be received into inventory or stock.
- Instead of the user as a goods recipient, the plant becomes the valid recipient of the materials.
- As these products will be received into stock; there is no account assignment required for direct material orders in the shopping cart. Therefore,

the shopping cart Item Details section does not contain a Cost Assignment section, and the material master Accounting view takes control.

▶ The standard document of ECDP is used when creating the PO.

▶ These orders are created in the back-end materials management system, but any further changes are only possible in SRM.

Users decide when to order a product as Direct by selecting the **Order as Direct Material** button in the shopping-cart line item. This is available within the details of the individual line item. Once this option is selected, it cannot be reversed. Figure 3.43 illustrates the **Order as Direct Material** functionality.

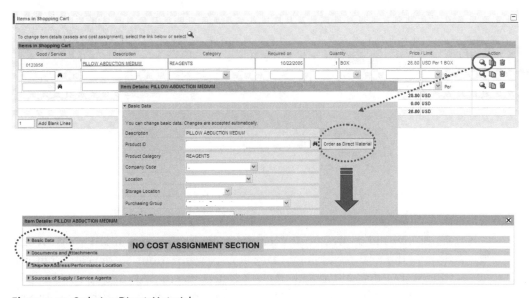

Figure 3.43 Ordering Direct Materials

If a valid and definite source of supply exists (for example, a contract, or vendor list) and the pre-defined approval criterion has been met, a PO will be automatically generated in SRM. Otherwise, the buyer will need to source this shopping cart to create a PO manually.

This concludes **STEP 1** of the self-service procurement scenario **Create Shopping Cart** that we started to discuss in Section 3.1.1. In Section 3.1.2, I will discuss **STEP 2** of the self-service procurement scenario as illustrated in Figure 3.5: **Approve Reject?**.

3.1.2 STEP 2: Approve Reject?

Automated and standardized approvals are the cornerstone of any e-procurement and SRM solution. Timely approvals and notifications help speed procurement execution and provide a documented audit trail. In SAP SRM, organizations can trigger one or more approval steps to gain approvals at different steps within the requisition-to-pay process.

Approval procedures are available upon creation, change, or deletion of a number of purchasing documents including shopping carts, POs, goods receipts, and invoice. Figure 3.44 illustrates **Step 2** of the self-service procurement scenario within operational procurement. You should have already created a shopping cart (Step 1) before this stage.

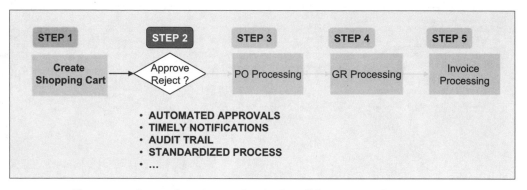

Figure 3.44 Approvals — Automating the Overall Procurement Process

Workflow and approvals provide key functionality within SAP SRM. Workflow is the SAP technology that allows organizations to develop approval procedures that align with their business need. SAP SRM provides predefined workflow templates for organizations to use out of the box. In SAP SRM all applications such as the shopping cart, PO, confirmation, contract, bid invitation, and others use workflow extensively.

A workflow needs to be triggered within the SAP SRM system in order to create a successful shopping cart, and a no-approval workflow can be triggered if approvals are not required. The main point to understand is that workflow play a very important part in the functioning of the SRM system. Chapter 10 introduces and explains role of workflow in SAP SRM. Readers can either directly jump to Chapter 10 now or continue to read the other sections in this chapter and then read Chapter 10 at a later time.

In Section 3.1.3, I will discuss **STEP 3** of the self-service procurement scenario illustrated in Figure 3.5, **PO Processing**.

3.1.3   STEP 3: PO Processing

In the self-service procurement scenario, purchasing professionals aim to empower the end users so they can request for goods and services easily and at the same time access and select from pre-negotiated sources of supply that users can select from. In doing so, they bypass the need for intervention by purchasing professionals. Some of the concepts woven into this section are listed as bullets in Figure 3.45.

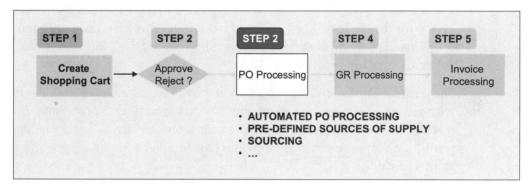

Figure 3.45 PO Processing — Completing and Ordering

Professional buyers can create contracts or vendor lists in the system for products or product categories that users then can select in the shopping cart. In addition, the commodity buyers are typically responsible for enhancing supplier relationships for adding more online catalogs or internal catalogs which users can use to search for goods and services. This allows the buyers to focus on transactions where the requisitioners are unable to find goods or services using the pre-defined sources.

Sourcing and professional procurement involves the core purchasing process of analyzing, qualifying, selecting suppliers, and processing orders. In this section, we're going to concentrate on the PO processing process. The other processes will be discussed in Chapter 4.

The concepts discussed in Section 3.1.3 are based on the idea that the purchasing professionals in your organization (also called buyers) are going to be processing the POs within the SAP SRM system instead of the back-end SAP R/3 system. If your organization plans to implement the Classic Scenario, then the PO processing will be handled in either the SAP R/3 or ERP back-end.

Purchase Order Processing and Order Management

The PO processing functionality in SAP SRM allows professional purchasers to create and maintain POs. Organizations that want to use this functionality need to implement the Extended Classic or Standalone scenario. This functionality is not relevant for the Classic scenario implementations, because in that scenario the professional purchaser's process POs in the SAP MM module.

There is usually confusion about what type of a shopping cart or PO is necessary for the business need of the organization. There are many different shopping carts such as Request, Shop, Shop with Limit, Purchase order. Table 3.1 aims to provide some clarity.

The Process Purchase Order application provides professional purchasers with a worklist containing incomplete POs that need further processing. An incomplete PO is one that requires attention from the buyer. It could be the result of a shopping cart created by the requisitioner needing a price and a source of supply.

The PO is either created automatically by the system or manually by the purchaser. Professional purchasers can select documents from their **Worklist** and either display them using the magnifying glass icon or change them using the pencils icon.

Business Need	Shopping Cart Type	PO Type	Self-Service, Service, or Plan- Driven Procurement
Departments request for items for consumption and expense	Shop	ECPO	Self-service
Purchasing agreement between organization and vendor that goods or services be delivered over a specified period of time for a specified dollar value	Limit	ECPO	Service procurement
Storeroom users that manage an inventory in SAP	Shop	ECDP	Self-service and plan-driven procurement

Table 3.1 Shopping Cart and PO Type

Business Need	Shopping Cart Type	PO Type	Self-Service, Service, or Plan- Driven Procurement
Departments within organization request items stocked within a central warehouse or storeroom within the enterprise	Shop	Reservation document created in R/3	Self-service

Table 3.1 Shopping Cart and PO Type (cont.)

This application also provides a **Find** function, which allows buyers to search from a variety of different criteria. Figure 3.46 illustrates the Process Purchase Order application. The purchaser can also create a new PO by first selecting the type of PO in the **Purchase Order with Transaction Type** drop-down menu and then clicking on the **Create** button.

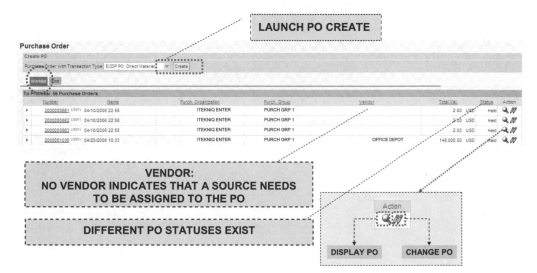

Figure 3.46 Process Purchase Orders

Similar to other documents in SRM, the Process Purchase Order application is split into a two tabs **Header Data** and **Item Data**. Let us begin with explaining the **Header Data** tab

▸ **Header Data**

On the PO header, there are a number of sections available that apply for the entire PO (all line items). These include Purchasing Organization, Purchasing Group, Vendor, etc. If the PO was created from a corresponding shopping cart, the purchaser can change the purchasing organization assignment on the PO if there are multiple purchasing organizations. Please note that the purchasing organization is not available for users to change in the shopping cart or for buyers in the Sourcing application. Figure 3.47 illustrates the **Basic Data** section of the PO header.

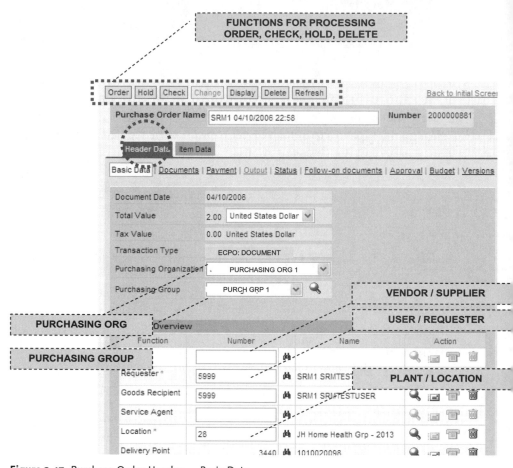

Figure 3.47 Purchase Order Header — Basic Data

A number of the sections on the PO are similar to other documents in SAP SRM, such as Document and Attachments, Approval, Budget, etc. We will discuss the **Payment**, **Output**, **Follow-on documents**, and **Version** sections of the **Header Data** tab in the following bullets:

► **Payment**
In the payment section, buyers can select and change the terms of payment that might be setup with a particular vendor for the PO. Typically,

these terms are defaulted based on the definitions in the vendor master however; these can be changed on a spot basis (illustrated in Figure 3.48).

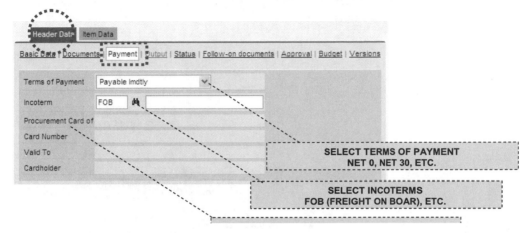

Figure 3.48 Payment Area

▶ **Output**

Once the PO is free of all errors, it can be ordered and sent to the vendor. Typically, the minmum of output is based on the definition in the vendor master record however. Occasionally, buyers might need to output the PO in a different medium or re-output an existing PO again (as shown in Figure 3.49). A output preview is available that displays the PO in a PDF format, and this can be viewed prior to the transmission of the manual POs. Organizations can define their own forms for POs in Customizing.

It is important for organizations to ensure that if the Extended Classic scenario is implemented, then the POs are created in SRM and a copy of the PO is sent to SAP back-end (R/3 or ERP). The output of the PO can only be triggered from the SRM system; no output is triggered from the SAP back-end system for these POs. In SAP SRM, the configuration setting needs to be completed in Customizing to enable document output.

▶ **Follow-on documents**

The follow-on documents section provides details on the documents that might be required post the PO creation. For example, if it is a requirement to receive a PO response from the PO vendor, then this would be selected. Again, typically this information is automatically defaulted based on the vendor master definition, but can be altered by the purchaser in this section. Figure 3.50 illustrates the follow-on documents section of the PO.

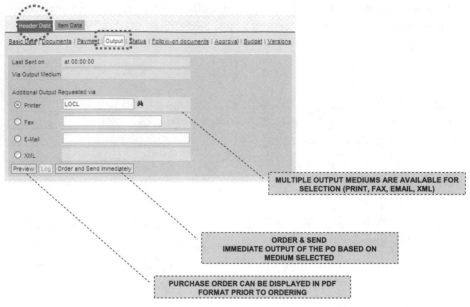

Figure 3.49 Output Area

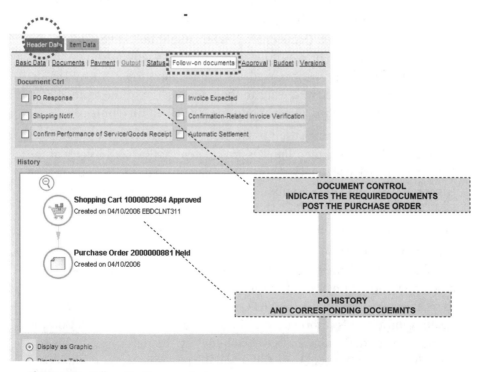

Figure 3.50 Follow-On Documents Area

This also displays the **History** of the PO document and corresponding documents such as the shopping cart, confirmations, etc.

▶ **Versions**

PO changes are made in SAP SRM using the Transaction Process Purchase Orders. Changes made directly to the PO result in the creation of a new version for the original PO. Buyers can then compare the different PO versions. Changes that are initiated by the vendor can be captured using the PO Response (POR) application.

Versioning is an important functionality available in many purchasing documents, including the PO. This allows the capturing of the needed trail of changes made to the PO and allows for quick comparison for changes.

Figure 3.51 illustrates the Compare function within the Versions section. Both the active and histrorical version of the PO has been selected for comparision. The changes are displayed at a header data and item data level. In our example, Version 2 of the purchase order contains a Quantity of 10 which is the change that was made compared to Version C1.

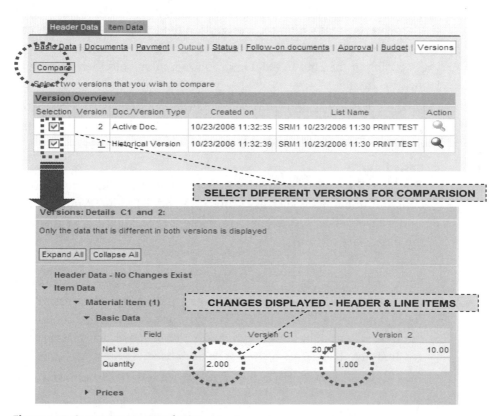

Figure 3.51 Comparing Versions for Documents

Now that readers are familiar with the sections within the **Header Data** tab, let us move on and discuss the **Item Data** tab and the sections that exist within it.

▶ **Item Data**

The **Item Data** tab on the PO can contain one or more line items. All the line items can only be for the same purchasing organization, purchasing group and vendor. The Item Data section is similar to the shopping cart document in SRM as it offers the functionality to create line items using multiple options such as catalogs, internal goods and services, or simply describe the product or service.

Figure 3.52 illustrates the **Item Data** tab within the PO. The line items within the PO Item Data tab contain a lot of fields and typically are not visible in the browser window; you will find yourself scrolling towards the right. Therefore, I have divided the line items so that they are visible on one screen in Figure 3.52.

In the Item Data tab, purchasers can create line items in the same way they do when creating a shopping cart, by entering a product ID in the Product field or entering text within the Description field. Also, the purchaser can add items using internal and external catalogs. This can be done by selecting a catalog in the Find in Catalog dropdown menu and then clicking to launch the catalog.

Once the purchaser is done with entering the line items in the PO, he or she can click on the magnifying glass to review the details of the PO line item. The sections within the item details are discussed next:

▷ **Basic Data**

The Basic Data section provides a detail view of the line item. It contains additional fields such as Incoterm, Vendor Product Number, and Under/Overdelivery Tolerance, to name a few. Figure 3.53 displays the Basic Data section.

▷ **Partner**

The Partner section provides information about the requisitioner (Requester), Goods Recipient, Location, and Ship-to Address. Typically, this information is entered in the Partner Overview section of the **Header Data** tab, but the purchaser can override that information at a line-item level. This section is seldom used.

Figures 3.53 and 3.54 illustrate the various areas within the **Item Data** tab on the PO.

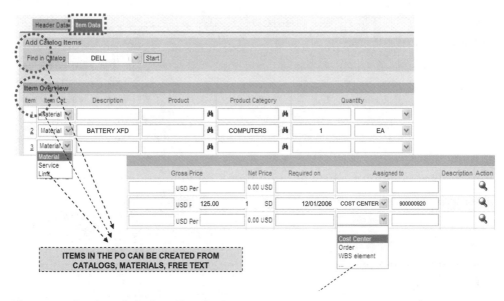

Figure 3.52 Purchase Order Item Data Section

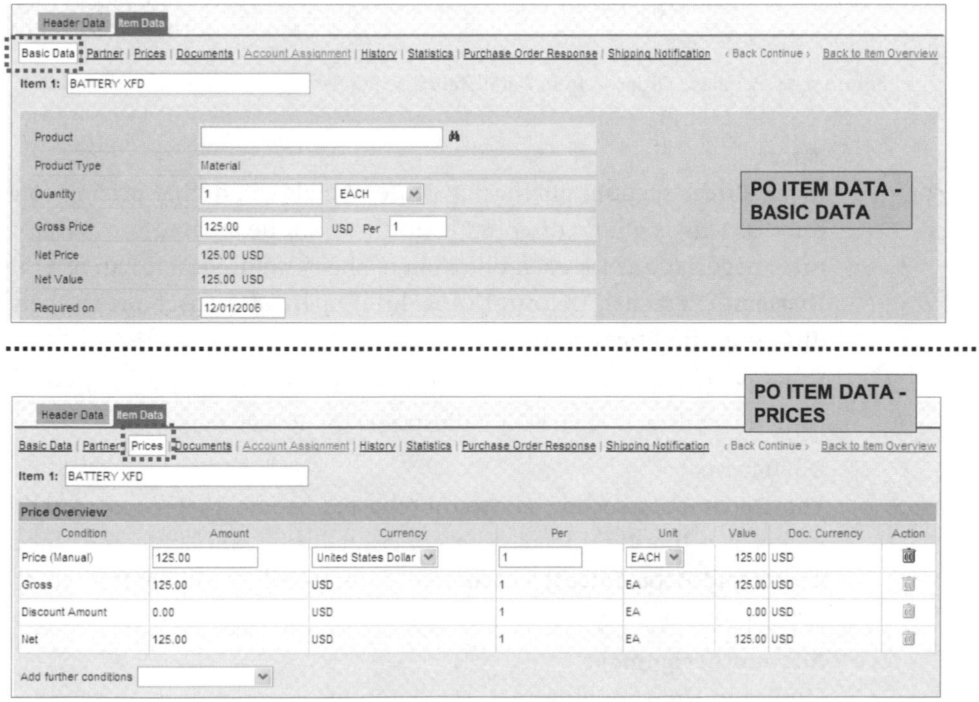

Figure 3.53 Purchase Order — Item Data: Basic Data, Prices

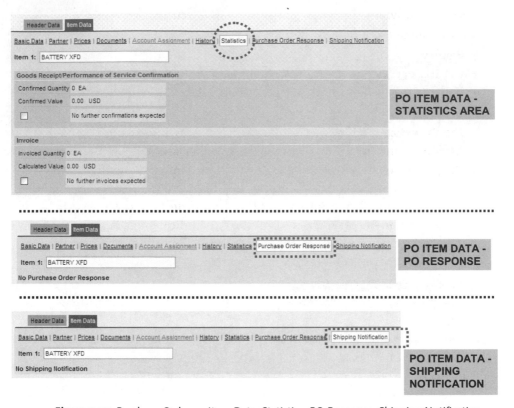

Figure 3.54 Purchase Order — Item Data: Statistics, PO Response, Shipping Notification

▶ **Prices**

In the **Prices** section, purchasing professionals can define pricing conditions. This is where discount conditions can be created for defining price negotiations for each line item of the PO. Purchasers can use the **Discount (Percent)**, **Discount (Absolute)** or **Header Discount (%)** conditions in the Prices section.

If the PO is sourced via a contract, the pricing conditions are adopted from the contract. Figure 3.53 illustrates the **Prices** section.

▶ **Documents**

The **Documents** section allows purchasers to add Notes and Attachments at a line-item level. This functionality is similar to the **Documents and Attachments** functionality discussed in the Shopping Cart application.

▶ **Account Assignment**

Similar to the shopping cart, the PO items can also contain multiple cost assignments with split distributions. The **Account Assignment** section provides the same functionality as discussed in the Account Assignment section of the Shopping Cart application.

▶ **History**

The **History** section provides a graphical and table view of all the documents that have been created relevant to the PO line item.

▶ **Statistics**

The **Statistics** section in the Item Data provides information on the confirmed and invoiced quantity for the particular line item. Purchasing professionals can select the **No further confirmations expected** check box to indicate that no further deliveries are expected from the vendor, essentially closing the PO line item. And they can select the **No further invoice expected** check box to indicate that no further invoices are expected from the vendor. This allows you to close the PO. The Statistics section is illustrated in Figure 3.54.

▶ **Purchase Order Response**

The **Purchase Order Response** (also called POR) functionality was introduced in the SAP SRM 4.0 release. This allows suppliers or purchasing professionals to enter a response from the vendor in regards to the PO sent. When a PO is sent to a supplier for goods or services, the supplier typically acknowledges the receipt of the PO. The supplier may respond for one or more goods or services to acknowledge its receipt, confirm the acceptance of the order with an agreement on delivery dates, quantities and prices, or to propose changes to the PO: Figure 3.55 illustrates the process flow for PO response.

> **Note**
>
> In previous releases, this functionality was termed Order Response/ Acknowledgement. Just as with a shopping cart, PO, the PO response is a separate application in SRM with a Business Object BUS2209.

Purchasers can create a POR manually to attach the changes indicated by the supplier such as delivery dates, prices, etc. This PO response gets attached to a specific PO that was transmitted to the supplier. From then on, creation of an auditable document can be tracked and followed up independently of the PO that was sent by the organization. Figure 3.56 illustrates the POR application. In the PO response application, the professional purchasers can search across multiple **Status** categories such as **Party Confirmed by Vendor**, **Rejected by Vendor**, **Variance in Purchase Order Response**, and others shown in Figure 3.56.

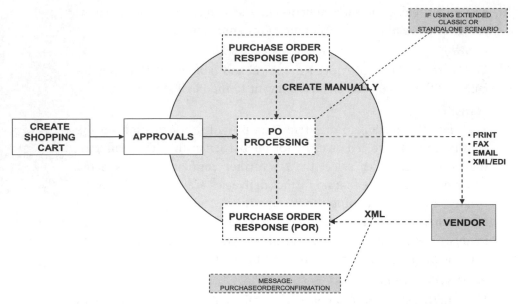

Figure 3.55 Purchase Order Response

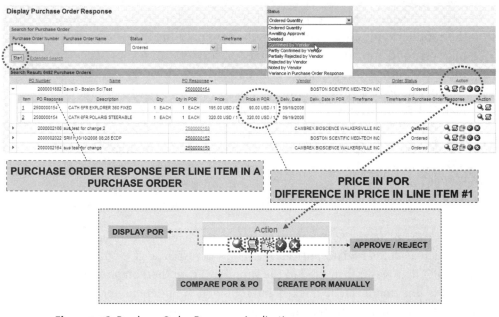

Figure 3.56 Purchase Order Response Application

When processing a PO response the professional purchasers have the capability to create a POR manually, approve or reject, or compare the PO to the POR.

If the purchaser selects the Accept all or Reject all icon in the **Action** column, a POR is automatically created with the status of Accepted or Rejected for all the line items in the PO. When comparing the POR against the PO that was sent to the vendor, a version log is available for tracking and comparison, as illustrated in Figure 3.57.

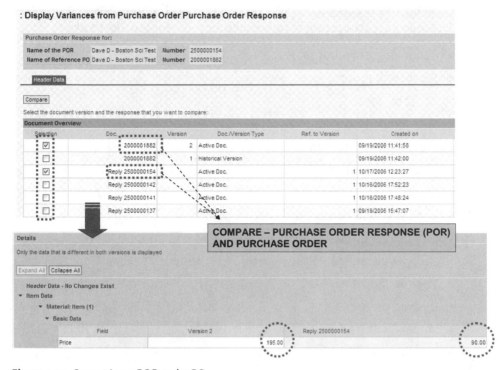

Figure 3.57 Comparing a POR and a PO

Alternately, if the suppliers have the ability to acknowledge the PO electronically, SRM can receive XML PO responses and display them automatically in the purchaser's worklist. This worklist also shows the document status such as **Party-confirmed** if there are changes by the supplier. This functionality is also available for suppliers to process in the Supplier Self-Services application (SUS). This application is a component within the SAP SRM solution and will be discussed in detail in Chapter 5.

Up to this point I have explained the header and item data tabs within the Purchase Order application in detail and you should be able to describe the different sections within these tabs.

I will conclude this section by addressing the splitting criteria used during the creation of a PO. In SAP SRM Purchase Orders can be created manually or via an existing document such as a Shopping Cart or External Requirement (e.g., Materials Resource Planning).

Manual POs are not affected by the splitting criteria, when only a PO is created using an existing document. If a local PO is generated in SRM from an existing shopping cart, it could result in one or more POs based on the line item detail of the shopping cart. This results from the split criteria of the POs. The following criteria are used for splitting a PO in SAP SRM 4.0:

▶ Purchasing organization

▶ Purchasing group

▶ Company code

▶ Procurement card company

▶ Procurement card number

▶ External quotation

▶ Logical financial system

▶ Logical system that is the source of an external requirement

▶ External requirement item number

▶ Subtype (extended, local scenario)

▶ Vendor

▶ Desired vendor

▶ Ship-to address fields

▶ Document type or process type

This concludes **STEP 3** of the self-service procurement scenario **PO Processing** that we started to discuss in Section 3.1.3. In Section 3.1.4, I will discuss **STEP 4** of the self-service procurement scenario illustrated in Figure 3.5: **GR Processing**.

3.1.4   STEP 4: GR Processing

Many organizations are lax about the process of goods receipt. A three-way match between a POs, goods receipt, and invoice is not mandated. However, companies implementing SAP SRM are realizing the value of implementing this process across their organization. This process provides a check and audit for the goods orders received and payments processed.

In this section I will discuss the goods receipt (known as confirmation) functionality in SAP SRM. Some of the key areas that I will discuss in this section are **Confirmation Entry**, **Express Confirmation** and **Returns** as illustrated in Figure 3.58.

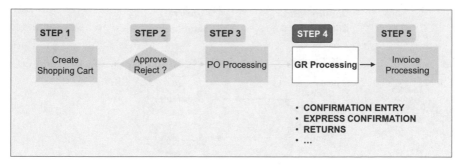

Figure 3.58 GR Processing — Entering Confirmations

In SAP SRM, a confirmation is synonymous with a goods receipt. Users can create a confirmation in SRM, and if a back-end SAP R/3 system is connected, a corresponding goods receipt is created. Depending on your implementation scenario, the organization can choose to create a confirmation in SAP SRM or a goods receipt in the back-end SAP R/3 system. Figure 3.59 illustrates the possible scenarios for creating confirmations in SAP SRM.

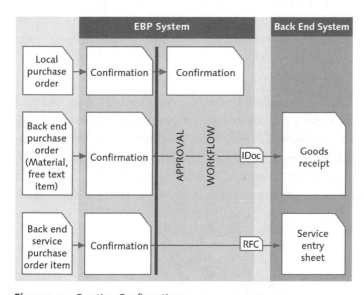

Figure 3.59 Creating Confirmations

Goods receipts and service entry (confirming service related purchases) are performed using the **Confirm Goods/Services** application in SAP SRM. Role-based authorizations control who can receive goods and services, as illustrated in Figure 3.60. The **SC Creator** in Figure 3.60 is the shopping cart creator.

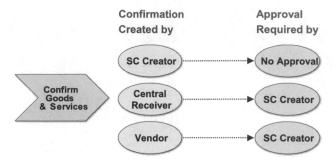

Figure 3.60 Who Can Confirm Goods and Services

Let us discuss the confirmation of goods and services by the shopping creator, central receiver, and vendor in further detail.

Confirmation for Goods and Services by Shopping Cart Creator

The shopping cart creator can confirm goods and services that they requested themselves or that others requested for them, where they are the goods recipient (for instance in the Shop For application). In the shopping cart or PO transactions, the user creating the document defaults as the **Goods Recipient** automatically. However, others can be assigned as recipients instead, as illustrated in Figure 3.61.

Users can either choose the **Confirm Goods/Services** application in SRM, or they can choose the express confirmation icon in the **Check Status** application. The **Confirm Goods/Services** application provides end users more flexibility in creating goods receipts. They can create receipts for multiple POs, multiple lines, receive partial quantities, and also perform cancellations and returns. The Express Confirmation functionality does not provide any of these capabilities. Also, the Express Confirmation icon only allows confirmation of a single item at a time. Figure 3.62 illustrates the **Confirm Goods/Services** application:

Figure 3.62 illustrates how the user can choose to either create a confirmation by selecting the **Confirm Goods Receipt/Services Performed** or display previously created confirmations by selecting the **Display/Process Confirmation**. The most commonly used selection when creating a confirmation is to search by the **Name of the Shopping Cart** or selection by **Purchase Order Number**.

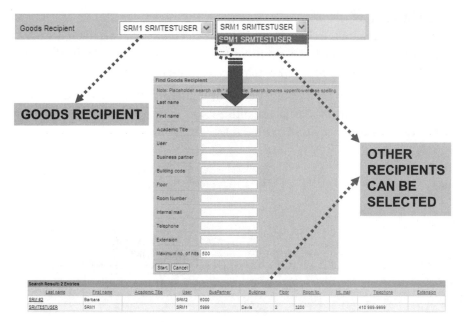

Figure 3.61 Goods Recipient

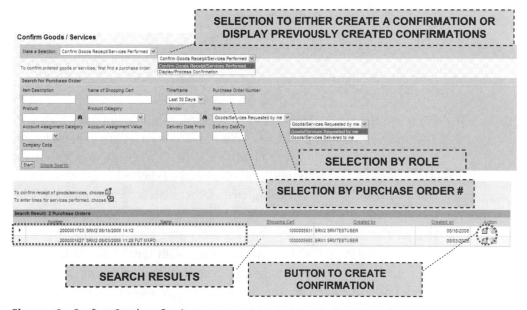

Figure 3.62 Confirm Goods or Services

Once a PO is available in the search results, the confirmation icon in the **Action** column can be used to begin the creation of a Confirmation. I will now explain the key areas within the confirmation application:

▶ **Item Data Tab**

When the **Create Confirmation** action is selected, as shown in Figure 3.62, the process for creating a confirmation is started. As a default, the **Item Data** tab is opened for the PO that needs to be confirmed.

Here the user can receive one or multiple line items at once and also can receive complete or partial quantities for each of the PO lines being received, as illustrated in Figure 3.63.

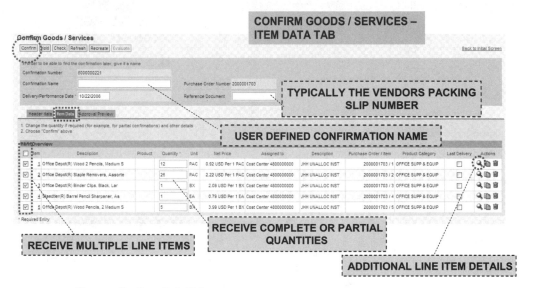

Figure 3.63 Item Data Tab

Users can also set the **Last Delivery** indicator in the **Item Data** tab as well. This indicator is useful when no additional deliveries are expected from the vendor. This is shown in Figure 3.64. In a three-way match scenario where the PO, Goods Receipt, and Invoice are expected, it is important to make sure deliveries are completed. Otherwise, a discrepancy will be found during invoice processing.

▶ **Header Data Tab**

The **Header data** tab allows users to enter additional information about the confirmation entry including the vendor's **Bill of Lading**, the **Goods Receipt Slip**. Additionally the **Header Data** tab allows the user to create notes and attachments in the **Documents** section. Figure 3.65 illustrates the **Basic Data**, **Partner**, and **Documents** section of the **Header Data** tab.

Figure 3.66 illustrates the History and the Status sections of the **Header Data** tab.

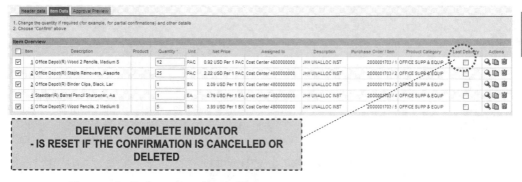

DELIVERY COMPLETE INDICATOR
- IS RESET IF THE CONFIRMATION IS CANCELLED OR
DELETED

Figure 3.64 Delivery Complete Indicator

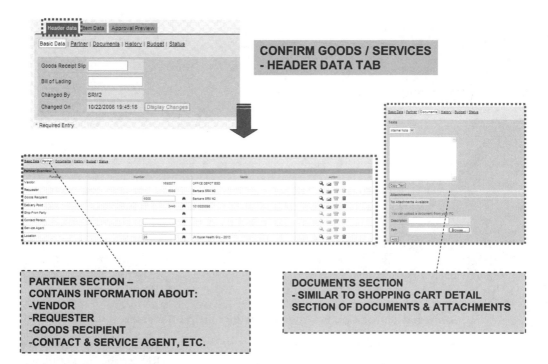

CONFIRM GOODS / SERVICES
- HEADER DATA TAB

PARTNER SECTION –
CONTAINS INFORMATION ABOUT:
-VENDOR
-REQUESTER
-GOODS RECIPIENT
-CONTACT & SERVICE AGENT, ETC.

DOCUMENTS SECTION
- SIMILAR TO SHOPPING CART DETAIL
SECTION OF DOCUMENTS & ATTACHMENTS

Figure 3.65 Header Data Tab

▶ **Approval Preview Tab**

Depending on whether or not the organization wants to use approvals for confirmation entry, the **Approval Preview** tab shows the preview of the approval process if required. Approvers can be added as well. The approval functionality in SAP SRM is discussed in detail in Chapter 10. Figure 3.67 illustrates the **Approval Preview** tab.

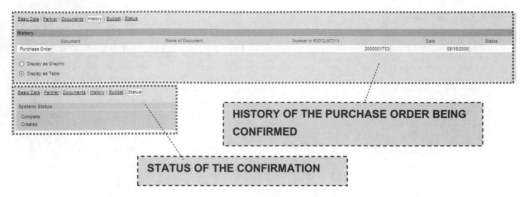

Figure 3.66 Header Data tab

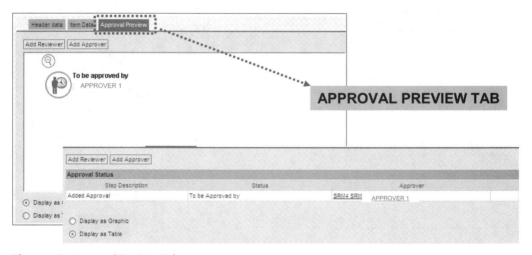

Figure 3.67 Approval Preview Tab

Confirmation for Goods and Services by Central Receiver

Users with the role of a Central Goods Recipient can perform confirmations for all POs. These POs could be ones originated in SRM or the back-end system.

Organizations need to be careful when assigning users' access to Confirm Goods/Services centrally, because there is no ability to restrict the POs that can be received. All POs across all departments and plants can be received by the individual having access to the central role. This role is typically given to users such as administrative assistants who are typically ordering for multiple people and who also serve as a central point for the delivery of goods and services.

If it is necessary to provide this transaction to many users, organizations can use a BAdI to restrict the POs that are available for the central receiver to confirm. BAdIs are development objects that need to be developed based on customer-specific logic.

Cancellation or Returns

Users also have the ability to cancel their confirmation or return goods using the Confirm Goods/Services transaction.

Once a determination is made that an item needs to be returned, the receiver or requisitioner contacts the vendor to obtain a return authorization number. A Return Goods Authorization (RGA) form is completed, indicating the return authorization number, reason for return, and any additional information required by the vendor.

When a return delivery is posted in SRM, a movement type of 122 is posted in the back-end SAP system (if the Standalone scenario is being used, then a local return is posted). It is important to note that this return only posts a transaction in SRM and has no correspondence to the RMA (Return Material Authorization) that needs to be obtained from the vendor. Typically, the individual posting the return should call the vendor to get the RMA number for the return prior to posting it in SRM. Figure 3.68 illustrates a sample process flow for returns.

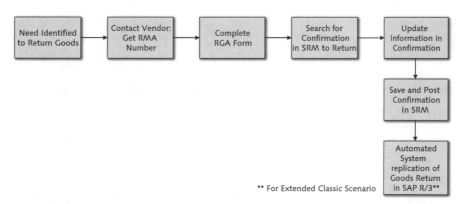

Figure 3.68 Return Goods Process Flow

Users can begin the process for return delivery or cancellation using the Display/Process Confirmation option in the Confirm Goods/Services application.

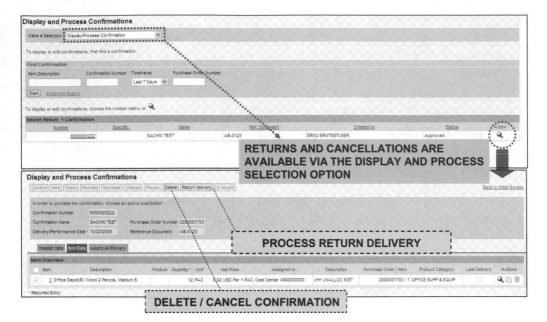

Figure 3.69 Cancellations and Return Delivery

Figure 3.69 shows that the **Return delivery** button can be used to return the previously confirmed product **Office Depot(R) Wood 2, Pencils, Medium 5**. Alternately, the **Delete** pushbutton can be used to delete or cancel confirmation number **6000000222**. Figure 3.70 illustrates the return delivery and cancellation confirmation.

> **Note**
>
> Only confirmations that have not yet been invoiced can be cancelled or changed.

Once the return of goods process is completed in SRM, the user can return the goods to the vendor or ask the receiving dock personnel to return the goods on the behalf of the requisitioner.

Express Confirmation

This functionality provides end users with the ability to quickly create a goods receipt (confirmation). This is especially useful for users who are casual requisitioners and do not want to create the regular goods confirmations. This function supports the self-service scenario in that it provides the end users with the ability to complete the entire purchase process from shopping cart to invoice-entry seamlessly.

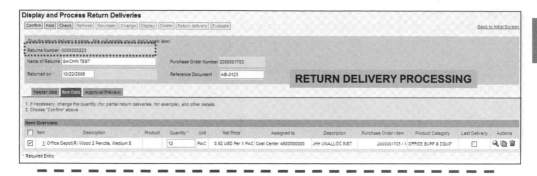

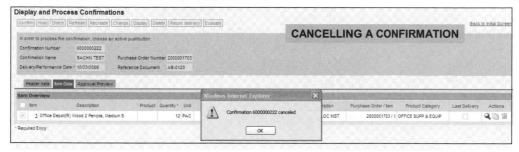

Figure 3.70 Cancel Confirmations and Return Delivery

The express confirmation can be accessed from the **Check Status** application, illustrated in Figure 3.71. From a process perspective, a goods receipt or confirmation is only available for entry after the PO is complete and transferred to the vendor. All shopping carts that have a corresponding PO are available for confirmation.

When the user selects the express confirmation truck icon, a goods receipt is automatically processed in the background. A message box is provided to the end user once the confirmation is created successfully. It is important to note that in this function there is no capability to enter any information such as bill of lading, etc. Therefore, users can only process the confirmation completely. Partial confirmations are not supported, for example if the PO was for quantity 10, and the express confirmation only needs to be created for quantity 6.

> **Note**
>
> You cannot create Express Confirmations or Express Invoices for unplanned items, nor can you create them for shopping cart items split between several POs.

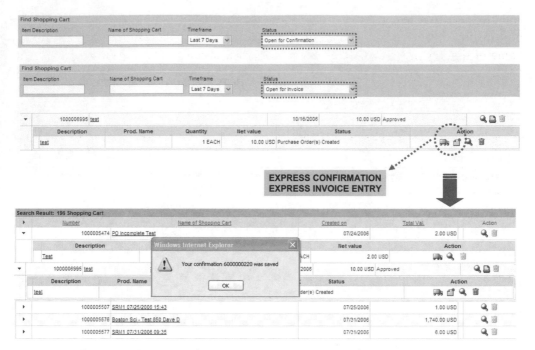

Figure 3.71 Express Confirmation

Confirmation for Goods and Services by Suppliers

Suppliers can use the confirmation function as well to create, edit, and send confirmations using the SAP SUS. The core advantage of this functionality is that small and mid-sized suppliers can be enabled by your organization to electronically respond to POs.

Using SUS, suppliers can create confirmation and invoices that are then sent to responsible users within your organization for approval. Not only does this reduce data-entry efforts for the customer, it allows for an electronic mechanism to collaborate on the entire procurement process. This functionality is discussed in detail in Chapter 5.

This concludes **STEP 4** of the self-service procurement scenario: **GR Processing** that we started to discuss in Section 3.1.4. In the next section 3.1.5, I will discuss the last step — **STEP 5** — illustrated in Figure 3.5: **Invoice Processing**.

3.1.5 STEP 5: Invoice Processing

An invoice is normally created after the goods receipt or service performance has been confirmed. It includes general invoice information, such as total amount, total tax, freight costs, vendor and invoice recipient, and detailed information (header information, item information, and approval preview). Some of the key areas that I will discuss in this section are **Invoice Entry**, **Credit Memo Entry**, **Partial Invoices,** and **Invoice with and without PO** as illustrated in Figure 3.72.

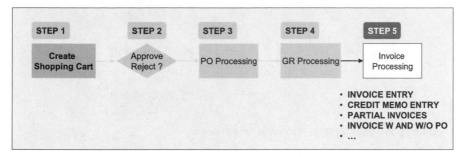

Figure 3.72 Invoice Processing — Entering Invoices and Credit Memos

In SAP SRM a single entry transaction is available for processing both invoices and credit memos. Invoices and credit memos are created using the *Enter Invoice/Credit Memo* transaction in SAP SRM, as illustrated in Figure 3.73.

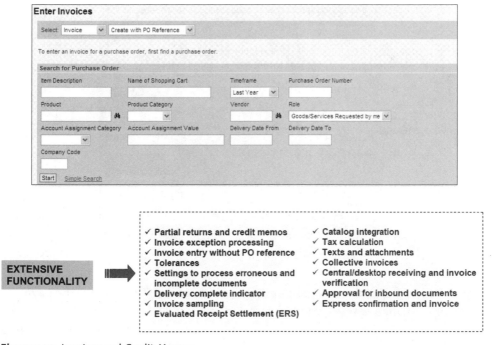

Figure 3.73 Invoices and Credit Memos

Role-based authorizations control who is allowed to access this transaction, as illustrated in Figure 3.74.

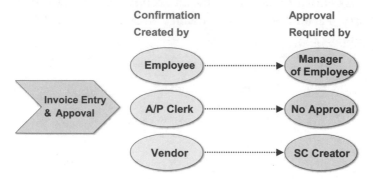

Figure 3.74 Who Can Enter Invoices and Credit Memos

In SAP SRM, users can create an invoice or credit memo in and if a back-end SAP R/3 system is connected, a corresponding invoice or credit memo is created. Depending on your implementation scenario, the organization can choose to create invoices in SAP SRM or directly enter invoices in the back-end SAP R/3 system. Figure 3.75 illustrates the possible scenarios for creating invoices in SAP SRM.

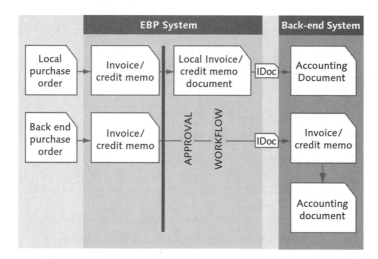

Figure 3.75 Creating Invoices and Credit Memos

When the invoice or credit memo is posted in the SRM system, the payment information is transferred to the corresponding SAP back-end financial system. Once the invoice is transferred to the back-end system, all accounting documents are updated and commitments are reduced. Additionally, an invoice or credit memo document is created in SAP MM and becomes visible in the PO history. Invoices in SRM can be created using one of the following options:

- Entering invoices with PO reference
- Entering invoices without PO reference
- XML invoice receipt
- Using Express creation

Let's explore these in more detail next.

Entering Invoices with PO Reference

As in SAP R/3 (or ERP), SAP SRM allows users to create invoices with reference to a PO or without reference. When creating invoices, one of the most important things an invoice processor needs is the ability to search using multiple criteria such as **PO Number**, **Vendor**, **and Product**, as illustrated in Figure 3.76.

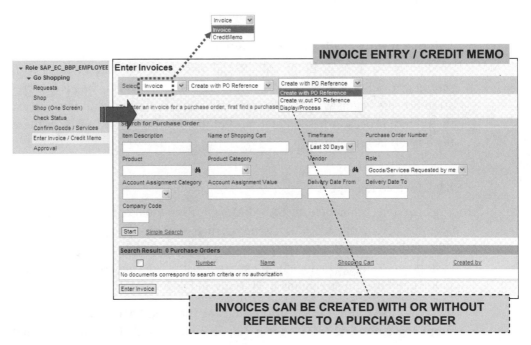

Figure 3.76 Enter Invoices with Reference to PO

As the PO is being referenced, all information in the invoice is pulled in from the corresponding PO. If all the criteria of total invoice value and PO value match, then the invoice can be posted. If there are discrepancies, the invoice processor has the ability to either put the invoice on **Hold** or send it for further approvals. The approval functionality available in SAP SRM is discussed in detail in Chapter 10.

When invoices are created with reference to a PO, the system automatically proposes the data from the system in which the PO was originally entered (local PO or back-end PO). This means that all the line items from the PO are automatically shown in the invoice for easy entry.

Invoices in SAP SRM can be entered for more than one PO at a time. This is called collective invoice processing. However, the PO needs to maintain the same:

▶ Vendor

▶ Company code

▶ Currency

▶ Back-end financial system

Entering Invoices Without a PO Reference

Similar to SAP R/3 (or ERP), SAP SRM allows users to create invoices with reference to a PO or without reference. When there is no PO, the invoice creation process begins with the selection of a vendor. Naturally, in this process the invoice processor has to enter most of the information manually as there is no reference document.

XML Invoice Receipt

Organizations implementing SAP SRM have also embarked on the electronic document exchange via XML. Vendors such as Office Depot, Fisher Scientific, and Dell are all examples of organizations that are encouraging their customers to engage in document exchange using Internet technologies such as XML in order to streamline operations and reduce costs.

Invoices in SAP SRM can be processed using inbound XML invoices from the suppliers. Since SAP SRM release 4.0, SAP has included functionality that allows organizations to process XML invoices even if no goods-receipt documents are processed.

Instead, the incoming invoice is created with a status of waiting and awaits the creation of a goods receipt. The status on the SRM invoice is: **Waiting for Preceding Document** as seen in Figure 3.77. A new program has been created (BBP_IV_AUTO_COMPLETE) that can be scheduled so that invoices are automatically posted once the corresponding goods-receipt documents are posted.

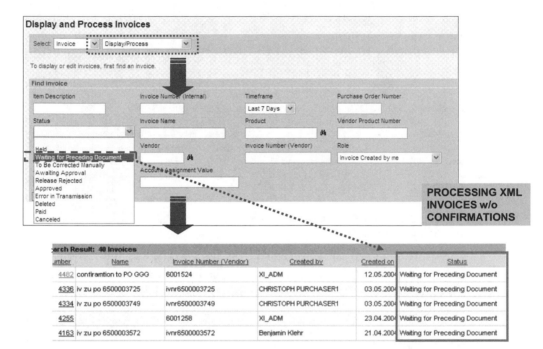

Figure 3.77 Processing XML Invoices Without Goods Receipts

When incoming invoices are received with errors, a status of **To Be Corrected Manually** is assigned to the invoice document, as illustrated in Figure 3.78. A background workflow notifies the responsible users, and they can manually correct the errors or send the invoice back to the vendor. In order to keep the original invoice intact, version-management functionality is available.

Express Invoices

This functionality gives end users the ability to quickly create an invoice. This supports the self-service scenario, in that it enables the end users to complete the entire purchase process from shopping cart to invoice entry seamlessly.

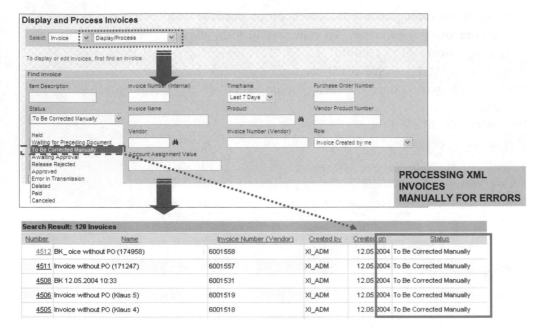

Figure 3.78 Processing XML Invoices to Correct Errors Manually

The express invoice can be accessed from the *Check Status* application, illustrated in Figure 3.79. From a process perspective, an invoice is only available for entry after the PO is complete and transferred to the vendor. All shopping carts that have a corresponding PO are available for invoice entry. If the PO requires a goods receipt as well, then the Confirmation/Goods Receipt step is mandatory prior to entry of invoices.

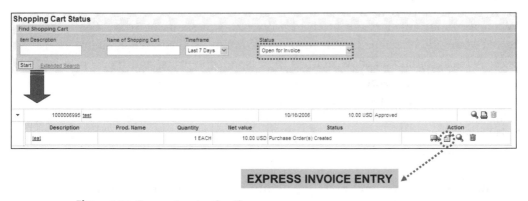

Figure 3.79 Express Invoice Creation

When the user selects the Express Invoice, an invoice is processed in the background automatically. A message box is provided to the end user once the invoice is created successfully. It is important to note that users can only process the invoice completely; partial invoices are not supported.

Remember that it is not possible to create express invoices for unplanned items, or for shopping carts that are split across multiple POs.

Processing Credit Memos

A credit memo is required when the goods or services that were provided by a supplier need to be returned because of defective product or other discrepancies. A credit memo allows the organization to reduce its liability for the goods or services received within its financial system. The credit memo transaction is the same as the invoice-processing transaction in SRM.

This concludes **STEP 5** of the self-service procurement scenario: **Invoice Processing**.

In Section 3.2, I will introduce the service procurement process within the operational procurement business scenario. In Section 3.2, readers will learn about the capabilities of SAP SRM for the procurement of services.

3.2 Services Procurement

In many organizations, spending on services consumes up to 50% of the overall procurement expenditure. Considering this huge number, it is imperative for organizations to focus on the services-procurement process and reduce costs for greater profitability. Some of the most important services that organizations procure are:

▶ Consulting

▶ Business and administrative services

▶ Marketing and advertising

▶ Building and maintenance services

▶ Legal services

▶ Technology services

▶ Air travel and transportation services

Services demand the same process controls as product procurement — such as budget and contract compliance — but add the challenge of service items that are mostly undefined at the time of requisition. Unplanned items are a significant cost within services procurement and can overrun budgets for projects unless they're allocated upfront.

Until recently, most SRM applications did not provide much support for procurement of services. Now that many organizations have realized the benefits of the non-service categories, they have started to focus on the opportunities to reduce cost within the procurement of services. SAP SRM supports the services procurement via the following three options:

▶ Creation of shopping carts with a value limit

▶ Request and ordering of external staff

▶ Creation of shopping carts with service products within the SAP MM module

Let us delve deeper into these options now.

3.2.1   Shop with Limit

In the Shop transaction, users with appropriate authorization can create a shopping cart with a value limit or validity period using the **Create with Limit** application. These could be used for creating orders for a limited period of service or dollar value. Some organizations refer to such purchases as a Blanket order. Confirmations for goods receipts or services, as well as invoices can be entered up to this limit.

This application gives the user flexibility to determine when creating a limit shopping cart whether only an invoice will be required as a follow-on document or both the confirmation and invoice will be required. This provides flexibility for simple service transactions such as snow removal, general landscaping, or cutting grass, where the service is performed on a regular basis and there is no one person responsible for the confirmation. Figure 3.80 illustrates the **Create with Limit** application.

In the Extended Classic implementation scenario, when creating shopping carts with more than one limit, separate POs will be created for each item when ordering, irrespective of the data (vendor, document type, purchasing group, company, location, performance period, etc.) in each item. For example, if a shopping cart with two limit positions is ordered, two POs always will be created but not one PO for two items.

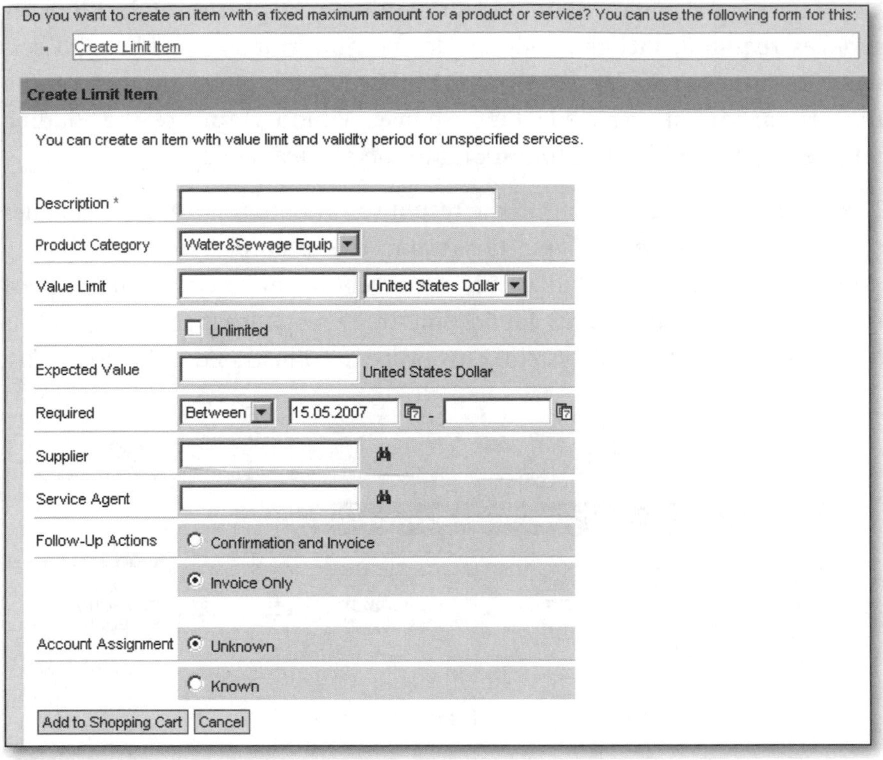

Figure 3.80 Create with Limit

3.2.2 Request for External Staff

In this section, we're specifically discussing the procurement of external staff, which was referred as *temporary labor* in earlier releases. The Requests application initiates a request for information/request for proposal (RFI/RFP) process to send a request for a service to a vendor before creating the actual PO. This allows organizations to find a better match of a service agent to their core requirement.

In SAP SRM, the service-procurement process can be initiated by an employee or purchasing assistant in the shopping cart or by the purchasing buyer in the SAP Bidding Engine component.

This scenario supports the process for both the request for information from a vendor and the actual purchase of the service. Depending on the service request, an organization might need to get detailed information from the vendor(s), prior to ordering the services. These could be a request for contracting or consulting service, for example.

Using the Requests application, users can initiate the process of detailing the services required, including adding detailed information on the skill sets needed for the service agents. Once the request it complete, it is then sent to the vendor via an email link for response. Vendors can use the Bidding Engine component in SRM to respond to the service requests.

The vendor can specify agents in the response, and can reject individual lines of the request. Upon receiving the response, the employee or purchasing professional can review and decide on accepting or rejecting the request from within the **Check Status** application. If the response is accepted, a PO is triggered in the SAP SRM system. This process is illustrated in Figure 3.81.

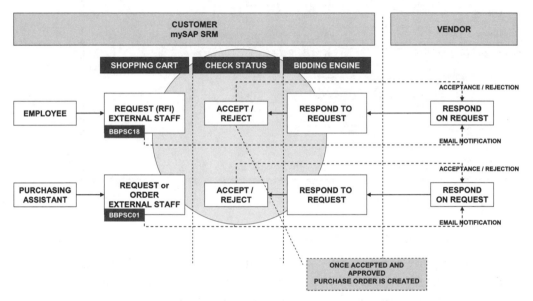

Figure 3.81 Request for External Staff — Process Overview

Because of the unique requirements of services procurement SAP introduced specific transactions for the request, receipt, and invoicing of service related purchases. These transactions contain specific containers for information that needs to be captured on a typical request for external services. Figure 3.82 illustrates the Service Request application in SRM.

The service request can be entered directly as free-form text or can be added from the service master if there are services defined in the product master. A performance period can be defined to identify when the service is to be performed.

Besides the usual additional information that you can include in the request using texts and attachments, organizations can also create a skills profile as a PDF form in the request. In this PDF form, you enter the prerequisites that a service agent must fulfill, and specific skill sets can be defined that are required for the service project. You can use a BAdI to modify the list of skills available for selection in the PDF form.

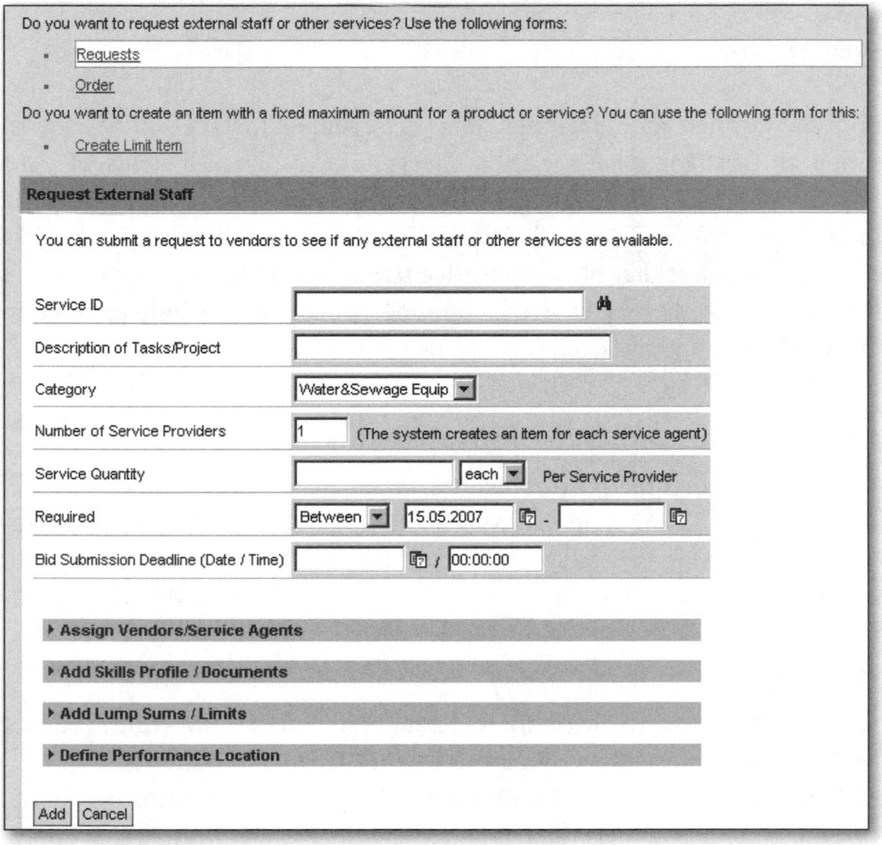

Do you want to request external staff or other services? Use the following forms:

- Requests
- Order

Do you want to create an item with a fixed maximum amount for a product or service? You can use the following form for this:

- Create Limit Item

Request External Staff

You can submit a request to vendors to see if any external staff or other services are available.

Service ID	
Description of Tasks/Project	
Category	Water&Sewage Equip
Number of Service Providers	1 (The system creates an item for each service agent)
Service Quantity	each Per Service Provider
Required	Between 15.05.2007 .
Bid Submission Deadline (Date / Time)	/ 00:00:00

- **Assign Vendors/Service Agents**
- **Add Skills Profile / Documents**
- **Add Lump Sums / Limits**
- **Define Performance Location**

Add   Cancel

Figure 3.82 Request for External Staff

The **Lump Sum** and **Limit** capability in the application enable organizations to allocate unplanned buckets (e.g., expenses or overtime) for the service request and assign specific not to exceed limits. These costs typically cannot be allocated explicitly, so a maximum limit is defined that can be charged during the entire duration of the service project. Both the Lump Sum and Limit categories provide free-text description fields that offer flexibility for a variety of uses.

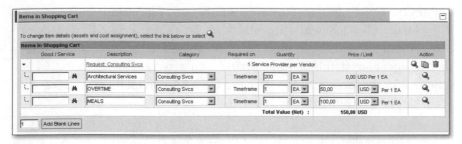

Figure 3.83 Request for External Staff — Adding Lump Sums and Limits

Both the planned and unplanned items are grouped together in the request shopping cart. For greater clarity, the system displays all items of your request combined in a hierarchy before you send the request. To display the individual items, you expand the hierarchy item, as illustrated in Figure 3.83. This ensures that planned service items and limit items for expenses that belong together are sourced from one vendor. This is only possible in the Standalone and the Extended Classic scenarios.

3.2.3 Services with MM-SRM Integration

SAP SRM supports the procurement of materials and service materials that are created in the SAP Materials Management (MM) module. Users can procure services using the shopping cart and PO and integrate the corresponding requisitions and POs within the SAP back-end (R/3 or ERP) system. This would be the scenario where services are created within MM and replicated to SRM.

The process starts with the creation of a shopping cart in SRM with a **Product Type** of Services as seen in Figure 3.84. In Figure 3.85, line item 1 is for **ENGINEERING SERVICE — ELEVATOR 1002**, which is a service material **102948**. Note that the **Product Type** for this item is **Services**, which allows the user to enter a **Timeframe** for the delivery date.

The **Required** field in the item details provides the ability to define a timeframe for the service performance using a **Between** or **Begin on** date. When the product type is **Goods,** the **Required on** field only allows user to enter a specific date for delivery.

Once the shopping cart is complete and ordered, based on system configuration, either a purchase requisition or PO of type Item Category **D** is created in SAP R/3, as illustrated in Figure 3.85.

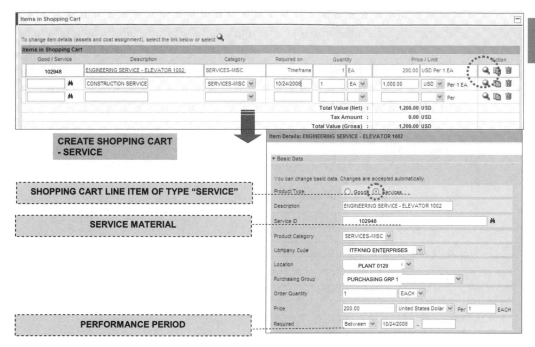

Figure 3.84 Shopping Cart of Type Service

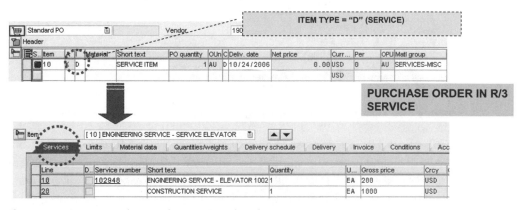

Figure 3.85 Service Purchase Order in SAP Back End

Once the PO is created, a service confirmation can be created in either the SAP back-end or in SAP SRM.

3.2.4 Confirmation and Invoice Entry

Once the service has been performed, a confirmation can be entered to record the services. Based on the original request or PO, confirmations and invoices posted for services can only be entered to the duration specified in the purchase request. At the time of confirmation, a timesheet can be maintained for capturing the detailed service documentation. The timesheet supports users when they enter a start date, start time, and end times for capturing hours worked. Please note that this time entry is not integrated in any way with the SAP Cross Application Time Sheet (CATS) solution seen in Figure 3.86.

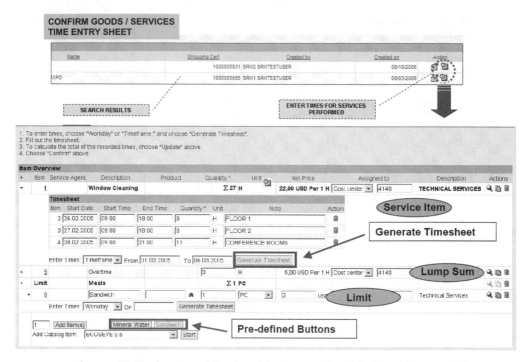

Figure 3.86 Confimation of Goods and Services — Time Entry Sheet (Source: SAP)

In Section 3.2, we discussed the services-procurement functionality within SAP SRM. In the next section, I will discuss the plan-driven procurement business scenario in SAP SRM, which allows organizations to integrate demand from other supply chain systems such as Project System (PS), Plant Maintenance (PM), or demand driven systems such as Materials Requirement Planning (MRP).

3.3   Plan-Driven Procurement

The plan-driven procurement business scenario integrates operational procurement with the existing Supply Chain Management (SCM), PM and PS applications. This is also sometimes referred to as *direct material procure-*

ment. In this scenario, requirements from external systems (both SAP and non-SAP) are transferred into the SAP SRM system for sourcing and PO processing. Figure 3.87 illustrates plan-driven procurement.

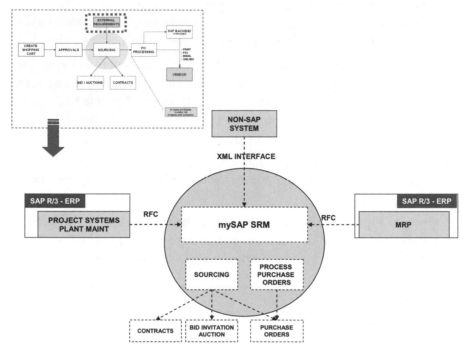

Figure 3.87 Plan-Driven Procurement — Overview

Organizations have the option in customizing to define whether the requirements that are transferred from external systems are processed in the Sourcing or the Process Purchase Order application. The sourcing application provides greater value, as the transferred requirements can then either be grouped into a single PO or used to initiate a bid invitation when no sources of supply are suitable.

Two of the key objectives of plan-driven procurement are:

▶ Improve supplier selection and efficiency compliance
▶ Centralize purchasing and integrate with external planning systems

The standard plan-driven procurement process is illustrated in Figure 3.88 Lets us walk through each of the steps illustrated in Figure 3.88 to understand the plan driven procurement business scenario:

1. Create a purchase requisition in the SAP R/3 system either from the MRP, Project System, or Plant Maintenance applications.

2. Based upon pre-defined conditions (product categories, etc.) a requisition is transferred from the SAP back-end to SAP SRM.

3. Based on configuration in EBP, the transferred requisition is converted into a shopping cart and is called an external requirement. It's important to note that the external requirements are transferred into SRM as shopping carts that are pre-approved. No additional approvals are possible.

4. Based on Customizing rules within SRM, the requirement is either processed in the Process Purchase Order application or in the Sourcing application. If unique sources of supply (contracts, vendor lists, etc.) exist, a PO is created automatically. Otherwise, the purchaser has to intervene and manually complete the requirement, as illustrated in Figure 3.89.

5. The purchaser processes the requirement in SRM, provided that a Source of Supply exists, or begins creating a Bid Invitation to request vendor quotes (RFQ).

6. Once the appropriate source is assigned to the requirement, a complete PO is created in SRM, an output is generated for the vendor, and a copy of the PO is transferred back to the original back-end system (SAP R/3 or ERP).

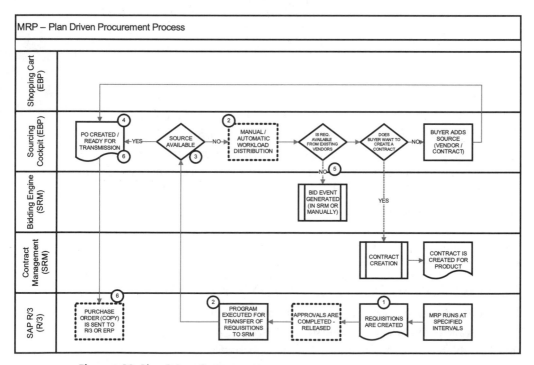

Figure 3.88 Plan-Driven Procurement

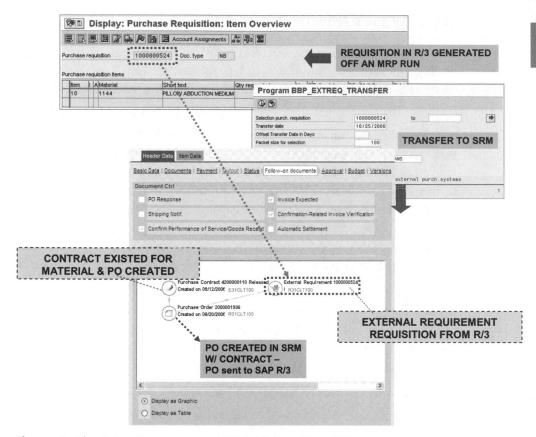

Figure 3.89 Plan-Driven Procurement — MRP requisition, PO in SRM

After the Step 6 shown in Figure 3.88, the goods receipt can be created in either SAP SRM or the SAP backend system. Once this is done, the inventory levels are automatically updated in SAP Inventory Management.

I have described the three business scenarios that exist within the operational-procurement business process: self-service procurement, services procurement, and plan-driven procurement. In Section 3.4, I will briefly discuss the new enhancements in the operational-procurement business process since SAP SRM release 5.0.

3.4   What's New in Operational Procurement?

SAP has been enhancing the SAP SRM solution every year. Each new release has brought forth a variety of rich and useful functionality. This section highlights some of the major functionality introduced in operational procurement scenario in the SAP SRM 5.0 release or beyond.

A new application has been introduced with the SAP SRM 5.0 release, which is the Invoice Management System (IMS). The primary goal of IMS is to provide a central system to manage all incoming supplier invoices. To explain it simply, the idea behind IMS is to create a central area where all invoice exceptions can be handled. Examples of some exceptions would be duplicate invoices, missing goods receipts, or price variances. The IMS solution is a part of the operational-procurement business scenario and uses the SAP SRM solution as its core platform. Review Figure 3.90 to get a detailed idea of IMS.

Invoice processing is probably one of the most time-consuming and error-prone processes within the procure-to-pay cycle. Organizations receive thousands of invoices via a variety of transmission media: paper, fax, EDI, or XML. Some of the major issues of this process are:

▶ The majority of invoices are paper based

▶ Invoices that are in error need to be managed and resolved manually

▶ Tracking capabilities are very poor

The IMS solution can make the invoice-management and error-resolution process more efficient and streamlined. Figure 3.90 illustrates the overall process flow in IMS and overview of functionality available.

Figure 3.91 shows that in the **Invoice Monitor** application in IMS, accounts-payable personnel can search for invoices that match a particular exception and process it accordingly. For example an exception of type **Duplicate Invoice** allows the user to compare the duplicate invoices side by side and then flag it to send to the vendor as a duplicate. IMS provides an end-to-end loop where the vendor can review the duplicate document and provide his responses. Similarly there are a number of other exceptions that can be processed within IMS.

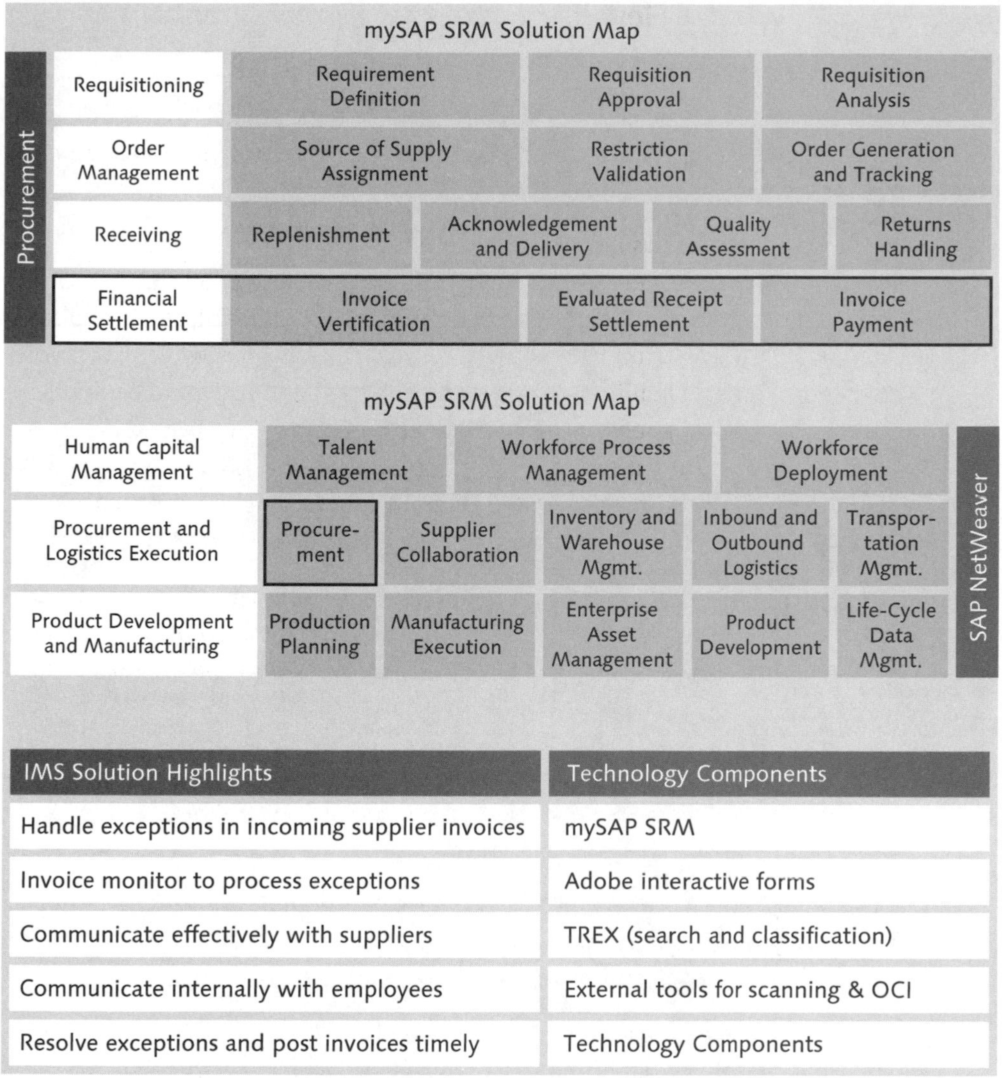

mySAP SRM Solution Map			
Requisitioning	Requirement Definition	Requisition Approval	Requisition Analysis
Order Management	Source of Supply Assignment	Restriction Validation	Order Generation and Tracking
Receiving	Replenishment	Acknowledgement and Delivery	Quality Assessment	Returns Handling
Financial Settlement	Invoice Vertification	Evaluated Receipt Settlement	Invoice Payment

(Procurement)

mySAP SRM Solution Map					
Human Capital Management	Talent Management	Workforce Process Management		Workforce Deployment	
Procurement and Logistics Execution	Procure-ment	Supplier Collaboration	Inventory and Warehouse Mgmt.	Inbound and Outbound Logistics	Transpor-tation Mgmt.
Product Development and Manufacturing	Production Planning	Manufacturing Execution	Enterprise Asset Management	Product Development	Life-Cycle Data Mgmt.

(SAP NetWeaver)

IMS Solution Highlights	Technology Components
Handle exceptions in incoming supplier invoices	mySAP SRM
Invoice monitor to process exceptions	Adobe interactive forms
Communicate effectively with suppliers	TREX (search and classification)
Communicate internally with employees	External tools for scanning & OCI
Resolve exceptions and post invoices timely	Technology Components

Figure 3.90 SAP SRM — Invoice Management System (Source: SAP America ASUG presentation)

Figure 3.92 shows an example of a **Duplicate Invoice**. The **Original** invoice and the **New** invoice can be compared side by side as seen in Figure 3.93. The accounts-payable clerk can mark the invoice as a duplicate by selecting the radio button for the question in the header: **Is this a duplicate invoice?** You can click the **Forward** button to send this response to the vendor along with the original invoice information.

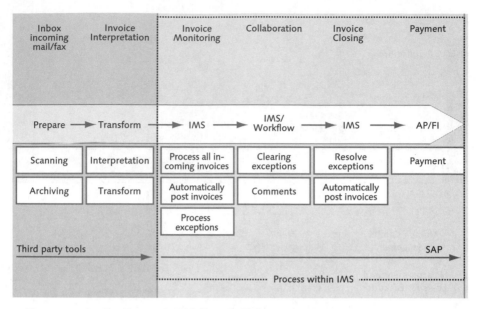

Figure 3.91 Invoice Process in IMS (Source: SAP)

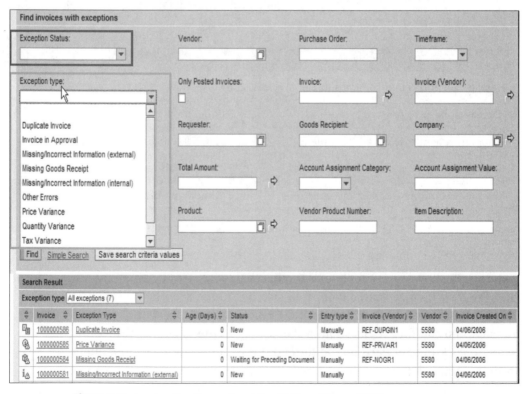

Figure 3.92 Invoice Monitor — Exception Options (Source: SAP)

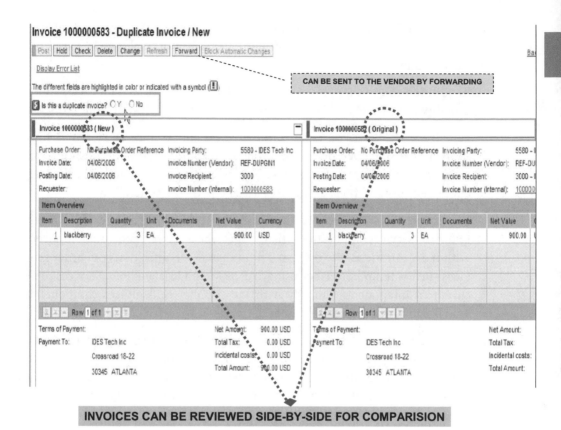

Figure 3.93 Invoice Monitor — Duplicate Invoices (Source: SAP)

The IMS solution can be deployed with all three implementation scenarios in SAP SRM.

3.5   Summary

This concludes the operational procurement chapter, which was an extremely long chapter due to the importance of the concepts that have been introduced, such as the shopping cart and purchase order applications. The concepts discussed in this chapter will create a baseline for the rest of the discussion within this book.

Let's quickly review what we learned in this chapter. We introduced the self-service procurement business scenario, which happens to be the most widely used business scenario in organizations that implement SAP SRM. In Section 3.1.1 we introduced the concept of a shopping cart, before which is the core of the procurement solution within SAP SRM. We discussed the different shopping cart forms that provide flexibility of deployment based on the needs of the end user.

In addition to the shopping cart, we briefly touched on the approvals functionality in SAP SRM. This will be discussed in detail within Chapter 10.

We also introduced you to the Confirmation and Invoice-entry functionalities in SAP SRM. We noted that user organizations have the flexibility to enter confirmations or invoices either in SAP SRM or continue to create goods receipts and invoices in the back-end SAP R/3 system.

In Section 3.2 we discussed the Create with Limit, Requests, and Order External Services applications that target the services procurement need within organizations. We discussed how answer Organizations can order services such as temporary labor using SAP SRM and learned how. Services procurement integrates seamlessly with the supplier self-services component, which will be discussed in Chapter 5.

In Section 3.3, we explained how organizations can integrate demand from external supply chain systems with SAP SRM. The plan-driven procurement business scenario provides the capability to integrate demand from MRP, project systems, and plant maintenance systems into the SRM system.

In Chapter 4, we will introduce the Strategic Sourcing and Contract Management capabilities of SAP SRM. You will learn about the Sourcing application, Bidding Engine, Live Auction, and the Contract applications within SAP SRM.

SAP SRM automates processes between sourcing and procurement, within the enterprise and across the supply base. It increases supply-chain visibility and gives you closed-loop insight into global spend.

4   Strategic Sourcing and Contract Management

Before proceeding with this chapter, let me define sourcing. *Sourcing* is the process of identifying, conducting negotiations with, and forming supply agreements with vendors of goods and services. In SAP SRM, sourcing is the core purchasing process of analyzing, qualifying, and selecting suppliers. It is also the process that enables compliance of purchasing strategies by creating contracts for goods and services that can be leveraged across the enterprise.

Sourcing has become the new buzzword now that e-procurement and SRM have become familiar terms within corporate procurement networks. However, the concept of sourcing is anything but new. Organizations that have already reaped the benefits of the process improvements of operational procurement are now getting ready to reduce costs further by focusing on their strategic sourcing processes and capabilities.

In simple terms, *strategic sourcing* is the process of identifying and qualifying suppliers that can provide the goods and services needed by the organization. It also includes the process of negotiating with suppliers using auction and bidding techniques to negotiate the best possible terms and conditions without sacrificing quality and dependability.

Contract management deals with the process of creating, maintaining, and monitoring contractual agreements between the buyer and supplier organizations. In SAP SRM, organizations can integrate data from request for proposals (RFP), request for quotations (RFQ), and auctions to create and update contract terms, conditions, and prices. These contracts can then be used as sources of supply to purchase goods and services.

In this chapter, I will discuss the capabilities of SAP SRM in the areas of strategic sourcing and contract management. I've combined the sourcing and contract management capabilities of SAP SRM into a single chapter. I have found that when we talk about strategic sourcing we should cover all aspects of the selection and negotiation processes with suppliers.

Once negotiations are complete with the supplier for the procurement of goods or services, the buying organization either enters into a contract with the supplier or just creates a one-time purchase order (PO). This chapter discusses the contract management capabilities in SAP SRM whereby contracts can be used as a valid source of supply by professional purchasers when making sourcing decisions.

4.1   Strategic Sourcing

In SAP SRM, Strategic Sourcing deals with the following aspects of supplier selection:

► Supplier screening and selection

► Source of supply determination (Sourcing)

► Request for qualification, bidding, and live auctions

Let us now look at these in some detail.

4.1.1   Supplier Screening and Selection

Supplier screening and selection is simply the process of choosing the right supplier for a certain product, service, or product category. This process allows organizations to pre-screen suppliers using detailed and customized screening questionnaires, allowing professional purchasers to determine whether those suppliers should be considered potential business partners.

The process of supplier screening begins when the organization invites potential suppliers to visit its external website and register as potential suppliers. A link on the organization's website can present potential suppliers with the registration process within SAP SRM. Once the supplier completes the required information and submits its information to the organization, it is sent to the designated purchasing professional for review and screening. The supplier registration process is discussed in further detail in Chapter 5.

During the screening process, the purchasing professionals can accept or deny a particular supplier. The suppliers that are accepted can then be available in the organization's supplier directory within SAP SRM. Note that suppliers contained in the supplier directory are not automatically available as sources within the SAP SRM applications (shopping cart, PO, etc.). These suppliers need to be transferred into the SRM system using the *Transfer supplier* action if you want them available in applications such as Bid Invitation..

Note
The supplier directory is contained within the SRM system and is not the same as the vendor master in the SAP R/3 or ERP system.

The supplier-screening process is triggered by using the transaction *Pre-select Vendors*. In this transaction, professional purchasers in the organization can accept or reject suppliers that have registered. Suppliers that are accepted can be transferred to the SRM system as business partners. Rejected suppliers cannot be transferred. Once the suppliers are accepted, they are added to the supplier directory, and can be accessed via one of the following applications:

▶ Sourcing

▶ Bid Invitations

▶ Vendor Lists

▶ Manage Business Partner

Figure 4.1 illustrates the supplier registration and screening process. This process is discussed in further detail in Chapter 5.

4.1.2 Source of Supply Determination (Sourcing)

In SAP SRM the *Sourcing* application provides the professional buyers with sourcing-relevant information that enables them to select the most appropriate source of supply for an open user requirement. If multiple sources of supply are available, the buyers can compare them and select the best source.

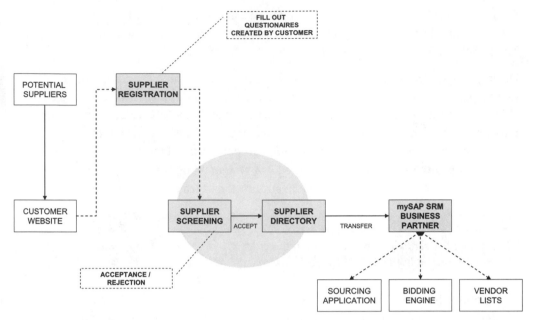

Figure 4.1 Supplier Registration, Screening, and Selection Process

According to SAP, *sourcing* is a central concept in SRM where open requirements from local or back-end systems are assigned sources of supply either in the Sourcing application or via SAP Bidding Engine. The resulting document (PO or contract) resides either in the local or back-end system, depending on the scenario being used.

Contracts, vendor lists and catalogs are considered approved sources of supply within the SRM system. When end users have requirements to purchase goods or services, they can select from these approved sources of supply without needing intervention from the purchasing department. However, organizations can have business rules that require intervention of the purchasing department for PO creation, and these rules can be defined in Customizing.

Therefore, the source determination is sometimes done automatically by the system when an exact match is found. Alternatively, professional purchasers can use the available sourcing options to determine the best source of supply for the requirement. Figure 4.2 illustrates the sourcing relationship in operational procurement and strategic sourcing.

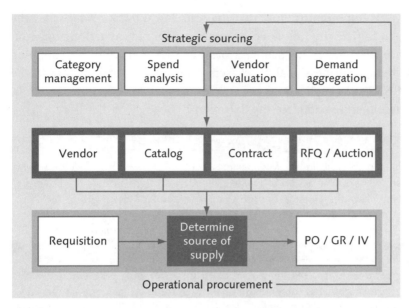

Figure 4.2 Relationship Between Sourcing and Operational Procurement when Determining Source

Organizations can choose when implementing SRM whether they want their professional purchasers to use the Sourcing application or work directly in the Process Purchase Orders application.

Reasons for Using the Sourcing Application

Because purchasing professionals can simply process shopping carts directly in the Process Purchase Order application, readers might wonder how they would benefit by adding a middle layer with the Sourcing application. Some of the key benefits of using the Sourcing application are as follows:

▶ Central repository for processing requirements from internal (e.g., shopping carts) and external systems (e.g.,requirements generated via MRP)

▶ Ability to access various sources of supply (e.g., the suggest sources of supply function)

▶ Capability to aggregate multiple requirements to create POs using grouping functionality (e.g., combine multiple shopping carts into a single PO)

▶ Ability to launch bid invitations and auctions directly

▶ Ability to create contracts from existing requirements

However, it is important to note that the sourcing application provides the capability to initiate the follow-on documents (PO, bid invitation, and contract). Once the follow-on document has been created from the shopping cart requirement, professional purchasers may need to work further in the individual SAP SRM applications of PO Processing, Bidding Engine, and Contract Management to complete the document.

Example 1

In the Sourcing application, the buyer selects a shopping cart, assigns an appropriate source and takes the action to create a PO. Any changes such as the *Terms of Payment* or *Purchasing Organization* on the PO can only be done within the Process Purchase Order application.

Example 2

This example deals with creating a contract from a shopping cart, when further detailed processing such as total release quantity or value on the contract can only be maintained within the Contract application. Figure 4.3 illustrates a simple flow for Sourcing and Process Purchase Order.

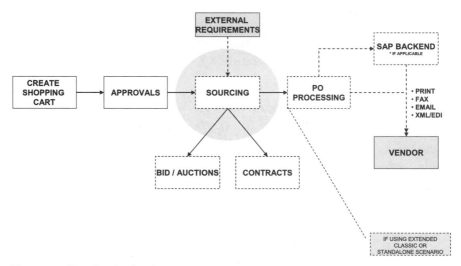

Figure 4.3 Sourcing Application

In essence, there are three key sources of supply that act as fixed sources. When a fixed source is selected in a shopping cart, the document is considered complete by the system and no buyer intervention is required for any subsequent PO processing. This is dependent on the business rules defined in Customizing (IMG). The following bullet points list the sources of supply that are considered as fixed in SAP SRM:

▶ Catalogs

▶ Contracts

▶ Vendor lists

In the SRM shopping cart, line items that require additional processing can be routed to the professional purchaser in the Sourcing application. All other line items that are complete with a fixed source or supply and price can generate a PO automatically. Alternatively, reservations can also be generated in R/3 for items that are subject to Inventory Management (if using the Classic or decoupled scenario). This can be controlled within Customizing.

When working in the Sourcing application, professional purchasers are provided with a *worklist* of requirements that need to be processed on a daily basis. Each worklist is segregated by a default product category of the requirement.

The main goal at this point is to process the requirements available within the worklist and create one of the follow-on documents of PO, contract, bid invitation or auction. In Figure 4.4, the **Worklist** tab in **Sourcing** provides an **Overview of Requirements**. The **Display** dropdown menu allows the purchaser to select a product category to filter the requirements; in our example the worklist is filtered by the **OFFICE SUPP & EQUIP** product category.

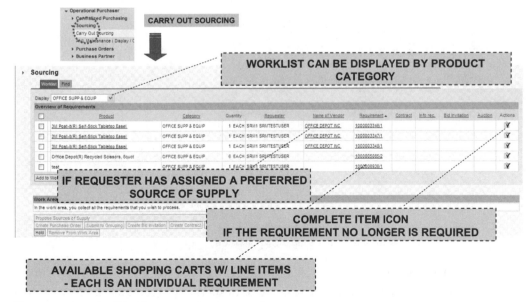

Figure 4.4 Sourcing Worklist

It is important to note that each shopping cart line item is individually listed in the **Requirement** column. Therefore, a shopping cart with multiple line items could be distributed to multiple purchaser worklists and eventually result in multiple POs. The **Actions** column contains a check- mark icon that can be used by the purchaser if the requirement is no longer required. Once this is selected, the requirement is removed from the **Sourcing** application and can no longer be processed.

Once the purchaser wants to process one or more items in the worklist, he or she can simply select the requirements and click on the **Add to Work Area** button for further processing, as illustrated in Figure 4.5. In our example, the shopping cart **1000005085/2** has been added to the work area. The purchaser can now enter a vendor number in the **Vendor** field or select the binoculars icon to search for a vendor in the Vendor database in SRM. Once the vendor and price information has been entered, the purchaser needs to select one of the action buttons; e.g., the **Create Purchase Order** button.

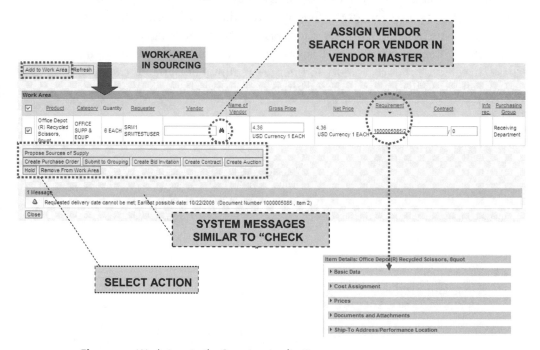

Figure 4.5 Work Area in the Sourcing Application

In the work area the professional purchasers can select one of the many actions to process the requirement further. The following bullets explain each of the action buttons:

▶ **Propose Sources of Supply**

Purchasers can search for negotiated sources of supply using the **Propose Source of Supply** button in the Sourcing application. The SRM system will propose any existing sources of supply and the buyer can assign a source to an open item. These sources will be from one of the following: contract items, vendor lists, or manual selection of a vendor at the buyer's discretion. If multiple sources of supply are available, the purchaser can compare them and select the best source. This can be seen in Figure 4.6

▶ **Create Purchase Order**

Once the buyer has assigned an appropriate source of supply or price to the open requirement item, a PO can be created. The purchaser can create an incomplete PO by leaving either the **Vendor** or **Gross Price** field blank and then clicking the **Create Purchase Order** button. This is required when the purchaser knows that additional information needs to be changed in the PO, such as terms of payment or maybe the purchasing organization. These fields are not available in the shopping cart and can only be changed in the PO.

▶ **Submit to Grouping**

This button allows multiple shopping carts or line items to be grouped into a single PO. Organizations that use the plan-driven procurement scenario to integrate the materials resource planning (MRP) requirements from SAP R/3 into SRM can also use the grouping functionality to automatically combine the multiple requisitions created from MRP.

▶ **Create Bid Invitation**

When an appropriate source of supply is not available for requirement(s), professional purchasers can create a bid invitation for the selected requirements directly from within the Sourcing application by clicking on the **Create Bid Invitation** button. Once the bid invitation is created, it can be further processed in the Bidding Engine application to enhance or send to selected suppliers.

▶ **Create Contract**

The buyers have the ability to create a contract instead of a PO via the Sourcing application and do so by clicking the **Create Contract** button.

▶ **Create Auction**

When an appropriate source of supply is not available for requirements,, professional purchasers can create a bid invitation for the selected requirements or Alternatively can create an auction event by clicking on the **Create Auction** button. You can see this in Figure 4.8.

▶ **Hold**

This button allows the buyer to **Hold** the requirement in the work area to process later. Requirements that are held will also appear in the worklist of the other members of the same purchasing group

▶ **Remove from Work Area**

This button allows the purchaser to remove the requirement from their work area so other buyers can process if required or work on the requirement at a later time. For example, let's say that while processing a requirement the purchaser needed to discuss the delivery information with the requisitioner. If the requisitioner is unavailable, the purchaser can remove the requirement from the work area to process at a later time.

In the Sourcing application, based on authorizations, professional purchasers can change the product, quantity, desired delivery date, goods recipient, or account assignment information on the shopping cart line item. This can be done by clicking on the document number in the Requirement column. For example, the purchaser can make changes to the **Requirement** number **1000005085/2** by clicking on the link as illustrated in Figure 4.5. All changes are noted in the Change History field of the shopping cart. Readers should note that no approval workflows are started for changes made to requirements in the Sourcing application.

Finding Requirements to Process

In the Sourcing application, professional purchasers can also process requirements for which they are not typically responsible. This could be a scenario when another buyer is not available or is on leave. The **Find** tab in the sourcing application allows buyers to search for requirements using a variety of criteria, as illustrated in Figure 4.6. For example, the purchaser could search by the **Number of Shopping Cart** and search for external requirements from a planning system by entering the requirement number in the **Ext. requiremt** field.

It is important to remember that all the requirements available in the Sourcing application are already approved, as illustrated in Figure 4.7. No further approval processes are triggered within Sourcing. Once the follow-on document (e.g., a PO) is created, additional approval workflows might apply.

The Sourcing application supports all of the implementation scenarios for SAP SRM (Classic, Extended Classic, or Standalone).

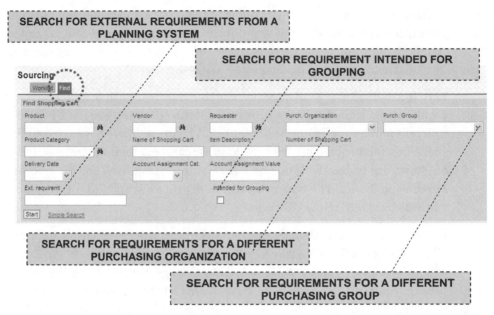

Figure 4.6 Searching for Requirements in Sourcing Application

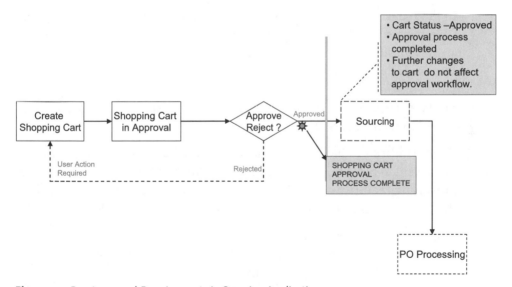

Figure 4.7 Pre-Approved Requirements in Sourcing Application

Workload Distribution (Reassignment of Workload)

From the SAP SRM 4.0 release, a new functionality has been introduced to assist with the re-assignment of purchaser workload. This process allows purchasing managers to distribute the workload of documents among the purchasers. This functionality is useful if the purchasing organization needs the capability to override the way documents are allocated to buyers in the standard solution. It is especially useful if a buyer is overburdened or is unavailable to process documents due to absence or other circumstances.

This functionality is available for changing the responsible purchaser for requirements (shopping carts or external demand), contracts, and POs to a different purchasing group. For example, in Figure 4.11 we have selected the check box for **Requirements** in the **Find Documents** section. Once we click on **Start**, the system will provide a list of all requirements for the relevant **Purchasing Group**. The buyer can also re-distribute workload for **Contracts** and **POs** by selecting the check box.

Based on roles and authorizations in SRM, purchasing managers can access all requirements that are passed on to the Sourcing application. In the Redistribute Workload application, purchasing managers have the ability to distribute requirements to the other buyers. This lets them control and allocate requirements based on the workload or the availability of buyers in their organizations.

In the standard solution, shopping cart requirements are sent to the responsible buyers based on the product commodities that the purchasing groups are responsible for. In other words, if there are five buyers and each is responsible for a particular product category (such as office supplies, lab suppliers, or construction), then in Customizing, organizations can assign these product categories to responsible buyers and those requirements are displayed in their buyers' worklist.

If the standard product category based solution does not work and organizations want to build their own business rules to distribute the work effort for processing requirements, they can use the Redistribute Workload application. Documents can be distributed via the following methods:

- **Manual Assignment**
  Purchasing managers can reassign the documents manually by accessing the Redistribute Workload application

- **Automatic Assignment**
  Based on business rules defined by the organization, documents can be assigned automatically to another purchasing group. This can be done using BAdI: BBP_PGRP_ASSIGN_BADI.

In the Redistribute Workload application, the purchasing manager can select from a variety of criteria and then select one or more documents that need to be redistributed from one purchasing group assignment to another. The results list displays any document that might already be undergoingprocessing by the responsible buyers.

Once the manager selects one or more documents to reassign, he or she can choose the new purchasing group from a drop down selection and click the **Start Manual Assignment** function to reassign the documents (as illustrated in Figure 4.8).

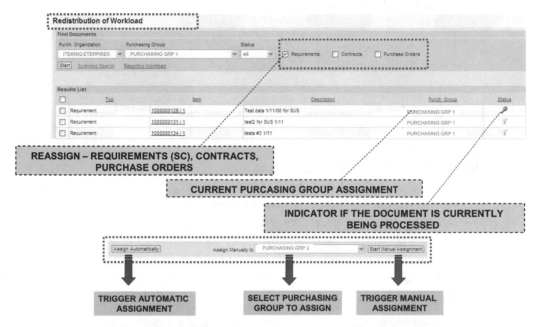

Figure 4.8 Redistribution of Workload

Notice in Figure 4.8 that there are three shopping carts in the **Results List** of the **Redistribution of Workload** application. The **Purch. Group** column shows the current purchasing group assigned to these shopping carts, which is **PURCHASING GRP 1**. To re-assign these shopping carts to another buyer, you need to follow these steps:

1. Select one or more requirements in the results list.

2. Select a new purchasing group in the **Assign Manually to** dropdown menu. In our example, this is **PURCHASING GRP 2**.

3. Click on the **Start Manual Assignment** button to manually assign the new purchasing group or click the **Assign Automatically** button to trigger automatic assignment based on pre-defined business rules.

Once this is done, the system provides a confirmation screen indicating whether or not the re-assignment was successful. These documents are then automatically available for processing in the worklist of the new buyer.

In the standard solution, organizations can determine in Customizing when Sourcing is triggered for a shopping cart line item. Figure 4.9 illustrates these options.

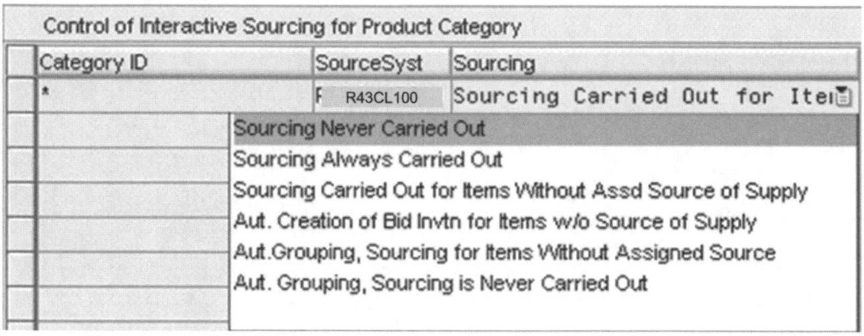

Figure 4.9 Control of Interactive Sourcing

However, this selection is based on the product category (**Category ID,** seen in Figure 4.12) of the shopping cart, which might not be a suitable criterion for determination. Organizations find themselves needing to determine business rules that can apply to determine whether a shopping cart is routed to the Sourcing application for buyer intervention. Table 4.1 provides some guidelines for this process.

Shopping Cart line item	Buyer Intervention in Sourcing
No fixed vendor in shopping cart	Yes
No price in shopping cart	Yes
Shopping cart for material reservations	No
High-dollar-value shopping carts	Yes (for reviewing source and any sole-source justifications)
Capital goods and leases	Yes
Replenishment of stock materials	No (if contract or vendor list exists)

Table 4.1 Guidelines for Developing Business Rules for Buyer Intervention (Sourcing)

Now that you understand the need for using the Sourcing application and are familiar with the different functions in Sourcing, I will begin to discuss the RFQ and bidding capabilities within SAP SRM.

4.1.3   RFQ and Bidding

The SAP Bidding Engine sits at the heart of the strategic-sourcing solution within SAP SRM and facilitates the request for qualification (RFQ) and bidding processes between the organization and the vendor. Purchasing professionals use the SAP Bidding Engine to create and process RFQs and bids for products and services. Contact persons (bidders) at the vendor organization in turn use the SAP Bidding Engine to submit bids in response to these bid invitations.

The RFQ and bidding functionality in SRM helps the purchasing professional negotiate the best possible prices, terms, and conditions with vendors.

In order to understand the bidding process, it is important to distinguish between the following two key terms:

▶ **Bid Invitation**
RFQ is typically the request a customer sends out to one or many vendors, inviting them to provide a quotation for a set of goods or services. The difference between the RFQ and RFI is that the RFQ requires a price, while the RFI does not require any prices on the response from the vendors.

▶ **Bid**
Also known as a quote, this is typically the response from the vendor based on the requirements outlined in the RFQ. Vendors that receive a bid invitation, can log on to the SAP SRM system and enter their bids against the product and service requirements outlined in the bid invitation.

In SRM, professional purchasers are able to initiate Bid Invitations from multiple different SAP SRM applications: Sourcing, Contract Management, and Bidding Engine, as illustrated in Figure 4.10.

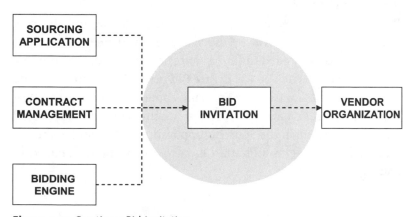

Figure 4.10 Creating a Bid Invitation

Figure 4.11 illustrates the same concept as Figure 4.13, but provides additional information regarding the processes that lead up to the creation of a bid invitation. For example, in the Sourcing application, a bid invitation can be created to source shopping carts that have gone thru the approval process. However, in the Bidding Engine application, a bid invitation can be created manually or using pre-defined templates. Let us discuss each of these three

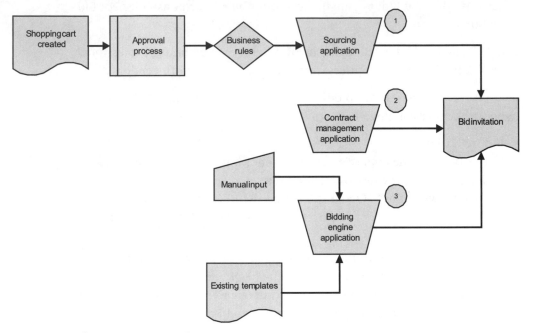

Figure 4.11 Initiate Bid Invitation

options in further detail.

Via the Sourcing Application

Using SAP Bidding Engine, buyers can create a bid invitation directly from the Sourcing application. This will be especially useful if there is an open requirement and the buyers need to find a source of supply. In the Sourcing application, the buyer will click on the **Create Bid Invitation** button to create a Bid Event for any item that is in the Sourcing application work area (illustrated in Figure 4.12). All data relevant to the bid invitation will be copied automatically from the item in the Sourcing application to the item in the bid invitation. Any additional texts and attachments will also be transferred to the bid invitation.

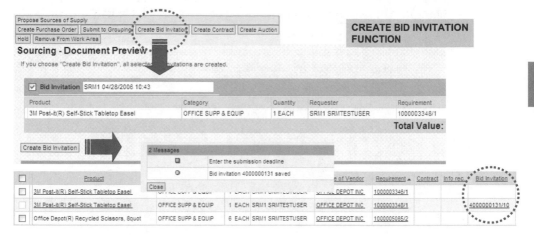

Figure 4.12 Create Bid Invitation via the Sourcing Application

At this point, no further activity can be performed on the shopping cart line items in the Sourcing application. Further processing will be handled in the Bidding Engine. Buyers will not be able to add any items to the bid invitation that have not been carried over automatically from the Sourcing application. Before a Bid Invitation is published, additional information, such as a submission deadline and chosen suppliers, have to be added in the Bidding Engine.

Any follow-on functions to either create a PO or contract will be performed from within the Bidding Engine application.

Via the Contract Management Application

Buyers can monitor contracts that are about to expire and can subsequently create a bidding event directly from the contract management application to renegotiate expiring contracts (illustrated in Figure 4.13). In releases prior to SAP SRM 4.0, this was termed the **Create Bid Invitation**; it is now called **Negotiate**.

The bid invitation is created automatically from the contract and all relevant information is auto-populated in it. Vendors will respond using the Bidding Engine, and a new version of the contract will be created if a supplier's proposal is accepted. Once the contract is approved, it can be released for use in other applications.

Figure 4.13 Negotiate Contracts

Via the Bidding Engine

Professional purchasers will be able to create bid invitations (RFIs and RFQs) directly from within the Bidding Engine (as shown in Figure 4.14). When an existing requirement such as a shopping cart request does not exist, buyers will proactively create Bid Events in SRM to initiate strategic negotiations for products and services, such as bidding for new computers for the organization.

In the Bidding Engine application, a bid invitation can be created in the following two ways:

► **Using Templates**
   This will help professional purchasers process recurring transactions more quickly and efficiently. In the Create Bid Invitation section, the purchaser can use the Create Template button to begin creating a bid invitation template.

► **Manually**
   Professional purchasers can initiate the RFQ process by creating a bid invitation directly in the Bidding Engine. As illustrated in Figure 4.17, the purchaser can select the type of bid from the dropdown menu and then click the **Create** button to create a new Bid Invitation, invite appropriate bidders, add products or services and free form requirements. Purchasers also can add attachments and notes relevant for the bid response.

Let's now move on to understanding the bidding Engine and how it works.

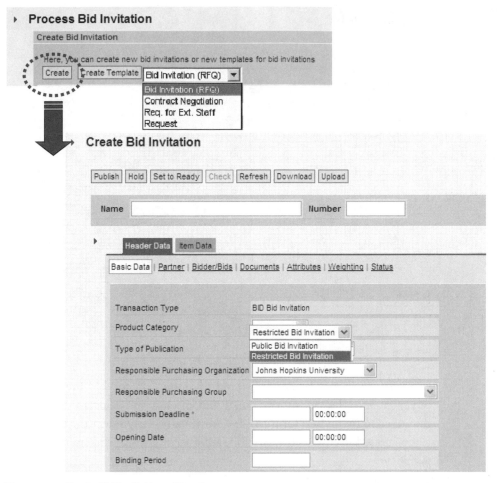

Figure 4.14 Create Bid Invitations Directly

4.1.4 The Bidding Engine — Bid Invitation in Detail

So far we have learnt that a bid invitation can be initiated from multiple different applications in SAP SRM. In this section we will discuss the Bidding Engine application in detail.

The bidding process in SAP SRM is initiated with the creation of a complete bid invitation. Using the Bidding Engine, suppliers are invited to submit their proposals as bids. Once their proposals have been submitted, buyers can compare and evaluate the proposals and accept the best bid or bids, which eventually result in a follow-on document such as a contract or a PO. Figure 4.15 illustrates the bidding process and the bullets after the figure explain each step in the process in greater detail.

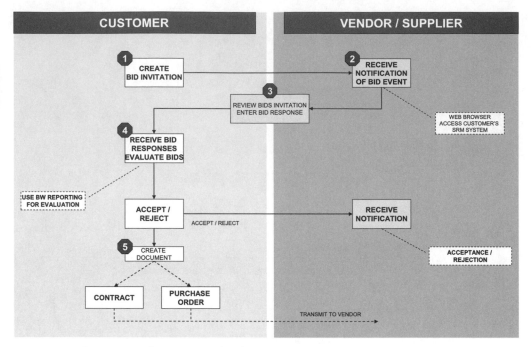

Figure 4.15 Bid Invitation and Bid Process

▶ In Step 1, we begin by creating a bid invitation. In the bid invitation the buyer enters relevant information about the bid and selects the suppliers that need to be invited for the bid. Additionally, they select the type of bid to be created. In SAP SRM, the following two types of Bid Invitations are supported:

   ▶ **Restricted Bid Invitations**

These are qualified, pre-determined suppliers that are active in the SAP Vendor Master and should have been replicated in SAP SRM.

   ▶ **Public Bid Invitations**

These are potential bidders that are not in the SAP Vendor Master and are invited to bid on requirements at the discretion of the professional purchasers creating the bid invitation. Notice of the bid invitation is published on marketplace bulletin boards.

▶ In Step 2 in Figure 4.15, the supplier(s) RECEIVE NOTIFICATION OF the BID INVITATION via email which includes a link to the bid invitation in SAP SRM (note: the Vendor Master in SRM needs to contain supplier information including email addresses). It is important to note that organizations might have to customize the information in this email as the standard email content might not be sufficient. Figure 4.16 shows you a restricted or private bidding option.

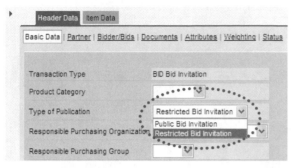

Figure 4.16 Restricted or Private Bidding

▶ In Step 3, the bidder or a contact person at the vendor organization logs on to the Bidding Engine application in SAP SRM to review the bid invitation (as shown in Figure 4.17). He or she is able to enter some of the following information on the bid response:

  ▶ Details on price and conditions, such as price scales

  ▶ Changes to quantity

  ▶ Vendor text and comments. The bidder can attach documents at header and item levels of the bid.

  ▶ Information on any customized attributes in the bid invitation; e.g., if the bid invitation contains an attribute of color. The vendor can provide information that is relevant to the attribute.

  ▶ Create additional line items, if this option has been allowed in the bid invitation

▶ In Step 4 in Figure 4.15 the strategic purchasers in SRM receive all the bid responses from the vendors with relevant information. By using evaluation tools in the Bidding Engine or the SAP BI solution, purchasers can compare all the bids before deciding on the best supplier. Figure 4.18 illustrates the comparision of a bid submitted by two vendors. **VENDOR1** has submitted their bid at a price of **20.00**, and **VENDOR2** has submitted the price of **23.00**. The system evaluates each criteria in the bid and automatically suggests the winning **Valuation Score** in green and others in red. Notice that Figure 4.18 shows an example of a simple bid comparision using **VENDOR1** and **VENDOR2** and the more complex bid comparision on the right between **C.E.B Berlin** and **BIDDERCOMP1**. I will discuss the bid evaluation capabilities in SAP SRM in detail in Section 4.1.5.

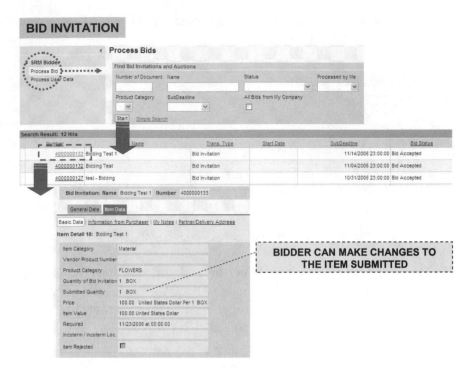

Figure 4.17 Bid Invitation Accessed by Supplier Contact

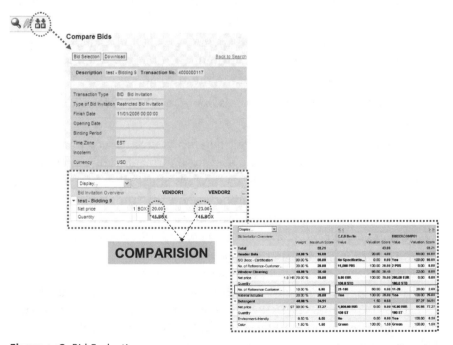

Figure 4.18 Bid Evaluation

▶ In Step 5, once the bid evaluation is complete and a bid is awarded to a supplier(s), the strategic purchaser can create a CONTRACT or PURCHASE ORDER document and transmit to the vendor.

4.1.5 Bid Evaluation in Detail

In the Bidding Engine, strategic purchasers can use the tools described in the following subsections to evaluate bids submitted by vendors.

Weighting and Ranking

In the Bidding Engine, organizations can use the Weighting and Ranking functions to evaluate and compare different bids that are submitted in response to a bid invitation. They can perform these evaluations at attribute and field, item, outline, and bid levels, a fact that provides flexibility in prioritizing the items and attributes in the bid invitation.

At the time of creating a bid invitation, the buyers will need to decide whether to use the weighting and ranking function. It cannot be used subsequently to analyze the bids in terms of their scores. By using the weighting and ranking function, buyers will be able to weight attributes or standard fields according to how important they are for the requirements, using a weighting factor. Figure 4.19 illustrates the process steps in creating attributes. Weighting is assigned and then used when evaluating bids.

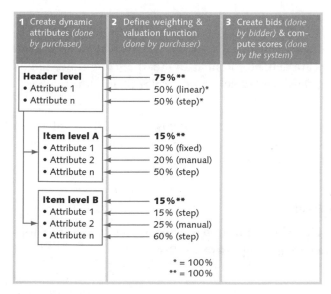

Figure 4.19 Dynamic Attributes — Concept

For example, weighting and ranking is useful if the delivery time is more important than the actual price of the item. In our example, we describe the weighting on standard fields of delivery date and price. However, dynamic attributes can be defined in the bid invitation and then analyzed based on the weighting and ranking. Dynamic attributes are specific characteristics of products and services that can be incorporated into the bidding process in the Bidding Engine. They are used to customize bid invitations and appear as additional fields requesting specific information. These attributes can be created and used for a specific bid invitation or made available to all bid invitations.

In addition to the weighting and ranking function, the following four functions can be used to calculate valuation factors (illustrated in Figure 4.20):

▶ **Linear**
This function is especially suitable for amount fields. The parameters of this function are minimum and maximum attribute values together with minimum and maximum function values. If a bidder enters a value that is outside the defined range, the minimum or maximum value is taken as the score value.

▶ **Step**
This function is especially suitable for information items such as delivery dates. When you are entering the intervals, you must ensure that the new interval begins where the previous one ends, for example 1–10 and 10–20.

▶ **Fixed**
This function is especially suitable for attributes with determined fixed values. If fixed values are defined for an attribute, the score values can be assigned to particular fixed values, such as the color of a product.

▶ **Manual**
This function is especially suitable for text fields with no fixed values. In this case, the purchaser will manually evaluate the contents of the fields in the bid document once received from the bidder.

Downloading Bids to Excel

Purchasers can use the **Download** button to download bids to their desktops for comparison and evaluation using Microsoft Excel.

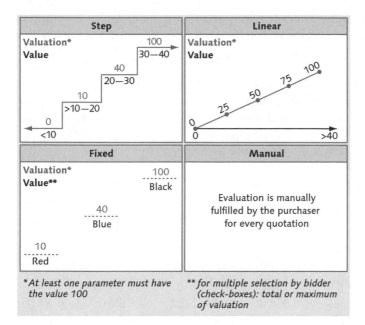

Figure 4.20 Bid Evaluation Factors

Using Reports in Business Intelligence (BI)

SAP NetWeaver Business Intelligence (SAP BI) is the reporting tool in SAP which was previously called Business Information Warehouse (BW). The following listed reports are examples of analytics available in the SAP BI that enhance a purchaser's ability to evaluate the bids received and determine a winner.

- Bidder history
- Vendor evaluation
- Price comparison List
- Detailed bid comparisons with attributes

Chapter 15 explains in detail the capabilities of SAP BI as it relates to SAP SRM. Let us now proceed with gaining an understanding of the live auction.

4.1.6   Live Auction

The live auction functionality in SAP SRM is an integral part of the SAP Bidding engine and replaces the previous functionality of reverse auction. It is implemented as a part of the SAP SRM strategic sourcing business scenario. In a typical auction, the buying organization creates an auction event for one or more products and services that it wants to purchase. Multiple suppliers bid for the products and services and depending on the nature of the auction (English, Dutch, or other), the winner is determined.

Most organizations use multiple criteria, not just cost alone, to select suppliers. The criteria could include quality of delivery, financial stability, supplier capabilities, and of course, total cost. Auctions foster competition among suppliers, as opposed to simply aggregating demand and then selecting the appropriate supplier.

Organizations have been able to gain huge savings by executing auctions. For example, in a success story published by SAP, SEA Containers Ltd., a logistics service provider, was able to leverage the auction capabilities in SAP SRM to generate savings of €1.4 million.

It is common for readers to question the core difference between the bid-invitation process of RFI and RFQs (discussed in Section 4.1.3) and the auction process, which also uses bid invitations. Figure 4.21 illustrates at a high level the difference between bid invitations and live auctions.

BID INVITATION	LIVE AUCTION
RFI & RFQ INVITATIONS INCLUDING PRICE AND NON-PRICE VARIABLES	BIDDING IS BASED ON PRICE ONLY EVALUATION CAN BE W/ OTHER VARIABLES
LONGER RESPONSE TIME FOR BIDDING VENDORS – DAYS TO WEEKS	TYPICALLY A SHORTER TIME-FRAME FOR BIDDING – HOURS TO DAYS
BIDDER'S ARE NOT ABLE TO SEE ANY INFORMATION ON COMPETITOR BIDS	RANK, BEST BID, AND NEXT BID CAN IS AVAILABLE IN REAL-TIME FOR BIDDERS
WELL SUITED FOR A LARGE VARIETY OF GOODS AND SERVICES, INCLUDING RAW MATERIALS, SERVICES, AND PROJECTS	WELL SUITED FOR COMMODITIES, OR GOODS AND SERVICES WITH STANDARDIZED ATTRIBUTES THAT VARY ONLY SLIGHTLY FROM ONE SUPPLIER TO ANOTHER SUPPLIER
TYPICALLY SOURCING IS BASED ON VALUE PROPOSITIONS (E.G. HIGH QUALITY, DELIVERY TIME) INSTEAD OF JUST PRICE	MARKET DYNAMICS OF AUCTION WORKS BEST WHEN THE BUYER / SUPPLIER RELATIONSHIP IS LOOSELY-COUPLED

Source: SAP America

Figure 4.21 High-level Difference Between Bid Invitation and. Live Auction

Strategic purchasers can use the Bidding Engine to create live auctions for products and services. Alternatively, auctions can also be initiated from either of the following sources (as illustrated in Figure 4.22):

- **Via the Sourcing Application**
  Shopping carts and external demand in the sourcing application can be directly converted into an auction event. It is important to note that auctions created from the Sourcing application do not allow to add additional items.

- **Convert a Bid Invitation**
  If a bid invitation has already been created or submitted, it can be converted into an auction as well for further processing.

- **Manually in the Bidding Engine**
  This can be done when there is no existing requirement and the strategic purchaser wants to initiate a strategic bid event. In this scenario, the resulting PO from the auction can only be saved locally.

SAP SRM delivers standard pre-defined auction profiles for organizations to use. These profiles use auction best practices; and are listed as follows:

- **English Auction**
  There is one simple rule, the lowest bidder wins the auction.

- **Rank-only Auction**
  Bidders can only bid lower than their last bid. The lowest bid from all suppliers ranks on top.

- **Blind-bidding Auction**
  Same as rank-only auction, but a bidder's rank is only displayed when that bidder is ranked first.

- **Company Best-bid Auction**
  Bids are validated against the best bid submitted so far by bidders from the same company.

The idea is that organizations can select an auction profile based on the type of auction being conducted, along with the supplier community being invited. For example, an English auction is effectively the reverse of the bidding event experienced on sites such as e-Bay, where the highest bidder wins. In the English auction, the lowest bidder wins, as the aim for the organization is to find the cheapest source for the product or service. Figure 4.23 illustrates the difference between these auction profiles.

Organizations can modify the auction profile in Customizing to change the validation rules and the information displayed to vendors during the auction process. These can be further changed dynamically when initiating the auction, as illustrated in Figures 4.24 and 4.25.

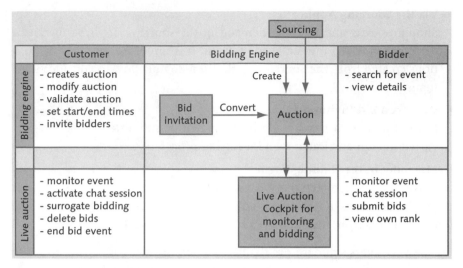

Figure 4.22 Creating an Auction

Profile type	Definition	Bidder sees (selection)	Bidder can'tsee (selection)
English	Basic reverse auction, bids validated against overal best bid, that is, the lowest bid ranks first	Rank Best bid Next bid Bid price No. of bidders	Bidder name Company best bid Company name First place
Rank-only	Bidder can submit a bid as long as it is lower than his own last bid, but it will not be ranked as first unless it is lower than all other bids.	Rank No. of bidders	Best bid First place Next bid Bid price
Blind bidding	Same as rank-only auction, excepted that a bidder's rank is only displayed when that bidder is ranked first.	First place	Best bid Rank Next bid Bid price
Company best bid	Bids are validated against the best bid submitted so far by bidders from the same company	Rank Rank in company Best bid Company best bid Bid price	First place Company name
Pre-defined profile types are delivered with mySAP SRM.			

Figure 4.23 Pre-Defined Auction Profiles

The interface for auction creation is very similar to the Bidding Engine. Figure 4.25 illustrates the **Basic Data** section within the **Header Data** tab of the auction. Organizations can select the type of auction to be created using the **Transaction Type** dropdown menu.

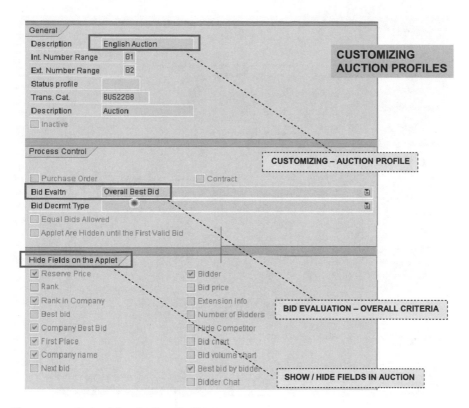

Figure 4.24 Customizing Auction Profiles

The strategic purchaser can also redefine the fields that are hidden from the bidders in the auction. This can be done in the **Bidder View** section of the auction header (shown in Figure 4.26 and Figure 4.27). This provides flexibility for organizations that want to determine dynamically during the auction creation whether certain information is valid for a particular auction event.

Similar to the dynamic attributes available in the bid invitation, the auction application contains *factored-cost* bidding. These allow for considering factors other than just the lowest price, such as the quality of the product or service or past performance of the supplier or vendor. In addition, organizations can assign bidding advantage or disadvantage to specific bidders while defining factors. The definition of factors is available at both the header and line-item levels of the bid event (auction). Figure 4.28 illustrates the factored-cost concept provided by SAP within SAP SRM.

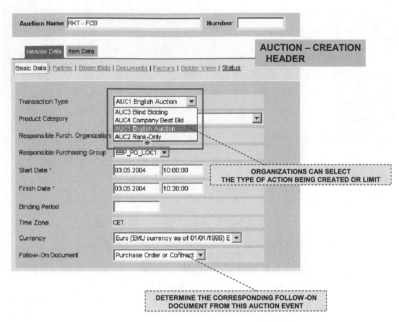

Figure 4.25 Auction Creation — Header

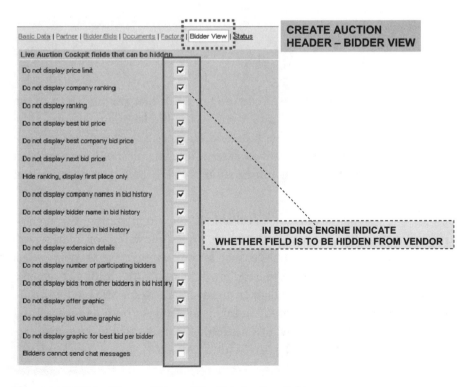

Figure 4.26 Bidder-View — Hide and Un-Hide Auction Fields

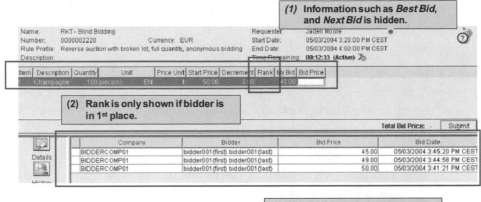

(1) Information such as *Best Bid*, and *Next Bid* is hidden.

(2) **Rank is only shown if bidder is in 1st place.**

(3) **Bidder can only see his own bids in the bid history. No price information is available from other bidders.**

Figure 4.27 Bidder's View in the Auction

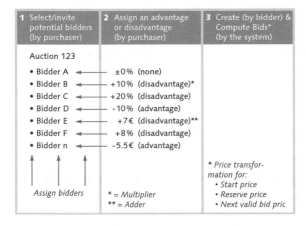

Figure 4.28 Factored-Cost Concept

Live auctions are started, ended, and extended automatically according to the parameters set during the creation of the auction. However, once the auction is started, the strategic purchaser has the capability to pause, extend, or end the auction at any point. Both purchasers and bidders can monitor the auction and bidding activity in real time. The purchaser's view of the auction is illustrated in Figure 4.29. The purchaser can view the **Best Bid** for each item in the auction. The purchaser can also initiate a chat session with any of the bidders to ask questions and provide additional information. The purchaser can also see the overall savings in the **Total Savings** field.

The bidder's view of the auction is illustrated in Figure 4.30. The bidder can view their overall rank in the **Company Rank** column. Additionally, they can also view the best bid and how it compares to their own bid. The **Bid Price** column allows the bidder to enter the next bid price.

Typically in the auction process the strategic purchaser(s) only monitors the auction to review the progress and status of the auction. However, there are times when the purchaser might have to intervene during the auction process, in one of the following ways:

▶ **Ban specific vendors**

This is required when you don't want a particular vendor to be a part of the auction process anymore.

▶ **Bidding on behalf**

Surrogate bidding might be required if the vendor is unable to bid. Although, the application provides this capability, there might be legal ramifications to this action.

▶ **Delete bids**

Sometimes a vendor might request the purchasing organization to delete a particular bid entered during the auction process. Although the application provides this capability, there might be legal ramifications.

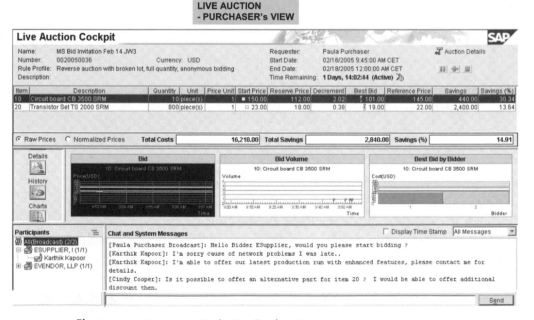

Figure 4.29 Live Auction Cockpit — Purchaser's View

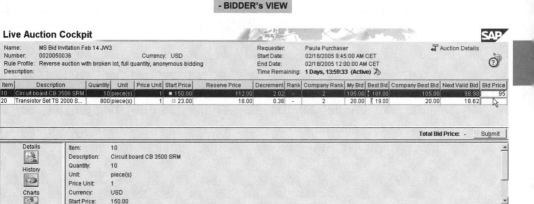

Figure 4.30 Live Auction Cockpit — Bidder's View

In Section 4.1, we discussed the strategic-sourcing capabilities in SAP SRM such as the Sourcing application, the Bidding Engine, and the Live Auction cockpit.

In the next section, I will cover the contract- management capabilities in SAP SRM.

4.2   Contract Management

Based on the current industry trends, contract management is one of the most talked-about processes within supplier relationship management. In 2005, Forrester Research concluded that:

Contract lifecycle management (CLM) applications will experience rapid growth of 40 % in demand in 2005, driven by the growing desire of enterprises to manage contract creation, negotiation, and compliance on an enterprise-wide basis, to help ensure compliance with Sarbanes-Oxley, and to capture savings buried in contracts with suppliers and sales or licensing revenues in contracts with customers or licensees of intellectual property.

That is underscored by recent research by the Aberdeen Group, which found that "…an astounding 80 % of enterprises are using manual or only partially automated processes to carry out contract-management activities."

It is very difficult for organizations to realize continuous cost benefits and achieve organization compliance in procurement unless a robust contract-management process and accompanying application is used within the over-all supplier relationship management system. Figure 4.31 illustrates some of the key issues and impacts of contract management based on a 2006 contract management benchmark report published by the Aberdeen Group.

Issue	Impact on Procurement
Fragmented procedures	• Increased maverick buying • Increased supply and financial risk • Under-leveraged spending
Labor-intensive process	• Long sourcing and contracting cycles • Less spend under contract / management • Non-competitive negotiations
Poor visibility into contracts and terms	• Poor compliance • Inconsistent and risky terms • Limited visibility into spending
Ineffective compliance monitoring and management	• Increased maverick buying • High purchase price variance, missed rebates, and discounts • Overpayments and performance risks
Inadequate performance analysis	• No view into category performance • Policy and regulatory violations • Under-leveraged spending and high risk

Figure 4.31 Impact of Poor Contract Management

In SAP SRM, the contract-management process deals with the development, negotiation, execution, and monitoring of contracts. Organizations can use these contracts to enhance their operational procurement processes, improve compliance, and achieve significant cost savings across the enterprise.

Contract management functionality in SAP SRM allows for a central reposi-tory of all the purchase contracts and pricing agreements of a purchasing organization. Purchase contracts represent long-term buying strategic agree-ments between the purchasing organization and suppliers to purchase cer-tain goods or services over a specified period. These contracts will provide the necessary flexibility for storing local exceptions, future prices, location-dependant prices, and minimum and maximum constraints as requirements demand.

Within SRM, contracts are used as a source of supply in shopping carts and POs. This allows organizations to empower requisitioners to order goods and services using pre-negotiated suppliers that have been selected as strategic for the product or commodity being purchased. Therefore, purchasing professionals don't need to intervene for purchases initiated with products and services that have active contracts in the system. In the SAP SRM Contract Management application, the following processes are supported, as shown in Figure 4.32:

▸ Contract development (create)

▸ Contract negotiation

▸ Contract execution (release and use)

▸ Contract monitoring

Figure 4.32 Contract Management Process

Sometimes, organizations tend to misunderstand the difference between contracts and catalogs. Although, they are both considered valid sources of supply in SRM, they differ in ways that are described in the following bullet points:

▸ **Contracts**
These are legal agreements between two parties, with detailed terms and conditions, clauses about penalty, warranty, and a determined validity period. A contract can contain products or product categories with specific discounts and other terms and conditions. In SRM, the contract is a document in the system, not the same as a PO and therefore users cannot receive or invoice against a contract. However, they can release POs against a contract.

▸ **Catalogs**
These contain products and list prices that are made available to users for easy searching and comparison. Catalogs are often supported by a contract to integrate the binding details existing in the contract. However, contracts are not required in the system to support catalogs. In the SAP SRM Catalog Content Management solution (CCM), organizations can transfer contracts from SRM into the catalog.

Purchasing professionals and users with appropriate authority have the ability to create contracts in SRM with the appropriate terms and conditions. In addition, they can assign to a contract an appropriate status: *Held, Approved or Released, Locked, Completed.* Requisitioners then have the ability to use the contracts that are in a Released status when creating their shopping carts as approved sources of supply to request for goods or services.

Contracts are used against purchases, and purchasing professionals have the ability to analyze and monitor the use of these contracts. This will assist in tracking vendor performance and overseeing internal contract compliance. Alert notifications via email allows professional purchasers to be aware of upcoming contract expiration dates.

Figure 4.33 illustrates the contract management process in SAP SRM. We will discuss each of these process steps in Section 4.2.1 thru Section 4.2.5.

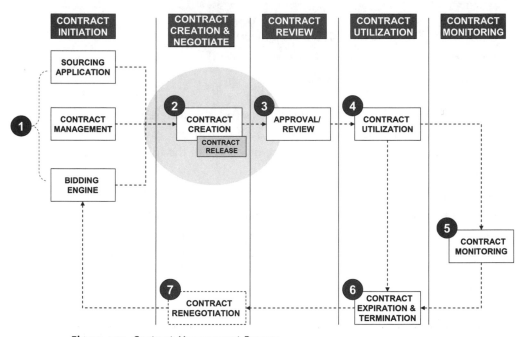

Figure 4.33 Contract Management Process

4.2.1 Contract Initiation

In Step 1 of Figure 4.33, we illustrate that in SRM professional purchasers have the ability to initiate contracts from any one of the following applications:

▶ From within the Sourcing application

▶ From directly in Contract Management

▶ From within the Bidding Engine

In Figure 4.34, we show the creation of a contract from **Sourcing**, **Process Contract,** and **Display Quotation** applications in SAP SRM.

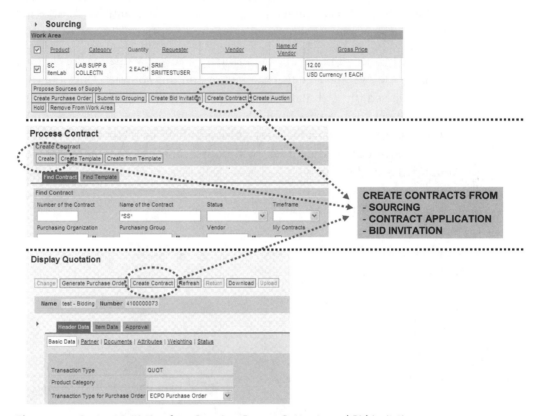

Figure 4.34 Contract Initiation from Sourcing, Process Contracts, and Bid Invitations

4.2.2 Contract Creation and Negotiation

In Step 2 of Figure 4.33, we show that once the contract is initiated, the contract-creation process begins. In SRM, organizations have the capability to create contracts or global outline agreements (GOA). A GOA is a purchasing document within SAP SRM created as a negotiated agreement with a vendor for the entire enterprise. It is typically created when multiple back-end systems are integrated within the landscape.

The contract application is similar in structure to the Process Purchase Order application discussed in Chapter 3. The application is divided between the **Header Data** tab and the **Item Data** tab.

Figure 4.35 illustrates the **Basic Data** section within the **Header Data** tab of a contract. In the Header Data tab, the contract administrator needs to complete the mandatory field marked with an asterisk next to the field. For example, **Vendor** is a required piece of data when completing the header tab of the contract.

Additionally, the administrator can maintain a **Target Value** for the contract indicating the overall value that can be used on this contract. Once the contract is released, the **Rel. Value** field is updated to indicate how much value in the contract has been used and what is remaining. Also, a tolerance can be defined in the **Under/Overdelivery Tolerance** field or the check box can be selected to indicate that the items within this contract can be received with **Unlimited** over-delivery.

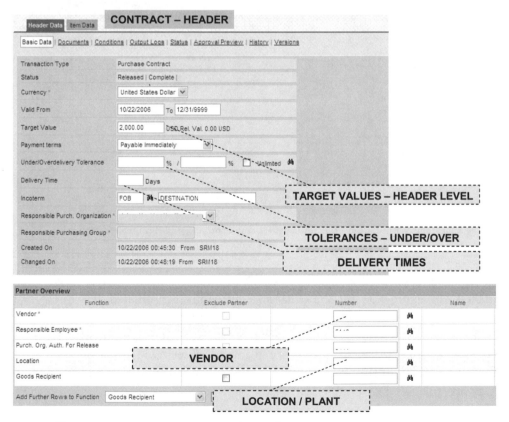

Figure 4.35 Contract creation — Header Level

Figure 4.36 illustrates the **Basic Data** section within the **Item Data** tab of a contract. The contract administrator can create a contract item that is a **Product** (material master-based) or **Description** based. In our example in Figure 4.36, the item is description-based called TEST.

It is important that when a description is used the administrator also enters the **Vendor Product Number** in the contract line item; this allows for sourcing the contract correctly. Now, when a shopping cart or PO is created, the end user needs to ensure that the same vendor product number is used in the shopping cart line item so that this contract will be available as a source of supply.

Notice that an **Under/Overdelivery Tolerance** can also be set at the item level as we saw in the Header Data tab. This allows more flexibility to set tolerances for individual items instead of the overall contract. The contract administrator can also set a **Minimum Order Qty** or a **Minimum Order Value** for each item within the contract.

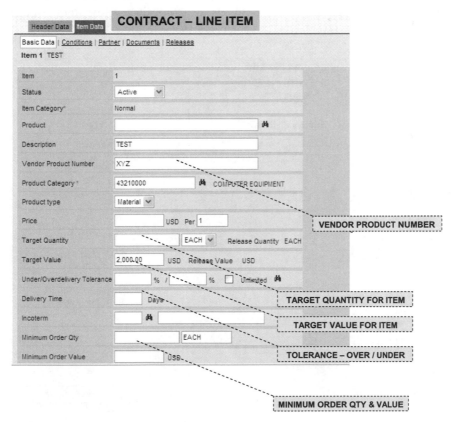

Figure 4.36 Contract Creation — Line-Item Level

During the creation and maintenance of contracts in SRM, the contract administrator has the ability to make use of the functions described in the following subsections.

Release Contracts

Using the **Release** button in the contract, the contract administrator can release complete (error-free) contracts. This contract can then be used as a source of supply for releases against POs. Remember that until a contract has the status of Released it cannot be used in shopping carts or POs.

Lock

Using this function, the contract administrator can lock an active document for releases. This way no POs can be made with reference to this document. For example, purchasers can set this status in order to temporarily remove a contract from Sourcing. If only a single item needs to be locked in a contract, it can be made **Inactivate** in the Basic Data section on the line item. Figure 4.37 illustrates this function.

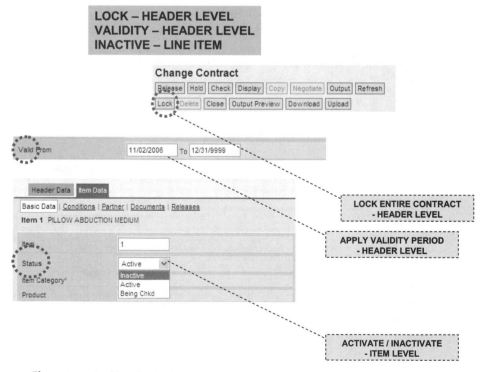

Figure 4.37 Locking Contracts

Download and Upload

Using this function, professional purchasers can download the contract documents to their PCs as files, process them locally, and then upload the changed document data to the SAP SRM application. From SAP SRM, a tabular file structure (in CSV format) is delivered. This provides additional flexibility for organizations to create and process contracts with a large number of items and also to make bulk changes.

> **Note**
>
> The download data file of the contract is not pretty to look at. The example illustrated in Figure 4.38 has been reformatted to make it more legible. SAP provides BAdIs with which organizations can apply additional business rules to augment or enhance the standard solution for upload and download (BBP_PD_DOWNLOAD).

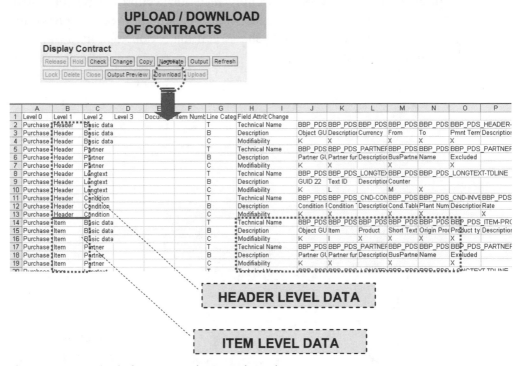

Figure 4.38 Download of Contract and GOA with Excel

Negotiate

Using this function, the contract administrator can create a bid invitation for an expiring contract in order to determine new vendors and possibly to negotiate improved conditions. Using SAP Bidding Engine, the contract administrator can then either create a new contract or update an existing one. This is discussed further in Section 4.2.6.

Attachments

Using this function, the contract administrator can attach terms and condition documents along with any electronic document used in the contract negotiation process. This will allow for a central repository for all pertinent documentation for a contract document.

Copy Contracts

The ability to copy contracts simplifies the process of renewing existing contracts or creating new ones. In addition, contract templates are available that can be used to quickly and efficiently create new contracts based on a standard format. Templates are linked to the standard approval process for the contract document. Figure 4.39 shows you the various options available is you nduring contract creation.

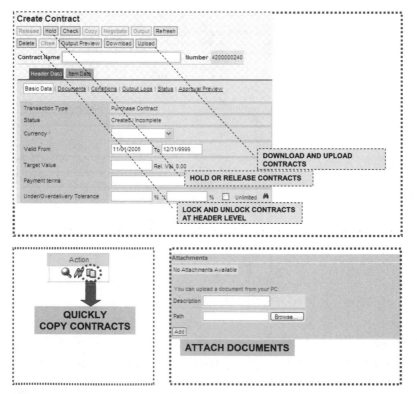

Figure 4.39 Contract Creation

Pricing

The contract administrator has the ability to manage item pricing conditions with conditions functionality, which is used in creating and maintaining contracts. These master conditions are used by the pricing functionality in SRM to determine a net price for products and services that are bought in the shopping cart or PO. The following standard SAP conditions are used in a contract:

▶ Fixed price

▶ Percentage discount

▶ Absolute discount

▶ Price dependent on location

▶ Discount (percentage) dependent on location

▶ Discount (absolute) dependent on location

For gross-price determination order, SAP provides the standard prioritization of condition types (according to the delivered calculation schema) as follows:

▶ Manual price-buyer override

▶ Contract price

▶ Catalog price

▶ Price from product

The pricing application guarantees that a manual price has priority over a contract price, which has priority over a catalog price, which in turn has priority over a price from product. This order illustrates how a price is derived when a source of supply is needed.

Restriction for Location

Organizations have the ability to allow for restricting **Location** reference globally. For contract items, the contract administrator can indicate that he or she is only authorized for release for specific locations. If this is the case, a location-dependent condition exclusive to these locations will be defined. In situations when the prices for products that are delivered from a vendor differ from one plant to another, this functionality makes it possible to define location-related pricing in a contract item. This is illustrated in Figure 4.40.

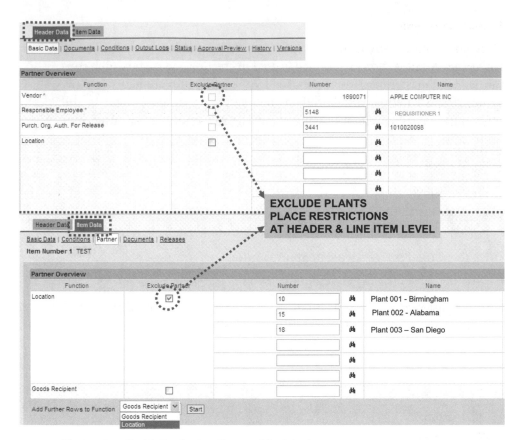

Figure 4.40 Restriction for Locations and Recipients

Quantity or Value Scales

The condition types used in contracts will provide for a scaling facility. In a separate sub-screen for scales, professional purchasers will be able to define scales based on prices or quantities. Figure 4.41 shows how scales can be used in the contract application.

Figure 4.41 Pricing Scales

Status Management

Using the status management functionality in SRM, purchasing professionals have access to the following document status categories, some of which they can manually assign and some of which are assigned automatically by the system. Figure 4.42 shows this functionality at work. Contract administrators can manage the following status categories in a contract:

▶ Held/Hold

▶ Released

▶ Locked

▶ Closed

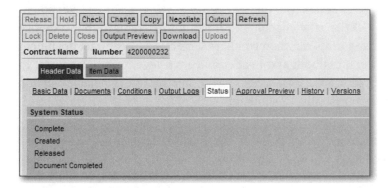

Figure 4.42 Status Management

In turn, the SAP SRM system then manages the following status categories:

▶ Created

▶ Document Completed

▶ In Negotiation

▶ In Renewal

▶ Deleted

▶ Archived

▶ Incomplete

▶ Complete

Version Management

When documents are modified, it is important that change history is maintained. In the Contract Management application in SAP SRM, version management provides the capability to keep track of changes made to contracts. In contrast to the change documents that retain a change history, a version displays the status of a document at a specific point in time. An example would be a situation in which you wish to display a PO in the form in which you transferred it to the vendor on a particular day. A version provides clarity in contract negotiations.

Once a contract is in *released* status and there are changes. These changes are saved in a change version of the original documents. They are subject to an approval process (based on business rules for your organization) before the changes are transferred to the active document. The change workflow is started once the changed version is released.

Once the changed version get the status *approved,* a historical version is saved as a copy of the active document. It cannot be changed, but only displayed. Authorized users can then compare versions of a contract document and list the differences both at a header and item level in tabular form. In Customizing, organizations can choose whether or not to enable version management for purchasing documents.

> **Note**
>
> SAP provides BAdIs for organizations to apply additional business rules to augment or enhance the standard solution for controlling the circumstances under which the system creates a version for contracts (BBP_VERSION_CONTROL).

Distribute Contracts to the SAP Catalog

Once contracts are created and released for use, they can be transferred to the SAP Catalog for easier search and selection. This is enabled using a standard process that integrates the contract application with the SAP Catalog (SAP CCM, SAP MDM Catalog) using the SAP NetWeaver Exchange Infrastructure (XI) solution.

Once the Customizing requirements are completed, all contracts that have a status of Released and have also been selected for transfer to the catalog (header level) are available for transfer to the SAP Catalog application.

4.2.3 Contract Review

Step 4 in Figure 4.33 showed that once a contract is created and released it may require approvals or review by others within your organization. For example, business rules in your organization might dictate that all contracts created in excess of $50,000 require the approval of the purchasing director. In this example, the contract will not be available for use as a valid source of supply until it has been approved by the purchasing director. Once all the required approvals are complete, the status in the contract changes to released.

In SAP SRM, a number of workflow templates are pre-delivered that organizations can use out-of-the-box without any development. As a part of the system set-up and configuration, project teams decide which workflows to activate and also define business rules within the workflow condition editor. Workflow in SRM and its use in the different documents such as contracts are explained in detail in Chapter 10.

4.2.4 Contract Utilization

Step 5 in Figure 4.33 illustrated that once contracts are created and released, they are available for use and execution within the system to create POs. Additionally, professional purchasers can use these contracts within the Sourcing application to assign contracted vendors as sources of supply when completing open shopping-cart requirements. As a contract gets used within the shopping cart or PO, the contract release gets updated subsequently and can be reviewed in the contract application. In this way, contract administrators can be aware of the use of the quantity or total value of the contract and make appropriate decisions. For example, let's assume that there is a contract created in the system for the purchase of computers with the Dell Corporation. The contract administrator can review the **Header Data** section of the Dell contract to check the **Release Value** of the contract.

4.2.5 Contract Monitoring

Contract monitoring is a continuous process of reviewing purchasing activity against the contract and contract budget. When monitored periodically, this activity ensures adequate performance and contract compliance. Industry research shows that although most organizations create and use contracts in some form with their vendors, they lack visibility into the way these contracts are used or complied with.

Step 6 of Figure 4.33 illustrates that released contracts are available for use in business documents such as shopping carts and POs, and once they are used the contract administrator can being the monitoring process. Using the contract monitoring functionality, contract administrators can monitor contract usage, contract renewal, volume of a contract, and overview of ordered products and categories. One of the key methods to ensure procurement compliance is for organizations to monitor purchasing activity periodically.

Progress should be matched with baseline metrics defined for the organization. When contracts are created, a validity period can be assigned to indicate the start and end dates of the negotiated terms and conditions in the contract. Once the contract end-date is reached, a contract attains status of *Expired.* Contracts with the expired status are not available as sources of supply for selection by end users or professional purchasers. In Step 7 in Figure 4.33, we showed that once a contract is expired the contract administrator needs to take action to either renegotiate the contract or terminate the contract. We will discuss the renegotiation of contracts in Section 4.2.6.

In SAP SRM, contract monitoring can be further enhanced by using the SRM alert-management functionality and reports in BI. In the previous paragraph, we explained that organizations can monitor individual contracts to review the contract use and expiration. To attain true contract monitoring, however, the BI solution provides access to pre-defined monitoring reports and alerts that can be triggered when contracts are about to expire.

From a process perspective, when specific events occur in SRM, alerts are generated and can be reported via the Contract Management content in SAP BI. This does not have to occur when a contract is nearing expiration; an alert could be configured for contract changes as well. The reporting capabilities of SAP BI as it relates to SAP SRM are described in detail in Chapter 15.

4.2.6 Contract Renegotiation

Contract administrators have the capability in SRM to renegotiate existing contracts directly with the vendor using the Bidding Engine. This is illustrated as Step 7 — **Contract Renegotiation** — as you saw in Figure 4.36.

Renegotiation is typically done to renew the terms and conditions of an existing contract. To initiate the negotiation, a bid invitation is generated directly from within the contract application, which can then be enhanced within the Bidding Engine before it is sent out as email request to preferred vendors. The vendor(s) can then submit new contract terms and conditions, such as target value or price conditions. If the professional purchaser or contract administrator accepts the vendor's bid, the data is transferred to the existing contract and it is renewed.

Contracts that are about to expire can be renegotiated via the SAP Bidding Engine, as illustrated in Figure 4.43. In this figure a GOA with the number **4200001316** is shown in display mode. The **Negotiate** button is used to begin the process of re-negotiation. Once this is clicked a pop-up box is displayed indicating that a bid invitation is created and held. In our example, the message is **Bid invitation 0000003316 Held**. The contract administrator can review the status of this contract at any time by clicking on the **History** link in the contract Header Data screen.

Figure 4.43 Negotiate Function in the Contract Application

Once the negotiation process is started, the system assigns different status based on the stage of the negotiation. This allows for flexible search capability. The **In Negotiation** status indicates that negotiations for a particular contract have started with the vendor. The **In Renewal** status indicates that a released contract has undergone negotiation and the bid invitation is currently in a **Held** status. This status tells the professional purchasers that additional work may need to be performed on the bid invitation before it can be published and sent to the vendor.

Once the generated bid invitations are enhanced and completed, a bid notification is sent to the supplier, who can then choose to change the bid by adding new items, change information on the target quantities or values for an item, the conditions or delivery times. The bid invitation and bid process are the same as described in the bidding section earlier in this chapter.

Once the bid is received by the customer, and accepted, the contract administrator has two choices: Create a new contract, or update the existing contract. Figure 4.44 illustrates that the **Update Contract** button can be used to update the contract that initiated the bid (a new version of the original contract is generated in SRM). The **Create Contract** button can be used to create a new contract from the bid award. Based on defined business rules, an approval for the contract update or creation might be required.

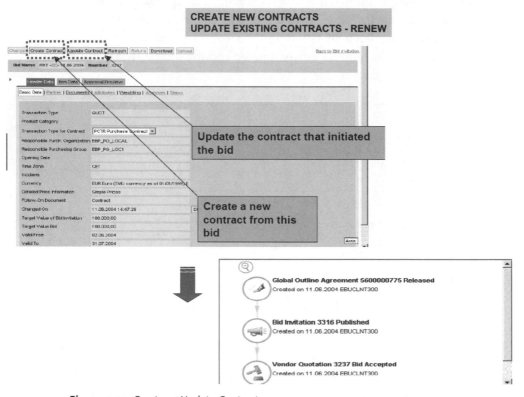

Figure 4.44 Create or Update Contracts

4.2.7 Contract Distribution

With SAP SRM, organizations can create contracts or GOAs. A GOA is a purchasing document within SAP SRM created as a negotiated agreement with a vendor for the entire enterprise; and is typically created when multiple back-end systems are integrated within the landscape. Once these GOAs are created, organizations can choose to distribute these documents to back-end SAP systems if needed. The back-end purchasing organizations can be notified about these new contracts via email, and at that point the purchasing organizations can register for these contracts and begin to use them for creating POs in the SAP back ends (as illustrated in Figure 4.45).

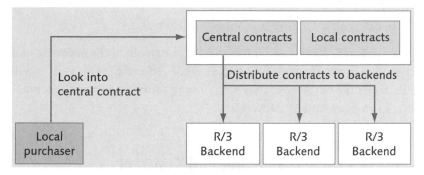

Figure 4.45 Distributing Contracts to Back-End Systems

> **Note**
>
> As of SAP SRM release 4.0, both the contract and scheduling agreement can be distributed compared to just the contracts in previous releases. It is important to note that organizations cannot create local contracts within SAP SRM and also distribute that same contract to a SAP back end. Only one of the options is allowed in release 4.0. Figure 4.45 illustrates **Central Contracts** separately than **Local contracts**.

When distributing the contracts or scheduling agreements, a separate document is created based on the purchasing organization and location (plant) defined within the contract document. The actual distribution is enabled using a standard IDoc: BLAREL — BLAORD03, COND_A02 — BLAREL02.

> **Note**
>
> SAP provides BAdIs for organizations to apply additional business rules to augment or enhance the standard solution for the contract distribution (BBP_CTR_BE_CRE-ATE in SRM; BBP_CTR in SAP R/3).

Organizations that want to distribute the contracts or scheduling agreements to the SAP back end need to be aware of the following restrictions (SAP SRM 4.0 release):

▸ Only releases R/3 4.0B or higher are supported.

▸ No distribution of central contracts to Enterprise Buyer are allowed.

▸ No automatic splitof target quantity and target value is allowed.

▶ Service items are not allowed for distribution from a GOA in SRM to a scheduling agreement in the SAP back-end.

▶ Contract hierarchies are not supported.

▶ Attachments are not transferred to the SAP back-end.

In Section 4.1 and Section 4.2, I introduced and explained the sourcing and contract management functionality in SAP SRM. In the next section, I will briefly discuss some of the new enhancements in sourcing and contract management since release of SAP SRM 5.0.

4.3   What's New in Sourcing and Contract Management?

SAP has been continuously enhancing the SAP SRM solution every year with new releases that have produced a variety of rich and useful functionality. This section highlights some of the new functionality introduced in Sourcing and Contract Management applications since SAP SRM 5.0.

4.3.1   Initial Upload of Contract from ERP to SAP SRM

A number of organizations that have been using the SAP R/3 solution use the Materials Management (MM) module within SAP for purchasing. As these organizations are moving towards the SAP SRM solution, they need to replicate the existing master data within these systems into the SRM system.

For example, the contract management functionality is now only being developed within SAP SRM. Therefore, it is beneficial for organizations to use SAP SRM to create and manage all contracts within SAP SRM and then distribute those of other systems within the organization if required.

A new report — BBP_CTR_INIT_UPLOAD — has been created as a standard tool to upload contracts and scheduling agreements from the back-end ERP system into SRM.

4.3.2   New Strategic Sourcing Offering — On-Demand Sourcing

On-demand solutions that assist in the overall delivery of Supplier Relationship Management are one of the key trends emerging in the marketplace. These solutions allow companies more flexibility and the ability to maximize their current technology investments. These solutions work with virtually any existing procurement or ERP system, including SAP, Oracle, PeopleSoft, and others. Some of the reasons on-demand is becoming a huge market lie in the following benefits driven by these solutions:

▶ Operational implementation is completed in a very short time compared to typical in-house solution installation and operation (typically within weeks).

▶ Implementation an start small and grow over time.

▶ Full payback and ROI occur within months because the costs of installation, set-up and ongoing maintenance are reduced dramatically.

▶ Start-up fees are dramatically lower than those for traditional software.

SAP acquired Frictionless Commerce, a leading on-demand supplier of e-sourcing solutions, in 2006. With this acquisition, SAP now offers a strategic sourcing on-demand solution. Frictionless Commerce's On-Demand edition offers e-sourcing capabilities available through a Web browser. Within days, organizations can run sourcing events and begin managing suppliers. The On-Demand edition offers shorter time-to-benefit, as well as measurable cost savings with a minimal investment in time, resources, and training.

The SAP e-sourcing on-demand functionality provides the following capabilities, referenced from the frictionless website:

▶ **Project management and reporting**
Manage activities, tasks, milestones and alerts. Capture supporting documents and files into one repository. Track a portfolio of savings opportunities.

▶ **RFx (RFI, RFQ and RFP) creation, management, and analysis**
Source simple-to-complex negotiation events in direct, indirect and services categories. Conduct multi-round sourcing events without re-entering data.

▶ **Wide variety of reverse auction capabilities and settings**
Manage advanced bidding rules such as bid visibility, automatic extensions, ranked-bidding format, weighted-bidding format, staggered line-item start and end times, and reserved prices.

The Frictionless offering was already NetWeaver compliant prior to the acquisition by SAP. Therefore, SAP advises that the migration path to SAP SRM for customers is fairly seamless.

> **Note**
>
> As of Q3 2007, SAP offers primarily two solutions for e-sourcing: Hosted and On Premise. The latter is installed within your firewall. Currently these two offerings are separate solutions. The Hosted solution is frictionless and the On Premise solution is SAP code. Currently, the Hosted solution offers integration of master data, executing RFx/Auctions and the creation of POs or contracts in SAP R/3 or ECC. The Hosted solution has no integration with SRM. SAP plans to offer a product later in 2008 that will integrate the solution offering for the Hosted and On-Premise solutions. The integration between E-Sourcing and SAP R/3 (ECC) is enabled using the Exchange Infrastructure (XI/PI).

4.4   Summary

In this chapter, I introduced readers to two key capabilities within SAP SRM: sourcing and contract management. I discussed how organizations can use the bidding and auction capabilities in SAP SRM to enhance their entire sourcing process to better identify and quality suppliers as well as to negotiate the best possible terms and conditions without sacrificing quality.

I also discussed in detail the contract-management functionality in SAP SRM. You should remember that contracts can be created from multiple different applications in SAP SRM. Contract management allows organizations to prepare, create, update, and monitor contractual agreements electronically within the system.

> **Note**
>
> In Q2 of 2007 SAP announced a new solution for Contract Management, branded as xCLM. The initial xCLM 1.0 release will be based on the legal contract authoring solution that controls the creation of contracts in MS Word, along with Duet. Contract management within SRM still remains, but xCLM will be a valuable tool for organizations that want the capability of authoring contracts using MS Word, which is made available using the Duet integration scenarios.

In Chapter 5, I will introduce you to the Supplier Enablement concept in SAP SRM. I will discuss in detail how buying organizations can integrate with suppliers for order collaboration and inventory replenishment. Chapter 5 will also introduce the Supplier Self Services (SAP SUS) component of SAP SRM.

The age of proprietary information systems is coming to an end, and the age of shared services is dawning. The traditional corporate boundaries are falling down giving way to cross–company sharing of business processes.

5   Supplier Enablement

According to Webster's dictionary, enablement means: "The act of enabling, or the state of being enabled; ability." When we generally talk about supplier enablement, we are referring to enabling the interaction, visibility, and collaboration between buying organizations and their suppliers.

While it's true that companies have done a great job streamlining their internal processes, their shared processes — those that involve interactions with other companies — are largely a mess. Think about your own procurement process. It's the mirror image of your supplier's order fulfillment process, with many of the same tasks and information requirements.

When your purchasing agent fills out a requisition form, for instance, she's performing essentially the same task the supplier's order entry clerk performs when he takes the order. Yet there is probably little or no coordination between the two processes. Even if you and your supplier exchange transactional data electronically, the actual work is still being performed in isolation, separated by a large inter-company divide.

Because cross-company processes are not coordinated, a vast number of activities end up being duplicated. The same information is entered repeatedly into different systems, the same forms are filled out and passed around multiple times, and the same checks are done over and over. When the activities and data make the jump between companies, inconsistencies, errors and misunderstandings routinely arise, leading to even more wasted work. Often scores of employees have to be assigned to manage the cumbersome interactions between the companies. Although all of these inefficiencies may be hidden from your accounting systems, which track only what happens within your own walls, the costs are real, and they are large. Today, efficiency ends at the edges of the company.

To better understand supplier enablement, let's take an example from the 2006 benchmark report published by the research company Aberdeen Group. This benchmark examined the supplier enablement processes, activities, benefits, shortcomings and technology use of 120 enterprises. Figure 5.1 provides some analysis of the data gathered from one question to customer organizations: How much data do you share with your supplier community?

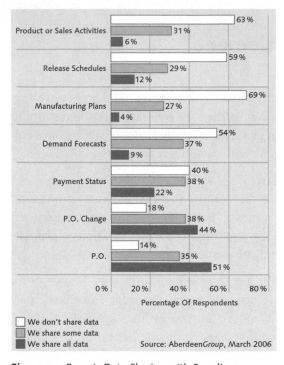

We don't share data
We share some data
We share all data   Source: AberdeenGroup, March 2006

Figure 5.1 Buyer's Data-Sharing with Suppliers

The data in Figure 5.1 illustrates that most companies that responded to the survey, exchange Purchase Order (PO) and Purchase Order Change data with the supplier electronically. 51 % of the respondents exchange all PO data electronically; 44 % of the respondents exchange PO Change data; 38 % of the companies share some payment status data and 22 % share all data related to payment status. Notice, however, that there is a big disparity for buying companies to provide visibility to suppliers about their demand forecasts and release schedules, with only 9 %–12 % of companies sharing all data in these areas.

Organizations are increasingly looking at technology for exchanging information with their suppliers. Based on the Aberdeen report, half of the respondent companies already use some form of Web-based supplier portal and Internet-based EDI, and about six of every seven enterprises will have programs in place within 12 months. Another interesting fact reported by Aberdeen was that in their 2004 benchmark report, the average e-procurement deployment had only 17 % of suppliers enabled. Today, that number has jumped to 29 %. This data is evidence that organizations are increasingly integrating their businesses processes with those in their supplier community.

Streamlining cross-company processes is the next great frontier to reducing costs, enhancing quality, and speeding operations. The leaders will be companies that are able to take a new approach to business, and who will work closely with partners to design and manage processes that extend beyond the traditional corporate boundaries.

This chapter focuses on how companies can use SAP SRM to closely integrate processes in order management, inventory and demand planning, and design collaboration. In Section 5.1, I will provide a brief overview of all of the integrated processes that exist within the SAP Supplier Collaboration solution.

5.1 Supplier Enablement Using SAP SRM

The SAP SRM application provides organizations with the ability to integrate with suppliers of all sizes. SAP provides this functionality to organizations using the core SAP SRM solution along with the SAP Supply Chain solution. Organizations can integrate their suppliers using a Web-based solution that is scalable and provides suppliers with immediate access to supply-side transactions and other relevant information. It provides a single point of entry where, among several other capabilities, purchasing organizations and suppliers can:

- Collaborate on exchanging orders and acknowledgements
- Share inventory and supply-demand plans
- Access uploaded supplier catalog data
- Check payment status
- Collaborate on new & existing product design plans

Over the last few years, SAP has enhanced their solution offering around supplier collaboration. Today, there are multiple components that integrate together to provide a holistic solution for Supplier Enablement. The main components are as follows:

- ▸ SAP Supplier Self Services (SUS, a component of SAP SRM)
- ▸ SAP Inventory Collaboration Hub (ICH, a component of SAP SCM)
- ▸ SAP NetWeaver Portal (a component of SAP NetWeaver)
- ▸ SAP Project Lifecycle Management (SAP PLM)
- ▸ SAP Supplier Network (an integrated component of SAP SRM)

Figure 5.2 illustrates how these components work together to enable collaborative processes along the entire supplier relationship lifecycle.

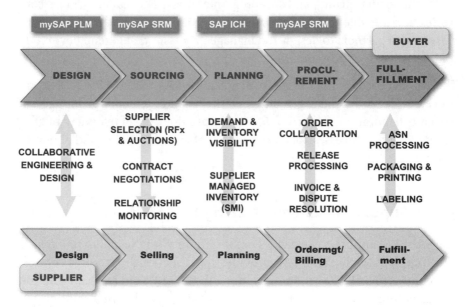

Figure 5.2 Integrated Processes Within Supplier Collaboration

This chapter focuses on the processes that are powered by the SAP SRM components (SAP SUS and Supplier Network), and, where appropriate, provides an overview of the functionalities available for Supplier Enablement using the other SAP components (ICH, SCM, PLM, etc.).

As mentioned earlier, suppliers only need a Web browser to access the SUS application. There are two main methods organizations can use to deploy SUS that I will discuss next:

5.1.1 Direct Access of SUS Application via BSP URL

In SAP SRM 4.0, the technical architecture of the SUS application was enhanced from that of prior releases. Now, the SUS application can be directly accessed via a Web URL that is based on the BSP technology within SAP NetWeaver. Readers should note that this access is different from accessing the EBP application, because EBP uses the ITS technology (which is now also integrated with SAP NetWeaver). SAP recommends that customers not access the SUS application in this manner, but instead utilize the SAP portal option described below. Figure 5.3 illustrates an example of accessing the SUS application directly via a BSP URL.

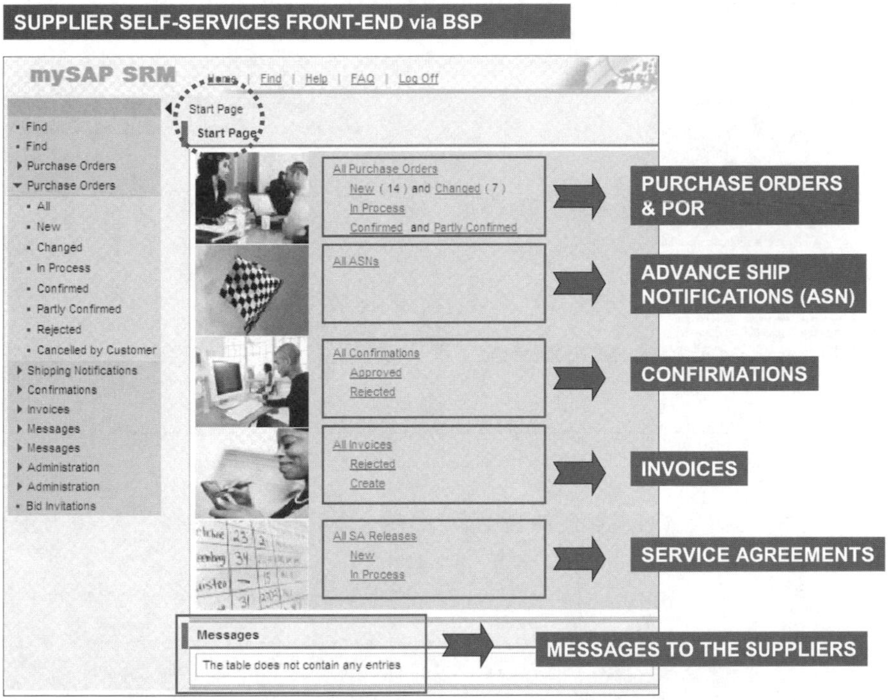

Figure 5.3 SUS Using Direct URL Access

5.1.2 Business Package or iView in the SAP NetWeaver Portal

This option is suitable for organizations implementing the SAP NetWeaver Portal solution, because they can then make use of the *supplier collaboration* business package provided by SAP for enabling supplier integration. The core benefit of using the SAP NetWeaver Portal is that the supplier is provided with a unified solution that could contain content from multiple SAP components.

For instance, let's say your organization wants to share several reports (from SAP BI) with a supplier for performance evaluation. You can easily add these reports into the portal environment and then the supplier can access the SUS component processes and the BW reports using a single login to the SAP NetWeaver Portal.

Additionally, if you invite the same supplier to a Bidding event, the portal can again be used as a seamless interface to the supplier. Further, the Bidding engine component can be integrated with the SUS application in such a way that the supplier view is unified. Figure 5.4 shows an example of the SUS application after accessing it via the SAP NetWeaver Portal.

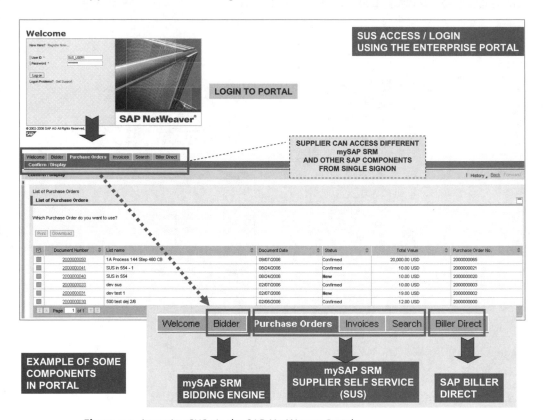

Figure 5.4 Accessing SUS via the SAP NetWeaver Portal

According to SAP America, the vision for supplier collaboration is: "Unified access to collaborative applications and information gateway, providing suppliers with a single point of access. This enables collaborative processes along the entire supplier relationship lifecycle."

After having gained an understanding of supplier enablement let us move on to supplier registration.

5.2   Supplier Registration

In an effort to enable organizations to reduce administrative overhead with the help of Supplier Enablement, SAP SRM provides multiple options to register prospective suppliers that are going to engage in collaborative processes with the organization. The Supplier Registration process is integrated with the overall supplier selection and use process in SAP SRM. This process is discussed below and also described briefly in Chapter 6. Suppliers can be registered in SAP SRM in the following ways:

▸ The buyer organization registers the supplier manually

▸ The supplier self-registers on the buyer's website

The process of self-registration in SAP SRM is enabled using the Supplier Registration concept, which utilizes the SAP SRM, Supplier Registration, and SAP SUS applications to complete the entire process. The process for manually creating the suppliers does not utilize the Supplier Registration application available in the SAP SRM system.

5.2.1   Buyer Organization Registers the Supplier

If your organization already has the necessary detail about a supplier's company, you can register the supplier manually. You can register the supplier either as a business partner in SAP SRM, or you can create a vendor master record for this supplier in the SAP R/3 or ERP backend. Once you've created the vendor or business partner (or replicated the organization from SAP R/3), a user ID and password is created for the supplier in the Supplier Self Services (SUS) application. This ID is automatically sent to the vendor or business partner via the email specified. This process is illustrated in Figure 5.5.

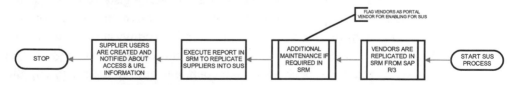

Figure 5.5 Buying Organization Registers Suppliers Manually

You need to create the appropriate supplier users (contact persons) in SAP SRM, in the SUS application. Additionally, the roles you assign to these users are SUS roles which are different from roles in EBP or SAP R/3. Many times organizations forget that these are different applications and therefore the security is independent in each of these applications. The security teams responsible for creating users need to know that the users need to be created with the User management application in SUS, and cannot be created using the **Create User** (SU01) transaction in the system. This is illustrated in Figure 5.6.

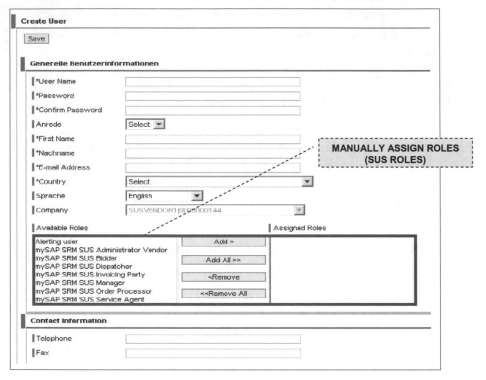

Figure 5.6 Creating Users in SUS User Management

5.2.2 Supplier Self-Registration

Organizations can invite selected suppliers to self-register on the organization's website. Suppliers can register using an anonymous user account (no logon required) on the website to fill out a basic application form. In addition to requesting standard information about the supplier, organizations can send category-dependent or -independent questionnaires to suppliers for gathering detailed information regarding the supplier's capabilities for providing goods and services for those categories.

The data in the registration application and the relevant questionnaires is used by purchasers to pre-screen suppliers. The supplier information and questionnaires are evaluated by the appropriate purchasing professional who decides to approve or reject a supplier. If approved, you can create a business partner for the supplier in SAP Enterprise Buyer and later replicate the business partner as a vendor in the SAP SUS application. This process is illustrated via a process flow in Figure 5.7. Each of these processes is further discussed in this section.

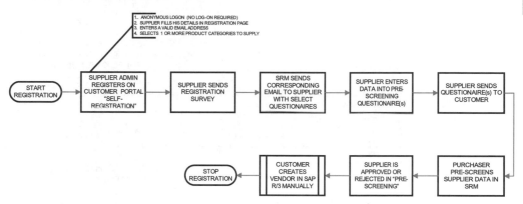

SELF-SERVICE REGISTRATION PROCESS

Figure 5.7 Supplier Registers via Self-Service

▶ **Self-Registration Application**
   To self-register, suppliers can fill out a simple application form to enter their company information. This form requests information that in the past was received from prospective suppliers via fax or mail and was then entered into SAP systems manually. Instead organizations can now leverage the Self Registration functionality to electronically receive supplier information. Figure 5.8 shows that the Supplier Registration form contains three main areas to capture supplier details: **Company Information**, **Address Data**, and **Which Commodities can you supply?**

▶ **Questionnaires**
   Organizations can also design specific questionnaires focused towards a specific product category that can then be used for the supplier pre-screening process. Figure 5.9 illustrates the customization area for Supplier Registration. You can use the **Create/Change Questionnaire** functionality to configure how the questionnaire should be created. Figure 5.9 shows the standard questionnaire available in SAP SRM, which contains three sections: **General questions**, **Certification**, and **Revenue**. This questionnaire is very generic and most organizations will find the need to use BAdIs available in SRM to modify the questionnaire and/or create a new questionnaire.

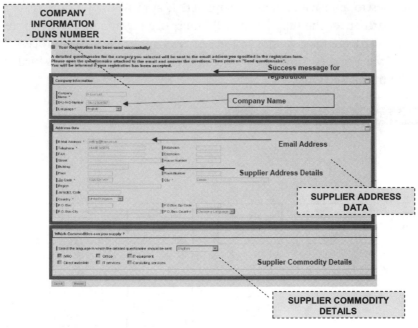

Figure 5.8 Supplier Registration Form

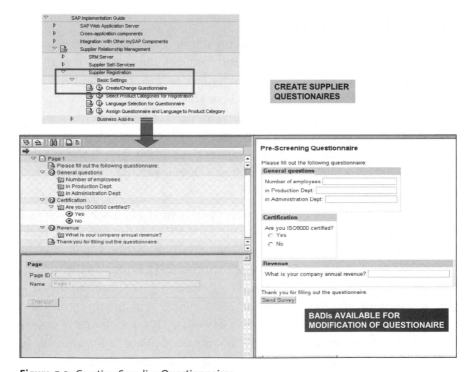

Figure 5.9 Creating Supplier Questionnaires

▶ **Supplier Pre-Screening**

Once prospective suppliers have submitted their registration applications and relevant questionnaires, the purchasing professionals in the buying organization can pre-screen the suppliers, and review their submitted details and questionnaires. Based on the evaluation, they can approve or reject a prospective supplier by clicking on the **Accept** or **Reject** buttons.

▶ **Transferring Screened Suppliers to EBP**

Once prospective suppliers have been screened and approved as accepted partners, purchasers can individually transfer these suppliers into the SAP SRM (EBP) application as business partners. The supplier can be selected from the list of approved Business Partners and then transferred to SAP EBP using the **Transfer** button. At this time, you can add information to this business partner record, if required. These business partners are then available to purchasers in EBP for selection in the sourcing, vendor lists, and other applications.

Note
Remember that the Supplier record is at this point only created in the SAP SRM (EBP) system as a business partner. Organizations using SAP R/3 or ERP as an enterprise backend might need to also create the supplier record in the Vendor Master in the SAP system for follow-up functions (PO, Invoice, etc.). The vendor master record needs to be created manually, as there is no process to create these automatically. In the EBP-SUS scenario, the supplier business partner is created in the EBP system. In the MM-SUS scenario, a supplier needs to be created in the SAP backend manually.

▶ **Transferring Business Partners from EBP to SUS**

Suppliers created in EBP are transferred to the Supplier Self Services (SUS) application using the SAP Exchange Infrastructure (XI). Once this is done, a sales organization is created in SUS and the supplier administrator (registered user) is sent an email containing a registration ID and password that they can use to create an administrator UserID for their company in SUS. The sales organization is then created in the Organizational Structure in SUS.

Once suppliers (business partners) are available in SRM, these supplier companies can be replicated to the Organizational Structure in SUS. This replication is carried out using standard programs in SAP SRM.

> **Tip**
>
> If organizations do not want to use the automated process of sending the registration ID via an email, they can deactivate the standard workflow for this process.

Once users are created in the Supplier Self Services (SUS) application, the buying organization and the supplier organizations can begin to collaborate on exchange of orders, inventories, invoices, payment status, etc.

5.3 Supplier Collaboration: Order Collaboration

The supplier collaboration process in SAP SRM utilizes the SAP Supplier Self-Services (SUS) component as its core application. The SUS application is, in simple terms, a hosted system that suppliers can easily access using a web browser. SUS provides collaboration capabilities for goods and service orders and integrates suppliers into the procurement processes of large buying organizations. Such suppliers do not require their own sales system for receipt and processing of orders; external suppliers can then access designated purchasing documents that have been sent from the buying organization for order management or collaboration.

> **Note**
>
> The objective of order collaboration and settlement is to provide an extended number of suppliers, specifically those without sophisticated technical capabilities, with self-service access to orders.

Figure 5.10 illustrates a very simple scenario for order collaboration using the SAP SUS application. Here, the process begins with the creation of a purchase order in SAP SRM. If the vendor is a SUS supplier, the purchase order is sent to the SAP SUS application for processing by the supplier. Orders can then be viewed and changed by the supplier to begin the process of order collaboration.

In this section, we'll discuss the detailed functionality available to organizations in SAP SRM for collaboration of purchasing documents with their suppliers. It is important to note that most organizations today exchange purchase documents with their suppliers using a variety of communication methods, including fax, EDI, XML, etc.

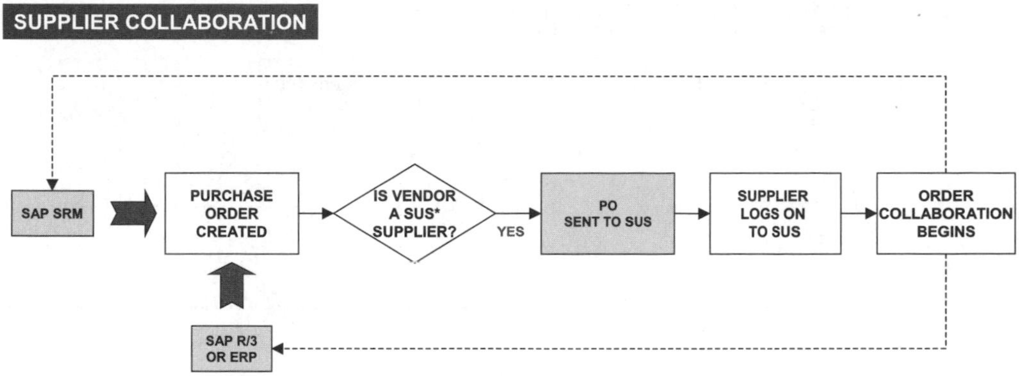

SUPPLIER COLLABORATION

Figure 5.10 Simple Process Illustration of Order Collaboration

The SAP SUS application is not a one-size fits all solution; organizations cannot expect all of their suppliers to forgo their existing electronic integrations and move to the SUS environment. Typically, this functionality is more relevant for suppliers that are smaller in size and can benefit from electronic order collaboration. Additionally, using this platform makes sense when organizations and suppliers can strategically integrate their inventory and design processes using real-time collaboration in a web-based environment. Typically organizations provide SUS access to only a select group of vendors.

You should remember that in Chapter 3, we discussed service procurement and plan-driven procurement business scenarios. An overview of the two processes is illustrated in Figure 5.11.

The Supplier Self Services (SUS) application provides capabilities for organizations to utilize the same business processes with select suppliers in a hosted environment (SUS) to collaborate on orders, RFIs, RFQs, etc (illustrated in Figure 5.12) Notice that in Figure 5.12, instead of communicating the **PURCHASE ORDER** directly with the **VENDOR**, you send the Purchase Order to the **SAP SUS** component. The supplier can then log in to SUS and access its orders.

In SUS, the following two order management scenarios are supported:

▶ Service procurement with Supplier Integration (also called *EBP-SUS*)

▶ Plan-Driven procurement scenario (Integration with SAP Materials Management, also called *MM-SUS*)

These order management scenarios are discussed in detail in Sections 5.3.1 and 5.3.2

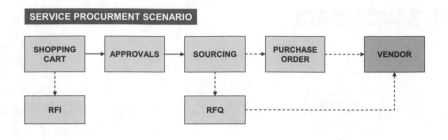

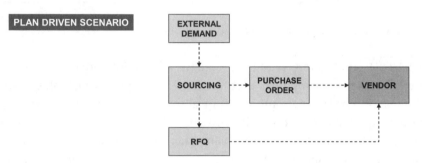

Figure 5.11 Service and Plan-Driven Procurement Scenarios in Operational Procurement

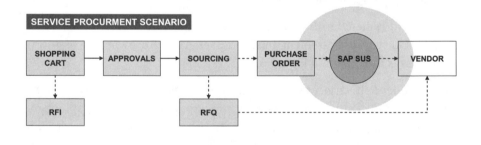

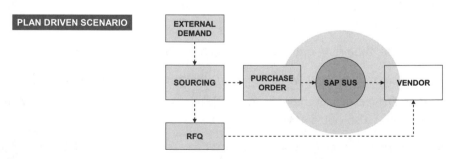

Figure 5.12 Service Procurement and Plan-Driven Procurement Scenarios in Supplier Enablement

5.3.1 Service Procurement with Supplier Integration (EBP-SUS)

Service procurement covers a wide range of services, such as temporary labor, consulting, maintenance, marketing, legal, printing, and facility management. It represents a significant opportunity for procurement cost savings. For services, processes are more complex and less standardized. SAP SRM incorporates the necessary flexibility, collaboration, and constraints for widespread services adoption. We discussed the service procurement process in detail within the chapter on operational procurement, Chapter 3.

This section discusses how the service procurement scenario is integrated with the SAP Supplier Self Services solution, enabling suppliers to collaborate electronically without having to invest in infrastructure or technology. The buying organization hosts the order management solution and suppliers simply use a Web browser for accessing and collaborating in the overall procurement process (as illustrated in Figure 5.13).

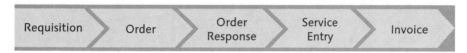

Figure 5.13 Supplier Collaboration in the Overall Procurement Process

It is important for organizations to realize that the processes described in Figure 5.12 are the same as those described in the Service procurement scenario in Chapter 3. The main difference is that in the Service procurement with Supplier integration scenario — which we'll call the EBP-SUS scenario — the supplier logs into a hosted environment of the buying organization to collaborate on processes such as responding to a service request, receiving orders, confirming goods or services, and entering invoices.

> **Note**
>
> All of these processes are illustrated in Figure 5.14. The difference between what you're learning in this chapter and what you learned in Chapter 3 is that here we discuss the capabilities suppliers have to perform collaborative functions in the context of a hosted Supplier Self Service (SUS) solution.

Organizations that are implementing the Extended Classic Scenario need to understand that the EBP-SUS scenario is not completely supported when Extended Classic is activated in SAP SRM. The scenario works for collaboration of purchase orders, purchase order response and change orders, but not for confirmation and invoice entry. If the Extended Classic scenario is activated in EBP and you send a purchase order from EBP to SUS, you cannot send the confirmation and invoice with reference to this purchase order back from SUS to EBP (Enterprise Buyer). However, some organizations have enabled this functionality using customizations and BADIs.

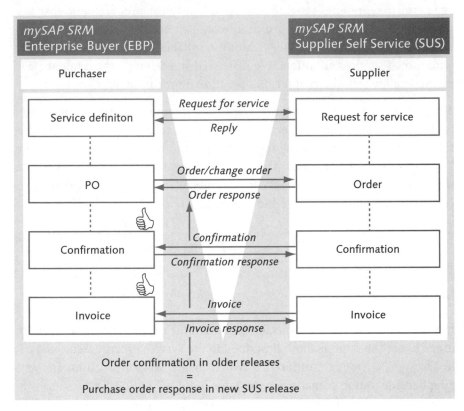

Figure 5.14 Service Procurement with Supplier Integration (EBP-SUS)

This chapter focuses specifically on the functionality available to the supplier for performing these functions. The functionality available to the purchaser is discussed in Chapter 3. Figure 5.15 shows that the **order, confirmation. service entry**, and **invoice** documents can be created in Enterprise Buyer (EBP) or in the Supplier Self Services (SUS) application for select suppliers. As mentioned earlier in this chapter, readers should note that the SUS application makes more sense for a select group of smaller suppliers, but not for all suppliers. Smaller suppliers can use SUS to communicate electronically with (larger) buying organizations.

The service procurement business scenario only supports the procurement of services and indirect materials; it does not support the procurement of direct materials or planned orders.

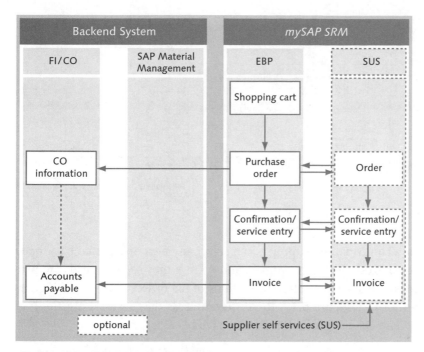

Figure 5.15 SUS Integration with EBP

EBP Purchase Orders

EBP purchase orders are converted into sales orders in the SUS application. This is because, technically, the hosted SUS application acts as a sales application for the supplier organization. Therefore, in SUS, each purchase order that is sent from EBP has a corresponding sales order number (generically termed as a document number). This is illustrated in Figure 5.16.

Once a Purchase Order is created in EBP for a SUS vendor, it is automatically sent to the SUS application via the Exchange Infrastructure (XI). In SUS the Purchase Order is available as a **New** order in the list of purchase orders section (illustrated in Figure 5.16). Suppliers can use a number of different criteria to search for new or existing purchase orders that require further processing for confirmation or invoice entry.

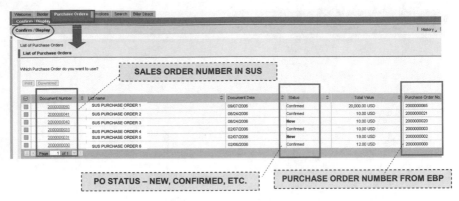

Figure 5.16 List of Purchase Orders in SUS

To create a confirmation, suppliers can select any new orders that have been sent to them from the buying organization. Once they select an order to process, they can display the different sections of the order, as shown in Figures 5.17 and 5.18. In Figure 5.17, the different areas that exist within the Process Purchase Order application in SUS have been collapsed.

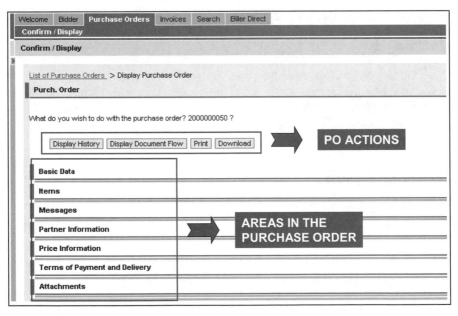

Figure 5.17 Purchase Order Sections

Figure 5.18 illustrates the different areas within a Purchase Order in SUS. The **Basic Data** section shows the sales order number (**2000000050**) in the **Document Number** field in SUS and the Purchase Order number

(**2000000065**) sent from EBP in the **Order Number** field. Remember, a PO sent by a customer becomes a sales order for the supplier. The **Items** section shows all of the items that are in the purchase order.

The **Messages** section enables the supplier to review any messages sent by the purchaser in the **Message from Purchaser** box or enter new messages in the **Message to Purchaser** box. The **Terms of Payment and Delivery** section displays the payment terms for the purchase order and the information on how any delivery charges will be handled. In the **Attachments** section, suppliers can review attachments sent by the purchaser, or they can attach any documents that should be reviewed by the buying organization.

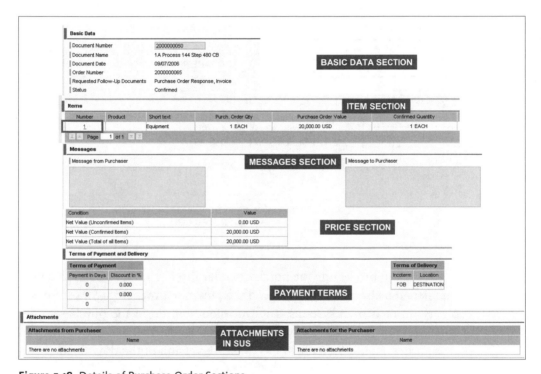

Figure 5.18 Details of Purchase Order Sections

While processing a purchase order in SUS, suppliers can accept the order partially by confirming some of the items or confirm the entire order. Additionally, they have the option to reject the items in the purchase order as well. Suppliers can also view the prices within the line items, and, if they disagree, change the price and then update the purchase order. The messages section in the PO enables the supplier to provide information to the purchaser. If additional documents need to be shared with the buying organization, the supplier can also attach documents in the attachment section. Figure 5.19, shows an example of the supplier processing purchase order number **2000000040** in SUS.

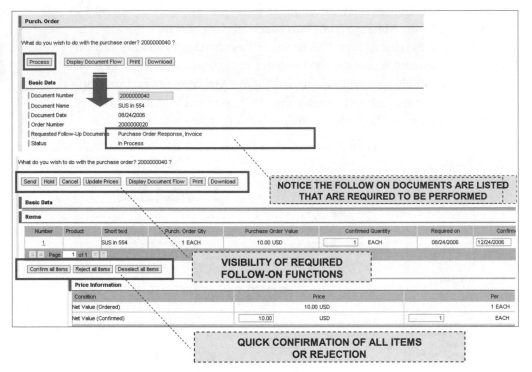

Figure 5.19 Purchase Order Processing in SUS

In addition to processing the purchase order directly in the SUS application, suppliers can also print or download the purchase order from SUS for possible use in their own systems. The **Download** button in the purchase order transaction in SUS enables suppliers to save an electronic copy of the purchase order. Figure 5.20 illustrates the XML version of the downloaded Purchase Order.

Purchase Order Response

Similar to the Purchase Order response transaction in the Enterprise Buyer (EBP) component, SAP SRM enables suppliers to create a PO confirmation/ acknowledgement using SUS. Once the supplier acknowledges the purchase order in SUS, the purchaser can review it in EBP. The PO response functionality was discussed in Chapter 3. You can see the purchase order response illustrated in Figure 5.21.

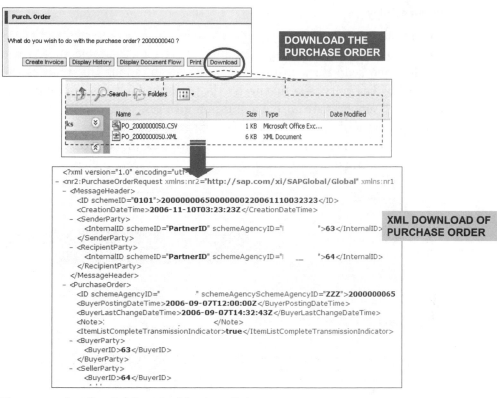

Figure 5.20 Suppliers Can Download Purchase Orders

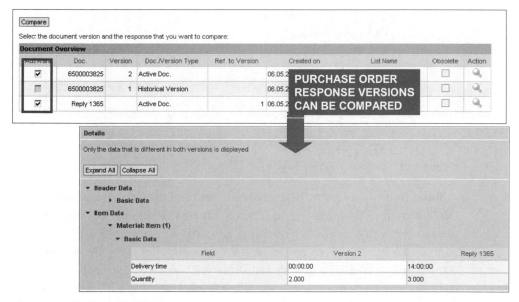

Figure 5.21 Purchase Order Response

Invoice Entry

Organizations can empower suppliers to enter invoices directly in the SUS application instead of having their internal accounts payable staff create invoices and send them to the purchasing organization. This reduces the number of data entry tasks that need to be performed in-house. Additionally, most small suppliers are unable to transmit invoices electronically. By allowing suppliers to create invoices in SUS, buying organizations can reap the benefits of automatically receiving these invoices in the SUS application directly. Confirmations are processed in the SUS as seen in Figure 5.22

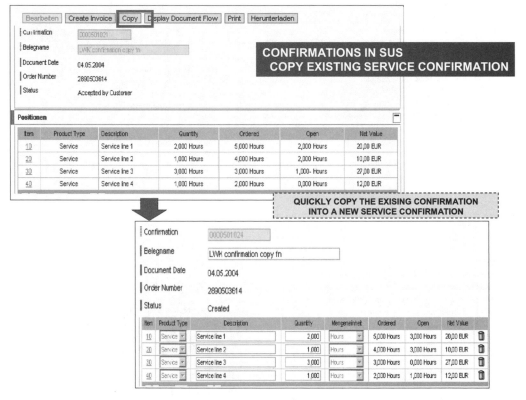

Figure 5.22 Confirmation Processing in SUS

Similar to the invoice entry functionality within Enterprise Buyer (EBP), SAP SRM provides capability for suppliers to create invoices in SUS. Invoices can be created with or without a reference to an existing purchase order. As illustrated in Figure 5.23, to create an invoice, a supplier uses the **With ref. to Order** link to create an Invoice with reference to a PO. To create an Invoice without any reference to a PO, suppliers need to use the **With ref. to Contact Person** link. If orders are being sent from EBP to SUS, then suppliers will be able to select the purchase order and directly create an invoice against it. This, however, depends on whether a confirmation or purchase order response is required before the invoice can be created.

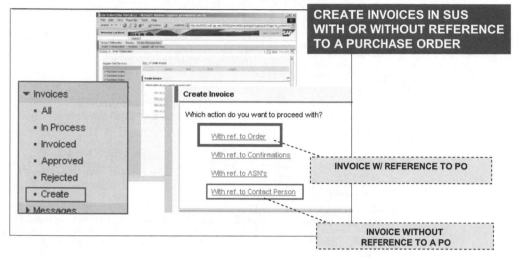

Figure 5.23 Creating Invoices in SUS With or Without PO Reference

When creating invoices, suppliers can also enter costs for unplanned delivery in the **Unplanned Delivery Costs** field within the invoice (illustrated in Figure 5.24). Unplanned costs are typically not known at the time of the creation of the purchase order. Therefore, this lets suppliers invoice the complete costs for the goods and services performed.

However, it is likely that this will create an invoice block if the total invoice value exceeds any tolerances created for posting an invoice. Figure 5.24 illustrates an example of creating an invoice in SUS. In our example, the supplier is has selected PO number **20000000081** and is creating an invoice using the **Create Invoice** button we saw in Figure 5.23. At this point s/he has the ability to invoice against all of the line items within the PO or create a partial invoice.

It should be noted that at first, many organizations are very hesitant to allow vendors to invoice via the SUS application, fearing that they lose control internally. Remember, however, that the SAP SRM application provides a number of standard workflow templates that facilitate the process of approvals prior to invoices being posted in the system. An approval can be triggered in the SAP EBP system for any documents posted in SUS.

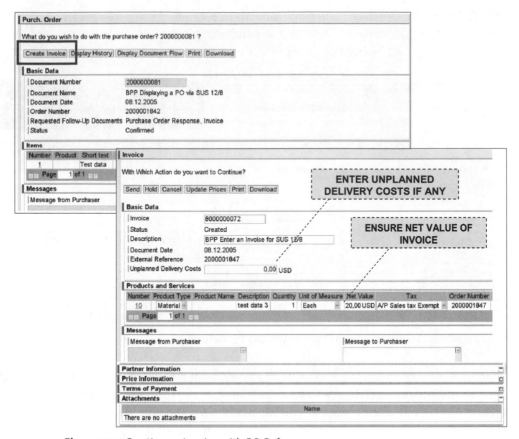

Figure 5.24 Creating an Invoice with PO Reference

For example, Figure 5.25 illustrates the approval of an invoice created in SUS. The invoice can always be **Approved** or **Rejected**, as shown in Figure 5.24, by the buying organization.

As mentioned earlier, the EBP-SUS scenario does not support the Extended Classic scenario. Many organizations that implement SRM still process invoices in the SAP back-end (R/3 or ERP) system. Therefore, an invoice entry by a supplier in SUS would not be possible in an EBP-SUS scenario, because invoices are sent to EBP instead of the SAP backend.

Organizations that have implemented the Extended Classic scenario and want to receive invoices in R/3 via SUS need to customize their configuration for the interfaces in the Exchange Infrastructure (XI) scenario (illustrated in Figure 5.26). In XI, development will be required to the outbound and inbound Invoice Request map so that instead of sending the invoice from SUS to EBP, it is sent from SUS to the **SAP R/3 OR ERP** back-end.

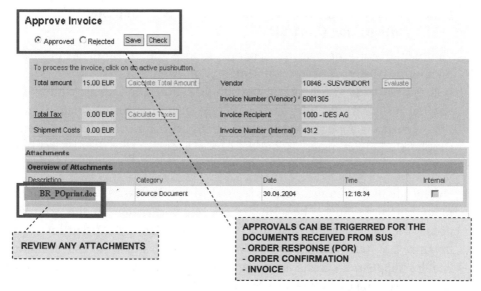

Figure 5.25 Approval of Invoice or Other Documents in EBP

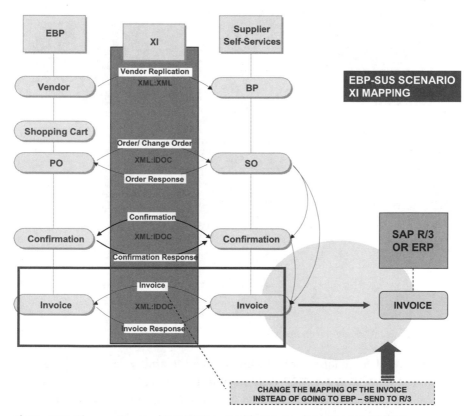

Figure 5.26 Changes Required in SAP XI to Enable Invoices being Sent to SAP R/3

5.3.2 Plan-Driven Procurement Scenario with Supplier Integration (MM-SUS)

The plan-driven procurement scenario supports the procurement of direct materials or planned orders with integration to SUS. This scenario is also called the MM-SUS scenario. In the supplier integration scenario, the SUS application is directly integrated with SAP materials management (MM). This scenario is applicable for organizations that want to collaborate with suppliers on direct materials and delivery schedules using the SUS application.

Organizations that implement this scenario do not necessarily have to implement Enterprise Buyer, because the document exchange in this scenario occurs only between the MM and SUS systems. Figure 5.27 illustrates the processes of the MM-SUS scenario. Notice that the MM-SUS scenario enables suppliers to create an Advance Shipping Notice (ASN) in SUS and send it electronically to the SAP R/3 backend.

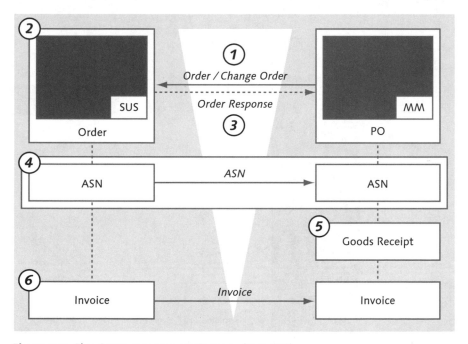

Figure 5.27 Plan-Driven Procurement Scenario (MM-SUS)

In the MM-SUS scenario, organizations have the ability to exchange orders created in the SAP R/3 or ERP systems with their suppliers. These orders are typically generated based on planned demand. Once a purchase order is generated, it is transferred to the SUS application via the Exchange Infrastructure (XI) layer. Suppliers have the same ability to search and process these purchase orders in SUS as discussed in the EBP-SUS scenario. Figure 5.28 illustrates a material-based PO created in SAP MM and the corresponding PO (2000000031) in the SUS application.

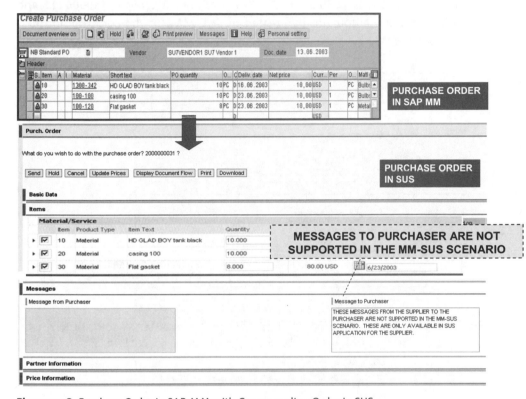

Figure 5.28 Purchase Order in SAP MM with Corresponding Order in SUS

After the supplier agrees to the goods or services in the purchase order, he or she can complete the PO response transaction in SUS. This provides an acceptance of the purchase order to the buying organization.

In the MM-SUS scenario, the supplier can create *Shipping Notifications* (also called ASNs) to indicate that the goods are being shipped. Shipping Notifications in the MM-SUS scenario are the same as *Confirmation* in the EBP-SUS application. Depending on your scenario, the supplier will be able to process either of the two documents. When processing the ASN in SUS, it defaults to the line items and quantities corresponding to the accepted purchase order (sales order) during the PO response process. Subsequently, the supplier can select the line items and quantities that will be confirmed.

The ASN is completed in SUS; it is then transferred to the SAP R/3 or ERP system via the exchange infrastructure. The ASN automatically creates inbound deliveries and the confirmation control key **LA** is included on the incoming confirmation line items. In Figure 5.29 you can see a confirmation (SUS ASN) that is posted in SAP R/3. Inbound deliveries **180000111** and **180000112** are automatically created in SAP MM for the confirmation performed in SUS.

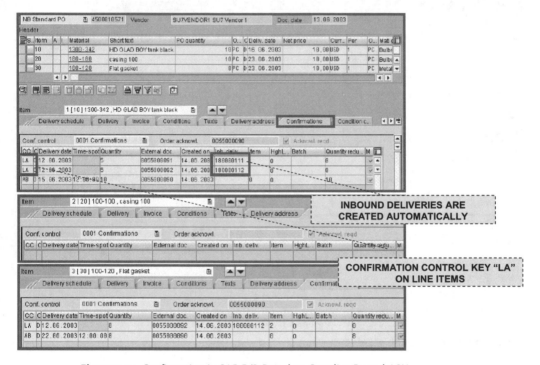

Figure 5.29 Confirmation in SAP R/3 Based on Supplier-Posted ASN

Once the ASN has been posted in SAP R/3, you can create an invoice in SUS per the ASN. Invoices can be created with a reference to the purchase order or directly against the ASN in SUS. Figure 5.30 shows creating invoices with a reference to ASNs in SUS. In SUS, the invoice will default to the line items and quantities that have been confirmed in the ASN. The SUS application provides the capability to post complete or partial invoices. For partial invoices, at a later time an invoice can be posted for the remaining amounts.

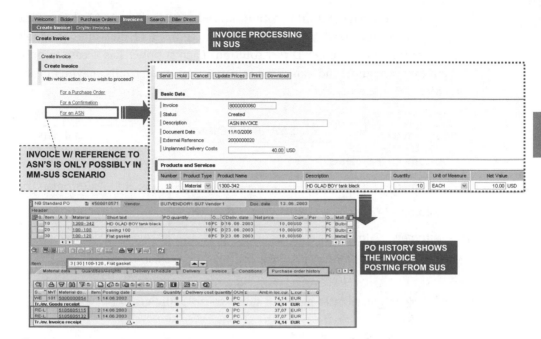

Figure 5.30 Creating Invoices for ASNs in SUS

5.3.3 Payment Status

The supplier collaboration solution lets suppliers review the status of an invoice submitted for payment. This functionality is provided by a new SAP solution offering called *SAP Biller Direct*. SAP Biller Direct is part of the SAP Financial Supply Chain Management (SAP FSCM) solution. The SAP Biller Direct application enables customers and suppliers to submit invoices, make payments, manage accounts, and settle and reconcile transactions via the Internet.

This solution has functionality to support both the customer and supplier in either the Buy-Side or Sell-Side of your enterprise Financial Supply Chain. Procurement functions fall under the Buy-Side functionality in Biller Direct, which enables suppliers to view accounts payable information via the Web. It also allows your suppliers to perform Web-based self-service account inquires and examine payment status.

Figure 5.31 shows the sell-side and buy-side of SAP Biller Direct. The sell-side provides capabilities used by customers and the buy-side provides capabilities for suppliers. This frees up an organization's accounts payable department from having to manage supplier questions about payment status, whether they come in by phone, e-mail, or fax. With SAP Biller Direct, suppliers can view payment information online, examine invoice and payment history, and view available supplier credit. Figure 5.32 illustrates the look and feel for the SAP Biller Direct solution. Each supplier has access to only their own accounts and can view information on any bills, payments, or credits.

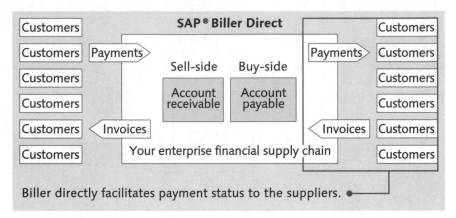

Figure 5.31 Biller Direct — Buy-Side

Figure 5.32 shows the **Bill History and Payments Overview** and **Payments History** information, which you can access by clicking on the **Bills** button. Remember, an invoice received from a supplier becomes a bill within Biller Direct; the buying organization then makes payments for any open bills for a supplier.

The Payment Status screen lets suppliers see the bills received (invoice), including information on due dates, open amounts and payment status. Additionally, suppliers can get information on the actual check that was posted by the buying organization for bill payment. For example, Figure 5.33 shows that for the supplier **Invoice 8000000210**, a **Check (1000000297)** was posted in the amount of **USD 144.00**. This information provides for self-service for suppliers and reduces the need for manual follow-up with the accounts payable department about invoice payments.

The Biller Direct application is very new and its Buy-Side solution has not been implemented at many organizations. Prior to being integrated into Biller Direct, a separate solution existed for the Buy-Side called Payer Direct. This solution is no longer supported. If you have short project timelines, you need to exercise some caution when implementing this solution. My experience at one organization was that SAP support for the application can be weak.

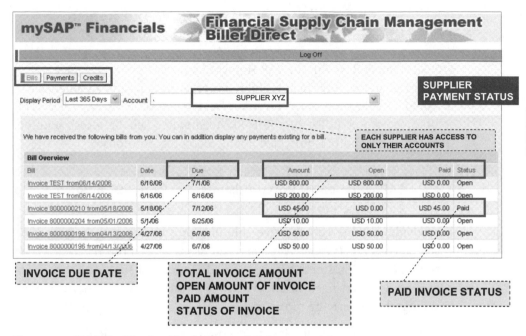

Figure 5.32 SAP Biller Direct — Vendor Payment Status

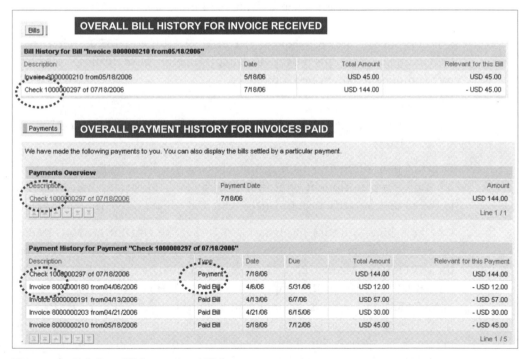

Figure 5.33 Detail on Bill Payment and History

5.4 Supplier Collaboration: Inventory and Replenishment

SAP SRM integrates with the SAP Supply Chain solution to provide automation and greater supply chain visibility for organizations and suppliers when it comes to collaboration of inventory and replenishment of orders. This solution does not utilize the SAP SRM (Supplier Self Services) solution. Instead this capability is provided by the following solutions:

5.4.1 SAP NetWeaver Portal Business Package for Supplier Collaboration

To provide a single collaborative solution for supplier management, SAP developed the *Supplier Collaboration* business package in the SAP NetWeaver Portal. The portal business package provides a unified solution for the supplier who does not need to understand the various SAP solutions that are providing the underlying capabilities.

In this scenario, the supplier logs into a supplier portal and all of the relevant information is pulled from all SAP systems and is displayed via the supplier collaboration business package. Figure 5.34 illustrates the SAP Supplier Portal concept. Note the different collaborative components that are used in this solution, such as the **SAP cFolder**, **SAP SUS**, **SAP ICH** and **SAP Purch. Direct**. Depending on your business requirements, one or more of these collaborative components might be required.

5.4.2 SAP Supply Chain Solution ICH (Inventory Collaboration Hub)

Organizations often find distinguishing between order collaboration and collaborative replenishment confusing. Figure 5.35 illustrates the difference between collaborative order management and collaborative replenishment.

One key thing to notice in Figure 5.35 is that the **ORDER MANAGEMENT** process is enabled by the **SUPPLIER SELF SERVICES (SUS)** component and the **INVENTORY MANAGEMENT** process is enabled by the **INVENTORY COLLABORATION HUB (ICH)** component. The **SAP ICH** component is not a part of **SAP SRM**; instead it is a component within the **SAP SUPPLY CHAIN** solution. Therefore, organizations that want to use the processes illustrated in Figure 5.35, such as **Supplier managed inventory**, will have to install and configure **SAP ICH** independent of SAP SRM.

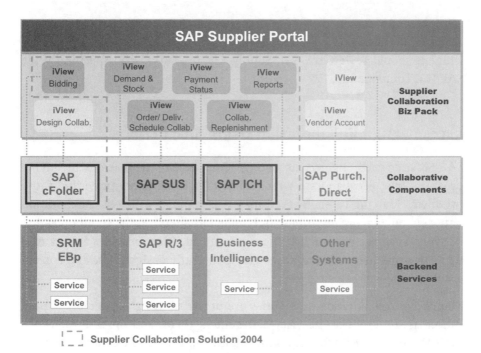

Figure 5.34 Supplier Portal or Supplier Collaboration

	SUPPLIER SELF SERVICES (SUS) mySAP SRM	INVENTORY COLLABORATION HUB (ICH) SAP SUPPLY CHAIN
	Order Management	**Inventory & Replenishment**
Process Focus	ORDER MANAGEMENT	INVENTORY MANAGEMENT
Supported Processes	• Supplier self registration • Bid invitations & auctions • Manage sales orders • Manage delivery schedules • Enter services rendered • Create invoices	• Supplier managed inventory • Manage delivery schedules • Create/ change order • Packaging & printing
	Demand & stock visibility, display financial status, reporting & alert handling	
Supplier Role	Sales assistent	MRP planner
Product Categories	• Indirect Materials • Direct materials, • Services	• Direct materials
Underlying components	• SAP SUS, • Supplier Collaboration (business package)	• SAP ICH, • Supplier Collaboration (business package)

Figure 5.35 Supplier Collaboration Order Management (SUS) vs. Collaborative replenishment (ICH)

Section 5.3 discussed the order management functionality. Organizations that are interested in the functionality identified under collaborative replenishment should review the SAP Supply Chain solution and specifically the SAP ICH component.

5.5 Design Collaboration Using SAP PLM

SAP SRM enables engineering and product development teams in buying organizations to collaborate with their strategic suppliers providing those products. Sourcing of engineered materials requires efficient collaboration between buying organizations and their suppliers. Early communication between engineering, purchasing teams, and suppliers provides an environment that optimizes product costs during the early design phase and considerably shortens time-to-market.

The design collaboration capabilities are provided using the **cFolders** application in SAP Product Lifecycle Management (**PLM**) and the SAP BIDDING ENGINE in the SAP SRM solution. Figure 5.36 illustrates the integration point between the **PLM** and **SRM** solutions.

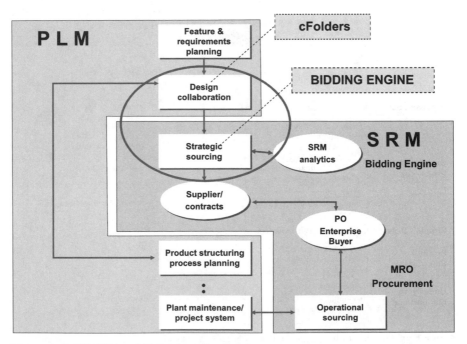

Figure 5.36 SAP SRM and PLM Integration Points

The SAP solution SAP Product Lifecycle Management (SAP PLM) contains a Web-based cooperation platform, referred to as the Collaboration Folders (**cFolders**). This platform is dedicated to promoting communication and collaboration between groups and people who need to work together but are regionally dispersed. Figure 5.37 illustrates cFolders in SAP PLM.

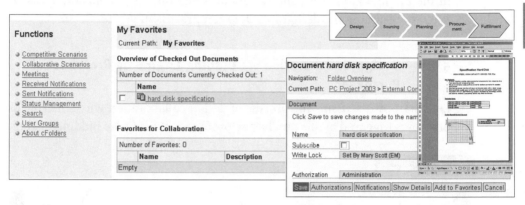

Figure 5.37 cFolders in SAP PLM

The cFolders application is integrated with SAP SRM for customers who want to extend design collaboration capabilities towards strategic sourcing and procurement for engineered goods (BOMs) and services.

The following bullets identify some of the benefits of using the SAP SRM design collaboration solution:

▸ Optimize product costs in the early design phase by bringing engineering and sourcing teams closer together.

▸ Increase process efficiency and shorten time-to-market through better communication between engineering, purchasing teams and suppliers.

▸ Ensure the right deals with the right companies while accelerating the ability to develop and deliver new products.

Let us now move on to discussing design collaboration using SAP SRM.

5.6 Design Collaboration Using SAP SRM

In SAP SRM, the design collaboration process can be triggered in two ways:

▸ Via the Bidding Engine by the professional purchaser

▸ Via the cFolders project by an engineering professional

Either of these two scenarios leads to collaboration between purchasing and engineering departments when creating a bid invitation that is sent to a select group of suppliers. The overall bidding process is the same as discussed in Chapter 6. However, in this scenario, the supplier has the ability to review the technical specifications in the cFolders application using a link provided in the bid invitation. This allows suppliers and buyers to collaborate easily. We'll now discuss the design collaboration process in greater detail.

5.6.1 Design Collaboration via Bidding Engine by Professional Purchaser

Let's start by discussing the process of design collaboration when the collaboration is triggered by the purchasing professional using the Bidding Engine.

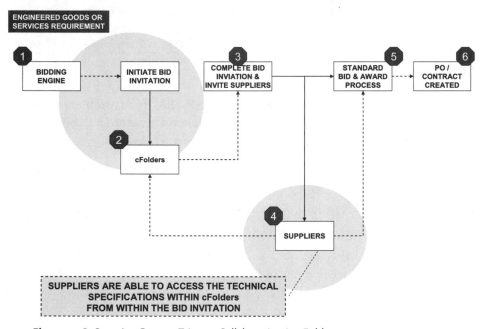

Figure 5.38 Sourcing Process Triggers Collaboration in cFolders

The following describes the process steps illustrated in Figure 5.38:

1. The purchasing professional initiates a bid invitation from within the BID-DING ENGINE application, based on requirements gathered from the engineering department.

2. The purchaser creates a collaboration project within the cFolders application in SAP PLM and invites engineers to add product specifications within cFolders for the particular good or service required.

3. Once all of the information is added in the cFolders project, the purchasing professional can complete the bid infitation and invite suppliers to participate in the bid invitation. Invited suppliers receive the notification about the bid invitation via email.

4. Suppliers can initiate a corresponding bid and access technical specifications and other documents available within the cFolders application using a link available in the bid invitation.

5. The standard bid and award process starts at this point, as described in Chapter 6 (Strategic Sourcing).

6. Once all bids are received, the purchaser and the engineer can evaluate the bids based on the criteria defined in the bid invitation and decide to create either a PO or a contract.

5.6.2 Design Collaboration via a cFolders Project by an Engineering Professional

Let's now discuss the process of design collaboration when the collaboration is triggered by an engineering professional using the cFolders application.

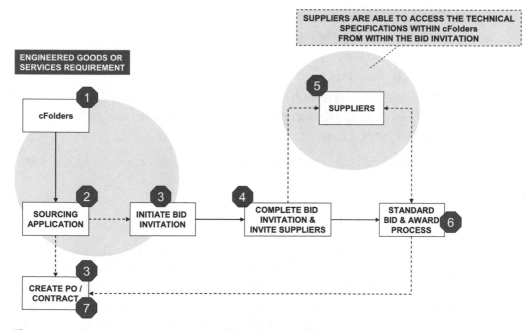

Figure 5.39 Engineering Process Triggers Collaboration in cFolders

Now you can review a description of the steps of the process illustrated in Figure 5.39:

1. An engineer with access to the SAP PLM application can create a collaboration project requirement in cFolders and upload any technical product information related to the goods or services that are required from a supplier.

2. The purchasing professional receives the requirement from cFolders as an open shopping cart in the sourcing application in SAP SRM, with a link to the respective cFolders collaboration.

3. The professional purchaser reviews existing sources of supply to source the goods or services required by engineering. If a source is found, the purchaser can inform the engineer to create a PO or contract. If no suitable sources are found the purchaser can initiate a bid invitation.

4. The purchaser can add information and evaluation attributes to complete the bid invitation and invite suppliers to participate in the bid invitation. Invited suppliers receive the notification about the bid invitation via email.

5. Suppliers can initiate a corresponding bid and access technical specifications and other documents available within the cFolders application using a link available in the bid invitation.

6. The standard bid and award process now starts, as described in chapter 06 (Strategic Sourcing).

7. Once all bids are received, the purchaser and the engineer can evaluate the bids based on the criteria defined in the bid invitation and decide to create either a PO or a contract.

We can now conclude our discussion of design collabration using SAP SRM.

5.7 Summary

In this chapter, I discussed the need for collaboration between buying organizations and their supplier community. I talked about how organizations can use the capabilities of SAP SRM to progress supplier enablement. The SAP Supplier Self Services (SUS) application is the core component within SAP SRM that enables organizations to collaborate both indirect and direct materials and services with suppliers.

Using SAP SUS, suppliers and buying organizations can exchange business documents such as Purchase Orders, Purchase Order Change, and Acknowledgements. In addition, using the MM-SUS business scenario, organizations can collaborate on direct material purchase orders and allow suppliers to perform Advance Ship Notifications (ASN) electronically using SUS and automatically integrate those ASNs within the SAP MM application.

I also discussed the portals-based supplier collaboration solution that allows organizations to further collaborate with suppliers. Using SAP solutions such as SAP ICH, SAP PLM, organizations can share planning and forecast information, allow suppliers to manage inventory levels, and involve strategic suppliers to collaborate on engineering and design documents.

In Chapter 6, I will address catalog and content management. I will begin the chapter by discussing the need for catalogs and explain how organizations can build a robust catalog strategy. Then I will move on to the SAP Catalog and Content Management (SAP CCM) solution, which enables organizations to create and manage internal (in-house) catalogs.

PART III
SAP SRM Implementation, Integration, and Upgrades

"Catalogs are a key necessity for all successful e-procurement and supplier relationship management projects. The mantra for catalogs is: If you cannot find it you cannot buy it; the quality of the content is a key to finding products and services in a catalog solution." —Source unknown

6 Catalog and Content Management — Crafting Your Catalog Strategy

In the year 2000, CommerceOne stated: "e-commerce, in its simplest form, comes down to one core component: *Content*. If there are no supplier catalogs, there is no e-commerce."

E-procurement evolved from automating procurement processes into an end-to-end supplier relationship management solution. Catalog management has seen a similar evolution over the past many years. In the late 1990s, some of the e-procurement market leaders such as Ariba, Requisite, and Ascent used electronic catalogs as the driver to elevate the value organizations obtained by implementing e-procurement solutions.

Sometime over the last few years the *e* was dropped from e-catalog, just as it was from many other applications that simply had added the *e* to indicate electronic. In this chapter we will simply use the term *catalog*. Let us define the terms catalog and catalog management:

▶ **Catalog**
A catalog provides users with a list of products and services in an organized and searchable format. This usually refers to the presentation of the content to the end users.

▶ **Catalog Management**
This is the process of consolidating and presenting goods and services offered for online purchase. The term usually refers to the authoring and management of the content that needs to be presented to the end users for searching.

Catalog content plays a vital role in procurement decision-making. Buyers require high-quality, up-to-date, and comprehensive content to make the right purchasing decisions more quickly and cost-effectively. On the other hand, suppliers want to ensure that the catalog content presented in their solution is easy for customers to search and navigate.

Over the past many years, the catalog solutions have seen an evolutionary growth from e-catalog to catalog management to the recent trend of master data management (Figure 6.1 illustrates this trend). The question is whether the catalog application your organization is using has caught up to this trend. SAP is in the process of doing so, as discussed in Section 6.2.9.

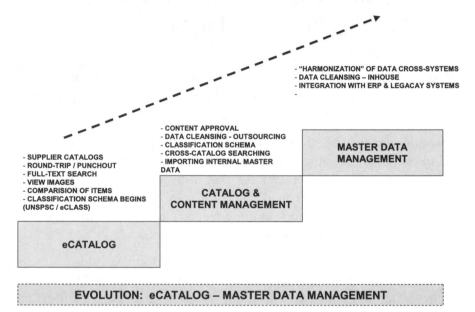

Figure 6.1 E-Catalog Evolution

In the early stages of e-procurement, organizations falsely assumed that accurate, appropriately formatted, and buyer-specific content was a given. The reality, however, is that content management is not so simple. Quality content doesn't just happen.

Moreover, supplier managed content is just one piece of the overall content management. Organizations need the capability to present consolidated harmonized content from disparate legacy and enterprise resource planning (ERP) systems. Therefore a more robust and complete solution is needed that addresses many of the following needs:

- ▶ Management of data across the enterprise applications, not just a quick upload of supplier data
- ▶ Cleansing data across disparate legacy and ERP systems
- ▶ Maintenance of a harmonized product data repository
- ▶ Consolidate multiple ERP instances into a single system of record
- ▶ Integrate with existing business processes enterprise back-end

According to Forrester Research master data management (MDM) is one of the key trends emerging in catalog and content management strategies for organizations.

Enterprises have long struggled with creating, maintaining, integrating, and leveraging enterprise master data. Furthermore, poor MDM gets in the way of successfully completing CRM, ERP, SCM, and other enterprise application initiatives. It can make it impossible to achieve promised returns on investment (ROI). To address these needs and support the move to services-oriented architecture (SOA), IT organizations are increasingly seeking cost-effective platforms that can support multiple master data entities outside of the core applications that use them.

This chapter is presented in two major parts. First, you will learn to build your catalog strategy. Then you will learn about catalog content management in SAP SRM.

6.1   Building a Robust Catalog Strategy

Before we dig into the SAP solution for catalog management, it is very important for readers to get at an understanding of catalogs and the different options available when building a catalog strategy for your SRM implementation. Once these are understood, all the concepts can be applied directly in the SAP SRM solution.

Most organizations in the beginning are unaware of the options available to them when it comes to creating catalog strategies that complement their overall SAP SRM implementations.

Therefore, it is important that the various types of catalogs are discussed in detail. This section aims to provide this information as an overview and should be discussed in further detail with your project teams. During the blueprint phase of the project it is very important that organizations discuss their true catalog needs in detail.

6.1.1   Types of Catalogs

I usually categorize catalogs into the different types: the supplier hosted, the broker hosted, and the buyer internally hosted. Let's examine these now.

Supplier Hosted Catalogs

These types of catalogs are hosted and managed by your supplier. Therefore the supplier is responsible for hosting and maintaining the catalog and its contents. The supplier offers you access to specific content and company specific pricing. **Examples are** Office Depot, Dell, and Grainger. While supplier catalogs are attractive, organizations need to keep in mind that every supplier has its own look-and-feel, and this can sometimes become a training issue for casual users.

Broker Hosted Catalogs

These catalogs are hosted and managed by content aggregators, brokers, or the marketplace. These catalogs combine content from a number of suppliers. The content aggregator or broker is responsible for setting up the catalog and maintaining its contents. Examples are ICG Commerce and SciQuest. This option provides organizations with access to a large number of catalogs quickly, but the associated costs are prohibitive for most organizations. The benefit for the suppliers in this option is that suppliers need only publish content to the broker once to make it available to the entire buying community.

Buyer Internally Hosted Catalogs

These are hosted and managed by your organization. This catalog is hosted, managed, and maintained within your own company's firewall. A catalog tool is installed, set up, and maintained within your organization. Typically organizations upload supplier data into this catalog, and internal master data from ERP systems is also uploaded into this catalog. Unlike the supplier hosted catalogs, the broker catalogs usually have a licensed subscription fee for accessing the content and usually quite expensive.

Example
The Requisite, SAP CCM, and SAP MDM option provides the most control of what users can see in the catalog. This requires dedicated support and maintenance staff for keeping the catalog content up to date.

Figure 6.2 provides a comparison between the different catalog types. Figure 6.2 illustrates how companies can use the different catalog types. The **INTERNALLY HOSTED** catalog can be accessed using a **SHOPPING CART** within the **FIREWALL** of your company. However, the **SUPPLIER HOSTED** and **BROKER HOSTED** catalogs exist outside of the company **FIREWALL,** and the users accessing these catalogs need authorization to access the Internet to search the products and services offered in these catalogs.

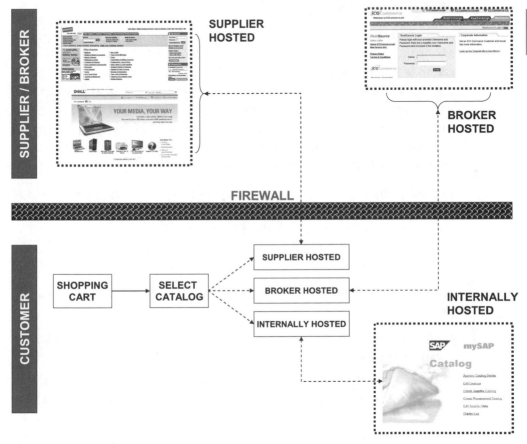

Figure 6.2 Accessing Supplier Catalogs

6.1.2 What are RoundTrip and Punch-Out?

The terms RoundTrip and Punch-out are synonymous. When the early e-procurement solutions were marketed around 1998, SAP and CommerceOne used the term RoundTrip, and Ariba used Punch-out. This difference in terminology remains. RoundTrip allows suppliers to maintain branded content on their own websites (supplier-hosted) or use a broker hosted system and extend their electronic catalogs to buying organizations.

Buyers can use a Web browser to connect to the supplier's website to select and configure products from the supplier's custom catalog. The supplier provides buyer specific items and pricing. One example of a RoundTrip catalog supplier is Office Depot. Customers can access the Office Depot catalog directly from their shopping carts and search for thousands of products offered by Office Depot.

After products are selected in the supplier catalog, the RoundTrip service automatically brings the required product details back into the buying application (e.g., the shopping cart in SAP SRM). At this point, the order is routed through the normal requisition and approval processes and eventually converted into a purchase order that is sent back to the supplier for order fulfillment. This provides organizations real-time up-to-date access to the suppliers' content while maintaining control of business processes and approvals within the SAP SRM application.

In SAP, the initial connection to the supplier catalog authentication and final return of the order information to SRM are all facilitated via RoundTrip. The RoundTrip function in SAP is the SAP Open Catalog Interface (OCI). The Open Catalog Interface (OCI) incorporates external product catalogs into the SAP SRM solution. OCI is described in detail in Section 8.2.

Let's take the flow illustrated in Figure 6.3 to highlight the RoundTrip buying process:

1. The end user searches for products and services by clicking on a link to launch the supplier catalog and jumps directly to the supplier's website.

2. Upon automatic authentication by the supplier, the end user can search and configure products using the website's resident capabilities. The user can then select one or more items from the catalog.

3. When the user is ready to order the items from the supplier, he or she clicks on the complete order or checkout button at the supplier's website (this can depend on the supplier's naming convention and differs based on the supplier).

4. The order request with information on one ore more line items is sent back to the buying application (SAP SRM). The system automatically brings selected product details back into the buying application. Organizations can configure what information is brought back from the supplier catalog to the buying application.

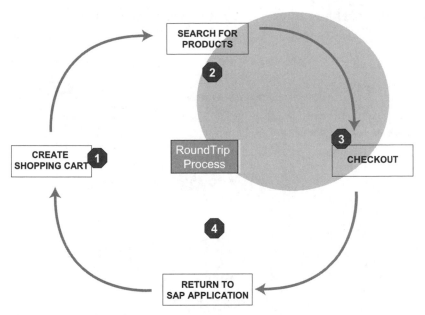

Figure 6.3 Round-Trip buying process

At this point, the RoundTrip process is completed. The resulting shopping cart can be routed through the usual approval workflow and is eventually converted into a purchase order. Once the purchase order is created, it can be sent to the supplier via a standard format (email, XML, EDI, paper, fax, etc.).

6.1.3 A Single Catalog Solution Might Not be Enough

The key to an effective catalog strategy is to drive the largest possible amount of spending via negotiated catalogs. After all, cost savings and compliance are two key reasons to implement the catalog solution in the first place. And users will only want to use catalogs if they know that they can get to the majority of products and services via the available catalogs. For this reason, it is important to on-board as many supplier catalogs as you can, which is only possible when using a hybrid approach between the different types of catalog solutions of supplier hosted, internally hosted or broker managed.

Organizations might feel that they only want to use the RoundTrip option to access catalogs, as that seems to require the least amount of effort for the internal staff on the project and ongoing maintenance. But this strategy does not prove very effective because each supplier needs to be onboarded separately. This is time-consuming and does not produce the expected results.

Figure 6.4 illustrates how companies can use a hybrid approach to meet their overall catalog and content-management needs. When choosing the right

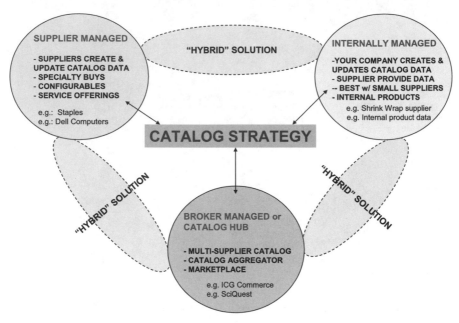

Figure 6.4 Adopting a Hybrid Catalog Strategy

catalog strategy for your organization, it is important to understand the cost and implementation effort required for each of these catalog options.

Figure 6.5 illustrates this via a matrix. Organizations that want to use the strategy to internally manage the catalog content need to be aware that there are high setup and implementation costs for this strategy.

	CATALOG STRATEGY	COST	IMPL.* EFFORT
1	INTERNALLY MANAGED - SETUP & MANAGE CATALOG INHOUSE	HIGH	HIGH
2	BROKER MANAGED - CATALOG HOSTING & MANAGEMENT SERVICES	MEDIUM	MEDIUM
3	SUPPLIER MANAGED - CONNECT TO SUPPLIER WEBSITE	LOW	LOW

*IMPL. - IMPLEMENTATION

Figure 6.5 Cost and Implementation Effort Matrix

However, this strategy provides the most control for the company in terms of making sure only select products are available to the end users. It also keeps the pricing for these products in check, as any updates to the catalog can be reviewed by the catalog manager or the buyer.

In comparison, the **SUPPLIER MANAGED** catalog strategy is fairly low in terms of cost and implementation effort. The supplier manages all the content for the catalog and maintains the product and price information on its website. This strategy enables companies to quickly set up access to multiple supplier catalogs with minimum effort from your organization. However, it also provides a minimum amount of control over when updates are made to the supplier catalog content; e.g., new product additions or price updates.

Figure 6.6 provides a list of some supplier-hosted catalog providers that already provide RoundTrip or Punch-Out capabilities and have successfully integrated with the SAP SRM solution. Organizations need to reach out to their supplier communities as a part of the supplier survey (onboarding process) to determine whether their suppliers are RoundTrip (OCI) compliant.

Figure 6.6 Some RoundTrip Capable Supplier Catalogs

Brokers

The following is a list of some of the leading aggregators or brokers: providers of catalog solution where the catalog provider hosts integrated catalogs for multiple suppliers in a single location. These catalogs are also accessed using RoundTrip capabilities. Many of these catalog providers started either as marketplace or industry vertical providers (e.g., SciQuest, a software provides solution for the higher-education market). The value of the broker is that the organization can get access to a large number of supplier catalogs. However, most catalog brokers do charge hefty sums for their catalog solutions. These include:

▶ SciQuest

▶ ICG Commerce

▶ Perfect Commerce

▶ Ariba

▶ SAP Supplier Network (Cc-hubwoo)

Organizations should note that most of these catalog solution providers also provide access to a supplier network solution, which enables companies to access thousands of suppliers and send and receive POs, invoices and other documents by using a Web browser or the latest XML-based or EDI integration technologies. All of these services have an extra cost.

6.1.4 Connect with Your Suppliers for Onboarding

One of the biggest pitfalls for organizations when implementing the catalog solution is that they forget to involve their business partners (suppliers) until much later in the project. Suppliers need to be informed and communicated with very early in project implementation. This allows the organization to determine which suppliers are ready for integration. The suppliers can project their resource requirements internally to meet the project deadlines for requirements gathering, analysis, testing, and go-live preparation.

Remember, your organization is not the only one that Dell Computers or Office Depot is integrating with. These suppliers have ongoing internal projects and integration projects with other customers as well. Getting on a supplier's timeline ensures a smoother implementation process.

The process of communicating with suppliers and getting them integrated into your overall solution is loosely termed as *supplier onboarding*. Each supplier that needs to be integrated into the SRM solution might have unique requirements and might have independent dependencies; therefore each supplier needs to be onboarded individually. Some integrations are simple than other based on the supplier and the requirements.

It is important to note that while many organizations are used to ordering goods and services on supplier websites, the orders are placed directly on the supplier website, not integrated to application supplier catalogs and websites to order goods and services. For example, when ordering from Office Depot, the order is placed directly on the supplier's website.

Once suppliers are onboarded in the SAP SRM solution, they expect to continue to receive their orders electronically. Therefore, many organizations also use the SRM implementation as a step towards implementing electronic means of communicating purchasing documents (e.g., purchase order and invoice) such as EDI or XML.

Figure 6.7 illustrates an approach for supplier onboarding that has been used by a large educational and healthcare organization. Organizations should be aware that there are a number of steps involved in onboarding a supplier, and it could take anywhere from eight to ten weeks or more to get a supplier catalog onboarded.

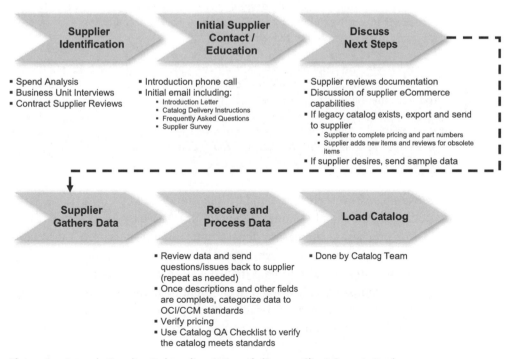

Figure 6.7 Example Supplier Onboarding Approach (Source: Client Organization)

6.1.5 Standardize Commodities

Garbage in is garbage out when it comes to master data and categorization. Organizations that take the time to cleanse and standardize the different master data elements are better able to report and analyze spending data. When it comes to catalog management, it is imperative that organizations truly review their product masters and categorization. It is amazing to see how badly the product master is categorized in organizations today. The same product could be created multiple times, and — even worse — categorized in entirely different commodities. Classifying products and services with a common coding scheme facilitates efficient commerce between buyers and sellers.

Many organizations that embark on SRM also look at the project as an opportunity to begin standardizing their products and services into industry relevant classifications. This means creating master data that is not only relevant to their internal organization but also easier for exchange with their supplier community.

Example

A user in the healthcare organization wants to purchase gloves. He or she searches the available catalogs, selects the desired gloves available from a supplier catalog, and adds them to the shopping cart. Once the relevant information is completed, an order can be generated to the supplier.

In this example, the supplier classifies the gloves under a category Lab Supplies, but your organization categorizes this item purchase, internally as Patient Examination Products. There is a discrepancy between how your suppliers would analyze your purchasing activity vs. the way your organization would analyze it. During contract re-negotiations or new contract discussions with other suppliers, there will be a situation of comparing apples to oranges if you and your suppliers cannot easily analyze the procurement activity.

This example shows where a standard taxonomy comes into play, as large corporations can get a harmonized view of purchases by using standardized codes for purchases. Purchasing departments should incorporate the codes in purchasing systems to help employees throughout the company find and purchase supplies and also to help themselves analyze the supplies expenditures of the company. This would enable them to analyze the specifics in the buying process at the level of detail that most suits the business needs in a timely and precise manner.

They can cut in half or less the time it takes to find the products needed by searching by commodity code through brokers, online exchanges, business partners, etc. across the globe. Organizations can spot buying patterns across departments or business units to leverage better conditions from suppliers and realize overall savings.

During the supplier onboarding process, organizations need to review the products and categories that will be available in the catalogs provided by the prospective suppliers. Then, they need to review how they will treat the products once they're returned from the supplier catalog into their internal shopping cart (as described in the RoundTrip process). What categorization or taxonomy will your organization use once the product is returned from the catalog? Are you going to use the supplier's categorization? Are you going to use your own categorization? Are they the same? All these are important questions to answer. Organizations implementing SRM will find themselves mapping their supplier categories to their internal categories unless they follow a common categorization standard.

Organizations that lack a standardized categorization in their current environment should look towards the industry for standardization and classification. Standards and initiatives include the United Nations Standard Products and Services Code (UNSPSC), RosettaNet, eCl@ss, North American Industry Classification System (NAICS), and Standard Classification of Transported Goods (SCTG). These aim to ease the information exchange between customers and suppliers by providing a framework to identify products and services in a global market. These classification systems provide a hierarchical system for grouping materials, products, and services.

UNSPSC is a commonly used classification schema widely used in the United States by customers and suppliers. e-cl@ss is a classification schema that is more widely used by organizations and suppliers across Europe. Large suppliers such as Office Depot, Fisher Scientific, Grainger, Dell, and catalog brokers such as SciQuest, ICG commerce, etc. already use the UNSPSC for classifying products and services with a common coding scheme. Therefore, if you're doing business with these suppliers, you can quickly benefit from using an industry classification such as UNSPSC.

UNSPSC is a hierarchical convention that is used to classify all products and services. It is the most efficient, accurate, and flexible classification system available today for achieving companywide visibility of spending analysis, enabling procurement to deliver on cost-effectiveness demands and allowing full exploitation of electronic commerce capabilities. Organizations can get an introduction to UNSPSC and how it can be used at *www.UNSPSC.org*.

Organizations can review their current classification schemes for products and services to see how they can convert to an industry classification, and get the following benefits:

▸ Searching tool for quickly and efficiently finding products and services

▸ Analysis tool for analyzing spending consistently

▸ Standardizing for consistent naming and coding conventions

Thus far in this chapter, we've been discussing how an organization should create a catalog strategy. In Section 6.2, we will delve into catalog and content management and how organizations can use SAP SRM to manage their catalog content.

6.2   Catalog and Content Management Using SAP SRM

SAP supported the catalog solution using software partner Requisite (now a part of Click Commerce) to provide support and maintenance for emerge and BugsEye solutions. In 2004, SAP introduced the SAP Catalog and Content Management (CCM) solution. SAP CCM provides the capability for organizations to create, cleanse, and manage their own catalog content. SAP designed CCM to be the unique catalog application for every SAP application (SAP SRM, SAP CRM, and SAP ERP). Prior to SAP CCM, there had been other attempts to create a catalog solution, but those never took off; customers always had a better option than the SAP offering.

In 2005, SAP advised its SRM customers that SAP would end its support for the Requisite products at the end of 2006. Customers that do not migrate to the SAP Catalog solution (SAP CCM) by the end of the maintenance period will need support and maintenance directly from Click Commerce for these solutions (review OSS Note 485884). This was the signal for organizations either upgrading from an earlier SAP SRM release or new customer implementations to review the SAP CCM offering instead of the earlier Requisite solution.

Today, there are a number of companies using the SAP CCM 1.0 or 2.0 versions integrated within SAP SRM as a single SAP solution. There are obvious advantages to the SAP CCM offering, as it's built on the same technology platform as the SRM solution. But, organizations that have used the Requisite or Ariba Catalog solution will find the SAP CCM offering a bit behind the curve.

SAP has recently announced that it will introduce a new solution for content management and eventually will phase out the SAP CCM offering. Although no new versions of CCM are expected, SAP will support and maintain the SAP CCM 2.0 release until 2013. The new solution is going to be based on the SAP NetWeaver MDM technology.

In this chapter, my primary focus is on the SAP CCM 2.0 release, which is integrated with SAP SRM 4.0 and 5.0 releases. I will also give you a brief overview of the new SRM-MDM catalog solution. The SRM-MDM solution has been designed to replace SAP CCM and support deep integration to core procurement business processes

6.2.1 SAP Catalog and Content Management (SAP CCM)

With the SAP SRM 4.0 release, SAP introduced its own catalog solution: SAP CCM 1.0. A new version — CCM 2.0 — was introduced in April 2005 with enhanced functionalities. This chapter focuses on the functionality available in the SAP CCM 2.0 release. There are two separate applications that are delivered as a part of SAP CCM. These are described in the following bullet points:

▶ **Catalog Authoring Tool (CAT)**
The authoring application allows organizations to create and manage content within the CCM Catalog. The CAT application is used by content managers.

▶ **Catalog Search Engine (CSE)**
The search application allows end users to quickly search rich content data that is created using the authoring tool. The CSE application is used by end users in shopping carts and professional purchasers when creating purchase orders or contracts in SAP SRM.

The CAT and CSE applications are illustrated in Figures 6.8 and 6.9. In Figure 6.8, you can see the CAT and CSE applications demonstrating the actual application screenshots. The **CATALOG AUTHORING TOOL (CAT)** provides a list of applications available to the catalog administrator: Approve **Catalog Entries**, **Edit Catalogs**, **Create Catalogs**, etc. These are based on the authorizations available to you. The **CATALOG SEARCH ENGINE (CSE)** provides end users the ability to search the catalogs created using CAT.

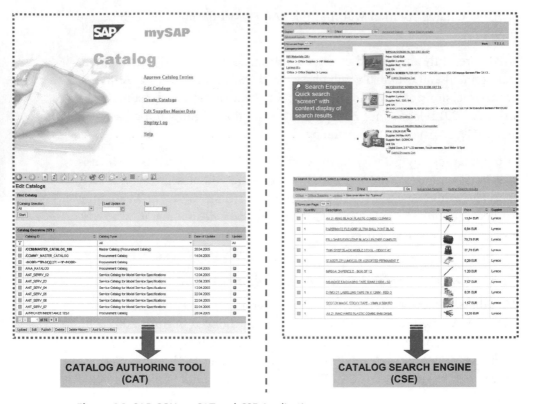

Figure 6.8 SAP CCM — CAT and CSE Applications

In Figure 6.9, you will notice the different functions available in CAT and CSE. The CAT tool provides the ability to import catalog data from external suppliers using the **Content Import** function, which can then be mapped to the **Master Catalog**.

The **Catalog Search Engine** allows users to **Search** and **Compare** products and services in the **Published Catalog**s that have been made available using the CAT application.

CCM allows organizations to create and manage unified catalogs, using tools that import data from internal and external sources, maintain consistent product schemas, and index products for faster search capabilities, this process is illustrated in Figure 6.10.

Each of the processes seen in Figure 6.10 is discussed individually in the following subsections.

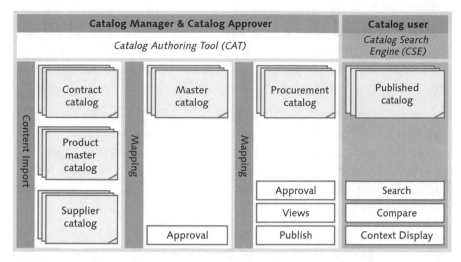

Figure 6.9 SAP CCM — CAT and CSE Functions

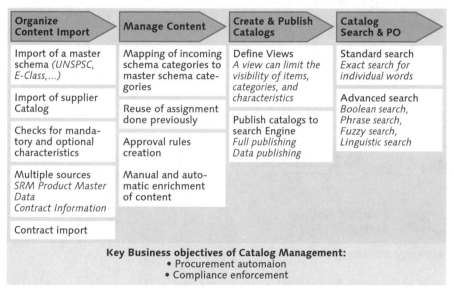

Figure 6.10 Process in CCM

6.2.2 SAP CCM — Organize Content Import

The main aim of the import process is to collect data from all possible sources into the CCM catalog. This could simply be a catalog file that you receive from your supplier or product information from your internal systems. Organizations need to first upload a master schema (categorization) for the catalog and subsequently import various catalogs.

The master schema is the classification that your organization wants to use to categorize the catalog content using an industry standard. Typically in North America the UNSPSC schema is widely used. In Europe, the eCl@ss schema is used by most of the suppliers to categorization content to uniform taxonomy.

The master schema is uploaded into the Master Catalog: a catalog type within CCM that is automatically created by the system when the authoring tool is accessed for the first time. All supplier catalogs are then mapped to this central catalog. Select the **/CCM/MASTER_CATALOG** and then select the **Upload** button to upload a master schema into the master catalog. The schema that is uploaded can be in different formats, e.g., UNSPSC.

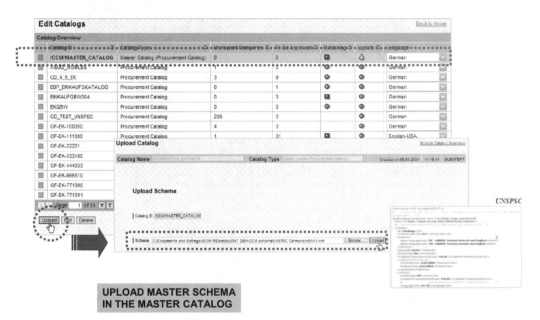

Figure 6.11 Uploading Master Schema

Once the schema is uploaded, the Master Catalog can be edited to view the structure of the uploaded schema (see Figure 6.11). To review the uploaded schema select **/CCM/MASTER_CATALOG** and then click the **Edit** button.

The CCM catalog can contain content from multiple different sources: content provided by external suppliers, material master data from a SAP backend or product master in SRM, and contract data (illustrated in Figure 6.12).

The following subsections explain further the different types of catalogs that can be uploaded into CCM.

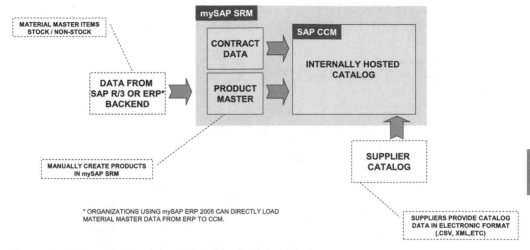

Figure 6.12 Uploading Data into CCM Catalog from Multiple Sources

Vendor-Supplied Content

Based on a predefined template, these are also called *upload supplier content*. Suppliers can provide a list of their products in a pre-defined template format provided. This product listing normally contains product attributes such as pre-negotiated contract price, description, picture (where allowable), manufacturer's part number, supplier's part number, and quantity in its container.

The format is typically in the form of a .csv, spreadsheet or XML file. Select the **Supplier Catalog** and then click on **Upload** to either upload or csv or XML file. If the supplier catalog is imported using the XML format, the SAP Exchange Infrastructure (SAP XI) application is required.

SRM Product Master

This is also called the *SRM product catalog*. The material master in SAP R/3 can be used to provide requesting departments a vehicle to request goods and services from an inventory or an internal provider respectively. Typically, in organizations with an SAP back-end (R/3 or ERP), the material master is created and maintained within SAP R/3 and then replicated into SRM as products.

The product master in SRM can then be merged into the SAP CCM catalog using standard programs (**BBP_CCM_TRANFER_CATALOG**) available in SRM (as illustrated in Figure 6.13). Organizations can also directly create product

259

masters in SRM and replicate those to the CCM catalog using this same process. The master data inclusion scenario requires SAP XI.

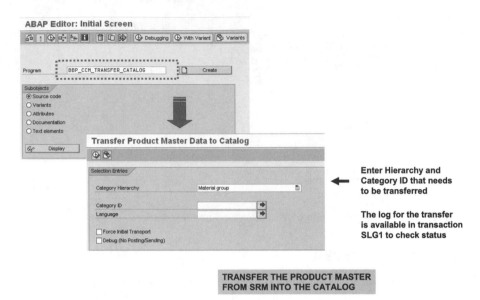

Figure 6.13 Master Data-Inclusion Scenario

Once the product master is transferred from the SAP EBP system into the catalog, a product catalog is created in CCM. The replicated products are available in the catalog within each product category hierarchy.

SRM Contract Upload

Organizations can transfer contracts created in SAP SRM into the SAP CCM catalog for users to search. This process is initiated by using a check field on the contract header that indicates that the contract should be distributed to the SAP CCM catalog. The contract has to be in *released* status before it can be transferred to the CCM catalog. The contract distribution scenario requires the SAP XI application. This is illustrated in Figure 6.14 and Figure 6.15. The transferred catalog is then available in the CCM application. In Figure 6.14, the **Distribute Contract to Catalog** check box is selected. This marks the catalog for distribution to the catalog.

Once the contract is distributed to the catalog, each contract can be individually selected to edit and view the line items in the contract. In Figure 6.15, we select the contract catalog **4400000765** to edit the line items within this contract.

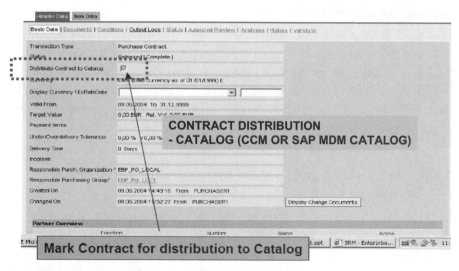

Figure 6.14 Contract Distribution to the CCM Catalog

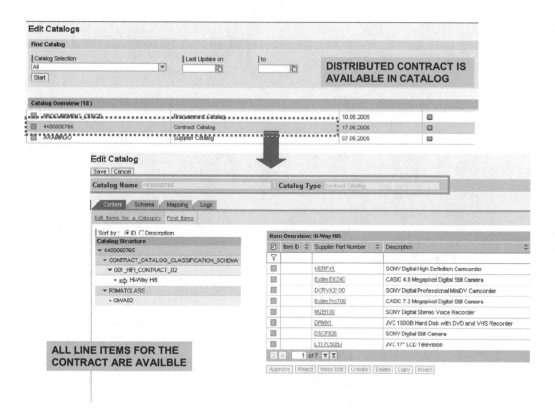

Figure 6.15 Contract and Line Items in CCM

Material Data from SAP ERP System

Organizations using the SAP ERP system can distribute the master data from the SAP ERP system directly into the CCM catalog. This is enabled using Transaction MECCM in the ERP system. The purchasing Info Record, contract and material master distribution is supported from the SAP ERP backend. This option is available for organizations that want to perform the purchasing process in the SAP ERP system.

6.2.3 SAP Catalog and Content Management (SAP CCM) — Manage Content

In the content management process, project teams map the source catalogs into the master catalog in CCM that contains the main catalog schema. This includes creating mapping rules to map the content from supplier catalogs, SRM product master, and contracts to the master catalog or to procurement catalogs (illustrated in Figure 6.16).

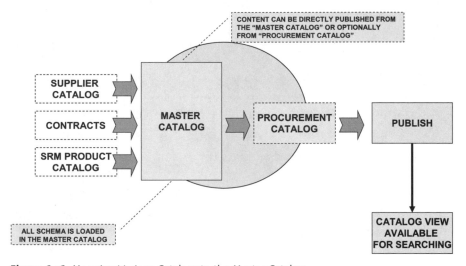

Figure 6.16 Mapping Various Catalogs to the Master Catalog

In Figure 6.16, notice that the **SUPPLIER CATALOG**, **CONTRACTS**, and **SRM PRODUCT CATALOG** are uploaded and mapped to the **MASTER CATALOG**. At this point, the content can be directly published from the Master Catalog or optionally from the **PROCUREMENT CATALOG**. Using the **PUBLISH** process the catalog data can be made available for search and comparison by end users.

This can be a fairly cumbersome process, especially if many categories need to be mapped. For each of the catalogs (supplier and product catalog) the source category needs to be mapped to the target category.

> **Example**
>
> If a supplier catalog has been uploaded, then the source category will be from the supplier's schema, which needs to be mapped to the target category in the CCM master catalog. The process of mapping the categorization (schema) used by the supplier to the buying organization can be fairly cumbersome, especially if your organization is not using a standardized categorization such as UNSPSC, e@CLASS, etc.
>
> If your supplier categorizes product 123 as Furniture and your organization categorizes this as Office Supplies, this is where mapping is required. If organizations use standardized categorization, they will be better able to analyze organizational spending and also cross-reference products and services with suppliers much more easily.

Once the categories are mapped, this does not have to be done again, unless new schema are introduced. The steps required to map the source category to the target category are listed in the following steps:

1. Select a catalog and open in edit mode. Then, select the source category that needs to be mapped in the **Source Catalog**.

2. Select target category into which the source category should be mapped (for example, **OFFICE_MATERIALS**).

> **Note**
>
> The target catalog is typically the master catalog **/CCM/MASTER_CATALOG**.

3. Select **Include Subcategories** if categories below the first level need to be mapped as well.

4. Click **Map Categories** button to establish the link between the **Source Catalog** and **Target catalog**.

Content management in CCM provides the capability to enrich the catalog content to make minor changes directly in the CCM catalog. In addition organizations can also create approval rules that can be used after catalog data has been uploaded. Let's discuss these now:

▶ **Enrich Item Data**
   In the master catalog and procurement catalog, managers can manually

enrich the product information by adding missing characteristics or characteristic values. CCM 2.0 allows mass editing of items, so that catalog managers can select a set of items and then perform functions such as change, delete, or copy. If required, the catalog manager can manually create additional items and characteristics directly in CCM. In CCM 1.0, new items or characteristics could only be added by uploading the supplier catalog again.

► **Approvals**

CCM provides an approval capability for organizations to review uploaded content and determine whether the information is appropriate before it can be published and made available to end users. Rules can be defined to determine automatic and manual approval of items.

The default status for all catalogs is delivered as **To Be Approved**. Organizations can change this option in Customizing. The approval functionality was enhanced in CCM 2.0. Designated approvers can now search for all items that are assigned to them and have an approval status *to be approved*. They can approve or reject single items or all selected items at once (illustrated in Figure 6.17). In addition, item history is available to view the changes made to a particular item over time. Approvers can view information such as who uploaded the item, when the approval status was changed, or who approved the item.

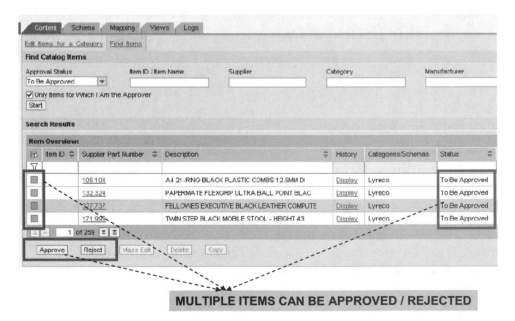

Figure 6.17 Approval of Items

6.2.4 SAP Catalog and Content Management — Create and Publish Catalogs

In this process the catalog manager can map the master catalog into multiple procurement catalogs, approve catalogs, define catalog views, and ultimately publish the catalog views to enable catalog search. Let's take a look at these now.

Procurement Catalogs

Procurement catalogs are subsets of the master catalog and can be created to divide the master catalog into separate division for regional or language dependent catalogs (or other business reasons). It is important to note that procurement catalogs are optional; content managers can create views directly from the master catalog and publish for searching. Procurement catalogs allow distribution of catalogs for specific procurement use.

Creating Views

Organizations can define views of the catalog before publishing for user search. Views are a subset of the overall catalog. This allows us to restrict the users in a particular department or organization to viewing the items that they're authorized to view.

As of SAP CCM 2.0, content managers can define rules to determine which items are included in a view. In release 1.0, this was a very cumbersome process as each item needed to be manually assigned if it was to be included in a catalog view. Conditions and characteristics can be defined to create the views. For example, a condition can be created such that all items in a particular product category create a view. You can also create a view for a particular supplier items. This is illustrated in Figure 6.18.

Once views are created, they also need to be assigned in the SAP role administration. Each view that needs to be made available for searching by end users in shopping carts or purchase orders needs to be assigned in the personalization object key /CCM/VIEW_ASSIGNMENTS of the role.

In Figure 6.19, we illustrate the example of a role in SRM **ZVIEW1**. In the Personalization tab of this role, the Catalog View ID **PRICE_BELOW_50** is assigned. At this point any user that has the Role **ZVIEW1** will have access to the PRICE_BELOW_50 view of the catalog.

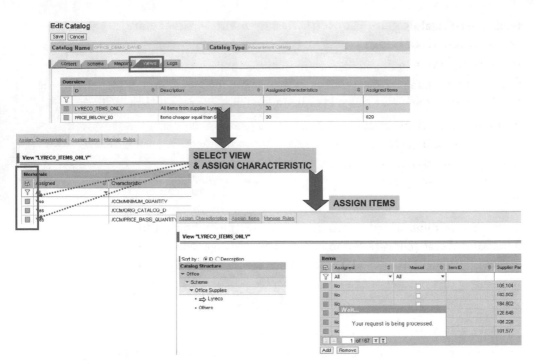

Figure 6.18 Assigning Characteristic to Views

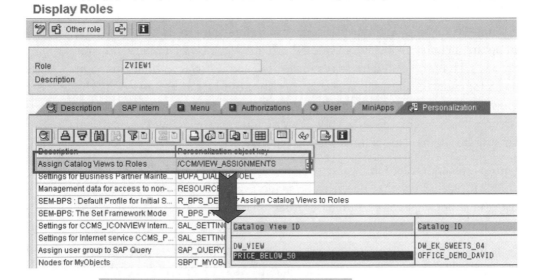

Figure 6.19 Assignments of Views in Roles

Publishing a catalog makes it available in the catalog search engine (CSE) for end users. Only the master catalog or the procurement catalogs can be published. Supplier catalogs, SRM product catalogs and contract catalogs cannot be published; these catalogs have to be mapped to either the master catalog or the procurement catalog to make them available for end user search in CSE.

Additionally, all items in status *To be approved* or *Do not publish* are not available for publishing. Organizations need to be aware that, depending on the number of items in your catalog, the publishing process might take a long time. For improving performance of publishing, parallel processing is available.

In the **Type of Publishing** section, the catalog administrator can use the radio buttons to either publish the entire catalog or just the new updates (delta) since the original catalog was published.

6.2.5 SAP CCM — Search

The catalog search process, illustrated in Figure 6.20, allows end users to search the published catalog views. Users have access to specific catalog views based on the catalog authorization in the SRM Organizational Structure. In SRM, users can access the CCM catalog from one of the following applications:

▶ Shopping cart

▶ Purchase order

▶ Contracts

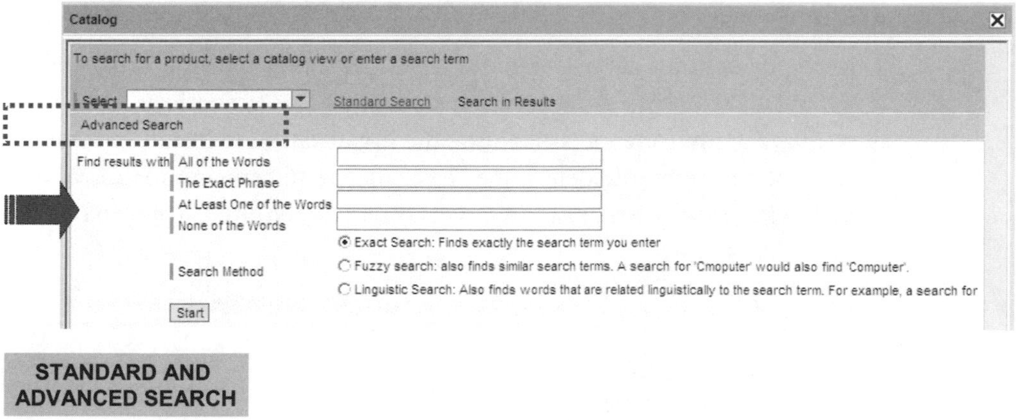

Figure 6.20 Standard and Advanced Search

From a process perspective, the end user selects the CCM catalog from one of these applications to launch the CCM-CSE application. Once the user is able to search and find the goods or services in the catalog, he or she can return to the SRM application along with all the items selected in the CCM catalog.

At this point they can either process the shopping cart, purchase order or contract further or send it for the follow-on step. In the catalog search engine (CSE), users can make use of the following capabilities:

▶ Free text search capabilities powered by TREX

▶ Switching between basic and advanced search

▶ Parametric search for refinement

▶ Item comparison

▶ Context display

▶ Minimum order quantity comparison and check

▶ Context display search results (search results are blocked)

6.2.6 SAP CCM — Architecture

SAP CCM is an add-on application to the SAP SRM solution. The application is built using the SAP Business Server Pages (BSP) technology. Therefore, it can be installed in the same client as SAP EBP. As described earlier, CCM is divided into two separate applications: CAT and CSE. Organizations have the flexibility to deploy these applications together or separately. Let's take a look at the various deployment options available for SAP CCM.

All-in-One Installation

This deployment scenario, combines the SRM server and the CCM add-on (CAT and CSE) on the same server installation. This scenario is ideal for a development environment as it allows the organization to install and test the configuration scenarios, determine the actual requirements for CCM, and then determine whether separate servers might be required. This can be seen in Figure 6.21.

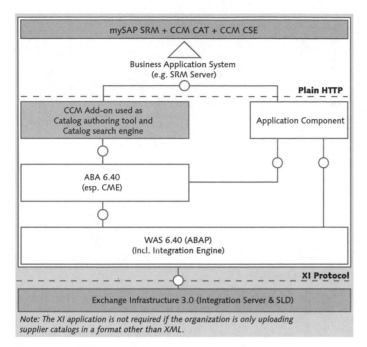

Figure 6.21 All-in-One Installation

Install CCM Applications on Same Server

In this deployment scenario, shown in Figure 6.22, both the CCM-CAT and CSE applications are installed on the same server, and SAP SRM is installed on a separate server. This deployment scenario can be especially useful if the WAS level for the application server (SRM) is different than for the CCM application. This would be the case if an organization was integrating CCM with an SAP SRM release older than SAP SRM 4.0.

Install CAT Application on SRM Server

In this deployment scenario, shown in Figure 6.23, there are a total of two servers in the environment; one for the SRM server with the catalog authoring tool and the other for the catalog search engine. This deployment is suitable if organizations want to provide a more independent environment for the search engine to ensure better performance.

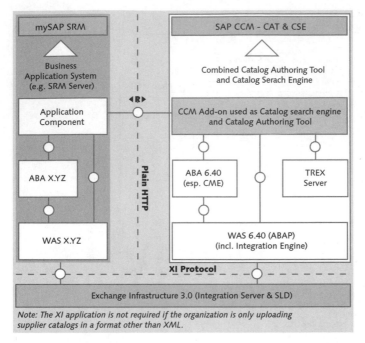

Figure 6.22 All-in-One installation: SRM and CCM on Separate Servers

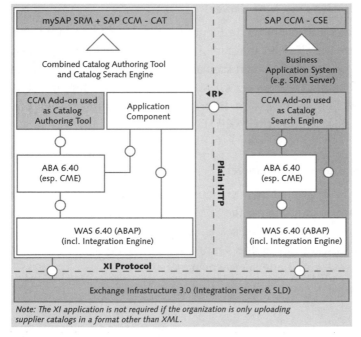

Figure 6.23 Installing SRM and CCM-CAT on the Same Server

Install all Applications on Separate Servers

In this deployment scenario, shown in Figure 6.24, the SAP SRM_SERVER, SAP CAT and SAP CSE are all installed on a separate server. This provides the most flexibility in deployment and performance. However, it is a costly option because in the overall landscape will involve development, QA, and production environments.

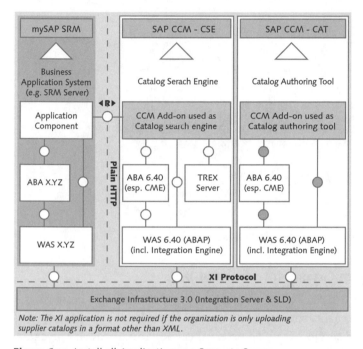

Figure 6.24 Install all Applications on Separate Server

Exchange Infrastructure (XI) Component

Organizations that install the SAP CCM catalog might be required to install and configure the SAP XI application. This is because of the different scenarios available in SAP CCM; depending on the scenario, your project might need XI or not. Figure 6.25 illustrates scenarios where XI is required for SAP CCM.

Scenarios	Scenarios			XI required ?
Content collection -	CSV 1.0			No
Load catalog file	CSV 2.0			No
	SAP XML			Yes
	BMECat			Yes
	eCX XML			Yes
Content collection -	Product Masters from SRM			Yes
Data Transfer	Contracts from SRM			Yes
	PIR from ERP			Yes
	Contracts from ERP			Yes
	Material Masters from ERP			Yes
Publishing	Distributed Deployment			Yes
	All-In-One Deployment			No
Feature		**CSV 1.0**	**CSV 2.0**	**XML**
Basic Content (flat structure, single value)		Yes	Yes	Yes
Hierarchical catalog schema		No	Yes	Yes
Multi-valued attributes (e.g.: price scales)		No	Yes	Yes
Description of IDs		No	Yes	Yes
Multiple language		No	Yes	Yes

Figure 6.25 When XI is Required for SAP CCM Scenarios

6.2.7 SAP Open Catalog Interface (OCI)

The Open Catalog Interface (OCI) determines the data exchange between the SAP SRM and external catalog applications. OCI enables the transmission of selected goods and services from an external catalog to SAP SRM. The external catalog can be located either behind your firewall or on the Internet.

In Section 6.1.1, we discussed the general process of using OCI-compliant supplier catalogs, also termed RoundTrip suppliers. In this section, we'll discuss the technical information related to the OCI interface and its setup in the SRM system. Figure 6.26 illustrates the OCI integration.

The catalog interface consists of two separate and distinct sections, the inbound section and the outbound section. Let's take a look at these next.

Inbound Section

The inbound section in OCI consists of the information being sent from the catalog application (supplier catalog, SAP CCM) to SAP SRM. This section contains data on the items selected in the catalog, such as the item descriptions, quantities ordered, and prices.

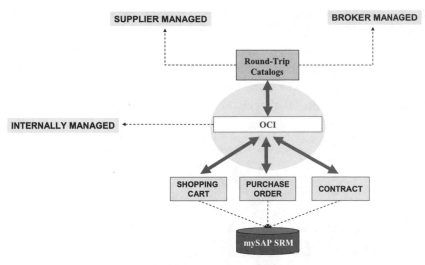

Figure 6.26 Integrate Internal and External Catalogs Using OCI Interface

The inbound data identifies the information that will be coming back from the supplier's catalog website and needs to be mapped to the shopping cart or purchase order fields in SAP SRM. Figure 6.27 provides a subset of the inbound and outbound OCI parameters available for SAP SRM release 4.0. A complete list of these is available in the SAP OCI document available on the Service Marketplace.

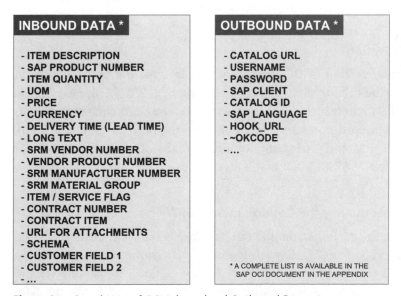

Figure 6.27 Sample List of OCI Inbound and Outbound Parameters

273

During the development and testing phase of integrating with a supplier catalog, there can be issues that result from the information coming back from the catalog. Project teams can quickly troubleshoot the root cause by reviewing the technical OCI Inbound parameters that are being passed back to the SRM application. This can be done by viewing the source code on the supplier's website at the time of checkout (as illustrated in Figure 6.28).

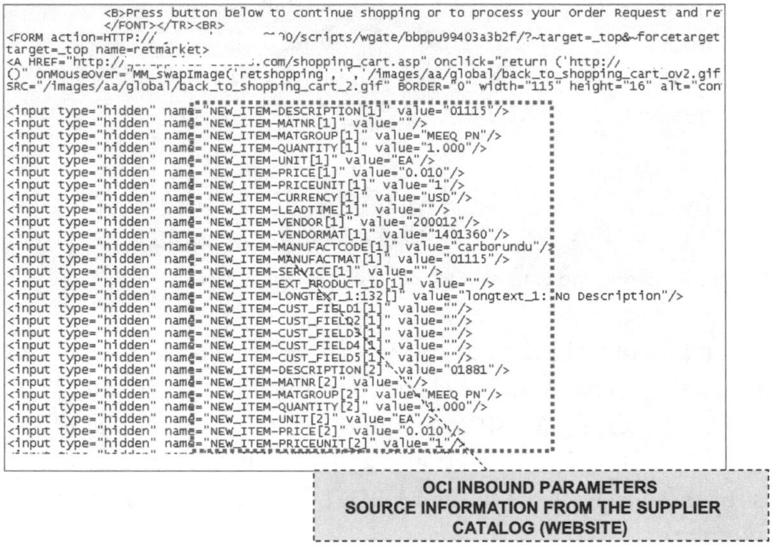

```
            <B>Press button below to continue shopping or to process your order Request and re
            </FONT></TR><BR>
<FORM action=HTTP://                  ~ ?0/scripts/wgate/bbppu99403a3b2f/?~target=_top&~forcetarget
target=_top name=retmarket>
<A HREF="http://                 .com/shopping_cart.asp" onclick="return ('http://
()" onMouseOver="MM_swapImage('retshopping','','/images/aa/global/back_to_shopping_cart_ov2.gif
SRC="/images/aa/global/back_to_shopping_cart_2.gif" BORDER="0" width="115" height="16" alt="con

<input type="hidden" name="NEW-ITEM-DESCRIPTION[1]" value="01115"/>
<input type="hidden" name="NEW-ITEM-MATNR[1]" value=""/>
<input type="hidden" name="NEW-ITEM-MATGROUP[1]" value="MEEQ PN"/>
<input type="hidden" name="NEW-ITEM-QUANTITY[1]" value="1.000"/>
<input type="hidden" name="NEW-ITEM-UNIT[1]" value="EA"/>
<input type="hidden" name="NEW-ITEM-PRICE[1]" value="0.010"/>
<input type="hidden" name="NEW-ITEM-PRICEUNIT[1]" value="1"/>
<input type="hidden" name="NEW-ITEM-CURRENCY[1]" value="USD"/>
<input type="hidden" name="NEW-ITEM-LEADTIME[1]" value=""/>
<input type="hidden" name="NEW-ITEM-VENDOR[1]" value="200012"/>
<input type="hidden" name="NEW-ITEM-VENDORMAT[1]" value="1401360"/>
<input type="hidden" name="NEW-ITEM-MANUFACTCODE[1]" value="carborundu"/>
<input type="hidden" name="NEW-ITEM-MANUFACTMAT[1]" value="01115"/>
<input type="hidden" name="NEW-ITEM-SERVICE[1]" value=""/>
<input type="hidden" name="NEW-ITEM-EXT_PRODUCT_ID[1]" value=""/>
<input type="hidden" name="NEW-ITEM-LONGTEXT_1:132[]" value="longtext_1:.No Description"/>
<input type="hidden" name="NEW-ITEM-CUST_FIELD1[1]" value=""/>
<input type="hidden" name="NEW-ITEM-CUST_FIELD2[1]" value=""/>
<input type="hidden" name="NEW-ITEM-CUST_FIELD3[1]" value=""/>
<input type="hidden" name="NEW-ITEM-CUST_FIELD4[1]" value=""/>
<input type="hidden" name="NEW-ITEM-CUST_FIELD5[1]" value=""/>
<input type="hidden" name="NEW-ITEM-DESCRIPTION[2]" value="01881"/>
<input type="hidden" name="NEW-ITEM-MATNR[2]" value=""/>
<input type="hidden" name="NEW-ITEM-MATGROUP[2]" value="MEEQ PN"/>
<input type="hidden" name="NEW-ITEM-QUANTITY[2]" value="1.000"/>
<input type="hidden" name="NEW-ITEM-UNIT[2]" value="EA"/>
<input type="hidden" name="NEW-ITEM-PRICE[2]" value="0.010"/>
<input type="hidden" name="NEW-ITEM-PRICEUNIT[2]" value="1"/>
```

**OCI INBOUND PARAMETERS
SOURCE INFORMATION FROM THE SUPPLIER
CATALOG (WEBSITE)**

Figure 6.28 Example of Inbound Parameters on Supplier Website

Outbound Section

The outbound section in OCI consists of the information being sent from SAP SRM to the catalog application (supplier catalog, SAP CCM, etc.). This is typically information such as the supplier's URL, user authentication parameters for login, and other session parameters required to maintain a link between the SRM and catalog application. Note that if an internal catalog is being used (e.g., SAP CCM), it is still accessed using the OCI mechanism.

6.2.8 Customizing the Catalog in SAP SRM

In SAP SRM, the catalog outbound call structure is set up in Customizing (as illustrated in Figure 6.29). Organizations can determine whether to set up the standard or integrated call structure for the catalog. The parameters and setup are the same for both the call structures. The difference is that the standard call structure opens the defined catalog in a new window and the integrated call structure opens the catalog within the same window. As of SAP SRM 4.0, the Hook_URL, OkCode, Target, and Caller parameters are no longer mandatory for maintenance. The system provides default values automatically.

SAP provides a standard BAdI BBP_CAT_CALL_ENRICH for organizations to enhance or modify the OCI interface parameters. This might be especially useful if the supplier catalog contains information that is captured using the customer specific parameters in the OCI inbound call structure. Project teams can then use the BAdI to move that data to specific fields within the SAP SRM document (shopping cart or purchase order).

The OCI interface is also able to process data in HTML and XML as input. Most organizations select the HTML method, as it does not have additional infrastructure requirements. For XML-based integration for OCI, you need to have SAP XI set up with your SAP SRM system. Most suppliers support the standard HTML OCI interface, so organizations do not need to worry about XML for catalog integration.

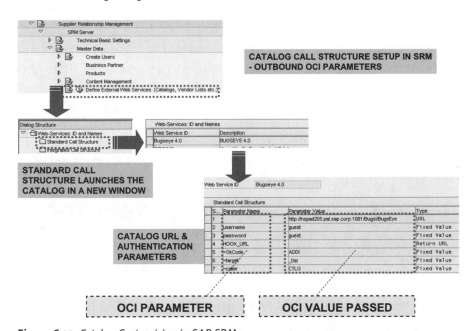

Figure 6.29 Catalog Customizing in SAP SRM

To become RoundTrip enabled, suppliers must make a few modifications to their website; many of the larger suppliers are already OCI compliant. Figure 6.6 provides a list of some of these supplier catalogs that are already OCI compliant. These changes include preparing the website to send and receive Open Catalog Interface requests for buyer authentication, session initiation, and shopping cart transmission back to SAP SRM.

> **Note**
>
> There have been no changes made to the SAP OCI structure since SAP SRM 4.0 release.

6.2.9 New Catalog Application — SRM MDM Catalog

In order to deliver the most valuable solution to its customers, SAP has decided to rely on SAP NetWeaver MDM technology to build the future catalog solution for SAP SRM. SAP MDM is a part of SAP NetWeaver platform and is already being used across SAP solutions to harmonize master data for organizations. For that reason, it probably did not make much sense for SAP to maintain a separate technology for product data in SRM (currently the SAP CCM solution). Therefore SAP has announced that there will be no further releases for SAP CCM, although **SAP CCM 2.0** will be maintained and supported by SAP up until the end of 2013, as illustrated in Figure 6.30.

This new catalog solution will be based on the SAP NetWeaver MDM technology and will be called the SRM-MDM catalog. In simple terms, the SRM-MDM catalog is a part of the SAP MDM solution with SRM-specific business content and data models. Essentially, customers that currently run SRM with Requisite or CCM and want to convert or migrate their data into SRM-MDM catalog will be able to use the import feature of SRM-MDM. This feature reads and compares data models and enables users to create maps between them to convert data.

> **Note**
>
> All customers implementing SRM 6.0 need to use the SRM-MDM catalog. Although CCM 2.0 is supported till 2013, it will not be supported with SAP SRM 6.0.

Figure 6.0 shows a timeline and Road-map for the SRM-MDM Catalog.

The **SRM-MDM Catalog** (SP1) is scheduled to be available for customers sometime towards the end of 2006. SAP SRM will be shipped together with the SRM-MDM Catalog component beginning with SAP SRM 6.0, which has a scheduled ramp-up delivery procedure beginning early 2007. Organizations need to be careful to implement the new SRM-MDM release because this not only includes a brand new catalog solution but also requires the underlying core MDM component and knowledge.

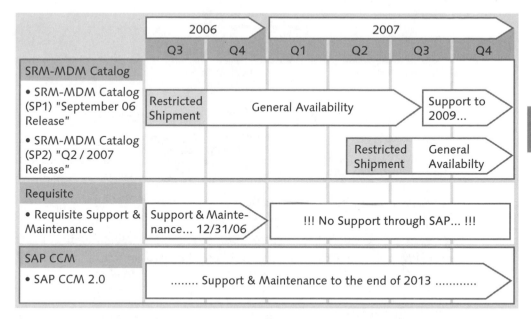

	2006		2007			
	Q3	Q4	Q1	Q2	Q3	Q4
SRM-MDM Catalog						
• SRM-MDM Catalog (SP1) "September 06 Release"	Restricted Shipment	General Availability			Support to 2009...	
• SRM-MDM Catalog (SP2) "Q2 / 2007 Release"				Restricted Shipment	General Availabilty	
Requisite						
• Requisite Support & Maintenance	Support & Maintenance... 12/31/06	!!! No Support through SAP... !!!				
SAP CCM						
• SAP CCM 2.0	.... Support & Maintenance to the end of 2013					

Figure 6.30 SRM-MDM Catalog Timeline (Source: SAP)

Figure 6.31 illustrates the catalog solution implementation recommendation for new and existing SRM and CCM customers. SAP is currently proposing that new customers implementing SAP SRM look at the **SRM-MDM Catalog** as the recommended catalog solution. SAP has advised that the SRM-MDM Catalog will be made available to SAP SRM customers with the same license and support conditions as currently defined for SAP CCM.

As SRM-MDM is an application built upon the SAP NetWeaver MDM application, organizations will have the opportunity to extend their licence from the SRM-MDM Catalog to SAP MDM. This will allow organizations the flexibility to expand beyond procurement-specific catalog management and deploy the SAP NetWeaver MDM application for managing any master data in the enterprise.

The SRM-MDM Catalog provides an existing repository structure for the business scenarios:

▶ Self-Service Procurement
▶ Service Procurement
▶ Contract Management

Current Catalog Solution	Proposed Solution
New Customer	SRM-MDM Catalog
Requisite Technology, willing to migrate before the end of 2006	SRM-MDM Catalog "September 06" Release
Requisite Technology, O.K. to wait 2007 or later	SRM-MDM Catalog "Q2/2007" Release
SAP CCM 1.0	SAP CCM 2.0*
SAP CCM 2.0*	Keep SAP CCM 2.0, then migrate to SRM-MDM Catalog later

*SAP CCM 2.0 is supported up until 2013

Figure 6.31 Implementation Recommendation

For each of these scenarios the integration of the MDM catalog is enabled with SRM using the OCI technology as I described earlier within this chapter.

6.3 Summary

In this chapter, I introduced the concept of catalogs and content management. You should remember that a well-thought-out catalog and content strategy is very important for any SRM initiative. Organizations should ensure that they do not pick a catalog strategy in a vacuum.

Internally managed, supplier-managed, and broker-managed catalogs each provide unique advantages. Broker-managed catalog providers such as SciQuest and ICG Commerce are different than supplier-managed catalogs because the broker hosts catalog data for multiple suppliers and typically charges an annual fee for accessing the catalog data. Typically, these providers also offer other services such as order collaboration and document transmission.

I also discussed in detail the capabilities of the catalog and content management solution introduced by SAP in 2004: SAP CCM. This solution replaces the existing Requisite BugsEye software that was bundled with prior SAP SRM releases. The SAP CCM solution provides content management capabilities that allow organizations to upload and manage their own product and contract data, along with supplier catalogs that can be hosted as an internal catalog. Organizations that are in the process of implementing the SAP SRM

4.0 or 5.0 solution should also review whether they should implement SAP CCM or the SRM-MDM catalog. The latter will eventually replace SAP CCM as the future SAP solution for catalog and content management. Organizations implementing SRM 6.0 need to implement SRM-MDM Catalog. A separate License is not required for MDM if it is only used for catalogs within SRM.

In Chapter 7 you will learn about the different implementation scenarios available for SAP SRM and understand the details of each scenario. That chapter will also equip readers with the information to make the decision on which implementation scenario to choose for their SRM implementation.

Is there a checklist to provide to clients when they are deciding to implement SRM, Classic or Extended? Is there any tool out there that can be shared in advising customers about which scenario is best for their business?

7   Choosing Implementation Scenarios

One of the biggest decisions in any SRM implementation, and one that continuously haunts project teams, is the selection of the appropriate implementation scenario. Even when you thoughtfully select the appropriate scenario, the questions still abound during and after implementation. The key reason is that, although SAP has provided flexibility for how organizations deploy the SRM solution using the different implementation scenarios, each scenario imposes known and hidden restrictions that organizations realize during their implementations. This chapter defines the available scenarios and provides the reasons for using one scenario over another.

7.1   Overview — SAP SRM Implementation Scenarios

SAP provides three main implementation scenarios (also sometimes called technical scenarios) that can be used to deploy the different SAP SRM business scenarios. These are:

- Classic
- Extended Classic
- Standalone

The selection of the implementation scenario is a key decision that determines the available functionality, unique configuration, and restrictions in the SAP SRM solution.

It is important for organizations and project teams to realize that the selection of implementation scenarios in SRM is really a two-fold decision: driven by business requirements driven and also by implications for the technical environment. Additionally, certain SRM functionality is only available based on the scenario implemented. Unfortunately, there is not one answer that fits all environments. This decision is entirely based on the organization's business requirements, business processes being implemented as a part of the current or future project(s), the current SAP environment (e.g., existing SAP landscape, new SAP implementation, or no SAP implementation), along with factors that are critical to the success of the project and user acceptance.

Most successful projects determine their implementation scenario during their blueprint phase of the project. This is when the project teams understand and share the "true" requirements and functionality so that a good choice can be made. However, in some cases its might be very clear which scenario to implement even prior to the blueprint phase. For example, suppose an organization already has a live SAP environment and it was decided as a part of the SRM project charter that there will be no major change to the core purchasing function that exists in their current SAP system. In this example, the SRM project teams will most likely choose to implement a *Classic* scenario. We discuss these choices in further detail later in the chapter.

Figure 7.1 provides a quick overview of the business processes that exist within the three different implementation scenarios and where each of the main processes occurs.

> **Note**
>
> In this book, I use the term back-end system generically to illustrate how the SAP SRM application can be integrated with SAP and non-SAP applications. For the vast majority of organizations, this back-end system correlates to their SAP R/3 or enterprise resource planning (ERP) system. For purposes of this book, I use the term back-end system interchangeably with the SAP back end, SAP R/3 or ERP system

Some examples of why organizations might use a back-end system are as follows:

- Checking the accounting information in SAP SRM against the information that exists in the back-end system.
- Creating a purchasing document in the back-end system; e.g., a purchase order (PO) or stock reservation
- Creating an invoice (Financial document) in the back-end system.

Now we can proceed further towards gaining an understanding of the various implementation scenarios.

	CLASSIC	EXTENDED CLASSIC	STANDALONE
CREATE SHOPPING CART	mySAP SRM	mySAP SRM	mySAP SRM
APPROVAL WORKFLOW	mySAP SRM or SAP R/3 or ERP	mySAP SRM	mySAP SRM
PURCHASE REQUISITION	Optional: SAP R/3 or ERP	N/A	N/A
PURCHASE ORDER CREATION	SAP R/3 or ERP	mySAP SRM and copy of PO in SAP R/3 or ERP	mySAP SRM
CREATE STOCK "RESERVATION"	Optional: SAP R/3 or ERP	N/A	N/A
CONFIRMATION ENTRY* or GOODS RECEIPT	mySAP SRM or SAP R/3 or ERP	mySAP SRM or SAP R/3 or ERP	mySAP SRM or SAP R/3 or ERP
INVOICE ENTRY	mySAP SRM or SAP R/3 or ERP	mySAP SRM or SAP R/3 or ERP	mySAP SRM or SAP R/3 or ERP

* A CONFIRMATION IN mySAP SRM is transferred to SAP backend and a GOODS RECEIPT (G/R) IS CREATED
BACKEND SYSTEM = SAP R/3, ERP OR NON-SAP SYSTEM

Figure 7.1 Quick Glance at the SAP SRM Implementation Scenarios

7.2   The Classic Scenario

The *Classic* scenario is by far the most widely adopted scenario among organizations that have implemented SAP SRM. In addition to the inherent virtues of the Classic scenario, there is another good reason for this adoption. When Enterprise Buyer was rolled out as a solution in 1999, the only scenario that was available for organizations was the Classic approach. Those were the days of the best-of-breed solution implementation. Many organizations that had SAP R/3 as an enterprise application still had implemented non-SAP best-of-breed solutions like Ariba for use within their procurement organization.

SAP along with its partner Commerce One targeted exactly those customers with an installed base of SAP R/3. The obvious selling point was simpler and tighter integration of Enterprise Buyer with SAP R/3 Materials Management (MM) and Financial Accounting (FI) modules.

In the classic or full-integration scenario, Enterprise Buyer is connected to a back-end system for MM, FI, and Controlling (CO). All MM documents, such as purchase orders, reservations, purchase requisitions, goods receipts and service-entry sheets are in the back-end system. Accounting and controlling systems with the relevant documents are also connected. The Enterprise Buyer system communicates all relevant business documents to the back-end systems, where they are then processed further.

This scenario relies strongly on the ERP back-end system(s), because all materials-management documents, such as purchase orders, goods receipts, service entry sheets, and invoices are located there. There may be one Enterprise Buyer Professional (EBP) system communicating with multiple ERP systems within this scenario. All financial checks and postings are made in the ERP system. The Classic scenario approach is illustrated in Figure 7.2.

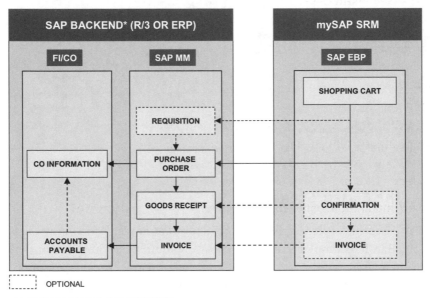

Figure 7.2 Classic Scenario Implementation in SAP SRM

In the classic scenario the process begins in SAP SRM with the creation of a shopping cart and ends with the entry of an invoice. Now let me walk you through this process as illustrated in Figure 7.2:

1. Create a **SHOPPING CART** in **SAP EBP** system with one or multiple line items.

2. Based on configuration and workflow customizing, the system determines whether an approval is required for one or more line items in the shopping cart.

Note

In this scenario organizations may either choose to use the approval/workflow capabilities that exist in EBP or use workflows in their back-end SAP R/3 system.

3. Once all the required approvals are complete in **SAP SRM**, based on the configuration and customizing set-up in **SAP EBP,** the system creates one of the following documents in **SAP MM: REQUISITION, PURCHASE ORDER,** or a reservation. Any changes required to these documents are entered within the SAP R/3 back-end system. The following functions take place in the **SAP MM** system:

   ▸ Source of Supply (Info Records, Contracts, etc.)

   ▸ Tax Determination

   ▸ Pricing Determination

   ▸ Output Determination

4. Goods Receipts (referred to as a **CONFIRMATION** in SAP EBP) and an **INVOICE** can be entered in SAP EBP. Based on workflow customizing, once all approvals are complete, the system will then trigger the appropriate postings within the back-end system. Alternately, companies could also choose to enter the **GOODS RECEIPT** and **INVOICE** directly in the SAP back-end (R/3 or ERP) system.

Standard integration between SAP *Enterprise Buyer* and the SAP back end ensures seamless status updates of the documents in both systems. Therefore, the end user can see whether an invoice is posted against his or her original shopping cart or purchase order.

Tip

If a confirmation or invoice entry is performed in SAP EBP, the corresponding goods-receipt and invoice documents are distributed to the SAP back-end system via means of Application Linking and Enablement (ALE) technology. A distribution model needs to be setup in Customizing, and — based on the release of your SAP R/3 system — you need to select the appropriate IDoc Message Type(s) as indicated in Table 7.1.

You should pay special attention to the fact that in Table 7.1 a message type could be different depending on the SAP R/3 release. For example, if your SAP R/3 release is newer than 4.0, then you should use the IDoc message type **MBGMCR** instead of **WMMBXY.**

Message Type	SAP R/3 System Release 3.1	SAP R/3 System Release 4.0	SAP R/3 System Release > 4.5
Goods Receipt (mat. doc.)	WMMBXY	WMMBXY	MBGMCR
Goods Receipt (acc. doc.)	ACPJMM	ACC_GOODS_MOVEMENT	ACC_GOODS_MOVEMENT
Procurement Card	ACLPAY	ACLPAY	ACLPAY
Invoice (CO)	BBPCO	BBPCO	BBPCO
Invoice	BBPIV	BBPIV	BBPIV

Table 7.1 ALE IDoc Message Types for Transferring Confirmations and Invoices from SRM to R/3

7.2.1 Impact of Classic Scenario When Integrating Enterprise Buyer with Supplier Self Services

Organizations that have implemented the Supplier Self Services (SUS) application to collaborate orders with their suppliers need to be aware that the implementation scenario in EBP has an impact on the standard functionality that is available. For example, the classic scenario does not allow for a purchase order to be sent to SAP SUS from SAP MM. Figure 7.3 illustrates the Classic scenario approach when SAP SUS is integrated with EBP. As you can see in Figure 7.3, the supplier enablement is not supported in SUS when using the classic scenario.

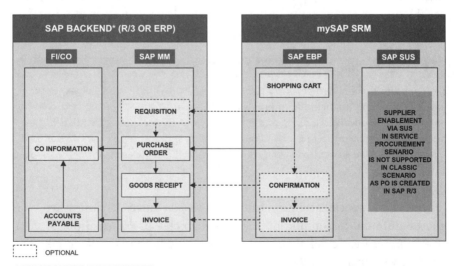

Figure 7.3 Supplier Self Services Integration with Enterprise Buyer (Classic Scenario)

7.2.2   Which Organizations Should Look at this Scenario?

You might ask, therefore, which organizations should consider the classic scenario. Some of these are:

▶ Organizations that have an existing (possibly large) installed base of users within the SAP R/3 environment.

▶ Organizations that already have users within their purchasing department using SAP R/3 MM/IM to procure goods and services and are comfortable with the solution.

▶ Organizations that want their purchasing professionals to continue to work and use the functionality offered in the SAP R/3 MM environment.

▶ Organizations that have already setup and want to continue to handle all supplier communication transmissions (EDI, faxc, email, print, etc.) via existing channels in the SAP R/3 system.

However, there are some restrictions of the classic scenario, that are examined next.

7.2.3   Restrictions of the Classic Scenario

Unfortunately, organizations implementing SAP SRM will find that restrictions exist when implementing a particular scenario. Therefore, project teams need to clearly understand their business requirements during the blueprint phase and review the following restrictions that exist in the scenarios in order to make an appropriate decision. These restrictions are:

▶ The integration of external requirements (plan-driven procurement) does not completely support a classic scenario, the following restrictions exist:

  ▹ You cannot procure direct materials using the Classic scenario.

  ▹ When you procure services, you cannot use the Classic scenario to process limits without an expected value. Additionally, the service packages transferred to SRM are not grouped together in SRM.

▶ The integration of the procurement card is not possible in the Classic scenario in the standard release.

▶ The service-procurement scenario deployment with SUS cannot be integrated with the SUS application. This scenario is also known as EBP-SUS scenario. Therefore the purchase orders are created in SAP Enterprise Buyer and sent to the SUS application.

7.2.4 Impact on the SRM Organizational Structure

The implementation scenario has an impact on the organizational structure setup, and project teams need to be aware of how to set up the organizational structure when the Classic scenario is activated. The organizational structure is described in detail in Chapter 10.

7.2.5 Technical Extras

As SAP SRM is a separate system than the SAP back-end system, there are standard functions and programs that are delivered by SAP to communicate between the two systems. It is often helpful to know the function modules and Business Application Programming Interface (BAPIs) that are used to communicate the Purchase Order information between EBP to the SAP back-end system.

Figure 7.4 illustrates the Function Module **BBP_REQREQ_TRANSFER** and **BAPI BAPI_PO_CREATE** that are used in EBP and SAP backend to create the purchase order.

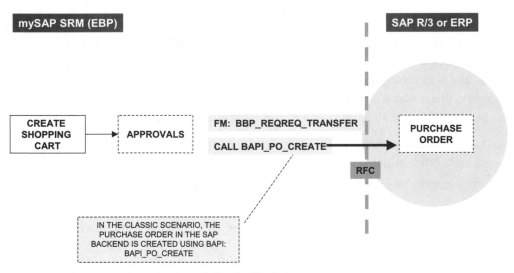

Figure 7.4 Create Purchase Orders in Classic Scenario

Often there are situations during projects where ambiguous errors are received when creating a purchase order in SAP R/3 using the shopping cart. Some errors can be deciphered, and for many others troubleshooting is required. The following step-by-step approach might be helpful when troubleshooting errors generated during creation of the purchase order in the SAP back end:

1. Create a shopping cart.

2. Execute **FM: BBP_REQREQ_TRANSFER** in debug mode.

3. Using break-points, troubleshoot the **BAPI BAPI_PO_CREATE** that creates the purchase order.

Now that we understand the classic scenario in SRM, let us discuss the Extended Classic scenario and how it differs from the classic approach.

7.3   The Extended Classic Scenario

The Extended Classic scenario came into existence when SAP customers began to request additional flexibility within their Enterprise Buyer implementations. Moreover, the Classic scenario required that the purchasing buyers work in the confines of the SAP R/3 MM environment. In the Extended Classic scenario, the entire procurement process takes place locally in SAP Enterprise Buyer and a copy of the data is replicated to the back-end system. In essence, this scenario is an extension of the classic scenario.

SAP introduced the Extended Classic scenario in 2002 with the release of EBP 3.5. Not many customers are now live with Extended Classic, but the use of this scenario is growing rapidly because of its inherent flexibility. It is being adopted by a number of organizations that are undertaking a new SAP SRM implementation or are upgrading their existing SAP Enterprise Buyer system.

Because purchase orders are created locally within SAP Enterprise Buyer, if the data in the shopping cart is insufficient to generate a complete purchase order, the data is supplemented manually within SAP Enterprise Buyer before being transferred to the back-end system. The Extended Classic scenario is illustrated in Figure 7.5.

In the Extended Classic scenario, the process begins in SAP SRM with the creation of a shopping cart and ends with the entry of an invoice. The following list walks you through this process, as illustrated in Figure 7.5:

1. Create a **SHOPPING CART** in **SAP EBP** system with one or multiple line items

2. Based on configuration and workflow customizing, the system determines whether an approval is required for one or more line items in the shopping cart

3. Once all the required approvals are complete in **SAP SRM**, based on the configuration and customizing set-up in **SAP EBP.** the system creates a complete or incomplete **PURCHASE ORDER** locally in **SAP EBP**. If an incomplete Purchase Order is created, a purchasing professional intervenes, completes the purchase order (e.g., a source of supply or price needs to be assigned) and transmits to the supplier. The following functions take place in SAP EBP:

   ▶ Source of Supply (vendor lists, contracts, etc.)

   ▶ Tax Determination (external System, EBP, custom rules)

   ▶ Pricing Determination (IPC, interlinkages, etc.)

   ▶ Purchasing Documents Output Determination (XML, email, etc.)

4. In the Extended-Classic scenario, the **PURCHASE ORDER** is created in **SAP SRM,** and a **READ-ONLY** copy of that PO is sent to the back-end **SAP MM** system. The purchase order in SAP EBP is the leading purchase order. Therefore, all subsequent changes to the purchase order can be made in the SRM system only.

5. Once the goods or services are received from the supplier, the end user can confirm the goods or services received either in the SAP EBP or SAP MM system. If a **CONFIRMATION** is created in EBP, a corresponding **GOODS RECEIPT** (GR) is created in the back-end SAP MM system. Therefore, organizations have the flexibility to choose where to perfom a goods receipt.

6. An **INVOICE** can also be entered within the **SAP EBP** system and corresponding invoice documents are created in the SAP back-end system. Most organizations however, continue to enter an **INVOICE** in the SAP back-end (R/3 or ERP) system.

The purchase order in the back-end system is a read-only copy that enables goods receipt, service entry, and invoice verification in the back-end system. This purchase order cannot be changed in the SAP R/3 or ERP systems. If you wish to make any changes to the purchase order, you must do so in the SRM system. Once you save these changes, they are transferred to the back-end purchase order. Therefore, in this scenario, the purchasing professionals operate primarily within SAP SRM instead of the SAP back end.

Most organizations that have a back-end SAP R/3 system continue to enter invoices within the back-end system. Even though SAP has provided increased support and functionality for invoice processing within SAP Enterprise Buyer, organizations tend to continue processing invoices in SAP R/3 because of their existing business processes, central focus, and enterprise accounts-payable functions. Review Chapter 5 to learn about invoice functionality in EBP, and also read the *What's New* section to see the Invoice Management Solution (IMS) that has been released by SAP with SAP SRM 5.0.

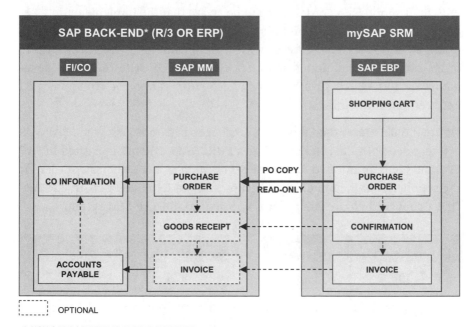

Figure 7.5 Extended Classic Scenario Implementation in SAP SRM

It is important to note that in the Extended Classic scenario the Purchasing Group is the key determinant for the resulting purchasing organization (POrg) on the PO sent to the supplier. If your company has multiple purchasing organizations, then the POrg will be determined based on the Purchasing Group used in the shopping cart.

However, in SAP MM (R/3 or ERP) the PO determines the POrg's value based on the plant in the purchase-order line item. This also causes an issue if, for example, there are multiple company codes, and where the POrg determined in SRM is not assigned to the company code or plant determined in SAP back-end. Therefore, it is important that the POrg determined in SRM is the same as in SAP R/3 so that the follow-on functions such as invoice entry are consistent. Review the OSS Notes referenced at the end of the chapter.

7.3.1 Impact of Extended Classic Scenario When Integrating Enterprise Buyer with SUS

Organizations that have implemented the SUS application to collaborate with their suppliers on orders need to be aware that the implementation scenario in EBP has an impact on the standard functionality that is available. For example, if the Extended Classic scenario is implemented, only the purchase order can be communicated between EBP and SUS. The follow-on documents such as PO confirmation or invoice entry cannot be communicated between EBP and SUS.

Figure 7.6 illustrates the Extended Classic scenario approach when SAP SUS is integrated with EBP. In Figure 7.6, a **PURCHASE ORDER** is created in **SAP EBP** and is communicated to the **SAP SUS** system as a **ORDER** (sales order for the suppliers). At the same time, because we're in Extended Classic, a **READ-ONLY** copy of the purchase order is also sent to the **SAP MM** system.

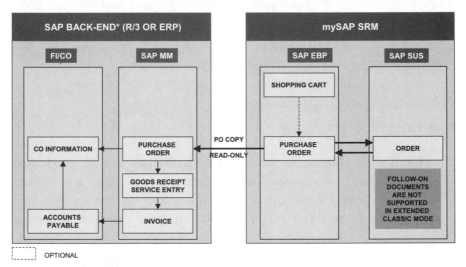

Figure 7.6 Supplier Self Services Integration With EBP (Extended Classic Scenario)

7.3.2 Which Organizations Should Look at This Scenario?

The following types of organizations might be interested in this scenario:

▶ Organizations that want to use the complete sourcing capabilities of SAP Enterprise Buyer.

▶ Organizations that want their purchasing professionals to operate primarily within the SAP Enterprise Buyer and maximize the streamlined purchasing functionality available within the system.

▶ Organizations that want to explore new communication channels for their suppliers (e.g.,XML). SAP Enterprise Buyer provides standard XML integration via the SAP Exchange Infrastructure (SAP XI).

▶ Organizations that don't have a business requirement to create a resulting requisition or reservation from the shopping cart.

Let's now explore the restrictions of this scenario.

7.3.3 Restrictions of the Extended Classic Scenario

Unfortunately, organizations implementing SAP SRM will find that restrictions exist when implementing a particular scenario. Therefore, project teams need to clearly understand their business requirements during the blueprint phase and review the restrictions that exist in the scenarios to make an appropriate decision. Let's take a look at these now:

▶ **Purchase Requisitions**
In the Extended Classic scenario, after a shopping cart is created, the subsequent document cannot be a purchase requisition.

▶ **Material Reservations**
In the Extended Classic scenario, after a shopping cart is created, the subsequent document cannot be a material reservation. A Business Add In (BAdI) to control the Extended Classic scenario can be used for achieving this functionality.

▶ **P-Card Functionality**
Organizations that want to use procurement cards (p-cards) as a mechanism of payment in SAP SRM, the Extended Classic scenario does not offer a solution. In the standard design this functionality is only provided in the Standalone scenario.

> **Note**
>
> In SRM 6.0 P-Card functionality is available within the Extented Classic scenario.

▶ **Shop With Limit Restriction**
In the Extended Classic scenario, when creating shopping carts with more than a one-item limit, separate POs will always be created for each item when ordering the shopping cart, irrespective of the data (i.e., vendor,

document type, purchasing group, company, location, performance period) in each item. For example, when a shopping cart with two limit positions is ordered, two POs will be created rather than one PO for two items.

▶ **Integration with SUS for Confirmation and Invoice Entry**
The Extended Classic scenario not completely released for SUS. The scenario works for collaboration of purchase order, purchase order response, and change order, but not for confirmation and invoice entry. If the Extended Classic scenario is activated in EBP and you send a purchase order from EBP to SUS, you cannot send the confirmation and invoice with reference to this purchase order back from SUS to EBP. Additionally, this scenario is only supported for free text items. The material-based scenario is not supported in Extended Classic and only supported for the MM-SUS integration (described in Chapter 5).

7.3.4   Impact on the SRM Organizational Structure

The implementation scenario has an impact on the organizational structure set-up, and project teams need to be aware of how to set up the organizational structure when the Extended Classic scenario is activated. The organizational structure is described in detail in Chapter 10.

7.3.5   Technical Extras

As SAP SRM is a separate system than the SAP back-end system, there are standard functions and programs that are delivered by SAP to communicate between the two systems. It is often helpful to know the function modules and BAPIs that are used to communicate the PO information between EBP to the SAP back-end system. Figure 7.7 illustrates the Function Module **BBP_PD_PO_CREATE** and **BAPI BAPI_PO_CREATE1** that are used in EBP and SAP back-end to create the PO.

Now that we understand the Extended Classic scenario in SRM, let us discuss the Standalone scenario and how it is different from the other two implementation scenarios.

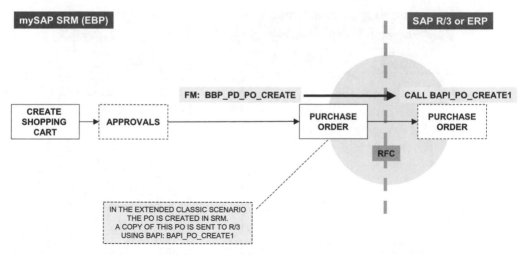

Figure 7.7 Create Purchase Orders in Extended Classic Scenario

7.4 The Standalone Scenario

Last but not the least, is the Standalone Scenario. This scenario was initially introduced by SAP with EBP 2.0 release in 2001. The primary reason SAP provided this implementation option was to capture a portion of the market that catered to organizations with non-SAP enterprise applications. This new approach had added benefits for organizations that had an SAP R/3 environment but also had divisions or companies within its enterprise that were not yet running SAP. For large, global organizations this provided a mechanism to provide its users an enterprisewide procurement solution that could integrate with SAP and non-SAP applications. The Standalone scenario has probably the smallest installed customer base, but nevertheless has key benefits.

This scenario handles the entire procurement process in SAP Enterprise Buyer. The shopping cart and follow-on documents, such as purchase orders, goods receipts and invoices, are created locally, and the whole procurement process is covered by SAP Enterprise Buyer. Validations and approvals are handled directly within SAP Enterprise Buyer.

All accounting validations are handled by one or more accounting back-end systems. At the same time, a commitment can be created in the FI/CO back-end system. Auxiliary account assignment checks, such as cost center checks and budget checks are also carried out in the back-end system. The Standalone scenario approach is illustrated in Figure 7.8.

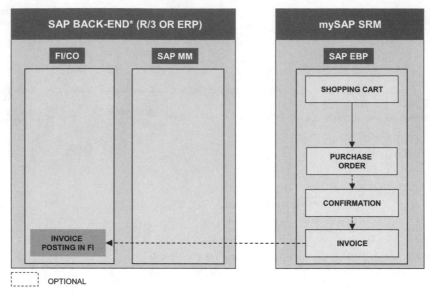

Figure 7.8 Standalone Scenario Implementation in SAP SRM

In the Standalone scenario, the process begins in SAP SRM with the creation of a shopping cart and ends with the entry of an invoice. All of the purchasing and accounts payable documents are created in **SAP EBP**. The following bullet points walk you through this process as illustrated in Figure 7.8:

1. Create a **SHOPPING CART** in **SAP EBP** system with one or multiple line items

2. Based on configuration and workflow customizing, the system determines whether an **approval** is required for one or more line items in the shopping cart

3. Once all the required approvals are complete, the system creates a complete or Incomplete **PURCHASE ORDER** locally in **SAP EBP**. If an incomplete PO is created a purchasing professional intervenes and completes the PO and transmits to the supplier.

4. Once the goods or services are received from the supplier, the end user can confirm the goods/services received and a **CONFIRMATION** is created locally in **SAP EBP**

5. An **INVOICE** can be entered at this point by a user in the accounts payable department. Once the invoice is entered, and unless any further approvals are required, the accounting information is transferred to the **FI/CO** system and all follow-on processes such as payments are processed there.

Now that the implementation is complete we can move on to understanding the impact of this scenario when integrating EBP with the SUS.

7.4.1 Impact of Standalone Scenario When Integrating Enterprise Buyer With SUS

Organizations that have implemented the SUS application in order to collaborate orders with their suppliers need to be aware that the implementation scenario in EBP has an impact on the standard functionality that is available. Figure 7.9 illustrates the Standalone scenario approach when SAP SUS is integrated with EBP.

Unlike the Classic and Extended Classic scenarios, the Standalone scenario provides a complete integration with SAP SUS and allows collaboration between SAP EBP and SAP SUS with respect to the **PURCHASE ORDER, CONFIRMATION**, and **INVOICE** documents.

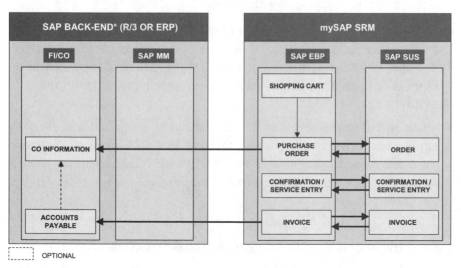

Figure 7.9 Supplier Self Services Integration with Enterprise Buyer (Standalone Scenario)

7.4.2 Which Organizations Should Look at This Scenario?

The following types of organizations might be interested in this scenario:

▶ Organizations that do not have a productive materials management system and want to handle the entire process locally within SAP Enterprise Buyer, integrating only to an accounting system.

- ▸ Organizations that want to use the streamlined purchasing functionality of SAP Enterprise Buyer for specific product categories, typically indirect materials and services.

- ▸ Organizations that want to use and implement the procurement card functionality within SAP Enterprise Buyer. This functionality is only supported within the Standalone scenario as the invoices are created locally.

- ▸ Organizations that want to free the back-end system of all purchasing activities by transferring a specific group of users to SAP Enterprise Buyer.

7.4.3 Restrictions of the Standalone Scenario

Unfortunately, organizations implementing SAP SRM will find that restrictions exist when implementing a particular scenario. Therefore, project teams need to clearly understand their business requirements during the blueprint phase and review the following restrictions imposed by the scenarios so as to make an appropriate decision:

- ▸ Any functionality relating to integration with an SAP back-end R/3 or ERP system, such as the creation of purchase requisitions, purchase orders, and material reservations is not possible in the Standalone scenario as there is no backend materials management system connected in this scenario.

- ▸ The plan-driven procurement scenario cannot be integrated with the SUS application. This scenario is also known as MM-SUS scenario. Therefore the purchase orders are created in the SAP back end and sent to the SUS application. In the Standalone scenario, no purchase orders are sent to the SAP backend.

7.4.4 Impact on the SRM Organizational Structure

The implementation scenario has an impact on the organizational structure set-up, and project teams need to be aware of how to set up the organizational structure when the Standalone scenario is activated. The organizational structure set-up is nearly the same as in the Extended Classic scenario. An exception is that no back-end organization units are set up, only an attribute for the accounting system. The organizational structure is described in detail in Chapter 10.

7.4.5 Technical Extras

Because SAP SRM is a separate system from the SAP back-end system, there are standard functions and programs that are delivered by SAP to communicate between the two systems. It is often helpful to know the function modules and BAPIs that are used to communicate the PO information between EBP and the SAP back-end system. Figure 7.10 illustrates the function module **BBP_PD_PO_CREATE** that is used to create a PO in **SAP SRM (EBP)**. As there is no back-end integration for purchasing documents, there is no need to use a BAPI for creating a purchase order in SAP R/3 or ERP as we do in the Classic or Extended Classic scenarios.

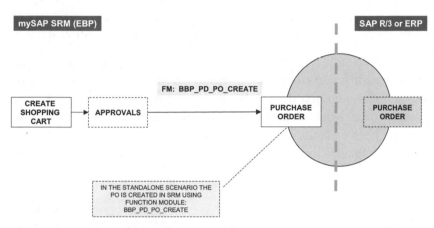

Figure 7.10 Create Purchase Orders in Standalone Scenario

7.5 Other Scenarios

In addition to the three scenarios defined in the previous sections, there is another option available for organizations with business requirements that warrant a combination of these scenarios.

7.5.1 Decoupled Scenario

One example would be an organization that wants to use the Extended Classic scenario but also has a business requirement to create a reservation in **SAP MM** from a shopping cart. Such a business requirement can only be satisfied if both the Classic and Extended Classic scenarios are combined. This scenario is sometimes referred as the *Decoupled* scenario. Readers should be aware that the majority of companies implement either Classic, Extended Classic, or Standalone scenarios.

7.5.2 Combining Scenarios

SAP Enterprise Buyer supports the functionality of implementing a combination of the scenarios. For example, a single SAP Enterprise Buyer system could allow for the creation of purchase orders resulting from shopping carts either in the EBP system or the backend ERP system. In the standard system, this determination is made based on the product category (material group) of the ordered item. We explain the decoupled scenario using Figure 7.11.

In Customizing, organizations can decide whether the requisition or purchase order is to be created in the SAP R/3 or SAP SRM system. As a standard, SAP provides the capability to make this decision based on the product category; however that will usually not be suitable for most organizations as a decision criterion. One example could be the case of the medical devices product category.

Your organization could stock some items in inventory for which you want to create a reservation in SAP MM. For all other non-stock items, a purchase order needs to be created and transmitted to an external vendor via the SAP EBP system. Therefore, the product category is not usually a good criterion. This is where organizations can make use of BAdIs and customize their own rules pertinent to their business requirements.

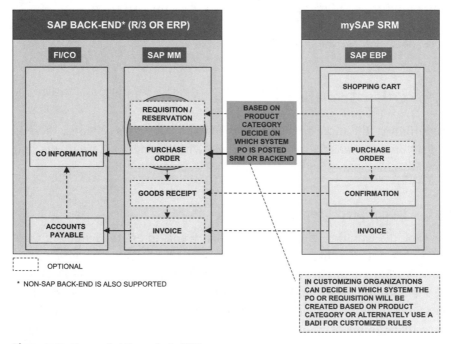

Figure 7.11 Decoupled Scenario in EBP

7.5.3 Running Scenarios in Parallel

The Classic, Extended Classic, and Standalone scenarios can be run in parallel. Here are some examples for when an organization might want to host multiple scenarios in the same EBP system:

▶ If the Extended Classic scenario was an appropriate fit for your organization but you wanted to use the reservations functionality in SAP R/3 for products (materials) that were stocked within a plant.

▶ The organization might have non-SAP back-end systems in addition to SAP, and the organization wants to roll out a single procurement front end using Enterprise Buyer. This suits customers who already might a productive materials management back-end system, but wish to handle the procurement of some supplies locally and others within the back-end system.

7.5.4 Technical Extras

In the standard system, the determination of which back-end system is used based on the product category (material group) of the ordered item. If your organization wants to use business rules that are different than the standard delivered product category method, SAP provides a BAdI called BBP_DETERMINE_LOGSYS. Here you identify the back-end systems and enter the information the system needs in order to choose the correct one.

For example, suppose your organization wants to use different back-end systems depending on the product category of the item in the shopping cart or purchase order. The project team can define each of these back-end systems using the Implementation Guide (IMG) activity *Define Back-end system for Product Category*. However, the organization wants a particular back-end system to be used whenever a specified employee orders an item. In this case, the project team would define a rule in the BAdI that applies whenever that user orders an item, thereby overriding the IMG settings.

7.6 Things to Remember and to Watch Out For

Now that we've discussed all the implementation scenarios, you will have to select the option that best meets the business requirements of your organization. The following is a list of things to remember when selecting your implementation scenario:

▶ In the Classic scenario, the PO is only available in the SAP back-end. In the Extended Classic and Standalone scenarios, the PO is created in SRM.

▶ Requisitions and or Material Reservations can only be created in the SAP back-end if the classic scenario is implemented (unless BAdIs are implemented).

▶ The Classic, Extended Classic, and Standalone scenarios can all co-exist in the same installation. Organizations need to use standard delivered BAdIs for enabling multiple scenarios, also called the decoupled scenario.

▶ In the Extended Classic scenario, the purchase order cannot be changed in the SAP back-end system; changes are only supported in the Enterprise Buyer system.

▶ In the Extended Classic scenario, all the purchasing documents (PO, Contracts, etc.) can only be transmitted to the vendor from the SAP SRM system. If the organization wants to output via the SAP R/3 backend, then it must use the Classic Scenario or customize.

▶ Purchasing Cards (PCards) can only be used in the Standalone scenario. If other scenarios are used, organizations will have to customize using BAdIs and other developments.

▶ If the Extended Classic scenario is implemented, then during the cutover phase the legacy purchasing documents (PO, Contracts, etc.) need to be converted into the EBP system instead of the SAP R/3 system. Organizations will find challenges in creating shopping carts (converting from requisitions) and contracts in SRM. SAP does not provide any standard programs to create these documents. Organizations will have to use eCATT or other tools such as Mercury.

Keep these mind during your implementation. Now let's review some relevant OSS Notes.

7.7 Relevant OSS Notes

In Table 7.2, I've provided a list of important OSS Notes available on the SAP Service Marketplace that are relevant for organizations implementing one of the implementation scenarios discussed in this chapter. For example, OSS Note 861889 provides an explanation of the limitations in SRM when creating Limit and service POs in an Extended Classic implementation.

Note	Description
861889	Limitations on limit and service PO's in case of ECS
543544	SUS: Extended Classic Scenario for EBP not supported
505030	Restrictions for the integration of external requirements
900825	Shopping cart commitments
946201	Using back-end P Org/ P Grp directly in ECS local PO
752586	Customer fields in extended classic scenario
627542	Grouping not supported in Classic scenario
841277	Limit items not created in the back-end system
841141	Valuated goods receipt in SRM

Table 7.2 OSS Notes in the SAP Service Marketplace

7.8 Summary

In this chapter, I've introduced the three main implementation scenarios: Classic, Extended Classic, and Standalone. Choosing an implementation scenario is an important decision for any organization as it forms a basis for the functionality that is available and the limitations for the business scenario selected.

In Chapter 8, I will introduce the concept and relevance of the organizational structure in SAP SRM. I will answer questions such as: "Why do we need an organizational structure?" and "Can we not use the organizational structure in SAP HR?" I will also discuss how the organizational structure acts as a security mechanism to control what users can see and do, using the concept of attributes.

An organizational structure is a hierarchical view of information about your company's divisions, departments, and positions. These positions, together with the individuals that fill them, create the reporting structures defined within your company.

8 Organizational Structure

Structure, whether hierarchical or linear, exists within every corporation. In SAP, the organizational structure is contained within the Human Resources module (HR). Organizational Management (OM) is the structural foundation upon which all other Human Resource and Payroll processes are based. The Organizational Management module is the central component that provides representation of the Enterprise's organizational structure and enables the administration and planning of this structure. Additionally, the Organizational Management structure provides the framework upon which to build the security and authorization accesses for SAP end users. This structure also provides a representation of the task-related, functional structuring of the enterprise used to enable SAP Business Workflow.

The organizational structure in SRM has largely been designed based on the Organization Management (OM) module in SAP R/3, known as SAP HR. SRM primarily facilitates procurement and strategic sourcing; therefore the OM functionality available in SRM does not make use of the complete SAP R/3 OM functionality. For example, in SAP R/3, the OM module facilitates the hiring of employees. Although SRM contains transactions for personnel management (e.g. PP01), there is no core functionality when using these transactions. In SRM, this functionality has been enhanced to provide for the unique needs of procurement that are not captured within the core R/3 organizational structure.

Let's look at an example of typical scenarios and the questions that arise on SRM projects.

Scenario
We already have SAP HR and maintain a large organizational structure. Why do we need another structure for SAP SRM? Can't we just use the one in HR? Do we have

> to use the organizational structure that is in SAP HR? Can we maintain a separate organizational structure in SRM? If we maintain a separate organizational structure in SRM, what happens post go-live? That is, who maintains the organizational structure in SRM? Is this the responsibility of the HR team or the procurement team?

This chapter contains information that will enable managers and consultants to answer these questions and chart a successful SRM implementation.

Let's start by highlighting the key differences between the organizational structure used in SAP R/3 vs. the organizational structure used in SAP SRM (see Figure 8.1). It is important for You to understand these differences because this is one of the confusing aspects of SAP SRM projects. Many individuals mistakenly consider the organizational structure in SRM to be the same as in SAP R/3 or disregard the organizational structure's importance. In SAP SRM, the organizational structure is one of the most critical elements of control that enables approval hierarchies and procurement attribute maintenance.

Organizational Structure in SAP HR	• … is primarily used to maintain the overall enterprise relationship between the **departments**, **positions**, **jobs** and **employees.**
	• … is purely structured around employee reporting hierarchy – actual approval responsibility for operational procurement could be very different.
	• … the structure further drives Human Resource functions key for the enterprise (e.g. Payroll, Time & Expense, etc.)
	• … the hierarchy built in Org Management (OM) is utilized extensively to for organizational reporting purposes (employee – manager relationship).

Organizational Structure in mySAP SRM	• … is primarily setup to define the **operational** hierarchy within the organization; it additionally drives the **approval** hierarchy & **responsibility**
	• … provides a core element of **control** in SRM via use of "**attribute**" maintenance (**Purchase Organization**, Purchasing Group, Plant, etc.) not available in the SAP HR Organizations Structure.
	• … the structure further **drives the procurement functions** for the enterprise (Indirect and Direct procurement, Bidding, etc.)

Figure 8.1 Comparing the Organizational Structure in SAP HR and SAP SRM

Before proceeding further, it is important to gain an overview of the organisational structure in SAP SRM.

8.1 Overview of the Organizational Structure in SAP SRM

The organizational structure in SAP SRM provides the base platform for executing most of the business transactions in the system. Unless a basic form of the organizational structure is available with relevant attributes, users in the SRM system are unable to perform tasks such as creating shopping carts or approvals. Why do we need an organizational structure in SRM? The following points aim to answer that question:

▸ By design, EBP requires at least a basic organizational structure setup.

▸ The organizational structure constructs the hierarchy in which the various organizational units of an organization are arranged, according to tasks and functions.

▸ The purchasing organizations and groups responsible for shopping carts and purchase orders can be determined.

▸ Operational attributes necessary for procurement need to be defined, such as company code, plants, and material groups. These are typically a part of the R/3 MM module.

▸ SAP Business Workflow can determine which agents are responsible for approving documents based on the hierarchy or approval limits defined within the organizational structure elements.

▸ The organizational structure acts as an extension to the SAP user master (SU01). It also acts as a security mechanism to control the authorization a user has to various cost centers, product categories, catalogs, etc.

Organizations implementing SAP SRM will learn that one of the very first things they need to set up is the organization's structure. Prior to this setup, no business transactions can be executed in SRM. Unfortunately, this is one area where one size does not fit all. Each organization normally has a varied organizational structure and an even more varied purchasing organization. In SRM, the structure that needs to be set up needs to contain not just the hierarchy of the division and departments within an organization, but also the structure of the purchasing department(s) within the organization.

Depending on the culture of an organization, purchasing can be a centralized or a de-centralized function. This can strongly impact how you design the organizational structure in SRM. Many organizations take the implementation of SAP SRM as an opportunity to seek centralized procurement. Therefore, they might change the organizational structure to accommodate the changes within the blueprint and realization phases. Figure 8.2 illustrates by example the organizational structure for a global company.

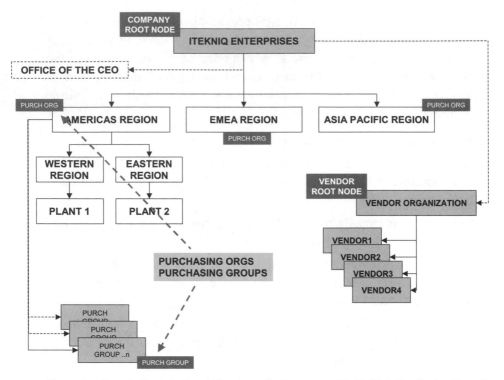

Figure 8.2 Sample Organizational Structure of a Company with Multiple Purchasing Organizations

Once the project teams have gathered an organizational structure with which to begin, the next step is creating this structure within the SRM system. (Typically this information is gathered from the HR department and then validated by individual departments with enhancement for procurement functions.)

Depending on the size of the organization and the scope of the implementation (whether SRM is being implemented within a region or globally), creating this structure within SRM can be a daunting task. For example, in Figure 8.2, the company **ITEKNIQ ENTERPRISES** has three purchasing organizations: **AMERICAS REGION**, **EMEA REGION**, and **ASIA PACIFIC REGION**. Each of these would serve as the top organizational node for the organization's global regions. The example further expands the **AMERICAS REGION** into the **WESTERN REGION** and **EASTERN REGION**.

Creating a similar structure and all of the positions within the regions can be a large task. This is especially true because SAP SRM, just like other SAP solutions, is implemented in a three-tiered landscape (development, QA, and production). Therefore, you will need an organizational structure in each of these environments (and individual clients). Not only is it challenging to create such a structure; gathering the information needed to create the organizational structure is also a separate task. SAP provides best practices to assist organizations with options to transport the organizational structure from one environment to another; we discuss these in a later section of this chapter.

Figure 8.3 illustrates the transaction used in SRM for creating and managing the organizational structure. There are three different transactions with which you can access the organizational structure, as seen in Table 8.1.

Transaction Code	Description
PPOCA_BBP	Create the root organization nodes
PPOMA_BBP	Change the organizational structure/attributes
PPOSA_BBP	Display the organizational structure/attributes
PPOMV_BBP	Manage external partners in SRM 5.0

Table 8.1 Transaction Code and Descriptions

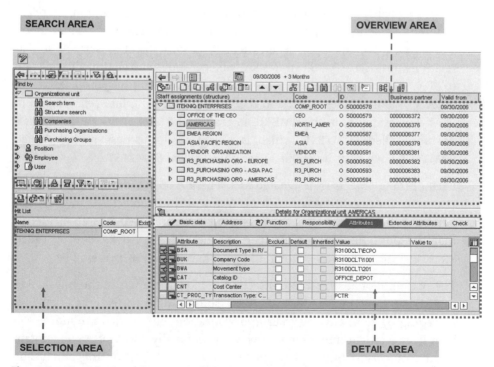

Figure 8.3 Organizational Structure in SAP SRM — PPOSA_BBP

Prior to the release of SRM 1.0 (EBP 3.0), you accessed the organizational structure transaction via the PPOMA_CRM; a scenario had to be selected before you could define user attributes. Since then, an independent transaction has been designed for SRM </PPOMA_BBP>.

As Figure 8.3 illustrates, the organizational structure transaction is divided into four parts: The *Search Area* (also called **Find by**), which lets you search by different objects in SAP (**Organizational unit**, **Position**, **Employee**, and **User**). The *Selection Area* (also called **Hit List**) displays the search results. Once you select a record, the *Overview Area* shows the structure available for that object. In Figure 8.3, the overview area displays the structure of the company **ITEKNIQ ENTERPRISES**, a fictitious company. Once you select an organizational unit, (in our example the **AMERICAS** region), then the *Details area* provides information on all relevant attributes assigned to that object.

Before we move forward, it is important to define the word *object*, as we will use it frequently throughout this chapter. Within any organization, there are different elements that bring structure to the organization — a department, a position, a job, an employee, etc. In SAP, various objects describe a similar relationship. Figure 8.4 illustrates SAP objects and their relationship relevant to SRM. The organizational unit, position, business partner and user are all objects that are inter-related and together form a complete relationship in SRM. For example, in the **AMERICAS** region, the **SAN DIEGO PLANT** has a position called **SRMTEST**, which is linked to a business partner called **SRMTEST /**, which is linked to a user object called **SRMTEST**.

Each of these objects is designated as a separate object in the organizational structure. The organizational object is **O**, the position object is **S**, the business partner is **BP**, and the user object is **US**. Please note that it is co-incidental that the position, business partner and user in Figure 8.4 are all called SRMTEST; normally, they would likely all have different names.

The organizational structure transaction in SRM is similar to the transaction in SAP HR. However, in SRM, there are some additional features — such as searching by company, purchasing organization, etc, — that are more relevant from a procurement point of view. Additionally, SRM lets you maintain organizational attributes, a key functionality in SRM that controls purchasing elements such as plants, catalogs, product categories, etc.

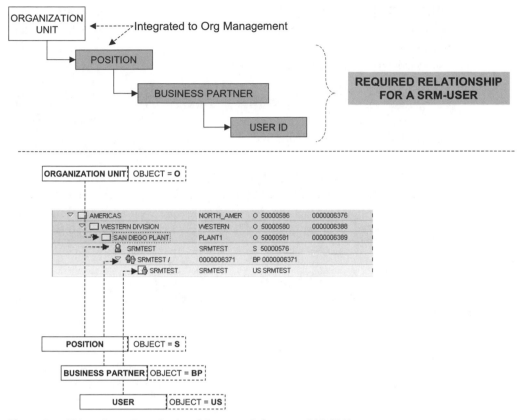

Figure 8.4 Objects in an Organizational Structure Relevant to SAP SRM

We explain the concept of attributes in detail later in this chapter. You can assign attributes to organizational units and positions relevant for purchasing. Figure 8.5 illustrates how you can perform different searches in the organizational structure in SRM that are relevant to procurement. As you can imagine, a search by purchasing groups in the SAP HR organizational structure would not be relevant. However, in SRM, it could be relevant to quickly search across all purchasing groups in the structure and either maintain or display the attributes within the purchasing groups.

Once a basic structure of the organizational plan is set up, it needs to be synchronized in such a way that the appropriate business partners are created for all of the organizational units created. This synchronization needs to take place on a regular basis via a background job. Project teams should note that unless an organizational unit is consistent, you can't assign positions or employees to that unit. You can use transaction BBP_BP_OM_INTEGRATE to synchronize the organizational structure, as illustrated in Figure 8.6.

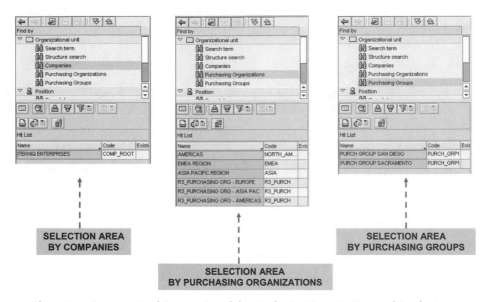

SELECTION AREA BY COMPANIES

SELECTION AREA BY PURCHASING GROUPS

SELECTION AREA BY PURCHASING ORGANIZATIONS

Figure 8.5 Organizational Struture Search by Purchasing Organizations and Purchasing Groups

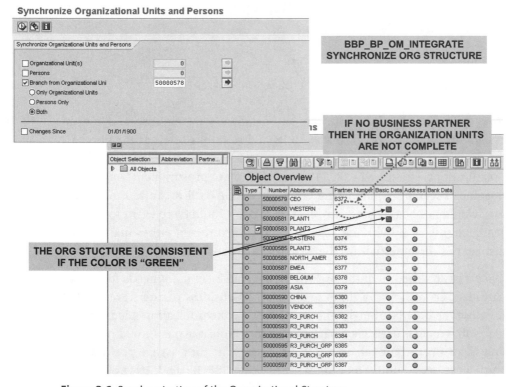

Figure 8.6 Synchronization of the Organizational Structure

You need to perform the synchronization procedure for each organizational unit that does not have a business partner number assigned, as illustrated in Figure 8.7.

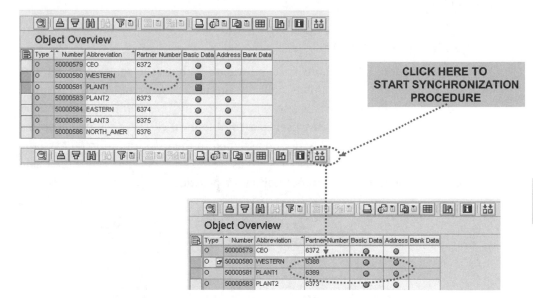

CLICK HERE TO START SYNCHRONIZATION PROCEDURE

Figure 8.7 The Synchronization Procedure for an Organizational Plan

SAP provides a very good step-by-step tutorial on how to create the structure of your organizational plan to reflect the structure and HR environment of your company. Project teams can access this tutorial via the URL:

http://help.sap.com/saphelp_erp2005/helpdata/en/fb/135990457311d189440000e829fbbd/frameset.htm.

Now you have an overall idea about organizational structures. In the next section we'll dive deeper to give you an understanding of the Details area of the organizational structure, including the Basic data, Address, Function, Responsibility, Attributes, Extended Attributes, and Check areas.

8.2 The Details Area of the Organizational Structure

In Section 8.1, we briefly discussed the Search Area, Selection Area and Overview Area of the organizational structure in transaction PPOSA_BBP. In this section, we will discuss in greater depth the Details area of the organizational structure transaction. One of the reasons I am putting greater emphasis on this section is that the attributes and functions for the entire organizational structure are maintained within this area. The *Details area* of the organizational structure contains configurable attributes organized within seven different tabs. We will discuss each of these tabs and their usage below.

8.2.1 Basic Data Tab

The **Basic data** tab contains basic information about the selected object. For organizational objects, this is typically the name of the object; for position objects, the **Basic data** tab also lets you specify the validity period of the position. Because the SRM user is a combination of the position, business partner and user, a validity period assigned to the position indirectly assigns the validity period to the user record as well. Figure 8.8 illustrates the **Basic data** tab for an **organizational unit** and a **position**.

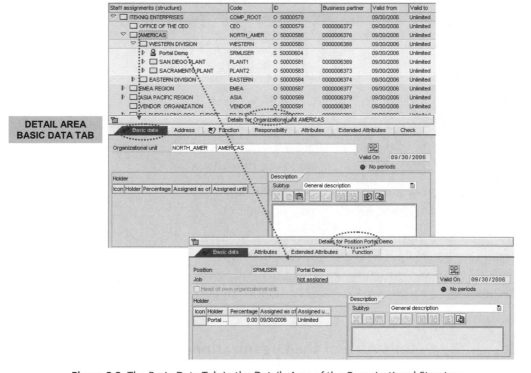

Figure 8.8 The Basic Data Tab in the Details Area of the Organizational Structure

8.2.2   Address Tab

This tab displays basic information about the organizational unit object, such as the address and telephone numbers for the organizational unit. Addresses are maintained at an organizational unit level. If the organizational unit is also classified as a company, the address specified for the organizational unit becomes the default hierarchy address for all departments within that company. When internal (company) addresses are created in SAP SRM, such as delivery addresses that users can select in the shopping cart, those addresses can be created under this main address.

An address is required for each organizational unit created in SRM. Otherwise, the organizational unit is not considered consistent for employee assignment, as illustrated by the **Organizational unit 50000587 is not consistent** message, seen in Figure 8.9.

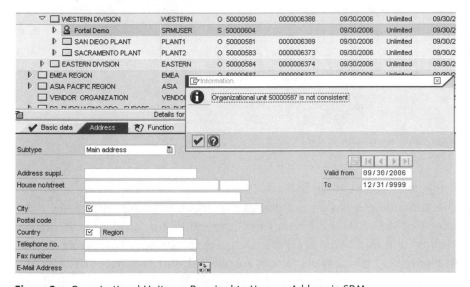

Figure 8.9 Organizational Units are Required to Have an Address in SRM

Readers should note that addresses are not required for positions and other objects in the organizational structure, as shown in Figure 8.10. In this figure, with the organizational unit **ITEKNIQ ENTERPRISES** selected, the Details area shows an **Address** tab with an address of **1000 HELLO STREET**. However, when the position **Portal Demo** is selected, the Details area does not show an **Address** tab (because, as we mentioned earlier, it isn't required).

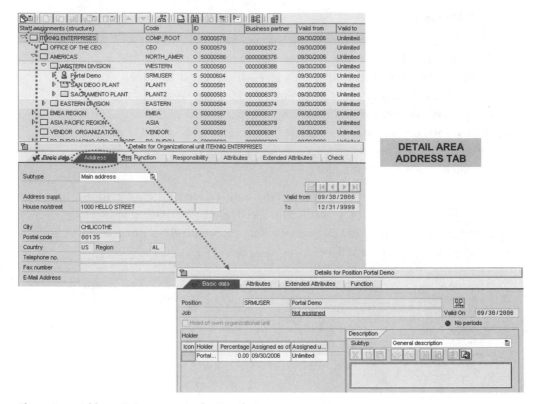

Figure 8.10 Address Maintenance in the Details Area

8.2.3 Function Tab

The **Function** tab has been a part of the organizational structure since the release of SRM 3.0. This tab provides a structured way to identify an organizational unit as a Company, Purchasing Organization or Purchasing Group. In Figure 8.11, the **Details for Organizational unit ITEKNIQ ENTERPRISES** illustrates the Function section. Here, you can identify an organizational unit as a Company or Purch. Organization by selecting the appropriate checkbox.

To create purchasing documents, the elements of **Company Code**, **Purch. Organization** and **Purchasing Group** are required in SAP R/3 as well as in SRM. Readers should also note that the **Company Code 1001** has a secondary field with the value **R3100CLT**, which indicates the RFC destination for the SAP R/3 backend connected to the SRM system. In the classic scenario implementation of SRM, a value is required in both the Company Code and backend system fields. Similar values are required for the elements **Purch. Organization** and **Purchasing Group**.

However, companies implementing the Extended Classic scenario don't have to enter a value for **Company code**, **Purch. Organization** or **Purchasing Group** in this section. Selecting the appropriate checkbox is sufficient.

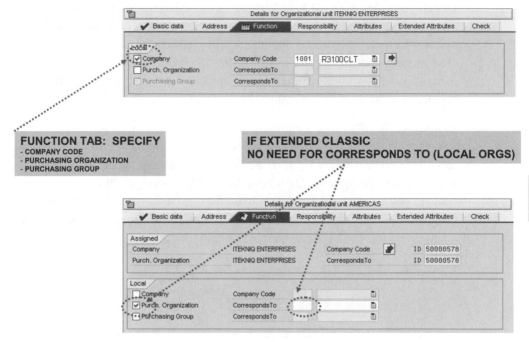

Figure 8.11 The Function Tab in the Organizational Structure

At a minimum, one organizational unit within the structure needs to be set up as a company. This attribute identifies an organizational unit as an independent legal entity. This flag can also be set for subsidiaries.

> **Note**
>
> You can only assign the ship-to and bill-to addresses to organizational units that are flagged as a Company. If there is more than one bill-to address in the organization, then you need to set multiple organizational units as Company, and they cannot be within the same hierarchy because the attribute is inherited down the structure.

The **Purch. Organization** attribute identifies an organizational unit as a purchasing organization for the company. It is important to note that the Purch. Organization identification is inherited by subordinate organizational units and positions. Therefore, a second **Purch. Organization** cannot be set up within the same hierarchy. Within the organizational structure, the Purch.

Organization must be set at either a level higher than Purchasing Groups or at the same level.

Let's look at an example. In Figure 8.12, we have selected the **WESTERN DIVISION** under the **AMERICAS** region. Notice that the **Assigned** area on the **Function** tab contains the **Purch. Organization AMERICAS**, and the **Corresponds To** field contains ID **50000586**. Here, **50000586** is the system-generated number for the organizational unit object **AMERICAS**. All other subordinate organizational units automatically inherit their purchasing organization as AMERICAS (50000586).

In addition to marking an organizational unit as a Purchasing Organization, you need to define the **Corresponds To** field and the back-end RFC destination. In the classic scenario, you must enter the corresponding 3–4 character backend purchasing organization, as well as the corresponding RFC destination. If you're implementing the Standalone or Extended Classic scenario, you can leave this blank. The checkbox is enough for identification, because no backend is verified, as illustrated in Figure 8.12.

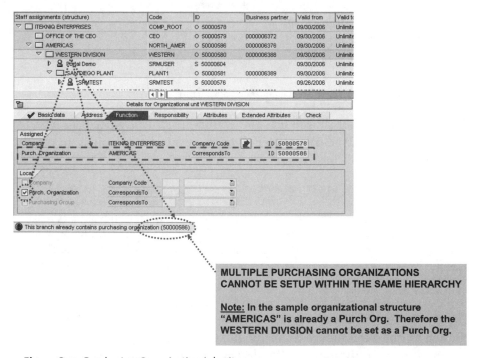

Figure 8.12 Purchasing Organization Inheritance

It is important to note that in the shopping cart and purchase order transactions, the purchasing organization and purchasing group name is shown exactly as the name of the organizational unit that is flagged as a purchasing or organization and purchasing Group. In our example, for instance, an end-user would see the name of the purchasing group as **PURCH GROUP SAN DIEGO** in the basic data section of the shopping cart transaction (illustrated in Figure 8.13). Therefore, it is important to determine the names of these organizational units accordingly. This also becomes a challenge when HR integration is active, because SRM project teams typically have less leverage to impact the names of organizational units. Remember that the purchasing group name in the shopping cart is derived from the organizational unit that has been selected as the Purchasing group, as seen in Figure 8.13.

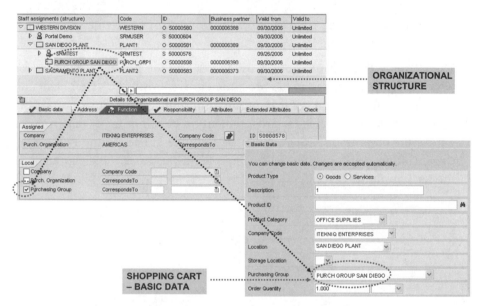

Figure 8.13 Purchasing Group Name in Shopping Cart

The **Function** tab is only available for Object type O, i.e., an organizational unit. This sometimes can become an issue if project teams want to assign positions the attribute of Purchasing Groups. From an HR perspective the position makes best sense to identify with a purchasing group. If HR integration is active, new organizational units might need to be created to accommodate the purchasing group attribute.

8.2.4 Responsibility Tab

The **Responsibility** tab is specifically designed for organizational units identified as a Purchasing Group. You can therefore assign this property only to objects of type O.

In an enterprise, a purchasing group (sometimes referred to as a buyer) might be responsible for more than one commodity (product category), and might also be responsible for purchases made by individuals in different purchasing organizations. The **Responsibility** tab has been designed to set the product and organizational responsibility of a purchasing group.

Example

Buyer A might be responsible for the office supplies and furniture product categories. Therefore, when a user creates requests (shopping carts) to order goods or services belonging to these two product categories, buyer A will receive the open shopping carts to source to the appropriate vendor. The Responsible Purch. Organization and Purchasing Group attributes are determined based on a user's organizational unit assignment when they create the shopping carts.

The attribute **Product Category** is used to define the product categories for which the purchasing group has procurement responsibility. If left blank, no restrictions are applied to that group. Additionally, because purchasing groups can be responsible for procurement on behalf of many departments within the organization, there might be multiple entries in the **Purchasing Organization** responsibility field. Figure 8.14 illustrates the assignment of the **Responsibility** tab.

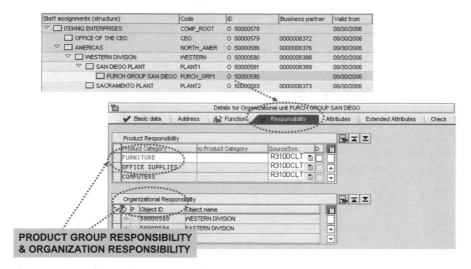

Figure 8.14 Product and Organizational Responsibility

In instances when more than one purchasing group is responsible for the same product category, the system defaults to the first entry in the table. However, users can change this in the shopping cart. This can be troublesome for organizations because users will have to perform this action every time. SAP provides BADI BBP_PGRP_FIND to enable organizations to determine the responsible purchasing group(s) in the shopping cart using their own business rules.

8.2.5 Attributes Tab

The **Attributes** tab in the organizational structure provides the elements of control for a user and position. In SRM, users require organizational attributes in addition to their security roles so they can create purchasing documents such as shopping carts, purchase orders, etc. Figure 8.15 provides an explanation of user attributes in SRM.

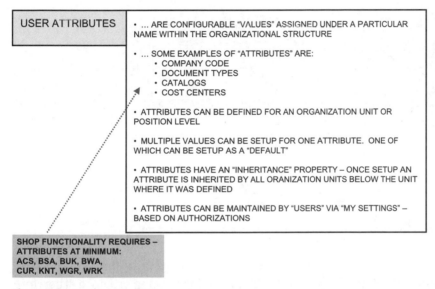

Figure 8.15 Attributes in SRM

You can define attributes at any level of the organizational structure (for objects O and S). To avoid redundant work, maintain attributes at the highest possible level. This way, subordinate units and positions can inherit the attributes set above their level in the structure.

A lot of attributes are available for assignment in the organizational structure. Once an attribute is assigned, it is inherited within the organization chain. Therefore, if all attributes are defined at the top-level ROOT node of the organizational structure, every subordinate organizational unit, position and employee will inherit applicable attributes. Examples of an inheritable attribute are Company Code (**ACS**) or Currency (**CUR**), given that there is only one company code in the organization and a single currency is used. Users are typically linked to a department or plant in the organizational structure. Maintaining attributes at the department or plant level automatically assigns the value of the respective attribute for all users in that department or plant.

Figure 8.16 illustrates the **Attributes** section for the organizational unit **AMERICAS**. In the **Value** field for the **BSA** attribute, a backend RFC destination and SAP R/3 document type need to be assigned; in our example this is **R3100CLT\ECPO** (R3100 is the RFC destination and ECPO the SAP R/3 document type). Other attributes, such as Catalog ID (**CAT**) have also been assigned.

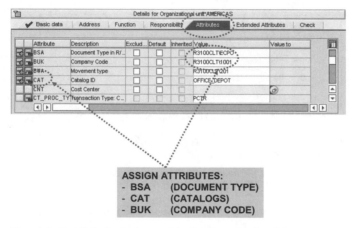

Figure 8.16 Attribute Assignment in the Organizational Structure

The value of this attribute, **OFFICE DEPOT**, illustrates that for the **AMERICAS** organizational unit, the **OFFICE DEPOT** catalog is being provided. Therefore all users that reside within the hierarchy of the **AMERICAS** organizational unit will inherit the **CAT** attribute value of **OFFICE DEPOT** and have the ability to use the office depot catalog in the shopping cart and other purchasing documents.

Depending on a user's security role, a different set of attributes might be required. For example, if a user is performing the role of a Contract Administrator, the attribute CT_PROC_TY (transaction type assignment for contracts) will be required so that the contract document type can be determined when a contract is being created.

Project teams will find that not all of the attributes available in SRM are valid for their implementation. For example, the attributes TEND_TYPE, PM_

WGR ACC_FUND_ACC_GRANT might not be relevant for your implementation because your scope for SRM might not cover the Bidding Engine or Plant Maintenance or be subject to a public sector overlay requiring Fund and Grant accounting objects. Therefore, your project team should extract the list of all of the attributes available for your SRM release and select the ones that are relevant for your implementation. A list of organizational structure attributes is available in Appendix J.

In SAP R/3, users are aware of the Parameters (PIDs) available in their user master record. These let users seamlessly insert default information into fields commonly used in transactions, for example the Company Code. In SRM, users can change their own attributes in the my settings </BBPAT05> application. These attributes are configured within the organizational structure in SRM, and allow users to control defaults within their shopping cart transactions.

Let's look at an example using Figure 8.17, which illustrates the **Change Settings** application (BBPAT05). If a user always assigns charge codes against a cost center, they can use the attribute **Account assignment category** and select **Cost Center** as the default value. As a result, the Account assignment category of Cost Center will always be pre-selected in the shopping cart. Similarly, if a user wants to set their default plant value, they can use the **Plant** attribute.

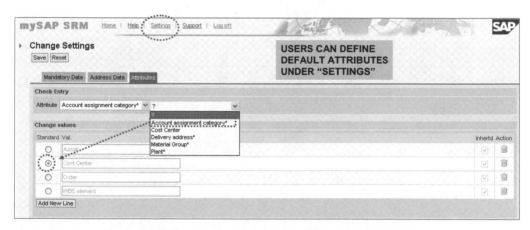

Figure 8.17 Users Can Define Defaults in the Change Settings Transaction BBPAT05

8.2.6 Extended Attributes Tab

The Extended Attributes tab in the organizational structure was introduced with the release of SRM 3.0. This provided more structure and simplified assignment of attributes to the various organizational units and positions. This tab lets you place restrictions on the following attributes:

▸ Product Categories and Locations

▸ PO Value Limits and Storage Locations

Product Categories and Locations

Product categories in SRM are synonymous with material groups in SAP R/3. Project teams can restrict users to a specific list of product categories by assigning them on this tab. For example, if the IT department is responsible for the purchasing of computer equipment, then the category **Computer Equipment** should only be allowed in the organizational units and positions relevant to the IT department. If the **Product Category** field is left blank, then no product categories are available for users to select in the shopping cart.

Locations in SRM are synonymous with plants in SAP R/3. Similar to enabling restrictions by product category, in SRM you can also enable location-based restrictions. For example, you can specify that only users working at a specific plant are able to select that plant as a location in their shopping cart transactions. Figure 8.18 illustrates attribute assignments on the **Extended Attributes** tab.

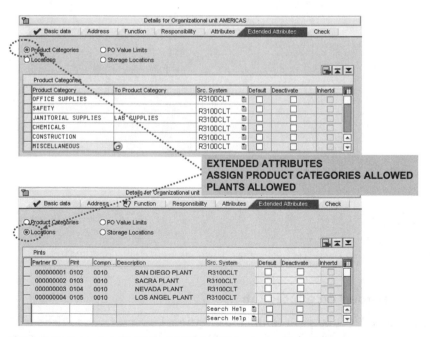

Figure 8.18 Extended Attributes — Product Category and Locations

PO Value Limits and Storage Locations

PO Value Limits let project teams that want to use approval workflow define value limits for the budget and spending limit approval workflows. Storage Locations are assigned in conjunction with Locations in SAP SRM. If direct material procurement is enabled in SRM, users can select the appropriate storage locations within their shopping cart line items.

8.2.7 Check Tab

The **Check** tab lets you check the consistency of the selected object. Consistency means that the organizational structure expects that you have defined required elements before they are used in business transactions. If the required attributes are not defined, the check will be inconsistent. For example, an address is required for each organizational unit in the structure, as we explained in the **Address** tab section. If an organizational unit does not have an address defined, or other required attributes are not defined, then the **Check** tab for that organizational unit will show an inconsistency. Figure 8.19 illustrates the **Check** tab. With the **EMEA REGION** organizational unit selected in the Overview area, the **Check** tab in the Details area provides an analysis of consistency for the organizational unit.

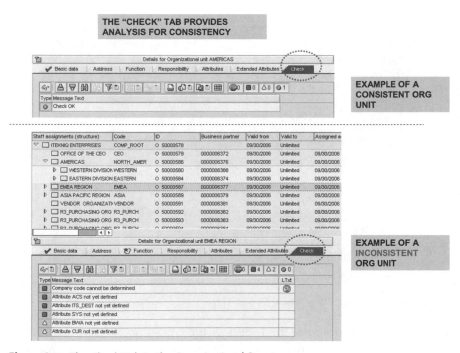

Figure 8.19 The Check Tab in the Organizational Structure

As you can see in Figure 8.19, when an object is not consistent, the system provides messages on the **Check** tab in the form of errors (red icons) or warnings (yellow icons). If all checks for that object are consistent, a message displays with a green icon.

The Check function within the organizational structure transaction </PPOSA_BBP> only provides a check for the selected organizational unit. It is recommended that project teams execute the standard report provided by SAP that allows a consistency check across the entire organizational structure. There are two options available for this check, transaction BBP_ATTR_CHECK or report BBP_CHECK_CONSISTENCY. In Figure 8.20, we illustrate an example of report BBP_CHECK_CONSISTENCY.

In the **Selection** area, you can select how the check will be performed, at the level of **Company**, **Department** or **User**. In the **Check Type** area, you can identify whether a check should be conducted for object consistency or to determine whether all attributes for the organizational object have been maintained for the business transaction, such as the shopping cart. This is important because although an object (organizational unit, position or user) might be consistent, a user still might not be able to create a shopping cart if all of the required attributes are not maintained.

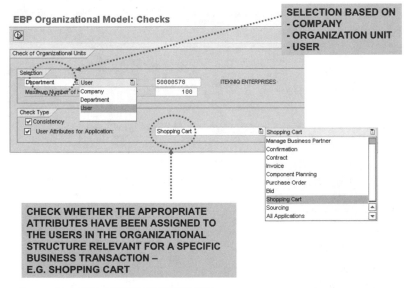

Figure 8.20 Transaction BBP_CHECK_CONSISTENCY

In Figure 8.21, you can see the results of the check; notice that the **Consistency check** section shows that the organizational unit is inconsistent because certain attributes are not defined. In addition, the User attribute check for application: Shopping Cart section shows that the user SRMUSER does not have the required authorization to create shopping carts because the required roles for creating a shopping cart are missing.

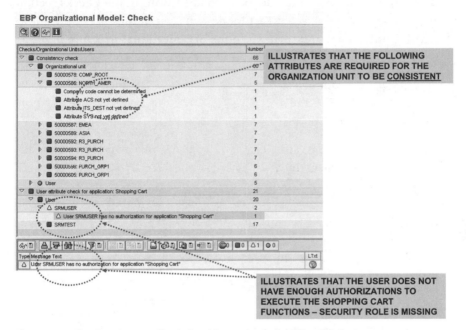

Figure 8.21 The Consistency Check Provides an Analysis of Possible Issues

Depending on the size of your organizational structure, the project team might need to maintain attributes using a program instead of performing maintenance manually. In the next section, we talk about the functionality available to you to reduce manual efforts in maintaining attributes.

8.3 Uploading Attributes via a Function Module

Maintaining attributes in the organizational structure can be a daunting task, especially given the interface of the Detail area in the organizational structure. In addition, many organizations want to provide financial controls by restricting which cost center users can display and use when shopping; this can be accomplished by using the CNT attribute. For any large organization, there could be hundreds of cost centers and the assignment of those at a user or department level in the organizational structure could be a very maintenance intensive task.

To help with this, SAP has provided a standard program B_UPLOAD_COST_CENTER_ATTRIBUTE that lets you upload the cost center attribute into the organizational structure. The program can also be modified to flag the default cost center. For example, in Figure 8.22, we've selected a text file in the **File Name** field under the **File for Upload** section. In the **Checks** section of the program, we've selected **Test Mode**, which indicates that we want to test the file upload without saving it to the organizational structure.

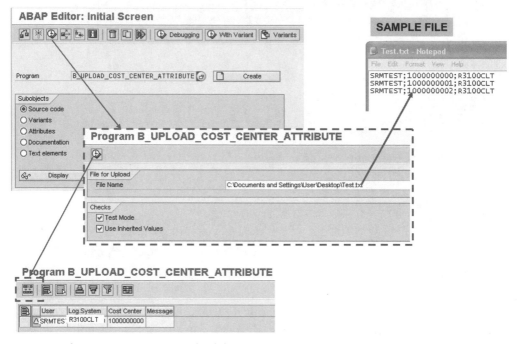

Figure 8.22 Program to Upload the Cost Center Attribute

The standard program only lets you update the cost center attribute. However, project teams can modify this program to enable updates of other attributes as well. As an alternative, you can also use the function module BBP_UPDATE_ATTRIBUTES to build a customized report. This function module lets you update most of the attributes in the organizational structure available on the **Attributes** tab. Figure 8.23 illustrates this function module.

> **Note**
>
> In Figure 8.23, the Function module lets you set attributes based on import parameters such as the user ID (**USER_ID_P**) and organizational unit (**ORGUNIT_ID_P**). In the **Tables** section, you can set the attribute in the **ATTR_ID** field along with setting attribute characteristics, such as indicating an attribute as a default in the **DFT_FLAG** field.

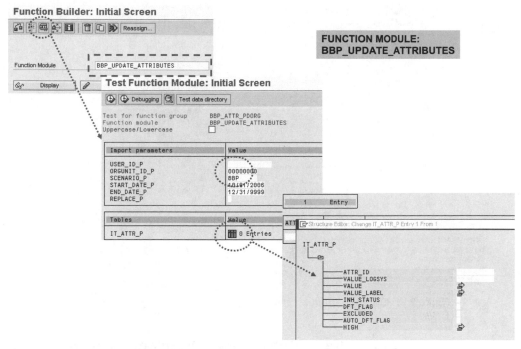

Figure 8.23 Function Module to Update Attributes

In the next section, we'll discuss how project teams can customize attribute maintenance.

8.4   Customizing Attribute Maintenance

SAP delivers a set of attributes in SRM with pre-delivered logic such as whether an attribute can be inherited from the top organization level to subordinate levels, whether search help is provided for an attribute, etc. Project teams may, however, find it necessary to customize the standard delivered properties for attributes.

8.4.1   Customizing Delivered Standard Attributes

If necessary, you can customize the functionality of the delivered attributes in the standard system. You do this by using transaction </SM30> and table T77OMATTR, or by using transaction </OOATTRCUST>. Figure 8.24 illustrates this transaction.

Dialog Structure
- ☐ Attributes
- ▽ ☐ Scenarios
  - ☐ Attributes/Scenarios
  - ☐ Object Types

Attributes/Scenarios

Scenario	Attribute	Inherit. type	Invisible	Seq.	Req. attribute	Search help-FM	Check module
BBP	C_CHITEM	Normal inheritance (additiv…	☐		☐	BBP_ATTR_F4_ACC	
BBP	ACC_FCAREA	Normal inheritance (additiv…	☐		☐		
BBP	ACC_FCENTR	Normal inheritance (additiv…	☐		☐		
BBP	ACC_FUND	Normal inheritance (additiv…	☐		☐		
BBP	ACC_GRANT	Normal inheritance (additiv…	☐		☐		
BBP	ACS	Local values overwrite inhe…	☐		☐	BBP_ATTR_F4	
BBP	ADDR_BILLT	Local values overwrite inhe…	☐		☐		
BBP	ADDR_SHIPT	Local values overwrite inhe…	☐		☐		
BBP	AN1	Normal inheritance (additiv…	☐		☐	BBP_ATTR_F4_ACC	
BBP	AN2	Normal inheritance (additiv…	☐		☐		
BBP	ANK	Normal inheritance (additiv…	☐		☐	BBP_ATTR_F4	
BBP	ANR	No inheritance	☐		☐	BBP_ATTR_F4_ACC	
BBP	APO	Normal inheritance (additiv…	☐		☐		
BBP	APPRV_LIM	Local values overwrite inhe…	☑		☐		
BBP	AUN	Normal inheritance (additiv…	☐		☐	BBP_ATTR_F4_ACC	
BBP	BSA	Normal inheritance (additiv…	☐		☐	BBP_ATTR_F4	
BBP	BUDGET	Normal inheritance (additiv…	☑		☐		
BBP	BUK	Normal inheritance (additiv…	☐		☐	BBP_ATTR_F4	
BBP	BWA	Normal inheritance (additiv…	☐		☐	BBP_ATTR_F4	
BBP	CAT	Normal inheritance (additiv…	☐		☐	BBP_ATTR_F4	
BBP	CNT	Normal inheritance (additiv…	☐		☐	BBP_ATTR_F4_ACC	
BBP	COCODE	Local values overwrite inhe…	☑		☐	BBP_ATTR_F4	
BBP	COMPANY	Local values overwrite inhe…	☑		☐		
BBP	CT_PROC_TY	Local values overwrite inhe…	☐		☐		
BBP	CUR	Normal inheritance (additiv…	☐		☐	BBP_ATTR_F4	

TRANSACTION: </OOATTRCUST>
ATTRIBUTE MAINTENANCE CAN BE CUSTOMIZED
- INHERITANCE
- SEARCH HELP
- MANDATORY / INVISIBLE

Figure 8.24 Changing Attributes and Scenarios

8.4.2 Create a New Attribute in the Organizational Structure

Organizations can define new attributes for use within their implementation and give users the ability to select these attributes within their my settings transaction. This gives organizations the power to use custom attributes in the organizational structure and gives users the flexibility to set these attributes individually. Figure 8.25 illustrates the process of creating new attributes:

1. Execute transaction </OOATTRCUST>.

2. Click on **New Entries.**

3. Select the scenario **BBP** and create a new Z* attribute (for example, **ZNEW**, as illustrated in Figure 8.25).

4. Assign any maintenance attributes of inheritance or search and then save the new entry.

5. Make sure to assign which object types are allowed to maintain this attribute (i.e. can this attribute be maintained at the organizational unit or position level or both).

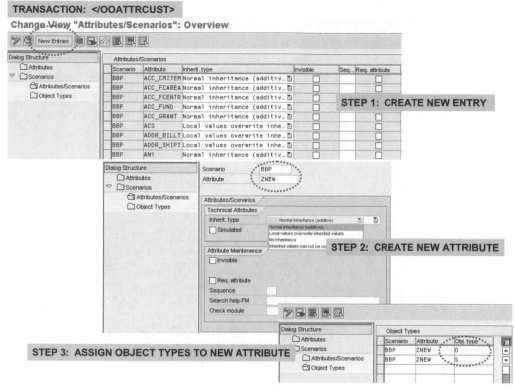

Figure 8.25 Creating New Attributes for Use in the Organizational Structure

8.4.3 Maintaining Attribute Rights by Role

SRM lets you configure whether users assigned to a particular role are authorized to display or change an attribute in my settings. Therefore, if the organization does not want users to be able to set the cost center attribute, they can limit this access using the IMG path: **Supplier Relationship Management • SRM Server • Cross-Application Basic Settings • Roles • Maintain Attribute Access Rights by Role**. This is illustrated in Figure 8.26.

In the standard system, these access rights are controlled using the SAP delivered roles. As most organizations copy standard roles into customer specific roles, keep in mind that this setting needs to be changed as the customer Z roles are not there by default. Project teams will have to configure the attributes' definitions here based on each ZRole created (Typically the Employee, Manager and Purchaser Roles).

The organizational structure comprises the heart of the operational and strategic functions within EBP. Therefore, only a select group of personnel should be authorized to change and modify this transaction. As a best practice, always access this transaction in display mode via transaction PPOSA_BBP. This also prevents problems caused by table locks, particularly when creating users. In addition, make sure that the organization admin closely tracks all changes made to the organizational structure — otherwise, things can get out of hand very quickly. Chapter 11 provides information on how to secure the organizational structure in a decentralized maintenance environment where multiple groups maintain the organizational structure.

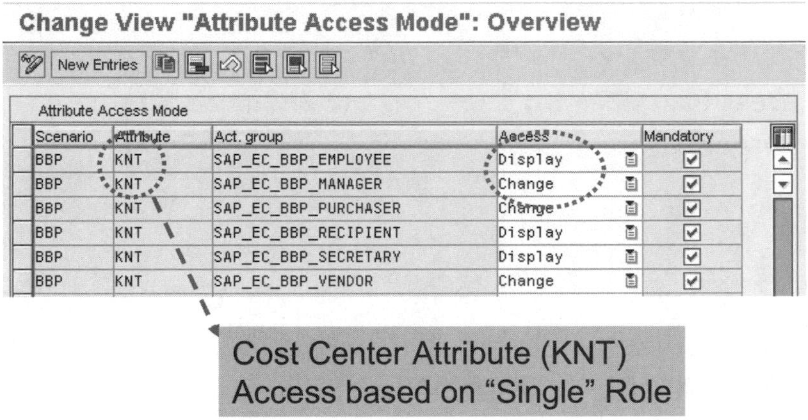

Figure 8.26 Maintain Attribute Access Rights by Role

In the next section, I'll talk about how to delete objects within the organizational structure, such as organizational units, positions and business partners.

8.5 Deleting Organizational Objects in SRM

You might at times during the SRM implementation process need to delete organizational structure objects. One example would be when you create the organizational structure from a legacy file using an upload program or possibly when integrating with SAP HR. It could happen, for example, that the structure was loaded incorrectly and needs to be deleted and re-loaded.

The following process provides a guide to deleting objects from the Organizational Management and Personnel Planning in SRM:

1. Execute report RHRHDL00 in transaction </SE38>.

2. Enter the objects that need to be deleted, e.g. **O** for organizational units, **S** for positions, etc. You can provide a range for the object numbers.

3. Make sure the **Test** checkbox is selected to verify the results the first time.

4. Once you are satisfied with the test simulation, deselect the **Test** checkbox and execute the deletion(s).

5. The objects listed will be deleted from the database.

In the next section, we will discuss how companies can use best practices for the creation and management of the organizational structure in SRM.

8.6   Best Practices for Creating and Managing the Organizational Structure

As with any SAP implementation, the SRM solution is typically implemented within a 3-tier landscape; in some implementations it can get up to a 5-tiered landscape with a sandbox and training environment added to the other three environments. Creating and maintaining an organizational structure within each environment (sandbox, development, quality, training, production, etc.) can be a very resource-intensive activity. In addition, it is a difficult task to maintain all of the attributes and keep them in synch across each environment, not to mention the different clients possible in each environment.

8.6.1   Key Organizational Structure Challenges

It is important for readers to understand the challenges revolving around managing an organizational structure. Some of you might be familiar with the organizational structure in SAP HR and the number of changes that a typical HR department needs to make to keep up with constantly changing positions, jobs and employee roles of an organization. The following bullets aim to summarize some of the key challenges of managing an organizational structure in SRM:

▶ Dual maintenance of organizational data (in the HR system and the SRM system).

▶ Maintainance as a result of frequent organizational changes.

▶ Creation and maintainance of organizational nodes and attributes.

▶ Sensitive data exposure within the organizational structure.

▶ Lack of well-defined financial approval structures (spending limit approval).

▶ Security (with large implementations).

▶ Keeping the organizational structure simple.

▶ Using the inheritance functionality for attributes from existing organizational nodes. Inheritance is configurable, but it can be difficult to decide on the best configuration.

From a best practices perspective, the following options are available:

▶ Transport the organizational structure from one environment to another (i.e. from quality to production for example).

▶ Integrate the HR organizational structure with the structure in SRM (only applicable if SAP HR is also implemented).

We will discuss these two best practices in detail in the next sections.

8.6.2 Transport the Organizational Structure

Creating and managing the organizational structure in SAP SRM can be a time consuming activity. Although many organizations choose to maintain the organizational structure in each of the development, quality and production environments individually, it is a best practice to transport the structure from one environment to another.

The challenge is that most companies are unable to define a clean organizational structure in the development environment and constantly use that as an experimental structure. Or, even if the development environment is strictly controlled for clean data, the complete structure is often nonetheless not defined because of the amount of time it takes to create the entire organizational structure.

The quality environment is a good environment to re-build the structure. However, many project teams are unable to gather all of the data in time or spend the time creating the entire structure. However, it is a best practice that organizations create a production-like organizational structure in the quality environment and then transport that to the true production environment. Figure 8.27 provides a best practices guide to creating and maintaining key objects in the organizational structure within EBP. SAP provides a detailed document that explains the best practices defined in Figure 8.27, which can be downloaded from the SAP Service Marketplace (Transporting SAP EBP Systems vers. 1.4.pdf).

	Development System	Quality Assurance of Consolidation System	Production System
Organizational model (organizational units only)	• Set up test orga-nizational structure manually	• Set up company org structure manually • Transfer from a HR backend using ALE	• Transfer from the Q system using ALE • Transfer from HR backend using ALE
Attribute mainte-nance in org. model	• Manually	• Manually	• Transfer from the Q system using ALE
Product categories	• Download from theR/3 MM back-end using CRM middleware	• Download from theR/3 MM back-end using CRM middleware	• Transport from the Q system using transport request
User (SU01 user)	• Manually • CUA (Central User Administration) • Download from R/3 using reports	• CUA • Download from R/3 using reports • Manually	• CUA • Client copy • Download from the Q system using reports • Manually
EBP user (user in the organizational model)	• Manually • Download from R/3 using reports	• Transfer from a HR backend using ALE • Download from R/3 using reports	• Transfer from HR backend using ALE • Download from Q system using reports • Download from R/3 using reports
RFC connections and logical systems	• Manually	• Manually	• Manually (if they have also been trans-ported, they must be accepted.)
Other customizing settings	• Manually	• Manually, in some cases using transport requests	• Client copy, transport request

Figure 8.27 Best Practices for the Organizational Structure

8.7 Integration with SAP HR — A Key Decision

A number of corporations that have implemented SAP R/3 have chosen to turn on only certain modules within the SAP suite (e.g., Financials, Materials Management, Inventory Management, Project Systems, etc.). That is, not everyone has SAP HR. It is also possible that your company uses a legacy sys-tem, or a competitive application like Peoplesoft, to manage HR functions. This section is aimed at organizations that have implemented SAP HR or are planning to implement SAP HR along with the SAP SRM solution.

8.7.1 Need for SAP SRM Integration with the HR Organizational Structure

On every project, the following questions come up: Why do we need to integrate the HR organizational structure into EBP? What are the benefits?

The obvious benefit is to leverage existing efforts and implement standardization. If you have SAP HR, the organizational units, positions, employees, etc. are already available in a standardized format. A previous or separate implementation team has taken the time to gather the organizational data, strategize on the structure and align departments and positions closely with the reporting relationships within the corporation. What you need to do now is integrate this structure with the EBP system and identify what organizational structure maintenance is still required after the integration. We'll expand on this later.

Another key benefit is that the HR system becomes the system of record and changes. For example, when an employee is relocated within the organization and the changes are entered and executed in the SAP HR system, the same changes are reflected within the SRM system as well. Or, take the example of an employee who has been terminated.

The HR department is notified first and takes the necessary steps to ensure that the employee information is updated correctly within the SAP HR system. If the organizational structure is integrated within SAP HR and SRM, this information is then also automatically updated in the SRM organizational structure and authorization for the terminated employee will be restricted seamlessly in SRM.

Another benefit revolves around frequent organizational changes, which are common in any large organization. Most organizational structure changes are not pleasant and a lot of time and effort is spent in restructuring and re-aligning various departments, positions and employees. An integrated HR structure at least ensures that you maintain these changes only once, in the HR system, and that the changes are propagated automatically to all other systems (e.g. SRM).

8.7.2 HR Integration Scenarios — When To Integrate

It is not always feasible for project teams to integrate the SAP HR organizational structure with SRM. In this section, I will explain different scenarios where HR integration is feasible, some with ease and others with difficulty. In Figure 8.28, we illustrate different levels of complexity for integrating the

HR organizational structure with SRM. The figure also illustrates when it is ideal for organizations to integrate the SAP SRM structure with SAP HR. For example, the most complex scenario to implement is number **1** in Figure 8.28, where the organizational structure already exists in both the SAP HR and SRM systems. In the paragraphs below, I will explain all four scenarios as illustrated in Figure 8.28.

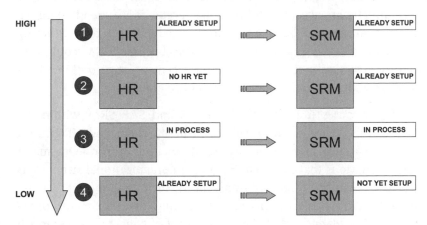

Figure 8.28 Feasibility of Integrating with the SAP HR Organizational Structure

Scenarios 1 and 2

Scenarios **1** and **2** illustrated in Figure 8.28 are quite complex to implement because an organizational structure has already been set up within the EBP system. In these scenarios, all of the organizational objects (O, S, P, etc) have a different number range; for example, the organizational unit object (O) in R/3 would contain a number range that is entirely different than the available number range for the O objects in SRM.

Integrating SAP HR in this scenario would mean deleting the existing EBP organizational structure and overwriting it with the structure from SAP HR. In a production environment, this could have a large effect on existing users with functions already in place, such as shopping carts, purchase orders, vendors, business partners, etc. The standard integration process of HR to SRM will not suffice in this scenario; a significant custom development effort would be required.

Scenario 3

Scenario **3**, as illustrated in Figure 8.28, shows a situation where SAP is possibly being implemented across the entire enterprise. In this scenario, both

SAP HR and SAP SRM could be in the process of being implemented and both have their individual timelines for completion. The HR team and the SAP SRM team might each have goals and requirements of their own. One disadvantage in this scenario is that HR is the leading system of record; therefore SRM is always dependent on the timeline of the HR implementation.

For example, in a project implementation schedule, if the HR team is behind schedule, it directly impacts the SRM timeline because it is dependent on the HR organizational structure being available. Typically, the HR data gathering process is slower than what is required for SRM, because SRM requires an organizational structure that supports the procurement organization. However, the HR team has to gather data for the entire enterprise.

If your organization is implementing SAP HR and SAP SRM within the framework of this scenario, make sure the supply chain and HR project teams are in a very close loop. Define expected timelines upfront. One major issue in this scenario is that SRM requires that an organizational structure is in place before it can begin its core transactions, such as shopping cart creation. In this scenario, project teams end up creating a manual organizational structure in SRM independently to being the proof-of-concept process for all other pieces and wait until a sizable organizational structure is created in HR to being the distribution process and utilize that as the organizational structure in SRM.

The key advantage of this scenario is that both the HR and SRM teams have the opportunity to collaborate on requirements, and build an organizational structure strategy that is closely aligned to meet the needs of both business processes.

Scenario 4

The least complex scenario to implement and integrate SAP HR with SRM is illustrated in scenario **4** in Figure 8.28. In this scenario, SAP HR has already been implemented within the company and SAP SRM (EBP) is yet to be implemented or is currently being implemented. This provides an opportunity for the implementation teams to review the existing HR organizational structure, understand the maintenance strategy, and better define the blueprint strategy for the EBP organizational structure.

From a timeline perspective, there is no pressure and no need to wait for data gathering efforts from the HR teams. The SRM team can review the existing organizational structure and determine possible gaps upfront. This allows for a better design and prevents surprises later.

The main disadvantage of this scenario is that the HR and SRM teams don't have much opportunity to collaborate on requirements. As the HR organizational structure and business processes are already built and available in a production environment, there is less desire for change.

8.7.3 Distributing the HR Organizational Plan

SAP provides a standard interface for the distribution of organizational structure objects from SAP HR into the SRM system. However, organizations need to determine what organizational structure objects need to be distributed from SAP HR into SRM; for example, should roles be distributed from HR to SRM, or, as another example, does address and bank information need to be distributed for employees. The process and setup of this distribution is covered in Chapter 18.

8.7.4 Maintenance of Organizational Structure After HR Integration

Integrating the SAP HR organizational structure with SRM does not eliminate maintenance requirements within SRM. On the contrary, there is still a significant amount of maintenance required in SRM after the integration. For example, in the HR organizational structure, there are no infotypes that are relevant for purchasing, such as purchasing organization, purchasing groups, plants, catalogs, etc. These attribute settings all need to be maintained in the SRM organizational structure once it has been distributed from HR.

Additionally, new organizational units are also necessary, such as the Vendor Root Organization, where all vendors are replicated from the backend SAP system. Further, for organizations implementing the Extended Classic scenario in SRM, additional organizational units are required that represent the backend SAP purchasing organization and purchasing group.

If the Direct Material scenario is being implemented, then the organizational units are required to map the entry point for the requirements being transferred from the external system into SRM.

Figure 8.29 illustrates some of the organizational units created manually in the SRM organizational structure. If the supply chain project teams are able to persuade the HR teams to create additional organizational units like the **R/3 Purchasing Org** in the HR structure, then these could be distributed via the ALE model as well.

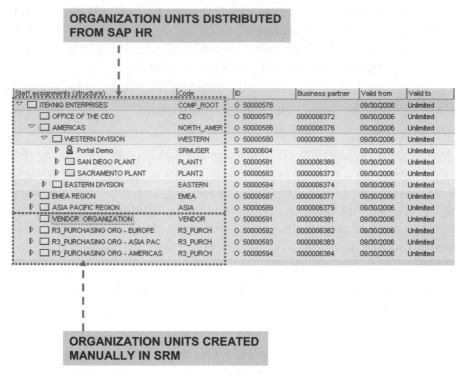

Figure 8.29 Organizational Structure — Manual Object Maintenance

The following is a list of several key attributes and master data elements that you must maintain in SRM:

► Company Code
► Purchasing Organization
► Purchasing Groups
► Internal and External Web Catalogs
► Product Categories
► Plants and Storage Locations
► Technical System Links (backend financial system, materials management system, etc.)

8.7.5 Responsibility Matrix for Setting Up the Organizational Structure During an Implementation

During the blueprint and realization phase, typically the consultants on a project will be responsible for designing the organizational structure model and the actual creation of organizational units and attributes. Remember, the organizational structure is a key element; therefore it is imperative that an appropriate knowledge transfer takes place between the consultants and business owners. As a best practice, business owners should set up the organizational structure in the quality and production environments. This ensures that the appropriate knowledge transfer has occurred.

8.8 Pros and Cons of Creating an Organizational Structure in EBP or Distributing from HR

In this section, I will provide a comparison between maintaining the organizational structure in SRM and distributing the organizational structure from SAP HR. Section 8.8.1 covers the pros and cons of creating an organizational structure in SRM. Section 8.8.2 covers the pros and cons of integrating and using the HR organizational structure.

8.8.1 Creating an Organizational Structure in SAP SRM

This section explains, with the help of Figure 8.30, the pros and cons of creating an organizational structure in SRM. One of the main pros of creating the organizational structure in SRM is that the project team has full control to create a structure that will serve the purposes of organizational procurement. The team is also in control of managing the overall timeline because there is no dependency on another team for the management of the organizational structure. However, for companies that also have implemented SAP HR, the long-term strategy and SAP best practice points in the direction of integrating the SRM organizational structure with HR.

8.8.2 Integrating and Using the HR Organizational Structure

This section explains, with the help of Figure 8.31, the pros and cons of integrating the organizational structure in HR with SAP SRM. One of the biggest advantages of integrating the organizational structure in HR with SRM is that it reduces the duplication of efforts in the management of organizational structure objects. Because HR is the system of record for changes in positions and employees (e.g. terminations or new hires), these objects can be managed in HR and be distributed to SRM in a timely manner. However, organizations need to keep in mind that even after integrating to HR, additional attributes need to be maintained in SRM because they are only available in SRM (for example a plant or purchasing organization attribute).

CREATING AN ORGANIZATIONAL STRUCTURE IN SRM	
PROS	• ...Allows the implementation team to have **better control** of the Organizational Structure setup. **Eliminates any dependencies**.
	• ... SRM Org Structure requires a subset of overall HR Org – **Minimize** Initial Setup & reduction of **complexity**
	• ... Allows flexibility to develop a custom structure if required for SRM
	• ... Typically adheres to the timeline allocated for the project
CONS	• ... **Long-Term strategy** for many organizations is to integrate HR Org with SRM
	• ... **Dual maintenance** of Organizational Structure in SRM and HR
	• ... **Not synchronized** with the latest org changes in HR (could have someone not working for the organization anymore in SAP, but still be able to order within SRM)
	• ...FTE's required for **maintenance** of **ongoing** Organizational Structure and changes
	• ...If determined later to integrate with the HR org structure, a large amount of re-work will be required. (see figure 11.28)

Figure 8.30 Creating an Organizational Structure in SRM

INTEGRATING & USING THE ORGANIZATION STRUCTURE IN HR	
PROS	• ... No Duplication of Organization Setup
	• ... Less FTE's required to maintain the Organizational Structure in SRM. Need to concentrate on attribute changes only.
	• ... Real-Time synchronization of HR Org structure with SRM Org structure
	• ...Initial SRM implementation best suited for SAP HR-SRM integration
	• ...If the corporation is using position based security, then Roles and authorizations can be assigned directly in SAP HR and distributed to the SRM system.
CONS	• ... Even after HR Integration, attribute maintenance is still required in SRM. HR Integration does not eliminate SRM org maintenance
	• ... Although HR integration is available as standard solution, issues can result based on the SAP HR org design.
	• ... Possible risk to overall project timeline if resources are not dedicated or are unavailable
	• ...If SAP HR is being implemented at the same time as SRM, there is a greater risk to project timelines. As SRM cannot function without the Organizational Structure, the SRM project team is highly dependent on the HR Organizational Structure availability

Figure 8.31 Integrating and Using the Organizational Structure in HR

8.9 Impact of the Extended Classic Scenario on SRM Organizational Structure

In Chapter 7, we discussed the different implementation scenarios for SAP SRM, including the Extended Classic scenario. This section provides a brief description on how to set up the organizational structure in the Extended Classic scenario.

If you are implementing the Extended Classic scenario, the organizational structure needs to be set up a little differently. The key point to remember is that because all purchasing documents (shopping cart, purchase order, etc.) are created in the SRM system, a local purchasing organization and local purchasing group is required in the organizational structure. However, because the purchase order is also sent to the R/3 backend, a mechanism needs to be there to identify the backend purchasing organization and purchasing groups. Therefore, a small structure is also needed for the backend purchasing organization and purchasing groups. Notice that in Figure 8.32, both the local purchasing organization and the backend R/3 purchasing organization are created. The local organization setup is illustrated in the shaded box for **LOCAL PORG/PGRP** and the backend R/3 setup is illustrated in the shaded box for **R/3 PORG/PGRP**.

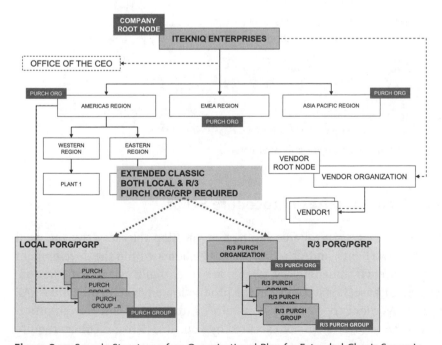

Figure 8.32 Sample Structure of an Organizational Plan for Extended Classic Scenario

In Figure 8.33, you can see an organizational structure in SRM that matches the illustration in Figure 8.32. Notice that the **AMERICAS** organizational unit is a purchasing organization but does not have a value entered in the **Corresponds To** field, because it's not required for local purchasing organizations. However, the **R3_PURCHASING ORG — EUROPE** is also set as a purchasing organization but contains a value in the Corresponds To field. This indicates the R/3-based purchasing organization **101** and the appropriate RFC destination **R3100CLT**.

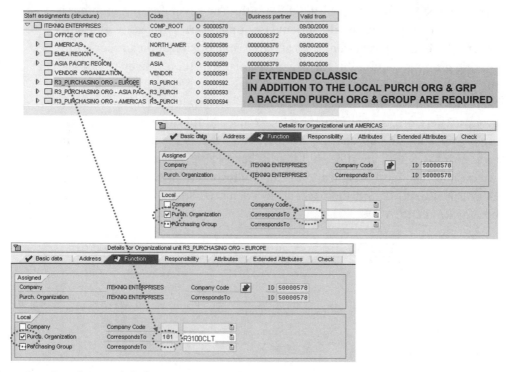

Figure 8.33 Sample Extended Classic Organizational Structure

8.10 System Refresh Procedure Steps

Enhancements, system rollouts and new application releases drive the need to create new clients, and/or refresh existing clients within the development and quality environments. New clients are often built using configuration, master and transactional data from the production environment. Unlike SAP R/3, an SRM client copy or refresh requires a number of post-refresh procedures. Some of these steps are executed by your BASIS team. Others require execution by the functional teams.

Once the system is refreshed, the organizational structure information needs to be reset based on the new system information (e.g. production environment copied onto a quality environment). A number of attributes in EBP contain references to the backend MM or financial system, including purchase order document type, cost center and material groups. For example, if the production system is copied over the quality system, then the cost center and material groups in the quality (QA) system organizational structure would still reference the backend destination of the production system. These will need to be changed to reflect the RFC and logical destinations of the QA system.

SAP provides a standard report in EBP, RHOMATTRIBUTES_REPLACE, to reset many of the system-specific attributes. This report provides a mass change capability so that all of the attributes can be changed quickly. Note that once the RHOMATTRIBUTES_REPLACE program has been executed, you can define attributes in the next screen, such as the CNT attribute shown in Figure 8.34.

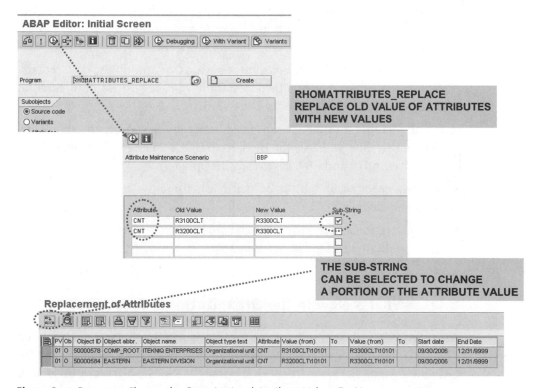

Figure 8.34 Report to Change the Organizational Attribute Values En Masse

In the Old Value field, enter the RFC destination for the source system and in the New Value field, enter the RFC destination of the copy system. Once all of the attributes are defined and the program is executed, the results page displays all of the corresponding objects where an attribute match was found and a mass change can be executed.

OSS note 447651 provides additional information on what to do when a system copy is done in SRM.

8.11   Things to Remember

Now that we've discussed the importance of the organizational structure in SRM and also the impact of integrating the structure with SAP HR, I'd like to leave you with some key points to remember:

▶ When integrating with SAP HR, remember that the HR organizational structure might be much larger than your EBP organizational structure needs to be. For example, you might only be rolling out EBP to a select group of users in the organization and do not require the entire population of positions and employees found in SAP HR.

▶ Maintenance of additional attributes such as commodities, cost centers, catalogs and so on will still be necessary in EBP, regardless of integration with SAP HR.

▶ Number ranges must be synchronized between the various environments. Remember, integrating with HR becomes a challenge if organizational structures in HR and EBP are already set up.

▶ Security needs to be built in so that HR is the only source for modifications and changes.

▶ Changes made in the EBP organizational structure cannot be replicated into the HR organizational structure.

8.12   What's New in the Organizational Structure?

As of SAP SRM version 5.0, an enhanced organizational (org) model called ERP-ORG has been provided. Because the org model was enhanced in the SAP ERP system, the same has been adopted for SAP SRM. This impacts both the EBP and SUS systems. There are two key differences in the organizational model in version 5.0, compared to previous releases:

▶ The organizational model has been split between internal and external business partner management. A new transaction </PPOMV_BBP> has been created for managing external business partners (vendors, bidders, etc.), as opposed to managing them in </PPOMA_BBP>. Therefore, external business partners cannot be represented in a company's own organizational model that is using SRM.

▶ For organizations using the integrated scenario with HR, the creation of internal business partners, which were in previous releases created as a result of the HR ALE integration model, are now created in SRM as they are created in the HR-ORG in ERP system (assuming same client).

The standard transaction </PPOMA_BBP> used to maintain the organizational structure also has been enhanced with a large detailed view for maintenance. You can access this view via the **Go-To • Large Detailed view** menu path.

Organizations that are upgrading from previous releases need to migrate the existing organizational structure. SAP provides a standard report, BBP_XPRA_ORGEH_TO_VENDOR_GROUP, to assist with this migration. The report deletes all of the organizational units and positions of vendors and bidders and groups them together into new organizational objects (vendor groups) that can be accessed in transaction. A vendor group is created for multiple vendors using the same attributes.

8.13   Summary

In this chapter you were introduced to the concept of an organizational structure in SRM, which is also a core component of control within SRM. The organizational structure provides the necessary authorization for users to create shopping carts, purchase orders and other documents. Attributes, such as purchasing organization, purchasing group, plants, web-based catalogs, cost center information, etc. are all examples of master data elements that are assigned to positions and employees in the organizational structure. I also discussed the importance and need of integrating the organizational structure in SAP HR with SRM and the best scenarios for this integration.

In Chapter 9, I will discuss the integration of SAP Financials, with SAP SRM. Purchasing documents such as shopping carts and purchase orders contain multiple integration points with master data in SAP Financials; budget checks and real-time account validation are a competitive selling point for the SAP SRM solution.

Tight integration between SAP's ERP system and the SAP SRM suite is a distinct advantage for customers. Integration of financial and procurement systems offers opportunities for both strategic and operational changes that improve overall efficiencies and reduce costs.

9 Integration with Financials and Project Systems

ERP systems are the backbone of enterprise financial information management, handling all data associated with financial transactions. Company-wide control and integration of financial information are essential to strategic decision making of any company. According to SAP, SAP ERP gives you the ability to centrally track financial accounting data within an international framework of multiple companies, languages, currencies, and charts of accounts. For example, when raw materials move from inventory into manufacturing, the system reduces quantity values in inventory and simultaneously subtracts monetary values for inventory accounts in the balance sheet. This chapter covers SRM integration with Financials and Project Systems.

SAP SRM leverages the tight integration between the SAP Financials (FI) system and the SRM suite, thereby creating a distinct advantage for the overall solution. Real-time integration with SAP's Financial Accounting (FI) module streamlines the entire supply-chain process from the accounting perspective and creates a document audit trail that helps in establishing the controls as required by new compliance regulations such as Sarbanes-Oxley (SOX). This integration also helps in validating the finance master data when processing any procurement transaction. The integration helps in real-time checking of available budget and creates real-time posting of procurement transactions into financial accounting.

All accounting-relevant transactions made in SAP's Logistics (LO) or Human Resources (HR) components are posted in real-time to FI by means of automatic account determination. This ensures that logistical goods movements (such as goods receipts and goods issues) are exactly reflected in the value-based updates in accounting. Financial integration occurs at different levels:

enterprise structure, master data, and transaction data. Figure 9.1 illustrates at a high level the SAP components that integrate with SAP Financials.

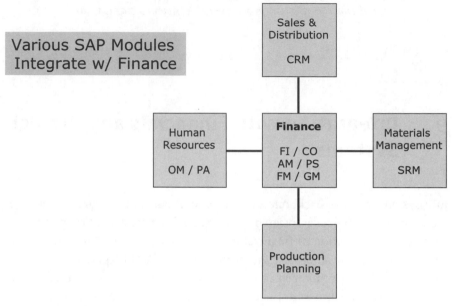

Figure 9.1 Integration with SAP Financials

In the next section, I will explain the basics of Financials in SAP to lay a foundation for the later sections in this chapter.

9.1 Financial Accounting in SAP

The SAP ERP 2005 solution map provides a listing of all the core business processes within an organization. SAP provides solution maps so that organizations can easily visualize and plan for the different business processes covered within the SAP solution and also plan the processes required to successfully run their operations. Figure 9.2 illustrates the major business processes that exist in SAP ERP 2005, and highlights the financial processes of Financial Supply-Chain Management, Financial Accounting, Management Accounting, and Corporate Governance.

Figure 9.3 gives a more detailed view of the functionality required within each of the financial processes. Procurement integrates at a number of touchpoints in FI, such as **General Ledger (G/L)**, **Accounts Payable**, **Fixed Assets Accounting**, and **Inventory Accounting**.

End-User Service Delivery				
Analytics	Strategic Enterprise Management	Financial Analytics	Operations Analytics	Workforce Analytics
Financials	Financial Supply Chain Mgmt.	Financial Accounting	Management Accounting	Corporate Governace
Human Capital Management	Talent Management	Workforce Management		Workforce Deployment
Procurement and Logistics Execution	Procure-ment / Supplier Collaboration	Inventory and Warehouse Mgmt.	Inbound and Outbound Logistics	Transportation Management
Product Development and Manufacturing	Production Planning	Manufacturing Execution	Product Development	Life-Cycle Data Mgmt.
Sales and Service	Sales Order Management	Aftermarket Sales and Service		Professional-Service Delivery
Corporate Services	Real Estate Mgmt. / Enterprise Asset Mgmt.	Project and Portfolio Mgmt. / Travel Mgmt.	Environment Health and Safety / Quality Mgmt.	Global Trade Services
mySAP ERP Solution Map — Financial				

Figure 9.2 SAP ERP 2005 Solution Map — Financials

Financials	mySAP ERP Solution Map Financial Accounting		
Financial Supply Chain Management	Financial Accounting	Management Accounting	Corporate Governance
Credit Management (S.4, S.1)	General Ledger (S.1)	Profit Center Accounting (S.1)	Audit Information System (S.1)
Electronic Bill Presentment and Payment (S.4, S.1)	Accounts Receivable (S.1)	Cost Center and Internal Order Accounting (S.1)	Management of Internal Controls (S.1)
Collection Management (S.4, S.1)	Accounts Payable (S.1)	Project Accounting (S.1)	Risk Management (S.1)
Dispute Management (S.4, S.1)	Contract Accounting	Investment Management (S.1)	Whistle Blower Complaints (S.1)
In-house Cash (S.1, S.5)	Fixed Assets Accounting (S.1)	Product Cost Accounting (S.1)	Segregation of Duties (S.12)
Cash and liquidity Management (S.1, S.16)	Bank Accounting (S.1)	Profitability Accounting (S.1)	
Treasury and Risk Management (S.1, S.5)	Cash Journal Accounting (S.1)	Transfer Pricing (S.1)	
Bank Relationship Management	Inventory Accounting (S.1)		
	Tax Accounting (S.1)		
	Accrual Accounting (S.1)		
	Local Close (S.1)		
	Financial Statements (S.1)		

Figure 9.3 SAP ERP 2005 — Financial Accounting

351

SAP Financials is integrated across all the other functional SAP modules. In the SAP system, you define the relevant organizational units for each component that you are implementing. For example, for *Sales and Distribution*, you define sales organizations, distribution channels, and divisions (product groups). Similarly, for *Purchasing*, you define purchasing organizations, evaluation levels, plants, and storage locations. The organizational units are independent of one another at this stage.

To transfer data between the individual components, you have to assign the organizational units to each other. You only need to make these assignments once in the system. Whenever you enter data subsequently, it is automatically transferred. Figure 9.4 illustrates the integration of the finance area at an enterprise level.

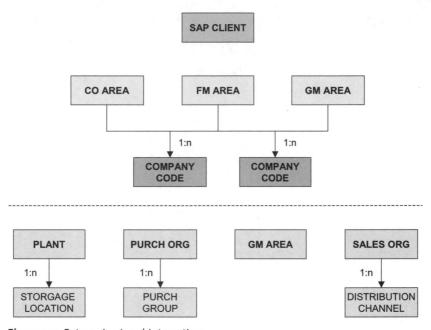

Figure 9.4 Entrerprise-Level Integration

Now that I have provided an introduction to SAP Financials, let us dive into the integration of SAP Financials with SAP SRM.

9.2 Integration of SAP Financials with SAP SRM

SAP SRM provides real-time integration with SAP Financials. Integration can happen at different levels: enterprise structure, master data, and at a business transaction level. Section 9.1.1 briefly discussed enterprise-level integration in SAP. This section will focus on the integration touch points in SAP SRM where financial master data elements (cost center, G/L account, etc.) interact with business transactions (shopping cart, purchase order, etc.)

9.2.1 Integration at the Master Data Level

Integration at the master-data level means that the master data used in SRM is integrated to master data in financial accounting via configuration within each individual area. To achieve optimum integration, master data must be designed very thoughtfully and mapped in a meaningful manner. If designed correctly, it reduces reconciliation and maintenance issues.

From an accountant's point of view, whenever any purchase is made, it needs to be posted either as an expense, asset, or inventory in financial accounting based on the nature of the item purchased. A combination of attributes such as account assignment category and the characteristic of the item purchased (e.g., consumable, material, or service) is used in directing the posting to the appropriate classification of this expense.

Some customers design the shopping cart approval workflow to include a finance validation, so as to validate the buyer's choice of the appropriate account assignment. Getting this right the first time reduces the subsequent expense reclassification effort. The idea is to capture all the data correctly the first time and carry it through till the end of the process in order to reduce reconciliation and data re-entry.

Figure 9.5 illustrates how SAP SRM integrates at a master-data level with the CO, Funds Management (FM), and Grant Management (GM) modules within SAP Financials. In SRM, users can utilize account assignments such as cost center, internal order, or fund in the shopping cart and purchase order documents.

These account assignments map to the cost center, internal order, and fund within Controlling **(CO)** and **FM** and **GM** modules. Figure 9.6 illustrates how this mapping should be done in the account assignment customizing transactions in SAP SRM.

Figure 9.6 illustrates the configuration setting in SAP SRM that allows organizations to map the SRM account assignment type to the SAP R/3 account assignment. Notice that in SRM the **COST CENTER** account assignment is delivered by SAP as **CC**, however, in SAP R/3 the cost center is delivered as **K**.

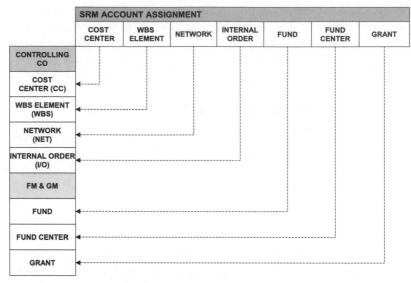

Figure 9.5 SAP SRM Integration at Master Data Level with CO, FM, and GM

SRM	SRM	R/3
COST CENTER	CC	K
INTERNAL ORDER	IO	F
WBS ELEMENT	WBS	P
ASSET **	AS	A

** SAMPLE ACCT ASSIGNMENTS IN SRM & CORRESPONDING IN R/3

▽ 🗋 Account Assignment
   📄 ⊕ Define Account Assignment Categories
   📄 ⊕ Define G/L Account for Product Category and Account Assignment Category
   📄 ⊕ Maintain Local Accounting Data

CONFIGURATION IN SRM

Account assignment categories

Account Assignment ...	Description	Active	Backend acct ass. cat.	
AS	Asset	☑	A	⬆
CC	Cost Center	☑	K	▼
FI	Finances and Funds	☐	K	
NET	Network	☑	N	
OR	Order	☑	F	
SO	Sales order	☐	X	
STR	Generic account assignment	☐		
WBS	WBS element	☑	P	

Dialog Structure
▽ ☐ Account assignment catego
    ☐ Acct assignment fields

AcctAssgmtCateg   CC   Cost Center

Acct assignment fields

Acct assignment field (technical name)	Description	Leading acc...	
ACC_STR	Generic Account Assignment	○	
CMMT_ITEM	Commitment Item	○	
COST_CTR	Cost Center	◉	
FUNC_AREA	Functional Area	○	
FUND	Fund	○	
FUNDS_CTR	Funds Center	○	
GRANT_NBR	Grant	○	

Figure 9.6 Account Assignment Category in SAP SRM

This mapping between the account assignments in SRM and R/3 is done in the customizing section Account Assignment in SRM. Additionally, project teams can choose to activate only a select few account assignments; e.g., if asset procurement is not going to be allowed via the shopping cart in SAP SRM, then leave the check-box under the Active column blank for account assignment **AS** which is used for assets.

Again from the accounting perspective, the purchase should be posted not only to the right type of classification, but also to the correct G/L account from the chart of accounts. How can the user make sure he picks the right G/L account when making the purchase? With the kind of integration available between SAP SRM and the financial accounting, the user just picks up the item to be purchased from the catalog and the back-end configuration and integration makes it post to the correct G/L account. How does this happen?

The use of product categories in SRM allows the linking of the G/L accounts from the company's chart of accounts to the product categories and catalogues in SRM. Let's take an example of this mapping. Say a product category, *pencils and pens* is mapped to a G/L account office supplies. When a buyer is processing a shopping cart and chooses the product category pencils and pens, the system automatically pulls up the G/L account as *office supplies*.

This way, the users do not have to keep thinking about the choice of G/L account, and the accountant doesn't have to validate whether each and every posting has been posted to the correct G/L account. This ensures a great element of control and at the same time greatly reduces validation and subsequent re-classification work.

Figure 9.7 provides an illustration of the configuration that makes this integration available in SAP SRM. Notice, in Figure 9.7, the **Category ID** (or Material Group) **STATIONERY** is mapped to a Cost Center (**CC**) and an Asset (**AS**) in the **AcctAssCat** field. A corresponding G/L account is mapped in the **G/L account no.** field. Organizations have the option of providing a different G/L account per account assignment; e.g., the CC is assigned to G/L **600100**, and the AS is assigned to G/L **100255** in Figure 9.7.

The mapping illustrated in Figure 9.7 requires the purchasing team to work in conjunction with the finance team to determine the appropriate level or classification relevant for both procurement needs and financial budgeting. Many project teams find this classification agreement a difficult task. The procurement department needs classification for analysis of spending across the various commodities purchased. Finance needs the G/L account classification from a budgeting perspective.

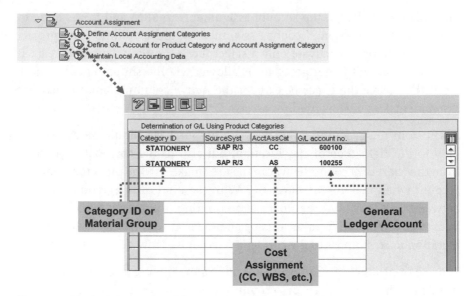

Figure 9.7 Product Category to G/L Account Mapping in SAP SRM

Allocate time during the design and configuration phase of the project to determine this activity. If no G/L account is mapped in the G/L account number field shown in Figure 9.7, then the user can enter any valid G/L in the shopping cart. In the shopping cart, users with appropriate authorization can search for all available G/L numbers in SAP R/3 and select from this list of accounts.

Organizations using material-based (product-based) procurement in SAP SRM have the ability to control the G/L account assignment via the valuation class within the material master in SAP R/3. For example, the material master record is linked to a G/L account via valuation class configuration. A material master is linked to a valuation class, which in turn is linked to a G/L account (illustrated in Figure 9.8).

So any time a business transaction relevant to financial accounting occurs for that material, a posting is made to the associated G/L account in the G/L. In the shopping carts if organizations want to limit the users from being able to change the G/L account when using products, they can do so using the Business Add-In (BAdI) BBP_DETERMINE_ACCT.

The various financial modules are tightly integrated amongst themselves, so that once a posting updates any of the modules all the remaining modules are updated automatically when necessary. Figure 9.9 shows you how the data is mapped in the different modules.

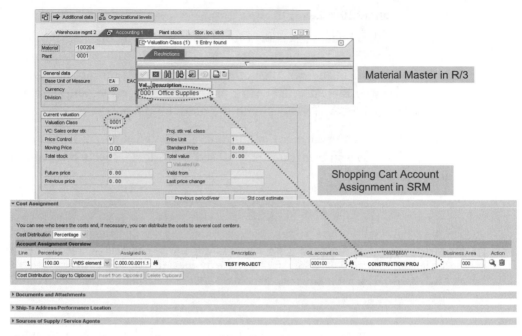

Figure 9.8 Material Master Valuation-Based G/L Control

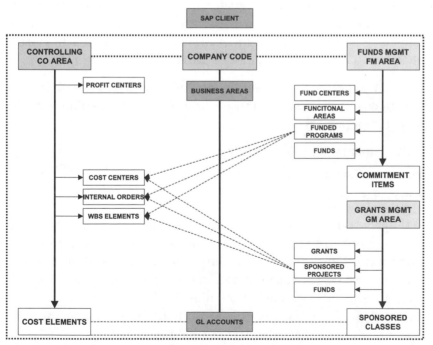

* For illustration purposes – does not reflect interaction between all master data and ledgers

Figure 9.9 Sample — Interaction of Master Data and Related Ledgers in SAP Financials

9.2.2 Transaction Level Integration

When we talk about transaction integration, we mean that the business transaction processed in one functional area has an impact or an automatic update or posting in another functional area in real time. For instance, when a purchase order is created in SRM or in SAP R/3, a corresponding commitment is created in SAP FM to commit the funds on the purchase order.

Different modules in financial accounting are designed to aid in multiple views of financial information that is used in various aspects of financial decision-making.

Example

The G/L is used for external financial reporting, whereas CO is used for internal management reporting, and so on. Each of these sub-modules has a different purpose and is updated differently for the same business transaction. Each also has its own master data but it is tightly integrated with other sub-modules based on configuration.

The updates and postings in the different financial modules depend upon the extent of implementation and the type of transaction processed. Figure 9.10 illustrates the transaction-level integration between SAP SRM and the different financial modules. In SRM, when **SHOPPING CART** is created there is no corresponding posting in SAP Financials. However, a **REQUISITION** created in SAP R/3 has a corresponding **PRE-COMMITMENT** posting in FM.

In SAP SRM there are three main options of validating financial account assignment data at the time of a processing a business transaction (e.g., the shopping cart or purchase order):

- Locally within Enterprise Buyer (EBP)
- Real-time validation of FI data in SAP R/3
- No validation at all

In the shopping cart, users can assign cost assignments at a line-item level. If the system of financial record is SAP R/3 and a Classic or Extended Classic scenario is being implemented, a real-time validation occurs in SRM against the back-end SAP system. If an invalid account assignment is used, the end-user gets an error prior to order creation in the shopping cart. Figure 9.11 provides a view of the Cost Assignment section in the shopping cart. The purchase order in SAP SRM provides the same functionality.

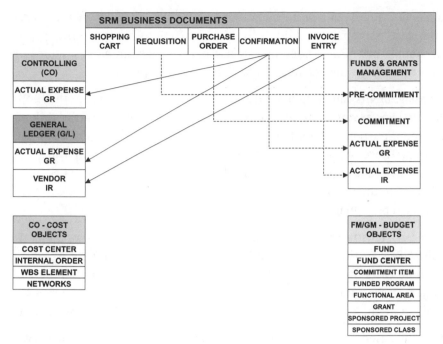

Figure 9.10 Integration at a Transaction Level

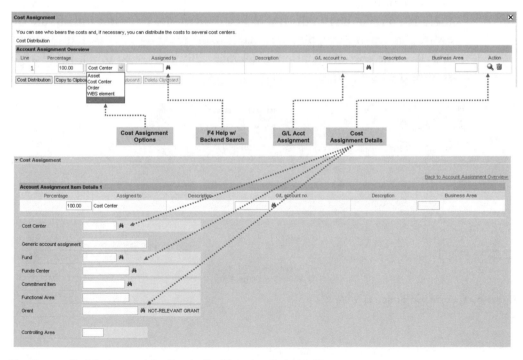

Figure 9.11 Cost Assignment Section in the Shopping Cart Line Item

Notice, in Figure 9.11 that the magnifying glass icon lets you view the details of the cost assignment. Additionally, if organizations are using the FM or GM module in SAP FI, shopping cart users might need to enter a **Funds** or **Grant** number on the details section of the cost assignment.

Cost assignments can be split across multiple lines and accounts in the shopping cart. For example, suppose a user is creating a shopping cart to order a large multi-purpose printer that will be used by multiple departments in the building. The cost for this printer will be shared across multiple departments. The cost-assignment section in the shopping cart provides the ability to distribute the costs across multiple accounts. Costs can then be assigned based on a percentage basis, quantity basis, or by value.

Figure 9.12 illustrates how cost distribution can be done in the shopping cart in SAP SRM. In the **Cost Distribution** dropdown menu, users can select to distribute costs by **Percentage**, **By Qty**, or **By Value**. Costs can then be distributed across multiple account assignments; in our example in Figure 9.12, we illustrate the cost distribution by Percentage and by using a Cost Center.

The value-based cost distribution is only available in SAP SRM. If the Classic or Extended Classic scenario is being implemented, then the purchase order is also sent to SAP R/3. In the Materials Management (MM) module of SAP, there is no capability to distribute based on value. Project teams should be aware that when a shopping cart that is distributed by value is transferred to SAP R/3, the cost distribution is automatically converted into a percentage split in the MM purchase order.

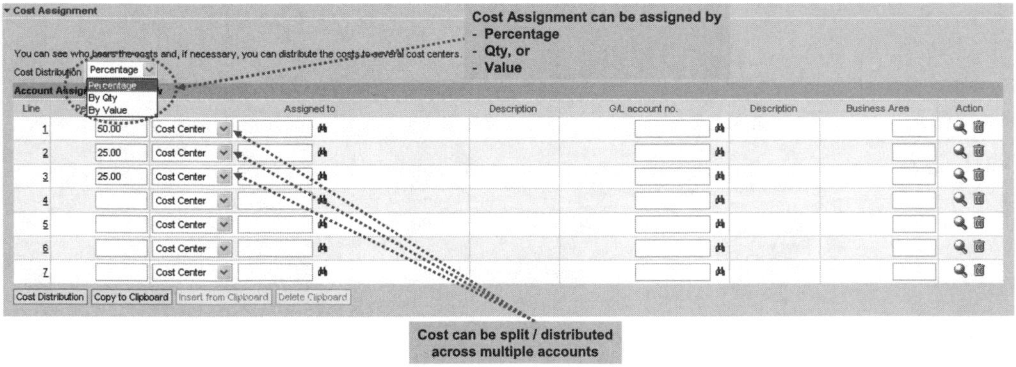

Figure 9.12 Cost Distribution in SAP SRM

9.2.3 Account Determination Based on Expense vs. Stocked Items

In SAP SRM, at the time of shopping-cart creation the system requires an account assignment category, account, and a G/L account. Unless valid accounting data is provided, the user cannot order the shopping cart. SAP SRM can be used for both expense and direct material (stock) procurement scenarios. Figure 9.13 illustrates what happens when a user in SAP SRM orders expense goods as opposed to goods to replenish stock.

Free Text Items including Catalogs	• Account Assignment Category is defaulted in the shopping cart from user's "my settings" or the Organization Structure in SRM • The G/L account assignment is determined based on the Product Category, based on the account assignment mapping in the IMG in SRM
Inventory Items	• Material based items, subject to inventory management. • The "Order as Direct" button is used in the shopping cart to order products for replenishment. • Account assignment information is not required in the shopping cart. This information is utilized from the accounting screen on the material master. • Account determination is handled in SAP R/3 for the inventory management, GR/IR reconciliation account or other postings
Planned based requirements (MRP)	• Plan based requirements, such as demand based requisitions in MRP, PS, PP are transferred from R/3 into SRM for sourcing • In SRM no account assignment information is passed, Account determination is handled in SAP R/3

Figure 9.13 Account Determination in SAP SRM and SAP R/3 MM

As discussed in Chapter 7, SAP SRM can be implemented in different scenarios: Classic, Extended Classic, and Standalone. It is important to understand the differences in the financial postings when different implementation scenarios are used in SRM. The next section describes the impact of SRM implementation scenarios on financial postings in the different sub-ledgers of FI.

In the next section, I will discuss how documents created during the purchase to pay cycle within SAP SRM and SAP R/3 impact the financial postings in SAP FI and FM.

9.3 Overview of the Purchase-to-Pay Cycle

In SAP SRM, the *purchase-to-pay* cycle starts with the step of creating a shopping cart and ends with the posting of an invoice. This process and its impact on SAP Financials modules is illustrated in Figure 9.14.

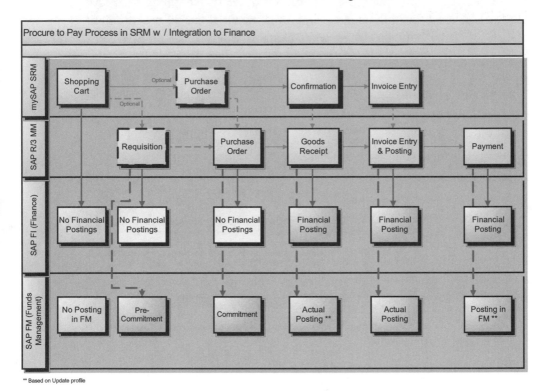

Figure 9.14 Procure- to-Pay Process in SAP SRM with Integration to Finance

As illustrated in Figure 9.14, once a shopping cart is created, it is either routed for approval or converted into a purchase order. At this time, there are no postings that occur in financial accounting. In certain scenarios, there is an option of creating a purchase requisition in SAP MM. If this option is chosen, a pre-commitment document is posted in FM. No other postings occur in any other financial modules.

Moving a step further, when the shopping cart is converted into a purchase order, a commitment document is posted within FM, with no postings to other modules. At this stage, if a pre-commitment document was previously created via a purchase requisition, it is liquidated.

Upon receipt of a purchase order, the vendor transmits the goods or services to your organization. At this time in the procure-to-pay process, a confirmation can be entered within SAP SRM for receiving and accepting the goods or services. Confirmations in SRM are seamlessly converted into a goods receipt document in SAP R/3. At this time, postings are created in the various submodules of FI. The expense or inventory posting is made in the G/L and an expense posting is made in CO. In FM, the previously posted commitment (based on the purchase order) is liquidated against the actual expense posting

At the time of goods receipt, the ownership of the goods passes from the seller to the buyer so the expense and the provision for the liability to pay the seller are posted in FI. All these entries are posted automatically in FI on a real time basis when the user makes an entry for receiving the goods.

This reflects a tight integration between purchasing and accounting. Several other ERP vendors have not been able to achieve this kind of integration between purchasing and FI modules. For example, organizations using the Ariba Buyer solution are unable to attain the tight integration with SAP Financials as available in SAP SRM.

It is important to note that confirmations in SRM are not exactly the same as a Goods Receipt document in SAP R/3. The confirmation document allows users to indicate the receipt of goods and services from a vendor.

Depending on the organization and configuration, subsequent approvals might be required. Once the **System Status** of the confirmation is **Approved**, a corresponding Goods Receipt document is created in SAP R/3. Figure 9.15 illustrates the system status.

> **Note**
>
> The confirmation document number in SRM is a different number than the Goods Receipt document in SAP R/3.

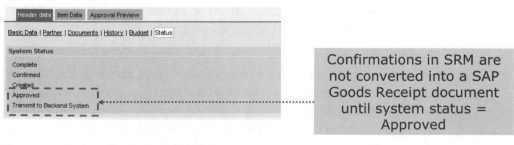

Figure 9.15 Confirmation Status in SAP SRM

The final step in the procure-to-pay process in SRM is the processing of vendor invoices. Once an invoice is entered in SRM, it can be subject to subsequent approvals. If no approvals are required or once all required approvals are completed, the invoice is transferred to SAP R/3 via standard ALE IDocs.

In SAP R/3, a three-way match of the invoice, goods receipt, and the purchase order can occur in order to check the accuracy of the quantity invoiced and the rate at which it is invoiced. If there is a match, the invoice is posted without any payment blocks. If there is a mismatch on either front, the invoice is posted with a block for payment.

The invoice posting creates posting in the various sub-modules of FI. It posts a vendor liability in G/L, and updates FM with the actual expense posting depending upon the update profile configured in funds management.

Once invoices are posted in SAP, the next step is to make a vendor payment for the goods/services rendered. In SAP R/3 the payment program can be used to transmit payment to the vendor by appropriate payment media (check, ACH, etc.).

9.3.1 Classic Scenario: SAP SRM and Back-End System is SAP R/3

In the Classic scenario implementation, the purchasing documents (requisition and purchase order) are created within the SAP R/3 system. However, Goods Receipts (confirmation) and Invoices can be created in either SAP R/3 or SAP SRM. Figure 9.16 illustrates the impact of the classic scenario on financial postings in SAP.

As illustrated in the Figure 9.16, once the shopping cart is created in SRM, no postings occur in either SAP FI or in SAP FM. Depending on the configuration in SAP SRM, organizations can choose to create requisitions as the follow-on document to shopping carts or skip the requisition and directly create a purchase order. If the purchase requisition is created, there is no posting in SAP FI, but a pre-commitment document is posted within FM for organizations using the public-sector solution..

If business rules determine that a purchase order is to be created as a follow-on document, there are still no postings created in FI, although but for organizations using the public-sector solution, a commitment document is posted within FM. The subsequent financial postings when creating confirmations, invoices, and vendor payments remain the same as described in Section 9.3.

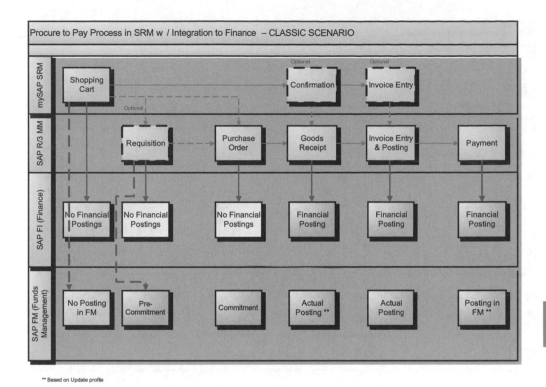

Figure 9.16 Classic Scenario Impact on Financial Postings

9.3.2 Extended Classic Scenario: SAP SRM and Back-End System is SAP R/3.

In the Extended Classic scenario implementation, the Purchase Order document is created within SAP SRM. Once this document is complete (with approved status), a copy is transferred to the SAP R/3 system. The system of record is SRM. Goods receipts (confirmation) and invoices can be created in either SAP R/3 or SAP SRM. Figure 9.17 illustrates the impact of the Extended Classic scenario on financial postings in SAP.

As illustrated in the Figure 9.17, once the shopping cart is created in SRM, no postings occur in either FI or FM. In this scenario, unlike the Classic, there is no option of creating purchase requisitions as follow-on documents to the shopping cart.

Therefore, the first time any document is posted in FI is at the time of posting the purchase order. In this scenario, the purchase order is created in SRM and copy is sent to MM. The posting of a purchase order creates a commitment document in funds management.

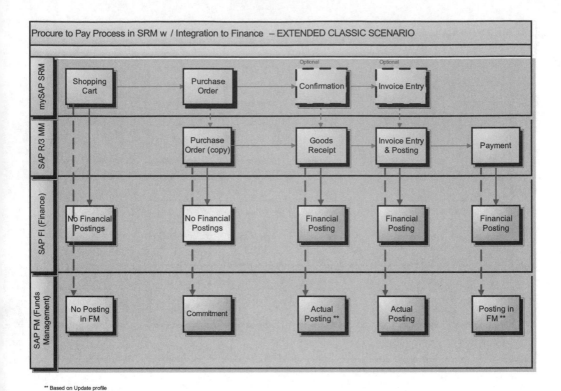

Procure to Pay Process in SRM w / Integration to Finance – EXTENDED CLASSIC SCENARIO

** Based on Update profile

Figure 9.17 Extended Classic Scenario Impact on Financial Postings

The rest of the processes from creation of the goods receipt to the payment of the invoice remain the same as described earlier in this section.

9.3.3 Standalone Scenario: SAP SRM with Non-SAP Back-End System

In the Standalone scenario implementation, the purchase order, confirmation, and invoice are created within SAP SRM. The SRM application is not integrated with the back-end accounting system apart from the creation of payments. In this case, the only time a posting from SRM into FI occurs is upon the posting of the vendor invoice so that it can be paid out of FI.

As illustrated in Figure 9.18 there is no financial posting when a **Shopping Cart**, **Confirmation,** or **Purchase Order** is created in SAP SRM. However, when an invoice is posted in SRM a financial positing happens in **SAP FI** and the actual posting happens in **FM**. Also, when the **Payment** is posted in **SAP R/3**, a corresponding financial posting is also done in **FI** and **FM**.

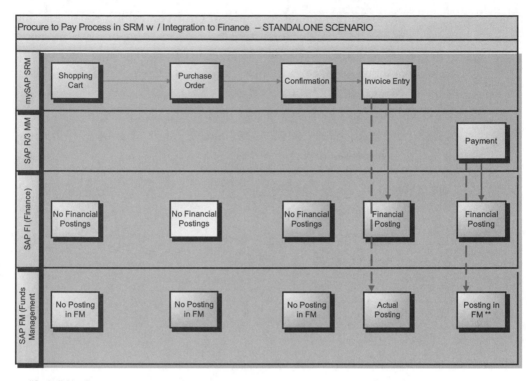

Procure to Pay Process in SRM w / Integration to Finance – STANDALONE SCENARIO

mySAP SRM	Shopping Cart	Purchase Order	Confirmation	Invoice Entry	
SAP R/3 MM					Payment
SAP FI (Finance)	No Financial Postings	No Financial Postings	No Financial Postings	Financial Posting	Financial Posting
SAP FM (Funds Management)	No Posting in FM	No Posting in FM	No Posting in FM	Actual Posting	Posting in FM **

** Based on Update profile

Figure 9.18 Standalone Scenario Impact on Financial Postings

In the next section we will discuss the real-time budget check functionality in SAP SRM.

9.4 Budget Check in SAP SRM

What do we mean by a budget check? A budget check means that every time any purchasing activity (for example, creation of shopping carts or purchase orders) is happening in SRM, the budget for the respective budget bearing object is checked in the R/3 financial back-end. If the budget is not sufficient, then — based on the configuration — a warning or error message is issued at the time of generating the commitment.

Budgeting is done in the CO module. In case the industry solution for public sector companies is implemented, budgeting can also be done in FM for internal funding sources and in GM for external or sponsored funding sources.

Various organizations implement budgeting for controlling expenses. This control can be achieved via monitoring through reporting or by then having system-based controls check the budget at the time of posting and issue a warning or error message to the user if the budget is not sufficient (this is called active availability control or AVC).

In SAP SRM, the budget availability check is available in the EBP system as of Release 2.0C and is triggered at the following points or with the following activities, as illustrated in Figure 9.19.

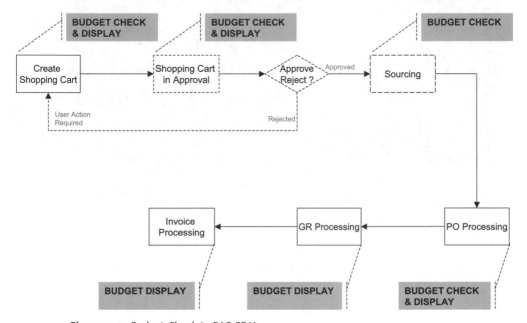

Figure 9.19 Budget Check in SAP SRM

In addition to the budget check, SAP SRM provides functionality for budget display in the various document types. The budget display functionality in SAP SRM provides an overview of the spent and available budget for an accounting object of a document. Users with appropriate authorizations are able to view the budget values and/or execute a BW report for further details.

The budget display provides a simulation of the budget consumed for a particular budget object at the time of the document creation, such as the shopping cart. The budget-display function compares the total value in the shopping cart with the total budget allocated and subtracts the budget used amount read from the FI/CO back end. Figure 9.20 illustrates the budget simulation in the shopping cart.

In the shopping cart overview, a **Budget** link is available within the **Additional Specifications** area. When you click on this link, the **Budget Overview** section is displayed. The Budget Overview provides a simulated view of the budget availability and allows the end user to visually see the budget consumption based on the shopping cart or purchase order value. The **Budget** field provides the overall budget available for the cost assignment in the **Assigned to** field.

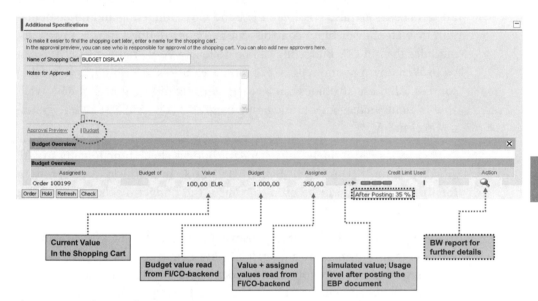

Figure 9.20 Budget Display in SAP SRM

In our example in Figure 9.20, there is a budget of **1.000,000** EUR and the shopping cart **Value** is **100,000 EUR**. The **Assigned** field displays the total budget value, which includes the shopping cart value plus the budget read from the FI/CO back-end system, in our case **350,000**. The **Credit Limit Used** field provides a simulated view of the budget usage. If the budget is exceeded, this field will show a simulated value in red.

> **Note**
>
> The budget check illustrated in Figure 9.20 does not take into consideration shopping carts that are awaiting approval or in the sourcing cockpit. As there is no posting in SAP FI or FM for shopping carts, the budget check will not be 100 % accurate until this shopping cart converts into a requisition or purchase order.

In SAP, budgets can be maintained in CO, FM, or GM. SAP SRM provides standard functionality for budget checks across all of these areas.

The budget checks in CO are available only if the cost object is an internal order or a Work Breakdown Structure (WBS) element. The budget check for cost centers is only possible via a workaround of creating a statistical job order for a cost center or cost center group and then entering the cost center budget as a budget for this job order. Availability control will need to be activated for the job order and a CO substitution will need to be defined to post to the statistical order every time a posting is made to the cost center.

Budget checks are also possible in FM and GM. Budgeting and implementation of budget availability controls can be better defined in these two submodules than in CO. Budgeting can be done at a very granular level and can be broken down by the type of expense, area of responsibility, and funding sources. All these attributes can be defined using different master data available in funds management. Budgeting by grants is possible at a same granular level in GM.

Project teams can influence the standard budget check functionality in SAP SRM by using the BAdI BBP_BUDGET_CHECK. In addition, **Authorization for Budget Display** can be used to control the budget display using object BBP_BUDGET.

In the event that your organization uses a non-SAP back end where financials are managed, you need to understand how commitments are handled for shopping carts and other purchasing documents. In this scenario, a commitment is simulated and the budget is checked using a remote function call (RFC). No commitment is written to the database. After the shopping cart is saved, it is transferred to the respective back-end. A commitment is created depending upon the setting used in the back-end, for example **Purchase Requisition Commitment** or **Purchase Order Commitment**.

In the next section, we will discuss how SRM integrates with Project Systems and finance. Readers will learn that structural cost assignments in project systems such as WBS elements and networks can be used for purchase activity in SAP SRM.

9.5   Integration with Project Systems

Both large-scale projects such as building a factory and small-scale projects such as organizing a trade fair require precise planning of the many detailed activities involved. To be able to control all tasks in project execution, clear, unambiguous project structure is the basis for successful project planning, monitoring, and control. The Project Systems (PS) module in SAP provides the functionality to plan, execute, monitor, and control the various phases within a project. A project in SAP can be structured in two different views:

▶ By structures, using WBS

▶ By process, using individual activities (Work Packages)

Users in SAP SRM have the ability to use structural cost assignments created in project systems (WBS and Networks) when requesting goods and services in the shopping cart or purchase order. Figure 9.21 illustrates this within the shopping-cart transaction. In the **Cost Assignment** area of the shopping cart, users can select the **WBS element** or Network account assignment in the account assignment dropdown menu. In our example, the WBS element **C.000.00.0011.1** is used which is a **TEST PROJECT**.

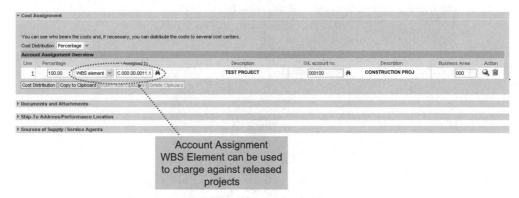

Figure 9.21 Cost Assignment — WBS for Project-Related Purchases

Organizations could have varying requirements when it comes to procurement of goods and services. Depending on the business requirement in project systems, there can be a few different methods of integrating PS with SAP SRM. Some options exist.

Let's describe each of these options aided by Figures 9.22, 9.23, 9.24, and 9.25. These figures contain the process flow, advantages, and disadvantages of each of the options listed for integrating PS with SAP SRM. Please note that these options are valid based on certain business requirements. It is entirely possible for project teams to define another option to fulfill the unique needs of their business processes. Let's review these options now:

▶ **Option 1: Create purchase orders in SAP R/3 directly, with no integration to SRM**

This is illustrated in Figure 9.22.

▶ **Option 2: Create shopping carts in SRM, with purchase order creation in SAP R/3 (Classic Scenario)**

This is illustrated in Figure 9.23.

▶ **Option 3: Create shopping carts and purchase orders in SRM (Extended Classic scenario)**

This is illustrated in Figure 9.24.

▶ **Option 4: Create requisition in SAP R/3 and purchase order in SRM (External Procurement business scenario)**

This is illustrated in Figure 9.25.

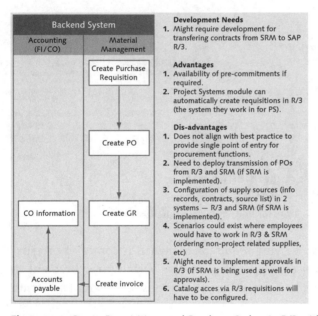

Figure 9.22 Create Requisitions and Purchase Orders in R/3 with No Integration to SRM

You should understand that when using the Extended Classic scenario a requisition cannot be created in SAP R/3. Therefore a pre-commitment cannot be created in SAP, and it is impossible to display funds usage.

In the next section, we will discuss the functionality gap in SAP SRM when implementing the Extended Classic scenario and the SAP Public Sector solution. I will also provide a workaround solution that companies can develop to overcome this gap in functionality.

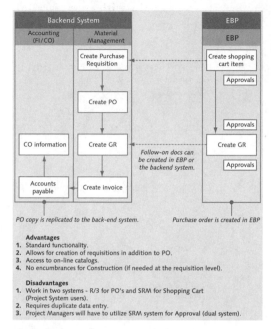

Figure 9.23 Create Shopping Carts in SRM, with a Purchase-Order Creation in SAP R/3

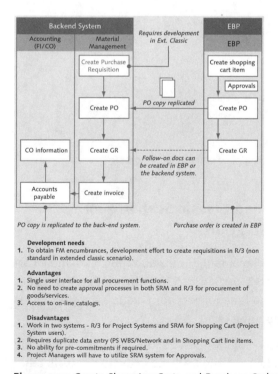

Figure 9.24 Create Shopping Carts and Purchase Orders in SRM

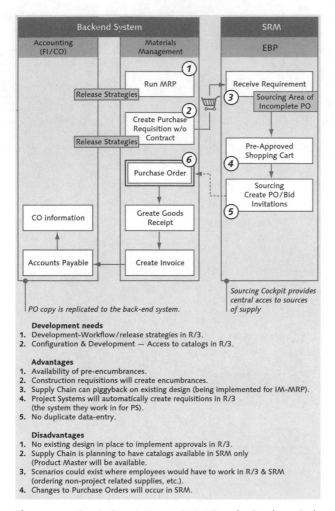

Figure 9.25 Create Requisition in SAP R/3 and a Purchase Order in SRM

9.6 Limitation of Extended Classic Scenario for SAP Public Sector Solution

In the Extended Classic scenario implementation, a shopping cart and a corresponding purchase order are both created in SRM. Only a purchase order copy is sent to SAP R/3. There is no functionality for creating a requisition as a follow-on document to the shopping cart.

Organizations using the Industry Solution EA-PS (Public Sector) typically implement the FM and GM modules within SAP and activate the availability control for budget check.

9.6.1 Identified Gap

The following bullet points explain the gap that exists for organizations that implement SAP SRM in an extended classic scenario and are using the SAP PS solution:

▶ Shopping carts do not consume budget in SAP R/3, only the documents transferred to R/3, such as purchase requisitions or purchase orders, consume budget.

▶ In Extended Classic, no purchase requisitions are allowed for creation in SAP R/3. Additionally, the shopping carts are not identified as a separate activity type within FM or GM availability control configuration in R/3. Thus, no special availability controls can be configured for a shopping cart.

▶ As the shopping carts are created in SRM and are not transferred to R/3, there is no visibility of these transactions in FM and GM reports.

9.6.2 Solution Approach

SAP does not offer any standard solutions for the identified gap, therefore organizations implementing the Extended Classic scenario will need to develop a customized solution to meet their pre-commitment and AVC needs.

One approach for development is to use the earmarked funds document (funds reservation) document in SAP R/3 for encumbrances based on the shopping carts created in SAP SRM. These funds reservations would provide the appropriate pre-commitment and visibility in SAP FM.

The essential aspect of this customized solution is that the shopping cart and funds reservation in R/3 have to be kept in sync at the various stages and statuses of the documents in SAP SRM. Figure 9.26 illustrates what happens when the funds reservation is updated in SAP R/3 at shopping cart creation, shopping cart change, approval, sourcing, PO creation, and PO change.

Organizations planning to undertake this development need to be aware that the most important phase of this development is testing. There are numerous scenarios when the shopping cart and subsequent documents in SRM are updated. The changes all need to be kept in sync with the corresponding funds reservation document in SAP R/3. The largest single amount of time in this solution is spent during the testing phase.

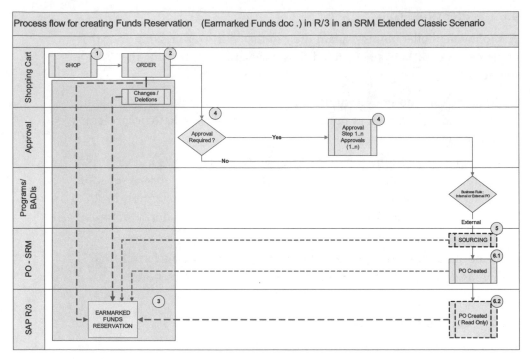

Figure 9.26 Process Flow for the Customized Solution Approach

If you are interested in funds reservation/encumbrance as it relates to shopping carts and SAP SRM Extended Classic scenario you should review Chapter 17. Here you will find information about the planned functionality for shopping cart-based encumbrances in the Government Procurement solution.

In the next section, I will review relevant OSS notes that deal with the integration of SAP SRM with SAP Financials.

9.7 Relevant OSS Notes

Table 9.1 lists important OSS Notes available on the SAP Service Marketplace that are relevant for readers when working with the Account Assignment, Budget Check, and Commitment in SRM. For example, OSS Note 815849 provides a FAQ on the system behaviour when using the Account Assignments in SAP SRM.

Note	Description
815849	FAQ: Account assignment system response
520717	Budget Check in EBP
828231	Commitments in SRM
524670	Budget display in EBP

Table 9.1 OSS Notes and Descriptions

9.8 Summary

In this chapter, I discussed the integration of SAP SRM with SAP Financials. I also reviewed the integration of SRM with SAP Funds Management and Grants Management. The real-time integration of SAP SRM with SAP Financials is the core strength for the solution; G/L validations and Budget checks are examples of the close integration between the two solutions.

In Chapter 10, I will introduce the concept of workflow in SAP SRM. We will begin with a discussion on what workflow means and then delve into how SAP SRM uses workflow to promote seamless and efficient work processes.

The efficient flow of work processes within an organization can not only improve how business documents and actions are processed, but can also provide the controls necessary for businesses today.

10 The Role of Workflow in SAP SRM

An efficient flow of work processes within an organization can create wonders in optimizing the entire process. It provides consistency, reduces wasted follow-up time, enables process standardization, and provides organizational audit and control. Software-based workflow in its simplest terms is: automated flow of work processes, where-by events, actions and documents are routed to responsible users and groups for their review or action.

A simple workflow example in a procure-to-pay process could be the routing of a purchase order (PO) for a computer purchase to your departmental team for review and to your manager for approval or rejection, as shown in Figure 10.1.

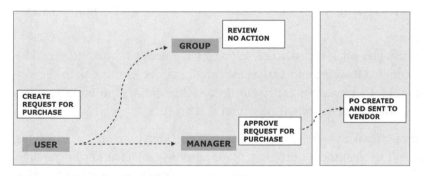

Figure 10.1 Example of Workflow in Procure-to-Pay Process

In many organizations, the routing of the requisition or PO as shown in Figure 10.1 is a paper-based non-automated process. This process at times could take one to two weeks for completion. A supplier relationship management system automates such work processes to reduce the wasted time and retain an electronic audit trail that can be reviewed at any time. Automating this process using workflow can reduce the approval time to less than one day. This achieves an efficiency factor of more than 10 days.

Let's review Figure 10.2, which is similar to Figure 10.1 but depicts a technical process flow. In this example, multiple parts of a workflow work together to define a concise and legible process flow.

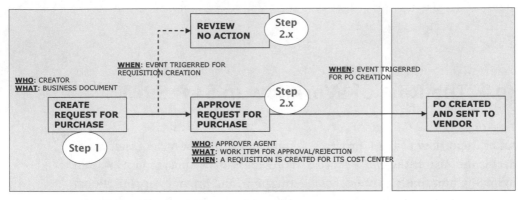

Figure 10.2 Event-Driven Workflow

The end user creating a purchase request is triggering an event (*When*). This event causes workflow to take action and determine *What* needs to be done next, which creates a new task of creating a work-item for the manager to approve or reject the request. The manager in this scenario then is the *Who* and is responsible for executing the task. Each of the *whats, whens,* and *whos* need to be determined. In addition to tasks that need to be executed by users, there are a number of tasks that execute in the background based on events.

In our example, once the manager approves the user's request to purchase the computer, a **Background Task** is executed that passes the task to the system program to create a purchase order. At this point, the workflow has completed all the steps contained within this process.

A common mistake made by organizations embarking on a project involving workflow is to treat the workflow activities on the project as entirely technical or development related. Too often, only development resources are allocated for this effort; the functional processes that make up the work effort are left unrecognized. It is important to recognize that the technical or development aspect of workflow only provide automation.

Unless the underlying core process are thoroughly reviewed and designed by the business, however, the workflow automation could be a waste. The functional knowledge experts need to build the process maps with detailed workflows of documents, events, and actions with the assistance of their workflow experts. Remember: Unless you can clearly define what a manager does with a time-entry workflow activity, the workflow itself is useless.

Workflow in SAP is an event driven chain of process that answers the questions of who, what, and when as discussed in the example seen in Figure 10.2. Each link in the chain, once completed, leads to the next step or task and a request for action (user-driven or system-driven).

Figure 10.3 provides an overview of the activities that work together within the SAP Business Workflow. In SAP SRM, there are a number of **Business Objects** such as the shopping cart business object BUS2121 or the PO business object BUS2201. In these business objects, an **Event** such as ordering a shopping cart or changing a PO could trigger the start of workflow. At this point, the **Attributes** of the business object are checked, and the workflow system will **Evaluate Starting Conditions** to check whether a workflow **Task** should be generated.

Example

When a shopping cart is ordered, the workflow system evaluates the start conditions for the shopping cart business object BUS2121 to evaluate whether an approval task is required. The workflow system then makes a decision to generate either a **user decision task** or a **background task**. The user decision requires an action from an end user (lets say a department manager) and the background task assigns a specific status to the Business Object. At this point the workflow process is complete until the next **Event** is triggered.

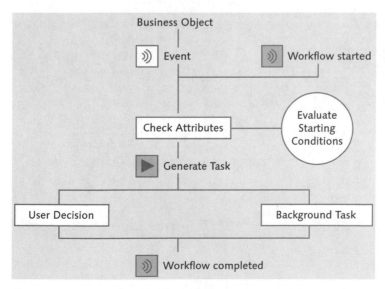

Figure 10.3 SAP Business Workflow (Source: SAP America)

This chapter will focus on the role of workflow specifically in SAP SRM. It will provide an understanding of how the various processes in SAP use workflow. SAP provides a number of standard workflow templates for SAP SRM which can be used out-of-the-box without any development. For a detailed learning on workflow development, read the SAP PRESS book *Practical Workflow for SAP* by Alan Rickayzen.

10.1 Workflow in SAP SRM

If you are familiar with business workflow in SAP, you will find some pleasant changes in the workflow delivered in SAP SRM. The workflow design is much more user-friendly and intuitive within SRM. SAP has created many standard workflow templates for different processes existing in SAP SRM. Organizations can select the appropriate templates, activate them, and be ready to use automated workflow without writing a single line of code. In other words, SRM offers out-of-box workflows.

In addition to the standard templates, SRM offers a graphical start-condition editor that does not exist in the core SAP R/3 system. This condition editor provides the ability to start a particular workflow template via configurable business rules. Figure 10.4 shows a preview of the condition editor. This figure shows that, unlike typical R/3 workflow, no development is required but only logic based on operators.

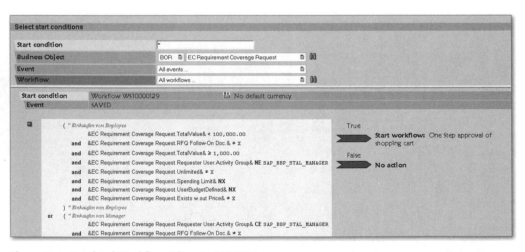

Figure 10.4 Graphical Workflow Editor in SAP SRM

Hence, I tend to use the term *workflow* when the requirement in SRM is configurable and does not necessarily require development. On the other hand, if the standard templates are not sufficient for your organization approval requirements, then development is inevitable. In order to allow organizations to enhance the standard delivered workflows in SRM, SAP has provided a few workflow Business Add-Ins (BAdIs). These BAdIs enable the use of standard delivered workflow templates but still enhance them using additional business rules applicable to the organization.

Another distinguishing factor of workflow in SRM is the ability for users to easily enhance the workflow process at runtime. Users can supplement the process by using a standard delivered anchor concept called *ad-hoc* approval. This anchor concept enables the addition of approval steps; users can add approvers and reviewers on the fly. Figure 10.5 provides an example of the ad-hoc approval functionality.

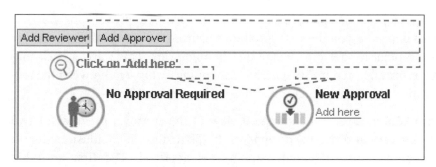

AD-HOC APPROVAL:APPROVAL PROCESS DID NOT REQUIRE APPROVAL, -
BUT AN APPROVER/REVIEWER CAN BE ADDED USING ANCHOR CONCEPT

Figure 10.5 Ad-Hoc Approval Functionality; Anchor Concept in SAP SRM

In the approval preview, the approval status shows **No Approval Required**, which means that no system generated approvals have been determined. At this point, the end user can click the **Add Approver** or **Add Reviewer** buttons to add an approver. All standard delivered workflow templates are pre-delivered with the functionality of ad-hoc insertion. Organizations that want to leverage the standard workflow templates and don't want any additional custom development can use the ad-hoc functionality to provide flexibility to their users to add approval steps at any point in the approval process.

The basic premise in SRM is self-service for the end user; it aims to empower end-users so that they not only can initiate the purchasing process but also determine the status of their purchasing documents at any given time. An example of the end user could be a requisitioner who creates a shopping cart to request office suppliers. Using the **Approval Preview** function in the **Shop** and **Check Status** application, the requisitioner can review the status of the approval steps for their shopping cart. Workflow in SRM contains a graphical Java applet for status visualization, which provides a simplified view of workflow in the Web browser.

This applet allows the end user see the current status of the entire approval process and if necessary determine who to follow up with or review any roadblocks. No additional changes or setup are required on the user's desktop; the SAP NetWeaver platform provides the required Java runtime engine.

The ability to preview the approval workflow provides an additional opportunity for users to make changes to the approvers prior to executing the work item. Figure 10.5 provides an example of the approval preview status visualization applet. During the creation of a shopping cart, a preview of the approval is available.

After saving the shopping cart, one of the active approval workflows is started depending on the start conditions. During the approval, the approver and the requisitioner can change the shopping cart. This starts a back-and-forth approval functionality where the shopping cart is sent between the requisitioner and the approver until approved or rejected.

Figure 10.6 illustrates the graphical view of the approval preview for two shopping carts and two PO documents. In the first example, illustrated by **1**, the shopping cart triggered a multi-level approval. The first level has approved and is shown as **Shopping Cart Approved by** along with the name of the approver, date, and time. The next approver is shown under **In approval since,** along with date and time. In the third example, illustrated by **3,** the PO was approved by the first approver in the chain but rejected by the second approver and the final status of the shopping cart is shown as **Result: Rejected**. Beginning from SAP SRM 6.0 the graphical view is no longer supported.

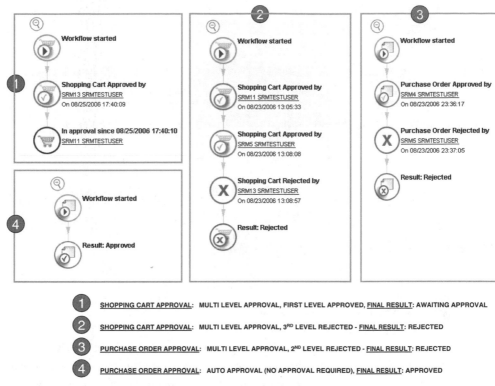

1. **SHOPPING CART APPROVAL:** MULTI LEVEL APPROVAL, FIRST LEVEL APPROVED, FINAL RESULT: AWAITING APPROVAL

2. **SHOPPING CART APPROVAL:** MULTI LEVEL APPROVAL, 3RD LEVEL REJECTED - FINAL RESULT: REJECTED

3. **PURCHASE ORDER APPROVAL:** MULTI LEVEL APPROVAL, 2ND LEVEL REJECTED - FINAL RESULT: REJECTED

4. **PURCHASE ORDER APPROVAL:** AUTO APPROVAL (NO APPROVAL REQUIRED), FINAL RESULT: APPROVED

Figure 10.6 Example of Visualization of the Approval in SAP SRM

Beginning with SAP SRM Release 4.0, a tabular view of approval preview is available as an alternate to the graphical Java applet view. The main aim of the graphical or tabular view in SRM is to provide an end user with an easy to understand approval flow. Figure 10.7 illustrates the tabular view of the Approval Preview function. The view in Figure 10.7 shows the same example as shown in Figure 10.6 but in a table format. In the first example, illustrated by **1**, the approval preview shows that **Level 1 Approval** approved the shopping cart and the shopping cart **Status** is **Awaiting Approval by**.

In the fourth example, illustrated by **4**, there was no approval needed and therefore the **Approval Preview** shows **Document Approved** which is a system status.

One aspect of workflow in SRM that users find confusing is that there are a number of business transactions based on the workflow process. In other words, the workflow engine is a requirement for the core business transactions to function at all.

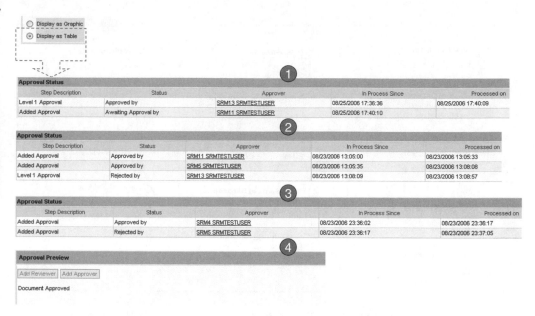

Figure 10.7 Example of Visualization in Table Format

A good example is the basic shopping cart transaction "shop." Let's say that the organization decides not to introduce any shopping cart workflow processes during the sandbox phase in order to quickly build a demo environment. The shopping cart transactions will not function until the standard workflow environment is set up and a specific "no-approval" workflow is configured to indicate that no approvals are required for the shopping cart application. This is not the case when working in the SAP R/3 environment creating requisitions or POs.

With SAP Business Workflow, you can define whether shopping carts are subject to an approval procedure in the Enterprise Buyer (EBP) system and the criteria that decide which shopping carts are to be approved. Similarly, there are conditions for approval of POs, confirmations, PO responses, invoices, contracts, and other business documents.

In the start conditions in Customizing, you can define which workflow is started under what conditions. As SAP offers multiple workflows for the same business transaction (e.g., shopping cart), a selection needs to be made to activate workflows used and inactivate workflows not being used. This way the system is able to provide flexibility in selection and use of approval workflows. Figure 10.8 illustrates this in a simple diagram.

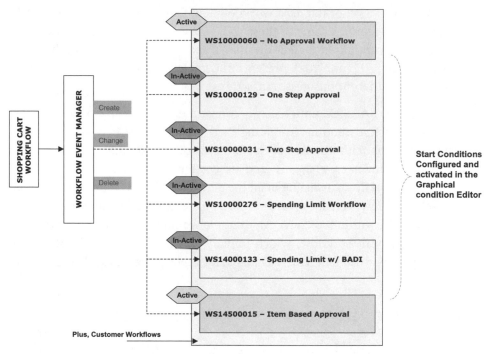

Figure 10.8 Activation of Workflow Templates to Trigger Required Workflows

In the example shown in Figure 10.8, I show that there are active and in-Active workflows within the system. The starting conditions were only activated for the WS14500015 and WS10000060 workflows. Therefore, when the shopping cart is created, changed or deleted, the WORKFLOW EVENT MANAGER reviews the conditions defined to determine the active workflow template and rules to be triggered. This process of activation and in-activation is required to setup many of the business transactions in SRM.

Now that I have provided an overview of the workflow functionality, let us learn about the standard workflow templates that are pre-delivered in SAP SRM.

10.2   Standard Delivered workflows in SRM

As discussed earlier, SAP provides a standard set of workflow templates that can be used out-of-the-box in SRM without the need for any development. Before we discuss the standard workflows, let's briefly review the business transactions in SRM from which the events and workflow engine are triggered.

SAP provides a set of standard workflow templates ready for use. The workflow system requires some of these to be activated while others can be activated and configured based on the organization's needs and business requirements. Figure 10.9 presents the major workflow templates used within the different business transactions.

Workflow in SAP SRM until recently concentrated on the approval templates within the requisitioning (shopping cart) process more than on any other process. Although there had been a basic workflow for shopping carts, confirmations, invoices, etc., SAP and its customers had not really used the approval workflows available in all the SRM processes. Over the past couple of releases, however, approval workflows have expanded in all the purchase-to-pay cycles within SAP SRM. An example would be the introduction of the n-step approval workflow, which initially was used only for the shopping carts. The approval template is available for other processes such as purchase orders.

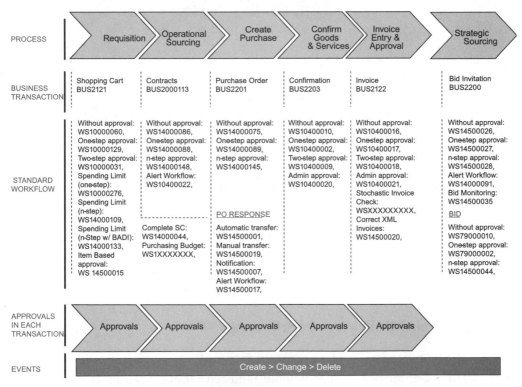

Figure 10.9 Standard Workflow Templates

The n-Step approval workflow enabled organizations to create a multi-level approval process, not restricted to just a single step or two steps. Using the n-Step workflow template, organizations can use their own business rules to determine how many approvers will be triggered in the approval chain: 1 through n. Notice in Figure 10.9 that for some applications SAP still provides one-step and two-step templates as a standard.

Let us review the approval flow within the purchase-to-pay process. Figure 10.10 provides an illustration of this approval flow.

Approval Process Flow

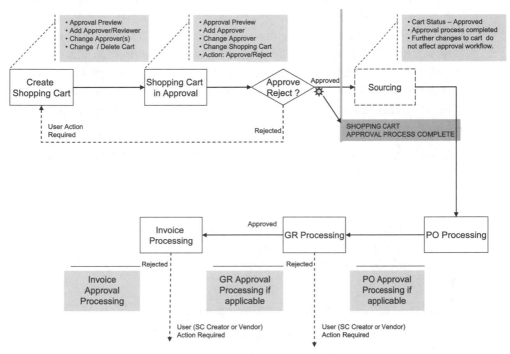

Figure 10.10 Self-Service Procurement Business Scenario Approval Process

In Figure 10.10, the functionality available in the shopping cart approval (**Approval Preview**, **Add Approver/Reviewer**, **Change Approver(s)**, etc.) is also available during **PO Processing**, **GR Processing**, and **Invoice Processing** steps that are not shown in the figure.

> **Note**
>
> During the sourcing step, the shopping cart status is approved, and the approval process is complete for the shopping cart. Any changes that are done to the shopping cart in the sourcing application do not affect the approval workflow.

10.2.1 Shopping Cart Workflows

In Figure 10.9 I provided a list of all the standard workflow templates pre-delivered in SAP SRM. In this section, I will concentrate on the workflow templates pre-delivered for the Shopping Cart application.

I will discuss each of the standard shopping cart workflows in detail, beginning with the No Approval workflow.

No Approval Workflow (WS10000060)

In SRM, business documents such as shopping carts, POs, and confirmations require the workflow environment to be configured whether approval workflows are going to be used for that document or not. The No Approval workflow, also called *workflow without approval*, allows the creation of a shopping cart without the need for any subsequent approval or manager intervention. Once the requisitioner completes the shopping cart, the status of the document is changed to approved, and the control is passed to the follow-on function of sourcing or PO creation.

Most organizations use the No Approval workflow for purchases that are usually below a certain dollar threshold (e.g., all purchases of less than $500). Also, shopping carts that involve the purchase of direct materials for inventory or reservations are usually not subject to any approvals. Figure 10.11 illustrates the flow for the **Without Approval** workflow template (WS10000060). Note that the **Business Rules** signify the workflow starting conditions that are defined as a part of Customizing.

One-Step Approval Workflow (WS10000129)

The One-Step Approval workflow template (WS10000129) triggers the approval by a manager or supervisor of the shopping-cart creator. When this approval template is used, only a single approver step is determined by the system. All additional approvers need to be added to the approval flow using the add approver functionality discussed earlier in this chapter. Figure 10.12 illustrates that, based on the workflow Business Rules, the One-Step workflow is started and the system determines the requestor's manager as the shopping cart approver. The manager or supervisor is determined based on the hierarchy defined in the organization structure in SRM. The One-Step approval does not take into account any spending or approval limits.

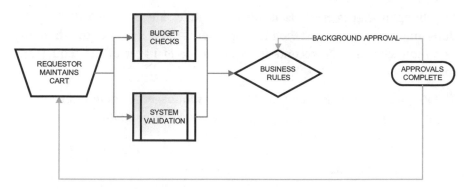

NO APPROVAL WORKFLOW (Without Approval)

1. NO APPROVAL IS REQUIRED
    - BUSINESS RULES DEFINE CONDITIONS
    IN WHICH NO APPROVALS ARE NEEDED

2. STATUS OF THE SHOPPING CART SET TO *'RELEASED'*

3. THE SUBSEQUENT DOCUMENT "FOR EXAMPLE A
    PURCHASE ORDER" IS CREATED

Figure 10.11 No Approval Workflow (Workflow Without Approval)

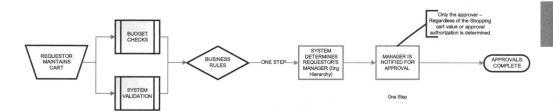

ONE STEP HIERARCHY WORKFLOW

1. THE REQUESTOR'S MANAGER APPROVES THE
    SHOPPING CART

2. THE REQUESTOR MANAGER IS DETERMINED
    BASED ON THE HIERARCHY DEFINED IN THE
    ORGANIZATION STRUCTURE

3. USER SPENDING AND APPROVER LIMITS ARE NOT
    TAKEN INTO CONSIDERATION FOR APPROVALS

4. IN ORGANIZATION STRUCTURE– THE "ORG CHIEF"
    FUNCTIONALITY IS UTILIZED TO DETERMINE
    MANAGERS

**WORKFLOW TEMPLATE:
WS10000129**

Figure 10.12 One-Step Approval Workflow

Two-Step Approval Workflow (WS10000031)

The Two-Step Approval workflow template (**WS10000031**) functions exactly the same as the One-Step Approval workflow except that the system determines two system approvers instead of one. Figure 10.13 shows that once the shopping cart is created and Business Rules are evaluated, the system determines two approvers: the first approver is the manager of the shopping cart requestor, and the second approver is the manager of the requestor's manager.

The **Requestor's Manager** and the **Manager's Manager** are determined based on the hierarchy defined in the organization structure in SRM.

TWO STEP HIERARCHY WORKFLOW

1. THE REQUESTOR'S MANAGER APPROVES THE SHOPPING CART

2. THE MANAGER OF THE REQUESTOR'S MANAGER IS APPROVES THE CART AS A SECOND APPROVER

2. THE REQUESTOR MANAGER & MANAGER'S MANAGER ARE DETERMINED BASED ON THE HIERARCHY DEFINED IN THE ORGANIZATION STRUCTURE

3. USER SPENDING AND APPROVER LIMITS ARE NOT TAKEN INTO CONSIDERATION FOR APPROVALS

4. IN ORGANIZATION STRUCTURE– THE "ORG CHIEF" FUNCTIONALITY IS UTILIZED TO DETERMINE MANAGERS

WORKFLOW TEMPLATE: WS10000031

Figure 10.13 Two-Step Hierarchy Workflow

Spending Limit for Shopping Cart (WS10000276)

This approval workflow was introduced in EBP 3.0 and was very well accepted within organizations, as they valued the ability to assign approval and spending thresholds to individuals within the organization. Most organizations have financial structures already in place, typically within the controller's office, that provide a spending authorization matrix based on structure within the organization (e.g., job levels or categories).

Figure 10.14 illustrates that once the **BUSINESS RULES** are evaluated and the **SPENDING LIMIT APPROVAL** workflow is started, the workflow system determines the approver based on the total value of the shopping cart and the spending limit of the approver. This workflow is also known as *Single-Step Approval Over Limit* because only a single approver is determined with the final authority for approval based on his or her approval limit.

In the Organizational Structure in Enterprise Buyer, each user is assigned a **SLAPPROVER** attribute. This attribute is used to designate the Spending Limit Approver (SLA).

In addition, each requisitioner is assigned a spending limit, and each approver is assigned an approval limit. The limits can be assigned to users either directly in the user master Transaction (SU01) or via a role assignment. SAP provides two object keys BBP_APPROVAL_LIMIT and BBP_SPENDING_LIMIT to capture the actual values for the approval and spending limit. These object keys are within the personalization tab that exists in the user master or user role.

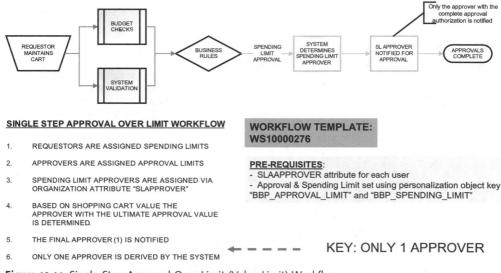

SINGLE STEP APPROVAL OVER LIMIT WORKFLOW

1. REQUESTORS ARE ASSIGNED SPENDING LIMITS

2. APPROVERS ARE ASSIGNED APPROVAL LIMITS

3. SPENDING LIMIT APPROVERS ARE ASSIGNED VIA ORGANIZATION ATTRIBUTE "SLAPPROVER"

4. BASED ON SHOPPING CART VALUE THE APPROVER WITH THE ULTIMATE APPROVAL VALUE IS DETERMINED.

5. THE FINAL APPROVER (1) IS NOTIFIED

6. ONLY ONE APPROVER IS DERIVED BY THE SYSTEM

WORKFLOW TEMPLATE: WS10000276

PRE-REQUISITES:
- SLAAPPROVER attribute for each user
- Approval & Spending Limit set using personalization object key "BBP_APPROVAL_LIMIT" and "BBP_SPENDING_LIMIT"

← − − − − **KEY: ONLY 1 APPROVER**

Figure 10.14 Single-Step Approval Over Limit (Value Limit) Workflow

I use Figures 10.15 and 10.16 to illustrate an example of how the spending limit workflow works in SAP SRM. In Figure 10.15, a matrix has been provided which contains 10 roles. Each role has been assigned the same spending and approval limit. Therefore, the user assigned the role of **Spending/Approval limit Role 3** has a spending limit of $50,000 and an approval limit of $5,000. Therefore, if this user creates a shopping cart with a total value of $5,000, no approval workflow will be required.

Now, let us review Figure 10.16. It illustrates a hierarchy of an organizational structure where the **Requisitioner** has an SLAPPROVER attribute as the **HR Department Administrator** who has an SLAPPROVER attribute as the **HR Department Manager** and so forth.

Role Name	Spending and Approval Limit
Spending/Approval limit Role 1	$0.00
Spending/Approval limit Role 2	$2,500.00
Spending/Approval limit Role 3	$5,000.00
Spending/Approval limit Role 4	$25,000.00
Spending/Approval limit Role 5	$50,000.00
Spending/Approval limit Role 6	$100,000.00
Spending/Approval limit Role 7	$250,000.00
Spending/Approval limit Role 8	$500,000.00
Spending/Approval limit Role 9	$1,000,000.00
Spending/Approval limit Role 10	> $1,000,000.00

Figure 10.15 Example: Spending or Approval Limit Matrix for Single-Step Approval Workflow

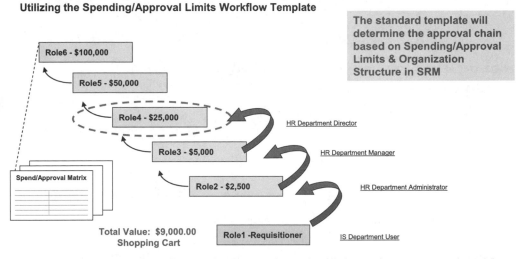

Figure 10.16 Example: Spending/Approval Limit Matrix for Single-Step Approval Workflow

The requisitioner has been assigned **Role 1**, which according to Figure 10.15 assigns a $0.00 spending and approval limit to this user. Now, assume that the requisitioner creates a shopping cart with a **Total Value** of **$9,000**. As the requisitioner has a $0.00 spending limit, an approval is required. The workflow system will evaluate the role hierarchy illustrated in Figure 10.16 and determine that only a user with **Role 4** has the authorization to approve this shopping cart because users with **Role 3** only have authorization to approve up to $5,000. Therefore the **HR Department Director** will receive the shopping cart for approval action.

The spending limit workflow template gives organizations an avenue to not just rely on the organizational structure hierarchy but also use the financial authority matrix that is prevalent in many organizations.

The obvious shortcoming of this workflow template is that only one approver is eventually determined; this shortcoming can be overcome with the N-Step Spending Over Limit workflow template introduced in EBP 3.5 (illustrated in Figure 10.17).

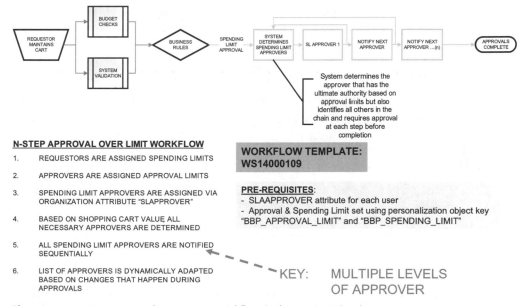

N-STEP APPROVAL OVER LIMIT WORKFLOW

1. REQUESTORS ARE ASSIGNED SPENDING LIMITS

2. APPROVERS ARE ASSIGNED APPROVAL LIMITS

3. SPENDING LIMIT APPROVERS ARE ASSIGNED VIA ORGANIZATION ATTRIBUTE "SLAPPROVER"

4. BASED ON SHOPPING CART VALUE ALL NECESSARY APPROVERS ARE DETERMINED

5. ALL SPENDING LIMIT APPROVERS ARE NOTIFIED SEQUENTIALLY

6. LIST OF APPROVERS IS DYNAMICALLY ADAPTED BASED ON CHANGES THAT HAPPEN DURING APPROVALS

WORKFLOW TEMPLATE: WS14000109

PRE-REQUISITES:
- SLAAPPROVER attribute for each user
- Approval & Spending Limit set using personalization object key "BBP_APPROVAL_LIMIT" and "BBP_SPENDING_LIMIT"

KEY: MULTIPLE LEVELS OF APPROVER

Figure 10.17 N-Step Approval Over Limit Workflow (Value Limit, N-Step)

N-Step Value Limit Approval Workflow (WS14000109)

The N-Step Approval workflow is based on the same concept as the Spending Limit Approval workflow template WS10000276. The SLAPPROVER attribute, the object key's BBP_APPROVAL_LIMIT and BBP_SPENDING_LIMIT are required to assign users' spending and approval limits. The difference is that the N-Step Approval Over Limit workflow provides a multi-step approval.

If we use the same example illustrated in Figure 10.16 and use the N-Step Approval template, the $9,000 shopping cart will result in three approvers instead of just one. Basically, the shopping cart will require an approval from the **HR Department Administrator** and then the **HR Department Manager,** and the final approver will be **HR Department Director**.

Item Level Approval Workflow (WS14500015)

With each release of SAP SRM, new workflows have been introduced. Beginning with the SAP SRM 4.0 release, SAP has provided support for shopping-cart approval functionality at an item level instead of for the total as in previous releases. This is a direct result of development requests entered by many organizations that were already using SAP SRM and recognized the need to determine approvers for individual items within a shopping cart. In item-level approval, only approvers responsible for their respective items act on it. Organizations that are using the item-level approval workflow are most commonly using it for determination of approvers by one of the following criteria:

► Cost center-based approver at individual item level
► Product category-based approver for selected commodities such as safety and radiation, capital items, etc.

Table 10.1 compares the item-level approval with the classic shopping cart approval.

Classic Shopping Cart Approval	Item-Level Approval
All items in the shopping cart require approval from each approver determined.	Approvers are only responsible for select items in the shopping cart and act on those individually.
Approvers receive all items.	Approvers receive select items.
Either the entire shopping cart requires approval or none.	Certain items in the shopping cart might not require any approval and are presented as *status approved*.
The follow-on documents (e.g., requisition, PO) are not created until the entire shopping cart is approved.	As with the classic approval, a follow-on document is created only after all the items in the shopping cart are approved

Table 10.1 Item-Level Workflow Compared to Standard Shopping Cart Workflow

Figure 10.18 illustrates the item-level approval in comparision with the standard shopping-cart approval. Note how the approvers are sequentially determined in the classic approval logic and in the item-level approval, approvers are determined based on the individual items.

In order to use the Item Level workflow, the template WS14500015 needs to be triggered in the workflow Customizing (TCode: /SWB_COND). Also note that this workflow can only be used if implemented in conjunction with the BAdI: BBP_WFL_APPROV_BAdI. The BAdI allows organizations to specify required business rules to determine approvers such by cost centers and product categories.

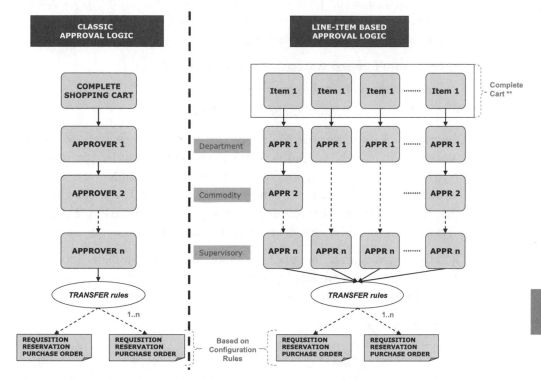

Figure 10.18 Item Level Approval Workflow

Tip

One key aspect of this workflow that project teams need to be especially aware of is that the Item Level workflow is never restarted. In other words, the authorization levels of LOW and MEDIUM in BBP_WFL_SECURITY personalization object key do not have relevance in this workflow.

Note

In SAP SRM 6.0, The BBP_WFL_APPROV BAdI is obsolete. A manual migration will be required by organizations.

Shopping Cart Completion Workflow (WS14000044)

In the procurement process, there are a number of scenarios where the requisitioner is only able to define the need for a particular item, and is unable to determine the appropriate price and vendor. In such cases, the professional buyers need to intervene. The Shopping Cart Completion work-flow — WS1000044 — provides the functionality for buyers to intervene in such scenarios and complete the shopping cart with the appropriate informa-tion prior to other approvals, such as financial approval. The following sce-narios can be considered for this workflow:

▶ Items with free text (vs. catalog or product based)

▶ Items where no price has been identified

▶ Items where no vendor has been identified

Figure 10.19 illustrates the Shopping Cart Completion workflow. In this workflow, the workflow Business Rules determine whether the shopping cart is complete. If the shopping cart is not found complete, an approval workflow is sent to the purchasing professional (buyer) who can complete the shopping cart. Once this is done, the requisitioner receives the shopping cart for review and can accept or reject the changes made by the purchaser.

It is important to note that once the shopping cart is complete, subsequent approval workflows can be triggered. Therefore, a secondary approval work-flow template can be determined based on the business rules in the system.

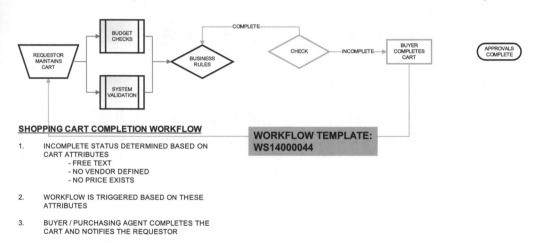

SHOPPING CART COMPLETION WORKFLOW

1. INCOMPLETE STATUS DETERMINED BASED ON CART ATTRIBUTES
   - FREE TEXT
   - NO VENDOR DEFINED
   - NO PRICE EXISTS

2. WORKFLOW IS TRIGGERED BASED ON THESE ATTRIBUTES

3. BUYER / PURCHASING AGENT COMPLETES THE CART AND NOTIFIES THE REQUESTOR

4. REQUESTOR AGREES & SUBSEQUENT APPROVALS ARE STARTED

WORKFLOW TEMPLATE: WS14000044

Figure 10.19 Shopping-Cart Completion Workflow

User Defined Budget Workflow (WS10000129)

The User Defined Budget workflow template was provided as an alternate workflow for organizations that need to trigger approvals based on individ-ual user budgets. It is important to recognize that these budgets have no relevance to the budgeting functionality in SAP-CO or SAP-FM. The user budget is set directly in SAP SRM. The system calculates the amount of budget spent for each user in a table (BBP_USRBDGT) and only when that exceeds the budget amount allocated for the user is an approval required. Figure 10.20 illustrates the User Defined Budget workflow.

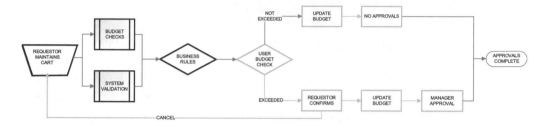

USER DEFINED BUDGETS

1. ARE DEFINED:
   - PER MONTH
   - PER QUARTER
   - PER ANNUM

2. USER'S SPEND TOTAL IS CAPTURED IN A TABLE AND ALL CARTS ARE CUMULATED AGAINST THIS TOTAL

3. WHEN BUDGET IS EXCEEDED A MESSAGE IS USED TO NOTIFY THE REQUESTOR

** THIS BUDGET CHECK IS DIFFERENT FROM THE FICO BUDGET CHECK AGAINST INTERNAL ORDERS or WBS ELEMENTS

WORKFLOW TEMPLATE:
WS10000129

PRE-REQUISITES:
- Define BUDGET Limit in Org Structure Extended attributes
OR in the
- User Budget personalization object key "BBP_USER_BUDGET"

Figure 10.20 User Defined Budget Workflow

I have explained the workflow templates available for the shopping cart application. In the upcoming subsections I will briefly introduce the workflows templates available for the other applications such as PO, and confirmation. The core concept of how these workflows operate is very similar to that used for the shopping cart.

10.2.2 Purchase Order Approval Workflows

Figure 10.21 illustrates three workflow templates that are pre-delivered in SAP SRM for approval of PO and PO changes (versions).

All these approval workflow templates are similar to the shopping cart workflow templates illustrated in the section above. The functionality for changes during approval, ad-hoc approver additions, etc. is similar to that for the shopping cart workflows. Using the start conditions in BBP_COND, organizations can set up business rules to trigger one of the above workflows.

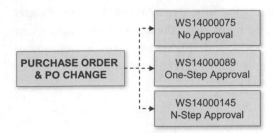

Figure 10.21 Approval Workflows for Purchase Orders and Changes (Versions)

The templates in Figure 10.21 can be triggered for both the PO creation and the PO changes. Each change to the PO can be saved into a different version document that can be compared.

> **Tip**
>
> The workflow template WS14000145 requires a BAdI implementation to enable the N-Step approval determination.

10.2.3 Confirmation Approval Workflows

Confirmations in SAP SRM can be entered by the shopping cart creator, a central receiver or even by a vendor. Based on who enters the confirmation, a specific workflow template can be triggered. Figure 10.22 illustrates four workflow templates that are pre-delivered in SAP SRM for approval of confirmations.

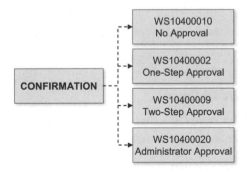

Figure 10.22 Standard Approval Templates for Confirmations

Organizations can use the start conditions in Transaction BBP_COND to set up business rules to trigger one of the workflows shown in Figure 10.22. In the standard solution, if a confirmation is created by the shopping cart creator, no approval is required. If the confirmation is created by the central receiver, an approval is required by the shopping cart creator. Finally, if the external vendor creates a confirmation, an approval of the confirmation is required by shopping cart creator. This is illustrated in Figure 10.23.

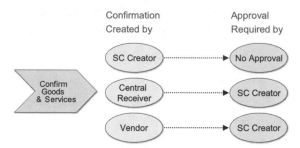

Figure 10.23 Confirmations in SAP SRM

10.2.4 Invoice Entry Approval Workflows

Most organizations that use SAP SRM still continue to use their SAP R/3 system to post and process invoices. However, organizations that use the invoice-entry functionality in SAP SRM can benefit from the standard workflow templates that come pre-delivered. The standard workflows templates pre-delivered in SAP SRM for approval of invoices are displayed in Figure 10.24.

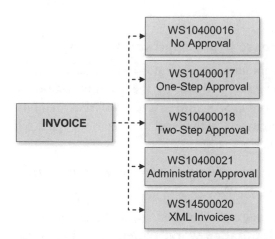

Figure 10.24 Standard Approval Templates for Approval of Invoices

Starting of the approval workflows above depends on the completion status, invoice category (credit memo or invoice), role, and total value of the invoice. Organizations can use the start conditions in Transaction BBP_ COND to set up Business Rules to trigger one of the workflows shown in Figure 10.24.

Invoices in SAP SRM can be entered by the shopping cart creator, an accounts-payable clerk, or even a vendor as illustrated in Figure 10.25. Based on who enters the confirmation, a separate workflow template can be triggered.

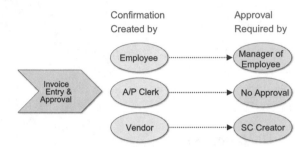

Figure 10.25 Approval of Invoices — Standard logic

If your organization receives electronic invoices in SAP SRM via XML, a separate workflow template can be triggered to handle the erroneous invoices. Instead of just sending the erroneous XML invoices back to the vendor, those invoices can be processed by the responsible employee using the **WS14500020** workflow template.

10.2.5 Purchase Order Response (POR) Approval Workflows

The PO Response (POR) document allows the vendor to provide a notification on the acceptance of the PO goods and service, the quantity and prices. These confirmations can be entered in SAP SRM in a few different methods: manually by the professional purchaser; by the vendor using the supplier self services component, or electronically via XML.

The standard workflows templates pre-delivered in SAP SRM for approval of PO response are illustrated in Figure 10.26

The workflow template **WS14500007** can be used as an alternative to the **WS14500019** template. If the **Notification** workflow template is used, the professional purchaser can be notified that a PO response is awaiting approval. An email is sent automatically to the responsible purchaser, and using the link in the email, he or she can review the PO response and take appropriate action.

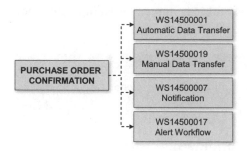

Figure 10.26 Purchase Order Confirmation Approval Workflow

Using the start conditions in the BBP_COND transaction, organizations can set up Business Rules such that the POR data is either transferred to the PO automatically or manually by the purchaser. For example, a tolerance can be set up in the starting conditions such that only PO responses with a variance above the tolerance are sent to the buyer for approval. All other PO responses are automatically transferred to the PO using the **Automatic Data Transfer** workflow.

10.2.6 Contracts and Contract Changes (Version) Workflows

The standard workflows templates pre-delivered in SAP SRM for approval of contracts or contract changes (versions) are illustrated in Figure 10.27

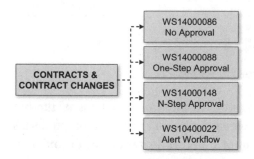

Figure 10.27 Contracts and Contract Changes (Version) Approval Worflows

The Workflow templates of **No Approval**, **One-Step**, and **N-Step** are similar in processing as the other shopping-cart workflows. For example, the One-Step Approval requires approval by the manager of the responsible purchasing organization to which the contract is assigned. Similar to the shopping cart one-step workflow, the entire contract needs to be approved and not just selected line items.

However, the Alert Workflow (**WS10400022**) is implemented in conjunction with SAP NetWeaver BI reporting and the Alert Monitor.

> **Tip**
>
> The Workflow template **WS14000148** requires a BAdI implementation to enable the N-Step Approval determination.

10.2.7 Bid Invitations and Bid Workflows

The standard workflow templates pre-delivered in SAP SRM for approval of bid invitation and bids are illustrated in Figure 10.28.

The **Alert Workflow** is used only when using external bid invitations in the context of auctions. When an auction event is in progress this workflow can keeps the bid-invitation creator notified of any errors during the auction or about the completion of the auction.

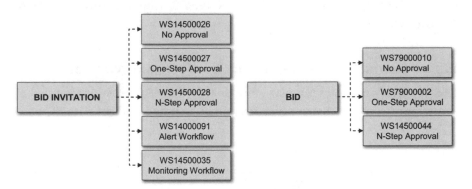

Figure 10.28 Bid Invitation and Bid Approval Workflows

The **Monitoring Workflow** is responsible to monitor the status of the bid invitation. This workflow is started when the buying organization publishes a bid invitation. At this time the Monitoring Workflow waits for the bid invitation to end. Once that happens, the system triggers a notification to the creator that the event has ended.

The **No Approval**, **One-Step,** and **N-Step** workflow templates work similarly to the shopping cart approval templates explained in Section 10.2.1.

10.2.8 Procurement Card Workflows

SAP SRM provides the functionality to use procurement card as a method of payment in the shopping cart. This allows organizations to streamline their processes of procurement and payment for small-dollar transactions. The following standard workflows are supplied by SAP in SAP SRM for approval of procurement card transactions.

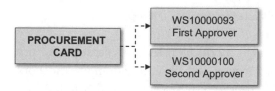

Figure 10.29 Approval Templates for Procurement Cards

The requisitioner is responsible for all approvals until the settlement value exceeds the limit specified in the customizing. All others are approved by the manager.

10.2.9 User Master and Vendor Master Workflows

Organizations that have many employees can reduce the work for their security team by allowing the employees to create their own user records. In this scenario, the employee can create a user record for himself or herself but requires the approval of his or her manager. If the manager approves the request, the user record is released and the employee receives the login information in his or her email. In this scenario, the manager within the organization decides whether their employees need access to the SAP SRM system. A standard workflow template called **New User** is provided for this scenario.

On the login page for SAP SRM, users have the ability to select the change password application. There are two approval templates available in SAP SRM for handling of password changes. The Forgotten Password Without Approval workflow (WS10000224) allows the user to request for the password change and receives a new password in email. Alternatively, the Forgotten Password Approval (**WS10000223**) is used, and a workflow is sent to the person defined in Customizing for approving password changes. If approved, an automatically generated password is sent to the user via email or else a rejection email is sent.

The standard workflow templates pre-delivered in SAP SRM for approval of user master records and vendor records are illustrated in Figure 10.30.

Figure 10.30 User Master and Vendor Master Approval Workflows

It is important to note that the majority of organizations already have processes in place for creation of user master records and seldom use the workflows illustrated in Figure 10.30. These are applicable to a few unique scenarios.

So far, we have talked about the need for workflow in SAP SRM and the pre-delivered templates that are available to organizations out-of-the-box. In the next section, I will explain the different options available for actually approving or rejecting the work items generated by these different workflows.

10.3   Online and Offline Approvals

So far we have been talking about the many different workflows that are available in SAP SRM. Assuming that you have selected the workflows that are relevant for use in your organization, we now need to learn how to actually take action when a work item is sent to an approver.

The term work item refers to a single workflow request on which the receiver needs to take an action. The action could be of approval, rejection, or simply forward to another individual.

There are a number of ways an action (i.e., approval or rejection) can be taken. Figure 10.31 illustrates three different ways in which an approval or rejection can be performed in SAP SRM. The most common option is via the SRM Inbox. With the second option, an approver receives an email notification with the URL link to the work item. The third option is direct approval in the email client using the approval and rejection buttons.

We will begin this section by discussing **Option #1: Approval in SAP SRM Inbox**.

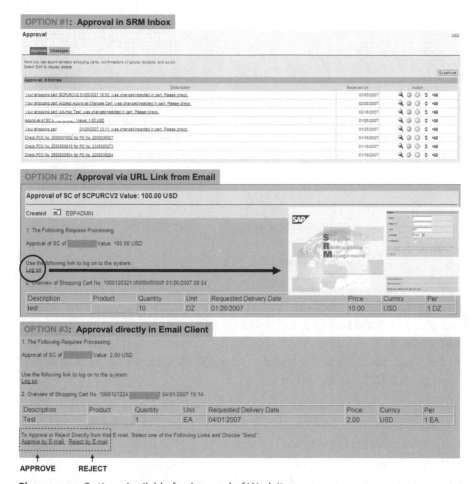

Figure 10.31 Options Available for Approval of Work Items

10.3.1 Approval in SAP SRM Inbox

In order to approve or reject a shopping cart, PO, or other documents, the user needs to have the approval role assigned. Based on the role assignment, approvers will have access to the Approval application. This is also called the SRM Inbox. All users with the employee role also have the **Approval** inbox but do not have the authorization to approve or reject work items.

Figure 10.32 illustrates the overview screen of the **Approval** application which has two tabs: **Approval** and **Messages**. The **Approval** tab contains a list of work items that require action (approve or reject) from the approver. The **Messages** tab contains notifications that the system generates to provide additional information but that do not require an action from the approver.

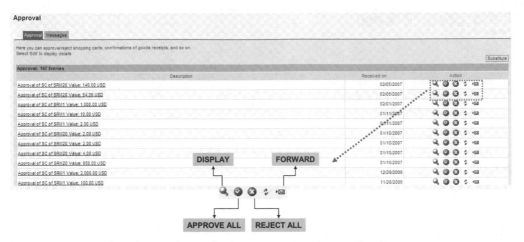

Figure 10.32 Approval Application (SRM Inbox)

Approvers have the option of directly taking an action on the approval work items in their inbox using the buttons that exist in the **Action** column. In Figure 10.32 the **DISPLAY** function is illustrated by a magnifying glass icon. The **APPROVE ALL** function is illustrated by a green check-mark icon. The **REJECT ALL** function is illustrated by a red x-mark icon and the **FORWARD** function is illustrated by an email icon.

The approver can take action directly in the overview window of the Approval application by clicking on the **APPROVE ALL** or **REJECT ALL** buttons. This is useful if the information visible in the overview screen is sufficient for the approver to make a decision. In most cases, the approver needs to see more information to be able to make an educated decision. This is one reason why some organizations restrict the APPROVE ALL and REJECT ALL buttons in the overview screen of the **Approval** application. This can be restricted using workflow Customizing.

In order to view additional information about the work item, the approver can click on the DISPLAY function illustrated by the magnifying glass. Figure 10.33 illustrates the detail screen of the Approval work item. Readers will notice that the Approval detail looks very similar to the shopping cart overview screen. This is because during approval of a shopping cart, the approver is able to review exactly the same information as the requisitioner.

As shown in Figure 10.33, the approver can select the Approved or Rejected radio buttons and click the **Save** button to complete the approval process. If the information available on this screen is not enough, he or she can click the magnifying glass to review the details of each line item in the shopping cart.

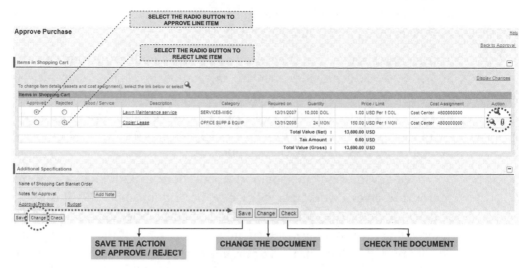

Figure 10.33 Approve Purchase — Work Item Details

Alternately, if the approver needs to change some information in the shopping cart (or other document approval), he or she can click on the **Change** button to begin the process of editing. At this point, the approver can change information such as Quantity, Price, or can click on the magnifying glass to change information in the details of the line item. One example would be if the approver wanted to change the General Ledger (G/L) account for the item he or she is approving. The user will need to do this in the details of the line item.

Once all changes are complete, the approver can ensure that the correct radio button is selected for approved or rejected and click on the **Save** button to complete their action.

This completes the approval or rejection of a work item. If there are additional work items in the approver's inbox, the approver can continue to take action on the remaining work items.

Let us now look at the second option that approvers have for approving or rejecting work items in SAP SRM.

10.3.2 Approval via URL Link from Email

Most users do not like logging into multiple inboxes. Similarly the SRM Inbox and the Approval application that we mentioned in Section 10.3.1 would be considered as a separate inbox for the approvers to check on a daily basis to see whether a work item is there for them to process; e.g., a work item to approve a shopping cart.

Instead, organizations can choose to use the email notification functionality in SAP SRM. SAP provides standard integration to email clients such as Microsoft Outlook, Lotus Notes, and GroupWise. Therefore, the work items that are sent to the SRM Inbox can also be simultaneously sent to the email application used by the approvers. This way, the approvers get notifications in regular inboxes that they check regularly.

An added advantage of the approval notifications in SAP SRM is that the approver receives a work item with a brief description and a URL link to the actual work item. The email notification contains a brief description of the items within the shopping cart work item and the value of the shopping cart. The approver can click on the **Log on** link provided in the shopping cart to launch the SAP SRM approval inbox, as illustrated in Figure 10.34. A login is required once the URL is accessed.

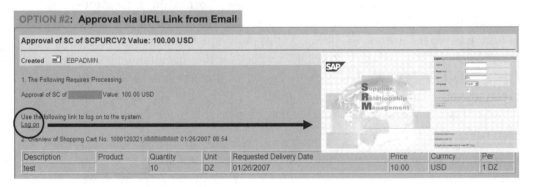

Figure 10.34 Approval Email with Login URL

Once the user logs into the SRM system, he or she is directly taken to the respective work item, where he or she can click on the approve or reject buttons as explained in Section 10.3.1.

Email integration is achieved using a standard report RSWUWFMLEC. This report collects all the work items that require approval and sends them to the SAP Connect component. A second report, RSCONN01 can then be scheduled to take all the items waiting in the SAP Connect component and send them to the respective email addresses of the approvers.

Let us now learn about the third option of approving in SRM, which is also sometimes called offline approval.

10.3.3 Approval Directly in Email Client (Offline Approval)

The third option for approving shopping carts and other documents in SAP SRM as illustrated in Figure 10.31 introduces the concept of offline approval. In this option, approvers receive email notification in their mail clients such as Outlook or Lotus Notes as they did in the second option discussed in Section 10.3.2. But in addition to the login URL in the email, the approver also receives two additional HTML links in the email: Approval per Email and Rejection per Email. Figure 10.35 illustrates a sample email containing these two links.

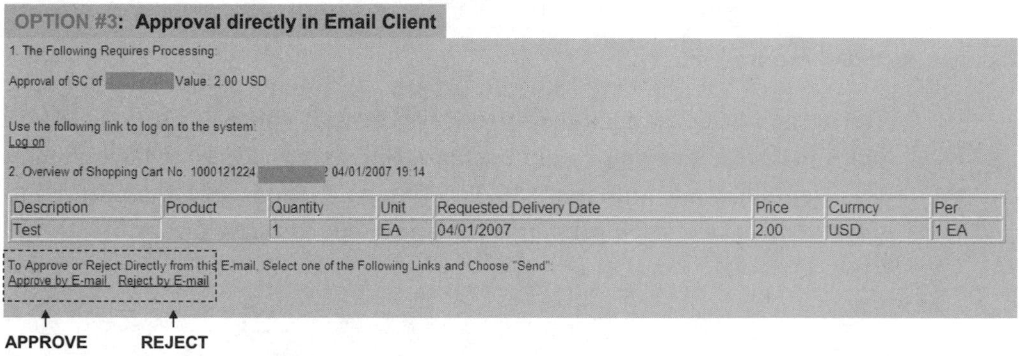

Figure 10.35 Offline Approval

The reason this option is sometimes also called offline approval is because in this option the approver does not have to log on to the SRM system and can process the work item directly in the email by clicking on the **Approval per Email** or **Rejection per Email** links. Once the approver clicks on either of these links to complete their action, an email is generated with the action (approval or rejection) and sent to the SAP SRM system with the approval result.

This option is ideal for departments or individuals who are mobile and do not have access to the system all the time. They can then access their approval emails offline, take action (approve or reject) and then synchronize with the SAP system once they're back online.

Note
In this scenairo the approver needs to approve or reject the entire document and does not have the ability to approve or reject by line item.

In SAP SRM, the offline approval functionality is enabled using two reports *RBBP_NOTIFICATION_OFFAPP* and *RBBP_OFFLINE_EVAL*, as described in Figure 10.36.

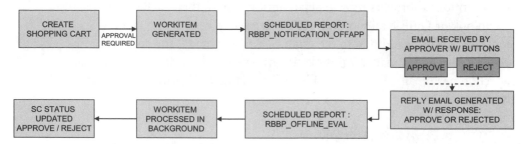

Figure 10.36 Offline Approval Process

Transaction </SOST> in Enterprise Buyer (SAP EBP) contains a list of all work items that are either waiting to be sent to the external system or have already been sent (illustrated in Figure 10.37). This transaction can be monitored to see whether the email work items are being sent correctly or not.

	Status	Send Method	Doc. Title	Sender	Recipient	Send date	Send time	Msg
	■	via Telefax	Purchase Order No.: 2000001798 Purch.OrdDate	WF-BATCH	US 410628-7058	09/07/2006	10:50:45	816
	◇	via Internet	Purchase Order No.: 2000001797 Purch.OrdDate 09/01	SRM1 SRMTESTUSER	sbenkow1@jhmi.edu	09/01/2006	20:56:53	718
	■	via Telefax	Purchase Order No.: 2000001788 Purch.OrdDate	WF-BATCH	US 410559-2244	08/31/2006	14:25:12	816
	◇	via Internet	Approval of SC of SRM12 Value: 14,000.00 USD	SACHIN SETHI	srmappvr@jhmi.edu	08/31/2006	11:40:07	718
	◇	via Internet	Approval of SC of SRM20 Value: 150,000.00 USD	SACHIN SETHI	srmappvr@jhmi.edu	08/31/2006	11:40:07	718
	◇	via Internet	Your shopping cart 'SRM20 08/09/2006 16:16' was	SACHIN SETHI	srmappvr@jhmi.edu	08/31/2006	11:40:06	718
	◇	via Internet	Approval of SC of SRM1 Value: 8,100.00 USD	SACHIN SETHI	srmappvr@jhmi.edu	08/31/2006	11:40:05	718
	◇	via Internet	Your shopping cart 'SRM1 08/23/2006 11:57' was c	SACHIN SETHI	srmappvr@jhmi.edu	08/31/2006	11:40:05	718
	◇	via Internet	Approval of SC of SRM1 Value: 5,002.00 USD	SACHIN SETHI	srm11@jhmi.edu	08/31/2006	11:40:05	718
	◇	via Internet	Your shopping cart 'SRM1 08/23/2006 13:14' was c	SACHIN SETHI	srmappvr@jhmi.edu	08/31/2006	11:40:04	718
	◇	via Internet	Approval of SC of SRM1 Value: 2,050.00 USD	SACHIN SETHI	srmappvr@jhmi.edu	08/31/2006	11:40:04	718

Figure 10.37 SAP Connect Transmission Log

Organizations can choose to either include or exclude the email buttons **Approve** and **Reject** using a variant for the report RSWUWFMLEC (displayed in Figure 10.38).

Most organizations implement the three methods to approve in phases as discussed in Sections 10.3.1 through 10.3.3 and shown in Figure 10.31. The option of **Approval in SRM Inbox** as discussed in Section 10.3.1 is standard out-of-the-box functionality. There is no additional effort required from the project team to implement.

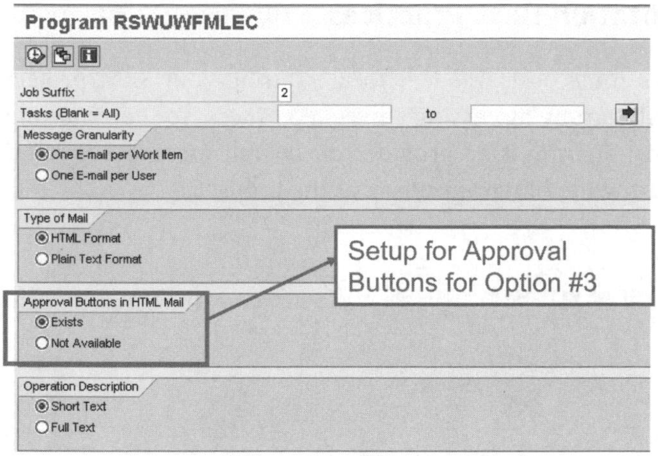

Figure 10.38 Report RSWUWFMLEC

The option of **Approval via URL link from Email** as discussed in Section 10.3.2 provides the greatest approval flexibility because the approvers can choose to either process the work items in their SRM Inboxes or wait till a work item is sent to them in their regular email clients (Outlook, Lotus Notes, etc.). They then approve the work items using the login URL provided in the email. Readers should note that, all users should have an email address maintained in the user master record.

Almost everyone waits to implement the **Offline approval** functionality discussed in Section 10.3.3 as a last option. The benefits of offline approval also bring complications; organizations should minimize those within their initial phase of their implementations.

> **Note**
>
> Organizations implementing SAP SRM 6.0 should review The Universal Worklist (UWL) functionality, which provides a single place for accessing all approval/alerts/notifications for SAP SRM and ERP. So users can go to a single location and process all work items.

In the next section, you will learn about best practices for implementing approval worklows in SAP SRM.

10.4 Implementation Best Practices

This section provides some best practices to use during your SRM project implementation. I will start by discussing a five-step process for determining your workflow needs. Figure 10.39 provides an overall methodology and strategy to follow during the blueprint phase of the project.

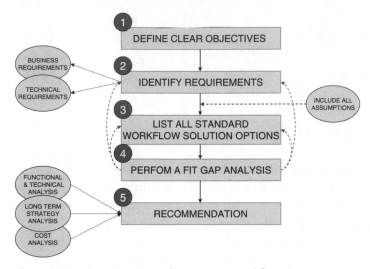

Figure 10.39 Five-Step Process for SAP SRM Workflow Projects

The process begins with the definition of clear objectives for the project. Let's review the steps now.

Define Clear Objectives

It is extremely important to define very clear objectives for the project and the role of workflow. SAP Business Workflow provides very rich functionality, and not all available functionality may be relevant for this project.

Identify Workflow Requirements

Project teams that do a good job of capturing most of workflow requirements end up more successful than others. This is true especially if it is determined that the standard workflow templates are not sufficient and workflow needs to be customized. The impact on timeline, resources, and cost is more tremendous when requirements are not captured completely and accurately. Here are some workflow requirements:

▶ Ability for all approvers to modify, approve, or reject shopping carts

▶ Ability for all reviewers to display shopping cart requests, although without the ability to modify, approve, or reject the shopping cart.

▶ If a shopping cart is rejected, the requisitioner receives a notification via email, informing them of the rejection. The requisitioner should have the opportunity to accept, modify, and resubmit the shopping cart.

▶ Modifications that result in a change to the shopping cart will trigger a notification to the requisitioner and a request to generate the re-approval process

▶ All approvers and reviewers receive email notification when a shopping cart approval is required.

▶ Ability to substitute another approver as a delegate approver for a period of absence

▶ Ability to add additional approvers to the approval process before and after the system generated approvers

List all Standard Solution Options

This should include all and any assumptions. Custom workflow development is a costly endeavor; especially in a rapidly changing solution like SAP SRM. In each new release, the workflow capabilities in SRM have been enhanced greatly. Therefore it is of upmost importance to review and exhaust the capability of standard delivered workflow templates in SRM. Remember that implementing what your organization does today is an easy user decision but not a strategic management decision. Instead, companies that have decided to implement SAP SRM need to take the time and opportunity to explore the best practices used at leading organizations. SAP-delivered workflows are a result of research and development of industry best practices. For most organizations, the implementation of SRM is not only a change in technology but also a change in the business processes existing in their entire value chain. Organizations are well advised to make use of the standard workflow templates delivered in SRM and if necessary add business rules using the delivered BAdIs.

Identify all the standard workflow templates for all the business documents relevant for workflow and list any assumptions when discussing with the business and technical implementation teams. The different sections in this chapter describe the standard workflows delivered, so review those. Here are some assumptions that should be captured and discussed:

▶ If spending limit and approval limit by dollar thresholds are required, they will remain common across the enterprise.

▶ A requisitioner will provide appropriate account assignment and product category information in the shopping cart to drive approvals.

Perform Fit-Gap Analysis

Custom workflow development is a costly endeavor; especially in a rapidly changing solution offering like SAP SRM. Over the past six years, the SRM solution has seen tremendous growth and with that has come a large array of enhancements. Organizations that have opted for highly customized workflows have realized when they had to upgrade that it these kinds of workflows are very time consuming and costly to maintain.

Just as with any other development effort within the SAP environment, a fit-gap analysis should be conducted for the workflows in SAP SRM. Figure 10.37 shows how to do a fit-gap analysis for your project. In a fit-gap analysis, we list all of the possible options and then map each option against the following questions:

▶ Is the option a SAP standard functionality?

▶ What is the level of development effort required to achieve the option?

▶ What is the ongoing maintenance effort and cost for this option?

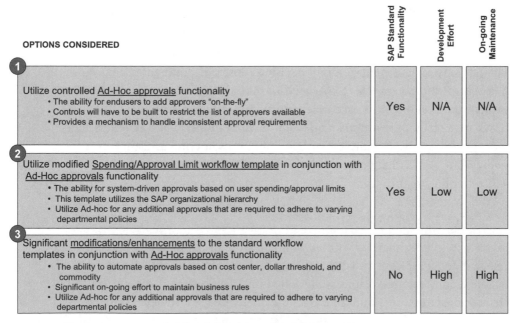

Figure 10.40 Example of High-Level Fit-Gap Workflow Analysis

Recommendations

Eventually each project team needs to determine the path of endeavor. A recommendation needs to be made using the information gathered in the four previous steps. Ideally, your recommendation along with the information gathered in the fit-gap analysis step should allow the management team to select an appropriate option for the implementation and long term viability.

In the next section, I will briefly discuss security and authorizations as they related to workflows in SAP SRM.

10.5   Security and Authorizations in Workflow

When we talk about workflow and agents (the individual(s) who are to receive work items), the audit departments pay close attention. They are interested in knowing all about who can approve what, how the approvers are determined, and what authorizations they will have for changing or adding to the business documents. A common question asked by auditors is: "Can the approver determined by the SRM system be changed by the end-user or further approvers?"

SAP offers authorizations and BAdI(s) in SRM to provide such flexibility for organizations. These allow changes to approvers or give specific users ability to make such changes.

Transaction <PFTC_CHG> makes it possible to assign specific processors for workflow templates. In the standard system, if there is no specific processor assigned, then that workflow task is considered a General Task; i.e., one that anyone is allowed to process. Alternatively, specific processors can be assigned based on user, role, Organizational Unit, position, etc. Authorization can be provided for changing and or inserting an approver or reviewer.

Table 10.2 provides a list of workflow templates that can be configured in Transaction <PFTC_CHG> for either change or insertion. Here you can configure who can be changed or inserted as an approver.

Workflow Template	Description	Change-Approver	Insert Approver/Reviewer
WS10000129	Approve shopping cart (one-step)	x	
WS10000031	Approve shopping cart (two-step)	x	
WS10000060	Workflow without approval (shopping cart)	x	
WS14000133	N-step approval of shopping cart	x	
WS14000109	N-step approval of shopping cart over value limit	x	
WS10000271	Approval of shopping cart		X
WS14000089	Approval of purchase order (one-step)	x	
WS14000075	Workflow without approval (purchase order)	x	
WS14000145	N-step approval of purchase order	x	
WS14000154	Reviewer workflow for purchase order	x	
WS14000002	Approval of purchase order		X
WS10400002	Approval goods receipt (one-step)	x	
WS10400009	Approval goods receipt (two-step)	x	
WS10400010	Workflow without approval (goods receipt)	x	
WS10400020	Approval of goods receipt by administrator	x	
WS10400008	Approval of goods receipt		X
WS10400017	Approve invoice (one-step)	x	
WS10400018	Approval invoice (two-step)	x	
WS10400016	Workflow without approval (invoice)	x	
WS10400021	Approval of invoice by administrator	x	
WS10400014	Approval of invoice		X
WS14000088	Approval of contract (one-step)	x	
WS14000086	Workflow without approval (contract)	x	
WS14000145	N-step approval of contract	x	

Table 10.2 Workflow Templates in SAP SRM

Workflow Template	Description	Change-Approver	Insert Approver/ Reviewer
WS14500010	Approval of contract		X
WS14500027	Approval of bid invitation (one-step)	x	
WS14500026	Workflow without approval (bid invitation)	x	
WS14500028	N-step approval of bid invitation	x	
WS14500022	Approval of bid invitation		X
WS79000002	Approval of Bid (one-step)	x	
WS79000010	Workflow without approval (bid)	x	
WS14500044	N-step approval of bid	x	
WS14500040	Approval of bid		X

Table 10.2 Workflow Templates in SAP SRM (cont.)

In addition to removing the classification of workflows as General Tasks; i.e., assigning specific processors of work-items, you can define whether a business transaction such as a shopping cart can be changed during the approval process.

Additionally, the standard workflow(s) can be influenced by Personalization Objects available for shopping cart workflows. In User Maintenance (SU01) on the Personalization tab, there are several Personalization Objects available for workflows: BBP_WFL_SECURITY, BBP_SPENDING_LIMIT, BBP_APPROVAL_LIMIT.

These objects can be used to restrict the authorizations of users or to define values limits for control of approval workflows. These objects can be assigned at a user or role level. The best practice calls for set up of this authorization within the user role instead of individual user personalization. This provides reduced overall maintenance and consistency across the user base. If several roles are assigned to the user, then the system uses the highest available authorization level during runtime.

For example, the BBP_WFL_SECURITY object can be used to define the authorization level used in workflow action once something is changed in the shopping cart. Table 10.3 provides a listing of the different workflow authorization levels and the behavior of the shopping cart workflow during the approval process.

Authorization level	Effects on approval	Workflow behavior
NONE	Not possible to change a shopping cart during approval process	Workflow continues.
LOW	Possible to change the shopping cart	The entire approval workflow restarts after each shopping cart change is made.
MEDIUM	Possible to change the shopping cart	The system evaluates the workflow start conditions and starts the approval workflow again if the change necessitates a new approval. If this is not the case, the approval workflow continues.
HIGH	Possible to change the shopping cart	Workflow continues

Table 10.3 Workflow Authorization Levels and Behavior During Approval

The different authorization levels enable organizations to control the behavior of the shopping cart workflow. A user with the authorization level of **NONE** can view or display the shopping cart but cannot change it.

If the user has the authorization level **Low,** then changes to the shopping cart are allowed, but the workflow process re-starts every time a shopping cart change is made, independently of which field of the shopping cart was changed. Organizations need to be careful when selecting the Low authorization level. Although it addresses the audit concerns of re-approval, it can be an unnecessary burden for the approvers and delay the procurement process just because a G/L account change is made. Figure 10.41 illustrates the Authorization Level object key that controls the approvers' authorization level.

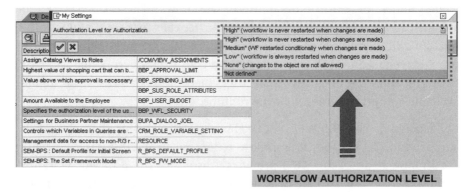

Figure 10.41 Authorization Level of the User in Approval

In the authorization level **Medium**, the workflow behaviour depends on the type of changes made to the shopping cart. After each change, the workflow system evaluates the starting conditions in SRM to determine if a new workflow needs to be triggered.

> **Example**
>
> A user creates a shopping cart of value $2,000. Based on the start conditions, a single-step approval workflow is triggered. During approval, the manager, changes the shopping cart value to $5,500. The workflow system re-evaluates the start conditions and determines that for all shopping carts worth more than $5,000 a two-step approval workflow is required. At this time the workflow system starts this new approval and completes the old single-step approval.

The authorization level **High** allows users to make changes to the shopping cart and does not impact the further processing of the workflow. Approvers are not re-determined, so that if the user was the last in the chain of approvers, the workflow will complete after approval. If there were other approvers in the chain after this approver, the workflow continues. I have seen more organizations use the High authorization approval level than used any of the other levels.

In addition to the personalization object key, a BAdI BBP_WFL_SECURE_BADI is available for organizations to develop business rules and override the settings of None, Low, Medium, or High authorization levels. With the BAdI BBP_WFL_SECUR_BADI, and method SET_SECURITY_LEVEL, one can change the workflow security level and override the value determined from role personalization. Using this BAdI, an organization can further determine whether to allow changes to the shopping cart or define how the workflow is to behave once the changes are done. A list of BAdIs available in SRM is available in Appendix D.

In the next section, I will introduce readers to the concept of rule resolution in workflow and compare responsibility rules to commonly used Z tables. Project teams usually create Z tables when the standard approval templates do not provide sufficient capabilities for approval routing. Also, many project teams create Z tables when they want to use the item-level approval workflow template. Readers can use this comparison to determine whether a Z table or a responsibility rule should be used to find workflow agents for their implementation.

10.6   Responsibility Rules vs. Custom Z tables

In workflow, the determination of agents (approvers or owners or recipients) can be derived in many different ways. A common method is agent assignment in the workflow template in SRM. Transaction <PFTC_CHG> provides the ability to assign specific processors for workflow templates as discussed in the security section above. But it is often not possible to just use agent assignment on projects, as it might not be possible to determine approvers for a particular workflow (e.g. shopping cart) using a role, position, job, organization unit, etc. It could instead be based on cost-center ownership or even on the wish of each individual department in the company to determine its own approvers.

This is when the common question arises: "Can we just use a custom z table to list all our approvers and have the workflow driven off the custom table?" Yes, just like any other ABAP program in SAP, workflows can use a custom table as well. SAP delivered workflows using a BAdI and customer-developed workflows. Custom tables might be the first thought but definitely not the best or only option when it comes to SAP Business Workflow.

	RESPONSIBILITIES	CUSTOM TABLE
STANDARD SAP DELIVERED FUNCTIONALITY	YES	NO
DEVELOPMENT EFFORT REQUIRED	LOW	HIGH
LOAD EFFORT	HIGH	HIGH
MAINTENANCE COMPLEXITY	HIGH	LOW
MAINTENANCE: CENTRAL / DISTRIBUTED	CENTRAL	CENTRAL OR DISTRIBUTED
SECURITY	LOW	COULD BE HIGH
GLOBAL VISIBILITY	POOR	GOOD
TROUBLESHOOTING	POOR	GOOD
TRANSPORTABLE	PARTIALLY *	YES
LONG TERM IMPACT	LOW MAINTENANCE	HIGH MAINTENANCE

* ONLY THE RESPONSIBILITY RULE CAN BE TRANSPORTED AND NOT THE ACTUAL DATA (APPROVERS), THOSE NEED TO BE ENTERED IN EACH ENVIRONMENT/CLIENT

Figure 10.42 Responsibility Rules vs.Custom Tables

Responsibility rules in SAP offer similar functionality to custom tables and are better suited for SAP Business Workflow. It is, however, always challenging to persuade project teams to use responsibility rules instead of a custom table. Figure 10.42 provides a comparison between the two to provide information project teams can use to make educated decisions.

The next section provides useful extras that readers might find interesting.

10.7 Extras

Figure 10.43 aims to provide an explanation for the different icons in the graphical workflow visualization in SAP SRM. Readers can use Figure 10.43 as a legend for the graphical view of the Approval Preview. Organizations can also replace these images to reflect their own by simply overwriting these .gif files. Project teams should work with their development teams to replace images.

> **Note**
>
> These images could differ from one SRM release to the other

Note: <Document> = Shopping Cart, Purchase Order, Confirmation, etc.

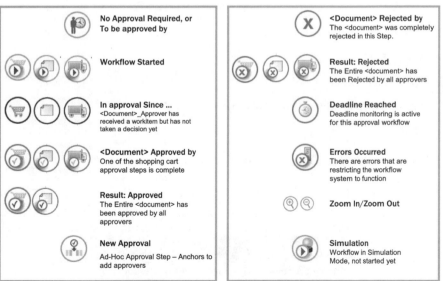

Figure 10.43 Workflow in SRM — Approval Visualization Icon Legend

Figure 10.44 provides a brief timeline of workflow in SAP SRM. This timeline can be useful for organizations using older SAP SRM releases. Here, they can get a quick overview of the workflow enhancements in the current SAP SRM release.

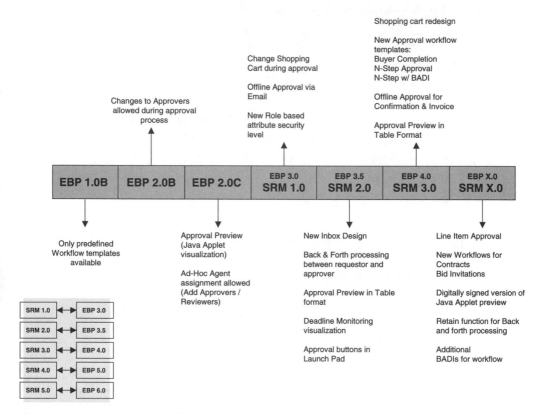

Figure 10.44 SAP Business Workflow in SAP SRM — Timeline

10.8 Relevant OSS Notes

Table 10.4 provides a list of important OSS Notes available on the SAP service marketplace that are relevant when managing workflow in SAP SRM.

Note	Description
547601	FAQ workflow, runtime environment and troubleshooting
903200	Workflow tracing for problem detection

Table 10.4 OSS Notes from the SAP Service Marketplace

Note	Description
322526	Analysis for workflow problems
391674	How to build ad-hoc agents in customer workflows

Table 10.4 OSS Notes from the SAP Service Marketplace (cont.)

10.9 Summary

In this chapter, I introduced you to the concept of workflow in SAP SRM. The chapter started with a discussion on the importance of workflow and how organizations can achieve efficiency by implementing workflow processes using SAP SRM. Readers are now aware that a number of workflow templates are pre-delivered in SRM and can be used in applications such as shopping carts, purchaser orders, contracts, and confirmations.

Note that SAP SRM 6.0 (SRM 2007) is going to introduce a new functionality for workflow and considerable changes. A number of the existing SRM workflow BAdIs and functions will become obsolete.

In Chapter 11, I will discuss the role of security in SAP SRM and how SAP security administrators can manage roles and authorizations within SAP SRM. I will also discuss why and how security is different in SAP SRM and the impact of Organizational Structure in security.

As businesses grow, their information systems support whole communities of users: customers, suppliers, partners and employees, all of whom count on the secure exchange of a wide variety of information. Managing the security of ERP information into and out of your organization has never been more critical — or more challenging.

11 Managing Security in SAP SRM

In today's environment, organizations are not just looking for a technical solution to thwart viruses, hackers, and information theft. They are looking for software companies to provide the most secure enterprise solutions, built on rigorous security standards and industry best practices, to help them manage governance, risk, and compliance. So let's start by defining security. The following are some security definitions:

▸ A secure system is a system which does exactly what we want it to do and nothing that we don't want it to do, even when someone else tries to make it behave differently: — *www.wikipedia.com.*

▸ In the computer industry, refers to techniques for ensuring that data stored in a computer cannot be read or compromised by any individuals without authorization — *www.Webopedia.com*

▸ A process of system screening that denies access to unauthorized users and protects data from unauthorized uses — *www.ask-edi.com*

▸ Work that involves ensuring the confidentiality, integrity, and availability of systems, networks, and data through the planning, analysis, development, implementation, maintenance, and enhancement of information systems' security programs, policies, procedures, and tools — *www.opm.gov.*

The gist of most of these definitions is that application security is required to restrict sensitive and important data within an organization. Based on an individual's job or responsibility, the security developers need to determine what transactions they should access, display, or execute.

SAP provides an enterprise solution for integrating the various aspects of organizations: internal operations, external business networks, regulatory compliance, etc. In its annual report for 2005, SAP states that SAP products include security features that are intended to protect the privacy and integrity of customer data.

Despite these security features, these products may be vulnerable to attacks and similar problems caused by Internet users, such as hackers bypassing firewalls and misappropriating confidential information. Such attacks or other disruptions could jeopardize the security of information stored in and transmitted through the computer systems of SAP customers and lead to claims for damages against SAP from customers. However, SAP technologies have not been significantly exposed to security attacks so far, and SAP provides extensive security functions, so means the risk can be classed as very unlikely.

The focus of this chapter is to discuss security as it relates to SAP SRM, but we'll start by briefly discussing the basic security concepts in SAP. In the SAP system, security is administered for objects (profiles and authorizations). Users are only authorized to display or change the areas of the system in ways made necessary by their respective job responsibilities.

11.1 Overview of Security in SAP

SAP has been implemented at more than half of the Fortune 500 companies, has approximately 44,500 installations at 32,000 customers in more than 120 countries, with more than 10 million users. Given this customer landscape, SAP is constantly driving to provide the best security practices available.

SAP is built upon the role-based security concept. Each user within the organization is assigned one or multiple roles that are deemed necessary for the functions they are supposed to perform, based on assigned organizational responsibility. The core of application security in SAP is the authorization concept," and and the three pillars of authorization in SAP are transactions, authorization objects and roles. Figures 11.1 and 11.2 illustrate this concept:

▶ **Transactions**
These are what users execute to perform functions in SAP. For example: MEPO is the transaction for purchase-order creation.

▶ **Authorization Objects**
An authorization object groups up to 10 fields that are related by AND.

Authorizations allow users to perform an operation in the SAP system. For an authorization check to be successful, all field values of the authorization object must be appropriately maintained in the user master.

▶ **Roles**

These are ultimately assigned to a user. Transactions and authorization objects are not directly assigned. Instead, authorizations are combined in an authorization profile that is associated with a role.

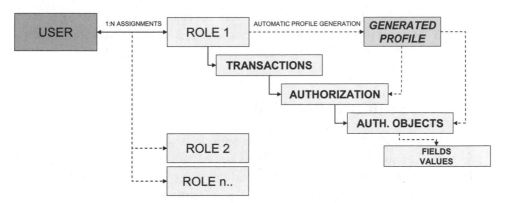

Figure 11.1 Security Hierarchy in SAP

Prior to SAP R/3 Release 4.0, companies used to go through the painstaking efforts of building user profiles and creating individual transactions with required authorizations involving field- and value-level checks. SAP has since provided many standard roles for different functional areas, such as the SAP_MM_PUR_PURCHASEORDER role available for users who need to have the function of creating purchase orders.

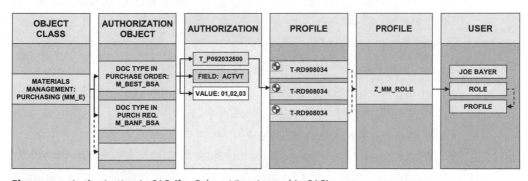

Figure 11.2 Authorization in SAP (for Colors, View Legend in SAP)

The best practice for creating specific user roles would be to copy the standard delivered SAP roles into Z roles in the customer namespaces and then modify the transactions and authorizations to conform to the organization's needs and requirements.

However, most organizations still seem to disregard the delivered roles and start off their security project by building these roles from scratch. This can be a very long and tedious process, although it does ensure the highest form of security development because it is based precisely on the organization's requirements and needs.

In this section, I introduced the security concept as it relates to SAP. Now let's move on to specifically discuss security in SAP SRM and some similarities and differences between security in SAP R/3 and in SRM.

11.2 Security in SAP SRM

On most projects, the security teams seem to be aware of the security processes, set-up, and best practices from an SAP R/3 perspective, but SAP SRM is normally a new solution for them, and the functionality within SRM is varied enough to create a steep learning curve for many security teams. The core advice for project managers is to involve and educate the security team on the SAP SRM solution, beginning with the blueprint phase. The security professionals need to know what questions to ask and what issues to worry about from a security perspective. If these professionals are not offered adequately training, security will lapse.

11.2.1 Common Questions About SRM Implementations

It is natural that questions arise during SAP SRM implementations. Some of these are listed here:

- Is SRM another module in SAP R/3?
- Are there roles in SRM as in SAP R/3?
- Can I execute SU53 in SRM to provide the authorization information to the security team?
- When I log in to SRM using my SAP Uuer ID, why do I get an error?
- What are these BSP transactions, and how do I include them in the role?

It might help you answer some of these questions more satisfactorily if you understand some important issues. To start with, SAP SRM is built leveraging the core SAP NetWeaver technology platform and shares the same robust security organizations have been using in the enterprise SAP R/3 solution for years.

The very first thing security professionals and organizations that have been working on the core SAP R/3 solution need to understand is that SAP SRM is an independent solution offered by SAP. It is an entirely separate system, installed on its own box, with its own database, and with an independent architecture and landscape.

Organizations need to manage security within the SRM environment and its components independent of the security in the SAP R/3 environment. The SAP ERP 2005 version is an exception to this rule, as SRM can be installed within the ERP system as an add-on component. Figure 11.3 illustrates this by using a simple diagram showing that SAP has many different solutions and that application security is required in each system.

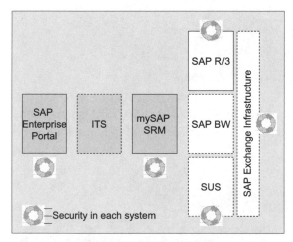

Figure 11.3 Security Requirements in SAP Solutions

11.2.2 Similarities Between SAP R/3 Enterprise and SAP SRM

It is important for security professionals to realize that, although SAP SRM is a separate application than SAP R/3, it does offer many similarities to R/3. It is not a stretch to say that the security-development environment in both the applications is pretty much the same. Therefore, let's get the basic similarities out of the way:

▶ The configuration and set-up GUI for SAP SRM looks just like the core SAP R/3 GUI (called the SAP GUI), as illustrated in Figure 11.4. The distinction here is between what a configuration expert does vs. what an end user does. The end users working with SAP SRM use the Web browser (IE, Firefox, etc.) as their user interface to create transactions like shopping carts and purchase orders in SAP SRM.

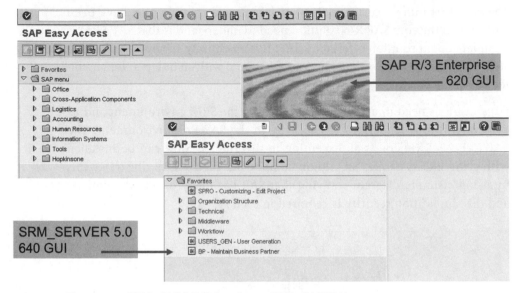

Figure 11.4 GUI in SAP R/3 Enterprise vs. GUI in SAP SRM

▶ The role-maintenance transaction in SAP R/3 and SAP SRM is the same and is accessed via Transaction </PFCG>, as illustrated in Figures 11.5 and 11.6.

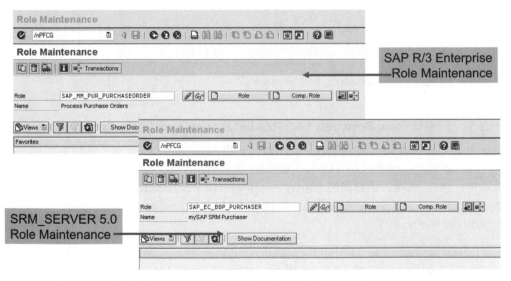

Figure 11.5 Role Maintenance in R/3 Enterprise and in SAP SRM

In Figure 11.5, we illustrate the **Role Maintenance** transaction **PFCG** in SAP R/3 Enterprise. Using this transaction, the **SAP_MM_PUR_PURCHASEORDER**

Role can be maintained in SAP R/3. Notice, that in SRM the same Transaction PFCG is used to maintain roles. As an example, in SRM a security expert can maintain the purchaser role **SAP_EC_BBP_PURCHASER** using the same process as in R/3.

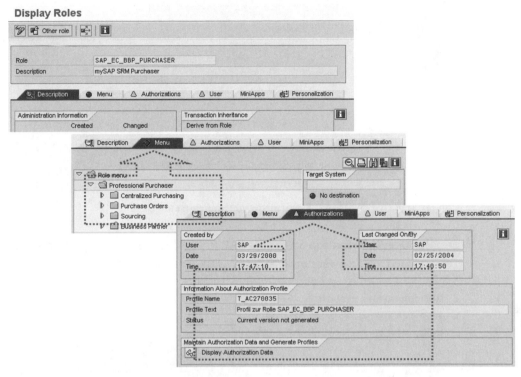

Figure 11.6 Detail of Maintenance of a Role in SAP SRM

In Figure 11.6, we illustrate that detail within the SAP SRM purchaser role in Transaction PFCG in SRM. Even though the PFCG transaction is being executed in SRM, the tabs within this interface to maintain roles is the same. Notice the **Menu** tab, **Authorization** tab, and **User** tab all look similar to the role maintenance transaction in SAP R/3 enterprise:

▶ The user-management maintenance transaction in SAP R/3 and SAP SRM is the same and is accessed via Transaction </SU01>, as illustrated in Figure 11.7. Notice that the **Display User** transaction in **SAP R/3 Enterprise** and the **SRM_SERVER 5.0** look exactly the same. However, be aware that, unlike SAP R/3, the Transaction </SU01> alone does not create a complete SRM user (this will be discussed in Section 11.2).

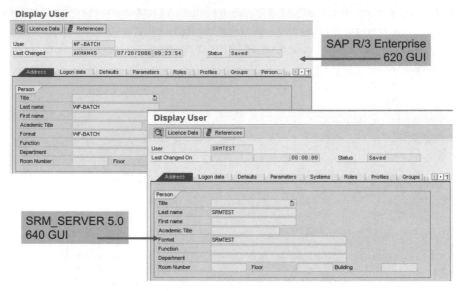

Figure 11.7 User Creation </SU01> in SAP R/3 and SAP SRM

► The **User Information System** in SAP R/3 and SAP SRM is the same and is accessed via **Transaction** </SUIM>, as illustrated in Figure 11.8.

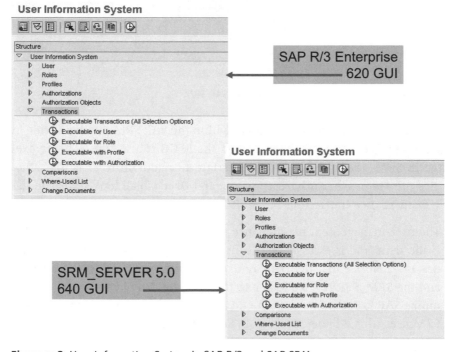

Figure 11.8 User Information System in SAP R/3 and SAP SRM

11.2.3 Security Related Differences in R/3 vs. SAP SRM

The obvious question after reading the previous section is: What is the real difference in security between what's in R/3 vs. SAP SRM? All of the key transactions we reviewed in the section above are the same and are accessed the same way. Where is the learning curve?

Although, the core environment for security management and development in SAP SRM is similar to what consultants and project teams might be used to in SAP R/3 Enterprise or earlier releases, there are a number of unique differences and requirements.

The very first thing to realize is that SRM project teams and consultants use the SRM GUI to configure the system, but the end users only use a Web browser to access the SRM application, as illustrated in Figure 11.9.This is very important to understand. Once the SRM system is configured, all end-users of the system can execute all their functions within the browser.

User access in SRM provides each user with a list of transactions available for them to execute; these are the only transactions they are able to execute. Unlike SAP R/3, in SRM the end users do not enter transaction codes to execute business functions. We will continue to discuss this topic in the section on security roles in SRM.

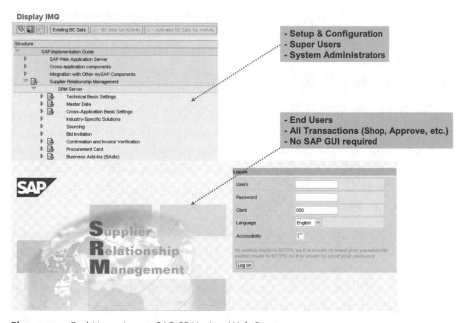

Figure 11.9 End Users Access SAP SRM via a Web Browser

In order to understand the security within SAP SRM, there are two main points to clarify for the reader.

First let's discuss the user-creation process in SRM. Unlike SAP R/3, where users can be created by using transaction SU01, SRM has just one step in its user-creation process. In SRM there is key user information that can only be stored as attributes in the organizational model.

Therefore, the user must be integrated in the organizational model. Figure 11.10 illustrates what a valid SRM user looks like. As illustrated in the figure, the required relationship for users in SRM is a **Position**, **Business Partner**, and **User ID** relationship. We will discuss the user-creation concept in SRM in more detail in Section 11.3.

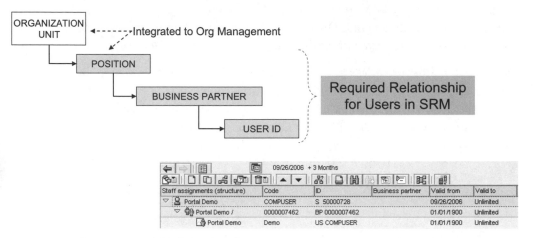

Figure 11.10 Valid Relationships for Users in SRM (Enterprise Buyer)

The second key to understanding security in SRM is that the assignment of roles to user ID in SRM does not enable a user to perform functions such as creating shopping carts, creating purchase orders, etc. For this, the user also must be a part of the Organizational Structure in SRM. Each user is assigned a position, and each position is attached to an Organizational Unit, as illustrated in the figure above.

The SRM environment only supports 1:1 assignments between users and their positions. When users are deleted objects *Position*, *Business Partner*, and *User* are managed as a common EBP user object. Positions and Organizational Units are objects of the Organizational Structure in SRM and are setup by the organization-management team.

Therefore the two key take-aways from our brief discussion above are:

▸ Users in SRM cannot be created just using the SU01 transaction. Further processing is required.

▸ Users in SRM need to be integrated into the Organizational Structure or else they will not be able to perform their functions in SRM.

One caveat to the two bullet points is that there is a distinction between users who are going to configure the SRM system and end users who are going to use the SRM system. The concept above does not necessarily pertain to user IDs required to configure the system.

Because of the nature of the SRM application, there is a need for both internal and external users. Internal users are typically employees of the organization and typically work within the system firewall. External users are partners of the organization engaging in business with the organization, such as vendors and bidders. SRM contains functionality within Supplier Self Services (SUS), Bidding Engine, and the Live Auction applications that might require your security teams to create external users. In Section 11.3, we'll discuss the process of creating both internal and external users in SRM.

11.3   User Creation in SRM for Enterprise Buyer (Internal)

Users in SRM can be created in multitude of ways. One of the prerequisites for mass user creation in SRM is to have at least a basic Organizational Structure. Figure 11.11 illustrates a simple process flow.

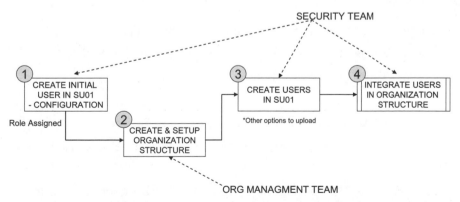

Figure 11.11 Simple Process Flow for User-Creation Requirement

In the flow seen in Figure 11.11: the security team in Step **1** creates a configuration user in SRM using the standard SU01 transaction. Let's assume that a configuration role has been assigned to this user, which allows him or her to create a simple Organizational Structure within the SRM system in Step **2**. Users created in this manner are only used for configuration or user administration but cannot be used for creation or approval of shopping carts. In Step **3**, the security team can create users in SRM using Transaction </SU01> for user management and then in Step **4** integrate the users in the Organizational Structure created.

In Step **4**, there are multiple ways to integrate users in the Organizational Structure. This aspect depends on which of the following options the organization is planning to use:

▶ Using SRM as a standalone system

▶ Using the HR Integration scenario

▶ Using Central User Administration (CUA) within SRM

▶ Depending on the options above, the plan to create users can be very different.

11.3.1 Using SRM as a Standalone System

We first need to ensure that readers do not confuse this option as the Standalone implementation scenario in Enterprise Buyer Professional (EBP).This option basically means that all the security is maintained only within the SRM system. In SRM, users are created via three main methods, which are listed below:

▶ Via the user self-service function in the Web browser

▶ Via the Manage User Data administrator function in the Web

▶ Via the USERS_GEN transaction

Creating New Users via the Web Self-Registration Service

Let us now review how to create new users via the web self-registration service.

Users access the SRM system via a Web URL in a browser. On the initial logon page, a user can either log in using his or her assigned user ID and password or can request for a new user ID by choosing the **Request User ID** link, as illustrated in Figure 11.12. This option is only available if organizations want to make the user creation process as self-service. Users are required to enter a **User ID**, **First name**, **Last name**, **E-mail address**, and **Approver**. In addition, the users are also required to enter their manager or supervisor's information. Once these required fields are entered, an approval email is sent to the user's manager for approval .

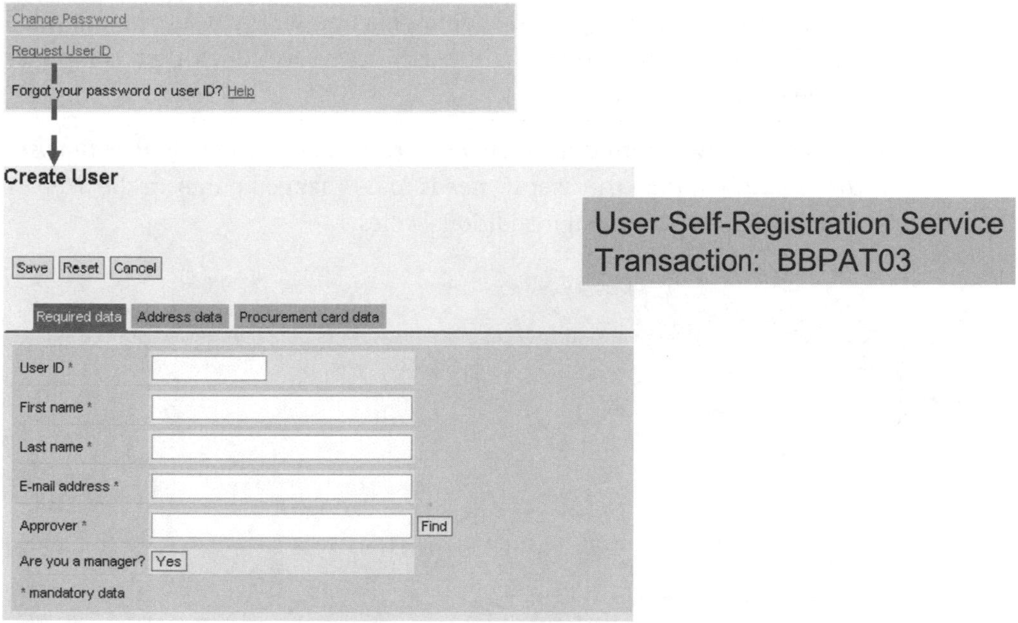

Figure 11.12 User Self-Registration Service — Transaction BBPAT03

A standard approval template is delivered for a manager's approval when new users are created. Organizations can choose to activate or deactivate this workflow. See Chapter 10 for details on workflow.

As you can imagine, there are obvious issues that organizations can face if they choose this method of creating users.Standardization is one big issue, and data integrity is another. Moreover, security teams tend to dislike this option because most organizations have an existing user-creation process and SAP seems like just another application that needs to be included within the existing security processes.

Creating New Users via the Manage User Data Web Service

The Manage User Data service is a Web-based transaction, which for all practical purposes should only be executed in a Web browser. In order to get access to this service, the Role SAP_EC_BBP_ADMINISTRATOR has to be assigned to the user. Figure 11.13 illustrates this transaction. When a user is created using BBPUSERMAINT, a corresponding position, business partner, and user master record are created in SRM. Therefore the objects S, BP, and US are created, which completes the requirement for a user in SRM, as shown in Figure 11.10. Please note that a Organizational Unit is required when creating users via this transaction. This unit will typically be provided by the functional team requesting the user creation. Which then completes the Step 4 shown in Figure 11.11.

When creating the user initially, only one role can be assigned.Once the user record is created, then the user ID needs to be changed either in the Web or in Transaction SU01 to assign additional roles.

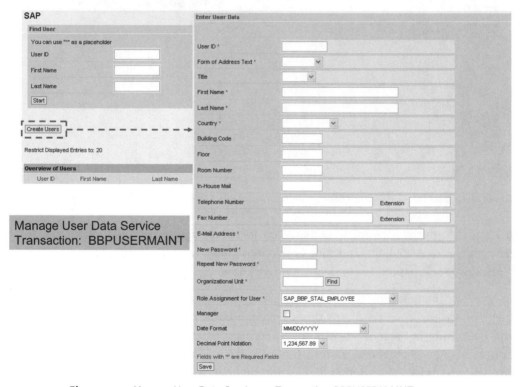

Figure 11.13 Manage User Data Service — Transaction BBPUSERMAINT

Most organizations shy away from the BBPUSERMAINT Web transaction as it becomes a tedious function that only allows the creation of one user at a time. They use this transaction more for deletions (which is explained later), and end up using Transaction USERS_GEN transaction because it allows more flexibility and the ability to create multiple users at one time.

Creating New Users via the USERS_GEN Transaction

Since SRM 2.0 release, SAP has provided a standard transaction that allows creation of individual and mass users in SRM. Transaction <USERS_GEN> is executed in the SAP GUI instead of the Web browser. Figure 11.14 illustrates this transaction.

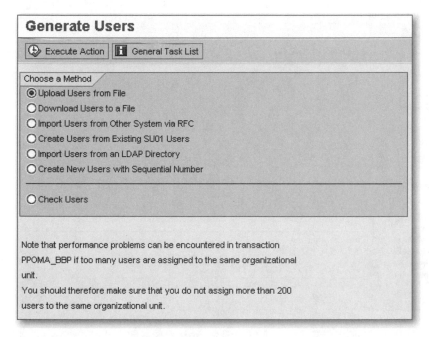

Figure 11.14 Generate Users Transaction (USERS_GEN)

This transaction is used for the initial creation of SRM users, but once the users are created they can be maintained in Transaction <SU01> t or the Manage User Data service.

In the **Generate Users** transaction (USERS_GEN) illustrated in Figure 11.14, security administrators can **Choose a Method** to generate users. The various methods available are listed next and then explained in greater detail:

▸ Upload Users from File and Download Users to a File

▸ Import Users from Other System via RFC

▶ Create Users from Existing SU01 Users

▶ Import Users from an LDAP Directory

▶ Create New Users with Sequential Number

Upload Users from File and Download Users to a File (ASCII)

Organizations can use the **Upload Users from File** method to create users from a flat file (ASCII) that contains details about the users, including the **User ID**, **Last Name**, **Organizational Unit**, and **E-Mail Address** as illustrated in Figure 11.15

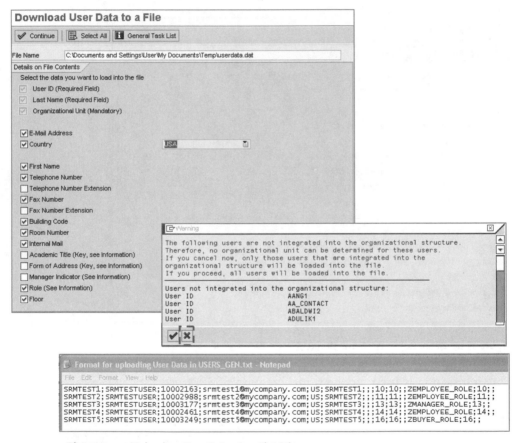

Figure 11.15 Uploading User Data via a Flat File

The data fields in the upload file should contain a separate row for each user record and the fields separated via a semicolon. It is important that the order of the data fields in the file have to be in the order specified in the **Details on File Contents** section as illustrated in Figure 11.15.

Security administrators can select the Download Users to a File method to create a download of the file, as it then provides the appropriate format for an Upload file that can then be used as an input file for the Upload Users from File method. Figure 11.16 illustrates an example of how a file can be generated using the **Download User Data to a File** method.

This method allows selecting the data fields that you want to download into the file. In our example in Figure 11.16, notice that if users are not integrated into the organizational structure, a **Warning** is displayed indicating that certain users are not integrated in the Organizational Structure and whether those users should be included in the downloaded file.

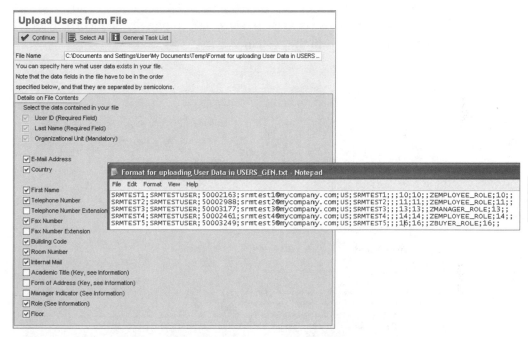

Figure 11.16 Downloading User Data to a Flat File

Note

The Organizational Unit is required for each user record. This information needs to be provided by the SRM functional team creating the Organizational Structure. This is an iterative process as the Organizational Structure within SRM continues to change as additional data is gathered by the organization. Organizational Units could be added and deleted. Therefore this upload file would change over time.

In the standard system, if the user record contains an email address, the system creates a password and sends it to the user's email address.

Import Users from Other Systems via RFC

It is possible to create users in SRM by importing user information from another R/3 system via Remote Function Call (RFC) as shown in Figure 11.17. Assuming that the appropriate RFC destinations are already created in Transaction SM59, the users can be uploaded from the corresponding system.

If the user record in the standard system contains an email address, the system creates a password and sends it to the user's email address. Some security administrators like this functionality because the users are automatically notified and the security team can expend less effort reaching out to users. Many security administrators are wary of this functionality, however, as they do not want passwords sent via email, especially if incorrect email addresses are captured in the system.

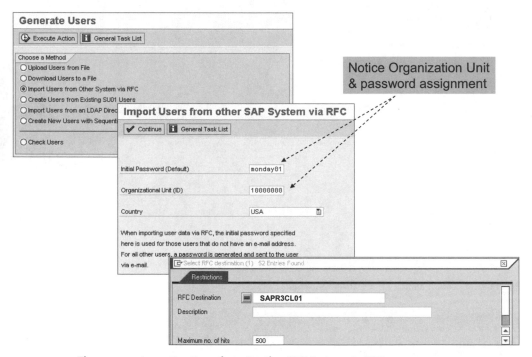

Figure 11.17 Importing Users from Another SAP System via RFC

You need to enter a default **Initial Password** and **Organizational Unit (O)** as a prerequisite, which then becomes a default Organizational Unit where all the users are created. Once the user creation is complete, a record from Position (S) to Business Partner (BP) to User (US) is created, which can then be moved within the Organizational Structure. Note that this can be a very tedious process depending on how large the Organizational Structure is for the organization.

It is important to note that a subsequent step is required after this function to assign any additional roles to the users. The standard transaction assigns the BBP*EMPLOYEE role to the user records as a default. Role assignment thus can be done via Transaction </PFCG>.

Create Users from Existing SU01 Users

Using this method, organizations can convert existing SU01 users into SRM users. This is especially useful if the user record is already created in SRM or possibly created using the CUA application. In Figure 11.18, we illustrate how users created in SU01 can then be integrated within the Organizational Structure.

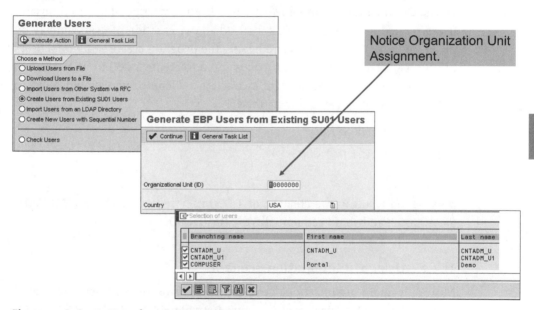

Figure 11.18 Create Users from Existing SU01 Users

It is required to enter an **Organizational Unit (O)** as a prerequisite, which then becomes a default Organizational Unit where all the users are created. Once the user creation is complete, a Position-Business Partner-User relationship is created, which can then be moved within the Organizational Structure. Remember, that this can be a very tedious process depending on how large the Organizational Structure is for the organization.

Import EBP Users from an LDAP Directory

In this method, LDAP users are imported into SRM to create Transaction SU01 records. A secondary step is executed to assign the individual Organizational Units to the users to integrate in the Organizational Structure. The second step is similar to what has been explained in the method Create Users from Existing SU01 Users.

Most large organizations use a corporate LDAP directory to maintain all the users in the organization and their appropriate authorizations. Using the Import EBP Users from an LDAP Directory method, organizations can quickly create users in SRM from an existing data source.

Create New Users with Sequential Number

This scenario is useful when mass-creating a number of users for testing purposes. Uses include performance or stress testing, when you need a thousand users created in the system. This method allows creation of users quickly by providing a basic convention and having the program create sequential users in EBP. Let's take an example. If you wanted to create 1,000 users beginning with the name as SRM, of eight-characters in length, you would need to enter the following using this method:

▶ Leading Initial: SRM

▶ Number part: 1 to 1,000

▶ Length: 8

This would result in the creation of 1,000 user records such as SRM00001, SRM00002, and so on sequentially to SRM01000.

11.3.2 Using HR Integration Scenario

More and more organizations are planning to use the SAP best practice of integrating the Organizational Structure between SAP R/3 HR and SAP SRM. In Section 11.3.1, we described the scenario where the Organizational Structure was being maintained independently in SRM with no integration with the HR Organizational Structure. In this section, we'll cover the scenario where the Organizational Structure is being maintained in SAP R/3 and periodically being distributed to SRM.

What impact does this have on security? When distributing the Organizational Structure from R/3, organizations have the option of distributing the

Organizational Unit, Positions and also the employees, as illustrated in Figure 11.19.

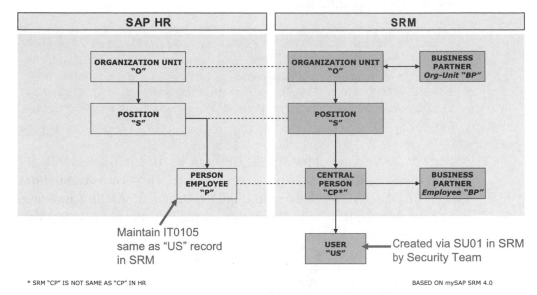

Figure 11.19 Distribution of Organizational Units, Positions, and Employees from SAP R/3 HR into SAP SRM

The HR integration scenario follows SAP best practices, as it reduces maintenance across a multitude of functions. The Organizational Structure is only being maintained primarily in SAP R/3, and dual maintenance is reduced in SRM. HR is usually the system with data of record for the organization anyway. From a security perspective, this scenario reduces the maintenance of user records dramatically. When HR Integration occurs, the only prerequisite for security teams is to create the standard user record in SRM prior to the distribution of the employees from the HR system.

Figure 11.19 illustrates that the User record Object US needs to be created in SRM. One additional important point is that the Info Record IT0105 for the employee Object P in SAP HR has to be exactly the same as the User ID in SRM. Once the value in IT0105 in HR matches the User ID in SRM, a business partner record is created. The process of distributing the Organizational Structure is discussed in detail in Chapter 8.

If the organization is planning to use position-based security, then security roles can be assigned directly to the **Position** in SAP R/3. Using the distribution model, the roles can be transferred to SAP SRM along with the Organizational Unit, position, and employee. This further reduces the maintenance effort required for the security teams. Please note however, that in this scenario, the roles have to be created in SRM as the Web services transactions and corresponding authorization objects are only available in SRM.

> **Note**
>
> When HR Integration is active, all employee personal data must be managed in the HR personnel management transactions, and therefore the SRM transactions BBPUSERMAINT and USERS_GEN are deactivated. Users are only allowed to change certain fields for default assignment under the **Settings** section (Transaction BBPAT05).

Figure 11.20 illustrates how USERS_GEN can be used in SRM even if HR Integration is active. This is not a best practice. However, organizations might find the need for this option if the HR Organizational Structure does not have certain positions and users that are required in the SRM Organizational Structure.

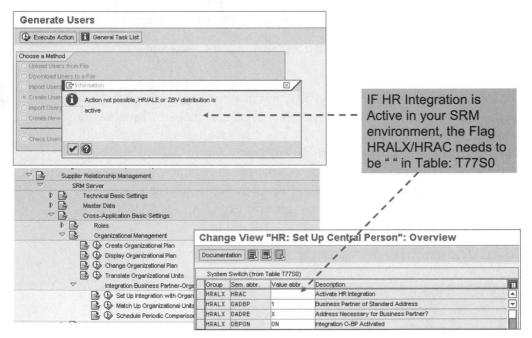

Figure 11.20 Alternate Method to Activate USERS_GEN When HR Integration is Active in SRM

11.3.3 Using CUA Within SRM

CUA allows security teams to create and manage SAP users centrally within one system and distribute the user records to all the connected systems via ALE. SRM can be operated together within a CUA environment, but there are certain restrictions. In this section we will explain how SRM can be used with SAP CUA. Central user administration in SRM can be integrated in two scenarios:

▶ HR Integration is active, as described in Section 11.3.2

▶ Users are managed in SRM using the user-management transactions Manage Users (BBPUSERMAINT or BBPUM01), as was explained in Section 11.3.

When HR Integration is active, all employee personal data must be managed in the HR personnel management transactions, and therefore the SRM transactions Manage Users and My Settings are deactivated. Figure 11.21 illustrates how CUA can be used in this scenario. Let's review these steps now:

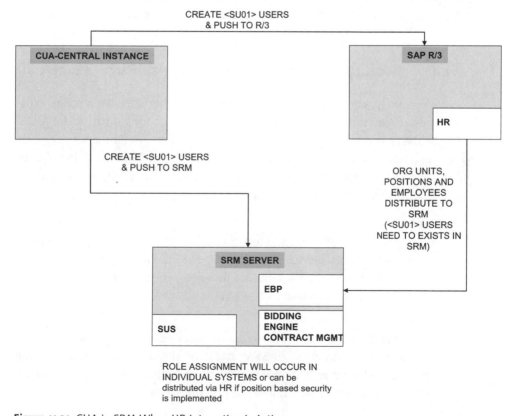

Figure 11.21 CUA in SRM When HR Integration is Active

1. **Users Created Locally Within CUA System**
   All users are created locally within the **CUA-CENTRAL INSTANCE** system and are distributed to the **SAP R/3** and **SRM SERVER** system via ALE IDocs. This creates the user record object US in both R/3 and SRM.

2. **HR Data Distribution from SAP R/3 to SAP SRM**
   Once the users are distributed in the **SRM SERVER**, the Organizational Units, Positions, and Employee data can be distributed from **SAP R/3** HR into SRM. This creates the required business partner (BP) to User (US) relationship record required in SRM. It is important that the IT0105 Infotype in the Employee record in SAP R/3 contains the user value that is exactly the same as the User ID in SRM.

It is not possible to create external users in SRM within a CUA environment. SRM 4.0, SUS 3.0 is currently not integrated with the CUA.

So far, we've concentrated on the creation of users in SRM that are internal to the organization. As the SRM solution is tightly integrated with external business partners like vendors and bidders, we will discuss in the next section the process of creating users that are external to your organization.

11.4   User Creation in SRM for Enterprise Buyer (External)

As we already know, SRM contains business scenarios where an external business partner needs to access and perform functions within SAP SRM. Therefore, it is necessary to create user records for external business partners — e.g.,company data for vendors and bidders — and master data for individual contact persons from the external vendor. In SRM, the following applications require external business partner access:

▶ **Bidding Engine**
   Bidding Engine in SRM is used for external vendors to submit competitive bids on goods and services required by the purchasing organization. A contact person is created as a bidder for each vendor that needs to receive bid invitations and create bids in SRM.

▶ **Supplier Self Service**
   In Chapter 5, we discussed how organizations can use the Supplier Self Service (SUS) component in SRM to drive supplier enablement. Using SUS, business partners external to your organization can collaborate in the procurement cycle to streamline the procure-to-pay process.

In SRM, there a two ways external business partners can gain access. These are explained in the following bullet points:

▶ **Self-Registration**

Master data for external business partners (such as bidders and vendors) can be created based on a registration application from an employee of the business-partner company. Once the user completes the self-registration, the purchaser or system administrator receives a work item with a link to the *Manage Business Partners* application. The employee responsible can see the data that the requesting user entered and can complete it. Once external users have been created or maintained, contact persons receive e-mails containing their User IDs, and passwords.

▶ **User Creation via SAP SRM**

This is accomplished by using the administrator service *Manage Business Partners* (BBPMAININT). In SRM, a separate transaction is used to create bidders; the Manage Business Partner transaction </BBPMAININT> is used to create bidders, as illustrated in Figure 11.22.

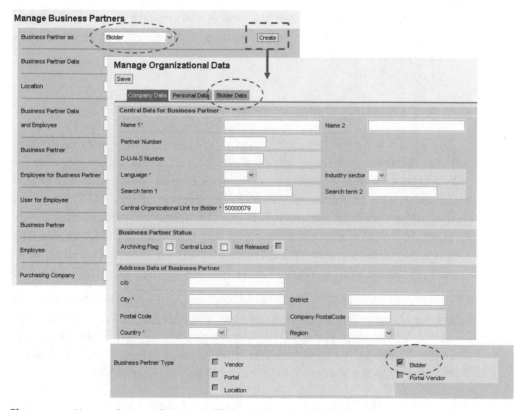

Figure 11.22 Manage Business Partners in SRM — Transaction BBPMAININT

Once bidders and/or contact persons are created in SRM, editing their user data is also done via the BBPMAININT transaction. In order to maintain the bidders in the BBPMAININT transaction, **Business Partner** and **Employee** numbers are required, as illustrated in Figure 11.23.

Business Partner Data

and Employee   Edit

Figure 11.23 Edit Business Partners (Bidders) using BBPMAININT

> **Note**
>
> Both Bidding Engine and SUS require the vendor contact persons to gain access to these applications hosted inside of your organization firewall. Additional security might be required to enable SAP Enterprise Portal to provide access or require SSL certificates for authentication. Most organizations today are implementing the bidding and SUS applications via the SAP Enterprise Portal.

In Section 11.4, we discussed the process of creating users within SRM. Equally important is the discussion on how to delete users in SRM, which is the subject of the next section.

11.5   Deleting Users in SRM

You sometimes need to delete users in the SRM system. A user could have been created incorrectly, for example, or test users might need to be removed from the system. As we discussed earlier, a complete user in SRM is a combination of the objects Position (S), Business Partner (BP), and User (US). When security administrators use the User Management transaction, SU01, to delete a user, the only object that is deleted is the US object. The remaining objects S and BP are incorrectly left undeleted. Therefore, deletion of users in SRM using the Transaction SU01 is not correct.

Deletion of users in SRM should only be carried out using the administration service Manage User Data (Transaction BBPUSERMAINT). When you do this, all the relationships for the US object are deleted, as well as the BP and US objects. Figure 11.24 illustrates the Manage User Data application (BBPUSERMAINT), which also allows us to delete users in SRM.

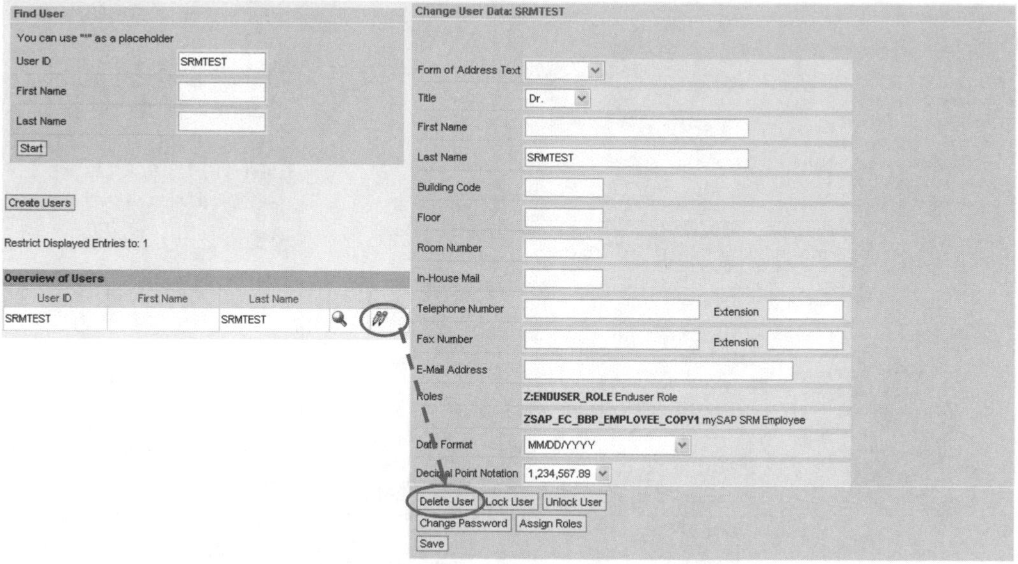

Figure 11.24 Deleting Users via Manage User Data — Transaction BBPUSERMAINT

In the example illustrated in Figure 11.24, the **SRMTEST** User ID can be deleted by clicking the change button (pencils) in the **Overview of Users** and then clicking on the **Delete User** button in the **Change User Data** section.

> **Tip**
>
> SAP recommends that users in SRM be deleted using the transaction illustrated in Figure 11.24.

As users in SRM need to be integrated into the Organizational Structures, it is often necessary to check users to ensure their consistency. In the next section we discuss the process of checking users in SRM.

11.6 Checking Users in SRM

SAP delivers a standard transaction USERS_GEN to check the consistency of users in SRM. This same transaction also makes it possible to repair any defective users. In Figure 11.25 I illustrate how the user check can be conducted. Once the **Check Users** radio button is selected, the **Execute Action** button is used to begin the process of checking users. In the subsequent **Check and Repair EBP Users** screen, we can either **Check Individual Users** or **Check Multiple Users** as illustrated in Figure 11.25.

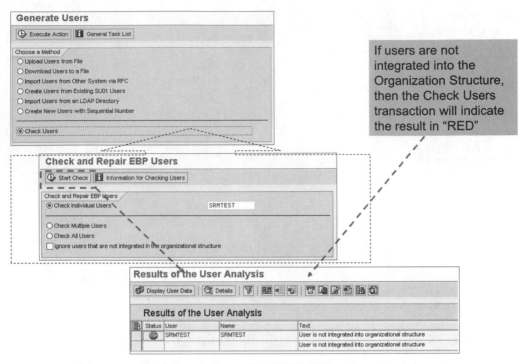

Figure 11.25 Check Users in Transaction USERS_GEN

In the example illustrated in Figure 11.25, we we wcheck an individual user **SRMTEST**. The result of the user analysis is that the user **SRMTEST** is not integrated within the Organizational Structure and therefore is not consistent. This user needs to be repaired prior to using executing any SRM transactions for shopping cart, approvals, etc. However, this user cannot be repaired unless integrated into the Organizational Structure.

Figure 11.26 illustrates the scenario where the same user SRMTEST has been integrated into the Organizational Structure via the Transaction </USERS_GEN> option to create users from existing SU01 users. When the check user's function is executed again, the user analysis shows that the **SRMTEST** user is now consistent. If the users are displayed with green traffic light icons in the list of results, that indicates consistency. It is also important that the Organizational Unit where the user is being integrated is also consistent. This can be checked in Transaction CRM_OM_BP_INTEGRATE. Only when the traffic light icon for the entire Organizational Unit is green is the Organizational Unit consistent.

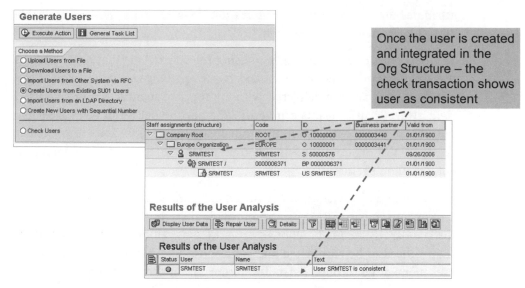

Figure 11.26 Check Users in SRM — Example of a Consistent User

The Check Users function should be executed on a periodic basis in the SRM environment. When users are found to be inconsistent, this transaction also provides a mechanism to repair the users.

> **Tip**
>
> If you have HR/ALE distribution active, users cannot be repaired in SRM using the USERS_GEN transaction. To repair the user data, you must redistribute using HR/ALE replication.

In the next section, we will discuss roles and authorizations within SAP SRM and the best practices organizations can use to manage this security.

11.7 Roles and Authorizations in SRM

SAP SRM comes delivered with a large number of predefined role templates that organizations can use directly or customize for their organization's requirements. Each user in the SRM system is assigned one or more roles that provide authorization to execute specific transactions.

When talking about roles and authorizations, it is important to understand that along with a role assignment, users in SRM are also required to be integrated in the Organizational Structure. This allows them to inherit specific attributes that further enhance or restrict their access in SRM. This is discussed in greater detail in Section 13.8.

SAP best practice when it comes to using roles in SRM is that organizations use the standard delivered roles and create customer specific Z roles. The standard roles are pre-delivered with appropriate menus that can be used right away. Security teams can verify whether the delivered roles meet the business requirements. If not, they can create roles tailored to the particular needs of the organization, assign transactions to them, and generate an authorization profile.

For sandbox and development environments, the quickest option is to create Z roles for standard SRM roles and provide these to the project team. Once the standard system is functional, project teams can decide on which transactions need to be eliminated and can choose to just delete those from the user menu or go through a detailed authorization check activity.

Remember, end users in SRM access SRM using a standard Web browser, so they are not executing the transactions directly. Rather, they are using the services available in their user- menu in the Web and executing only those services (see a caveat regarding this further in this section). The key lesson here is that users cannot execute the SU53 transaction in the Web, which is widely used in SAP R/3 to get details on the authorizations missing for an end user. Security administrators therefore will need to use other tools to get information on missing user authorizations.

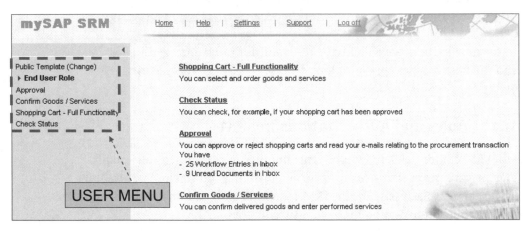

Figure 11.27 Example of a User Menu in SRM

Table 11.1 provides a list of standard roles delivered in SRM release 5.0. This includes the most-used roles on SRM project implementations.

Role	Role Description
SAP_BBP_STAL_EMPLOYEE	SAP SRM Employee
SAP_BBP_STAL_PLANNER	SAP SRM Component Planner
SAP_BBP_STAL_PURCHASER	SAP SRM Professional Purchaser
SAP_BBP_STAL_MANAGER	SAP SRM Manager
SAP_BBP_STAL_BIDDER	SAP SRM Bidder
SAP_BBP_STAL_VENDOR	SAP SRM Vendor
SAP_BBP_STAL_RECIPIENT	SAP SRM Goods Recipient
SAP_BBP_STAL_ADMINISTRATOR	SAP SRM Administrator
SAP_BBP_STAL_SECRETARY	SAP SRM Purchasing Assistant
SAP_BBP_STAL_ACCOUNTANT	SAP SRM Accountant
SAP_BBP_STAL_PURCHASE_MANAGER	SAP SRM Purchasing Manager
SAP_BBP_STAL_CONTENT_MANAGER	SAP SRM Manager Catalog Content
SAP_BBP_STAL_OPERAT_PURCHASER	SAP SRM Operational Purchaser
SAP_BBP_STAL_STRAT_PURCHASER	SAP SRM Strategic Purchaser

Table 11.1 List of Standard Roles in SAP SRM 5.0

The standard roles delivered in SAP SRM can be used across the different business scenarios. Most organizations that implement SAP SRM begin with the operational procurement business scenario. However underlying business requirement and the return on investment (ROI) entirely drive the various business scenarios implemented. Figure 11.28 illustrates the relationship between roles, business scenarios, and the underlying SAP components that power those business scenarios.

This list of these standard roles can be found in the Role Maintenance transaction, Transaction </PFCG>. For all composite relevant SRM roles, search for **SAP_BBP_STAL*** as illustrated in Figure 11.29.

The Application Security Guide for SAP SRM contains detailed information on the standard roles in SRM and the corresponding transactions and authorization objects within the roles. This information is useful for all project teams, as it is one of the first tasks conducted to gather security requirements on the project. Figure 11.30 illustrates the level of detail provided in the Application Security Guide, available for download from the SAP Service Marketplace.

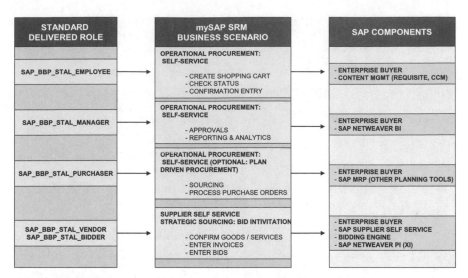

Figure 11.28 Sample Business Scenarios in SAP SRM and Roles Used

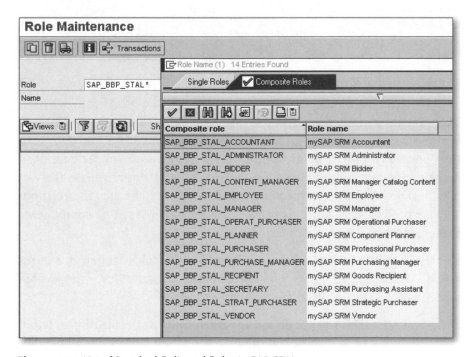

Figure 11.29 List of Standard Delivered Roles in SAP SRM

If organizations decide to create their own roles, the best practice is to always use the composite roles (**SAP_BBP_STAL***), which contain several single roles. Copying the composite roles helps to maintain the synchronization in the menu's built for SRM roles; otherwise, users will get the same menu entry multiple times in the browser. Figure 11.31 illustrates the standard menu for the Employee role.

Roles/Technical Names	Services (Menu Entry)	Transaction	Authorization Group	Authorization Objects	S_RFC	S_TCODE
Employee	Request	BBPSC18	AAAB	B_BUPA_RLT (02,03)	ARFC	BBP_BGRD _APPROVAL
SAP_EC_BBP _EMPLOYEE	Shop	BBPSC02		B_BUPR_BZT (ACTVT02; RELTYP BUR010)	BBP_ATTR_ MAINT	BBP_CTR _DISP
SAP_BBP_STAL _EMPLOYEE	Shop (one screen)	BBPSC03		S_ME_SYNC (38)	BBP_BD_ME TA_BAPIS	BBP_CTR _DISPNR
SAP_BBP_MUL TI_EMPLOYEE	Check Status	BBPSC04		S_PRO_AUTH (03)	BBP_BS_POD	BBP_CTR _EXT_PO
	Confirm Goods/Services	BBPCF02		S_RFC	BBP_BS_RQD	BBP_CTR _WF_APP

Figure 11.30 Sample Role — SAP_BBP_STAL_EMPLOYEE and Corresponding SAP SRM Authorization Objects

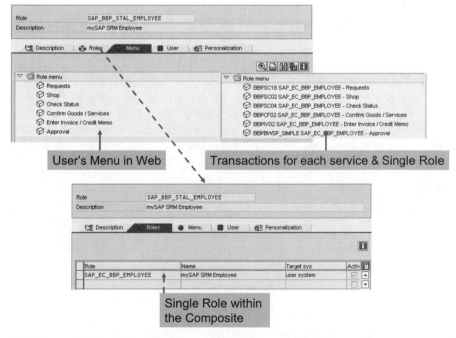

Figure 11.31 Standard Composite Role in SAP SRM

In SRM, the employee role is the most widely used role, as it contains transactions that are for creating shopping carts (which employees use to request goods and services). There are three different layouts of the shopping cart transaction, as shown in Table 11.2.

Shopping Cart Type	Transaction Code
Wizard Based	BBPSC02
Single Screen — simplified	BBPSC03
Extended form — professional users	BBPSC01

Table 11.2 Three Types Of Shopping Cart Forms and Corresponding GUI Transactions

However, the transaction </BBPSC01> is not available in the BBP_SAP_STAL_EMPLOYEE role. In the standard delivery, it is only available in the Operational Purchaser role </SAP_BBP_STAL_OPERAT_PURCHASER>. When organizations copy the standard Employee role, they will be unable to get access to the Extended Form BBPSC01 transaction unless they merge from the Purchaser role. Organizations planning to use Enterprise Portal and the standard business packages need to be aware that the same process will have to be done in the portal roles as well.

> **Note**
>
> This is a security caveat. SRM is accessed via a URL provided to all users. In the URL that provides access to SRM, knowledgeable users might be able to determine what services to execute (similar to executing a transaction in R/3). Figure 11.32 provides an illustration of a sample URL to access SRM. Here, if end users change the "BBP-START" service to "BBPIV02," they can launch the Invoice Entry transaction. If this is done, then users can possibly access additional transactions that might not be available in their user menu. This is only possible if the SRM application is being accessed directly and not via business packages within Enterprise Portal.

Figure 11.32 Example URL to Access the SRM Application

11.7.1 Authorization Objects in SRM

Beginning with SAP SRM release 4.0, the authorization check has been changed and new authorization objects have been added that include authorization parameters and authorization fields. In previous SRM releases, users where only able to create/edit/display business documents (purchase order) according to their organizational unit dependencies (which means only one purchasing organization) inherited within the Organizational Structure in SRM.

Document Checks Using Authorization Objects in SRM determines whether a user can access a specific document (e.g., purchase order) and what functions (display, change, and so on) the user can carry out.

The Application Security Guide for SAP SRM contains detailed documentation on the standard roles in SRM and the corresponding transactions and authorization objects within the roles. Authorization objects that have been extended or newly created for SRM 5.0 are also included in this guide, which is available from the SAP Service Marketplace. A list of authorization objects relevant for SRM is available in Appendix G of this book.

SRM 5.0 Tip

From SRM Release 4.0 onwards, users have the ability to use **F4** help for available account assignments in the shopping cart and purchase-order transactions. Both the number and the description of an account assignment object or general-ledger account are displayed for back-end systems. In SAP SRM Release 5.0, organizations can customize whether a user is allowed to use **F4** help. This can be restricted in the single role SAP_EC_BBP_EMPLOYEE (or the customer specific employee role created for your organization), and by changing the values for authorization object **BBP_FUNCT**. Un-check entry **BE_F4_HELP**.

11.7.2 Roles Containing BSP Transactions Instead of ABAP Transactions

A few transactions within SRM are developed using the Business Server Pages (BSP) technology available in the Web Application Server (Web AS). These are HTML services that can only be executed over the Web and do not have corresponding transactions that can be executed within SRM. Remember, SRM transactions that we discussed previously, such as the shop transaction, are executed in the Web but do contain a corresponding ABAP transaction; e.g., BBPSC01.

These BSP transactions are delivered with SRM applications that are built using the BSP technology. Currently, the SUS and Catalog Management (CCM) applications are delivered using BSP technology.

Security teams have a challenge with creating roles based on these, as there are no corresponding ABAP transactions; see the illustration in Figure 11.33.

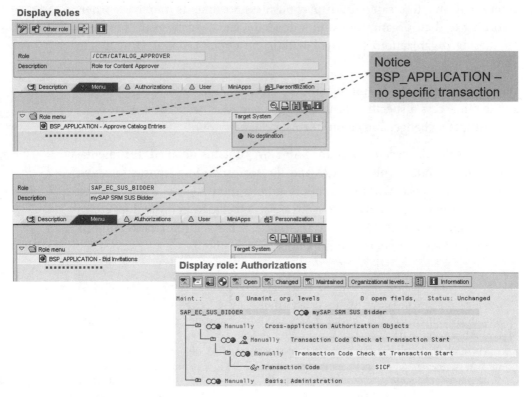

Figure 11.33 BSP-Based Transactions in SUS and CCM

In order to view the actual BSP that is being triggered, click on **Display details** in the BSP_APPLICATION service, as illustrated in Figure 11.34. These BSP applications are built using services that can be accessed via the BASIS transaction </SICF>.For example, the Approve Catalog Entries BSP can be accessed via service:/CCM/CAT_CDC/CDC_MAIN.do.

In Chapter 8, I introduced the concept of Organizational Structure in SRM. In the next section we will discuss the impact of the Organizational Structure on security. It is very important for security administrators to read the next section as the Organizational Structure in SRM provides a lot of controls such as catalog access, plants, purchasing groups, etc., which are relevant for security.

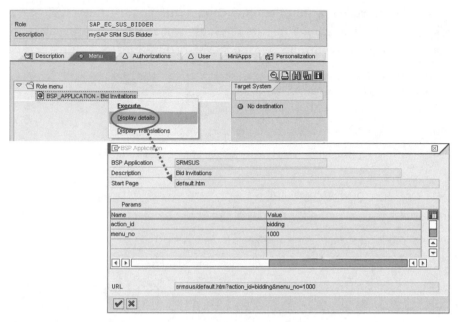

Figure 11.34 Display URL Accessed via the BSP Application

11.8 Impact of Organizational Structure in SRM on Security

The Organizational Structure is the heart of SAP SRM. Users cannot process any of the SRM functions such as creating shopping cart, approvals, or processing purchase orders until an Organizational Structure is created. It is very important for security professionals to understand the organizational structure in SRM because the Organizational Structure contains attributes that provide an additional level of security in addition to the SAP roles and integrated authorizations.

11.8.1 Organizational Structure as a Security Mechanism

The Organizational Structure in SRM acts as a security mechanism to control the authorization a user has to various operational attributes such as company codes, cost centers, plants, etc. Sometimes we refer to it as an extension to the SAP user master.

Typically in SAP R/3, organizations secure the purchasing values such as Purchasing Organization, Plant, etc., using the SAP role assigned to the end user, making use of fields and values in the authorization objects. In SRM, many of these are controlled within the SRM Organizational Structure. Table 11.3 gives a list of user attributes that are relevant from a security perspective that are maintained and controlled via the SRM Organizational Structure.

Attribute	Description
BSA	Purchase Order document type
BUK	Company Code assigned to users
CAT	Catalog ID — Name of catalog an organization or user is allowed to access
CNT	Account Assignment (Cost Center) object allowed
ITS_DEST	The URL used to access the SRM Web front end
PURCH_GRP	Purchasing Group assignment to users
PURCH_ORG	Purchasing Organization assignment to users
ROLE	All roles that can be adopted by a person within an Organizational Unit
SLAPPROVER	Indicates the approver used in shopping cart workflows based on spending limit
SPEND_LIM	Spending limit assigned for a user.Once this limit is exceeded, approval workflow is triggered
WRK	Plants that users are allowed to access and assign for procurement

Table 11.3 Examples ofAttributes Within the Organizational Structure in SRM

Figure 11.35 illustrates an example of attributes assigned in the Organizational Structure. In our example, the **SLAPPROVER** attribute is selected in the **Attributes** tab, which contains a value of the approver who will get the approval notification for shopping carts. In addition to the SLAPPROVER attribute, security teams need to be aware of all the possible attributes that are planned for use within the SRM environment. They also must be aware of how the controls are going to be implemented within the organizational structure for audit compliance.

Most security teams are very sensitive to the accessibility of any user ID and password information within the SAP system outside of security transactions. In SRM, the catalog-management configuration contains explicit access information with **username** and **password** information that can be accessed by anyone having access to the IMG, as illustrated in Figure 11.36.

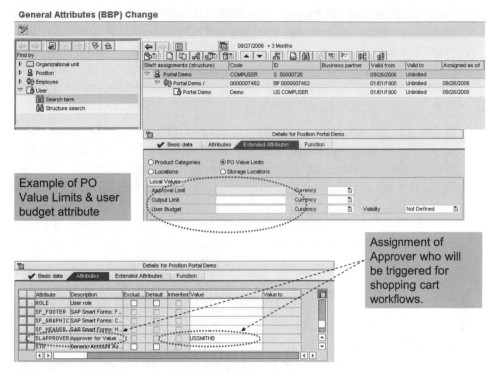

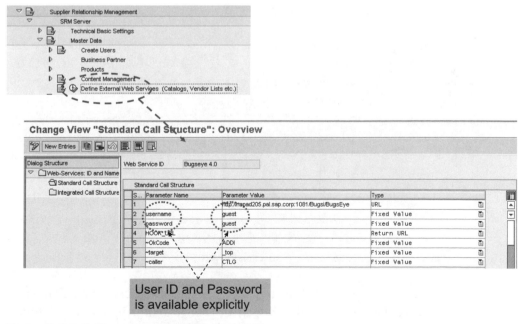

Figure 11.35 Attribute Assignment Within SRM Organizational Structure

Figure 11.36 Definition of Catalogs Within SRM IMG

Catalogs are a key functionality in SRM. Users can access catalogs within their shopping carts and view products and services offered by various vendors. The CAT attribute in the Organizational Structure controls who gets access to what catalogs within SRM. Security teams need to work with their functional project teams to decide which individuals need access to this setting.

In SAP R/3, users are aware of the parameters (PIDs) available in their user master record. These allow users to seamlessly default information into fields commonly used in transactions, for example the company code. In SRM, instead of using PIDs within the user master record, users can set attributes in the My Settings transaction </BBPAT05>. These attributes are configured within the Organizational Structure in SRM, and allow users to control defaults within their shopping cart transactions.

For example, if a user always assigns the charge codes against a cost center, he or she can use attribute Account assignment category and select Cost Center as a default value. This way, in the shopping cart, the **Account Assignment category Cost Center** will always be pre-selected. The same can be done if users wants to set their default plant value, they can use the **Plant* Attribute** as illustrated in the **Settings** transaction (also called **Change Settings**) shown in Figure 11.37.

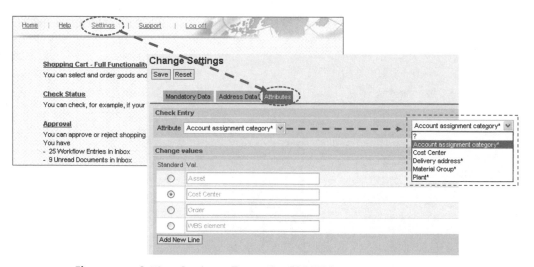

Figure 11.37 Settings Service — Transaction BBPAT05

You can configure SAP SRM to specify whether the users assigned to a particular role are authorized to display or change an attribute in My Settings.

Therefore, if the organization wants users to be able to set the **Cost Center** attribute, it can enable this access in the IMG.

The menu path is: **Supplier Relationship Management • SRM Server • Cross-Application Basic Settings • Roles • Maintain Attribute Access Rights by Role**. This is illustrated in Figure 11.38.

Notice in the figure the Cost Center Attribute **KNT** contains the **Access** of **Display** and **Change** depending on the role assignment in the **Act. Group** column. This means that all users with the role assignment of **SAP_EC_BBP_EMPLOYEE** can display the Cost Center, and users with the **SAP_EC_BBP_MANAGER** role have the access to change the Cost Center.

Security administrators should keep in mind that if customer-specific roles have been created, then those should be used instead of the standard SRM roles supplied by SAP as illustrated in Figure 11.38.

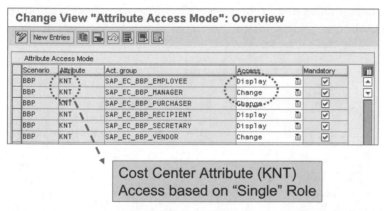

Figure 11.38 Maintain Attribute Access Rights by Role

In the next section we will discuss how organizations can secure the Organizational Structure maintenance in SRM. This can be especially useful for large organizations that might have a decentralized organization, such as one divided by geographical regions including Americas, EMEA, and Asia Pacific. Imagine a global organization that has a single SRM instance. For such an organization it's often impractical for a single department to maintain the Organizational Structure. Therefore, it is especially important to secure Organizational Structure maintenance transactions such that only specific groups are able to maintain specific portions of the structure.

11.8.2 Securing the Organizational Structure in a Decentralized Environment

In most SRM implementations, project and security teams forget that in addition to developing and managing security for all the end user roles, there needs to be a tight security on who should access and manage the Organizational Structure. This is true especially if the Organizational Structure is going to be maintained in a decentralized environment after go-live.

The core issues are as follows:

▶ The Organizational Structure in EBP is currently wide open to anyone who has authorization to access the Organizational Structure.

▶ Display and Change of the Organizational Structure need to be separated based on the Department/Organizational Unit.

The Organizational Structure can be secured using Transaction OOSP to create authorization profiles and Transaction OOSB to assign appropriate profiles to users who need to maintain the Organizational Structure, as illustrated in Figure 11.39.

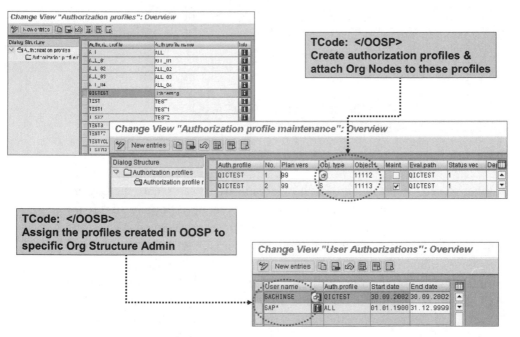

Figure 11.39 Securing the Organizational Structure

Users in SAP require roles to execute transactions and access data in the SAP system (SAP and SRM are synonymous here). In SAP, roles are either assigned directly to a user record or to a position object in the Organizational Structure. So far in this chapter, we have discussed how security roles are assigned to users directly via the role maintenance transaction, PFCG. In the next section, I will introduce the concept of position-based security in SAP and how it works with SRM.

11.9   Position-Based Security in SRM

Let's start by answering the most commonly asked question: Does Position Based Security work in SRM? The answer is yes. Now, let us explain what position-based security really means.

Position-based security aims to simplify the process of assigning roles to users in an organization. In position-based security, roles are assigned to a position in the Organizational Structure and then are applicable to any user that occupies that position. It is therefore important to state that position-based security is relevant only for organizations that implement the SAP HR module.

Let's take an example to explain this concept.A manager in a department has a particular SAP role. When this manager leaves the department, the same role will be assigned automatically to the new manager hired into that position. The role-assignment process will occur automatically in SAP with no action required by the security teams.

When role assignment is based on positions, the activity to assign roles is no longer triggered by routine turnover of employees, but instead by changes to processes, to positions, or to the department. Organizations either implement role-based security or position-based security, which also requires role assignment. Figure 11.40 provides a quick comparison between role based and position-based security.

Position-based security is relevant for SRM implementations when the HR organization structure is being integrated into SRM and the organization is implementing position based security in SAP. Chapter 8 discussed in detail the process of integrating the Organizational Structure in HR with SRM. In the HR integration scenario, the Organizational Units, positions, and employees' objects are distributed from SAP HR into SRM. In addition to distributing these objects, SAP roles assigned to those positions can also be distributed to SRM.

Role Based Security	Position Based Security
• Initial Setup is less involved	• Initial Setup is more involved.
• Process must be defined to add and remove Roles when people move in and out of organization. Employee mobility causes constant maintenance for security role assignment.	• At some organizations HR positions are not directly proportional to user's activities
	• Simplifies the process of granting user roles, organizations can assign roles to the position a user occupies in his or her department rather than to the person. Security maintenance is greatly reduced.
• Security & Role assignment typically lies within the Security team.	
• If approval workflow is being utilized within the SAP environment, the workflow to user assignment would be hard coded	• Position based role assignment limits role assignment activity caused by employee mobility.
	• Position maintenance is becomes the responsibility of HR and thus role assignment can be done by the HR team with assistance from Functional owners.
	• Security team is responsible for technical changes to the Roles.
	• If approval workflow is being utilized within the SAP environment, the workflow to user assignment can be via positions in HR

Figure 11.40 Role-Based vs. Position-Based Security

The HR Organizational Structure is distributed from SAP R/3 into SRM via a standard report, RHALEINI (or via Transaction PFAL). As part of customizing, organizations can maintain distribution filter(s) indicating the type of information that is to be distributed from the Organizational Structure in R/3 into SRM. For example, the payroll or bank-account information for a user in the HR master has no use in SRM and therefore is not distributed. However, the roles assigned to the position in which a user resides can be distributed via the object type **AG** in the filter definition. This is illustrated in Figure 11.41.

Notice, in Figure 11.41, that the **Infotype 1001** contains multiple object types: **O** for Organizational Unit, **P** for Person, **S** for Position, **C** for Job, and **AG** for Role. All the objects included in this filter are distributed from SAP HR into the SRM Organizational Structure.

Figure 11.42 provides a sample process for distributing the positions and roles from R/3 into SRM when position-based security is implemented. As illustrated, the role object AG is assigned to the position object **S** in the Organizational Structure in SAP HR. Note that one or more roles can be assigned to a single position.

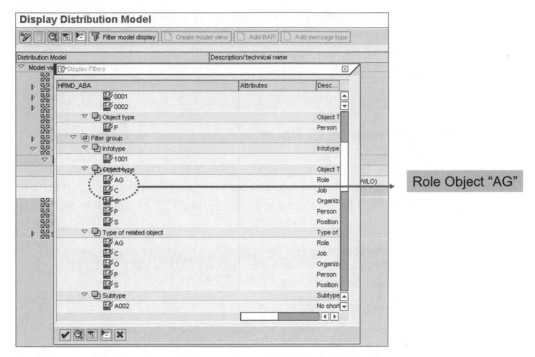

Figure 11.41 Distribution of Role Object (AG) Using ALE Distribution

Once all role assignments are complete, a standard job can be scheduled to execute the position to a role-synchronization process using the RHPROFLO and PFUD transactions in SAP R/3. At this point the Organizational Structure can be distributed to SRM using a filter to send the objects **O**, **S**, **P**, and **AG**. The last step in the process is to then execute the **PFUD** transaction in SRM to synchronize the user with the role assignment in SRM.

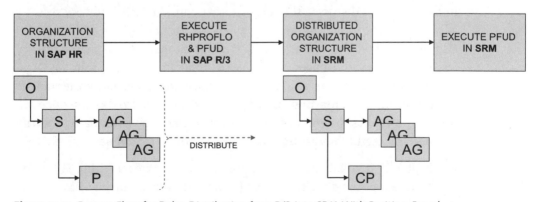

Figure 11.42 Process Flow for Roles Distribution from R/3 into SRM With Position-Based Security

471

In this section, we discussed the concept of position based security. This concept can be very beneficial for organizations that implement SAP HR and integrate the HR Organizational Structure with SRM.

Let us move on to review important OSS Notes for managing security.

11.10 Relevant OSS Notes

In this section, I've provided you with a list of important OSS Notes available on the SAP Service Marketplace that are relevant when managing security in SAP SRM. Table 11.4 lists the important notes and then describes what they entail.

Note	Description
501797	Check all EBP users
419423	Repairing incorrect EBP users
402592	SRM in the environment of a Central User Administration
548862	FAQ: EBP user administration
644124	EBP: Managing access rights to attributes per user role
857745	Generation of User Authorizations in EBP/CRM/SRM environment

Table 11.4 Important OSS Notes and Descriptions

11.11 Summary

In this chapter, I discussed the role of security in SAP SRM and how security administrators can manage security roles and authorizations within SRM. I also discussed why and how security is different in SRM and shared the key lesson that a functional user in SRM needs to be integrated within the Organizational Structure with a link to the position and business partner (a user master record in Transaction SU01 is not sufficient). I also discussed the difference on role vs. position-based security and how position-based security is especially useful to organizations using the SAP HR module.

In Chapter 12, I will discuss the importance of master data within SRM. You will learn about the different types of master-data elements in SRM and the strategy for maintaining master data on your SRM project.

U.S. businesses lose more than $600 billion each year from operational and staffing costs directly related to dealing with poor data quality and management. The need to clean, manage, process, and maintain master data is more than a best practice. It is imperative for business success. — The Data Warehousing Institute

12 Dependency of Master Data in SAP SRM and SAP R/3

SAP SRM is tightly integrated with the SAP R/3 and ERP solutions. The various components of HR, FI, MM, and other SAP modules all provide critical master data elements that provide a basis for an integrated solution. Many organizations manage their master data in various IT and business systems. Discrepancies between vendor, products, business partners, and other master data across the various systems lead to delays in processing time and incorrect decision-making. Harmonization of this data enables organizations to reduce costs and improve efficiency within their business processes.

In Figures 12.1 and 12.2, you can see an overview of the different types of master data that exist in SAP SRM and SAP R/3 or ERP. As master data can exist in both the SAP SRM and back-end systems, the figure also identifies elements that are *maintained, replicated,* or *distributed* from the back-end, and *used* in SAP SRM.

Master data elements such as vendors, locations, products, and product categories can be maintained in either the SAP SRM system or the SAP back-end. However, organizations with SAP R/3 or ERP back-ends maintain this master data in the SAP Enterprise system and replicate it to the SAP SRM system. SAP provides transactions and middleware to download this master data.

There also are objects such as general ledger (G/L) accounts, account assignments, purchasing organizations, and purchasing groups, which could be maintained in the SAP Enterprise system but are used in SAP SRM.

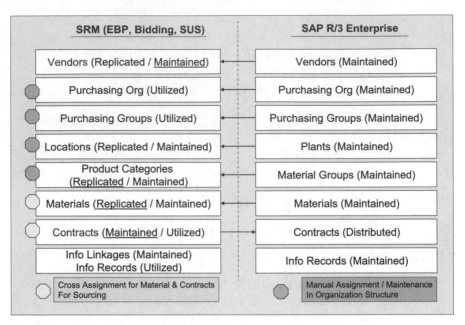

Figure 12.1 Master Data in SAP SRM and SAP R/3 Enterprise — I

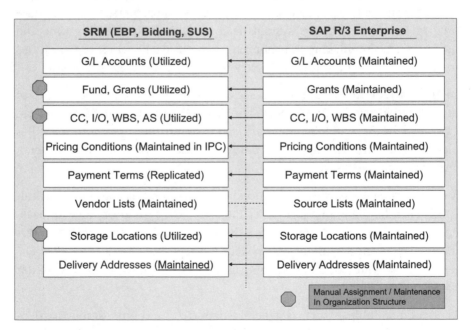

Figure 12.2 Master Data in SAP SRM and SAP R/3 Enterprise — II

A real-time validation occurs within the SAP back-end to check whether the master data being used in SRM is correct. G/L accounts are an example of such a validation. An error message is displayed in the SRM shopping cart if the G/L account used is not valid in the SAP back-end. Similarly, if an incorrect purchasing group is used in the SRM organization structure, a validation check occurs and an error is provided prior to purchase-order creation.

The organizational structure in Enterprise Buyer (EBP) is home to a number of the master data objects seen in Figure 12.1 and 12.2. The Purchasing Organization, Groups, Locations, Storage locations, and Delivery Addresses are all manually referenced in the Organizational Structure. These provide a mechanism of user defaults and attribute inheritance in business transactions, for example, a shopping cart, a purchase order, or a contract.

In the upcoming sections of this chapter, we will discuss each of these master-data elements.

12.1 Middleware

Products and categories can either be created manually in the SRM system or be replicated from the SAP back-end system. The middleware is a set of programs that exist partly in the EBP system and partly in the SAP back-end. This software is pre-delivered in the SAP system and is responsible for the replication of a number of master data objects.

Figure 12.3 shows how the middleware functions within SAP and the EBP. Essentially, a plug-in is installed within the SAP R/3 Basis layer and an adapter on the EBP system communicates with this plug-in. It is important to install the plug-in corresponding to your SAP SRM release.

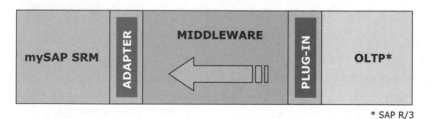

Figure 12.3 Middleware Function in SRM

The two main master data objects transferred from the SAP back-end into SRM are:

▶ Material Masters
▶ Material Groups

The data in SRM is downloaded from the back-end system using two mechanisms:

▶ **Initial Download**
The initial download allows for downloading all the required data (based on filter settings) for products (materials) and product categories (material groups).

▶ **Ongoing Delta Download**
Subsequently, a delta download occurs, whereby during the normal processing and operation the online transaction processing (OLTP) system sends the updated data for materials automatically. As an example, when a Material Master record is changed in the R/3 system, and if that material record is subject to the filter settings, the record is automatically sent from R/3 into SRM via the qRFC mechanism.

During the setup and configuration of SRM, filters can be configured in SRM to identify which products and categories should be downloaded from SAP R/3. These could be based on number ranges, material types, etc. Suppose, for example, that an organization wants to use SRM only for indirect goods and services procurement, and wants to continue the procurement of raw materials within the SAP ERP system. In that case, a filter should be set up within SRM that restricts the replication of raw-material type products from R/3 into SRM. Figure 12.4 shows an example of a material filter in SRM.

However, the delta download is only available for business objects and is not available for product categories, considered as a Customizing object. After the initial download, as new product categories are created in the back-end system, they need to be replicated manually using the initial-download mechanism. The relevant Customizing objects in SRM are given below:

▶ DNL_CUST_BASIS3: Basis CRM online

▶ DNL_CUST_PROD0: Material number conversions

▶ DNL_CUST_PROD1: Product categories

▶ DNL_CUST_SRVMAS: Customizing: service master

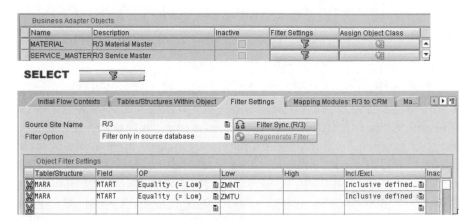

Figure 12.4 Material Filter in Transaction R3AC1

The relevant Business Adapter Objects in SRM are:

► MATERIAL R/3: Material Master

► SERVICE_MASTER R/3: Service Master

The initial download is triggered in SRM using the transaction <R3AS>. Once the parameter **Load Object** is specified with the customizing or business objects, and the sender (SAP back-end) and receiver (EBP/CRM) systems are specified, the download can be triggered.

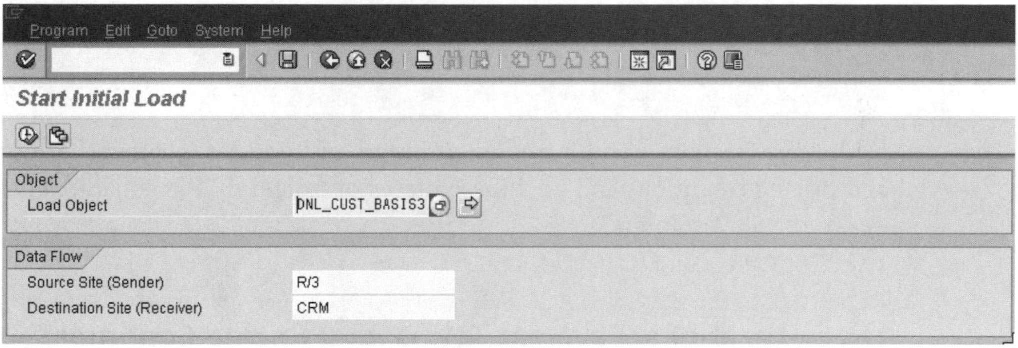

Figure 12.5 R3AS — Start Initial Download

The **Load Object** can contain more than one Customizing or business object for download. It is important to distinguish which objects have dependencies; only independent objects can be downloaded in parallel. For example, the MATERIAL business object cannot be downloaded before the DNL_CUST_PROD0 Customizing object is downloaded.

Once the objects have been downloaded, they can be accessed in the following transactions:

► <COMMPR01> (product master or materials)

► <COMM_HIERARCHY> (product categories or material groups)

Products and categories are stored internally in the SRM system as Global Unique Identifiers (GUIDs). End users do not come in contact with GUIDs, but configuration, technical and support analysts need to be aware of their function. Most function modules, programs, and Business Add Ins (BAdIs) use and access information in the SRM system with the use of GUIDs. In addition to products and categories, other objects in SRM such as shopping carts, purchase orders, vendor masters, etc. are all stored as GUIDs as well.

SAP provides documentation on the set up and replication of the middleware objects, which can be downloaded from the SAP Service Marketplace. In addition, Chapter 18 walks through the setup in SAP SRM to download the products and categories from SAP R/3 into SRM.

> **Note**
>
> The middleware concept in SAP SRM was a legacy of the SAP CRM solution. CRM, just like SRM, has master data needs that integrate back to the SAP R/3 core system (e.g., sales organizations, sales materials, etc.) The middleware for SRM was detached from the SAPCRM solution since release of SRM 4.0. This provided efficiencies and simplicity to the SRM solution as the CRM middleware objects were eliminated. In addition, this also made the download object Plant (DNL_PLANT) and the CRM-specific download objects (DNL_CUST_BASIS3 and DNL_CUST_BASIS5) obsolete.

In the next section, I will introduce concepts of locations, payment terms, and pricing conditions and how these pieces of master data enable capabilities in the SRM solution.

12.2 Locations, Payment Terms, and Pricing Conditions

In this section, I will cover some unrelated but integrated elements of master data: locations, payment terms, and pricing conditions. Locations and payment terms are mandatory master data elements that are needed for the procurement functionality in SRM. Locations define physical entities within an organization. Payment terms, though unrelated, are required to define the legal terms of agreement between the customer and the supplier. Let's discuss each of these in further detail.

12.2.1 Locations

In SRM the term *location* is synonymous to the term *plant* in SAP R/3. The function of a location in SRM is to define a physical entity of an organization. A standard program is used to replicate the locations (plants) existing in the SAP back end into SRM.

Once the locations have been replicated within the SRM system, an attribute assignment needs to be maintained in the Organizational Structure. The location attribute is maintained in the **Extended Attributes** tab in the Organizational Structure. This allows the end users to have access to one or many locations while creating shopping carts or purchase orders.

The location(s) are available for end users in their shopping carts basic data section. In the Classic or Extended Classic scenario, the location is sent to the R/3 purchase order as a plant.

> **Note**
>
> In SAP R/3, the plant determines the purchasing organization on a purchase order. However, in SRM the purchasing group determines the purchasing organization on a purchase order. Locations (plants) are only used to define a user's location. This is of great significance if multiple purchasing organizations are being used within the purchasing process.

12.2.2 Payment Terms

The procure-to-pay process in SAP uses the payment terms to determine the payment terms agreed upon between the vendor and the purchasing organization. These can be created locally in SRM (Standalone scenario) or can be replicated from the SAP back-end (Classic or Extended Classic scenario).

SAP provides the BBP_UPLOAD_PAYMENT_TERMS program/report to download the payment terms (see Table 12.1). The BBP_PAYTERM table in SRM can be used to verify and analyze the payment terms. Additionally, the payment terms can also be created manually in SRM by using this table. However, there is no procedure to replicate these from SRM to the SAP back-end. Also, ensure that the terms of payment texts are maintained in the tables.

SAP R/3 Back End	SAP SRM
T052	BBP_PAYTERM
T052U	BBP_PAYTERM_TEXT

Table 12.1 Maintenance of Payment Terms Texts

The terms of payment are available on the purchase order in SRM and can be changed during purchase order creation or processing. In the Classic or Extended Classic scenario, the terms are sent to the R/3 purchase order.

12.2.3 Pricing Conditions

In SAP SRM, pricing for purchase orders have the following priority:

- Manual price
- Contract price
- Catalog price
- Price from product linkage or from product

Organizations using an SAP back-end that want to transfer the pricing conditions from the SAP back-end (SAP R/3 or ERP), can use the standard report EBP_GET_BACK END_PRICES in SRM. Figure 12.6 illustrates this report. Notice that **Product ID** is a required field in this report. Additionally, organizations can choose to replicate prices based on an **Average value of all prices** or **Use first price**.

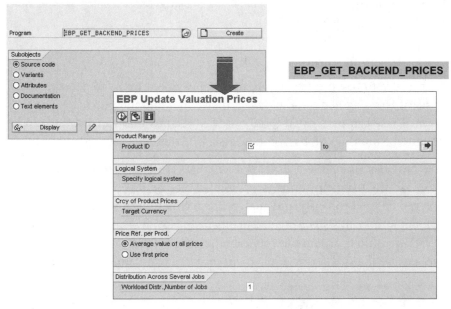

Figure 12.6 Transfer of Conditions from SAP Back End to SRM

In the next section, I will discuss the roles of interlinkages and vendor lists in SRM.

12.3   Interlinkages

In this section we talk about master-data element *interlinkage*. At the very basic level, an interlinkage provides the ability to create a relationship between a product, vendor, and price in SRM. This allows us to create a vendor-specific price for a particular product. Let's discuss this in further detail.

12.3.1   Interlinkages and Info Records

In SAP R/3 an Info Record is used significantly within the material procurement scenario. However, in SRM there are no Info Records that are created locally or replicated from the SAP back-end. In the SRM Standalone scenario the Info Record is not available for use. Only in the Classic or Extended Classic Scenario, if the Info Records are maintained in the SAP back end, can they be used for sourcing of shopping carts in SRM.

Interlinkages in SRM are similar to Info Records in SAP R/3. They are based on a product and vendor relationship and provide a mechanism to determine vendor-specific pricing for products while creating purchasing documents in SRM. The product linkage is created manually in transaction <COMMPR01>. Interlinkages are not as robust as Info Records and provide only minimal functionality. Most SRM projects do not use Interlinkages as master data.

In the next section, we introduce the concept of a vendor list, contract, and catalog in SRM and how they are related. Vendor lists create the relationship between a product or product category and a vendor. This way, organizations can create lists of preferred vendor relationships as sourcing criteria, which can be used when creating shopping carts, purchase orders and other documents. Let us discuss the relationship between a vendor list, contract, and catalog in detail.

12.4   Vendor Lists, Contracts, and Catalogs

In this section, I will uncover the relationship between vendor lists, contracts, and catalogs. The key between all of these master data elements is that all of them can be used as *fixed* sources of supply in the different purchasing documents. On most projects, there always seems to be confusion on the relationship between these applications. Figure 12.7 aims to clarify this confusion by illustrating the interaction between a vendor list, contract, and catalog.

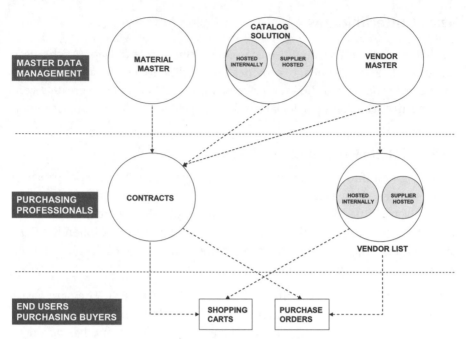

Figure 12.7 Understanding Master Data — Vendor List, Contracts, Catalogs

In most organizations, the material master and vendor master applications end up as the responsibility of the master data management team. For organizations that have in-house catalog applications, the support and management of the catalog are best handled by the master data management team as well. Using these master data objects, professional purchasers can create contracts and vendor lists in SAP SRM. Both contracts and vendor lists can be created using a material master or catalog item, and the vendor (business partner) is a required object.

Once contracts and vendor lists are created, they can be used as sources of supply in the shopping carts and purchase orders by end users or purchasing buyers. In addition, catalogs can be directly used in shopping carts and purchase orders.

12.4.1 Vendor Lists

Vendor lists in SRM correspond to source lists in SAP R/3. The vendor list provides a mechanism to create a sourcing relationship between a product or product category and a vendor. The purchasing organization can create preferred lists of vendors valid for a particular product or product category. Users can employ these vendor lists when searching for sources of supply for their purchases. Product-vendor lists take precedence over product-category vendor lists. The following information is required when creating a vendor list:

▶ A product or product category

▶ A vendor or back-end contract

The vendor list is integrated into every application that contains a vendor search help and in which you can display sources of supply such as the following:

▶ **Shop and Shop with Value Limit**
You can specify that only vendors maintained in the vendor list can be selected or just have them highlighted in the sources of supply overview.

▶ **Sourcing Application**
Professional purchasers can assign vendor lists as a source of supply when completing open requirements, but is not limited to these. If the Open Partner Interface (OPI) is connected, sourcing can be extended to cover external vendor lists.

▶ **Bidding Engine**
Strategic purchasers can search for bidders via defined vendor list for a product or product category.

In the vendor list, one or more vendors can be assigned as preferred sources of supply, and can be marked as active or inactive. This provides the flexibility to have access to the preferred suppliers for a particular product or product category and activate them when desired (illustrated in Figure 12.8). For example, if the active supplier is unable to provide the goods for a defined period of time due to back-ordering, the professional purchaser can activate an inactive supplier already available as a substitute in the list.

Using hierarchically arranged product categories (e.g., eCl@ss and UNSPSC), buyers can create a vendor list for a hierarchy subtree; i.e., combine multiple product categories. This vendor list is then valid for several product categories. Once the vendor list is released, all requirements that contain the hierarchical product category can use this vendor list as a source of supply.

Figure 12.9 illustrates an example of a hierarchy based vendor list. In this example, a product category of 008* is used to show how a wildcard-based category can be used to create a vendor list. Once this vendor list is created and released in SRM, purchasing professionals can use a wild card search of 008*, and all vendor lists that have been created for this hierarchy of categories is available.

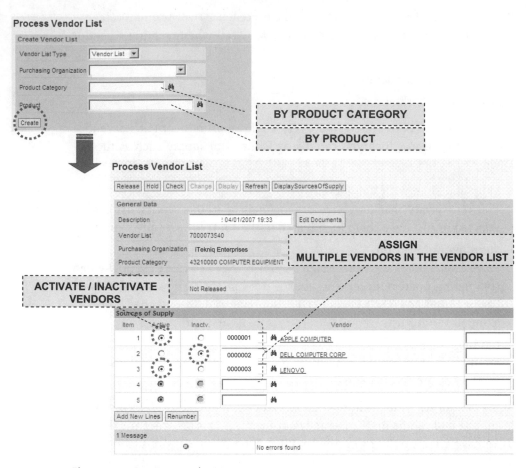

Figure 12.8 Creating Vendor Lists

If a purchasing organization is not specified in the vendor list, all purchasing organizations in the SRM system are allowed to use this business partner as a source of supply within the shopping cart and sourcing transactions.

The Classic scenario also allows contracts that exist in the SAP back end to be used within the SRM vendor list. Local contracts used in Extended Classic or Standalone scenario are not supported in the vendor list as of SAP SRM 4.0.

> **Note**
>
> Vendor lists in SRM do not provide any functionality for validity based on dates like source lists in SAP Materials Management (MM). An active or inactive radio button is available to activate various sources of supply. Additionally, a vendor list requires at least one source record active.

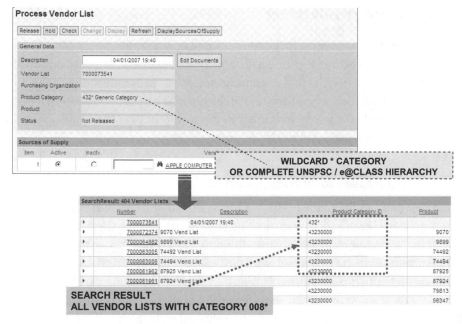

Figure 12.9 Vendor List Hierarchy by UNSPSC

12.4.2 Contracts

SRM provides the functionality to create value and quantity-based contracts that determine price and act as sources of supply in shopping carts and purchase orders. Additionally Global Outline Agreements (GOAs) for the entire organization can be created in SRM.

Contracts and GOAs can also be distributed from SRM to one or more backend systems, and can be used there locally. Contracts are discussed in detail in Chapter 6.

12.4.3 Catalogs

SRM provides the functionality for requisitioners and purchasers to access online and hosted catalogs to search for goods and services quickly and efficiently. These catalogs also make it possible for the organization to maintain compliance by offering access to selected products and services that have been pre-screened by the purchasing organization.

Catalogs and the concept of content management are discussed in detail in Chapter 8.

12.5 Delivery Addresses

In this section, I will discuss the need of delivery addresses in SRM. When we talk about procurement of goods and services, one of the key pieces of information that needs to be communicated to a vendor is a delivery address. In SRM, delivery addresses can be created by the SRM administrator and are available for use by end users in the different purchasing documents such as shopping carts and purchase orders.

12.5.1 Addresses for Business Partners

In SRM, you can maintain a ship-to address during the creation of a shopping cart on item level and to transfer this ship-to address to the SAP back-end system. It is important for organizations to know that the system behavior for ship-to addresses changed with SAP SRM 3.0 (EBP 3.5) release. Since then, a default ship-to-address is required for the shopping cart user in the organization structure. Then users have the ability to overwrite the default delivery address in the shopping cart (illustrated in Figure 12.10). Review OSS Note 701321.

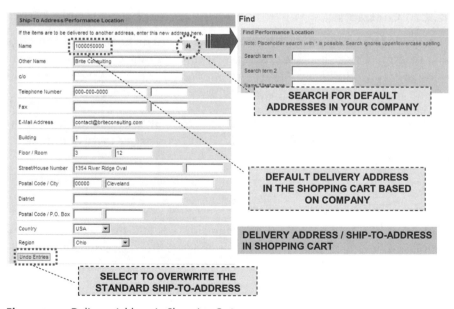

Figure 12.10 Delivery Address in Shopping Cart

In the standard solution, if the shopping cart line items have a delivery address (default or manually created), then the delivery address of the back-end purchase order is the same as the shopping cart. If no delivery address is specified in the shopping cart line item, the address in SAP R/3 is defaulted based on the plant data that was transferred from the shopping cart.

Project teams can create standard delivery addresses in SRM, which users can select from while creating their shopping carts. This simplifies the need for users to re-enter the standard delivery addresses manually. In SRM, addresses can be created for Organizational Units (in the Organizational Structure in PPOMA) that are marked as COMPANY under the function tab.

This allows the flexibility to create separate delivery addresses for one company vs. another (note that a company in SRM is not the same as the company code). The company could be any logical separation of the organization. Figure 12.11 shows the Organizational Structure transaction in SRM where the **Function** tab provides the ability to indicate an organization unit as a **Company**. SRM makes it possible to create one or more delivery addresses for each organization unit marked as a **Company**. This is illustrated in Figure 12.11.

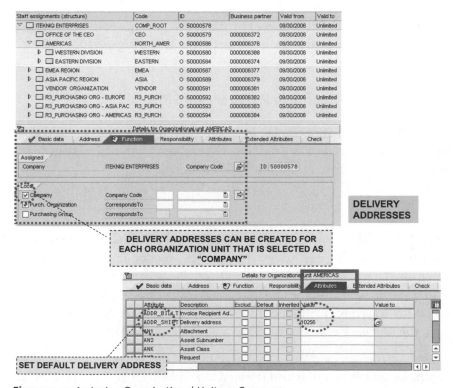

Figure 12.11 Assigning Organizational Units as Company

In SAP SRM, addresses can be created using the Maintain Internal Addresses application (BBPADDRINTC), shown in Figure 12.12.

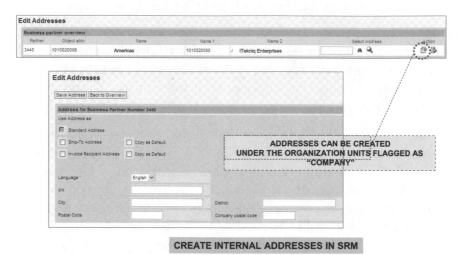

Figure 12.12 Creating Internal Addresses

Now that we've looked at addresses in your SRM system, let us proceed to a discussion of business partners in SRM external to the organization.

12.6   External Business Partners in SRM

Business partners in SRM can be internal to the organization or external to the organization. Vendors and bidders are considered external business partners. Let's discuss these business partners in detail.

12.6.1   Vendors

Similarly to products and categories, vendors can be maintained either in the SAP back end or the EBP system locally. The vendor in SRM is attached within the Organizational Structure and receives a corresponding business partner record similar to the Organizational Units. In SAP SRM, the concept of a business partner is introduced and a number of master data objects existing in the SAP back end correspond to a business partner in SRM.

Vendors, plants, and bidders are all examples of business partners. In SRM, the vendor master record is also referred to as a *business partner*. In SRM, an internal or external business partner is created for every person, organization, or group of people who could be involved in a business transaction (e.g., a purchase order or bid invitation).

Figure 12.13 illustrates the Manage Business Partner application (transaction BBPMAININT) in SRM. This application allows the creation and management of business partners in SRM. For example, a vendor can be flagged with status of **Central Lock** in the **Business Partner Status** section of this application.

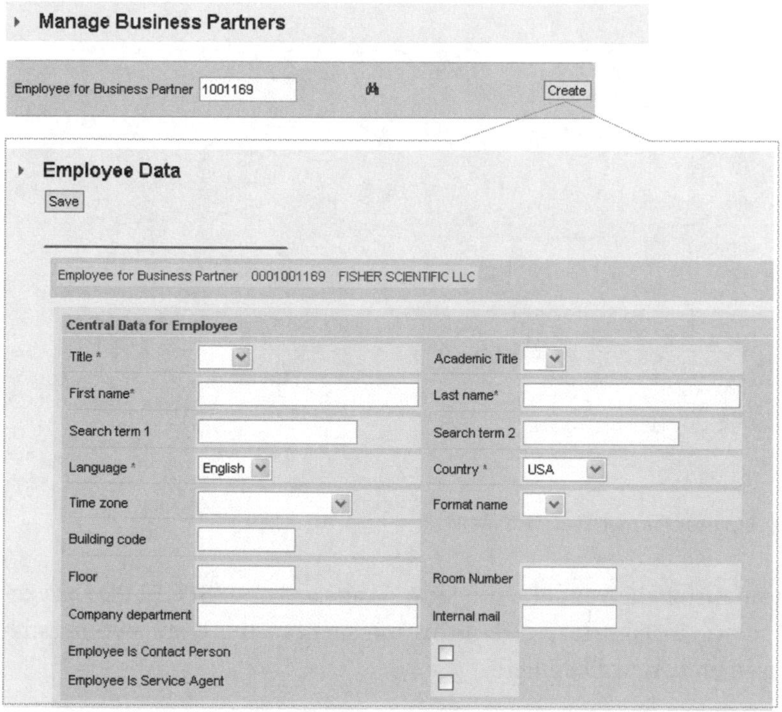

Figure 12.13 Managing Business Partner (Vendor) Transaction

Business partners, internal and external, can also be accessed via the Business Partner transaction (transaction BP) as shown in Figure 12.14. Notice that in the BP transaction, the **Display in BP role** field contains the type of business partner: Bidder, Business Partner (Gen), Financial Services BP, Organization Unit, and Vendor.

Several organizations using SRM maintain the vendor master in the back-end SAP system and replicate them within the SRM system. The core reasoning here is the existing processes for vendor maintenance in the enterprise system. SAP delivers a standard set of programs and transactions to replicate the vendor master from the back-end R/3 system to SRM. There are two different transactions that are available for the transfer of the vendor master: initial transfer of vendor master records, and the update/comparison of vendor master records.

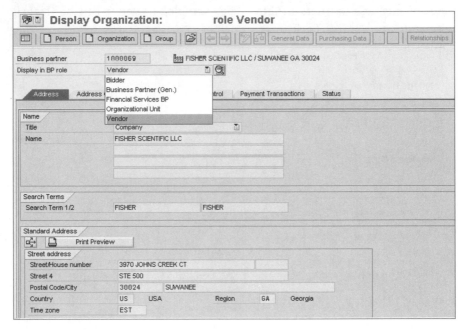

Figure 12.14 Business Partner Transaction <BP>

In order to transfer the vendors into SRM, Transaction <BBPGETVD> is executed, as shown in Figure 12.15. In this transaction, there are two mandatory requirements, described here:

▶ **Source System Information**
The source system is the back-end system where the vendor master record is maintained. The value specified in the **System** field is the RFC destination of the back-end client.

▶ **Target Organization Unit for Vendor**

The second mandatory element, **Object ID**, is the value for the **Vendor Root Organization** in the Organizational Structure, as shown in Figure 12.16.

In order to limit the selection of vendors for replication, additional fields are available in Transaction <BBPGETVD>. Once the values are maintained, it must be decided whether to keep the back-end number assignment or internally assign within SRM.

Transfer Vendor Master Records

Identification of Source Data

System ☑ _____

Limit Vendor Selection
Vendor   From   _____   To   _____
Purchasing Organization   From   _____   To   _____

Without Reference to Backend Purchasing Org.   ☐

Transfer Information Number (LFA1-KRAUS) from Dun & Bradstreet   ☐

Take Uniform Resource Location (LFA1-LFURL) as E-Mail   ☐

Address Comparison to Identify Duplicates   ☑

Only Transfer Vendors for the Following Roles   ☐

Organizational Unit for Vendor

Object ID   ☑ _____

○ Internal Number Assignment Only
◉ Only Transfer R/3 Numbers
○ If R/3 Number Assignment is not Possible: Internal Number Assignmnt

| Start Transfer | Cancel |

Figure 12.15 Vendor Master Replication Transaction <BBPGETVD>

General Attributes (BBP) Display

06/06/2006 + 3 Months

Find by
▽ ☐ Organizational unit
  📋 Search term
  📋 Structure search
  📋 Companies
  📋 Purchasing Organizations
  📋 Purchasing Groups
▷ 👤 Position

Hit List

Existence | Name | Chief
Vendor Root Organization

Staff assignments (structure)	Code	ID		Business partner	Valid from	Valid to	Assigned as of	Assigned until
▽ ☐ Vendor Root Organization	VEND_ORG	O 50000002		0000002861	11/10/2005	Unlimited		
▽ ☐ D2005111000001	D00001	O 50000009			11/10/2005	Unlimited	11/10/2005	Unlimited
☐ AJ STATION	AJ STATIONER	O 50000010		0001000001	11/10/2005	Unlimited	11/10/2005	Unlimited
☐ AM OFFICE	AMERICAN OFF	O 50000011		0001000002	11/10/2005	Unlimited	11/10/2005	Unlimited
☐ BECKMAN	BECKMAN COUL	O 50000012		0001000003	11/10/2005	Unlimited	11/10/2005	Unlimited
☐ BECKMAN	BECKMAN COUL	O 50000013		0001000004	11/10/2005	Unlimited	11/10/2005	Unlimited
☐ CARDINAL	CARDINAL HEA	O 50000014		0001000005	11/10/2005	Unlimited	11/10/2005	Unlimited
☐ CHESA OFF	CHESAPEAKE O	O 50000015		0001000006	11/10/2005	Unlimited	11/10/2005	Unlimited
☐ CLARK CONS	CLARK CONSTR	O 50000016		0001000007	11/10/2005	Unlimited	11/10/2005	Unlimited
☐ DENNETT	DANIEL DENNE	O 50000017		0001000008	11/10/2005	Unlimited	11/10/2005	Unlimited
☐ DENVILLE	DENVILLE SCI	O 50000018		0001000009	11/10/2005	Unlimited	11/10/2005	Unlimited
☐ DOURON	DOURON OFFIC	O 50000019		0001000010	11/10/2005	Unlimited	11/10/2005	Unlimited
☐ HANOVER	HANOVER UNIF	O 50000020		0001000011	11/10/2005	Unlimited	11/10/2005	Unlimited
☐ AUER	TIMOTHY AUER	O 50000021		0001000012	11/10/2005	Unlimited	11/10/2005	Unlimited
☐ MCKESSON	MCKESSON COR	O 50000022		0001000013	11/10/2005	Unlimited	11/10/2005	Unlimited
☐ OR SPECIAL	OR SPECIALTI	O 50000023		0001000014	11/10/2005	Unlimited	11/10/2005	Unlimited

Figure 12.16 Vendor Root in the Organizational Structure — Object ID

Prior to the actual transfer of the vendor records, a summary is provided to ensure that the appropriate records are being transferred, as shown in Figure 12.17. If there are discrepancies in the master data (e.g., purchasing view or incomplete vendor master), the program provides a list of the vendors that will not be replicated (number of vendors lost). The total number of vendors that will be replicated is also provided. Once the transmission is started, an application log captures the results for the transfer, which can be viewed in Transaction <SLG1>.

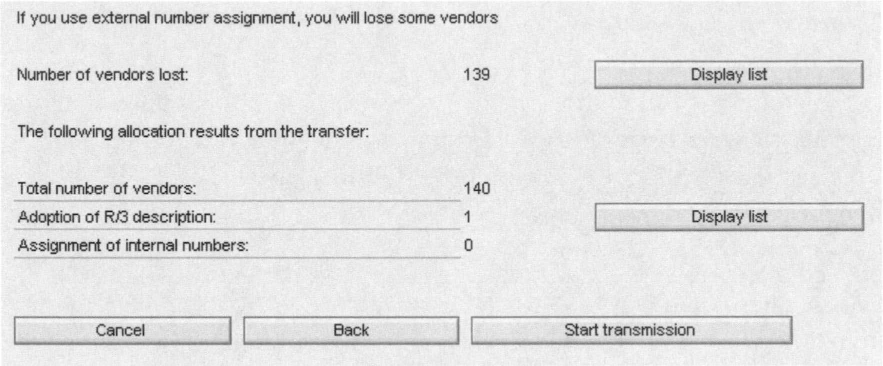

Figure 12.17 Summary of Vendor Transfer in BBPGETVD

> **Note**
>
> Only purchasing-relevant vendors are available for replication into SRM. Therefore, in many implementations the organizations have to go through the process of extending their existing vendor masters with purchasing views. Therefore A/P vendors can remain in the R/3 back end and only purchasing vendors are replicated in SRM.

At the technical level, the SRM supplier/vendor data can be found in tables VENMAP and BUT000. The VENMAP table contains the GUID for the business partner (vendor), and the BUT000 table contains additional vendor details.

> **Note**
>
> Make sure you set the business partner number range prior to the replication of vendors or the creation of any other business partners in SRM. Because vendors, organization units, plants, bidders, etc., are all business partner objects, it is important to review and set up the business partner number range before any records are created. (IMG: **Supplier Relationship Management • Cross-Application components • SAP Business Partner • Basic Settings • Number ranges and groupings**).

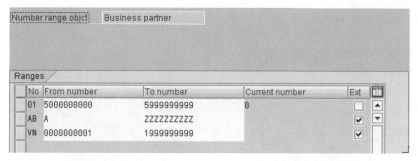

Figure 12.18 Business Partner Number Range

Once the number ranges are defined (see Figure 12.18), they can be assigned to the groupings to indicate internal vs. external. Grouping **0001** indicates **Internal Number Assignment**. This number range will be used for internal Organizational Structure (PPOMA_BBP) business partners and vendors created locally in SRM.

Grouping **0002** indicates **External Number Assignment** (see Figure 12.19). This number range will be used for external vendors that will be replicated from R/3. Typically, the R/3 number range for vendors will either be numeric or alphanumeric.

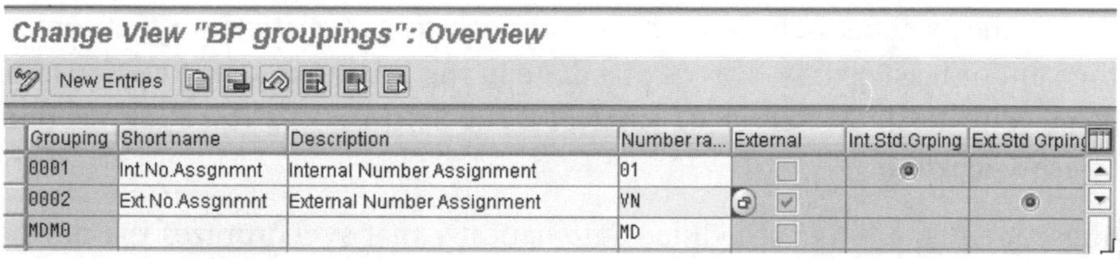

Figure 12.19 Business Partner Groupings

The vendor master can also be created manually in SRM using the transaction <BBPMAININT>, as shown in Figure 12.20. SAP does not provide a reverse process to transfer the vendor master records created in SRM back to SAP R/3. However, the replicated vendor records (i.e., those created in R/3 and replicated to SRM) that have been modified in SRM can be updated in R/3 via a standard XI scenario in SRM 5.0 release.

Once the vendor records have been replicated into SRM, any updates to the vendor master in SAP R/3 can be updated in SRM either using the Update transaction or a synchronization job can be scheduled. The update transaction <BBPUPDVD> compares the R/3 vendor record to the SRM record and replicates any changes.

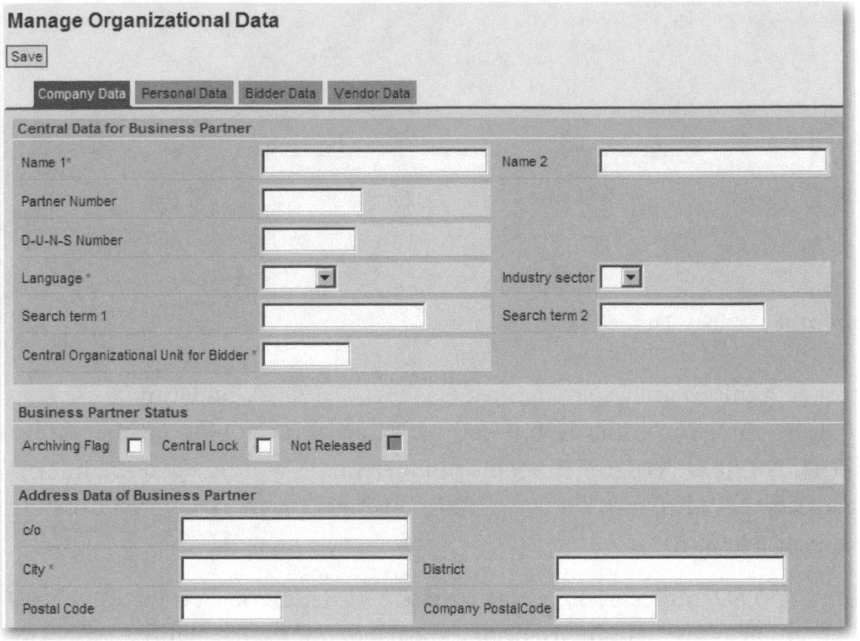

Manage Organizational Data

Save

| Company Data | Personal Data | Bidder Data | Vendor Data |

Central Data for Business Partner

Name 1*   Name 2

Partner Number

D-U-N-S Number

Language *   ▼   Industry sector   ▼

Search term 1   Search term 2

Central Organizational Unit for Bidder *

Business Partner Status

Archiving Flag ☐   Central Lock ☐   Not Released ■

Address Data of Business Partner

c/o

City *   District

Postal Code   Company PostalCode

Figure 12.20 Create Vendor Master Record in SRM <BBPMAININT>

As an alternative, using customizing for vendor synchronization, you can define the systems between which you wish to automatically synchronize the vendor master data. This can be done in the IMG: **Supplier Relationship Management • SRM Server • Technical Basic Settings • Settings for Vendor Synchronization**.

Subsequently, a job is scheduled automatically that synchronizes the newly created or changed vendor master data in the back-end and updates regularly in the EBP System. In addition to updates to the vendor master records, the **Create New Vendors Also** check box, allows for the transfer of new vendor master records in SRM as they are created in the R/3 back end (Figure 12.21)

Note

Table 12.2 contains information about the synchronization job.

BBP_VDSYNC_CUST	information about the last synch
BBP_NEWVD_LOG	new vendors added
BBP_SNEW_SYNCVD	new vendor added

Table 12.2 Synchronization Jobs

Change View "Global Settings for the Vendor Synchronization": Details

New Entries

☐ Create New Vendors Also

If vendors are to be created also, check the following details
☐ Carry Out Address Comparison to Determine Duplicates
Organizational Unit in EBP for the Vendor   ☑
Vendor Number Assignment Type   Only Assign R/3 Numbers

Figure 12.21 Vendor Synchronization

Vendor Replication in Extended Classic Scenario

In the Extended Classic scenario, local purchasing organizations and purchasing groups are required to create shopping carts and purchase orders. In this scenario, when the vendors are replicated from the SAP back-end using BBP-UPDVD program (vendor replication) or the vendor-synchronization programs, the vendor update in SRM is only for the R/3 purchasing organization. Because the local purchasing organizations are required in SRM for the Extended Classic or Standalone scenario, these replicated vendors (business partners) needs to be extended to the local purchasing organizations.

Organizations can use Transaction BBP_UPDATE_PORG for extending the vendors to the local purchasing organization (illustrated in Figure 12.22). Please also see OSS Note 390546.

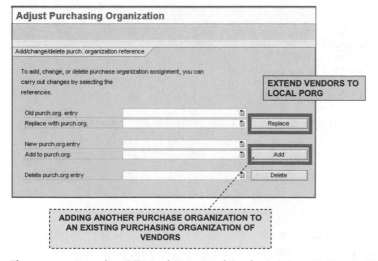

Figure 12.22 Extending R/3 Vendors to Local Purchasing Organizations in SRM

12.6.2 Bidders

A *bidder* is synonymous with an external vendor partner and is a subset of the vendor record in SRM. The vendor in SRM is a business partner (supplier or a service provider). A contact person or service agent is created in SRM for the external vendor organization that needs to engage in bidding or request-for-proposal functions with the purchasing organization. A contact person represents an end user in the vendor or bidder organization. Once a contact person (user ID) is created, vendors can log in via a pre-defined URL, access Bid Invitations, and enter their bids.

SAP security administrators need to be aware that bidders cannot just be created via the standard Transaction <SU01> (Create User), instead Transaction <BBPMAININT> is used to create bidder records (**Manage Business Partners**).

In BBPMAININT, the bidder's user ID, password, email address, and other details are specified. Once the record is saved, SRM creates an automated email containing the system access details that can be sent to the vendor. An example is shown in Figure 12.23. Notice, in our example illustrated in Figure 12.23, this email contains the **User** and **Password** information for the bidder. External partners (bidders) can click on the **links** specified in the email to access your SRM system.

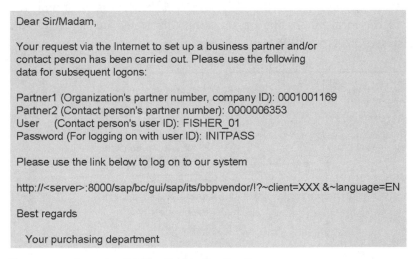

Dear Sir/Madam,

Your request via the Internet to set up a business partner and/or contact person has been carried out. Please use the following data for subsequent logons:

Partner1 (Organization's partner number, company ID): 0001001169
Partner2 (Contact person's partner number): 0000006353
User   (Contact person's user ID): FISHER_01
Password (For logging on with user ID): INITPASS

Please use the link below to log on to our system

http://<server>:8000/sap/bc/gui/sap/its/bbpvendor/!?~client=XXX &~language=EN

Best regards

  Your purchasing department

Figure 12.23 Example of Bidder Registration Email

SRM uses role-based authentication and therefore requires appropriate roles assigned to each user in the system. During the creation of a bidder, the system administrator can assign a default role for the bidder. However, only a single role assignment is allowed. If additional role assignment is required, a further manual step will be required.

SRM also provides the functionality of self-registration for external business partners. This functionality is described in detail in Chapter 5.

Although bidders are external users they still reside within the Organizational Structure in SRM. Position, business partner, and user records are created for each bidder contact person/service agent with the vendor organization in SRM, as shown in Figure 12.24. In our example, the business partner is **FISHER SCIENTIFIC** and the user record for the bidder is **FISHER_01**. Note that the user specified in Figure 12.23 is FISHER_01. Therefore when this user was created, an email is generated for the external business partner, in our example FISHER_01.

However, it should be noted that if HR Integration is active; i.e., the Organizational Structure is being distributed from HR to SRM, the vendor position, business partner, and user are only available in SRM and not in SAP HR. Therefore, these objects have to be created locally in the SRM Organizational Structure. HR Integration with SRM provides the ability to distribute the organization (**O**), position (**S**), and employee (**P**), etc. automatically. These objects are then only maintained in the SAP HR system.

Staff assignments (structure)	Code	ID	Business partner	Valid from	Valid to
▽ ☐ FISHER	FISHER SCIEN	O 50000381		04/04/2006	Unlimited
▽ 👤 SP		S 50000561		01/01/1900	Unlimited
▷ 🏢 FISHER SCIENTIFIC /	0000006353	BP 0000006353		01/01/1900	Unlimited
🏢 FISHER SCIENTIFIC	SCIENTIFIC	US FISHER_01		06/07/2006	12/30/9999

Figure 12.24 Business Partner and Contact Person Record for a Vendor

12.6.3 Portal Vendor

The Supplier Self Services (SUS) scenario allows vendors to perform a number of collaborative functions such as purchase-order processing, confirmation, invoice entry, and payment status inquiry. A portal vendor is a business partner that also exists as a business partner record in SUS.

The portal vendor is created in a similar fashion as a bidder. In the Manage Business Partner transaction, a field for *Portal Vendor* flags a vendor to be enabled for SUS.

12.7   Relevant OSS Notes

In this section, in Table 12.2, I have provided a list of important OSS Notes available on the SAP Service Marketplace that are relevant for master data in SAP SRM.

Note	Description
744359	ECS: Deactivate transfer of delivery address to back end
427906	Transfer of the delivery address to the back-end system

Table 12.3 OSS Notes

12.8   Summary

This chapter introduced you to a number of master data elements within SRM. We discussed business partners, replication of products and categories, contracts, vendor lists and other topics. Master data is a key component for any enterprise solution, and clean and harmonized master data is essential for enabling the true benefits of SRM.

Chapter 13 will introduce you to the architecture of SRM. We will review the different business-process scenarios and how each scenario might have a unique requirement from the architecture.

SAP SRM leverages the powerful capabilities of the SAP NetWeaver platform to integrate seamlessly with both third-party and SAP solutions. The SRM solution uses components within the NetWeaver platform, such as BI and MDM, to create a powerful strategic, operational and analytical supplier relationship management solution.

13 Architecture and Technology of SAP SRM

SAP SRM is built on the core SAP NetWeaver technology, the application and integration platform of SAP. SRM was one of the first SAP products that was launched on the SAP NetWeaver platform and it has been leveraging the power of NetWeaver ever since. The SRM solution is designed to harmonize processes both internal and external to the organization. The NetWeaver platform provides the flexibility in the SAP SRM solution to integrate the self-service, sourcing, catalog management, and supplier collaboration processes that drive the efficient processes within supplier relationship management.

The business scenarios in SAP SRM provide a range of functionality including global spend analysis, self-service procurement, strategic sourcing, content and master data management, and collaborative supplier processes such as order collaboration. These business scenarios are made possible by the software infrastructure delivered by SAP NetWeaver.

> **Note**
>
> It is important for you to understand that SAP NetWeaver is not a single product but rather a single platform. SAP NetWeaver provides a platform where a number of different components are included. Figure 13.1 illustrates the components within the SAP NetWeaver platform and how SAP Supplier Relationship Management (SRM) leverages the power of SAP NetWeaver.

In order for organizations to leverage the full opportunity within the SAP SRM solution, the SAP NetWeaver integration is a must. NetWeaver applications such as SAP NetWeaver Portal, Business Information Warehouse (BI), and the Exchange Infrastructure (XI) are key components of the SAP SRM solution. Figure 13.2 provides a simple illustration of the components that are used in SAP NetWeaver for SAP SRM.

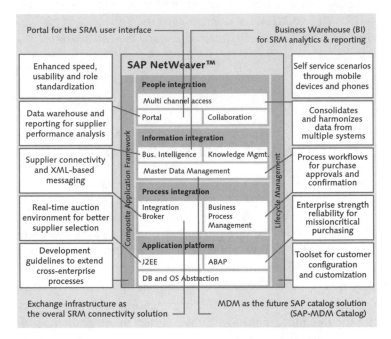

Figure 13.1 SAP SRM Leverages Integration Platform of NetWeaver

mySAP Business Suite / Solutions	SAP components						SAP NetWeaver					
	SAP R/3 Enterprise	SAP SCM	SAP CRM	SAP SRM	SAP SEM	SAP KW	SAP Web AS	SAP BW	SAP Enterprise Portal	SAP Exchange Infrastructure	SAP Mobile Infrastructure	SAP Master Data Management
my SAP Business Suite	✓	✓	✓	✓	✓	✓	✓	✓	✓	✓	✓	✓
my SAP CRM	✓	✓	✓		✓	✓	✓	✓	✓		✓	
my SAP SRM				✓			✓	✓	✓	✓	✓	✓
my SAP SCM	✓	✓	✓	✓		✓	✓	✓	✓	✓		
my SAP PLM	✓		✓	✓		✓	✓	✓	✓			
my SAP ERP	✓			✓	✓	✓	✓	✓	✓	✓	✓	✓

Figure 13.2 SAP and NetWeaver Components Used in SAP SRM

Remember that SAP SRM is a separate solution, independent of the R/3 or ERP solution offered by SAP. It is common for people to forget that SAP SRM is installed and implemented within its own three-tiered architectural landscape, independent from the SAP R/3 or ERP landscape. However, it is still an SAP system; the GUI for SRM is the same as for native SAP R/3, with an IMG for core-configuration. The difference lies in the user interface for SRM: End users only require a Web browser to access all the transactions.

13.1   SAP SRM Components and Matrix

The overall SRM solution is based on several different SAP components, integrated to provide a comprehensive solution offering. Some components are core to the SRM system; others are integrated with the SRM server to provide the solution offering.

13.1.1   Definition of Components

Before we discuss the integration of these components further, it is important that you understand the terminology and brief definitions of some of the components that make up the SRM solution:

▶ **SAP SRM or SRM Server**
  This solution has many names, which creates confusion for users. Figure 13.3 illustrates by example the different terminology for SAP SRM. SAP Supplier Relationship Management Server (SAP SRM Server) comprises SAP Enterprise Buyer (EBP), SAP Bidding Engine, and Supplier Self-Service (SUS).

▶ **SAP CCM**
  The Catalog and Content Management (CCM) solution replaces the earlier catalog offering from Requisite Technology SAP has offered CCM since 2004.

> **Note**
>
> Starting from SAP SRM 5.0 the SAP-MDM Catalog has been introduced based on the NetWeaver SAP MDM Solution.

▶ **SAP ITS**
  The Internet Transaction Server (ITS) is the link between the Internet and SAP applications. It enables users to access SAP transactions (including

SRM) using a Web browser. The ITS is a required component to access most of the transactions in SAP SRM. Since SAP SRM 4.0, the ITS is integrated within the Web AS layer.

▶ **SAP IPC**
The Internet Pricing Configurator (IPC) is a tool for product configuration and pricing in the Internet. In SAP SRM, it is a required component if the Extended Classic scenario is implemented.

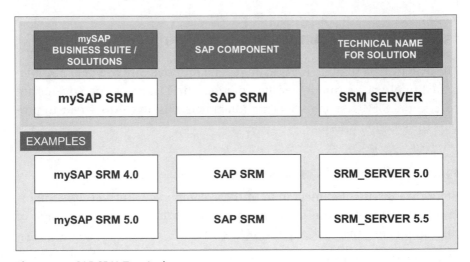

Figure 13.3 SAP SRM Terminology

▶ **SAP TREX**
This is the search and classification engine used across many SAP applications. It is actually a technical component of SAP NetWeaver that provides solutions with a wide range of functions for intelligent search, retrieval and classification of textual documents. The TREX engine is primarily used for catalog and contract management solutions in SRM.

▶ **Exchange Infrastructure**
As a part of SAP NetWeaver, SAP Exchange Infrastructure (XI) is the product for the message-based integration of all internal and external systems. It becomes a required component for organizations that want to use SUS, the CCM master-data inclusion scenario, transmission of purchasing documents via XML from SRM server, and other functionality.

In general there has been a shift in terminology for the NetWeaver components since the SAP NetWeaver 2004s release, which is integrated in the SAP SRM 5.0 release and higher. This is illustrated in Figure 13.4.

Previous SAP NetWeaver "compo-nents" providing certain capabilitys	Usage Type with SAP NetWeaver 2004s	Short name
SAP NetWeaver BI (SAP BW)	Business Intelligence	BI
SAP BW + SAP Web AS (Java)	BI Java Components	BI Java
SAP NetWeaver AS (SAP Web AS) + certain Java components	Development Infrastructure	DI
SAP NetWeaver AS (SAP Web AS)	Mobile Infrastructure	MI
SAP NetWeaver Portal (SAP EP)	Enterprise Portal	EP
SAP NetWeaver XI (SAP XI)	Process Integration	PI
SAP NetWeaver AS (SAP Web AS)	Application Server ABAP	AS ABAP
SAP NetWeaver AS (SAP Web AS)	Application Server Java	AS Java

Figure 13.4 SAP NetWeaver Components Terminology Shift

13.1.2 SRM Server Components — Overview

The SRM Server contains a combination of a few different components, such as EBP, Bidding Engine, and SUS. Figure 13.5 provides a very simple view of the components that make up the core SRM server. Depending on your implementation, these components can be installed on one or more servers and within separate clients. For example, **EBP** and **SUS** can be installed on a single server, but are always installed within separate clients.

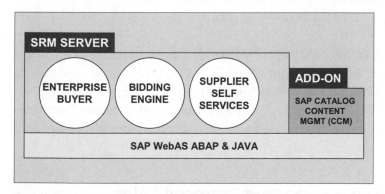

Figure 13.5 Main Components of the SRM Server

In addition to the components above, there are a number of other integrated SAP components that make up the SAP SRM solution. These components are typically installed separately and require their independent environment and landscape. This is illustrated in Figure 13.6 for SAP SRM 5.0.

Within the overall SRM components illustrated in Figure 13.6, there are: SAP SRM Server 5.5, SAP NetWeaver BI 7.0, TREX 7.0 and SAP NetWeaver Portal 7.0 and more. Depending on the business scenario being implemented, one or more of these components are mandatory. The next section discusses the business scenario and component matrix in greater detail.

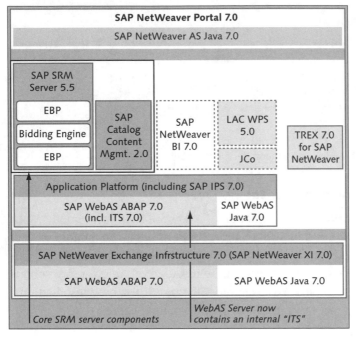

Figure 13.6 SAP SRM 5.0 — Components Overview

It is important to know that with SAP SRM 5.0, organizations can no longer use SAP XI 3.0 because it is not compatible. This means that organizations upgrading to SRM 5.0 and already using XI will need to upgrade the XI component as well. Organizations that might have created custom interfaces within XI will need to pay special attention to the interfaces when upgrading the XI environment.

13.1.3   Business Scenario-Based Component Matrix

As described throughout this book, the SRM solution is implemented based on the many business scenarios, such as self-service, strategic sourcing, etc. Each of these business scenarios require one or more of the components illustrated in Figure 13.6 above. In order to assist organizations in determining what components are required, SAP provides a standard components matrix.

This matrix allows the functional and technical teams to determe easily the technology components required for implementing specific functional business scenarios. Based on the project blueprint, the functional teams should be able to determine the *business scenarios* that are going to be required to meet the requirements gathered during blueprinting.

Based on these scenarios, the technical teams should be able to use the matrix shown in Figure 13.7 to determine all the components that might be required to support these business scenarios. Figure 13.7 illustrates the component matrix for SAP SRM 4.0. Figure 13.8 illustrates the matrix for SAP SRM 5.0. Contract management is a new scenario in the 5.0 release.

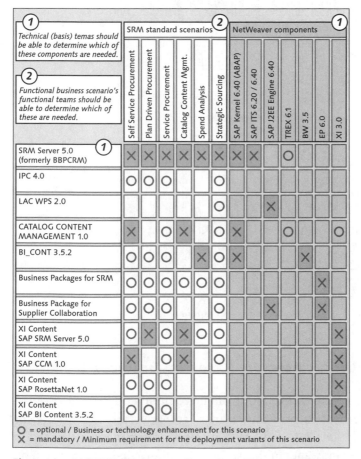

Figure 13.7 SAP SRM 4.0: Business Scenario — Component Matrix

Organizations using SRM 4.0 or 5.0 can use the component matrix to determine which SRM and NetWeaver components are required or are optional, based on the business scenario being configured. For example, it is evident from Figure 13.8 that the SRM Server is a required component for implementing SRM no matter what business scenario. In another example, if your organization is planning to implementing the spend analysis business scenario, the NetWeaver BI component and BI Content are required.

① Technical (basis) temas should be able to determine which of these components are needed.

② Functional business scenario's functional teams should be able to determine which of these are needed.

	SRM standard scenarios ②							NetWeaver components ①						
	Self Service Procurement	Plan Driven Procurement	Services Procurement	Catalog Content Mgmt.	Spend Analysis	Strategic Sourcing	Contract Management	WebAS ABAP 7.0	SAP ITS 7.0	WebAS Java 7.0	TREX 7.0	BW 7.0	EP 7.0	XI 7.0
SAP SRM Server 5.5 ①	X	X	X	X	X	X	X	X	X	O				
Live Auction Cockpit (LACWPS) 5.0						O				X				
SAP Catalog Content Management 2.0	X		O	X		O		X		O				O
SAP NetWeaver® BI_CONT 7.0.2	O	O	O		X	O		X			X			
Business Packages for SRM	O	O	O	O	O	O							X	
Business Packages for Supplier Portal	O	O	O			O				X			X	
XI Content for SAP SRM Server 5.5	O	X		X	O	O								X
XI Content for SAP Catalog Content Mgmt. 2.0	X			X	O									X
XI Content for RosettaNet 1.0	O	O	O											X
XI Content for SAP NetWeaver BI Content 7.0.2	O	O	O											X

O = optional / Business or technology enhancement for this scenario
X = mandatory / Minimum requirement for the deployment variants of this scenario

Figure 13.8 SAP SRM 5.0: Business Scenario — Component Matrix

13.2 SAP SRM Architecture Based on Business Scenario

In Section 13.1, I explained that SRM contains a number of business scenarios, and to implement each of the business scenarios the technical teams need to determine the SRM, and SAP NetWeaver components that need to be installed in the landscape. In this section, I will provide further detail on the architecture needs based on the business scenario that needs to be implemented for SRM.

13.2.1 Self-Service Procurement Business Scenario

In Chapter 3 we discussed in detail the self-service procurement scenario in SRM and described the functions that employees in an organization would execute. For example, they could create and manage their own requisitions for procuring indirect materials, operational and strategic MRO materials, and services. In Figure 13.9, we illustrate the different SRM components that are typically required to support the processes within the self-service procurement scenario.

> **Tip**
>
> It is important to know that the **ITS** application is required for **SAP SRM Server 5.5**. Although SRM can be also accessed via SAP NetWeaver Portal, the business packages within the portal application access SRM using the ITS technology.

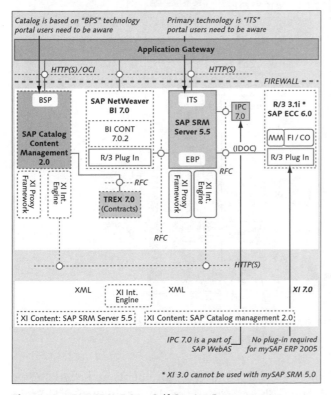

Figure 13.9 SAP SRM 5.0 — Self-Service Procurement

Also note that, beginning from SAP SRM 5.0, the IPC application has been integrated within the SAP Web AS. Therefore organizations do not require a separate installation for IPC. Organizations implementing SRM in the Extended Classic scenario are required to use the IPC.

13.2.2 Plan-Driven Procurement Business Scenario

In Chapter 3, we discussed the capabilities of the plan-driven procurement scenario in SRM. Within this scenario, organizations typically either integrate the requirements generated in the SAP R/3 planning modules (MRP, PM, etc.) with EBP for sourcing or the SUS component. If planning requirements from R/3 are sent to EBP for sourcing and procurement, the SAP R/3 or ERP system needs to be connected with the EBP system using standard remote function call (RFC) and IDoc connections, as illustrated in Figure 13.10.

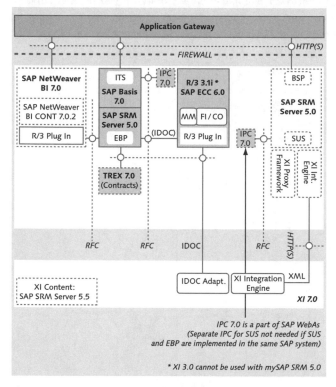

Figure 13.10 SAP SRM 5.0 — Plan-Driven Procurement

Organizations can also integrate the planning requirements in the SAP R/3 or ERP with the SUS component. This scenario is explained in Chapter 5. From an architecture and technology standpoint, SAP XI is required in this scenario to communicate between the business document in the SAP R/3 system and SUS. The SAP R/3 system uses the IDoc Adapter to communicate with the XI system, as illustrated in Figure 13.10.

13.2.3 Service Procurement Business Scenario

From the SAP SRM 4.0 release, SAP has been continuously enhancing the functionality for the procurement of services using SRM. More organizations are now interested in using the service-procurement business scenario. Users can create service requests in EBP and using XI to communicate those to the SUS component. Vendors or suppliers can then review these service requests in SUS and provide responses. It is important to note that the technology that powers the user interface for **EBP** is still **ITS**. Since the release of SAP SRM 4.0, ITS is available as an Integrated application within the SAP Web AS layer. Organizations do not have to install ITS as a standalone application.

SUS, on the other hand, uses **BSP** as the technology to provide the end user interface. BSP is also a native technology within the WebAS layer and is automatically installed as a part of the SRM Server.

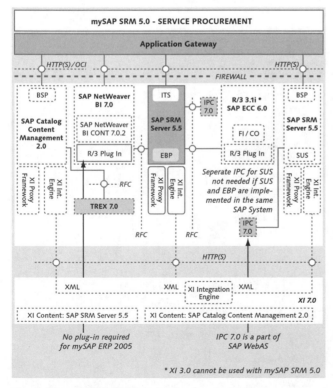

Figure 13.11 SAP SRM 5.0 — Service Procurement

Figure 13.11 illustrates the integration between SRM, SAP R/3, and NetWeaver components in the service-procurement scenario. Also note that beginning with SAP SRM 5.0, the IPC application has been integrated within Web AS, therefore organizations do not require a separate installation for IPC. Organizations implementing SRM in the Extended Classic scenario are required to use the IPC.

13.2.4　CCM Business Scenario

SAP introduced SAP CCM solution in 2004. I have explained the capabilities of **CCM** in detail in Chapter 6. At a basic level, CCM acts as the catalog solution for applications within SRM, enabling end users to use catalogs to search and order goods and services maintained by the organization. The user interface in CCM is powered by the **BSP** technology within Web AS.

Also, the SAP **TREX** engine is a required component installed when using CCM. TREX provides a powerful search and retrieval capability within the catalog. Organizations using contract management in SRM should note that a separate TREX installation is required to provide extended search capabilities in contracts, as illustrated in Figure 13.12.

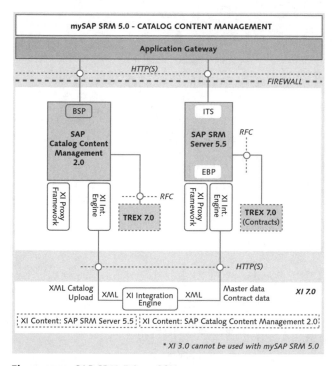

Figure 13.12　SAP SRM 5.0 — CCM

In addition to the architecture illustrated in Figure 13.12 for CCM , Chapter 6 provides a few different deployment options for implementing SAP CCM. The XI Integration Engine is a requirement if specific scenarios are implemented for CCM. For example, Figure 13.12 illustrates that master data and contract data can be integrated between **EBP** and **CCM** using the **XI Integration Engine**. Review Chapter 6 for additional details.

13.2.5 Strategic Sourcing Business Scenario

In many ways the strategic-sourcing business scenario uses all of the SRM and NetWeaver components. In addition to the components described in the sections above, strategic sourcing also introduces the Live Auction Cockpit (LAC) component in SRM. Organizations using the SAP Bidding Engine can utilize the LAC to perform real-time online auctions.

The LAC is an integral part of SAP Bidding Engine and replaces the previous reverse auction functionality. Depending on your SRM implementation design, some of the components illustrated in Figure 13.13 might not be required. However, this figure provides a comprehensive illustration of the different components that work together to enable the strategic sourcing business scenario.

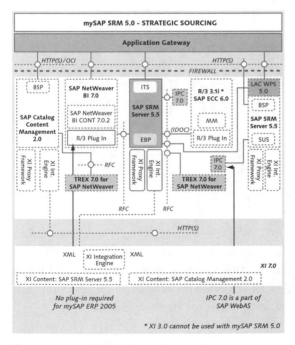

Figure 13.13 SAP SRM 5.0 — Strategic Sourcing

13.2.6 Spend Analysis Business Scenario

A key objective for organizations implementing SAP SRM is to be able to analyze their overall spending. Too many organizations fall under the trap of implementing operational procurement and forget to realize the true value of SRM as they overlook spend analysis. Leaders in the market are constantly analyzing their spending to find ways of strategic sourcing, contract management, and reduction of maverick spending, to name a few opportunities.

In SRM, the BI solution provides the avenue for reporting and spend analysis. In BI, SAP provides pre-built reports and queries for SRM that can be activated and used out-of-the box. In the spend-analysis business scenario, both the SAP R/3 and SRM systems are connected. BI integrates with both R/3 and SRM to extract master data and transactional data to populate the reports and queries available in BI. Figure 13.14 illustrates the architecture for spend analysis in SRM.

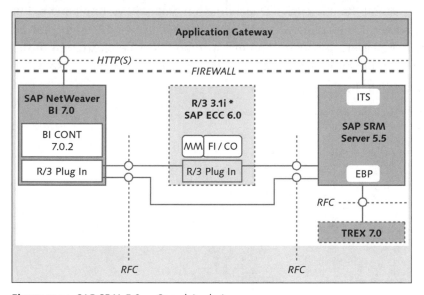

Figure 13.14 SAP SRM 5.0 — Spend Analysis

In most of the business scenarios described in this chapter, the XI integration engine is used as an underlying architecture layer. This is because XI is an integral part of the underlying technology platform for all SAP solutions including SRM. The next section will provide users with an understanding of when XI becomes a mandatory component for functionality in SRM.

13.3 SAP SRM Business Scenarios Using SAP NetWeaver XI

The XI component of SAP NetWeaver is highly integrated within the overall SAP SRM solution. However, it is not a required component for all business scenarios. Organizations need to review the business scenarios that they want to implement and use the information in this section to determine whether they need the XI component installed and configured. The following bullet points will help readers determine situations when the XI component will become mandatory in their SAP SRM implementations:

▶ **Output of purchasing documents from SAP SRM in XML format**
In general, if there is a need to input or output any document (inbound or outbound) in the SRM system using XML technology, SAP XI becomes a required component. If, for example, the *Extended Classic* or *Standalone* scenario is being implemented; this requires transmission of purchase orders from SRM. If there is a requirement to transmit purchase orders to suppliers in XML format, XI will be required. If documents need to be transmitted from SRM in EDI format, XI is required along with a third-party EDI adapter (e.g., Seeburger EDI Adapter).

▶ **Plan-driven procurement with supplier integration**
Organizations that have a requirement to exchange planning documents (purchase orders with material items) from the SAP R/3 or ERP system to the SUS system will require XI. This scenario is also called the SUS-MM deployment.

▶ **Service procurement with supplier integration**
Organizations that have a requirement to exchange service orders with suppliers using the SUS component. This scenario is also called the SUS-EBP deployment.

▶ **SAP CCM scenario**
If organizations are just uploading supplier catalog files into SAP CCM in formats other than XML, XI is not required. However, it is required when:

▷ CCM authoring and searching (CAT and CSE) applications are installed in different clients or servers.

▷ Contract distribution is made from SAP SRM to the SAP CCM catalog

▷ Product master data from SAP SRM is included in the SAP CCM catalog

The SRM-MDM scenario also requires XI if the contract distribution or product master distribution scenario are implemented.

If any of these described scenarios are used, then a separate business system is configured on the XI Integration Server. This is illustrated in Figure 13.15. Note that EBP, SUS, and MM are all separate business systems when it comes to integrating with the XI application. The Integration Server within XI contains a business system for all the other applications that need to interact with XI.

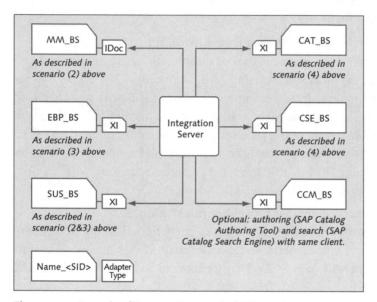

Figure 13.15 Example of Business Systems Definition in SAP XI

In Section 13.4, I will discuss a change in the ITS architecture and how organizations can benefit by use the integrated ITS within the SAP Web AS layer. This is especially important for organizations that are upgrading from a SRM 3.0 or earlier release and currently have large ITS architecture requirements to support the SRM application.

13.4 ITS as Part of Web AS

In earlier releases of SAP SRM, organizations had no choice but to have an independent landscape for SAP ITS. This caused organizations not only to support an additional software component, but also bear the cost of a separate environment (development, QA, production). Furthermore, some organizations had their core SRM servers installed on UNIX platforms and the ITS component installed on Windows platform to minimize costs, thus having to maintain and support different operating platforms.

Organizations that are implementing the SAP SRM 4.0 release or higher do not need to install the ITS on a separate hardware; it is now integrated into the SAP WebAS layer as an internal ITS. Although, SAP SRM 4.0, customers can still choose to install an external ITS, it is not recommended.

With the integrated ITS in the SAP Web AS, the Web browser now communicates directly with the SRM system. Furthermore, all ITS-related sources — such as service files, HTML templates, or MIME files — are now stored in the SRM system database rather than on a separate ITS server. ITS templates are published to an internal ITS site. Organizations using an array of ITS servers today will realize a total cost reduction when upgrading to SRM 4.0 or later releases, as they no longer need dedicated hardware for housing the ITS software, which in some organizations can require five to ten dedicated servers.

> **Note**
>
> From SAP SRM 6.0, the ITS technology is no longer used to web enable SRM. A new portal based Web Dynpro technology is utilized. ITS is obsolete for SRM functions from SAP SRM 6.0 onwards.

13.5 SRM Sizing

Just like any other SAP solution, the SAP SRM solution needs to be sized accordingly for optimum efficiency. Keep in mind that SAP SRM is a Web-based solution. Unlike the standard SAP GUI used on SAP projects, end users' access the SRM solution using an Internet browser. Not only are organizations faced with SRM server optimization but they need to be fully aware of the requirements for internet connectivity, secure socket layer (SSL), wireless connectivity, etc.

Project teams that do not spend the appropriate time in conducting accurate sizing may have issues in the performance of the application once the solution is rolled out to the user community. The system might not have the optimum hardware and capacity required to support the users involved or the processes and documents generated in your SRM environment. Project teams need to clearly understand the business scenarios and the components that are planned within the scope of their SRM implementation to correctly size the application.

Often there is misunderstanding between the functional teams and the technical teams when it comes to determining all the components that are required for implementing a particular business scenario. This is where the detailed component matrix comes handy for reference. SAP publishes the procedure shown in Figure 13.16 for sizing the SAP SRM solution.

Typically, the SAP Basis or technical team on the project is responsible for downloading the sizing questionnaire from SAP Service Marketplace as illustrated in Step 2 in Figure 13.16. The functional teams are responsible for providing the business scenarios and information about the number of business documents expected from their daily and yearly operations.

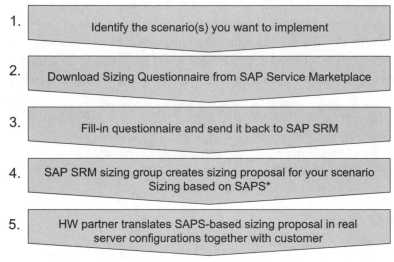

1. Identify the scenario(s) you want to implement

2. Download Sizing Questionnaire from SAP Service Marketplace

3. Fill-in questionnaire and send it back to SAP SRM

4. SAP SRM sizing group creates sizing proposal for your scenario Sizing based on SAPS*

5. HW partner translates SAPS-based sizing proposal in real server configurations together with customer

* SAP Application Benchmark Performance Standard

Figure 13.16 SAP SRM Sizing Procedure

For instance, if the SRM business scenario is self-service procurement, then it is important for the sizing questionnaire to capture the number of requisitioners and buyers, shopping carts and purchase orders expected, etc. This information collectively is used by SAP or another sizing partner to determine the hardware requirement for your SAP implementation.

13.6 Summary

This chapter covered the architecture and technology that power the SAP SRM solution. I also discussed the importance of the various NetWeaver components such as BI and XI and how they enable a holistic SRM solution.

Project teams can use the architectural illustrations provided in this chapter to map out the technology requirements on their project, based on the selection of business scenarios.

In Chapter 14, I will discuss upgrades to your SRM system. The chapter will explain why organizations need to upgrade and describe approaches for SRM upgrades.

SAP is continuously enhancing its SRM solution, and over the last seven years there have already been more than eight product releases. This chapter provides an overview for organizations on what it means to undertake an SRM upgrade initiative.

14 Upgrade — A How-To Approach

What is an upgrade? An upgrade is a new or enhanced version of a software product that is considered to have major enhancements or improvement to its features or functionality. Usually, upgrades are denoted by a version number.

If you are an organization currently in the process of implementing SRM, be ready. You are going to upgrade in the next two to three years. Based on a SRM upgrade presentation by Kodak at the annual ASUG conference in 2006, the company already has upgraded SRM three times since it first installed SRM in 2000. Kodak implemented Enterprise Buyer Professional (EBP) 2.0B in Dec 2000, EBP 3.0 in June 2002, and SRM 4.0 in December 2005.

Although SAP SRM has consistently evolved over the last six years (as illustrated in Figure 2.1 in Chapter 2), SRM is still a relatively new solution for many companies. Many organizations still operate only portions of the overall SAP SRM suite, with the majority using only EBP.

Organizations that implemented the core SAP R/3 solution are more accustomed to a four- to five-year window of upgrades, but they realize that in order to continually stay competitive and optimize their business processes they need to leverage the major enhancements and improvements provided in the software upgrades provided by SAP. In the next section, I will help to answer the question that many companies ask: Why should we upgrade?

14.1 Why Upgrade?

This is the million dollar question is. As an organization, if we just made a large investment in the SRM implementation, then is there justification for an upgrade two to three years in the future, given that SAP supports the releases for a number of years. The answer eventually boils down to the age old decision of Build vs. Buy. Luckily, standard software upgrades from SAP are already included within the maintenance and support fees of the SRM solution. However, the organization should confirm this with their SAP account representative. Licenses and contracts are specific for each company, and it is important to understand what is covered in the software upgrades.

Therefore the true costs in an upgrade are the implementation costs and possible hardware costs, which can be significant. An upgrade project is very similar to a new implementation, such that a project methodology is still required. The environments for sandbox, development, and test are still required. A dedicated technical, functional, project-management team is still needed. In other words, the upgrade project needs to be executed like an SAP project. Organizations that have experience with the initial implementation will realize the time commitment they can expect.

Many organizations that have implemented SAP R/3 for a while have circumvented the upgrade path and chosen to customize the required functionality in-house. This is partly due to the large undertaking the core SAP R/3 solution upgrade requires and partly to the fact that the product releases are spread-out over a number of years. Organizations that required functionality not available within their SAP releases went ahead and developed it internally; they could not afford to wait for the next available SAP release. The SAP SRM solution has evolved at a very rapid pace over the last several years.

SAP has released a new version of the my SRM solution almost every year. Customers have seen advantages and disadvantages from this rapid release strategy of SAP's. The advantage is that SAP has been able to incorporate customer requirements and new functionality and market them very quickly, providing organizations with the ability to leverage the best practices developed by SAP in the new release. The disadvantage is that customers would have to upgrade to the newer SAP SRM release to attain the major enhancements. Figure 14.1 provides a comparative look at the software releases by SAP for the core R/3 solution vs. SAP SRM over the last six years. It can be clearly seen that SAP has released a new version for SAP SRM almost every year.

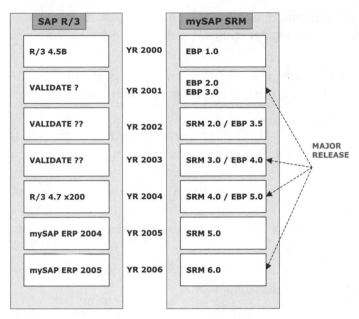

Figure 14.1 SAP SRM Solution Release Timeline

The complexities involved in an implementation for SAP SRM could be similar to those of an SAP implementation, but the impact to the organization might be vastly different. SAP SRM focuses on procurement and strategic sourcing; a typical SAP implementation could involve FI, HR, SD, to name a few solution areas.

The impact to the organization is huge, involving everything from requirements gathering, gap analysis, organization change, training, and deployment. This is one reason why some organizations have been able to undertake an SRM upgrade two to three times over the last five to six years rather than upgrading their core SAP R/3 system once at most. Another reason why many organizations have upgraded SRM multiple times is because of the enhanced functionality that SAP has provided with every new release. It is more beneficial for organizations to upgrade and benefit from this new functionality.

There are probably as many reasons to upgrade as there are companies. However, let's take a look at the top eight identified reasons in the bulleted list below:

▶ The maintenance and support is ending for your current release of SAP SRM. As an example, the Requisite catalog that was previously bundled with the SRM solution will no longer be supported past 2006. This would require companies to either upgrade to the new SAP catalog solution of CCM or MDM or have a separate contract maintenance and support with Requisite.

▶ The business functionality your organization needs is available in the newer release of SAP SRM, and you recognize the limitations of your current environment.

▶ The total cost of ownership (TCO) of your existing SAP SRM solution is reduced greatly by the upgrade. For example, organizations operating on SAP SRM 3.0 or earlier typically have a separate Internet Transaction Server (ITS) infrastructure for each of their SRM sandbox, development, quality, and production environments. Beginning with SAP SRM 4.0, a separate ITS infrastructure is no longer required; an internal ITS is available within the SRM server.

▶ Your organization is upgrading the back-end SAP R/3 solution, and therefore the entire landscape is being upgraded

▶ Minimize customizations thus reducing the need to implement enhancements

▶ The upgrade release provides significant functionality improvements for additional rollouts to your user community.

▶ The upgrade release increases user acceptance (error reduction, user interface, process time improvements)

▶ The upgrade strategy is in line with the organization's strategy to constantly leverage enhancements in software and technology to gain a competitive advantage in the industry.

After reviewing the reasons for upgrading, let us move on to the decision methodology.

14.1.1 Decision Methodology

An upgrade is an important and major undertaking for any organization. I have come across a number of organizations that started to build a business case for an upgrade but then were unable to quantify the return on investment (ROI). Therefore, these organizations either stopped the upgrade effort and jumped on an enhancements initiative or strategically decided to wait for another year based on either the effort involved or the value foreseen. A detailed assessment is very important.

14.1.2 Working with a Decision Methodology

Figure 14.2 illustrates a five-step decision methodology that I've seen prove successful at many organizations. Let's review these steps next:

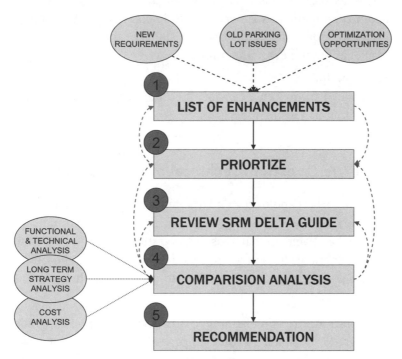

Figure 14.2 Upgrade Decision Methodology

▶ **Step 1: Create a List of all Enhancements**
These could be requirements gathered from the user community to post to your initial SRM implementation, issues that were put on a parking lot for review after go-live, or optimization/user acceptance opportunities.

▶ **Step 2: Prioritize the List**
Once an exhaustive list of enhancements has been created, prioritize it. One strategy would be to create high, medium, and low priority groupings, and then to divide all the enhancements within these groups.

▶ **Step 3: Review SRM Delta Guide**
As a new SRM release is introduced, SAP provides customers with release notes and delta guides. The resources enable project teams to understand the functionality in the new release and act as a metric for comparison with the existing releases. This step can either be performed after the first two or can be performed independently.

▶ **Step 4: Comparison Analysis**
Once steps 1, 2, and 3 are complete, comprehensive gap and comparison analyses should be conducted. A gap analysis is required to understand the enhancements/requirements that may not be available in the new release. A comparison analysis is necessary to identify the opportunities existing for an upgrade, especially when 75 %-80 % of the enhancements might be available in the new product release.

▶ **Step 5: Recommendation**
The results obtained from Step 4 can then become the basis of your recommendation for a management decision.

14.2 Answer the Question: Technical or Functional?

An upgrade is an important and major undertaking for any organization and is not a trivial effort by any means. At the end of the day it's another SAP implementation. What I find is that most organizations struggle with the scope definition in upgrades. It is very important to define scope and not to allow it to slip. To define scope, it's important to understand the goal and objectives of the upgrade.

I like to ask the question: Are you planning to do a purely technical upgrade or a functional upgrade? At first it's a confusing question for many, but as we delve further, answering this question provides a framework for defining the overall scope of the project.

A technical upgrade focuses purely on upgrading the core release and architecture of the product. These tend to be more focused and shorter-duration projects. One example would be a situation where SAP stops providing support for a particular release of SRM; there is end to maintenance. Organizations will then want to upgrade to the release that is supported within the maintenance strategy offered by SAP.

Although the organization might not want to spend the money and resources on the upgrade, it would make a strategic decision to just upgrade the product release. The focus of a technical upgrade is not new functionality or enhancements; instead it's to migrate to the newer product release as quickly as possible.

A functional upgrade, on the other hand involves a technical upgrade plus with an additional goal of mining the new functionality offered and revisiting existing business processes. Figure 14.3 provides a simple view of the difference between a technical and functional upgrade. A functional gap analysis would be a common practice, and business processes are outlined that might require blueprinting.

Managing scope on a functional upgrade is typically tough. During the upgrade, the project team realizes new benefits and functionality and constantly struggles to keep focus on the scope boundaries. In the next section, I will explain why it's important for project teams to understand what they have in their existing SRM environment. Unless you understand what you already have, it is difficult to decide what you want in an upgrade.

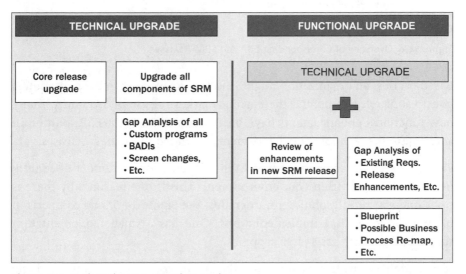

Figure 14.3 Technical or Functional Upgrade

14.3 Understand Your Current Environment

Understanding your current SAP SRM environment is very important for adequately analyzing the potential impact of the newer release. Typically, once the consultants that implemented the initial SRM release have gone, so does the technical know-how. Organizations that manage this situation well, using project methodology for the ongoing knowledge transfer, usually can eliminate this issue.

As the SAP SRM solution has gone through a change in branding, many organizations might be more familiar with their EBP release instead of the SRM release. Figure 14.4 provides a quick correlation between the SRM and EBP releases.

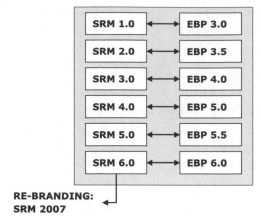

Figure 14.4 Overview of Corresponding EBP and SRM Releases

Based on this, an organization might find that its existing implementation is two to four releases behind the current market release of SAP SRM. Many new functional enhancements have been made to the SRM/EBP solution in addition to the technology enhancements provided in the new releases.

Depending on the scope of your SRM implementation, a number of components could exist within your environment. This is one reason why there is not a one-size-fits-all solution for upgrades. See Figure 14.5 for a comparison of two different SRM implementations. One has a small implementation scope, and another has a large scope.

It is evident from this example that the small scope contains only a single business-scenario implementation. Therefore, the underlying software components used are limited. However, in the larger scope, as more business scenarios are being implemented, additional software components are required.

This example illustrates that the level of effort in an upgrade project for a SAP SRM implementations will depend on the current environment. It is important to realize the dependency on the software components; more components means upgrading each of the components individually. Out of each component arises an independent opportunity for issues.

In an upgrade, it is imperative that the project team(s) understand the current environment well, in addition to the vision of the future. Figure 14.6 illustrates the specific components used in an organization's current EBP environment and shows the changes in the technology landscape within the SRM 4.0 solution.

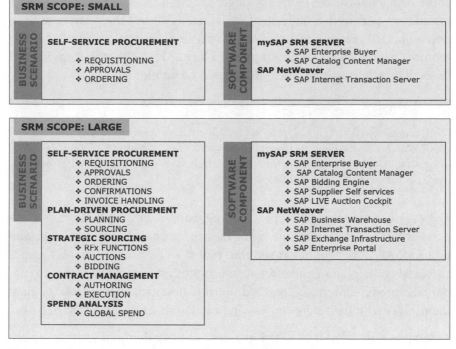

Figure 14.5 Scope Comparision for Two SAP SRM Implementations

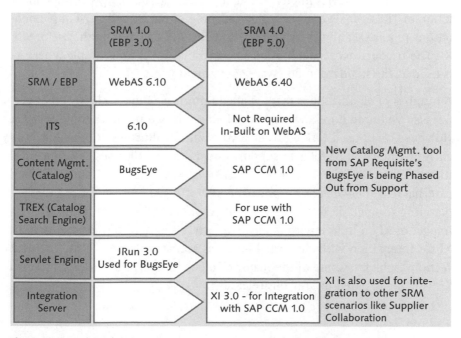

Figure 14.6 Technical Comparison Between SRM 1.0 and SRM 4.0

Some components like ITS are no longer required from a separate hardware installation perspective (reducing the overall TCO) but there are new additions, like SAP Catalog and Content Management (CCM) in SRM, that can require an independent architecture including SAP's TREX search engine and its Exchange Infrastructure (XI.) integration component.

> **Note**
>
> SAP announced a strategic shift in its content-management strategy in May 2006. SAP MDM Catalog will be the strategic content-management offering by SAP beginning Q4 2006. SAP CCM will be supported for a while but new functionality will be added to SAP MDM Catalog.

The organization in our example could be using Requisite BugsEye, a third-party software solution for managing electronic catalogs, as its catalog solution for SAP SRM. SAP has announced that it will no longer support Requisite Catalog integration, therefore organizations must decide whether to support the product internally, pay additional maintenance fees to SAP or align themselves with the future content and catalog strategy supported by SAP.

A detailed discussion is required to determine whether you want to replace the SAP BugsEye solution and replace with SAP CCM and to review the pros and cons. If SAP CCM is implemented, it requires additionally the implementation of TREX for search and SAP XI for integration. Not all CCM implementations require XI; however, specific scenarios in CCM require the use of SAP XI. The product master replication scenario in CCM is an example where XI is used as the standard middleware component.

A number of organizations that installed Enterprise Buyer release 3.0 or earlier also ventured into new methods of electronic communication like XML. However, they used SAP's earlier XML solution, Business Connector. The current strategy for SAP is to support integration of all types. That includes internal integration between other SAP systems, (e.g., SUS and EBP) and external (e.g., between business partners) via SAP XI.. Organizations that are planning to upgrade to the newer release of SAP SRM need to analyze the impact of XI on their environment. SAP offers standard business content in XI for integration with supported business scenarios in SAP SRM. The next section highlights some of the major changes that have been introduced in SAP SRM compared to previous releases.

14.4 Expected Changes in New SRM Release

During the analysis or blueprint phase of the project, a gap analysis of the SRM releases will provide the project team with the major changes that need to be reviewed and addressed. Figure 14.7 provides a quick overview of some changes between SRM 4.0 and previous releases.

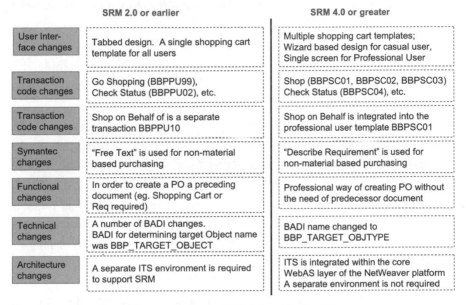

	SRM 2.0 or earlier	SRM 4.0 or greater
User Interface changes	Tabbed design. A single shopping cart template for all users	Multiple shopping cart templates; Wizard based design for casual user, Single screen for Professional User
Transaction code changes	Go Shopping (BBPPU99), Check Status (BBPPU02), etc.	Shop (BBPSC01, BBPSC02, BBPSC03) Check Status (BBPSC04), etc.
Transaction code changes	Shop on Behalf of is a separate transaction BBPPU10	Shop on Behalf is integrated into the professional user template BBPSC01
Symantec changes	"Free Text" is used for non-material based purchasing	"Describe Requirement" is used for non-material based purchasing
Functional changes	In order to create a PO a preceding document (eg. Shopping Cart or Req required)	Professional way of creating PO without the need of predecessor document
Technical changes	A number of BADI changes. BADI for determining target Object name was BBP_TARGET_OBJECT	BADI name changed to BBP_TARGET_OBJTYPE
Architecture changes	A separate ITS environment is required to support SRM	ITS is integrated within the core WebAS layer of the NetWeaver platform A separate environment is not required

Figure 14.7 Overview of Changes Between SRM 4.0 and Earlier Releases

Compared to SRM 2.0 (EBP 3.0) the following major changes have been introduced in the SRM application that are noteworthy:

▶ The user interface (UI) has been completely changed. In addition to provide usability enhancements in the shop application, new navigational designs have been introduced to accommodate the needs of the casual user, the frequent user, and the purchasing user.

▶ Sourcing and Bidding Engine functions have been enhanced. The Sourcing Cockpit has been introduced. Additionally, demand aggregation is provided to reduce the number of purchase orders generated and thus lowering processing costs.

▶ PO Cockpit allows for manual purchase-order creation and processing of incomplete purchase orders; approval workflows have been introduced.

- ▶ Extended Classic scenario is more stable than before.More organizations are implementing this scenario to leverage the rich functionality offered. The PO data transferred to the back-end R/3 system has been enhanced.

- ▶ Requisite Emerge and BugsEye products are no longer offered as a bundled product within SRM. Maintenance support for requisite products ends 2006. SAP CCM has been introduced as the catalog application for SAP SRM. CCM is a WAS 6.40 add-on based on ABAP Object and BSP technology.

- ▶ Shopping Cart, Purchase Order and other transactions have been changed, therefore all custom modifications will become obsolete. For example, the shopping cart transaction in SRM 4.0 is "bbpsc01" vs. "bbppu99" in earlier releases.

- ▶ HTML templates, services, and document-storage tables model have been changed. This again could have a large impact on custom programs, workflows, and UI enhancements. Major re-work could be required in your upgrade.

- ▶ ITS is now integrated in the core WAS 6.40 kernel; no additional standalone ITS servers are required, reducing TCO. For some organizations this could involve four to five environments across Sandbox, development, QA, and production. However, If specific ITS flow-logic services were changed, they will probably not be supported by the internal ITS.

- ▶ The Internet Pricing Engine (IPC) is a mandatory component for all organizations implementing the Standalone or Extended Classic scenario. For Classic scenario implementations, a Business Add-In (BAdI) can be implemented as a workaround.

- ▶ Organizations using XML will be introduced to SAP XI instead of the Business Connector. SAP XI is also a required component if certain business scenarios are configured; e.g., the master-data inclusion scenario in SAP CCM requires the use of SAP XI, and all SUS-to-SRM scenarios require the use of SAP XI.

- ▶ SAP has introduced a ton of new BAdIs in the newer SRM releases, allowing organizations to reduce the core modification to the SAP release and instead building business logic using release-supported BAdIs (similar to User Exits).

Organizations upgrading to the SRM 5.0 release need to remember to convert their existing Organizational Units for vendors into vendor groups. In previous releases of SRM, a single organization-management transaction was used: PPOMA_BBP. This was used to maintain both internal and external organization units and business partners. Vendors were maintained within a single hierarchy using this transaction.

Beginning with the SAP SRM 5.0 release, a new transaction, PPOMV_BBP, has been developed to create and maintain vendor organization units. The concept of vendor groups (VG) has been introduced and is used for grouping; it is no longer obligatory to have one VG per vendor, as was previously the case for organizational units. If several vendors (who previously were assigned to an organizational unit) have identical attributes, they are now assigned directly to a common VG. During the upgrade, organizations can execute the report: BBP_XPRA_ORGEH_TO_VENDOR_GROUP to create vendor groups.

To delete all organizational units and organizational plans of the vendors from the internal organizational plan (transaction PPOMA_BBP) and group these according to their attributes in new organizational objects (transaction PPOMV_BBP).

After an upgrade to SRM 5.0, this report must be executed in each client for each central organizational unit for vendors (root organizational unit). This applies both to EBP and to SUS systems. So far, we have discussed the need organizations have to upgrade their SRM systems. In the next section, I will highlight some of the tools that project teams can use during their upgrade initiative.

14.5   Upgrade — Tools and Resources

A common question that comes up regarding upgrade projects is: Where do I start? Let's take a look at what you can do to ease your upgrade process.

14.5.1   SAP Documentation

SAP provides invaluable documentation for the execution of your upgrade project. Figure 14.8 provides an overview of the major documentation provided by SAP within the upgrade phase.

The Upgrade Master Guide, available at the SAP Service Marketplace, is the starting point for upgrading the business scenarios of the SAP SRM solution. It provides scenario-specific descriptions of preparation, execution, and follow-up of an upgrade. It also refers to other documents, such as the Component Upgrade Guides and SAP Notes. Only specific components may be valid for the SRM upgrade within your organization.

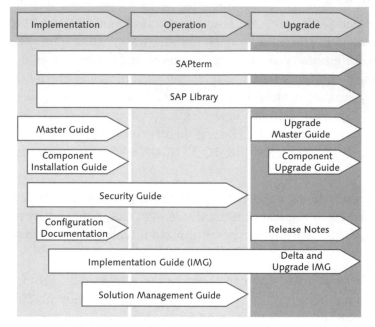

Figure 14.8 Documentation for SAP Software Life Cycle — Focus: Upgrade

> **Tip**
>
> If your organization does not use the plan-driven procurement business scenario in SRM, then those aspects of the upgrade guide can be skipped.

The Component Upgrade Guide describes the technical upgrade of an SAP component, taking into account the combinations of operating systems and databases. It does not describe any business-related configuration.

Release notes are documents that contain short descriptions of new features or changes in an SAP component since the previous release. Release notes about ABAP developments enable the SAP system to generate delta and upgrade IMGs.

The master guide, component guide, and release notes will all help to get you started in the right path. In addition, there are standard tools used for the application of support packs and notes, all of which are valuable utilities that are used within the upgrade process.

14.5.2 Modified Objects

During an upgrade, existing objects of the SAP standard system are overwritten with the objects re-delivered in the new release. To help customers retain the development objects modified in their existing (previous) release, SAP provides the newly modified objects re-delivered in the upgrade adjustment of Transactions SPDD and SPAU.

Organizations can use these transactions during an upgrade to select these objects and modify them manually. The SPDD and SPAU transactions are commonly used by the BASIS teams in the upgrade process. Let us look at these more closely now.

SPDD Transaction

This is a standard SAP transaction that allows you to process ABAP Dictionary objects. It is important to realize that the process of reconciliation of SPAU and SPDD objects can be extremely time consuming. Contrary to what is commonly understood, this is not purely a technical or development activity. This process does begin with the technical team but then requires your functional experts to analyze and research the reason for existing changes and decide whether they should be kept as current or be overridden by the new changes from SAP. For instance, if a modification was implemented to meet a business requirement in your current SRM environment but has provided a standard solution in the SRM upgrade SAP to meet that business requirement, your functional experts need to provide direction to the technical team on how to move forward with the SAP update.

SPAU Transaction

This is a standard SAP transaction that allows you to adjust programs, function modules, screens, interfaces, documentation, and text elements after an upgrade. One common example in SRM upgrades is HTML template changes. Organizations that implemented SRM early on struggled with the user interface, and for user acceptance changed a number of the standard HTML templates provided by SAP. Transaction SPAU would identify those template objects and request an action to accept changes in the SAP upgrade or analyze the existing templates. Other examples would be standard programs, screen and menu painter, and text elements.

Basically, when your upgrade is complete, you check Transactions SPDD and SPAU, which will indicate all standard SAP objects changed in previous version (e.g., customer modifications like HTML screens or OSS notes, etc.). Typically, the basis team will provide the SPAU list, and the SRM upgrade team will have to determine in each object change whether to accept a new version (RESET TO ORIGINAL). For organizations that have made many modifications in their SRM system, this activity will be one the most important post upgrade tasks.

Note Assistant (SNOTE)

This is a standard SAP transaction provided to automate the process of applying SAP OSS Notes. This tool (shown in Figure 14.9) allows you to download SAP Notes into your SAP environment and then automatically implement the corrections contained in the notes into your SAP system. The Notes assistant works well when there is code insertion or deletion into existing ABAP objects. However, notes that contain HTML or Java scripting corrections cannot be implemented via the SNOTE transaction; they have to be implemented manually. This tool is very useful to quickly apply OSS Notes that earlier required a lot of manual development effort.

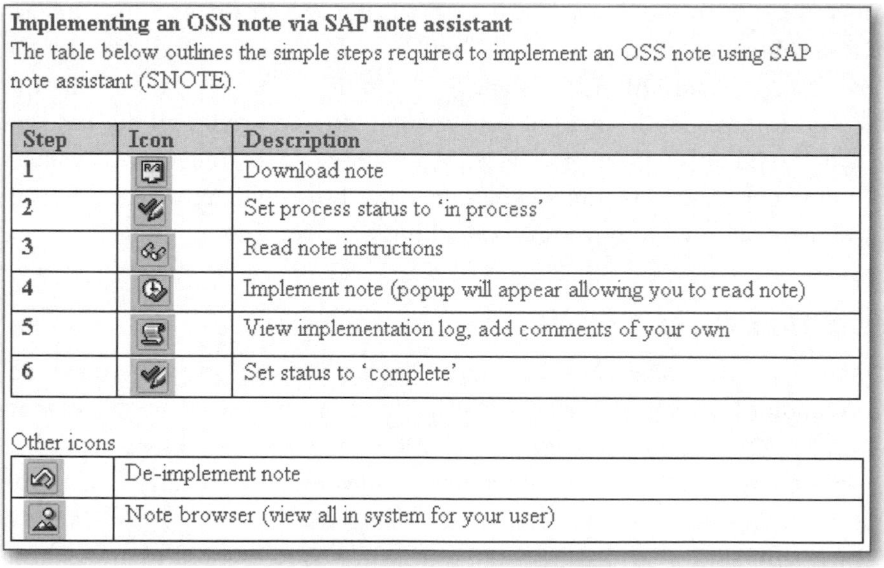

Implementing an OSS note via SAP note assistant
The table below outlines the simple steps required to implement an OSS note using SAP note assistant (SNOTE).

Step	Icon	Description
1		Download note
2		Set process status to 'in process'
3		Read note instructions
4		Implement note (popup will appear allowing you to read note)
5		View implementation log, add comments of your own
6		Set status to 'complete'

Other icons

	De-implement note
	Note browser (view all in system for your user)

Figure 14.9 Implementing an OSS Note via SAP Note Assistant

eCATT

SAP users have long used the Computer Aided Test Tool (CATT) heavily during the testing and conversion phases of a project implementation. CATT scripts are frequently used to upload master data or to make changes to master data records. In an upgrade, this tool comes in very handy as it can be used for testing transactions, reports, and business scenarios. The SRM system is based on the NetWeaver platform, and transactions run on the SAP Web Application Server (Web AS), for which the CATT tool does not work. However, the extended Computer Aided Test Tool (eCATT)) can be used in SRM and other Web Application Server 6.20 or higher systems for the same. In SAP, eCatt can be executed using the standard transaction SECATT.

In the next section, we will discuss the best practices to keep in mind during your upgrade project.

14.6 Best Practices — Upgrade Impact

Upgrade projects are notorious for getting out of hand when it comes to scope. Therefore it is extremely important that your project-management team create clear boundaries on the goals of your upgrade and the overall scope. Is your upgrade project a purely technical upgrade? Or is it both a functional and a technical upgrade? A purely technical upgrade would have a strict guideline for the project that only current functionality will be implemented; i.e., new functionality and components will be out of scope. The system will be upgraded to the newer release of the software but only functionality existing in the "current production environment" will be tested and supported.

A functional upgrade, on the other hand, is initiated with the expectation that the software release will be upgraded to make use of the rich functionality in the new release of the product. One example would be that in your current environment the SRM Service Procurement business scenario has not been implemented. But in the upgrade your organization would like to roll out this new functionality.

It is very important for an organization to understand the impact of an SRM upgrade project. Users, training, change management, system architecture, and maintenance and support all are important areas for impact analysis.

14.6.1 Upgrade Assessment — Process-Based Impact to User Community

Each upgrade release brings new enhancements and changes to the core solution. Ideally, the changes in the new SRM release should be for the better, but as with any change it has to be managed. An assessment is required to define the processes that are being used in your SRM implementation and map any new changes to those processes, so user impact can be determined.

The SAP SRM solution map provided by SAP is a good place to start; it provides an overview of all the business scenarios within the new SRM release. The impact of these process changes will be different for each organization, depending on the functionality implemented in their current SRM environment.

Figure 14.10 shows an example of a Self-Service Procurement process chain. During your upgrade assessment, the project team should map out all the sub-processes (new and existing) that will promote a change within the current processes. The sample depicted in Figure 14.10 shows an example SRM implementation that does not include Invoice Entry and Approval within the existing implementation and future scope of the SRM upgrade. Therefore there are no sub-processes listed as being affected by the upgrade. Each sub-process needs to be further broken down and listed as either an enhancement or a new functionality.

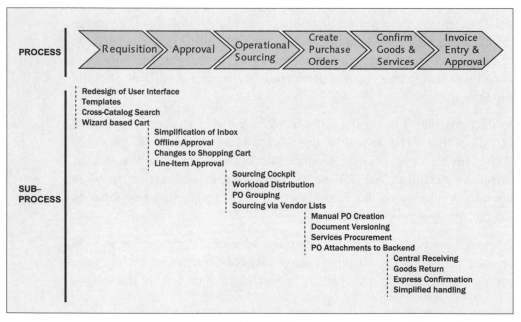

Figure 14.10 Sample — Processes Impacted by the Upgrade

Typically SRM upgrades tend to have a considerable impact on the end-users. SAP has been enhancing the user interface for SAP SRM in almost each new product release. Depending on your current SRM release, an upgrade to SAP SRM Release 5.0 or 6.0 could be a major change in user interface (apart from functionality). User acceptance and usability impacts need to be assessed along with impacts to training and user guides.

Figure 14.11 shows an example of user impact during a SAP SRM upgrade. In our example, the suppliers were originally collaborating with the organization using a custom-developed application. The upgrade scope included the implementation of SUS, and hence had a considerable impact to the supplier community as well.

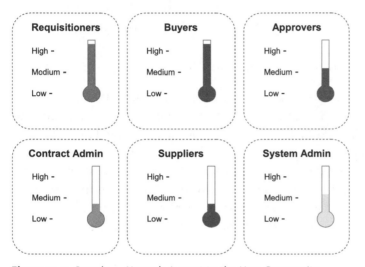

Figure 14.11 Sample — Upgrade Impact to the User Community

14.6.2 Upgrade Assessment — Technical and Development Impact

One of the core processes within any SRM upgrade is the analysis of the development objects within your system. In your initial SRM implementation, there might have been a lot of customized changes to the user interface (especially in the older SRM releases such as 2.0), workflows, business rules driven BAdIs, etc. All of these are development objects that are affected when an upgrade is performed.

The functional teams work closely with the development teams to determine the plan of action to upgrade the different objects that are customized in your environment. These are typically activities conducted during the blueprint and build phases of the upgrade project. The following key areas require the functional and development teams to work together to determine the appropriate action to take when it comes to upgrading objects such as HTML templates, Workflows, and BAdIs.

HTML Templates

Since SAP SRM 3.0, the user interface has changed. If your organization made changes to the HTML templates for EBP, you will need to analyze these one at a time and determine whether you still require those customizations or the new user interface (which is dramatically user-friendly) is sufficient for the user acceptance. If customizations are still required, then the development team needs to customize each of the existing HTML screen changes in the new screens provided by SAP. This can be time consuming.

Workflows

In the earlier SRM releases, many organizations customized the standard SAP delivered workflow templates to meet their business requirements for approvals. As of SAP SRM 5.0, there are more than 30 standard SAP delivered workflow templates. Organizations will find that their need might have been met by SAP and they can do away with their existing custom development. Or, if changes are required, they will be able to use new BAdIs to enhance the delivered workflow templates, instead of copying or modifying the templates. This provides a better framework for future upgrades.

BAdIs

SAP has built upon their strategy to deliver a standard SRM solution that can be used across various industry organizations, and it has been able to deliver on this strategy by allowing companies to adapt their business requirements into the standard SAP solution by using BAdIs. A BAdI is a standard exit within SAP programs whereby organizations can change SAP programs without carrying out any system modifications. During an upgrade, organizations will need to review the existing BAdIs that they are using and check to see if those have been changed by SAP in the new release. A change could be that the BAdI has been enhanced or it could be completely replaced with a new BAdI. The functional and development teams need to work on this activity together.

Table 14.1 provides an abridged list of the back-end purchasing documents related BAdIs introduced in SAP SRM 5.0. A complete list of BAdIs in SAP SRM is available in Appendix D. Also, this appendix provides users a more detailed understanding of BAdIs and new changes that have been introduced to BAdIs in the SRM 4.0 and 5.0 releases. This is especially important as any new business logic that needs to be developed should be done using the new BAdIs and also the existing code should be moved into the new BAdIs for appropriate support.

BAdI Description	SAP SRM 5.0	Earlier Releases
Purchase Order in Back-end system	BBP_CREATE_BE_PO_NEW	BBP_CREATE_PO_BACK
Purchase Requisition in Back-end system	BBP_CREATE_BE_RQ_NEW	BBP_CREATE_REQ_BACK
Reservation in Back-end system	BBP_CREATE_BE_RS_NEW	BBP_CREATE_RES_BACK
Grouping of Shopping cart items for follow-on documents	BBP_BS_GROUP_BE	BBP_SC_TRANSFER_BE, BBP_RESERVATION_GRP
Determine target objects in Backend system	BBP_TARGET_OBJTYPE	BBP_TARGET_OBJECTS

Table 14.1 New BAdIs in SAP SRM 5.0 for Follow-On Documents

OSS Notes

Anyone who has gone through an SAP upgrade before knows the importance of OSS Messages and application of SAP Notes (corrections). When you encounter a problem during your upgrade, it is very possible that other organizations might have experienced the same. This is where the SAP Service Marketplace (also known as SAP OSS) is of great help. Before you end up spending hours troubleshooting the issue it is advisable to search your issue on the Service Marketplace. If you are unable to find a similar issue, then you should create a Customer Message with SAP. Figure 14.12 provides a simple template to manage your OSS Messages.

Short text	Long Description	Working in Previous Release	System ID	Installation	Message Number	Component	Priority	Status	Created on	Changed on	Reporter name
EBP 30: upgraded vendors are not updated in new tables	After the upgrade the Vendors are not updated in the new tables. When the shopping cart is created the vendors are not displayed as a search result in the Preferred Vendor search.	Yes	EBS	XXXXXXXXX	12567	SRM-EBP-ADM	Medium	In Processing by SAP	1/1/2006	1/1/2006	MIKE

Figure 14.12 Template to Manage OSS Messages

14.6.3 Upgrade Assessment — Impact on End User Training

A number of organizations embarked on the SRM upgrade project recently due to maintenance ending for SRM Release 3.0. Extension of mainstream maintenance was extended from end of June 2006 to end of December 2006, at no extra fee. Some are also upgrading from SRM 2.0. There have been major functional, technical, and architectural changes over these releases.

Training is serious business. Depending on your current and upgrade release, there might be major design and functional changes. Capturing those changes and adequately training users is not an easy task.

During the initial SRM implementation, many organizations embarked on Web-based e-training; e.g., video, sound, and multimedia. The upgrade brings changes making the existing training content obsolete. Now organizations are faced with a new question: Do we continue to develop extensive multimedia-rich training only to see if become obsolete in a few years? The SRM solution has changed almost every new release from a new player to a key player. Today SRM is a best of class e-procurement solution, but there are no guarantees that major changes will not happen in the upcoming releases.

Organizations upgrading will find themselves faced with major rewrites of their existing training materials. A best practice is to build delta training guides targeting your largest audience. Typically, the Requisitioners and Approvers are by far the biggest SRM user segments in most organizations, and also the most dispersed. Building the training material can be a daunting task; the best practice would be to begin this activity during the development phase of your upgrade.

Sample Project Plan

Figure 14.13 provides a sample project plan, one that is in no way all-inclusive. Use it as an example of a plan used during an upgrade project. Notice that one of the first activities that needs to be accomplished is the review of existing business processes and beginning of blueprinting the new processes utilizing the enhanced functionality in the new release. The next and major activity is the gap and impact analysis. A detailed analysis needs to be conducted on the functionality available in the new release and what impact it would have on the user, configuration, training, support, and landscape for your organization.

Go-Live Strategy — Some Thoughts

Although each implementation has its own goals and objectives and no two upgrades might be the same, the following thoughts will help you with your go-live strategy.

▶ As a best practice, all end users in the current system should go live with an upgrade at the same time. Sometimes, this might be a challenge to implement when a single SAP is instance is being used across a global user base.

▶ A phased roll-out by plant, geographical region, or functional areas creates the need to support two or more production systems and makes huge demands on technical and functional dependencies.

▶ Once the project phase is in integration testing, parallel roll-outs of the existing release would have to be stopped.

▶ The project cutover should typically occur over a holiday period or long weekend. Organizations that operate on a 24x7 schedule are unable to sustain long system downtime. Many organizations aim to achieve a two-day downtime period during their upgrade.

▶ Understand that although you are implementing an SRM upgrade, it impacts your entire environment. The SAP ERP system, the BW system, and the Enterprise Portal system are just examples of what might be affected in the overall SAP SRM solution by an upgrade. Ensure the availability of the dependent systems.

Project teams need to be aware of the changes and enhancements that are available in the new SRM release. This is especially relevant if, for example, your organization has built a number of custom function modules or remote function call (RFC) programs to achieve some business requirements. In the new SRM release, it could be that SAP has provided standard Business Application Programming Interfces (BAPIs) that accommodated those business requirements. It is important for your project team to be aware of such new functionality and secondly, it needs to be clear within your project charter whether conversion of existing custom code to new BAPIs is within the scope of your upgrade project. If your project timeline is aggressive, it is advisable not to undertake such activity; instead, define a separate project focused towards similar efforts.

In an assessment for the SRM upgrade, organizations should also consider using SAP Enterprise Portals for the overall user interface. SAP recommends that portals be used as the single user interface to provide access to the various components integrated within SRM (shopping carts, BW reporting, SAP R/3, etc.). Again this becomes a scoping question. Implementation of SAP Enterprise Portals is typically a strategic direction for the organization and would be advisable to be implemented and as a separate project.

In the next section, I'll discuss some of the lessons I have learned from implementing SRM upgrade projects.

14.7 SAP SRM Upgrade — Lessons Learned

Every project provides lessons that can and should be leveraged in the next engagement. Unfortunately, in the world of SAP, each organization has implemented SAP and SRM to accommodate its business requirements and environment. Therefore, a one-size-fits-all approach cannot be used. However, lessons can be gained from previous experiences or other organization's experiences. Here are the top lessons learned from my experience with SRM upgrade projects:

▶ Keep an eye on the functionality being delivered in the upcoming releases of the product; aim toward less custom development.

▶ Do not treat an upgrade as a technical effort. Enlist your business users for analysis from the very beginning.

▶ Define your scope. A new release from SAP offers hundreds of new functionality; define the overall scope of the project upfront.

▶ Do not forget the external systems; new software releases provoke changes in all areas of the product.

▶ Programs that contains variants need to be reviewed.

▶ Do not underestimate the role of security in your upgrade effort. Each new release of SRM provides tons of new transactions which need to be analyzed with existing user authorizations. The SAP SRM solution is notorious for changing transaction codes for the same function.

▶ Training is serious business. Depending on your current and upgrade release, there might be major design and functional changes. Capturing those changes and adequately training users is not an easy task.

▶ Staying current with support packs is important during the upgrade. In the new release, especially ramp-up, SAP provides corrections via OSS Notes and support packs.

> **Note**
>
> SAP SRM release 3.0 the Shop transaction is "BBPPU99", and the SAP SRM release 4.0 the Shop transaction is "BBPSC01".

In the next section, I have provided an upgrade assessment questionaire that can be very useful for organizations prior to beginning their upgrade initiatives. This questionaire will help to answer questions that are typically not very intuitive and prompt organizations to think through the different areas relevant for any upgrade project.

14.8 Upgrade Assessment — via a Questionnaire

An upgrade is an important and major undertaking for any organization. Asking the right questions upfront not only provides a clear picture of the various opportunities, challenges and risks involved, but also saves a great deal of time in planning and execution.

The following list of questions can be used as an assessment for your e-procurement upgrade and enhancement project. In order to answer the following questions, input will be required from different functional and technical teams in your organization. Once you are able to complete this assessment, your project team can analyze the answers in the different section to create a starting point for building your upgrade vision and scoping document:

1. **Goal**
   - What is the reason for the upgrade?
   - Current release going out of support
   - Would like to leverage features available in new release
   - Due to internal infrastructure standardization
   - System consolidation
   - Other
2. **Current Implementation**
   - What is the current release of SRM/EBP implemented?
     - Release xxxx
   - Which of the following components of SRM are implemented?
     - Enterprise Buyer (EBP)
     - Bidding Engine

- ▶ Contract Management
- ▶ Supplier Self Services
- ▶ Requisite BugsEye
- ▶ Requisite Emerge
- ▶ SAP CCM
- ▶ Internet Transaction Server
- ▶ Other xxxx
- ▶ When was the current implementation installed or upgraded to?
  - ▶ Year xxxx
- ▶ Which integration scenarios are currently implemented?
  - ▶ Classic
  - ▶ Extended Classic
  - ▶ Standalone
  - ▶ If a combination of above scenario's exist, please advise the functionality used for the scenario xxxx
- ▶ Which functional scenarios are implemented?
  - ▶ Self-Services Procurement
  - ▶ Plan-Driven Procurement
  - ▶ Strategic Sourcing
  - ▶ Auction/Bidding
  - ▶ SAP HR Integration to SRM
  - ▶ Plant Maintenance Integration
  - ▶ SAP BW for Spend Analysis
  - ▶ XML PO to Suppliers
- ▶ Do you have any custom workflow implemented?
  - ▶ Yes No
- ▶ What type of workflow (e.g., cost-center based)
- ▶ Which catalogs are used and how many?
- ▶ Any internal catalog?
- ▶ Number of suppliers in internal catalog
- ▶ Number of roundtrip catalogs — xxx
- ▶ Is P-card function implemented?

- ▸ Yes No
- ▸ In SRM or R/3 x
- ▶ How many Business Add-Ins (BAdIs) have been used?
- ▶ Please provide a list if possible
- ▶ Have you customized the front-end user experience (modified standard SAP HTML templates)?
  - ▸ Yes No
- ▶ If yes, could you please advice if minor or major?
- ▶ Is SRM system integrated to multiple R/3 bac-end systems?
  - ▸ Yes No
- ▶ Is SRM system integrated to non-R/3 back-end systems?
  - ▸ Yes No
- ▶ Do you have multi-currency, multi-language implemented?
  - ▸ Yes No
- ▶ If Yes, what currencies and languages:
- ▶ How many sites are using SRM?
  - ▸ xxx
- ▶ How many users are using SRM?
  - ▸ xxx
- ▶ Please list any major limitations/shortcomings/problems in current system
  - ▸ xxx
- ▶ How many environments in current SRM system landscape?

3. **Additional Functions/Features in Upgrade**

- ▶ Please list new functions and features you are planning to include in the upgrade
  - ▸ xxx xxx xxx xx
- ▶ Please list functions and features you are planning to enhance in the upgrade.
  - ▸ xxx
- ▶ Please list functions and features you are planning to discontinue after the upgrade.
  - ▸ xxx

- ▶ Are you planning to replace your internal catalog with SAP CCM?
  - ▶ Yes No N/A
- ▶ Are you planning to use SAP Business Connector with SAP XI?
  - ▶ Yes No N/A
- ▶ Please explain the planning and study already done for scope of the upgrade activity.
- ▶ Are you planning to increase any environment for SRM system? Introduce Pre-production, add QA etc.
  - ▶ Yes No N/A
- ▶ Do you currently use the SAP Enterprise Portal?
  - ▶ Yes No
- ▶ Do you plan to utilize the SAP Enterprise Portal with SRM?
  - ▶ Yes No
- ▶ If you currently do not integrate with SAP HR for Organizational Structure, do you plan on integrating that in the upgrade?
  - ▶ Yes No
- ▶ Will there be additional sites/users rolled out as part of the upgrade?
  - ▶ Yes No

14.9 Summary

The goal of this chapter was to provide you with an understanding of how to approach SRM upgrade projects. Readers need to remember that it is very important for project teams to continuously consider the scope-creep threat in an upgrade project. Also, it is vital to treat an upgrade project as another SAP implementation. Depending on the SRM release, new enhancements and changes at various areas of the product could affect the application usability, architecture, training, and possibly change management.

Now, we can proceed to Chapter 15, which addresses performance reporting via SAP BI.

Every organization strives to find tangible information — amid mountains of data — that provides true competitive differentiation. This information allows you to make timelier, more accurate, and fiscally advantageous decisions that drive improved corporate performance.

15 Performance Reporting via SAP NetWeaver Business Intelligence

Organizations implement SAP solutions all the time; sometimes it takes years to complete their initial ERP implementation. Scope is adjusted, resources are strapped, the timeline is always the ugly child, and what gets scrapped are performance reporting measures. These were the same performance measures that were discussed in the beginning of the project and that probably were a key factor for implementing the enterprise solution.

Time and time again, organizations plan to implement performance reporting but lag in the delivery of that reporting. Part of the issue is that when requirements are being gathered, the functional teams are bombarding the performance reporting teams with the existing requirements and customized reports they have available in the legacy systems.

The performance reporting team seeks to meet the desired needs by struggling in a dark cloud for a few months trying various methods to produce the requested customized reports that were deemed go-live critical. Not until after the project realization phase does realization dawn that the overall business processes will be changed as a part of the new solution implementation, and the customized reports might be nice to have rather than critical.

A business-intelligence survey by IDC found that: "...only 15% of managers agree with the statement that most reports developed in their organizations deliver the right data to the right people at the right time."

Unfortunately, what both the functional and performance reporting teams forget during this process is the real needs of the new business environment. What are the key performance indicators (KPIs) that are required to realize the immense value of the solution that was implemented? Most e-procurement and supplier relationship management (SRM) implementations face the situation described here.

Many organizations are bound by industry and governmental requirements and drive the reporting desired. Those situations aside, our argument applies to the non-regulated reporting needs.

Performance reporting in a supplier relationship environment is also multi-faceted. There are many business partners that need to analyze data and cannot operate efficiently without proper reporting mechanisms. In an organization, the departments have a need to report on purchases made and compare against open budgets and actual.

Professional purchasers need to analyze spend based on contracted and non-contracted sources, and review maverick procurement. Strategic buyers need to be able to view supplier history and performance in order to negotiate better contacts and select the best sources of supply. The key requirement for all these business partners, internal and external to the organization, is to be able to analyze data for better decision-making.

According to Research Vice-President Frank Buytendijk at Gartner Research: "...if you ask organizations what they want to use business intelligence (BI) for, better decision-making is the top answer. The pressure from cost cutting and compliance has put a greater focus on BI..."

SAP SRM within itself does not provide many standard reports, only a few reports that are far from serving any strategic or operational needs. However, the NetWeaver platform integrates SAP's business intelligence application (SAP NetWeaver BI, formerly known as Business Information Warehouse or BW) with SAP SRM to deliver a multitude of out-of-the-box reports that organizations can use in the standard delivery.

15.1 SAP NetWeaver BI with SAP SRM

In this section, I will describe the BI solution in general and how it integrates with the SAP SRM solution. At the very basic level, readers need to understand that BI acts as the reporting solution for SAP SRM. There are no reports available within the different components of SAP SRM (EBP, SUS, etc.). In Enterprise Buyer (EBP), there are a few administrator reports but none that are practically useful for end users.

The standard content in SAP BI, however, fills the gap for reports in SRM. SAP provides over a 100 standard reports that are available using SAP BI.

Organizations implementing SRM need to be aware that unless they implement BI they will be unable to adequately analyze their procurement spending. Analysis such as documents awaiting approval, open shopping carts for your departments, and purchasing workload analysis are all examples of the standard content available in SAP BI.

15.1.1 Business Intelligence within SAP NetWeaver

Before we move further, let us define the term *business intelligence* from an industry and an SAP perspective. You can review two definitions here:

- ▶ "Business intelligence (BI) is a broad category of applications and technologies for gathering, storing, analyzing, and providing access to data to help enterprise users make better business decisions." — searchSAP.com
- ▶ "SAP Business Information Warehouse (now SAP NetWeaver BI) provides data-warehousing functionality, a business intelligence platform, and a suite of business intelligence tools that enable businesses to attain these goals." — SAP Service Marketplace

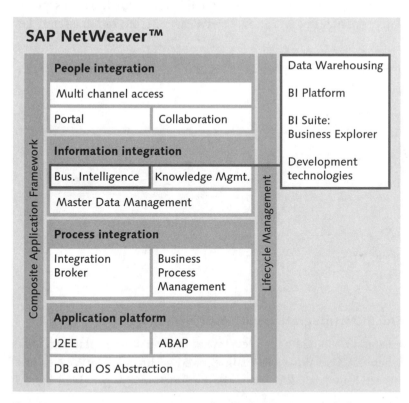

Figure 15.1 SAP Business Intelligence Within the SAP NetWeaver Platform

Most organizations might be familiar with the product name *SAP BW* that has been around for the past many years. The information-warehouse solution is now part of the SAP NetWeaver BI suite and functions as the core reporting module for all SAP applications, including SAP SRM.

All SAP technology components are now integrated within SAP NetWeaver, including NetWeaver Portal (EP), Master Data Management (MDM), Exchange Infrastructure (XI), and Business Intelligence (BI). In this chapter, when we use the term SAP NetWeaver BI, it is synonomous with SAP Business Information Warehouse or SAP BW. Figure 15.1 illustrates how the business intelligence solution is integrated within SAP NetWeaver.

15.1.2 Basic Reporting Concepts

Before we move forward, it is important to understand the following terms and definitions, as we'll use this terminology within this chapter. It is also important to get acquainted with these terms so you can speak knowledgeably when discussing and providing requirements to the performance reporting teams for your project. Please note that the following terms are not an all-inclusive list of terms within SAP NetWeaver BI, but rather a set of key concepts:

- ▶ DataStore Layer
- ▶ InfoCube Layer
- ▶ Multi-provider Layer
- ▶ DataSources
- ▶ DataStore Objects
- ▶ InfoSources
- ▶ InfoCubes
- ▶ Structures
- ▶ Web Templates
- ▶ Queries

15.1.3 SAP SRM Integration with SAP NetWeaver BI

Now that we understand at a high level what the NetWeaver platform looks like and where SAP NetWeaver BI is integrated within the NetWeaver platform, let us see how SAP SRM leverages the functionality provided by SAP NetWeaver BI.

The first thing that should be clarified is that SAP NetWeaver BI is installed and implemented on an independent environment separate from SAP SRM. The standard SAP technology of Remote Function Call (RFC) connects the two systems. Therefore, the first thing that is done is to create a connection is between the SRM and BI systems, as illustrated in Figure 15.2.

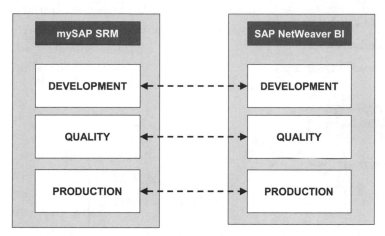

Figure 15.2 Typical Landscape for SAP SRM and Business Intelligence Integrated

Why is this important? First, when the business intelligence analyst asks you any questions about the requirement, you want to be sure you both understand that this is not you're not talking about the SAP R/3 environment, that SAP SRM is a separate system. Time and time again, project teams new to SRM assume that the source system for them will be the SAP R/3 (ERP) system.

15.1.4 Source System

Simply put, the main job of the business-intelligence system is to connect to all the systems in the enterprise landscape and collect data from the different places (sources). Figure 15.3 provides an example of what sources could be important in a typical SAP SRM–BI implementation. In this figure, SAP R/3 is a source system for BI, and SAP SRM is another source system. Basically the BI solution can pull data from any of these sources to create an appropriate report. The resulting report could provide information collected and aggregated from both of these source systems in a single analytic report.

One example of this scenario could be that in SAP SRM the organization is creating shopping carts and POs. And the goods receipts and invoices are being entered and posted in the SAP R/3 system. In this scenario, if a department manager wanted to know about the open items that still need to be received in the system, he or she could use an Open Items (Confirmations) report, which could provide information on the following:

- ▶ Cost center that ordered the goods or services.
- ▶ The PO number
- ▶ The open PO value outstanding
- ▶ The open delivery value
- ▶ And the open PO Quantity

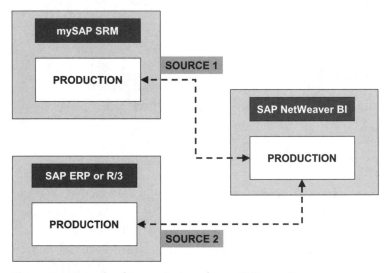

Figure 15.3 Example of Source Systems from a BI Perspective

> **Note**
>
> Confirmations in SAP SRM are similar to goods receipt entry in SAP R/3.

In such a report, the source system for the PO information is SAP SRM. The source system for the delivery, confirmation, or goods-receipt information is SAP R/3. This report then is not truly valuable unless the information is aggregated from both these sources and presented to the end user in a single format to analyze. This is where the power of SAP NetWeaver BI comes to play, and its integration with the SAP solutions provides an edge over the competition BI solutions.

Note that the transactional source systems are in fact the DataSources that define the structures and the data used for reporting in SAP BI. Figure 15.4 illustrates the sample scenario described above. In this illustration, the invoice entry is not used in SRM. We do not need to activate the DataSource, which transfers invoice data from the SRM to the BI system, because it does not contain any data.

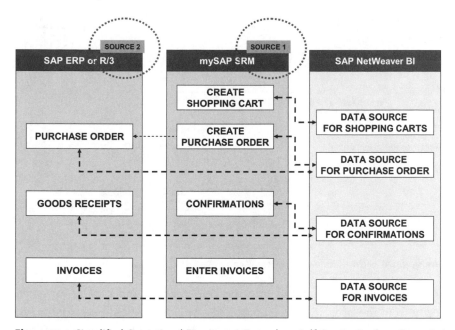

Figure 15.4 Simplified Operational ProcuremenExample -- Self-Service Business Scenario in Enterprise Buyer

> **Note**
>
> Organizations should be aware that competitors are gaining ground on SAP. BI competitors such as *Cognos* (Cognos 8 MR1 release) are stepping up their integration with the SAP solutions to provide an alternate solution for SAP customers.

15.1.5 Accessing Reports from SAP NetWeaver BI in SAP SRM

There are two key methods for users to access the analytics and reports created in the BI system in SAP SRM. Let's take a look at these now.

Directly Integrated in the User's LaunchPad in SRM

A simple way to integrate reports from SAP BI into SRM is via the user's LaunchPad. The LaunchPad is simply the menu provided to the end users within their browser once they've successfully logged on.

The role-based concept in SRM provides all users with a role and within each role there are specific Web services and transactions that they can execute, for example, **Shopping Cart-Full functionality,** or **approval.** These are typically presented to the end users via a menu in their Web browsers, as illustrated in Figure 15.5.

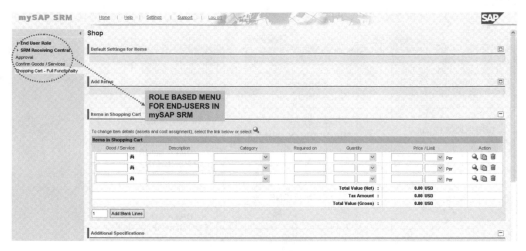

Figure 15.5 SAP SRM — Role-Based User Menu

The BI analyses are integrated into the role concept and can be executed directly from the browser LaunchPad. SAP provides pre-defined, role-based models in BI for SAP SRM that contain a set of standard templates for reporting and analysis. Figure 15.7 illustrates this concept. Some key benefits of this option are as follows:

▶ Users can analyze the reports without having to leave Enterprise Buyer.

▶ Option is suitable for organizations not using the SAP NetWeaver NetWeaver Portal.

▶ Standard roles in SAP BI and in SAP SRM can provide a out-of-the box solutions for accessing these reports quickly.

▶ Allows usage of pre-defined templates for reporting and analysis.

To illustrate this via an example, let us review the manager role (SAP_BIC_SRM_MANAGER) in SAP BI provided for the SRM operational procurement business scenario. This BI role contains standard templates and queries that a manager using SRM might want to access from a reporting and analysis perspective. The manager might want an overview of the purchasing history within his or her department or cost center and additionally might want to also know who requisitioned those purchases.

SAP provides three standard Web templates for use within the BI Manager role and for each of these templates a set of standard queries is available for use within SAP SRM. Figure 15.6 illustrates the scenario of the manager role within BI.

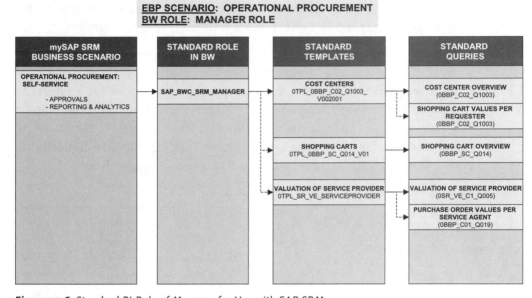

Figure 15.6 Standard BI Role of Manager for Use with SAP SRM

Figure 15.7 illustrates the access of queries within the SRM user LaunchPad.

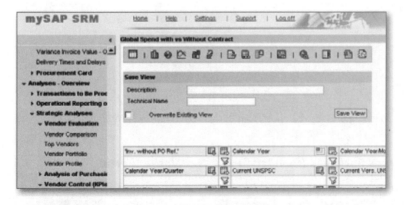

Figure 15.7 Analyses Within Launchpad in Enterprise Buyer

Note
A number of standard BI roles are provided for use with the various SAP SRM business scenarios.

Some of these reports are also directly accessible for professional purchasers to make decisions during sourcing, PO processing, or during contract management. An example would be a scenario in which a buyer needs to determine the best source of supply for a particular shopping cart in the *Sourcing* application. The buyer might want to compare different vendors for past performance. The buyer can launch a BI report directly from within the *Sourcing* application, allowing him or her to streamline the sourcing process.

In order to have buttons displayed to launch SAP BI reports from the different application contexts of reporting for Enterprise Buyer, special roles have to be assigned to a user. The buttons appear in the application contexts as icons in the form of a magnifying glass. One role that makes these buttons visible is SAP_EC_BBP_BUDGET_EXAMPLE. This role offers the overview information of the budgeting queries, as well as the possibility of displaying details of single accounting objects, as illustrated in Figure 15.8.

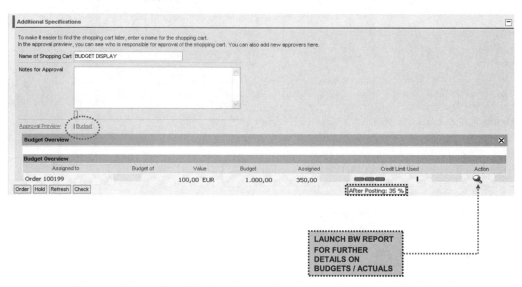

Figure 15.8 Launching BI Budget Report from Budget Overview in SRM Shopping Cart

Using Business Packages Provided in SAP NetWeaver Portal

This option is relevant for organizations that are using SAP NetWeaver Portal, with SAP SRM to leverage the portal Business Package for SAP SRM.

The Business Package for SAP SRM 4.0 is available for use with the NetWeaver Portal 60.2 release, and can be downloaded free of cost from *www.sdn.sap.com*. This Business Package contains worksets and iViews defined for all the standard SAP SRM roles, so that organizations using SRM can quickly incorporate SRM transactions within the portal.

So basically what project teams can do is to use the standard roles in NetWeaver Portal to get access to all the standard queries provided by SAP for SAP SRM. These standard queries are available in the portal as iViews. If an organization is using the roles in NetWeaver Portal and SAP SRM applications out-of-the-box, without modification, this solution provides end users a seamless and effortless access of standard queries within the NetWeaver Portal.

However, it is highly unlikely that organizations are going to use the roles without modification. The standard roles delivered by SAP are based on best practices but are not always practical for different organizations.

Example
There are two different standard roles for purchasing professionals: Operational Purchaser and Strategic Purchaser. Your organization might not differentiate between the two roles, and maybe the professional purchasers in your organization are responsible for all the transactions or activities that form these two roles. In this example, the project teams can no longer use the standard roles available in the portal, SRM, or BI. A new role would have to be developed and integrated across the three applications.

SAP provides the business-package roles illustrated in Figure 15.9 along with the back-end roles (SRM and BI) to which the business-package roles are mapped.

ENTERPRISE PORTAL ROLE	SRM ROLE	BW ROLE
EMPLOYEE / USER	SAP_BBP_STAL_EMPLOYEE	NO STANDARD BW ROLE EXISTS FOR THIS SRM ROLE
MANAGER	SAP_BBP_STAL_EMPLOYEE	SAP_BWC_SRM_MANAGER
	SAP_BBP_STAL_MANAGER	
PURCHASING ASSISTANT	SAP_BBP_STAL_EMPLOYEE	SAP_BWC_SRM_PURCHASING_ASSIST
	SAP_BBP_STAL_SECRETARY	
OPERATIONAL PURCHASER	SAP_BBP_STAL_EMPLOYEE	SAP_BWC_SRM_OPER_PURCHASER
	SAP_BBP_STAL_PURCHASER	
STRATEGIC PURCHASER	SAP_BBP_STAL_EMPLOYEE	SAP_BWC_SRM_STRAT_PURCHASER
	SAP_BBP_STAL_STRAT_PURCHASER	
CONTENT MANAGER	SAP_BBP_STAL_EMPLOYEE	NO STANDARD BW ROLE EXISTS FOR THIS SRM ROLE
	SAP_BBP_STAL_CONTENT_MANAGER	
COMPONENT PLANNER	SAP_BBP_STAL_EMPLOYEE	NO STANDARD BW ROLE EXISTS FOR THIS SRM ROLE
	SAP_BBP_STAL_PLANNER	
GOODS RECIPIENT	SAP_BBP_STAL_EMPLOYEE	SAP_BWC_SRM_RECIPIENT
	SAP_BBP_STAL_RECIPIENT	
ACCOUNTANT	SAP_BBP_STAL_EMPLOYEE	SAP_BWC_SRM_ACCOUNTANT
	SAP_BBP_STAL_ACCOUNTANT	
ADMINISTRATOR	SAP_BBP_STAL_EMPLOYEE	NO STANDARD BW ROLE EXISTS FOR THIS SRM ROLE
	SAP_BBP_STAL_ADMINISTRATOR	

Figure 15.9 NetWeaver Portal Roles Mapped to SAP SRM and BI Roles

For purposes of illustration, in Figure 15.9 the SRM roles only show composites; single roles and multiple roles are not displayed but are available for use. In order to implement this option, the following prerequisites need to be completed:

- SAP SRM 4.0 is installed
- SAP BI 3.5 is installed
- NetWeaver Portal 6.0 is installed
- NetWeaver Portal Plug-In is installed on the BI server
- Single Sign-On is configured for SRM and BI
- SAP SRM 4.0 Business Package is imported in EP
- All relevant Business Content in BI is activated

> **Note**
>
> Although the Business Packages provide out-of-the-box integration with SAP SRM, organizations end up spending considerable time to customize Business Packages to meet their own role and security requirements. The Business Packages reduce the overall time effort to integrate SAP SRM within the NetWeaver Portal application, but the organization-specific effort should not be underestimated.

Now let's go on to discuss the importance of the standard content available in NetWeaver BI for SRM. SAP provides pre-built reports and queries that organizations can use for SRM, and these are available by importing the content relevant to your SRM release.

15.2   Standard SAP BI Business Content for SAP SRM

One of the key competitive advantages that the SAP solution has over other data-warehousing solutions in the marketplace is that SAP provides a large amount of pre-delivered content for SAP SRM. When you talk to people in an organization who are responsible for managing a department's budget, or to audit personnel, procurement buyers, and others, they all typically have a ton of reporting requirements.

Building these reports manually from scratch can be time consuming. This is where the standard content in BI becomes a business advantage. SAP provides more than 100 standard reports that organizations can use directly out-of-the-box. Organizations can either choose to use these reports and queries as delivered or they can use them as a starting point to further enhance to meet business requirements.

When we talk about BI Content, we're referring to the software component in SAP NetWeaver BI that provides the content for all SAP applications including standard content for SAP SRM. The BI component has to be installed for using any of its functionality. Please note that as of its BW 3.1 release, SAP's solution has been split into two different software components: a business-warehouse component and a business-intelligence component.

15.2.1 Key Benefits for Standard SAP BI Content

There are several benefits for organizations implementing SRM to use the standard BI Content provided by SAP. Here are some key benefits:

▶ Out-of-the-box reports, data models, extractors, and transformations.

▶ A good starting point for extending the reports for use within your business needs and requirements.

▶ The standard reports provided, based on best practice researched from customer needs.

▶ Shorter project implementation timeline.

▶ Ability to use standard reports and analysis until actual requirements are determined based on new business processes implemented.

15.2.2 Release Compatibility for SAP SRM and SAP NetWeaver BI

As SAP NetWeaver BI and SAP SRM are separate solutions, they have their own independent release roadmaps. SAP is continually trying to get the release strategy for all components into uniformity, but until that actually happens organizations have to deal with the different release roadmaps.

It is important at the beginning of the project that release compatibility is accessed between SAP SRM and SAP NetWeaver BI. And since release 3.1 of SAP BW, the software components are divided; it is important to review whether the appropriate BI content is available for the SRM release. Figure 15.10 illustrates the release compatibility between SRM and SAP NetWeaver BI as of SAP SRM 5.0.

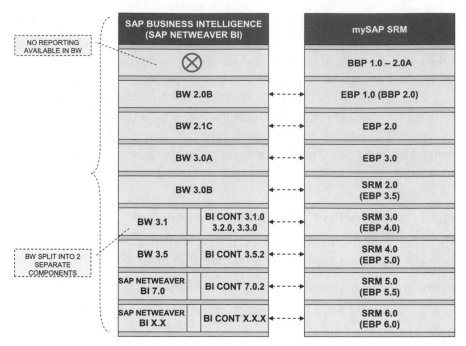

Figure 15.10 SAP SRM and SAP NetWeaver BI Release Compatibility

15.2.3 BI Content Delivered for SAP SRM

SAP provides standard business content that is delivered for many different SAP solutions including SAP SRM. The term *business content* is synonymous with the pre-delivered objects such as roles, templates, queries, data models, extractors, transformations, etc. It is important to understand that business content is delivered as an add-on to the core SAP BI solution. Therefore, for SAP SRM, SAP provides a specific add-on that is compatible with your SRM release, as was illustrated in Figure 15.9.

Figure 15.11 illustrates a timeline for the variously named SAP BW and BI solutions over the past several releases, including the BI Content available for each release.

SAP provides a list of all the available content dependent on the SAP SRM release, SAP BW, or SAP NetWeaver BI release and the BI Content add-on your organization is planning to implement. This is illustrated in Figure 15.12, and a complete listing is available on the SAP Service Marketplace.

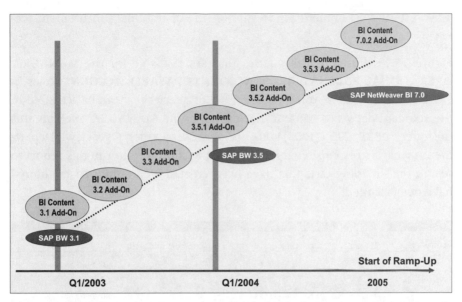

Figure 15.11 SAP Business Intelligence Product Release Timeline (Source: Service-SAP.com)

SRM Rele.	BW Tech R.	available since BI Content Release	Area	Query Name	Query-id	Backend	Target (ODS / Info- / Multi-cube)
SRM 2.0	3.0B	3.0B	eProcurement Account Assignment-Total Records	Purchase Values per Cost Center	0BBP_C02_Q007	MM* and SRM	0BBP_C02
SRM 2.1	3.0B	3.0B	eProcurement Account Assignment-Total Records	Purchase Values per Order	0BBP_C02_Q009	MM* and SRM	0BBP_C02
SRM 2.3	3.0B	3.0B	eProcurement Account Assignment-Total Records	WEB: My Cost Center - Current Procurement	0BBP_C02_Q1001	MM* and SRM	0BBP_C02
SRM 2.2	3.0B	3.0B	eProcurement Account Assignment-Total Records	SRM Manager - Cost Center Overview	0BBP_C02_Q1003	MM* and SRM	0BBP_C02
SRM 2.0	3.0B	3.0B	Goods/Services Confirmation-Single Documents	Overview of Return Deliveries	0BBP_CONF_Q013	MM* and SRM	0BBP_CON
SRM 2.0	3.0B	3.0B	Invoice - Single Documents	Invoices per Contract	0BBP_INV_Q012	MM* and SRM	0BBP_INV
SRM 2.0	3.0B	3.0B	Purchase Order - Single Documents	Purchase Orders per Contract	0BBP_PO_Q011	MM* and SRM	0BBP_PO
SRM 2.0	3.0B	3.0B	Shopping Cart - individual documents	Shopping Carts per Shopping Cart Number	0BBP_SC_Q001	SRM	0BBP_SC
SRM 2.0	3.0B	3.0B	Shopping Cart - individual documents	Shopping Carts per Shopping Cart Number with	0BBP_SC_Q002	SRM	0BBP_SC
SRM 2.0	3.0B	3.0B	Shopping Cart - individual documents	Shopping Carts per Requester	0BBP_SC_Q003	SRM	0BBP_SC
SRM 2.0	3.0B	3.0B	Shopping Cart - individual documents	Shopping Carts per Product / Product Category	0BBP_SC_Q004	SRM	0BBP_SC
SRM 4.0	3.5	3.5.2	FI-SL only; FI Global Spend Data for SRM	Top 15 Suppliers	0SR_FIC01_Q0004	** FI Special Ledger	0SR_FIC01
SRM 4.0	3.5	3.5.2	FI-SL only; FI Global Spend Data for SRM	Invoice Values per Category (Top 5)	0SR_FIC01_Q0006	** FI Special Ledger	0SR_FIC01
SRM 4.0	3.5	3.5.2	FI-SL only; FI Global Spend Data for SRM	Top 15 Categories	0SR_FIC01_Q0007	** FI Special Ledger	0SR_FIC01
SRM 4.0	3.5	3.5.2	FI-SL only; FI Global Spend Data for SRM	Invoices per Account	0SR_FIC01_Q0008	** FI Special Ledger	0SR_FIC01
SRM 4.0	3.5	3.5.2	FI-SL only; FI Global Spend Data for SRM	Invoice Values with PO and Contract Ref. (Con	0SR_FIC01_Q0009	** FI Special Ledger	0SR_FIC01
SRM 4.0	3.5	3.5.2	Contract Management	Contract Details	0SRCT_DS1_Q003	MM* and SRM	0SRCT_DS1
SRM 4.0	3.5	3.5.2	Contract Management	Expiring Contracts	0SRCT_DS1_Q004	MM* and SRM	0SRCT_DS1
SRM 4.0	3.5	3.5.2	Contract Management	Contracts per Product Category (current)	0SRCT_DS1_Q005	MM* and SRM	0SRCT_DS1
SRM 4.0	3.5	3.5.2	Contract Management	Contracts per Purchasing Organization / Purch	0SRCT_DS1_Q006	MM* and SRM	0SRCT_DS1
SRM 4.0	3.5	3.5.2	Contract Management	Contract Alerts	0SRCT_DS1_Q007	MM* and SRM	0SRCT_DS1
SRM 4.0	3.5	3.5.2	Contract Management	Contracts per Product and Vendor	0SRCT_DS1_Q008	MM* and SRM	0SRCT_DS1
SRM 4.0	3.5	3.5.2	Contract Management	Scheduling Plan Details	0SRCT_DS1_Q009	MM* and SRM	0SRCT_DS1
SRM 5.0	7.0	7.0.2	Procurement Account Assignment	Cost Center Overview	0SR_C02_Q002	MM* and SRM	0SR_C02
SRM 5.0	7.0	7.0.2	Auctions	Auctions Analysis	0SR_LAC1_Q0001	SRM	0SR_LAC1
SRM 5.0	7.0	7.0.2	Auctions	Auction Items Analysis	0SR_LAC1_Q0002	SRM	0SR_LAC1
SRM 5.0	7.0	7.0.2	Auctions	Bidders Analysis	0SR_LAC1_Q0003	SRM	0SR_LAC1
SRM 5.0	7.0	7.0.2	Procurement Overview (multicube aggregate)	Procurement Value Analysis	0SR_MC01_Q0001	MM* and SRM	0SR_MC01
SRM 5.0	7.0	7.0.2	Procurement Overview (multicube aggregate)	Procurement Values per Service Provider	0SR_MC01_Q0002	MM* and SRM	0SR_MC01
SRM 5.0	7.0	7.0.2	Procurement Overview (multicube aggregate)	Supplier Information	0SR_MC01_Q0003	MM* and SRM	0SR_MC01
SRM 5.0	7.0	7.0.2	Procurement Overview (multicube aggregate)	Key Performance Indicators	0SR_MC01_Q0004	MM* and SRM	0SR_MC01
SRM 5.0	7.0	7.0.2	Procurement Overview (multicube aggregate)	Price Trend Analysis per Product	0SR_MC01_Q0005	MM* and SRM	0SR_MC01
SRM 5.0	7.0	7.0.2	Procurement Overview (multicube aggregate)	Number of Suppliers per Country	0SR_MC01_Q0006	MM* and SRM	0SR_MC01
SRM 5.0	7.0	7.0.2	Procurement Overview (multicube aggregate)	ABC Analysis for Suppliers (Lorenz Curve)	0SR_MC01_Q0007	MM* and SRM	0SR_MC01
SRM 5.0	7.0	7.0.2	Procurement Overview (multicube aggregate)	ABC Supplier	0SR_MC01_Q0008	MM* and SRM	0SR_MC01
SRM 5.0	7.0	7.0.2	Procurement Overview (multicube aggregate)	Success of an SRM Project	0SR_MC01_Q0009	MM* and SRM	0SR_MC01

Figure 15.12 Standard Queries Based on SAP SRM, BI release, and BI Content Add-On

15.2.4 Operational Procurement Scenario

As discussed in Chapters 3, 4, and 5, there are a number of business scenarios in SAP SRM, with operational procurement scenario being a key engine for the rest. Figures 15.13 and 15.14 provide a list of reports available in SAP

SRM 4.0 using BI Content 3.5 to support the operational procurement scenario.

Figure 15.13 illustrates the queries that are available for the **MANAGER**, **OPERATIONAL PURCHASER**, and **ACCOUNTS PAYABLE ACCOUNT** Roles in SRM. For each of these roles, there is a set of queries that can be activated in the standard delivered content. For example, the MANAGER role contains the query **0BBP_C02_Q1003_V002** for the Cost Center Overview. Department managers responsible for a particular cost center can run this report to see all the shopping carts that have been created where their cost center(s) have been charged.

ROLE	WEB TEMPLATES	QUERIES
MANAGER SAP_BWC_SRM_MANAGER	COST CENTER INFORMATION 0TPL_0BBP_C02_Q1003_V002001	COST CENTER OVERVIEW 0BBP_C02_Q1003_V002
		OVERVIEW OF PROCURMENT VALUES PER REQUESTER 0BBP_C02_Q1003_V001
	SHOPPING CART INFORMATION 0TPL_0BBP_SC_Q014_V01	OVERVIEW OF SHOPPING CARTS 0BBP_SC_Q014_V01
	EVALUATION OF SERVICE PROVIDERS 0TPL_SR_VE_SERVICEPROVIDER	EVALUATION OF SERVICE PROVIDERS 0SR_VE_C1_Q005
		PROCUREMENT VALUES PER SERVICE PROVIDER 0BBP_C01_Q019
OPERATIONAL PURCHASER SAP_BW_SRM_OPER_PURCHASER	DEADLINE MONITORING 0TPL_0BBP_DS1_Q013_V002	DEADLINE MONITORING BBP_DS1_Q013_V002
	HELD PURCHASE ORDERS 0TPL_0BBP_PO_Q007_V02	HELD PURCHASE ORDERS BBP_PO_Q007_V02
	SHOPPING CART INFORMATION 0TPL_0BBP_SC_Q004_V02	SHOPPING CART INFORMATION 0BBP_SC_Q004_V02
	CONTRACT UTILIZATION 0TPL_0BBP_CT_Q004	CONTRACT UTILIZATION 0BBP_CT_Q004
		VENDOR EVALUATION 0BBP_C01_Q032
ACCOUNTS PAYABLE ACCOUNTANT SAP_BW_SRM_STRAT_PURCHASER	INVOICE VERIFICATION / MONITOR PAYMENTS 0TPL_BBP_DS1_Q002	OPEN ITEMS (INVOICES) 0BBP_DS1_Q004
		EXCESSIVE INVOICES 0BBP_DS1_Q005
		INVOICES PER VENDOR 0BBP_INV_Q002

Figure 15.13 Operational Procurement Scenario Queries

In addition to the roles in Figure 15.13, additional queries are available for the **PROCUREMENT MANAGER**, **PURCHASING ASSISTANT**, and the **GOODS RECIPIENT** roles, as illustrated in Figure 15.14. For example, a purchasing manager might be interested in analyzing the number of POs created based on a purchasing organization or purchasing group. They can use the 0BBP_PO_Q005_V02 query for **PURCHASE ORDER PER PORG or PGROUP**.

You should note that I often use the terms reports and queries interchangeably in this chapter. There is a difference however. One easy way to differentiate this is that a query contains a specific structure, designed for a specific requirement, and usually built from a single BI InfoCube.

ROLE	WEB TEMPLATES	QUERIES
PROCUREMENT MANAGER SAP_BW_SRM_PROC_MANAGER	EVALUATION CONTROLLING 0TPL_SRVE_CONTROL_01	SUBMITTED INVOICES FOR EVALUATION 0SRVE_IS1_Q003_V001
		SUBMITTED EVALUATIONS FOR GR / SERVICE CONF. 0SRVE_IS2_Q003_V001
		SUBMITTED EVALUATIONS FOR VENDORS 0SRVE_IS3_Q003_V001
	BID INVITATION PER PRODUCT CATEGORY 0TPL_SR_BIDC01_Q005	BID INVITATION PER PRODUCT CATEGORY 0SR_BIDC01_Q005
	UTILIZATION PER PURCHASING GROUP 0TPL_BBP_PO_Q005_V02	PURCHASE ORDER PER PORG / PGROUP 0BBP_PO_Q005_V02
		SHOPPING CARTS PER PORG / PGROUP 0BBP_SC_Q005_V02
		CONTRACTS PER PORG / PGRP 0SRCT_DS1_Q006
	PROJECT SUCCESS OF AN EBP IMPLEMENTATION 0TPL_BBP_C01_Q039	
PURCHASING ASSISTANT SAP_BW_SRM_PURCHASING_ASSIST	SHOPPING CART OVERVIEW 0TPL_BBP_SC_Q003_V0302	SHOPPING CARTS PER REQUESTER 0BBP_SC_Q003_V02
		SHOPPING CART STATUS 0BBP_SC_Q003_V03
		SHOPPING CARTS TO BE APPROVED 0BBP_SCA_Q003_V001
GOODS RECIPIENT SAP_BW_SRM_RECIPIENT	EVALUATE GOODS RECIEPTS 0TPL_SRVE_IS2_Q001	MANDATORY EVALUATION OF GR / SERVICE CONF. 0SRVE_IS2_Q001_V01
		OPTIONAL EVALUATION OF GR / SERVICE CONF. 0SRVE_IS2_Q002_V01
	GOODS RECEIPTS 0TPL_BBP_DS1_Q002009	OPEN ITEMS (CONFIRMATIONS) 0BBP_DS1_Q002
		DELIVERY DELAYS 0BBP_DS1_Q009
		QUANTITY RELIABILITY (10 WORST VENDORS) 0BBP_C01_Q032_V001
		TIMELINESS (10 WORST VENDORS) 0BBP_C01_Q032_V002

Figure 15.14 Operational Procurement Scenario Queries

A report (also known as template), on the other hand, can be constructed using one or more queries. For example, as a part of the PROCUREMENT MANAGER role, A Web report — UTILIZATION PER PURCHASING GROUP — is available. This report is built using three queries: 0BBP_PO_Q005_V02 and 0BBP_SC_Q005_V02, and 0SRCT_DS1_Q006. For content information on SAP SRM 5.0, you should also read Section 15.4.

High-level Activities for Integrating BI Reports in SRM

Before users can start to use the reports in SRM, the performance reporting teams need to configure the NetWeaver BI system and activate the relevant DataSources in SRM. Figure 15.15 illustrates at a high level the pre-requisites for using SAP NetWeaver BI reporting within SAP SRM.

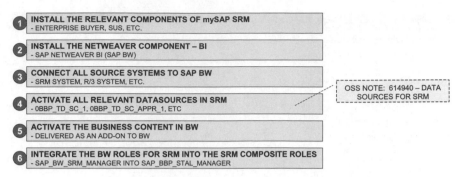

Figure 15.15 High-Level Activites for Integrating BI Reports within SAP SRM

15.2.5 Some Standard BI Reports for SAP SRM

As we've already discussed, there are many standard reports and queries available for SAP SRM in BI. Now, let's look a few examples of the reports available. Organizations can use these reports to analyze the procurement activity within their company. For example, a department manager can use the *Overview of Approved Shopping Carts* report to quickly analyze the shopping carts where all approval activity has been completed.

Overview of Approved Shopping Carts

This query provides information to a department manager concerning all the shopping carts that have been approved, along with who approved them, and the number of approval steps required to approve a shopping cart for a particular purchase amount. This is especially valuable for organizations auditing the approval process for purchase of goods or services. Figure 15.16 illustrates this query.

Shopping Carts per Catalog

Many organizations implement SAP SRM but do not follow up with the appropriate analysis of the value achieved after the initial project implementation. For example, catalogs may be implemented but value analysis forgotten when it comes to checking whether those catalogs are actually being used by the organization. This query shows an overview of the shopping carts that were created from a particular catalog. In addition the Vendor and Product Category fields are available in this report so the professional purchaser can analyze whether particular purchases in a product category should have originated from a vendor catalog onboarded by the organization. Figure 15.17 illustrates this query.

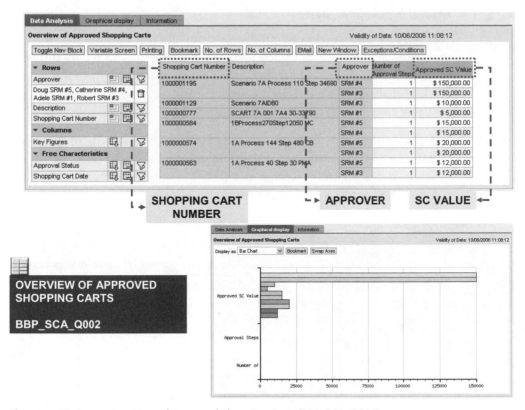

Figure 15.16 Query: Overview of Approved Shopping Carts (BBP_SCA_Q002)

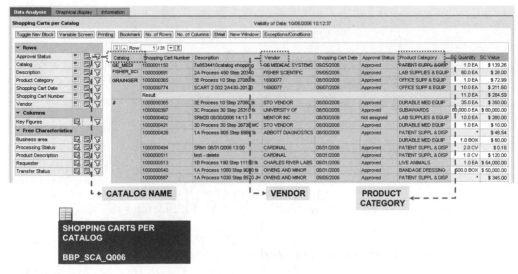

Figure 15.17 Query: Shopping Carts per Catalog (BBP_SCA_Q006)

Maverick Buying Analysis

This query allows purchasing professionals in an organization to review the purchases that do not conform to a strategic contract. The report provides information on POs that have resulted from contracts and the value of the POs that have not resulted from contracts. Additionally, the vendor data is available so that maverick purchases can be identified.

Organizations often will be able to analyze procurement activity to spot additional contract opportunity. Perhaps many goods or services are being ordered from a particular vendor, and there is an opportunity to enter into a contract. Figure 15.18 illustrates this query.

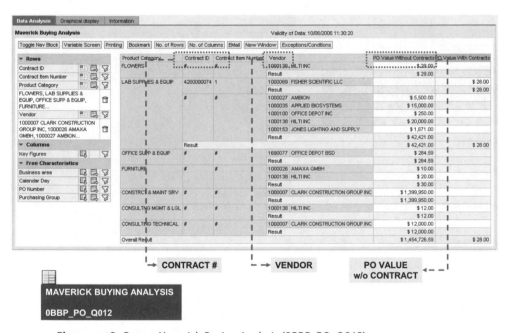

Figure 15.18 Query: Maverick Buying Analysis (0BBP_PO_Q012)

Purchase Order Detail by Line Item

Every organization needs reporting on the details of the purchases being made. This report or query provides detail information about the PO with line item and accounting details. Figure 15.19 illustrates this query.

Contracts per Product and Vendor

Organizations that use the contract-management functionality in SAP SRM can use this query to get an overview of the value-based and quantity-based contracts for particular vendors and products. This report can allow a strategic purchaser to analyze the total releases for the contracts open in the system. Figure 15.20 illustrates this query.

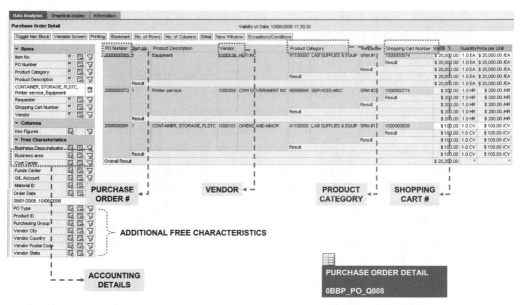

Figure 15.19 Query: Purchase Order Detail by Line Item (0BBP_PO_Q008)

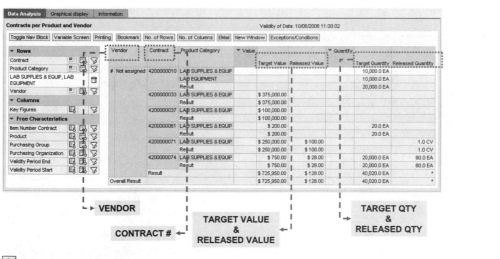

Figure 15.20 Query: Contracts per Product and Vendor (0SRCT_DS1_Q008)

In the next section, I will evaluate the impact of SAP SRM implementation scenarios on extracting and developing content in BI.

15.3 SAP SRM Implementation Scenario Impact on BI Reporting

As we've already discussed, SAP SRM can be implemented in different scenarios: Classic, Extended Classic, and Standalone. Based on the scenario implemented in SRM, the BI DataSources might change. For example, in the Classic scenario, the shopping cart is only created within SAP SRM, therefore transactional data for shopping carts can only be extracted from the SRM system. However, data for other purchasing documents such as POs, goods receipts, and invoices needs to be extracted from SAP R/3. In this example, at least two different source systems are needed to extract data into SAP NetWeaver BI and provide reporting. Therefore, it is important to understand the implication of SRM implementation scenarios on SAP NetWeaver BI.

Regardless of the implementation scenario, the DataSources (seen in Table 15.1) from SRM and the SAP back end (ERP or R/3) are needed in order to load the various DataStores in SAP NetWeaver BI to enable reporting in the operational procurement business scenario for SAP SRM.

SYSTEM	DATASOURCE	DATASOURCE USE
SRM	0BBP_TD_SC_1	Header and item-level information for shopping carts (e.g., product, product category, etc.)
SRM	0BBP_TD_SCA_1	Shopping cart approval information such as: approver of a shopping cart, the time of approval, and the approved value of a shopping cart
SRM**	0SRM_TD_PO	Information on header, item, and schedule line from SRM and ERP Pos
SRM**	0SRM_TD_PO_ACC	Header and item-level information on PO data with associated account assignment data
SRM**	0SRM_TD_CF	Header, item, and account assignment information on from confirmations in SRM
SRM**	0SRM_TD_IV	Header and item-level data on invoices created or parked in SAP SRM

Table 15.1 Relevant DataSources in SRM and SAP R/3

SYSTEM	DATASOURCE	DATASOURCE USE
SRM	0BBP_TD_CONTR_2	Header and item-level data for contracts created in SRM
SRM	0SRM_REL_CT	
ERP (R/3)	2LIS_02_HDR	Header information for a purchasing document (e.g., POrg, Vendor, etc.)
ERP (R/3)	2LIS_02_ITM	Item-level information for a purchasing document (e.g. Pgroup, Plant, etc.)
ERP (R/3)	2LIS_02_SCL	Schedule line information for a purchasing document (only if scheduling agreements are used)
ERP (R/3)	2LIS_02_ACC	Accounting information for a purchasing document (e.g., cost center, WBS element.)
ERP (R/3)	2LIS_06_IV	Header and item-level information for an invoice document (e.g.. invoice number, terms of payment)

Table 15.1 Relevant DataSources in SRM and SAP R/3 (cont.)

> **Note**
>
> The DataSources 0SRM_TD_PO, 0SRM_TD_PO_ACC, 0SRM_TD_CF, and 0SRM_TD_IV are only available as of SAP SRM 5.0 release and SAP ERP 2005 release.

All master-data texts that are relevant for account assignment are not located in Enterprise Buyer but in the ERP back-end system. If, for example, a cost center is uploaded and only Enterprise Buyer is connected, it is only possible to display the cost center number in a report (for example, 1000) and not the corresponding text. To get the master data text into SAP NetWeaver BI, you either have to connect your ERP back end to SAP NetWeaver BI to upload this part of the master data.

Figure 15.21 illustrates the overall data model in business reporting: extraction of data from the various DataSources, into the ODS (Operational Data Store) DataStores, to the InfoCube, to multi-providers, and finally to be made available for end user reporting.

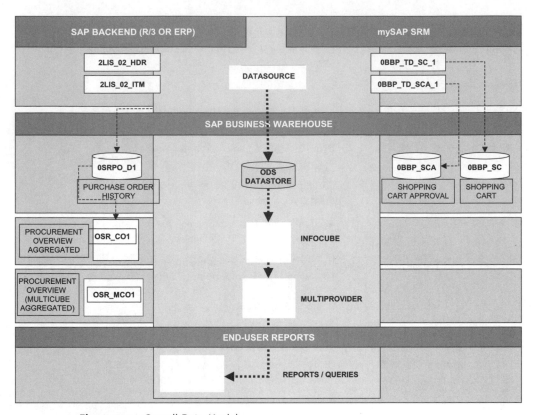

Figure 15.21 Overall Data Model

15.3.1 The Classic Scenario

In the Classic Scenario, the shopping cart document is created in SAP SRM. Based on business configuration, a purchase requisition or a PO is subsequently created in the SAP back end (R/3 or ERP). Follow-on documents such as goods receipt (confirmation) and invoices can be entered in SRM or the SAP back end. However, the transactional data for POs, goods receipts and invoices is extracted from SAP R/3. Figure 15.22 illustrates this scenario.

In this implementation scenario, both SAP SRM and ERP (or R/3) need to be connected to the SAP NetWeaver BI system as source systems, as illustrated in Figure 15.22. Figure 15.23 illustrates the data flow and mapping between the DataSources and DataStores based on the Classic implementation scenario of SAP SRM.

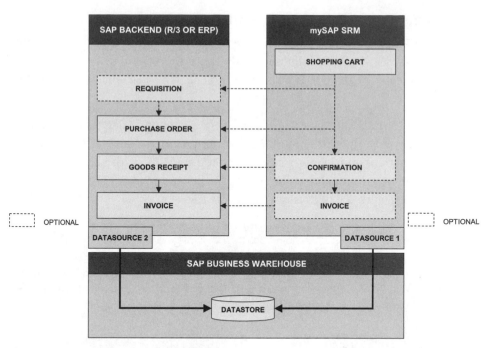

Figure 15.22 Classic Scenario in SAP SRM

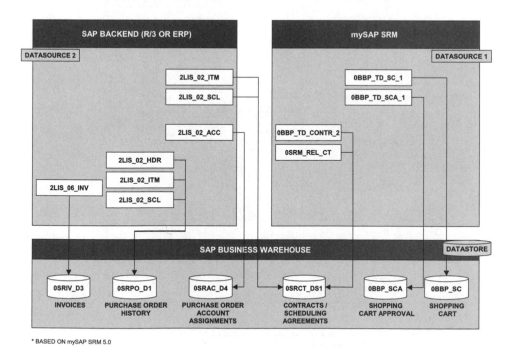

Figure 15.23 DataSource and DataStore Mapping in Classic Scenario

15.3.2 The Extended Classic Scenario

In the Extended Classic scenario, the shopping cart and the PO documents are created in SAP SRM. Subsequently, once the PO status is completed in SRM, a copy of this PO is transferred to the SAP back-end system (R/3 or ERP).

The PO in the SAP back-end is a read-only document; changes to this document are only allowed in SRM. Follow-on documents such as goods receipt (confirmation) and invoices can be entered in SRM or the back-end. However, the transactional data for goods receipts and invoices is extracted from SAP R/3. Figure 15.24 illustrates this scenario.

> **Note**
>
> In the Extended Classic scenario, the complete procurement process can take place locally within the SAP SRM system: shopping cart, purchase order, confirmations, and invoices. However, most organizations tend to continue executing the goods receipt and invoice functions within their SAP back-end system.

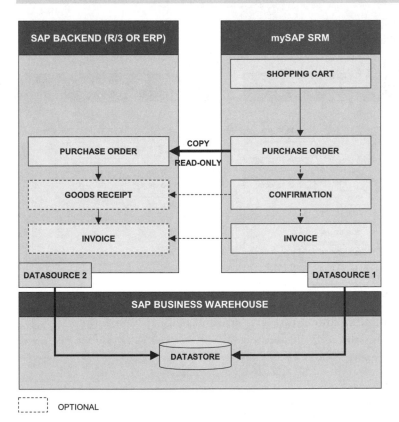

Figure 15.24 Extended Classic Scenario in SAP SRM

In this scenario, both SAP SRM and ERP (or R/3) need to be connected to the SAP NetWeaver BI system as source systems, as illustrated in Figure 15.24.

Figure 15.25 illustrates the data flow and mapping between the DataSource and the DataStore based on the Extended Classic implementation scenario of SAP SRM.

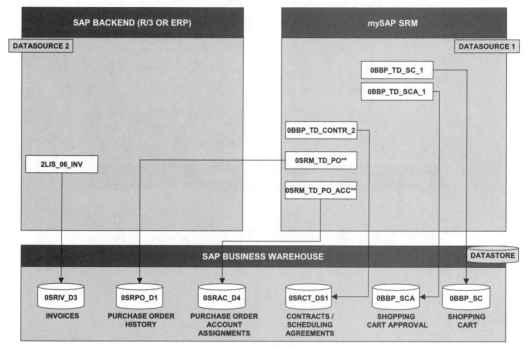

** BASED ON mySAP SRM 5.0

Figure 15.25 DataSource and DataStore Mapping in Extended Classic Scenario

15.3.3 The Standalone (Lean) Scenario

In the Standalone scenario (also described as *Lean* scenario), all the purchasing documents are only created in SAP SRM. The shopping cart, PO, confirmation and invoice documents are created in SAP SRM. In this scenario, all validations occur within the SRM system, while accounting processes such as financial accounting and controlling are still handled within the SAP back-end system. Invoice entry is completed in SAP SRM and posting of the invoice happens in the SAP back-end. Figure 15.26 illustrates this scenario.

In the standalone scenario, only the SAP SRM system needs to be connected to the SAP NetWeaver BI system as the source system, as illustrated in Figure 15.26. All transactional data is extracted directly from the SRM system.

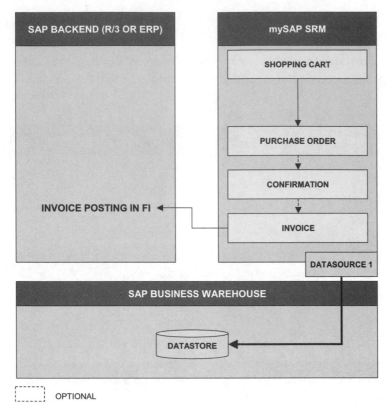

OPTIONAL

Figure 15.26 Standalone Scenario in SAP SRM

Figure 15.27 illustrates the data flow and mapping between the DataSources and DataStores based on the Standalone implementation scenario of SAP SRM.

15.3.4 The Decoupled Scenario

It is important for project teams to know that SAP SRM can also be implemented in a decoupled mode. In simple terms, this means that a combination of the scenarios listed above (Classic, Extended Classic, or Standalone) can be implemented in a single SRM environment.

A common reason why organizations do this is to separate the procurement activities within SAP SRM and the SAP back-end. The standard solution provided by SAP is based on product category. Based on this, the organization can determine whether it wants to create a PO locally within SRM or create it within the SAP back-end.

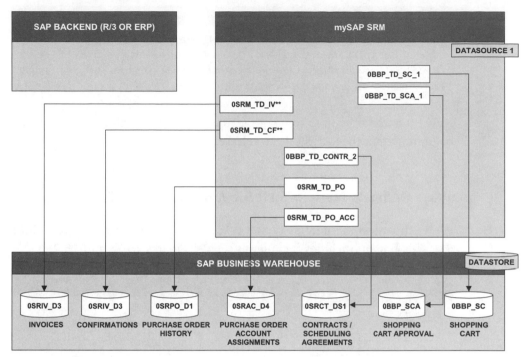

Figure 15.27 DataSource and DataStore Mapping in Standalone Scenario

However, it should be noted that most organizations do not use the product category option but instead use available Business Add-Ins (BAdIs) to implement their own business rules to determine in which system a purchasing document is created. One example would be an organization that wants to implement an "Extended Classic" scenario but also wants to use the functionality to create material-based shopping carts in SRM that create *reservations*.

Because SAP SRM does not have the functionality to create reservations, those documents can only be created in the SAP back-end (ERP or R/3). Therefore, a Classic scenario would have to be implemented for creation of reservations from a shopping cart. In our example, project teams can use the available BAdI to implement business rules so that when a material is used the Classic scenario is enable, but otherwise the Extended Classic scenario is enabled. This would be considered a decoupled mode. From a BI perspective, data is captured from the DataSources, SRM, and the SAP back end (ERP or R/3).

> **Note**
>
> The figures in this section provide the mapping information focused on the operational procurement business scenario. Review the documents available at SAP Service Marketplace for information on the other business scenarios such as strategic sourcing and plan-driven procurement.

Now I'll introduce you to some of the new Analytics functionalities available beginning from the SAP SRM 5.0 release.

15.4   What's New in SAP SRM 5.0 Analytics?

We've discussed the new BI Content 7.0.2 available for use with SAP SRM 5.0. This content includes the queries seen in Figures 15.28 and 15.29.

AREA	QUERY NAME	QUERIES	TARGET ODS / INFO / MULTI CUBE
PROCUREMENT ACCOUNT ASSIGNMENT	OVERVIEW OF PURCHASE ORDER VALUE PER REQUESTER	0SR_C02_Q001	0SR_C02
	COST CENTER OVERVIEW	0SR_C02_Q002	0SR_C02
PROCUREMENT DOCUMENT OVERVIEW (MULTICUBE)	PURCHASE ORDER DOCUMENT ANALYSIS	0SR_MC02_Q0001	0SR_MC02
	MAVERICK BUYING ANALYSIS	0SR_MC02_Q0002	0SR_MC02
	WORKLOAD PER PURCHASING GROUP	0SR_MC02_Q0003	0SR_MC02
	PARETO ANALYSIS ACCORDING TO PURCHASE ORDER VOLUME (CHART)	0SR_MC02_Q0004	0SR_MC02
	PARETO ANALYSIS ACCORDING TO PO VOLUME PER CATEGORY	0SR_MC02_Q0005	0SR_MC02
	CONFIRMATION DOCUMENT OVERVIEW	0SR_MC02_Q2001	0SR_MC02
	OPEN ITEMS (CONFIRMATIONS)	0SR_MC02_Q2002	0SR_MC02
	INVOICE DOCUMENT OVERVIEW	0SR_MC02_Q3001	0SR_MC02
	EXCESSIVE INVOICES	0SR_MC02_Q3002	0SR_MC02
	SALES HISTORY (FOR SUPPLIER)	0SR_MC02_SUS_Q1002	0SR_MC02
PROCUREMENT OVERVIEW (MULTICUBE AGGREGATE)	PROCUREMENT VALUE ANALYSIS	0SR_MC01_Q0001	0SR_MC01
	PROCUREMENT VALUES PER SERVICE PROVIDER	0SR_MC01_Q0002	0SR_MC01
	SUPPLIER INFORMATION	0SR_MC01_Q0003	0SR_MC01
	KEY PERFORMANCE INDICATORS	0SR_MC01_Q0004	0SR_MC01
	PRICE TREND ANALYSIS PER PRODUCT	0SR_MC01_Q0005	0SR_MC01
	NUMBER OF SUPPLIERS PER COUNTRY	0SR_MC01_Q0006	0SR_MC01
	ABC ANALYSIS FOR SUPPLIERS (LORENZ CURVE)	0SR_MC01_Q0007	0SR_MC01
	ABC SUPPLIER	0SR_MC01_Q0008	0SR_MC01
	SUCCESS OF AN SRM PROJECT	0SR_MC01_Q0009	0SR_MC01
	SALES VALUES (FOR SUPPLIER)	0SR_MC01_SUS_Q0001	0SR_MC01
	SALES VALUES PER SERVICE PROVIDER (FOR SUPPLIER)	0SR_MC01_SUS_Q0003	0SR_MC01

Figure 15.28 New Queries in SAP SRM 5.0 and BI CONT 7.0.2

Let's now proceed to learn about the new Analytics.

AREA	QUERY NAME	QUERIES	TARGET ODS / INFO / MULTI CUBE
ATTRIBUTES OF BIDS	LIST OF BID INVITATION ATTRIBUTES	0SR_QUODA_Q002	0SR_QUODA
AUCTIONS	AUCTIONS ANALYSIS	0SR_LAC1_Q0001	0SR_LAC1
	AUCTION ITEMS ANALYSIS	0SR_LAC1_Q0002	0SR_LAC1
	BIDDERS ANALYSIS	0SR_LAC1_Q0003	0SR_LAC1
	DETAILED ANALYSIS OF BIDS BY CATEGORY	0SRM_LADS1_Q0001	0SRM_LADS1
	AUCTION DETAILS	0SRM_LADS1_Q0002	0SRM_LADS1
VENDOR EVALUATION	VENDOR PORTFOLIO WITH PO VALUE AND OVERALL SCORE	0SR_VE_M1_Q001	0SR_VE_M1
	TOTAL EVAL. / PURCH. ORDER VALUE OF VENDOR OVER TIME	0SR_VE_M1_Q002	0SR_VE_M1
	EVALUATION OF VENDOR BY PRODUCT CATEGORY	0SR_VE_M2_Q001	0SR_VE_M2
	EVALUATION OF VENDOR BY PRODUCT CATEGORY AND PRODUCT	0SR_VE_M2_Q002	0SR_VE_M2
	SUBMITTED EVALUATIONS (VENDORS)	0SR_VE_M2_Q003	0SR_VE_M2
	MANDATORY EVALUATIONS FOR INVOICES	0SRV_IS1_Q001	0SRV_IS1
	OPTIONAL EVALUATIONS FOR INVOICES	0SRV_IS1_Q002	0SRV_IS1
	OPEN EVALUATIONS (INVOICES)	0SRV_IS1_Q003	0SRV_IS1
	MANDATORY EVALNS FOR GOODS RECEIPTS/SERVICE CONFIRMATIONS	0SRV_IS2_Q001	0SRV_IS2
	OPTIONAL EVALNS FOR GOODS RECEIPTS/SERVICE CONFIRMATIONS	0SRV_IS2_Q002	0SRV_IS2
	OPEN EVALUATIONS (GOODS/SERVICE CONFIRMATIONS)	0SRV_IS2_Q003	0SRV_IS2
	SUBMITTED EVALUATIONS FOR SUPPLIERS	0SRV_IS3_Q003	0SRV_IS3

Figure 15.29 New Queries in SAP SRM 5.0 and BI CONT 7.0.2

SAP SRM 5.0 officially only supports the new NetWeaver BI 7.0.2 queries. Because of the functional enhancements in Release 5.0, SAP developed new data extractors for PO data (order history, confirmation, and invoice and account assignment). This required the BI data model to be changed as well. Figure 15.30 shows the InfoProviders that have changed.

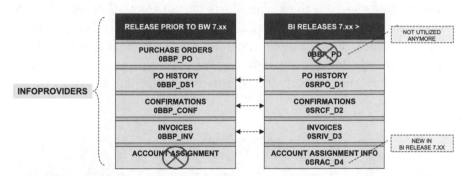

Figure 15.30 Changes in BI Content Data Model — SAP SRM 5.0

In order to use the new queries available in the BI Content 7.0, SAP recommends that organizations upgrade their SRM systems to SAP SRM 5.0, and also upgrade their corresponding BI Content to at least version 7.0.2.

15.4.1 SAP Analytics xApps for SAP SRM 5.0

In SAP SRM 5.0, SAP introduced a new application powered by SAP NetWeaver called SAP Analytics xApps. The application is based on SAP's new vision for the Enterprise Services Application (ESA) platform.

SAP Analytics xApps provides SAP SRM with embedded analytic composites designed with Visual Composer and based on SAP NetWeaver BI queries to support procurement executives with their analytic, transactional, and collaborative daily tasks.

The value of these xApps is that organizations can leverage pre-packaged analytic applications based on best practices in order to deliver more powerful analytics for Supplier Relationship Management. Project teams can use the xApps application to create queries using drag-and-drop and WYSIWYG functionality; no coding is required. There are three analytics applications available for SAP SRM 5.0. Let's examine them now.

Category Management

The Category Management analytics application has been developed based on four standard NetWeaver BI queries that provide information on monitoring product categories and vendors. The report gives an overview of the top 10 vendors, evaluation of vendor performance, procurement based on product categories, and the key products bought from all vendors. Figure 15.31 illustrates the Category Management dashboard. The Category Management analytics would be very useful for purchasing managers and directors who can quickly get a snapshot of the overall procurement spending across vendors and products in the different geographical regions of the organization.

Figure 15.31 Category Management Analytics Application

Contract Management

The Contract Management analytics application has been developed based on five standard NetWeaver BI queries that provide information to support the daily contract management tasks for strategic purchasers. The report provides information on maverick purchasing, potential savings on contracts, details on contract utilization, and expiring contracts that need re-negotiation.

Figure 15.32 shows the Contract Management dashboard. The Contract Management analytics would be very useful for purchasing professionals responsible for managing contracts within their organization. This dashboard quickly provides a snapshot of the utilization and compliance of contracts within the organization.

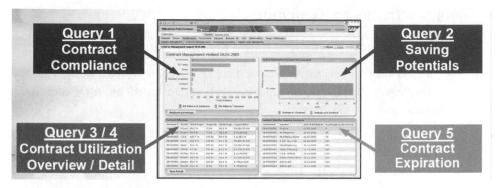

Figure 15.32 Contract Management Analytics Application

Supplier Order Management

The Supplier Order Management analytics application has been developed based on four standard NetWeaver BI queries that provide information on sales orders and statistics. This application is useful when organizations are using the SUS component of SAP SRM. The application is geared towards suppliers. It gives them valuable real-time information on sales history of the top 10 product categories supplied to customers, suppliers incoming sales orders, upcoming deliveries, and information on the deliveries that have been returned because of quality issues. Figure 15.33 shows the Supplier Order Management dashboard.

Figure 15.33 Supplier Order Management Analytics Application

Additional analytics applications for SAP SRM are currently under development by SAP.

15.5 Things to Remember

Let's review some of what you should remember during this process:

▸ Project teams need to remember that SAP NetWeaver BI, SRM, R/3 and NetWeaver Portal are all separate systems, installed on their individual landscapes.

▸ It is important to remember that the security roles are independent in each system; there are roles in NetWeaver Portal, roles in NetWeaver BI, roles in SRM and roles in R/3.

▸ Make sure that the functional teams allocate enough time to test the reports generated by the performance reporting teams. It is not just a matter of checking that the reports execute; the more important consideration is that the data within the reports is correct.

▸ The standard content provided by SAP provides a good starting point, but the standard queries are not typically sufficient, and modification is generally required by organizations. However, it is much easier to modify these delivered queries than to develop them from scratch.

▸ Do not forget about customized fields created in the different system (e.g., custom fields created for the shopping cart and PO documents in SRM). These need to be extracted as well in the queries. If organizations are not able to report on the customized fields, then it defeats the purpose of creating them. Make sure to let your performance teams know up front that you will have a need to report on customized fields.

▸ When testing the queries, make sure to review each characteristic and its values. Many of the custom queries are delivered with incorrect data. For example, the product characteristic may be delivered with the GUID value instead of the actual product number, or the purchasing group characteristic may be delivered with the organization unit value instead of the name of the purchasing group.

Let us now review important OSS Notes for implementing SAP Netweaver BI for SAP SRM.

15.6 Relevant OSS Notes

Table 15.2 lists important OSS Notes available on the SAP Service Marketplace that are relevant for organizations implementing the SAP NetWeaver BI solution for SAP SRM.

Note	Description
352814	Loading data from Enterprise Buyer into SAP NetWeaver BI
401367	Calling the BI Web Reports via the EBP LaunchPad
520131	Activation of SRM Roles for NetWeaver BI and SRM decision
614940	DataSources for Enterprise Buyer
955804	SRM 5.0 — BI Content data model changed

Table 15.2 OSS Notes from SAP Service Marketplace

15.7 Summary

In this chapter introduced the SAP NetWeaver BI reporting solution. The majority of the organizations implementing SAP SRM are going to find the need to implement SAP NetWeaver BI because there is a lack of reporting in SRM by itself. SAP provides all reporting and analytics capabilities in NetWeaver BI for use in SAP SRM. Standard content for SAP SRM can be imported into NetWeaver BI to provide out-of-the-box reports.

In Chapter 16, you will be introduced to the concept of NetWeaver Portal in SAP and you will learn how this NetWeaver component can become a key solution for your SAP SRM implementation.

Enterprise Portal provides the default user interface for all SAP SRM applications. Organizations implementing SAP SRM need to view Enterprise Portal as a key component that supports their overall procurement, sourcing, and collaboration strategy.

16 Enterprise Portals and SAP SRM

Enterprise Portal (EP) is a component within the SAP NetWeaver platform that unifies key information and applications to give users a single view that spans IT silos and organizational boundaries. Most organizations implementing SAP SRM today are also reviewing the need to implement Enterprise Portal as a part of their SRM deployment strategy. In this chapter I will discuss the integration of Enterprise Portals with SAP SRM.

SAP SRM leverages the NetWeaver Enterprise Portal application, seen in Figure 16.1, for a number of capabilities. First, the portal provides the front end to all SRM applications; users can access all SAP SRM components via single sign-on (SSO). Second, the simple navigation capabilities in the portal ensure a consistent user experience regardless of which application the user is accessing. The collaboration capabilities in the portal allow users to have access to an integrated inbox, which can receive work items from multiple applications. Users can also seamlessly access analytical reports that assist in their operational and strategic decision-making.

The components in SAP SRM, such as Enterprise Buyer (EBP), Catalog Content Management (CCM), and Supplier Self Services (SUS) are all available via a browser-based interface, and therefore do not necessarily require Enterprise Portal for deployment. However, the various SRM components, SAP applications, and other third-party applications can be deployed simply to the user community via the Enterprise Portal. By using Enterprise Portal's SSO approach, users can simply log on to a single application and access all the other applications they need for their respective functions without the need for secondary log-ons.

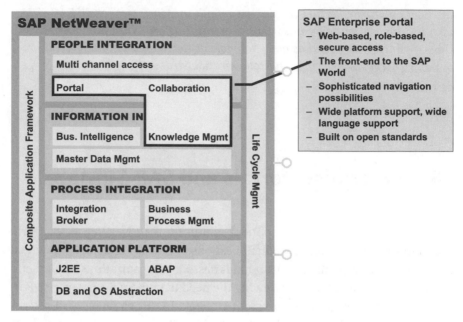

Figure 16.1 SAP SRM Uses the Power of SAP NetWeaver Enterprise Portal

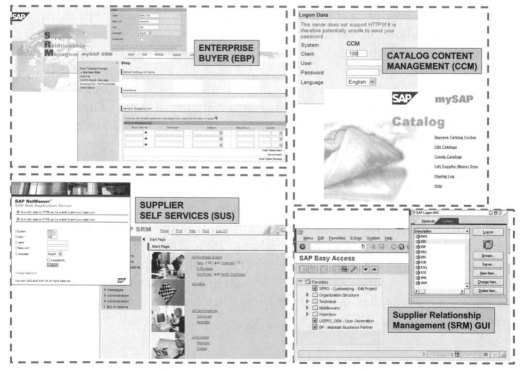

Figure 16.2 Accessing SRM Applications Individually

Enterprise Portal enables organizations to project a single user interface for distinct applications; this is illustrated in Figures 16.2 and 16.3. Figure 16.2 shows that if users need to access EBP, CCM, or SUS applications, they need to launch independent URLs and log on to each of these applications individually. Figure 16.3 shows that, using the Enterprise Portal approach, the user has access to all of these applications from a single interface and log on to the portal.

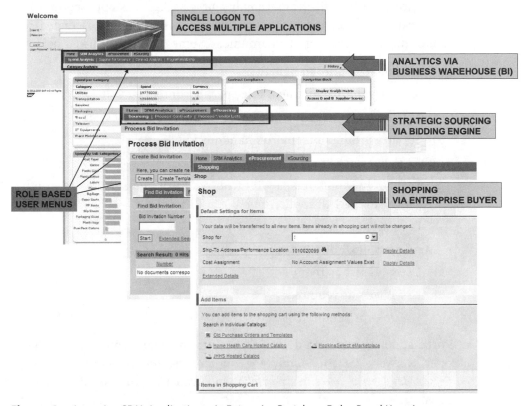

Figure 16.3 Accessing SRM Applications via Enterprise Portals — Role- Based User Access

SAP provides an integrated approach for the SAP SRM applications and the Enterprise Portal. From SRM Release 2.0 onwards, SAP provides portal users with role-based access to services of the SRM components. Organizations implementing SAP SRM can quickly integrate with the Portal by using standard business packages provided by SAP. These business packages contain SRM specific roles, worksets, and iViews that allow organizations to access SRM applications from within the Enterprise portal.

16.1 SRM Business Packages for Enterprise Portal

According to SAP, business packages provide users (both buyer and suppliers) with an integrated workplace and user-friendly role-based access to all tasks that are part of the procurement process in SAP SRM, available via iViews in Enterprise Portal (6.0). All integrated SRM components provide log-on-free access via SSO; you only need to log on to the Enterprise Portal.

There are many benefits from using business packages as opposed to manually creating content and then providing role-based access for created content in the Enterprise Portal environment. Some of these are listed below:

- **Faster Implementation Benefits**
  - SAP provides pre-defined, role-specific content
  - No development required (however, changes are inevitable)
  - Set up a production environment quickly
- **Built-in Business Processes Benefits**
  - Seamlessly integrate analytics from SAP BW and services from other SAP and non-SAP applications
  - Leverage the work done by SAP
- **Maximum Flexibility Benefits**
  - Use worksets as required
  - Use iViews as required
  - Use roles as required

Portal administrators can download business packages from the SAP Developer Network (SDN). Simply log on to SDN (*https://www.sdn.sap.com/ irj/sdn/developerareas/contentportfolio*) and search for the portal content on SRM.

Note that SAP creates business packages for a specific release of SAP SRM. Therefore, it is important to download the appropriate business package that is relevant to your SRM release. Once the business package is downloaded, it can be imported in your portal system and available for role assignment (prerequisites such as SSO are required prior to using the content).

Table 16.1 provides a guide towards choosing the right business package for your implementation. Also, note that roles and iViews for the SUS application are contained within a separate business package for SRM, called business package for supplier collaboration.

SAP SRM release	Portal Business package	Technical Requirements
SAP SRM 4.0	Business package for SAP SRM 4.0 — 6.02	▸ Enterprise Portal 6.0, SP 4 ▸ SAP SRM 4.0 ▸ BW 3.5 ▸ CCM 1.0
	Business package for supplier collaboration	▸ Enterprise Portal 6.0, SP 4 ▸ SAP SRM 4.0 (SUS) ▸ BW 3.5
SAP SRM 5.0	Business package for SAP SRM	▸ Enterprise Portal 7.0 (NetWeaver 2004s) ▸ SAP SRM 5.0 ▸ SAP BI Content 7.0.2
	Business package for supplier collaboration	▸ Enterprise Portal 6.0, SP 4, or 7.0 ▸ SAP SRM 4.0 (SUS), SRM 5.0 ▸ BW 3.5

Table 16.1 Business Package Compatibility

As users learn about the business packages available for SRM and the standard content within these packages, it is also important to understand portal security in SRM and how it differs from that in the other SAP applications.

16.2 Portal Security

Security in the portal environment is independent of the security maintained within the individual applications that are being integrated. Therefore, in addition to the roles and authorizations maintained in SRM or SAP R/3, additional roles and user authorizations must be maintained in the Enterprise Portal system.

Remember, EP is a separate solution with its independent architecture, therefore objects such as users, roles, etc., are required to be created in EP just as in any other SAP system. Security in Enterprise Portal is two-fold as discussed next.

16.2.1 User Authentication and SSO

As mentioned earlier, the user in EP is a separate object than the user in SRM. Organizations can choose to create distinct users within Enterprise

Portal, upload users from SRM or another SAP system, or authenticate the users accessing Enterprise Portal using a corporate LDAP environment.

16.2.2 Provide Roles and Authorizations for Accessing Content in Portal Environment

Roles can be either created manually in the portal or uploaded from an SRM or SAP system. Alternatively, roles can be assigned to user groups in the LDAP and the portal can authenticate against these user groups when users log on. Additionally, roles can be automatically created by importing the business package for SAP SRM.

Most organizations using SRM via the portal use the standard content provided by SAP in the business package for SRM. Portal administrators can work with the functional teams to determine which roles and portal content are relevant and then assign these roles to the users. Once a role has been assigned to a user in EP, the user can access the different SRM applications as long as he or she has a corresponding UserID, role, and appropriate authorization available in the SRM system.

It is important to understand that the role of portal security is to identify what applications should be visible to the end user in the portal. The role of security within SRM is to then check whether the user accessing an application from the portal has the appropriate authorizations to access those applications in the SRM system.

For example, an end user in Enterprise Portal may have been assigned a role: SRM Employee. This role contains iViews that allow users to access the shopping-cart application in SRM. Once a user clicks on this application, the security in the SRM system takes control. In SRM, a corresponding role and additional authorization objects then determine whether the user can create a shopping cart using a particular catalog. The controls within the SRM system determine what the user can do within the shopping-cart application.

> **Note**
>
> Security teams need to understand that they could be required to create users and roles in the Enterprise Portal system. Therefore it is important for organizations to train their security teams on Enterprise Portal and define a process for the creation of users and roles within the SRM and EP systems. Time and time again, I find that the security group is not provided appropriate training up front, and therefore a constant catch-up occurs all through the implementation.

In Chapter 11, we discussed the standard SRM roles provided by SAP. For each standard delivered role in the SRM system, a corresponding role is provided in the Enterprise Portal business package. Table 16.2 provides an example of the delivered roles. A complete list of roles can be found in the business package for SAP SRM document available when downloading the business package at the SAP Software Development Network (*www.sdn.sap.com*).

Business Package Roles for EP	Back-end System Roles (SRM)
Employee (SRM_Employee_showcase)	▸ SAP_EC_BBP_EMPLOYEE ▸ SAP_BBP_STAL_EMPLOYEE ▸ SAP_BBP_MULTI_EMPLOYEE
Manager (SRM_Manager_showcase)	▸ SAP_EC_BBP_EMPLOYEE ▸ SAP_BBP_STAL_EMPLOYEE ▸ SAP_BBP_MULTI_EMPLOYEE ▸ SAP_EC_BBP_MANAGER ▸ SAP_BBP_STAL_MANAGER ▸ SAP_BBP_MULTI_MANAGER ▸ SAP_BWC_SRM_MANAGER

Table 16.2 Business Package Roles and Roles in the Back-End

Portal administrators need to be aware that, although SAP provides standard content for SRM in the business packages, organizations will need to change contents of this business package to meet their requirements. For example, if the portal role "Employee" is used, it provides access to the Shop, Check status, Inbox, Confirmation and Invoice applications.

If the organization does not want to perform Invoice entry in SRM, then this application access needs to be removed from the Employee role in the portal. Therefore, the role and worksets in the portal will need to be changed to remove the Invoice iView to represent appropriate user access. Similarly, other changes might be required; therefore organizations should not consider the business-package approach to involve zero work effort. Instead, they should consider the content available via the business package as a good starting point.

Business packages provide organizations a starting point to quickly integrate the SAP solutions such as SAP SRM within their portal solution. However, business packages do not provide for a complete solution. Project teams will find a need to enhance the contents of these packages and integrate other components and applications that are not available as business packages. A well thought-out Enterprise Portal strategy is critical for any enterprise implementing SAP.

16.3 Considerations for Portal Strategy

Organizations implementing SAP SRM along with other SAP applications such as SAP R/3 or ERP need to review their overall portal strategy. I have come across a number of projects where the value of SAP Enterprise Portal was not realized because it was used just as a technical solution to integrate applications. Project teams did not think through their overall portal strategy, for the immediate and long-term use in the enterprise.

When implementing SAP Enterprise Portal, organizations need to allocate appropriate time and resources to build a robust implementation and business strategy. Some questions that need to be discussed are addressed here:

▶ **Are you going to provide iView based content only for SRM applications?**
Are you going to create iViews for all transactions within SAP R/3? The portal strategy needs to keep in mind both the immediate portal user and the long-term users.

▶ **How will the users access the SRM or SAP GUI?**
Does the user community only use a Windows OS or are there other users that use the Mac OS as well? Are all the portal based SRM applications supported on a Mac?

▶ **What will be the training strategy?**
Will there be a single portal instance for training that provides access for multiple SAP R/3 clients? If so, what happens with the business package-based content for SRM, given that ideally each portal content (iView) can only point to a single source client. Although users can launch the SAP GUI for multiple clients, the SRM iViews based on roles will be pointing to single source client.

▶ **Is supplier collaboration within your project scope?**
If so, then an external portal environment might be required. Are you planning to have certificate-based user authentication? What about LADP-based authentication or simple portal database login?

After this review of the Portal strategy we are now at the end of this chapter.

16.4   Summary

In this chapter, I discussed how the SAP Enterprise Portal solution can be used with SAP SRM to provide a single user interface for the entire organization. Users can log on once into the portal and automatically get secure access to all the SRM components without the need to log on again. Organizations can use standard business packages available for SRM to quickly provide role-based application access to users.

In Chapter 17, I will introduce the SAP Government Procurement solution that can be used with SAP SRM as a component add-on. The Government Procurement solution has been specifically designed for government organizations and other public-sector companies dealing with regulatory requirements.

PART IV
Industry Solutions for SAP SRM

Government entities responsible for maintaining public funds and public trust must adhere to strict regulations and guidelines. For them, the standard procurement solution offers only partial functionality. These organizations require a procurement solution that specifically addresses their unique needs and requirements.

17 Government Procurement — Public Sector

Government procurement as a generic term is used to describe the procurement activities of government entities such as federal, state and local governments. In addition, it covers activities of other public entities or enterprises and generally covers procurement of all goods and services including construction services. The types of transactions covered in this procurement are purchase, lease, rental, and hire purchase. Government Procurement (GP) is now known as Procurement for Public Services (PPS) though in this chapter it is still referred to as Government Procurement.

The goal for this chapter is to give readers an overview of the SAP Government Procurement solution (GP), and to briefly describe the highlights of the functionality within this solution offering. SAP GP is relatively new, and release 1.0 of GP has been generally available with the SAP ERP 2005 and SRM 5.0 releases. Development and testing of GP 2.0 is under way and is planned for completion in 2007 and release with SAP SRM 6.0.

17.1 SAP SRM and SAP Government Procurement

SAP GP is a relatively new solution that has been built to focus on the procurement processes of government organizations and other public sector entities. It is primarily a SAP SRM-based solution that fully integrates with SAP's Funds Management (FM) and Materials Management (MM) solutions.

Note
GP is not the same as the SAP Public Sector solution (IS-PS/EA-PS). Rather, SAP GP builds upon and enhances the standard capabilities within the SAP EA-PS solution.

The GP solution delivers a wide range of functionality for professional purchasers and contracting personnel and augments SAP SRM 5.0 standard capabilities. It also eliminates the need to operate and maintain multiple procurement solutions and associated interfaces. Traditionally, government entities using SAP had used SAP MM for procurement functionality.

The SAP GP solution combines the SAP SRM, SAP ERP, SAP Records Management, and SAP NetWeaver applications to collaborate and support public-sector customers. Public-sector organizations can use the capabilities of the GP solution to maintain Federal Acquisition Regulations (FAR) clauses and detailed FAR document and contracts, and integrate these with the enhanced sourcing and procurement capabilities within SAP SRM.

According to Wikipedia, the free online encyclopedia, FAR consists of a series of regulations issued by the US federal government concerning the requirements for contractors selling to the government, the terms under which the government obtains ownership, title, and control of the goods or services purchased, and rules concerning specifications, payments and conduct and actions regarding solicitation of bids and payment of invoices.

Therefore, it is imperative that the procurement and sourcing solution used by government and public sector organizations provide extensive capabilities for adhering to FAR regulatory requirements. The core functionality in SAP GP was defined based on the requirements generated by the US Defence Logistics Agency (DLA).

Figure 17.1 illustrates at a high level the various applications that make up the overall GP solution. In addition to functional enhancements made to SAP SRM, shown in Figure 17.1, the **Document Builder** is a major component of the GP solution.

Document Builder is available to organizations as a part of the SAP GP add-on to SAP SRM 5.0. The purpose of Document Builder is to allow creation of complex documents that can be used for a number of different business documents such as contracts and purchase orders. Organizations can create and manage FAR regulatory documents using the capabilities within Document Builder. Figure 17.2 illustrates the technical components within the SAP GP 1.0 solution.

Tip
It is possible to activate GP functionality with prior versions of ERP, though significant functionality is lost.

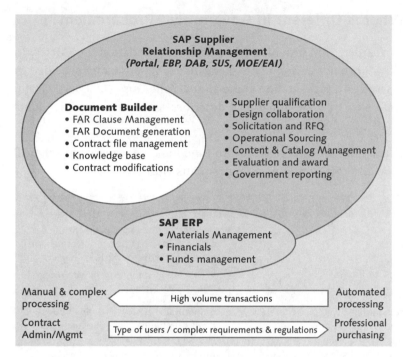

Figure 17.1 Government Procurement — SAP SRM, SAP NetWeaver, and SAP ERP applications

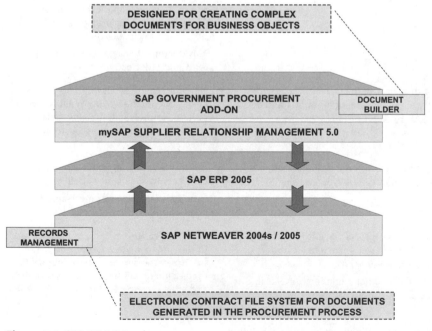

Figure 17.2 SAP GP 1.0 Landscape

17.2   What is Different in Government Procurement?

As discussed earlier, SRM provides the underlying foundation for SAP GP. In many cases, GP extends or augments the standard functionality provided in SAP SRM. Based on a presentation at the annual Americas' SAP Users' Group (ASUG) conference in 2006, Table 17.1 describes some of the key highlights of the SAP GP 1.0 solution.

Table 17.1 provides a comparison of the functionality available in the SAP SRM solution and corresponding enhancements within GP.

Provided by SAP SRM	Government Procurement
	▶ Introduction of SAP Document Builder application, a solution for creating complex documents for business objects ▶ Web-based user interface, with integration to SAP SRM
In SRM a standardized system- generated document numbering scheme is used. For example: Purchase orders will have a 10-digit sequential numbering scheme of 2000000000 — 2xxxxxxxxx	▶ Configurable customer-defined document numbering (Long Procurement Number) is introduced. ▶ Ability to assign a second, customer-defined document ID number to Bid Invitations, Contracts, and PO in SRM ▶ Complies with US FAR, DFARS, European Union, Canadian, and other numbering schemes, as well as local government and other public schemes. ▶ This document is available for search in SRM and ERP documents.
Confirmations (goods receipt) or Service Entry allow movement types 101 and 102 for SAP backend system.	▶ New movement types *107* and *109* have been added to SAP MM, to allow receipt of items at the vendor facility, before shipping, that also allows FM to be affected.
Sourcing application is available and customized rules can be created using BAdIs.	▶ Automated sourcing of requirements to contracts (with customer defined rules) ▶ User warning and error messsages have been improved
Standard PO History provides a fairly basic view of follow-on documents (Goods Receipt and Invoice). Primarily document numbers are available as a history.	▶ An *Extended History* tab has been added to the SRM Purchase Order transaction to display the complete transactional history including GR, IR, Payments, Credits, and even Clearing Documents, with subtotals and totals.

Table 17.1 Key Highlights for SAP GP Solution

Provided by SAP SRM	Government Procurement
Bid Invitations can be manually created in the sourcing application.	▸ Bid Invitations can be created automatically based on the requirements received from external planning systems. ▸ Document Builder introduction ▸ choice to auto-publish (0-step workflow) or manually publish after workflow approval
Confirmation of goods is entered once goods are received at buyer's location.	▸ New concept of acceptance of goods at vendor location (termed Origin Acceptance) ▸ This provides an ability to create a GR for items that are still at the vendor distribution facility ▸ Ability to trigger FM integration before physical receipt of items
Contracts do not encumber any funds and no financial postings are possible for contracts.	▸ Introduced new functionality for reservation of funds in SAP ERP based on SRM Contracts (Guaranteed Minimum) ▸ Ability to manually record a funds reservation (via earmarked funds) on an SRM contract header; ▸ Consumption of reservation amount is based on obligations of POs issued against the contract

Table 17.1 Key Highlights for SAP GP Solution (cont.)

Figure 17.3 illustrates an example of the customer defined, configurable, document numbering available in SAP SRM with the SAP GP add-on. In the purchase-order document, this number is illustrated in the **Doc. Name** field. Note that a secondary number that is system generated is displayed in the **Number** field as shown in Figure 17.3.

Figure 17.4 illustrates an example of the enhanced history available in the purchase order document within the **Payment History** area. Without the GP add-on, the purchase order in SRM only provides a basic view of follow-on documents (Goods Receipt and Invoice). The purchase-order document using the GP add-on solution display the complete transactional history, including **GR**, **IR**, Payments, Credits, and even Clearing Documents, with subtotals and totals

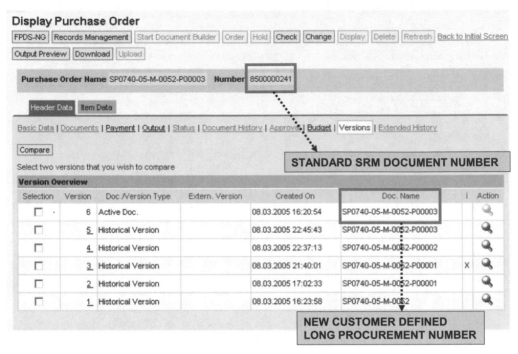

Figure 17.3 Long Document Number in the Purchase Order

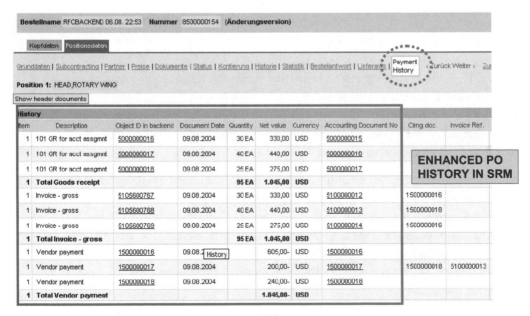

Figure 17.4 Enhanced PO History in SRM

Tip
SAP GP Release 1.0 is designed to run only within the SRM extended classic scenario.

17.3 Summary

In this chapter, I gave you an overview of the SAP GP solution and its integration within SAP SRM. The key lesson for users is that SAP GP is an add-on component of the SAP SRM solution specifically designed for organizations implementing the SAP public sector solution.

In Chapter 18, I will cover selective configuration in SAP SRM such as integrating the HR organization structure with SRM, workflow setup in SRM, catalog setup, etc. This configuration along with the business scenario configuration guides available for SRM at the SAP Service Marketplace will assist project teams in implementing their SRM solutions.

PART V
Selected Configuration in SAP SRM

In this chapter, we'll cover selected configuration settings found in SAP SRM, such as HR integration, workflow, and MRP integration. You will find these settings useful as most of them are not generally covered in other SAP resources.

18 Selected Configuration in SAP SRM

The purpose of my book was to arm you, the reader, with information I have gained over the years implementing SRM, and that is generally unavailable in print. In the final chapter of this book I want to give you some selected configuration settings in SAP SRM that you will find useful. Let us begin with SAP HR, now also called SAP Human Capital Management (HCM).

> **Note**
>
> The configuration settings covered in this chapter are meant to provide you with a guide on how to approach your configuration, but will need to be modified to meet the requirements of your specific project implementation.

18.1 Integrate Organizational Structure with SAP HR

This section provides a set of steps required to distribute the organizational structure from SAP HR or HCM to the Enterprise Buyer (EBP) system.

18.1.1 Prerequisites for Integration

The distribution of HR data into SRM expects that the following activities have already taken place:

▶ You have reviewed the following OSS Notes: 550055, 390380 (Composite SAP Note: HR/ALE distribution in EBP/CRM; check the Related Notes section).

▶ In the R/3 system, the HR data has been created (Orgs, Positions, Jobs, Employees) — check the filter information below to ensure that the required information exists.

▶ In R/3, an ALE distribution model has been created with *Filters defined*, as listed below, and distributed to the appropriate SRM system and client.

▶ For users that need to be created in SRM, in the R/3 system the corresponding Employees have been assigned infotype 0105. In SRM, the users (SU01) have been created — at least the ones that contain a corresponding infotype of 0105.

▶ Prior to the distribution process, please make sure that no additional updates or changes are being performed on the Organization Objects (O, C, S, P,) within the R/3 HR system, because the system will try to lock these objects during distribution.

The customizing table **T77S0** has been set up as seen in Figure 18.1.

Change View "HR: Set Up Central Person": Overview

System Switch (from Table T77S0)

Group	Sem. abbr.	Value abbr.	Description
HRALX	HRAC	X	Activate HR Integration
HRALX	OADBP	1	Business Partner of Standard Address
HRALX	OADRE	X	Address Necessary for Business Partner?
HRALX	OBPON	ON	Integration O-BP Activated
HRALX	OBWIG	X	Ignore Business Partner Warnings
HRALX	ONUMB	1	Business Partner Number Assignment (Org. Unit)
HRALX	OPROL	BUP004	Roles: Functional Description
HRALX	OSUBG		Business Partner Subgroup (Organizational Unit)
HRALX	PBPHR	ON	Employees Are Replicated from HR System
HRALX	PBPON	ON	Integration Employee/BP Activated
HRALX	PCATS		Integration P-BP for CATS Activated
HRALX	PNUMB	1	Business Partner Number Assignment (Employee)
HRALX	PPROL	BUP003	Roles: Employee Description
HRALX	PQUAL		Import Qualifications
PLOGI	PLOGI	01	Integration Plan Version / Active Plan Version
PLOGI	PRELI	99999999	Integration: default position

Figure 18.1 Integration Set-Up with Organizational Management

18.1.2 Filtering of Objects to be Distributed from R/3 into SRM

The technical set-up of the distribution model between R/3 and SRM in BD64 requires the following filters for message type HRMD_ABA (OSS Note: 312090).

Filter Group for Organization Objects

▶ Infotype:
  ▶ 1000   Existence of Org objects
  ▶ 1002   Description of Org objects

- Objects:
  - C   Jobs
  - S   Position
  - O   Organization

Filter Group for Employees:

These subtypes are required; otherwise, the Business Partner in SRM will not be created.

- Infotype
  - 0000   Actions — IT0000
  - 0001   Organization Assignment
  - 0002   Personal Data — IT0002
- Objects
- Person or Employee

Filter Group for Relationships

- Infotype
- 1001   Relationship between objects
- Objects
  - AG   Role
  - C   Jobs
  - O   Organization
  - P   Person
  - S   Position
- Type of related object (SCLAS)
  - AG   Role
  - C   Jobs
  - O   Organization
  - P   Person
  - S   Position
- Subtypes
  - A002   Reports to

- ▸ A007   Describes
- ▸ A008   Holder
- ▸ A012   Manages
- ▸ B002   Is line supervisor of
- ▸ B007   Is described by
- ▸ B008   Holder
- ▸ B012   Is Managed by

Filter Group for Employees

This is required; otherwise, the Business Partner in SRM will not be created.

- ▸ Infotype
- ▸ 0006   Address
- ▸ Subtypes
- ▸ Permanent Residence

This creates the relationship between the R/3 Employee and the SRM User. Note that as a standard, the relationship is only created if both infotype 0105 (in R/3) and UserID (in SRM) exist.

- ▸ Infotype
  - ▸ 0105   Communication
- ▸ Subtype
  - ▸ 0001   SY-UNAME
  - ▸ 0010   Email Address

Filter group for Employees — Relationship:

- ▸ Infotype
  - ▸ 1001
- ▸ Object type
  - ▸ P
- ▸ Type of related object
  - ▸ S
- ▸ Subtype
  - ▸ B008

Filter Group for Relationship with Linked Objects

(See OSS Note 312090)

▶ Infotype

   ▷ 1001   Relationship between objects

▶ Objects

   ▷ O   Organization

   ▷ S   Position

▶ Type of related Object (SCLAS)

   ▷ O   Organization

   ▷ S   Position

▶ Subtypes

   ▷ A003   Belongs to

   ▷ B003   Incorporates

18.1.3　Activating Change Pointers

You can activate change pointers in the HR system to avoid distributing the entire structure when you make changes to the HR-ORG model, and instead distribute only the changes you have made. Follow these steps:

1. In SAP R/3, go to Tcode and follow this path: **</SALE> • Modeling and Implementing • Master data distribution • Replication of Modified data • Activate change pointers — Generally**

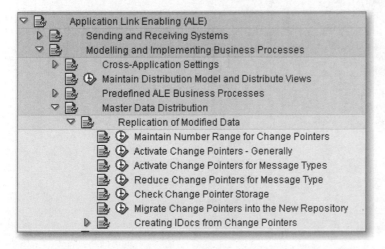

Figure 18.2　ALE Model — Activation of Change Pointers

2. Set the button for activating change pointers as shown in Figure 18.3. This is a transportable configuration; therefore the system will request a transport number.

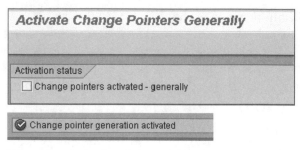

Figure 18.3 Activation of Change Pointers

3. Select **Activate change pointers for Message Types**, and select the message type for which the change pointer should be activated, as seen in Figure 18.4.

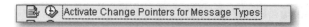

Figure 18.4 Change Pointer Activation Based on Message Type

4. Set the active indicator for message type **HRMD_ABA**, as shown in Figure 18.5.

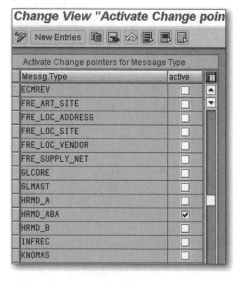

Figure 18.5 Select Appropriate Message Type

This is a transportable entry, therefore you should create a transport request. You can combine it with the earlier transport. Then, save your entries.

Job Scheduling for Transferring Changes or Deletions from HR to EBP.

So that master data changes from the HR system can be distributed to the EBP system, you must schedule a report. This report reads the change pointers activated previously and generates IDocs from it. You schedule this report in the **SAP R/3** system. To do so, the following steps are required:

1. Define variants for the program **RBDMIDOC,** as seen in Figure 18.6, and schedule the report on a periodic basis (e.g., once a day).

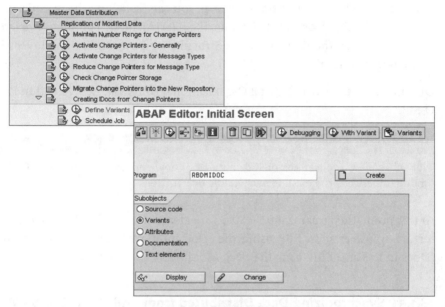

Figure 18.6 Define a Variant for Program RBDMIDOC

2. The variant you create should be for the message type selected in the previous steps. As such, enter **HRMD_ABA**, as seen in Figure 18.7.

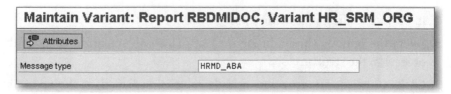

Figure 18.7 Maintain Variant for RBDMIDOC

3. Once you've created a variant, you can schedule a periodic job to run this report on a regular basis. Typically, a daily run is sufficient.

4. Change pointers can be manually executed using tranaction code BD21 and BD22.

18.1.4 Distribute the HR-Organizational Model (Initial Distribution)

For distributing the HR organizational model, follow these steps:

1. Execute Transaction </SA38 or SE38>.

2. Start the report RHALEINI, and specify the data that should be distributed. Be very careful with this transaction as you can distribute the organization model in INITIAL or UPDATE mode; the INITIAL mode completely deletes and re-creates the Organizational Structure or positions or employees in the target system.

One approach is to distribute all Organizational Units via the Evaluation Path O-S-P.

> **Tip**
>
> All subsequent replications or distributions (if any) should be done in UPDATE mode; otherwise, the existing data will be overwritten.

At this point, the Organizational Structure elements as defined in the ALE filter are transferred to EBP using the IDoc Interface. You can monitor the IDocs in R/3 and EBP using the IDoc Monitor in Transaction WE02.

18.1.5 Synchronizing Data Distributed from SAP R/3 HR to SRM.

The next step is to synchronize the overall Organizational Structure that has been distributed. The synchronization creates any business partners that have been missed and also provides a report for the organizational objects that have issues and need to be fixed:

1. In SRM, execute Transaction <BBP_BP_OM_INTEGRATE>

2. Select the options shown in Figure 18.8. This will synchronize all of the objects in the structure.

3. Click on the execute icon and a results table is displayed, as shown in Figure 18.9.

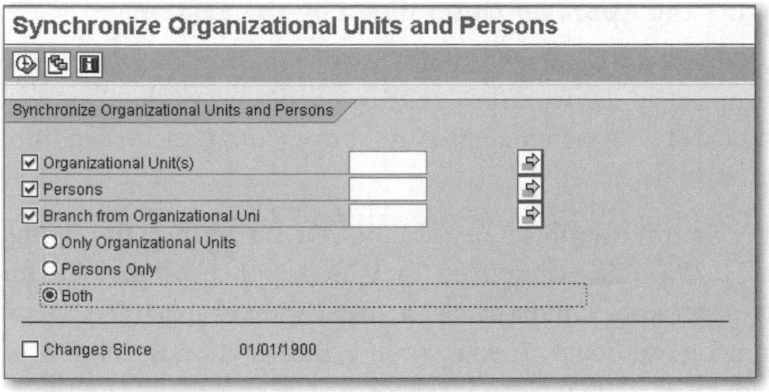

Figure 18.8 Synchronize the Organizational Structure

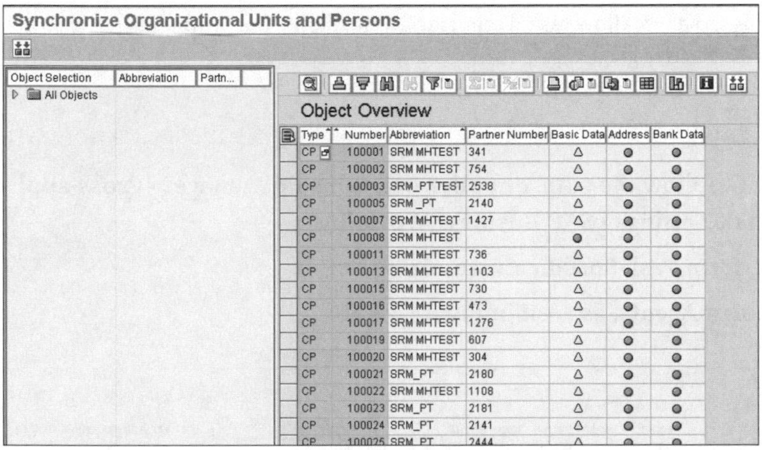

Figure 18.9 Synchronization of Organizational Units and Persons

Items with green lights are all set, items with red lights indicate an error, and items with yellow lights indicate that you need to take corrective action. Use the synchronize icon to fix incorrect objects. This activity can take some time, depending on the number of objects with a *yellow* or *red* status.

18.2 Workflow: Restriction for Changing and Adding Approvers in the Shopping Cart

In the Shopping Cart Approval Preview function, users can change the approver that is determined by the system. Also, users can add an approver ad hoc, using the Add Approver button. This section provides the configuration necessary to control this functionality.

18.2.1 Changing the Approver Determined by the System

As a standard in Enterprise Buyer (EBP), users are able to change the approver determined by the workflow starting conditions in the Approval Preview function. This can be an audit issue for organizations that do not want the approver to be changed.

To provide some control over this functionality, you can perform the configuration outlined below. Once completed, only users with a specific role, for example the Manager Role, will be available (in a list) to change the system-derived shopping cart approver. The key to this configuration is to limit the agent assignment on workflow task TS10008126.

Tip

To assign roles to a workflow task, your user ID must have the proper authorization to assign roles to user groups.

Follow these steps next:

1. In the IMG, follow the path: **Supplier Relationship Manager · Cross-application Basic Settings · SAP Business Workflow**.

2. Select **Perform Task-Specific Customizing**.

3. Select **Assign Agents**, as seen in Figure 18.10.

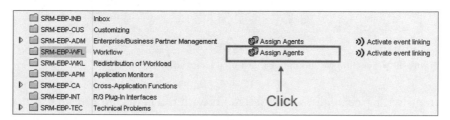

Figure 18.10 Selecting Assign Agents

4. Find and select workflow task TS10008126.

5. Click on **Attributes**.

6. Mark task TS10008126 as **General forwarding allowed**, as seen in Figure 18.11.

7. Assign the restriction on who should be able to be selected in the approval preview, as shown in Figure 18.12. (In our example it's by Role restriction of Manager.)

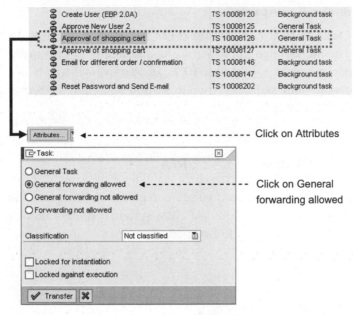

Create User (EBP 2.0A)	TS 10008120	Background task
Approve New User 2	TS 10008125	General Task
Approval of shopping cart	TS 10008126	General Task
Approval of shopping cart	TS 10008127	General Task
Email for different order / confirmation	TS 10008146	Background task
	TS 10008147	Background task
Reset Password and Send E-mail	TS 10008202	Background task

Attributes... ◄------------------------ Click on Attributes

Task:

○ General Task
◉ General forwarding allowed ◄----------------- Click on General
○ General forwarding not allowed   forwarding allowed
○ Forwarding not allowed

Classification   Not classified

☐ Locked for instantiation
☐ Locked against execution

✔ Transfer ✖

Figure 18.11 Configuring General Forwarding Allowed

8. Once the Manager role is assigned, in the Approval Preview function only users with the Manager role will display for selection and change.

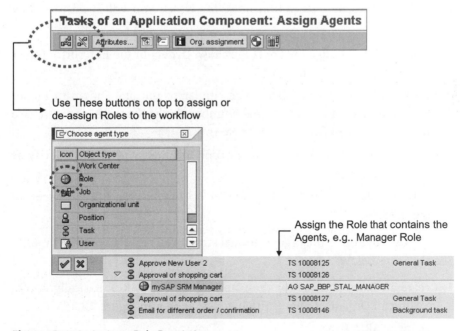

Figure 18.12 Assigning a Role Restriction

18.2.2 Adding an Ad-Hoc Approver

In the Shopping Cart Approval Preview, users can also add an approver in addition to the system-generated approver(s). As a standard in Enterprise Buyer (EBP), users can add any valid user ID as an approver. If this is not desired, then follow the same steps as shown in Section 1.2.1, but use work-flow task WS10000271 instead.

18.3 MRP Integration with SAP SRM

In this section, we'll examine the configuration required to integrate the MRP requisitions from SAP R/3 into the SAP SRM system. Configuration is required in the Enterprise Buyer and R/3 systems for:

▸ Number ranges

▸ Document types

▸ Organizational structure

▸ Sourcing decision

▸ MRP tables

▸ Jobs

Let's move on to the integration now, for which you will need to follow these steps:

1. **Define Number Range for Local Purchase Orders** in the Enterprise Buyer (EBP), as shown in Figure 18.13.

2. In SAP R/3, create a number range similar to the one shown in Figure 18.13 and mark it as an External Number Range, because. the purchase orders will be sent from the EBP system.

3. Create a transaction type document type in Enterprise Buyer. Specify as **ECDP** for direct procurement.

4. In the SAP R/3 system, create a similar document type **ECDP, as** seen in Figure 18.14.

Now, let's move on to the organizational structure Transaction PPOMA_BBP. See the steps below:

1. Create an Entry channel for the planning system (MRP). Basically you're creating an Organizational Unit object, as shown in Figure 18.15

2. Create an SRM **User**.

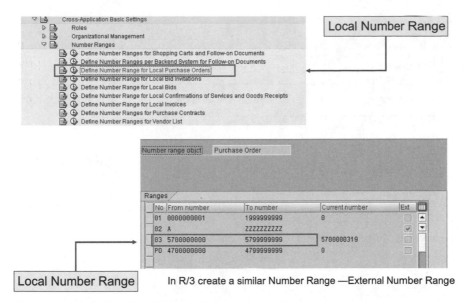

Figure 18.13 Defining a Local Number Range in Enterprise Buyer

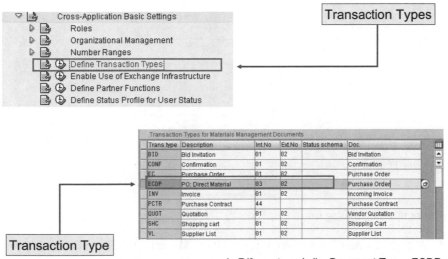

Figure 18.14 Create a Document Type ECDP

3. Place this user within the **Entry Channel**. This user will be used as an RFC user from R/3 into SRM, as shown in Figure 18.15.

4. Define the organizational responsibility for the entry channel you created. This should state which **Purchasing Group** will be responsible for this entry channel, as shown in Figure 18.16.

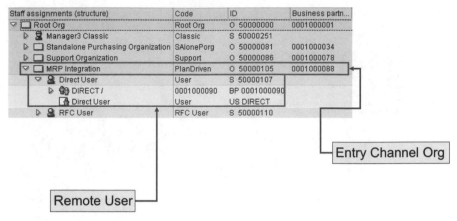

Figure 18.15 Creating an MRP Entry Channel and Remote User

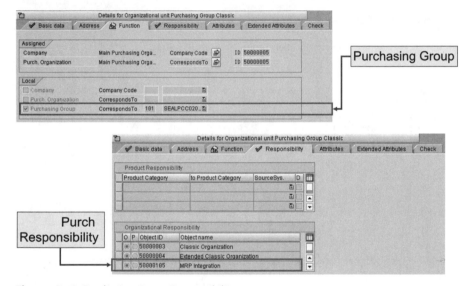

Figure 18.16 Purchasing Group Responsibility

5. Assign the Attribute of creating a Direct Material Purchase Order for this entry channel. Assign attribute **DP_PROC_TY** as **ECDP**. You can see this in Figure 18.17.

6. At any time you need to download the plants and **Replicate Plants from R/3**, as seen in Figure 18.18. In the example, the Category is **R3MATCLASS**.

7. Define how **Sourcing** will be carried out in EBP — either via the Sourcing Application or via the Purchase Order Application. This can be seen in Figure 18.19.

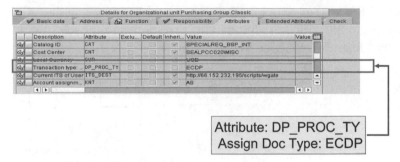

Figure 18.17 Assigning Attribute to Create Direct Purchase Order

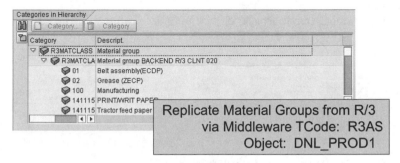

Figure 18.18 Replicate Plants and Material Groups

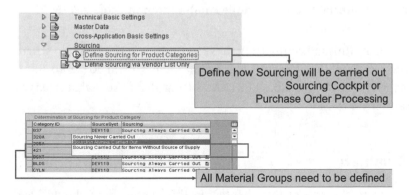

Figure 18.19 Define the Sourcing Decision

Let's take a look at what these options mean:

► **Sourcing Never Carried Out**
All external requirements will be sent as Incomplete POs in EBP.

► **Sourcing Always Carried Out**
All external requirements will be sent into the Sourcing Application in EBP.

8. In the SAP R/3 system, define a profile name and the corresponding RFC destination to EBP. The RFC destination corresponds to the RFC user of the Entry Channel. Define the View V_T160PR.

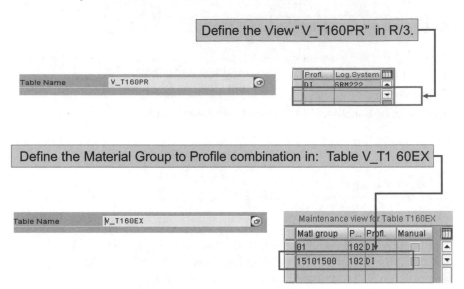

Figure 18.20 Define RFC Destination and Material Group Profile

9. Define the **Material Group to Profile combination in Table V_T160EX**, as shown in Figure 18.20

10. When you're finished configuring these settings, you can begin to schedule the program that transfers the requirements from R/3 into SRM. Report RPRSEL01 reads table EPRTRANS from R/3 to see what needs to be transferred to EBP.

18.4   Summary

This brings us to the end of this chapter. In this chapter you should have learned to integrate SAP SRM organizational structure with HR and also learned how to change approvers for the shopping cart and how to integrate MRP.

These integration issues are very important for you as you move forward in your procurement enhancement journey with SAP SRM. The key solution configuration information in this chapter was not intended to be comprehensive in scope. Rather it was to be a guide for key setup and configuration areas in SAP SRM.

18.5 Book Conclusion

We are also now at the end of this book. I hope you found this to be a practical and useful resource that you will return to from time to time, when you need solutions or advice. I intended this to be a practical guide for you and tried to keep a real-world focus throughout.

From gaining an overview of SAP SRM and understanding how it fits into the overall SAP landscape to getting information about detailed functionality and capability of this solution. I hope this book helps you enhance procurement in your company by giving you a detailed look into how SAP SRM works.

You should also now have a fairly good understanding of implementation, integration and updates. This section is largely based on my own experiences and contains valuable information not found in other SAP resources. This is where you should have received the answers to your commonly encountered problems, issues and needs.

To make this book a comprehensive and real-world guide I delved deep into some specific industry solutions. These included Government Procurement and generally highlighted the public-sector solution.

Then, we proceeded on to selected configuration issues, which was intended to be a guide for key setup and integration issues related to SAP SRM.

The appendices contain valuable extras which should greatly help you in your projects. Here you can get an SRM functionality matrix, job scheduling, a quiz to determine your SRM knowledge and more. I encourage you to read the appendices and use them as you need to.

I hope that you find this book useful and valuable for your needs. I know that I learned a lot while writing it and I hope I was able to pass on the sum of my knowledge and experience on to you.

Appendix

A SRM Functionality Matrix

The SAP SRM solution has evolved at a rapid pace over the last six years, with each release of the solution providing enhanced functionality. Each implementation team is faced with the task of gathering varied organizational requirements and then performing a gap analysis against the SRM release being implemented. The SRM scenario implementation type (Classic, Extended Classic, etc) has a considerable impact on this gap-analysis. SAP continually aims to offer comparable functionality across the different implementation scenarios but the inherent nature of each scenario results in restrictions.

SAP has developed an SRM functionality matrix that provides a comparative analysis for the different implementation scenarios, the functional processes and the solution releases. This document will be especially useful for organizations that want to compare — at a detail functionality level — which capabilities in SAP SRM are supported in the Classic, Extended Classic or Standalone scenarios. Organizations can review the matrix for each of the SRM core processes: strategic sourcing, operational procurement and supplier enablement. Let's look at an example.

If your organization wants to implement the Request for External Staff functionality available within the operational procurement process, it is important for you to know whether this functionality is supported within the Classic, Extended Classic or Standalone scenario. The SRM functionality matrix illustrates that this functionality is only available in the Standalone scenario. As you can see, this information becomes very valuable because it enables you to correctly blueprint and select your implementation scenario.

You can access and download the SRM matrix document from the following URL: *www.sap-press.com*

B   Jobs that Require Scheduling

As part of a production SAP SRM system, you need to schedule and execute several jobs on a regular basis. This appendix discusses these jobs and the parameters that are required for each job.

Table B.1 provides an example of the frequency for the jobs you must schedule in the SAP SRM system. Organizations can change these frequencies, based on their requirements.

B.1   Jobs Required in SAP SRM

JOB NAME	DESCRIPTION	STEPS (PROGRAMS)	FREQ
CLEAN_REQREQ_UP	This job executes report (SE38) CLEAN_REQREQ_UP to ensure that subsequent objects of shopping cart (SC) items and IDocs, which can be generated from confirmations and invoices, were updated successfully in the backend system. If the subsequent objects are created successfully, the report sets the status of the SC to 6 and deletes temporary data that is not needed anymore from the EBP system. (This is why it is called a CLEANER job.) Note: The entries in table BBP_DOCUMENT_TAB represent the worklist for report CLEAN_REQREQ_UP. This is why the runtime of the report increases with time. When the check is successful, the corresponding SC entries are deleted from table BBP_DOCUMENT_TAB.	CLEAN_REQREQ_UP	Every 15 minutes

Table B.1 Jobs Required for Scheduling in SAP SRM

JOB NAME	DESCRIPTION	STEPS (PROGRAMS)	FREQ
SPOOLER JOB	Similar to CLEAN_REQREQ_UP. You need to select either SPOOLER JOB or CLEAN_REQREQ_UP — Although SPOOLER JOB is not scheduled in SM37, it is still scheduled to execute in the system.. You configure the job in the IMG: **EBP • Technical Basic Settings • Set Control Parameters**. The spooler transfers shopping cart data to the backend system. The preferred method is scheduling CLEAN_REQREQ_UP.		
APPROVALS — SEND EMAIL TO EXTERNAL MAIL SYSTEMS	This job enables offline approval functionality in SRM and transfer of work-items in an SRM user's Inbox to their preferred email client (e.g. Outlook, Lotus Notes, GroupWise, etc.) There are two steps in this job: The initial step moves the approval work-item from the SAP Inbox to SAP Connect (TCode: SCOT). The second step moves the same work-item from SAP Connect to the organization's mail server, which then sends the email to the user's preferred email client.	Step 1: RSCONN01 Variant: SAP&CONNEC-TALL Step 2: RSWUWFM-LEC Variant: EMAIL_VARI-ANT Attributes: Type of Mail: HTML Approval Buttons: NO Operation: FULL TEXT Email Address: EMAIL ADDRESS@CO MPANY.com	Every 15 minutes

Table B.1 Jobs Required for Scheduling in SAP SRM (cont.)

JOB NAME	DESCRIPTION	STEPS (PROGRAMS)	FREQ
GET STATUS OF SRM DOCUMENTS	This job retrieves status information back from the backend system. Once a Req. or a PO is generated in EBP, the spooler transfers it over to the backend. This job then gets the status of the created object and provides the appropriate input to the Check Status Transaction of the end-user's shopping cart. If Check Status is not being updated in the shopping cart and the subsequent PO, GR or Invoice has been created, and then check whether this job is running.	BBP_GET_STATUS_2 Variant might be required post production	Every 15 minutes
ORGANIZATION MODEL CLEAN-UP & PROFORMANCE IMPROVEMENT	This job cleans up the buffers of the organizational structure, which helps with the performance of the system. Additionally, it schedules inheritance of attributes within the organizational structure to allow for quicker access.	RHBAUPAT (for release <3.0) HRBCI_ATTRIBUTES_BUFFER_UPDATE (for releases >= 3.0) Variant might be required post production	Every night
RSPPFPROCESS	This report provides the mechanism to output local purchase orders for automatic message output.	RSPPFPROCESS	Every 30 minutes
EVALUATED RECEIPT SETTLEMENT EXECUTION	When ERS is being used, you need to schedule this report. This allows the ERS procedure execution in SRM. Relevant for organizations using the local scenario. This executes the settlement. Assumption: Confirmation exists	BBPERS	1–2 times/day

Table B.1 Jobs Required for Scheduling in SAP SRM (cont.)

JOB NAME	DESCRIPTION	STEPS (PROGRAMS)	FREQ
WORKFLOW: RUNTIME PROGRAMS	There are a number of jobs that are required to run so that workflow in the SRM environment can be successfully executed. Typically these jobs can be automatically scheduled using the Automatic Workflow Customizing in TCode SWU3. A background job is scheduled for the following: ▶ Missed deadlines ▶ Work items with errors ▶ Condition evaluation ▶ Event queue ▶ Clearing tasks	The following jobs need to be running in a production environment: ▶ SWWDHEX ▶ SWWERRE ▶ SWWCOND ▶ SWWCLEAR	Every 15 minutes
INVOICE: STATUS SYNCHRONIZATION	This report synchronizes the status of invoices in the SRM system with the status in the corresponding SAP R/3 or ERP backend system. Once invoices are "Paid" in the backend, the SRM status is synchronized to show "Paid".	BBP_IV_ UPDATE_ PAYMENT_ STATUS	2–4 times/day
CHECK GOODS RECEIPTS FOR XML INVOICES	All invoices that come in via XML with a status of "Waiting for Preceding Document" to check if the preceding documents (such as Confirmations) have been posted and periodic attempts are made to post the relevant invoice.	BBP_IV_ AUTO_COMPLETE	2 times/day
CONTRACT EXPIRY CHECK	Organizations that use the Contract application in SRM can schedule this report to check on the status of the contract. The report provides selection parameters to identify contracts that might be nearing expiry or where the quantity or release value is nearing completion. Organizations using the Business Intelligence (BI) solution can use the Alerts functionality in SAP SRM to trigger contract expiry reports in BI.	BBP_ CONTRACT_ CHECK	Once/day

Table B.1 Jobs Required for Scheduling in SAP SRM (cont.)

JOB NAME	DESCRIPTION	STEPS (PROGRAMS)	FREQ
WORKFLOW: OFFLINE APPROVAL	Organizations using the Offline approvals functionality within Enterprise buyer can schedule this report to enable receipt of status of approvals from external mail systems.	RBBP_ NOTIFICATION _OFFAPP	Every 30 minutes

Table B.1 Jobs Required for Scheduling in SAP SRM (cont.)

B.2 Jobs Required in SAP R/3 or ERP

Table B.2 provides an example of the frequency for the job you have to schedule in the R/3 or ERP backend system. This job is only required if you have integrated the organizational structure in SRM with the organizational model in the SAP HR module. Organizations can change this based on their requirements.

JOB NAME	DESCRIPTION	STEPS (PRO-GRAMS)	USER	FREQ
HR CHANGE POINTERS	Assumption: HR Org. Integration is active. When Org/Position changes are executed in R/3 HR, then those changes/deletions need to be distributed to the SRM system. HR distributes the changes/deletions to SRM and other systems via the IDoc interface. This job executes a report that creates IDocs from the change pointers in the R3 HR system. It then sends them to the receiving system (SRM) and updates the organizational structure in SRM.	STEP: RBDMIDOC Variant: HR_ SRM_ORG Attributes: Message Type: HRMD_ABA		Once/day

Table B.2 Jobs Required for Scheduling in SAP R/3 or ERP

In a production SRM system that is linked to an SAP R/3 or ERP backend, the BBP_GET_STATUS_2 report needs to be scheduled as described in Table B.1.

It is important to note that for performance reasons, this report should be scheduled using a variant.

The BBP_GET_STATUS_2 report receives status information about documents that are pertinent to a backend system, e.g. purchase requisition, purchase order, reservation, goods receipt and invoice. The following parameters are available for setting up the variant:

▶ Shopping carts (interval)

▶ Logical system (if multiple backend systems are being used)

▶ Shopping carts in the last number of days (restrict variant based on range)

▶ Shopping cart status indicator (Deleted, Completed, etc.)

C   Using Different Browsers with SAP SRM

Every organization has policies regarding their support of applications used within the company, including Internet browsers. Probably the most used and supported browser is Microsoft Internet Explorer. However, other browsers such as Mozilla Firefox and Apple Safari are also used at a number of companies. It is important for organizations to know whether and to what extent the browser used in their company is supported by SAP for the SAP SRM application.

The main components within SAP SRM (Enterprise Buyer, Bidding Engine, Supplier Self Services, and Catalog Content Management) are all accessed via a Web browser. End users can access the components directly via a URL representing the ITS (for EBP and Bidding Engine applications) or BSP (CCM and SUS applications) technologies.

Alternatively, they can access these components seamlessly via the Enterprise Portal system. No matter how these applications are accessed, a Web-browser is used (except when using the Windows GUI for configuration). The following browsers are supported for use with SAP SRM 4.0:

- Microsoft Internet Explorer 6.0
- Mozilla Firefox 1.5

> **Note**
>
> At the time of writing, Microsoft Internet Explorer 7.0 is not supported. Also, the Netscape Navigator browser is not completely supported for use with SAP SRM.

Additionally, organizations that are using SAP SRM 4.0 on computers running MAC OS should use Mozilla Firefox as their browser.

For up-to-date information on using browsers with SRM, review SAP Notes 438481 and 838013.

> **Note**
>
> A new SAP BAdI repository has been introduced on the SDN by SAP with the collaboration of the SAP community. You can review it at www.SDN.sap.com/IRJ/WIKI and select the Supplier Relationship Management WIKI. The BAdI repository contains useful examples of BAdI code as implemented by other organizations.

D Using Business Add-Ins (BAdIs) with SAP SRM

From SAP 4.6A, and for all SAP SRM releases, SAP provided a new enhancement technique in the form of Business Add-Ins. Business Add-Ins (BAdIs) are object-oriented enhancement options. Enhancements represent customer requirements that have not been developed in the standard SAP software. A BAdI is a standard exit within SAP programs whereby organizations can change SAP programs without carrying out any system modifications.

A common saying in SAP SRM projects is that BAdIs are your best friend and that you need to get to know them. This is because there is hardly any SRM project where organizations have not utilized BAdIs to achieve their unique business requirements. A number of projects begin with the charter of no development and then realize that the only way to achieve some of their business requirements by using BAdIs. Let's take a simple example: the *Shop* transaction BBPSC01 contains different options for end users to create shopping carts.

Users can create shopping carts to order temporary labor, request for external staff, etc. If you do not plan to utilize the Services procurement functionality in SRM implementation then you might not want to give users the access to this these options. In our example, the only way to remove these from the shop transaction is either by using a BAdI or making HTML modifications. SAP provides a growing number of BAdIs with each SRM release.

With the help of BAdIs, organizations can implement business specific logic to gain flexibility without creating Customer modifications, as BAdIs are completely supported by SAP. According to SAP, Release upgrades do not affect enhancement calls from within the standard software nor do they affect the validity of call interfaces. Also, BAdIs are not required to be registered in the SAP Software Change Registration (SSCR).

D.1 Implementing a BAdI

To implement a BAdI in SRM, development experts can navigate to the implementation through the IMG: (**Supplier Relationship Management • SRM Server • Business Add-Ins**) or use Transaction SE19 or SE18. To implement a BAdI the first steps are to give an implementation name adhering to the customer naming standards and to define the required attributes. There are basically two types of attributes in a BAdI implementation, which are:

▶ Multiple Use
▶ Filter Dependent

These are described below.

D.1.1 Multiple Use

Multiple use for BAdI definitions means that there can be several active BAdI implementations in a single environment. When there is a call, they are all called up though, in an unpredictable sequence. If you have multiple-use BAdI definitions, the sequence must not play any role therefore. It should be noted that although SAP provides the functionality around multiple use BAdIs attributes, most BAdIs available in SAP SRM are filter dependent and not available for multiple-use.

D.1.2 Filter Dependent

Filters allow SAP to provide one technical object that can be used across multiple business documents. As a default, each BAdI definition — method automatically has an importing parameter FLT_VAL assigned.

Let's take an example. The BAdI: BBP_VERSION_CONTROL has an attribute type filter dependent checked. This means that this BAdI will be triggered for specific object types that are defined in the standard system configuration. Therefore, this same BAdI can be triggered for different documents such as, purchase order (BUS2201), contracts, etc. Figure D.1 illustrates the filter dependency for the purchase order business object.

Usually a BAdI will have at least one method where a custom code can be written. Within this method there will be parameters. These parameters can be importing, exporting, returning or changing parameters. We can see the list of the available parameters during runtime by clicking the signature button within the Implementation or by simple double clicking any of the Interface names in the BAdI definition.

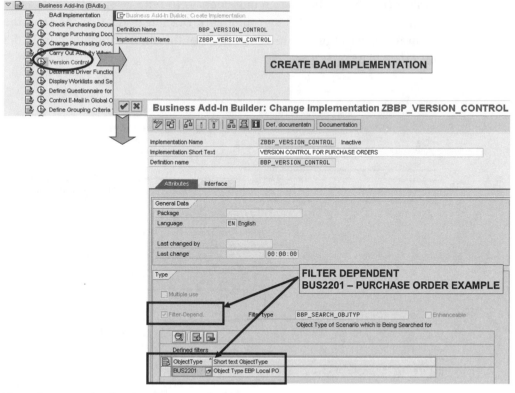

Figure D.1 Example of BAdI Definition and Filter Selection

D.2 Examples of BAdIs in SAP SRM

Each SRM implementation will experience a requirement of using BAdIs, based on their business requirements. This section provides a few examples where BAdIs can be implemented in SRM.

D.2.1 BAdI: Change Display in Shopping Cart (BBP_SC_MODIFY_UI)

The Shop transaction BBPSC01 in SRM was designed with professional purchasers in mind. Many organizations enable this transaction for casual end-users as well. However, most organizations want to remove specific access in this transaction from the casual users. This BAdI allows removing fields such as: Catalog Search, Catalogs, Limit Cart, Describe Requirement, Temporary labor, Product, Temp Labor Req, and Default Scr.

In this example, our business requirement is to remove specific fields from the shopping cart BBPSC01 screen. Figure D.2 illustrates that the Describe Requirement selection can be removed from the Shop transaction using the BBP_SC_MODIFY_UI BAdI.

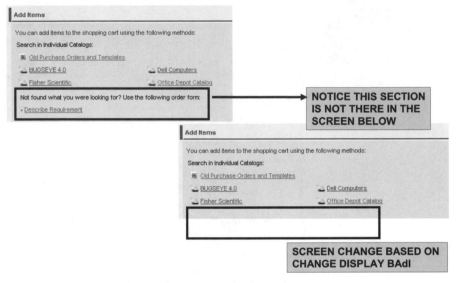

Figure D.2 Example of Change Shopping Cart display BAdI

Here is a sample code that organizations can use to remove specific fields in the shop transaction. In our sample code, the Limit Cart, Temporary Labor, Product and Catalog selections are cleared from user access. Let's take a look at the code now:

```
Definition: BBP_SC_MODIFY_UI
Method:SC_MODIFY_SCREEN
method IF_EX_BBP_SC_MODIFY_UI~SC_MODIFY_SCREEN.
   clear is_scr_itmchoice-LIMIT.
   clear is_scr_itmchoice-TEMP_LAB.
   clear is_scr_itmchoice-PRODUCT.
   clear is_scr_itmchoice-CATALOGS.
endmethod.
```

D.2.2 BAdI: Define Target Objects (BBP_TARGET_OBJECTS)

In SAP SRM when implementing the classic scenario, organizations have the choice to create a target document in the SAP R/3 or ERP back-end. A purchase requisition, purchase order or a reservation can be created in the back-end once the shopping cart is approved in SRM. In this example, our business requirement is to ensure that all shopping cart line items are converted into a purchase order.

Here is a sample code that organizations can use to force the target object in the backend system to be a purchase order. In this code the backend object is being set as 3 which indicates PO creation; this can be set to *1* or *2* to create a purchase requisition or reservation based on your business requirements. Here is the code now:

```
method IF_EX_BBP_TARGET_OBJECTS~DETERMINE_TARGET_OBJECTS.
 DATA: itM_data_OO TYPE bbp_bapipogn_eci,
 l_index TYPE sy-tabix.
* SET THE OBJECT TO BE GENERATED AS 3 FOR PO CREATION
 LOOP AT item_data INTO itm_data_OO.
 l_index = sy-tabix.
 itm_data_OO-obj_to_gen = '3'.
 MODIFY item_data FROM itm_data_OO INDEX l_index.
 ENDLOOP.
endmethod.
```

D.2.3 BAdI: Change Purchasing Document data (BBP_DOC_CHANGE_BAdI)

The change purchasing document data BAdI is probably the single most utilized BAdI in SRM implementations and can be utilized creatively to meet many unique business requirements. This BAdI allows organizations to change the data in the business document being created. For example, change data in the shopping cart, or purchase order transactions. This example illustrates how organizations can utilize this BAdI to convert a preferred vendor in the shopping cart to a *fixed* vendor.

When creating a shopping cart, users can select a preferred source of supply in the details of the shopping cart. If the business requirement empowers the end user to make the decision on the vendor selection and no further purchasing intervention is required, this preferred vendor would need to be converted into a fixed vendor in the system. This BAdI can be utilized for influencing this change in the shopping cart document data.

Here is a sample code that organizations can use to convert a **preferred** vendor in the shopping cart to a fixed vendor:

```
Method: BBP_SC_CHANGE(FILTER BUS2121)

DATA: ls_partner TYPE bbp_pds_partner,
  l_index type sy-tabix.
CONSTANTS:
    c_prt_19 TYPE bbp_pds_partner-partner_fct VALUE '00000019',
    c_prt_39 TYPE bbp_pds_partner-partner_fct VALUE '00000039'.
* MOVE PARTNER DATA TO WORK AREA
  LOOP AT it_partner INTO ls_partner.
  l_index = sy-tabix.
* CHECK IF THE PARTNER FUNCTION IS PREFERRED VENDOR
  IF ls_partner-partner_fct EQ c_prt_39.
* IF TRUE CHANGE IT TO FIXED VENDOR
  ls_partner-partner_fct = c_prt_19.
  ENDIF.
* APPEND THE CHANGING PARAMETER TABLE
  APPEND ls_partner TO et_partner.
  ENDLOOP.
```

D.2.4   BAdI: Check Purchasing Document (BBP_DOC_CHECK_BAdI)

The check BAdI is another BAdI that is utilized heavily on SRM projects. This BAdI allows the organization to ensure that the purchasing documents (shopping cart, purchase order, etc.) in SRM are checked for validation using business rules specific to your organization. This example checks the shopping cart document to ensure that users are not using the Service radio button on the shopping cart line item.

In the shopping cart, users can choose the service or product radio button. Many organizations do not want to use the service option when creating shopping carts. The check BAdI can be utilized to ensure that if user selects the service radio button during the creation of the shopping cart line item, the system should issue an error message. The example in figure D.3 illustrates the error message that a user receives if the **Services** product type radio button is selected in the shopping cart.

Here is a sample code that organizations can use to check the shopping cart if the Service radio button has been selected:

```
Method: BBP_DOC_CHECK
 DATA:
 wa_item TYPE bbp_pds_sc_item_d,
 wa_messages TYPE bbp_smessages_BAdI.
```

```
LOOP AT lt_item INTO wa_item WHERE del_ind NE 'X'.
IF wa_item-product_type EQ '02'.
CLEAR wa_messages.
wa_messages-msgty = 'E'.
wa_messages-msgv1 = 'Product type service not allowed'
APPEND wa_messages TO et_messages.
ENDIF.
ENDLOOP.
```

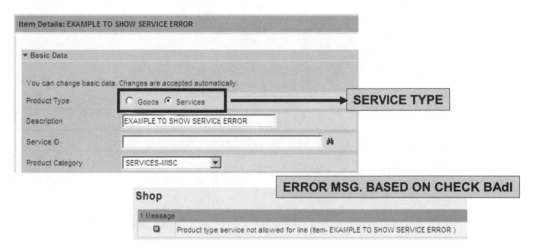

Figure D.3 Example of Document Check BAdI

D.3   List of BAdIs in SAP SRM

SAP provides a number of BAdIs that can be utilized in the SRM system as illustrated in the few examples in Section D.2. The purpose of this section is to provide users with a list of all the BAdIs that are available in SRM as of release SAP SRM 5.0.

The list of BAdIs is organized in a table format and when applicable are grouped together by function. For example, Table D.2 grouped the different BAdIs that are available for controlling the Extended Classic scenario.

The majority of the BAdIs are available within the Enterprise Buyer application. However, certain BAdIs are also applicable for SUS, and are seen in Table D.1.

Business Add-Ins (BAdIs)	Definition Name	SAP SRM Application	Release
Check Purchasing Document	BBP_DOC_CHECK_BAdI	EBP	
Change Purchasing Document Data	BBP_DOC_CHANGE_BAdI	EBP & SUS	
Change Purchasing Group Assignment	BBP_PGRP_ASSIGN_BAdI		changed in 5.0
Carry Out Activity When Saving	BBP_DOC_SAVE_BadI	EBP & SUS	
Version Control	BBP_VERSION_CONTROL	EBP & SUS	
Determine Driver Function Modules	BBP_DRIVER_DETERMINE		changed in 5.0
Display Worklist and Search Results Lists	BBP_WF_LIST		
Define Questionnaire for Vendor Evaluation in SRM	BBP_VE_QSTN_DET_BAdI		
Control E-Mail in Global Outline Agreement	BBP_CTR_MAIL_BadI		
Define Grouping Criteria for Local Purchase Orders	BBP_GROUP_LOC_PO		
Define External Print Formatting for Office Documents	BBP_DOC_PRINTPROC		
Archive SRM Documents	BBP_ARCHIVING_BAdI	EBP & SUS	4.0
Upload/Download SRM Documents	BBP_PD_DOWNLOAD		4.0
Further Authorization Check for SRM Documents	BBP_AUTHORITY_CHECK	EBP & SUS	4.0
Activation of Vendor Monitor	BBP_BAdI_SUPP_MONI		4.0
Create Skills Profile	BBP_SKILLS		
Transfer Additional Characteristics to SAP CCM	BBP_CCM_CHAR_MAIN		

Table D.1 Generic BAdIs in SAP SRM

Business Add-Ins (BAdIs)	Definition Name	SAP SRM Application	Release
Filter for Scheduling Agreement Releases	BBP_SUS_FILTER_SCHAR		
Download Documents	BBP_SUS_DOWNLD_FILES	SUS	
Customer Text for Registration Screen	ROS_CUST_WEL_TXT	Supplier Registration	
Definition of Required Fields for Customers	ROS_REQ_CUF	Supplier Registration	
Default Quantity for Items in the Confirmation	BBP_SUS_QUAN_PROPOSE	SUS	
Field Checks for Customer-Defined Required Fields	ROS_BUPA_DATA_CHECK	Supplier Registration	

Table D.1 Generic BAdIs in SAP SRM (cont.)

Table D.2 lists BAdIs for the Extended Classic scenario.

Business Add-Ins	Definition Note
Activate Extended Classic Scenario	BBP_EXTLOCALPO_BadI
Transfer Purchase Order Data to Logistics Backend	BBP_ECS_PO_OUT_BadI

Table D.2 BAdIs for Controlling the Extended Classic Scenario

Now, take a look at BAdIs for master data in Table D.3.

SAP SRM Application	Definition Name	Release
Customer Field Replication in Vendor Master Data	BBP_GET_VMDATA_CF	
Extension for Tax Number Mapping	BBP_SUS_BP_TAXNUMMAP	SUS
Extension for Duplication Check	BBP_SUS_BP_DUPLCHECK	SUS

Table D.3 BAdIs for Master Data

Table D.4 looks at BAdIs for shopping carts and requirements.

SAP SRM Application	Definition Name	Release
Shopping Cart: Determine Responsible Purchasing Group(s)	BBP_PGRP_FIND	
Determine Backend System / Company Code	BBP_DETERMINE_LOGSYS	
Determine Target Object in BE System	BBP_TARGET_OBJECTS	Changed in 5.0 (new BAdI added)
Monitor Shopping Cart: Selection and List Display	BBP_MON_SC	
Change Display in Shopping Cart	BBP_SC_MODIFY_UI	4.0

Table D.4 BAdIs for Shopping Carts and Requirement Items

Table D.5 lists them for external web services.

SAP SRM Application	Definition Name
Transfer Shopping Cart from Catalog	BBP_CATALOG_TRANSFER
Transfer Additional Parameters	BBP_CAT_CALL_ENRICH
Deactivate Cross-Catalog Search	BBP_WS_AGENT_SEARCH

Table D.5 BAdIs for External Web Services (Catalogs, Vendor Lists, etc.)

Table D.6 lists BAdIs for follow-on document generation for the back-end system, which is new in SAP SRM 5.0.

SAP SRM Application	Definition Name	Release
Determine Number Ranges and Grouping in Backend Documents	BBP_SC_TRANSFER_BE	Changed in 5.0 (new BAdI added)
Purchase Requisition in Backend System	BBP_CREATE_REQ_BACK	Changed in 5.0 (new BAdI added)
Purchase Order in Backend System	BBP_CREATE_PO_BACK	Changed in 5.0 (new BAdI added)
Grouping of Reservations	BBP_RESERVATION_GRP	Changed in 5.0 (new BAdI added)
Reservation in Backend System	BBP_CREATE_RES_BACK	Changed in 5.0 (new BAdI added)
Create Contract in Backend System	BBP_CTR_BE_CREATE	

Table D.6 BAdIs for Follow-on Document Generation in the Backend System

Learn about old and new definition names in Table D.7.

Business Add-Ins (BAdIs)	Old Definition Name	New Definition Name
Grouping of shopping cart items for follow-on documents	BBP_SC_TRANSFER_BE	BBP_BS_GROUP_BE
Purchase Requisition in Backend System	BBP_CREATE_REQ_BACK	BBP_CREATE_BE_RQ_NEW
Purchase Order in Backend System	BBP_CREATE_PO_BACK	BBP_CREATE_BE_PO_NEW
Grouping of Reservations	BBP_RESERVATION_GRP	BBP_BS_GROUP_BE
Reservation in Backend System	BBP_CREATE_RES_BACK	BBP_CREATE_BE_RS_NEW

Table D.7 New BAdIs in SAP SRM 5.0 for Follow-on Document generation in the backend system

Get a list of BAdIs relevant for sourcing in Table D.8.

Business Add-Ins (BAdIs)	Definition Name
Define Execution of Sourcing	BBP_SRC_DETERMINE
Define Sourcing via Vendor List	BBP_AVL_DETERMINE
Change Bid Invitation Data Before Transfer to Bidding Application	BBP_CREAT_RFQ_IN_DPE
Find and Check Sources of Supply	BBP_SOS_BAdI

Table D.8 BAdIs Relevant to Sourcing in SAP SRM

Table D.9 is your source for BAdIs that are needed for bid invitations.

Business Add-Ins (BAdIs)	Definition Name	Release
Dynamic Attributes in the Bid Invitation	BBP_DETERMINE_DYNATR	
Determine Bid Invitation Transaction Type	BBP_BID_DET_PROCTYPE	4.0
Control for Collaboration Folders	BBP_CFOLDER_BadI	4.0

Table D.9 BAdIs Relevant for Bid Invitations

If you are interested in account assignment you will find Table D.10 very useful.

Business Add-Ins (BAdIs)	Definition Name
Change Account Assignment Category when Creating Backend Documents	BBP_ACCCAT_MAP_EXP
Change Account Assignment Category when Importing Back-end Documents	BBP_ACCCAT_MAP_IMP
Determine G/L Acct	BBP_DETERMINE_ACCT
Deactivate Automatic Budget Check	BBP_BUDGET_CHECK

Table D.10 Account Assignment Relevant BAdIs

Those interested in tax calculation will find Table D.11 interesting.

Business Add-Ins (BAdIs)	Definition Name
Determine Tax Code	BBP_DET_TAXCODE_BadI
Change Tax Data	BBP_TAX_MAP_BadI
Calculate Tax for Freight Costs	BBP_FREIGHT_BadI

Table D.11 BAdIs Relevant for Tax Calculation

Gain important information about Controlling Pricing Configurator (IPC) in Table D.12.

Business Add-Ins (BAdIs)	Definition Name	Action
Switch On Simplified Pricing (Classic Scenario)	BBP_PRICEDATA_READ	
Switch off Buffer Refreshing IPC		REMOVED

Table D.12 BAdIs for Controlling Pricing Configurator

Confirmation and invoice verification BAdIs are found in Table D.13.

Business Add-Ins (BAdIs)	Definition Name
Define Target System for Sending of Confirmation	BBP_XML_CONF_LOGSYS
Send Confirmation via XML	BBP_XML_CONF_SEND
Control Default Values for Time Recording	BBP_TREX_BAdI
Control Entry Options for Unplanned Items	BBP_UNPLAN_ITEM_BAdI

Table D.13 BAdIs for Confirmation and Invoice Verification

Component Planning BAdIs are found in Table D.14.

Business Add-Ins (BAdIs)	Definition Name
Define Default Values for Component Planning	BBP_PM_DEFAULT_VAL
Check and Complete Component Data	BBP_PM_COMP_CHK

Table D.14 BAdIs for Component Planning

Direct material and plan-driven BAdIs are given in Table D.15.

Business Add-Ins (BAdIs)	Definition Name	Action
Control Direct Material Procurement	BBP_DP_PROD_CHK_BAdI	
Send XML Document to Planning System	BBP_XML_DET_SYSTEM	
Check Items for APO Relevance		REMOVED

Table D.15 BAdIs for Direct Material and Plan-Driven procurement

SAP SRM workflow related BAdIs are found in Table D.16.

Business Add-Ins (BAdIs)	Definition Name	Release
Authorization to Change During Approval	BBP_WFL_SECUR_BAdI	
Determine Approver (Administrator)	BBP_WFL_ADMIN_APPROV	
Determination of Approver for n-Step Dynamic Approval Workflow	BBP_WFL_APPROV_BAdI	
Determine Shopping Cart Value for Purchasing Budget Workflow	BBP_SC_VALUE_GET	
Control Workflow for Stochastic Document Check	BBP_STOCH_CUST_BAdI	
Allow Changes to Approvers	BBP_CHNG_AGNT_ALLOW	4.0
Select Users when Creating/Changing Approvers	BBP_CHNG_AGNT_GET	4.0

Table D.16 BAdIs relevant for Workflow in SRM

If you want to use BAdIs to create customer fields you will find Table D.17 of use.

Business Add-Ins (BAdIs)	Definition Name	Release
Customer Field Control	BBP_CUF_BadI	4.0
Customer Fields with Standard Table Control	BBP_CUF_BAdI_2	4.0

Table D.17 BAdIs for Creating Customer Fields

If you use BAdIs for SAP XML interfacing, Table D.18 will be of use to you.

Business Add-Ins (BAdIs)	Definition Name	Release
Change SAP XML Inbound Mapping	BBP_SAPXML1_IN_BAdIEBP & SUS	4.0
Change SAP XML Outbound Mapping	BBP_SAPXML1_OUT_BAdIEBP & SUS	4.0

Table D.18 BAdIs for Use with SAP XML Interfaces

For controlling document output you can use Table D.19.

Business Add-Ins (BAdIs)	Definition Name	Release
Output Shopping Cart with Customer Form	BBP_CHANGE_SF_SC	4.0
Output Contract with Customer Form	BBP_CHANGE_SF_CTR	4.0
Print Preview for Comparison of Purchase Order Versions	BBP_CHANGE_SF_POVERS	4.0
Change Smart Form for E-Mails Relating to Bids	BBP_CHANGE_SF_BID	

Table D.19 BAdIs for Controlling Document Output

To enhance user interface configuration you can use Table D.20.

Business Add-Ins (BAdIs)	Definition Name
Determine Screen Variants	BBP_SCREENVARIANT
Field Control in Purchasing Document	BBP_UI_CONTROL_BadI
Display of Input Helps, Search Helps, and Favourites	BBP_F4_READ_ON_ENTRY
Restrict the Display in Input Helps and Search Helps	BBP_F4_READ_ON_EXIT
Internal Temporary Storage of Favourites for Input Helps and Search Helps	BBP_F4_MEM_UPDATE
Final Saving of Favourites for Input Helps and Search Helps	BBP_F4_SAVE_DB

Table D.20 BAdIs to Enhance the User Interface Configuration

E   Customer Fields in SAP SRM

Every SAP project brings forth unique business needs and requirements; this is one of the reason for a common saying, "Every SAP Project is different". Same is the case with SRM projects. Organizations implementing SRM often find the need to define customer-specific fields to capture information driven by their business needs. SAP uses the term "Customer-specific Fields" or User-Defined fields to describe fields that are not delivered in the standard out-of-the-box solution, but organizations can create to meet their business requirements.

Organizations can use Customer-specific fields (CUF) in the SRM system to enhance the standard SAP structures and store additional information that might be unique to their business and can display, change, and search for these customer fields.

User-defined fields provide the flexibility to enhance SRM screens without MODIFICATION (or CORE MOD), as these fields are supported by SAP during application of notes, support packs and implementation of upgrades.

E.1   Customer-Specific fields in SRM document types

In SAP SRM User-Defined fields can be created at the Header and Item level for the different document types. As of SRM Release 4.0, user-defined fields are no longer specified in the CI includes but in the INCL_EEW_* structure. These are shown in Table E.1.

Document Type	Structure
Shopping Cart**	▸ INCL_EEW_PD_HEADER_CSF_SC ▸ INCL_EEW_PD_ITEM_CSF_SC
Purchase Order	▸ INCL_EEW_PD_HEADER_CSF_PO ▸ INCL_EEW_PD_ITEM_CSF_PO
Confirmation	▸ INCL_EEW_PD_HEADER_CSF_CONF ▸ INCL_EEW_PD_ITEM_CSF_CONF

Table E.1 Structures for SRM Document Types

Document Type	Structure
Invoice	▸ INCL_EEW_PD_HEADER_CSF_INV ▸ INCL_EEW_PD_ITEM_CSF_INV
Contracts	▸ INCL_EEW_PD_HEADER_CSF_CTR ▸ INCL_EEW_PD_ITEM_CSF_CTR
Quotations	▸ INCL_EEW_PD_HEADER_CSF_QUOT ▸ INCL_EEW_PD_ITEM_CSF_QUOT
Bid Invitations	▸ INCL_EEW_PD_HEADER_CSF_BID ▸ INCL_EEW_PD_ITEM_CSF_BID

Table E.1 Structures for SRM Document Types (cont.)

Additionally, customer-fields can also be created in the account assignment section within the shopping cart, purchase order and invoice document types.

As of SAP SRM 5.0, customer fields in the shopping cart can also be created that appear directly underneath the item overview. This allows for additional flexibility when users are creating shopping carts and don't have a need to navigate to the detail of the item level (illustrated in Figure E.1).

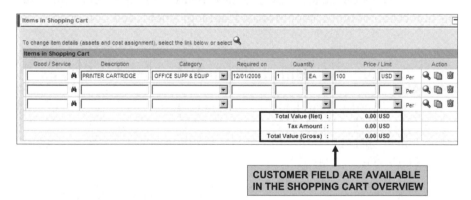

Figure E.1 Customer Fields in Shopping Cart Overview

E.1.1 Procedure for Creating a User-Defined Field

The following steps can be used as a guide for creating customer-specific fields in SRM:

1. Identify the structure(s) to be utilized; based on the document type that needs to be changed. (For example, if a new user-defined field needs to be

created in the shopping cart, the structure INCL_EEW_PD_ITEM_CSF needs to be used (we use the *ITEM_CSF* instead of "HEADER_CSF*, as the header fields cannot be displayed; the shopping cart is not displayed in a header and item level).

2. In transaction </SE11> append the structure identified in step1 with one or more user-defined fields. Append the structure(s) using the SAP proposed structure "ZAINCL*" (e.g. For shopping cart use ZAINCL_EEW_PD_ ITEM_CSF).

3. Define these document-specific fields in the append structures at the header (INCL_EEW_PD_HEADER_CSF) and item level (INCL_EEW_PD_ ITEM_CSF) for the document type where the user-defined field needs to be created, as illustrated in Figure E.2.

4. Repeat steps 1 through 3 above for each document types where this user-defined field needs to be available (for example, in the purchase order, and contract).

5. Activate all the appended structures.

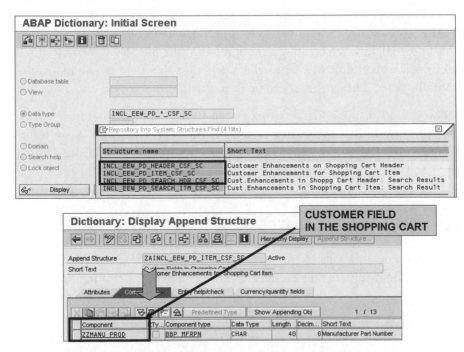

Figure E.2 Customer Field in Shopping Cart Document Type: View 2

Once the customer field is created, it is available in the document type, in our example the shopping cart document. It is important to note that the customer fields created in SRM are available in the **Default Settings for Items** section, as well as in the **Item Details: ITEM** section of the shopping cart.

A standard report BBP_CUF01 can be utilized to check the consistency and completeness of the user-defined fields. It is important to understand that contents of a user-defined field can be transferred from document to another only if the field is defined with exactly the same name in following document types.

The procedure for creating customer fields, defined in Section E.1.1 allows the creation of the customer-specific fields to store data in the SRM system. These fields are then available for additional "checks" or processing in the various SRM BADIs; in which case the individual BADI implementation would be required. Development experts can further enhance the user-defined fields by using the BAdI BBP_CUF_BADI_2 to control the changeability and the display of the fields. Additionally, other BAdIs can be utilized to further influence these Z fields. Let's take an example:

Assume that a new customer-specific field is created in the shopping cart (BUS2121) document, to capture the **Manufacturer Part Number**. Once this field is created, if you want to ensure to ensure that end users always enter this information when creating a shopping cart; the BBP_DOC_CHECK_BADI will need to be implemented to check whether this field is entered in the shopping cart, if not an error can be presented.

Organizations using a Classic or Extended Classic implementation scenario can also ensure that the Customer-specific fields created in SRM are transferred to the SAP R/3 or ERP backend. It is important that the fields created in SRM are then also created in the specific SAP backend for transfer.

E.2   Related OSS NOTES

Table E.2 contains a list of notes available at the SAP Service Marketplace that provide helpful details on the creation of customer fields in SRM.

Note	Description
458591	User-defined fields: Preparation and use
672960	User-defined fields 2
980074	Contents of old customer fields copied to new items

Table E.2 Relevant OSS Notes

Note	Description
809630	Customer field in bid invitation and bid — How does it work?
762984	SRM40-SUS: Implementation of customer enhancement fields

Table E.2 Relevant OSS Notes (cont.)

F Business Objects in SAP SRM

In SAP SRM, there are a number of business documents such as shopping carts, purchase orders, contracts, bid invitations, etc. These documents are described as business objects (BOR Object) in the system. The following tables provide a list of the business objects that exist in SAP SRM and SAP R/3 system. Table F.1 contains the business objects that exist in the Enterprise Buyer component of SRM.

Business Objects	Short Description
BUS2121	Shopping Cart
BUS2201	Purchase Order
BUS2209	PO Response
BUS2203	Confirmation/GR
BUS2205	Incoming Invoice
BUS2210	Invoice Default
BUS2000113	Purchase Contract
BUS2200	Bid Invitation

Table F.1 Business Objects in Enterprise Buyer (EBP)

Table F.2 contains the business objects that exist in the SUS component of SRM.

Business Objects	Short Description
BUS2230	PO in SUS
BUS2232	PO Confirmation in SUS
BUS2233	Confirmation in SUS
BUS2203	Confirmation/GR
BUS2231	Shipping Notification in SUS (ASN)
BUS2234	Invoice in SUS

Table F.2 Business Objects in Supplier Self Services (SUS)

Table F.3 contains the business objects that exist in the SAP R/3 or ERP system.

Business Objects	Short Description
BUS2093	Reservation in R/3
BUS2009	Requisition in R/3
BUS2012	Purchase Order in R/3
BUS2013	Scheduling Agreement in R/3
BUS2014	Contract in R/3

Table F.3 Business Objects in SAP R/3

G   Authorization Objects

In Chapter 11, I discussed the role of security in SAP SRM. I described roles, profiles, authorization objects, and transactions. The authorization concept protects transactions, programs, and services in SAP SRM from unauthorized access. This appendix contains a listing of the authorization objects that are available in SRM as of release 4.0. Organizations can use these objects to control the level of authorization available to users when creating business documents in SAP SRM, such as shopping carts, purchase orders ,and invoices.

For example, in the shopping cart application, you can select a cost center or G/L account by using the binoculars icon (the F4 search help) from the corresponding SAP R/3 or ERP back-end.

If you want to enable or restrict this option, your security team can do this via the authorizations in Transaction <PFCG>. This can be achieved by using the authorization object BBP_FUNCT (or M_BBP_SHLP for release SAP SRM 4.0). If the value BE_F4_HELP is activated, then the call for F4 help is enabled in R/3. (cont.)

Tables G.1 and G.2 give you information on authorization objects in SRM 5.0 and SAP SRM.

Authorization Object	Description
S_BBP_PID	Authorization check for PID tree maintenance
M_BBP_ASS	Authorization for Create Attachment Master
M_BBP_ADM	Authorization for administration of application layer BBP
BBP_BUDGET	Authorization for budget display
M_BBP_CTR	Authorization for contracts
M_BBP_SHLP	Authorization for search helps
M_BBP_VE	Authorization for vendor evaluation in Enterprise Buyer
BBP_PD_AUC	Auction
BBP_PD_BID	Bid Invitation
BBP_PD_CNF	Confirmation

Table G.1 Authorization Objects in BBP Component Class in SAP SRM

Authorization Object	Description
BBP_PD_CTR	Contracts
BBP_PD_PCO	Purchase order response
BBP_PD_PO	Purchase orders
BBP_PD_QUO	Quotations
BBP_PD_SC	Shopping carts
M_BBP_BID	Bid Invitation in Enterprise Buyer
M_BBP_I_EX	External invoice entry in Enterprise Buyer
M_BBP_Q_EX	External bid creation in Enterprise Buyer
M_BBP_SES	External PO confirmation in Enterprise Buyer
M_BBP_I_IN	Internal invoice entry in Enterprise Buyer
M_BBP_CONF	Internal PO confirmation in Enterprise Buyer
M_BBP_Q_IN	Internal bid processing in Enterprise Buyer
BBP_BUYER	Maintenance (create or change) of buying company in EBP systems
M_BBP_PC	Procurement card master data
M_BBP_PO	Purchase order in Enterprise Buyer
M_BBP_AUC	SRM Live Auction
BBP_PD_VL	SRM: Edit vendor list
BBP_FUNCT	SRM: General access authorizations in EBP
BBP_PD_INV	SRM: Process Invoices
BBP_VEND	SRM: Vendor activities in EBP
BBP_SUS_PD	SUS: Document access in SUS (replaced in SAP SRM 5.0)
M_BBP_IM_1	Web goods receipt against purchase order: Plant

Table G.1 Authorization Objects in BBP Component Class in SAP SRM (cont.)

Authorization Object	Description
BBP_CTR_2	Contracts (used in addition to the BBP_PD_CTR object)
BBP_SUS_AC	User authorization per SUS actions
BBP_SUS_P2	SUS documents (replaces BBP_SUS_PD authorization object)

Table G.2 Authorization Objects in SAP SRM 5.0

4. **True or False: SAP Enterprise Buyer Professional (EBP) and SAP SRM Server are essentially the same component.**

   a) True

   b) False

5. **Which of the following statements is correct regarding the relationship between SAP SRM and SAP R/3 (ERP):**

   a) SAP SRM can only work with SAP R/3 as the backend.

   b) SAP SRM can work with non-SAP backend systems.

   c) SAP SRM cannot be integrated with SAP R/3.

   d) SAP SRM requires SAP R/3 4.6C as a minimum.

6. **The classic scenario in SAP SRM implies that:**

   a) The shopping cart and the purchase order reside in SAP SRM.

   b) The shopping cart resides in SAP SRM and the purchase order resides in the backend.

   c) Both the shopping cart and the purchase order reside in the backend.

   d) None of the above.

4. **Which of the following reports update the status of the follow-on documents within the shopping cart history?**

   a) BBP_GET_STATUS_2

   b) CLEAN_REQREQ_UP

   c) RSWUWFMLEC

   d) BBP_BW_SC2

5. **What is the function of the RSWUWFMLEC report in EBP?**

   a) To transfer purchase orders from EBP to the back-end system in a standalone scenario.

   b) To allow printing of the shopping cart.

   c) To send notifications for work items via e-mail to e-mail recipients.

   d) To provide the ability for approval preview in the shopping cart.

6. **The following statements are true for the Extended Classic Implementation scenario:**

   a) The leading document is created in SRM and a copy of the document is transferred to the back-end SAP system.

   b) The follow-on documents of confirmation and invoice can only be entered in the SAP back-end system.

   c) The purchase order can be changed in SAP R/3.

   d) The SAP Portal is not compatible with the Extended Classic Implementation scenario of SRM.

7. **Which of the following statements are correct about the organization structure in EBP?**

   a) SRM users can be created simply by using the SU01 transaction.

   b) An organization structure is required. The self service scenario cannot be implemented without the organization structure.

   c) The inheritance administration of attributes from PPOMA can be configured in table T77OMATTR.

   d) The report BBP_CHECK_CONSISTENCY checks the consistency of the organization plan.

8. **What statement(s) is correct regarding Plan Driven Procurement in SRM?**

   a) It is one of the business scenarios in SRM.

   b) It only supports the sourcing or procurement of requirements generated in APO.

c) The requirements created in the back-end system can be transferred to EBP where a shopping cart is created, and can then utilize the workflow start conditions rules to get approval(s).

d) The report BBP_EXTREQ_TRANSFER is utilized in the SAP backend to transfer the relevant requisitions to EBP.

9. **Which of the following is true concerning the workflows in SRM?**

a) There is only one workflow template provided by SAP for the shopping cart workflow. All others need to be customized based on the project.

b) The approval preview allows the end user to visualize all required approvals in a graphical and tabular format.

c) As an alternative to the workflows supplied in the standard system, you can use the SLAPPROVER workflow to ensure more flexible assignment of users. This is a one-step approval workflow.

d) Ad-hoc approval functionality provides the ability to dynamically insert approvers or reviewers within the approval chain for a document.

10. **What elementary step(s) is/are associated with workflow customizing in SRM?**

a) The workflows to be used have to first be activated in customizing.

b) The organization buffer of the organizational plan has to be refreshed first, using the transaction SWU_OBUF.

c) The IMG activity, "Maintain Standard Settings for SAP Business Workflow" can be configured by any user with access to this transaction.

d) Workflow start conditions need to be configured by business objects (e.g. BUS2121 for the shopping cart).

11. **What does the transaction BBPGETVD do?**

a) It transfers the materials from the back-end SAP R/3 system into EBP.

b) It transfers the terms of payment of the vendors from the backend into EBP.

c) It replicates the vendors from the back-end system into the vendor organization (PPOMA_BBP).

d) All vendor master records are transferred from the backend and the business partner numbers are entered for these vendors in EBP.

12. **Which statement(s) concerning master data in SRM is/are correct?**

   a) Material Master Data is transferred from the SAP backend to EBP using middleware.

   b) Product Categories correspond to material groups in the SAP backend.

   c) Business partner master records correspond to the vendor master records in the SAP backend.

   d) The vendors are downloaded into SRM from the SAP backend via the middleware.

13. **What statements pertaining to the OCI interface are correct?**

   a) OCI allows organizations to connect their EBP systems with online catalogs like Office Depot, Dell, and Grainger and transfer their catalog data into the EBP shopping carts.

   b) OCI describes the data exchange between the EBP and external catalog applications.

   c) The OCI is the Open Content Interface that ensures that the correct content is transferred to EBP from the catalog.

   d) If products are contained in the catalog and are already maintained in the product master, EBP does not require any inbound parameters for transfer of the product data, since this data is already known in EBP.

   e) The OCI interface contains inbound and outbound parameters.

14. **Which of the following are correct as of release SRM 4.0?**

   a) Customer-specific fields can be created for the shopping cart, purchase order, and contract documents in SRM.

   b) The procurement card functionality in EBP can be implemented in the Classic and Extended Classic scenario.

   c) ITS can now be utilized integrated with the Web Application Server 6.40. This can decrease the total cost of ownership (TCO).

   d) Archiving documents is not supported in SRM.

15. **What statements pertaining to the account assignment in SRM are correct?**

   a) A real-time validation occurs in the SAP back-end system.

   b) A G/L account has to be assigned to the product category for the validation of the accounts.

c) A local validation in EBP independent of a back-end system is also possible.

d) The only account assignment categories available in SRM are Cost Center (CC) and Asset (AS).

H.2   Answers

You can check your responses and see how many you got correct by going through Table H.1.

Question	Correct Answer
1	B
2	D
3	A, B
4	A
5	C
6	A
7	B, C, D
8	A, D
9	B, C, D
10	A, D
11	C
12	A, B, C
13	A, B, E
14	A, C
15	A, C

Table H.1 Correct Responses

H.3   Explanations for the Answers

This section is designed to give you some insight into the correct answers and the thought processes involved in arriving at the correct response:

1. **True or False: The terms Supplier Relationship Management (SRM) and Enterprise Buyer (EBP) are the same, and can be used interchangeably.**

   Answer: B

   SRM and EBP are often used interchangeably, but they are not the same. Enterprise Buyer (EBP) is a component within the SAP SRM solution.

   SAP launched its e-Procurement solution in 1999 with B2B Procurement 1.0. later branded as Enterprise Buyer Professional (EBP). It started off as just a catalog-based Employee Self Service tool and evolved into a robust eProcurement solution. In 2003 SAP launched SRM, Supplier Relationship Management, which not only provided an eProcurement solution but also added a supplier collaboration engine. Since then SAP SRM has become a best of breed multi-purpose solution. Today SAP SRM focuses on the core supply processes of procurement, sourcing, contract management, and supplier enablement.

2. **Which of the following is not a standard scenario available for SRM?**

   Answer: D

   The Extended Classic Scenario is an Implementation Scenario for EBP. It is not a Business Scenario.

   In the Extended Classic Scenario, the purchase order is created locally within EBP. If the data in the shopping cart is insufficient to generate a complete purchase order, the data is supplemented manually within EBP before being transferred to the back-end system. The purchase order in EBP is the leading purchase order. Goods receipts (confirmations) and invoices can be entered in EBP or in the back end.

3. **The following technical component(s) is/are mandatory for the Self Service Scenario in SRM 5.0:**

   Answer: A, B

   The Self Service Scenario does not require XI or the Live Auction Cockpit as mandatory technical components. SAP XI is only required if XML-based communication/integration is required (e.g., CCM material master replication from SAP R/3 to SAP EBP to SAP CCM). The Live Auction Cockpit is also not a mandatory component for the Self Service Scenario.

   According to the SRM 5.0 Component matrix published by SAP, the CCM component is a required install. However, organizations that choose not to utilize the CCM solution would have the option of not configuring CCM.

4. **Which of the following reports update the status of the follow-on documents within the shopping cart history?**

   Answer: A

   The BBP_GET_STATUS_2 job is scheduled to retrieve the status from the back-end system. Once a Req. or a PO is generated in EBP, the spooler transfers it over to the backend. This job then gets the status of the created object and provides the appropriate input to the check status transaction of the end user's shopping cart.

   The CLEAN_REQREQ_UP job ensures that the subsequent objects of shopping cart (SC) items and the IDocs, which can be generated from confirmations and invoices, are updated successfully in the back-end system. If the subsequent objects are created successfully, the report sets the status of the SC to '6' and deletes temporary data in the EBP system, it is not needed there anymore (this is the reason why it is called a "cleaner" job).

5. **What is the function of the RSWUWFMLEC report in EBP?**

   Answer: C

   This job is scheduled to enable offline approval functionality in SRM and to allow the work items in the SRM user's inbox to be transferred to their preferred e-mail client (e.g. Outlook, Lotus Notes, GroupWise, etc.). E-mails are only sent to those users for which the user attributes (FORWARD_WI) "Flag: Forward work item," are maintained in PPOMA_BBP. This is useful for users that do not use the integrated inbox of the EBP system, so that another mail client can process work items in their usual mail client.

   There are two steps in this job:

   1. The initial step moves the approval work item from the SAP inbox to SAP connect (TCode: SCOT). This step is executed by report: RSCONN01.

   2. The second step moves the same work-item from SAP connect to the organization's mail server, which then sends the e-mail to the user's preferred e-mail client. This step is executed by report: RSWUWFMLEC.

6. **The following statements are true for the Extended Classic Implementation scenario:**

   Answer: A

   In the current SRM 5.0 release, SAP provides three implementation scenarios for use: the Classic, Extended Classic, and the Standalone. In the Extended Classic scenario, the entire procurement process takes place locally in EBP and a copy of the data is replicated to the back-end system. In essence, this scenario is an extension of the Classic Scenario.

   The purchase order in the back-end SAP system is a read-only copy that enables goods receipt, service entry, and invoice verification in the back-end system. The back-end purchase order cannot be changed. If you wish to make any changes to the purchase order, you must do so in EBP. Once you save these changes, they are transferred to the back-end purchase order.

7. **Which of the following statements are correct about the organization structure in EBP?**

   Answer: B, C, and D

   Users in SRM cannot simply be created using the SU01 transaction. For valid system access, users have to belong to an organization unit, a position, have a business partner ID, a central person and a SU01-User ID.

   An organization structure and a set of user attributes are required for working with EBP professional. Each user attribute represents a value that is stored under a particular name within the organizational structure. Depending on a user's role, a different set of attributes is required.

   The report BBP_CHECK_CONSISTENCY (that can also be called via transaction BBP_ATTR_CHECK), checks the consistency of the organizational plan. It also checks whether the attributes for companies, purchasing organizations, purchasing groups, and users are defined correctly for the individual applications.

8. **What statement(s) is correct regarding Plan Driven Procurement in SRM?**

   Answer: A, D

   The Plan Driven Procurement Scenario supports the sourcing and procurement of requirements from external planning systems within EBP. The requirements coming from an SAP back-end system could result from an MRP run, or a PM or PS document or could be created manually. In addition, requirements from APO can be transferred into EBP. Once the requirements are transferred, if the data is complete and unique, purchase order(s) can be created automatically in EBP. If data is missing, the professional purchaser has to complete the missing information in sourcing or via process purchase orders.

If customizing is set up for sourcing, the requirements appear in the sourcing transaction; technically an interim shopping cart (BUS2121 object) is created but this is not relevant for any approval(s).

Requirements from an SAP back-end are replicated via RFC into the EBP. The report BBP_EXTREQ_TRANSFER can either be executed manually or scheduled in the background to transfer these requirements into EBP.

9. **Which of the following is true concerning the workflows in SRM?**

Answer: B, C, and D

SAP provides multiple workflow templates for the shopping cart. One of the workflows is Single Step Approval Over limit, where the Requisitioners are assigned spending limits, approvers are assigned approval limits. Spending limit approvers are assigned via the attribute in the org structure SLAPPROVER instead of depending on the hierarchy of orgs, positions and users. Based on the shopping cart value, the approver with the ultimate approval value is determined.

In the SRM shopping cart, approval preview provides a user with an approval flow simulation. The user can be aware of the approval chain, and if required, add approvers in addition to the ones determined by the system.

The process of adding additional approvers on the fly is Ad-Hoc approval functionality. In the approval preview, employees can specify a different approver for a shopping cart or other document at runtime. This might be necessary, if, for example, a manager is temporarily absent and has not specified a substitute for shopping cart approval.

10. **What elementary step(s) is/are associated with workflow customizing in SRM?**

Answer: A, D

Prior to using any of the scenarios in SRM, the workflow environment needs to be configured. Even if no approvals are to be triggered in your business process, SRM needs to be configured for triggering the "no-approval" workflows.

We can configure the standard workflow environment in the **IMG • SRM • Cross-Applications • SAP Business Workflow**. Standard tasks and workflows can be activated for use.

A user who belongs to the super user group should perform the automatic workflow customizing activity. If you belong to the super user group, and the WF-BATCH user does not exist, it is created and automatically gets the maximum authorization of the current user (SY-UNAME). The system user must have the authorization SAP_ALL if the workflow system is to function without problems.

In the start conditions in customizing, you define which workflow is started under what conditions. The conditions always apply for the entire shopping cart, confirmation, or invoice. For example, you decide that shopping carts must be approved if the total value exceeds $1,000.

11. **What does the Transaction BBPGETVD do?**

Answer: C

Transaction BBPGETVD exists to download vendor information as business partner information from the back-end system into the EBP. You should take the following into account: whether the EBP is to assign numbers from the internal number range for business partners for the vendors to be copied; whether the vendor numbers are to be copied from the back-end system.

However, it cannot be scheduled to automatically synchronize vendor master data between SRM and R/3. Instead, in customizing for vendor synchronization, you define between which SAP or R/3 back-end systems and the EBP you wish to automatically synchronize the vendor master data. This setting is necessary in order to start a job-based execution of the synchronization, so that the vendor master data that is newly created or changed in the backend is updated regularly in the EBP System (SRM IMG: **SRM Server • Technical Basic Settings • Settings for Vendor Synchronization**).

12. **Which statement(s) concerning master data in SRM is/are correct?**

Answer: A, B, C

Master data in SRM can be downloaded from the SAP back-end. This data includes product master records, business partner master records, and product categories. products (material), service masters, and product categories (material groups) are downloaded via the middleware. The middleware is a set of programs that exist partly in the EBP and partly in the SAP back-end plug-in.

EBP uses the SAP business partner concept. An internal or external business partner is created in EBP for every person, organization, or group of people who could be involved in a business transaction. The vendor is an external business partner. Conversely, plant is an internal business partner. A shopping cart requester, a plant, an organization, a creditor, vendor, a bidder, or a marketplace are all business partners within SRM.

Vendors are not downloaded via the middleware -- instead using a transaction BBPGETVD or via the synchronization report.

13. **What statements pertaining to the OCI interface are correct?**

   Answer: A, B, E

   The Open Catalog Interface (OCI) describes the data exchange between the EBP and external catalog applications. OCI enables the transmission of selected goods and services from an external catalog to the EBP. The external catalog is located either within the Intranet or somewhere on the Internet. SAP's Open Catalog Interface uses standard Internet protocols.

   Punch-Out or Round-Trip allows suppliers to maintain branded content on their own Web sites and extend their e-commerce capabilities to buyers. By simply connecting to the supplier's Web site, buyers can select and configure products from the supplier's custom catalog. The supplier can provide buyer specific items and pricing.

   After products are selected, the Round-Trip service automatically brings the required item details back into the buying application. At this point, the order is routed through the normal requisition and approval processes and eventually converted into a purchase order that is sent back to the supplier for order fulfilment. The initial connection, authentication, and final return of the order information are all facilitated with the SAP Open Catalog Interface (OCI).

14. **Which of the following are correct as of release SAP SRM 4.0?**

   Answer: A, C

   Customer fields can be used in shopping carts, purchase orders, confirmations, invoices, and contracts at the header and item level, and for account assignment. Customer fields can be displayed in the standard interface or on a custom screen. A BADI is available for customer-defined sub screens.

In EBP, you can specify procurement card as the payment method when purchasing items. However, this functionality is only supported in the Standalone or Local implementation scenarios. The Classic and Extended Classic scenarios do not support this functionality. Some organizations have handled this limitation via development.

As of SAP NetWeaver '04, ITS is available integrated with the NetWeaver component, SAP Web Application Server 6.40, as an Internet Communication Framework (ICF) service. The integrated ITS runs on one machine, reducing the number of servers and decreases the total cost of ownership (TCO).

Archiving is a process to remove bulk or outdated data from your database that is no longer needed in your system. Many documents including the shopping cart, purchase order, confirmation and contracts can be archived in SRM. In SRM 4.0 the restoration of archived data is not yet possible.

15. **What statements pertaining to the account assignment in SRM are correct?**

Answer: A, C

In the EBP, account assignment validation can be done in the following environments:

▶ In the Enterprise Buyer Professional (local validation of FI data).

▶ In the back-end system (real-time validation of FI data).

▶ You can choose not to validate at all.

In the configuration you can enter the G/L account to be used based on product category and account assignment category.

The account assignment categories used in the EBP system are Asset (AS) — the local counterpart of the backend account assignment category A. Cost Center (CC) — the local counterpart of the back-end account assignment category K. FI — the local counterpart of the back-end account assignment category K. NET — the local counterpart of the back-end account assignment category N. Order (OR) — the local counterpart of the back-end account assignment category F. SO — the local counterpart of the back-end account assignment category C. And WBS — the local counterpart of the back-end account assignment category P.

I System Refresh Procedures

On many SAP SRM projects a need arises to copy one system landscape to another. For example, the project testing strategy might require multiple testing cycles and for each cycle a separate client landscape is required. In this example, the project might want to have a Golden Client in the QA environment, let's say as 400, where all configuration and master data is created. Now for testing purposes, the project team needs four additional clients: 410,420,430,440, each for a separate cycle of testing.

SAP SRM contains a number of different components and is often connected to one or more SAP backend systems. Therefore the client copy or system landscape copy requires a number of steps that need to be followed by the BASIS and Functional teams. There are obvious tasks that are required of the BASIS team; however in an SRM environment a number of steps might be required of the Functional teams as well. Therefore the project team needs to develop a task list and sequence of steps outlined that are owned by the BASIS and functional teams. It is my experience that often the BASIS teams are unaware of all the steps required.

Until recently a comprehensive guide did not exist for project teams to follow to complete this task. However, SAP has recently published an OSS Note that is fairly comprehensive and will serve very useful for project teams during this task. Project teams need to review this note and list all the activities that are relevant for their project scope. It is important to assign responsibilities between the BASIS and Functional ownership and the sequence of steps is important to follow. For example, the functional team cannot make changes to the Organization Structure until the BASIS team has made the RFC and Logical system changes.

> **Note**
>
> Review OSS Note: 995771 — System Landscape Copy for SAP SRM 4.0 and 5.0.

J   Organization Structure Attributes

The organizational structure is considered the heart of SAP SRM because it controls a number of different user and organizational attributes in SRM. Table J.1 contains a list of the attributes available in SAP SRM. These attributes are maintained in the organization maintenance transaction PPOMA_BBP in SRM.

Attribute	Example Value	Description	Manda-tory
ACS	BACKEND	▶ Key for the FI/CO backend. ▶ Required for Invoices without PO reference and ▶ Local Invoices. ▶ You should define the backend system in the Customizing. Path in the IMG ▶ Enterprise Buyer professional edition • Basic ▶ Settings • Define Backend Systems	X
ADDR_BILLT		Default bill-to party address in purchase order	
ADDR_SHIPT		Delivery address in purchase order. Specify at least one delivery address and set it as the default address.	
AN1		Account assignment (Asset) object permitted. Specifies the asset in the backend system.	
AN2		▶ Account assignment (Asset sub-number) ▶ Object permitted. Specifies the asset subnumber in the backend system	
ANK		▶ Account assignment (Asset class) object permitted ▶ Specifies the asset class in the ▶ backend system	

Table J.1 Attributes in SAP SRM Organizational Structure

Attribute	Example Value	Description	Mandatory
ANR		▸ Account assignment (Order) object permitted ▸ Specifies the order in the back-end system	
APO		▸ Account assignment (Sales Order Item) object permitted ▸ Specifies the sales order item in the back-end system	
APPRV_LIM		▸ Approval limit for manager roles. Currency should be specified ▸ Note that this attribute must be maintained in the *Extended Attributes* tab	
BSA	LOCAL\EC BACKEND\EC	▸ Document type in back-end/local system ▸ The document type you define here, has to be defined in the back-end system too	X
BUK	LOCAL\1234 BACKEND\1234	Company code in backend and/or local system if you are using back-end and/or standalone.	X
BWA	BACKEND\201	Movement type in back-end system. This is only required if reservations are being created in the backend system	X
CAT	CATALOG ID	▸ Name of the catalog an organization/user is allowed to use ▸ This attribute must have been defined during customizing	
CNT	LOCAL\1234 BACKEND\1234	▸ Account assignment (cost center) object permitted. Specifies the cost center in the back-end system ▸ If you are using only numerical cost centers in the backend system, you need to maintain leading zeros: <SYS>\0000001234 instead of <SYS>\1234	
COMPANY		▸ Company. Identifies a part of a company that functions as a separate legal entity ▸ Set by Type tab flag Company	
CUR	EUR	Key for the local currency	X

Table J.1 Attributes in SAP SRM Organizational Structure (cont.)

Attribute	Example Value	Description	Manda-tory
DP_PROC_TY		▶ Transaction type: Direct material ▶ Specifies the transaction type used when purchase orders for direct materials are created via BAPI, shopping cart, or bid invitation/bid ▶ This attribute MUST be maintained for the responsible purchasing group (see also TEND_TYPE) ▶ The specified transaction type must correspond to the document type used in the backend system for direct material purchase orders with external number assignment ▶ Path in the Implementation Guide (IMG): **Enterprise Buyer professional edition • Application-Specific Basic Settings • Define Transaction Types**	
ITS_DEST	http://<server>/scripts/wgate/	Needed for the administrator application monitors and for tendering	X
IS_COMPANY		▶ Flag that identifies the org. unit as an independent legal entity ▶ Define an organizational unit near the top of the org. plan as a company by setting this flag ▶ If other org. units at a lower level in the plan represent subsidiaries, the flag should be set for these too ▶ Set by Type tab, flag Company	
IS_PGR		▶ Flag that identifies an org. unit as a purchasing group ▶ Set by Type tab	
IS_POR		▶ Flag that identifies an org. unit as a purchasing organization ▶ Set by Type tab	
KNT	CC	▶ Account assignments (account assignment category) permitted ▶ Has to be previously defined in Customizing: Enterprise Buyer professional edition Account Assignment ▶ Define Account Assignment Categories	X

Table J.1 Attributes in SAP SRM Organizational Structure (cont.)

Attribute	Example Value	Description	Manda-tory
LAG		Storage location	
PRCAT		▸ Product category that an organizational unit or user is allowed to order. As opposed to the WGR attribute, PRCAT is displayed in readable form ▸ Note that this attribute must be maintained in the *Extended Attributes* tab	
PRI	XXXX	Key for the printer that an organizational unit or user is going to use by default. Has to be defined previously.	
PRO		▸ Account assignment (WBS) object permitted ▸ WBS element (individual structural element in a work breakdown structure representing the hierarchical organization of an R/3 project) in the backend system	
PURCH_GRP		▸ Number of the organizational unit that is indicated as the local purchasing group in the organizational plan ▸ Set by Type tab, Purchasing Group	
PURCH_GRPX		▸ Number of the organizational unit that is indicated as the R/3 purchasing group in the organizational plan ▸ Set by Type tab, R/3 purchasing Group	
PURCH_ORG		▸ Number of the organizational unit that is indicated as the local purchasing organization in the organizational plan ▸ Set by Type tab, Purchasing Organization	
PURCH_ORGX		▸ Number of the organizational unit that is indicated as the R/3 purchasing organization in the organizational plan ▸ Set by Type tab, R/3 purchasing organization	
REQUESTER	O 50000001	Ship-to party for which a user or organizational unit will be allowed to order	

Table J.1 Attributes in SAP SRM Organizational Structure (cont.)

Attribute	Example Value	Description	Mandatory
RESP_PGRP	O 50000001	▶ Only define for organizational units that are purchasing departments ▶ Organizational unit(s) or users for which this purchasing group is responsible ▶ This is a mandatory attribute for organizational units for which the attributes PURCH_GRP or PURCH_GRPX are defined ▶ See Responsible_POrg_PGrp	X
RESP_PRCAT		▶ Product category for which this department is responsible, in readable form (not GUID). Only define for organizational units that are purchasing departments ▶ This attribute works in conjunction with the PRCAT attribute. It also must be maintained in the *Extended Attributes* tab	
RESP_WGR	123	▶ Only define for organizational units that are purchasing departments: (optional)Product ▶ category for which this department is responsible. ▶ Maintain GUID — select product category via F4 search help. If system does not automatically convert product category into GUID, proceed as follows: <SM30> Table: T77OMATTR, choose ▶ Maintain, flag BBP, double-click on Attribute/Scenarios, go down to Attribute RESP_WGR and change the matchcode from BBP_ATTR_F4 to BBP_ATTR_F4_PROD_CAT ▶ See Responsible_Porg_PGrp	
ROLE	SAP_BBP_STAL_EMPLOYEE	▶ All role(s) that can be adopted by a person belonging to this organizational unit ▶ Not relevant for vendors or bidders ▶ Use only the SAP_BBP_STAL_xxx composite roles, or customer amended versions. See Roles	
SF_FOOTER		SAP Smart Forms: Footer line	

Table J.1 Attributes in SAP SRM Organizational Structure (cont.)

Attribute	Example Value	Description	Mandatory
SF_GRAPHIC		Company logo. Used by Smart Forms when purchase orders or contracts are printed.	X
SF_HEADER		SAP Smart Forms: Header line	
SLAPPROVER		Specifies the approver used in workflows based on a spending limit. i.e. If an employee with a spending limit of $500 orders a shopping cart with a total value of $600, the employee's spending limit has been exceeded and the spending limit approval workflow is started. The workflow determines the manager to approve the shopping cart on the basis of the value for the attribute SLAPPROVER.	
SPEND_LIM		▶ Spend limit for user. If this is exceeded the spending limit approval workflow is triggered ▶ Currency should be specified ▶ Note that this attribute must be maintained in the *Extended Attributes* tab	X
SYS	BACKEND	MM Backend system used (if backend system is used)	X
TEND_TYPE		▶ Bid invitation transaction type ▶ Specifies the transaction type for bid invitations created automatically in the PLM (collaborative engineering) scenario ▶ Define this attribute or the purchasing group responsible for the organizational unit of the entry channel ▶ Path in the Implementation Guide (IMG): **Enterprise Buyer professional edition • Application-Specific Basic Settings • Define Transaction Types**	
TOG		▶ Tolerance Group ▶ Using this attribute you define a user group for which tolerance checks are used when quantity or value tolerances for deliveries or invoices are exceeded	

Table J.1 Attributes in SAP SRM Organizational Structure (cont.)

Attribute	Example Value	Description	Mandatory
VENDOR_ACS	BACKEND	▶ Vendor Root: Accounting system for the vendor ▶ Specifies the backend system where the accounting for the vendor is checked	X
VENDOR_SYS	BACKEND and/or LOCAL	▶ Vendor Root ▶ System in which POs can be created for this vendor	X

WGR (GUID32)	123	▶ Product category that an organizational unit (or user) is allowed to order.
		▶ Define a default value. For example, if a user mainly purchases office materials, it would make sense to specify office materials as the default value.
		▶ Maintain GUID — select product category via F4 search help.
		▶ If system does not automatically convert product cat into GUID proceed as follows: <SM30> Table: T77OMATTR, choose **Maintain**, flag BBP, double-click on **Attribute/Scenarios**, go down to **Attribute** RESP_WGR and change the matchcode from BBP_ATTR_F4 to:
		  ▶ BBP_ATTR_F4_PROD_CAT
		  ▶ See also Create_Product_Hierarchies to
		  ▶ enable searching to return GUID results
			X

WRK	BACKEND\1234	Plant (in the back-end system)	

Table J.1 Attributes in SAP SRM Organizational Structure (cont.)

K Useful Transactions and Function Modules

In this appendix I have provided some of the most utilized transactions and function modules in the SAP SRM system. Readers will find that these will be extremely helpful during their SAP SRM project implementation and assist in troubleshooting issues.

This appendix is divided into multiple sections so it is easier for you to find transactions (TCode), function modules (FM), Programs or Tables based on the application area within SAP SRM. Transaction codes can be executed directly in the SRM Gui. The Function Modules are executed using transaction SE37 and then entering the individual function module. Programs are executed using transaction SE38 and then entering the individual program name. Tables are found using transaction SE16 and then entering the individual table name.

Let's begin with reviewing the different transactions, function modules and tables that assist with the Shopping Cart (SC) application (Table K.1). And then we will continue with the different application areas further below. Tables K.1 through K.6 cover the transaction or function modules and their codes.

Transaction or Function Module	Description	Type
BBPSC01	Shopping Cart — Extended Form	TCode
BBPSC02	Shopping Cart — Wizard	TCode
BBPSC03	Shopping Cart — Limited Functions Form	TCode
BBPSC04	Check Status	TCode
BBPSC05	Public Template — Create	TCode
BBPSC06	Public Template — Change	TCode
BBP_BW_SC2	Shopping Cart status Report in SRM	TCode
BBP_PD	SRM Document Report — SC, PO, etc.	TCode

Table K.1 Shopping Cart Application

Transaction or Function Module	Description	Type
BBP_MON_SC	Monitor Shopping Cart — This is accessed using the Web application monitor shopping cart. Typically in the SRM Administrator role.	TCode
BBP_PD_DOC_CHECK	Makes all checks for the document — SC, PO, etc	FM
BBP_PD_SC_GETDETAIL	Shopping cart details	FM
CRMD_ORDERADM_H	Shopping cart header details	Table
CRMD_ORDERADM_I	Shopping cart Item details	Table
BBP_DOCUMENT_TAB	Table with documents in relationship with POs and confirmations not yet cleared in SRM.	Table

Table K.1 Shopping Cart Application (cont.)

Transaction or Function Module	Description	Type
PPOCA_BBP	Create Organizational Structure	TCode
PPOMA_BBP	Maintain Organizational Structure	TCode
PPOSA_BBP	Display Organizational Structure	TCode
PPOMV_BBP	Create Vendor Organization	TCode
BBP_BP_OM_INTEGRATE	Synchronize / Verify Org Structure. Also used when integrating the HR Organizational Structure	TCode
RHOMATTRIBUTES_ANALYZE	Analysis of attribute inheritance	Program
RHOMATTRIBUTES_CONSISTENCY	Consistency check for attributes	Program
RHOMATTRIBUTES_REPLACE	Mass change of attributes in organizational structure	Program
BBP_ATTR_CHECK	Check organizational model checks for consistency (e.g. to check if user's attributes are complete for creating shopping carts or purchase orders.	FM
BBP_USER_GET_ATTRIBUTES	Get a list of all the attributes assigned to a user	FM
BBP_READ_ATTRIBUTES	Get a list of all attributes for a organizational object	FM

Table K.2 Organizational Structure Application

Transaction or Function Module	Description	Type
HRP1000	Organizational Structure objects	Table
HRP1001	Organizational Structure objects with relationships	Table
PFAL	Distributing the organizational structure from HR into SRM. This is a SAP R/3 transaction.	TCode
PP01	Maintain information for HR Objects such as employee, position, organizational unit in SAP R/3	TCode
PA30	Employee master maintenance in SAP R/3	TCode
BBPSC03	Shopping Cart — Limited Functions Form	TCode

Table K.2 Organizational Structure Application (cont.)

Transaction or Function Module	Description	Type
SWU3	Maintain standard workflow settings and configuration	TCode
SWB_PROCUREMENT	Workflow condition editor	TCode
SWI1	Workflow log	TCode
SWI5	Ability for administrator to review the list of workitem that are awaiting approval in a user's inbox.	TCode
SOST	Log for all workitem being sent to the external email address. This transaction is used for all external communication examples: Email, Fax, XML etc.	TCode
OOCU_RESP	Maintain Responsibility rules	TCode
SWUD	Workflow diagnosis for troubleshooting	TCode

Table K.3 Workflow Application

Transaction or Function Module	Description	Type
BBPGETVD	Download Vendors from SAP R/3 into SRM	TCode
BBPUPDVD	Update Vendors from SAP R/3 into SRM	TCode

Table K.4 Master Data & Business Partner Application

Transaction or Function Module	Description	Type
BBP_UPDATE_PORG	Adjust the purchasing organization in SRM when using Extended Classic scenario	TCode
BBPADDRINTC	Maintain addresses for the organization (Company)	TCode
BBPMAININT	Maintain external Vendor/Bidder	TCode
BBP_LOCMAP	Business Partner records for plants	Table
BBP_PD_SOS_FIND	Find all valid sources of supply	FM
BBP_VENDOR_READ_DETAIL	Get detail about a vendor	FM
COMM_HIERARCHY	Product Categories (or Material groups replicated from SAP R./3)	TCode
COMMPR01	Maintain Products (or Materials replicated from SAP R/3)	TCode
SMQ1	Outbound queue monitor when downloading master data from R/3	TCode
SMQ2	Inbound queue monitor when downloading master data from R/3	TCode

Table K.4 Master Data & Business Partner Application (cont.)

Transaction or Function Module	Description	Type
BBPUM01	User Maintenance transaction from SRM 5.0	TCode
BBPUSERMAINT	User Maintenance	TCode
BBPUM02	Settings for user data and attributes. New transaction in SRM 5.0	TCode
BBPAT05	Settings for user data and attributes.	TCode
USERS_GEN	Manage user and Employee data	TCode
BBP_USER_GET_DETAIL	Get details for a user	FM
SU01D	User master display	TCode
BBP_CHECK_USERS	Check users	TCode

Table K.5 Manage Users Application

Transaction or Function Module	Description	Type
SM12	Unlock user application sessions	TCode
ST22	View short dumps in the system	TCode
SXI_MONITOR	Monitor the XI log for documents in SRM	TCode
WE02	Monitor IDocs (e.g. confirmations)	TCode
SM21	Check logs for system issues	TCode
SLG1	Log for documents (e.g. download of vendor master)	TCode
WE20	Define partner profiles for EDI and ALE transfer	TCode
BD64	Create distribution model (e.g. for distributing Confirmations to R/3)	TCode
WE19 / BD84	Repost IDocs in error	TCode
RZ20	Application monitor errors captured in the system	TCode
SE10	Transport management	TCode
RBDMIDOC	Creating IDocs for change pointers. Used when transferring HR data from R/3 into SRM	Program
BBP_CLEANER	Starts synchronization with backend system	TCode
BBP_PROCDOC_CHECK	Makes all checks for the document	FM
BBP_PD_GETHISTORY	Get a history of all the documents	FM
BBP_PD_PO_TRANSFER_EXEC	Transfer purchase order data to backend after error in Extended classic scenario	FM
BBP_REQREQ_TRANSFER	Transfer the shopping cart to the backend after error	FM
BBP_PD_PO_DOC_FLOW	Document flow between Shopping cart, PO, confirmation, etc.	FM

Table K.6 General Administration

L About the Author

Sachin Sethi is an author, speaker, and agent of change for SAP SRM. He is the co-founder and Managing Partner of Brite Consulting, which provides business consulting and systems integration services for the SAP Public Sector, Retail, and other verticals.

Previously, he led the SRM practice for SEAL Consulting. A certified SAP SRM consultant, Sachin's track record includes serving global clients at Deloitte Consulting, Ernst & Young, MarchFirst, and IBM.

Sachin's services are sought by industry leaders in the healthcare, consumer products, automotive, retail, manufacturing, and higher education sectors. He has helped them build business cases for SRM, launch SRM ramp-up and upgrades, and analyze several e-procurement solutions.

Sachin's experience with SAP SRM and EBP products dates back to their inception, to the initial B2B release. He has addressed audiences at the Logistics and Supply Chain conference, annual SAPPHIRE, and ASUG conferences, e-business seminars, universities, and local ASUG chapters.

Sachin holds a dual degree in Computer Engineering and Business Administration from Case Western Reserve University. He also has an Executive MBA degree from Baldwin Wallace College.

He can be reached at *sachins@briteconsulting.com*.

Index

Understanding the SAP Logistics Information System

www.sap-press.com

Martin Murray

Understanding the SAP Logistics Information System

Gain a holistic understanding of LIS and how you can use it effectively in your own company. From standard to flexible analyses and hierarchies and from the Purchasing Information System to Inventory Controlling, this book is full of crucial information and advice.
Learn how to fully use this flexible SAP tool that allows you to collect, consolidate, and utilize data. Learn how to run reports without any ABAP experience thus saving your clients both time and money.